The Tomb of Jesu

The Tomb of Jesus and His Family?

Exploring Ancient Jewish Tombs
Near Jerusalem's Walls

*The Fourth Princeton Symposium
on Judaism and Christian Origins,
Sponsored by the Foundation on
Judaism and Christian Origins*

Edited by

James H. Charlesworth

WILLIAM B. EERDMANS PUBLISHING COMPANY
GRAND RAPIDS, MICHIGAN / CAMBRIDGE, U.K.

Published 2013 by
Wm. B. Eerdmans Publishing Co.
2140 Oak Industrial Drive N.E., Grand Rapids, Michigan 49505 /
P.O. Box 163, Cambridge CB3 9PU U.K.

Library of Congress Cataloging-in-Publication Data

Princeton Symposium on Judaism and Christian Origins
    (4th: 2013: Princeton Theological Seminary)
    The tomb of Jesus and his family?: exploring ancient Jewish tombs near
Jerusalem's walls: the fourth Princeton Symposium on Judaism and
Christian Origins / edited by James H. Charlesworth.
        pages   cm
    Includes bibliographical references.
    ISBN 978-0-8028-6745-2 (pbk.: alk. paper)
    1. Jesus Christ — Death and burial — Congresses. 2. Jesus Christ —
Family — Congresses. 3. Tombs — Jerusalem — Congresses.
4. Jerusalem — Antiquities — Congresses.   I. Title.

BT460.P75   2013
232.9 — dc23

                                                        2013024836

www.eerdmans.com

Dedicated to Admired Colleagues Who Shared Their Wisdom

Hanan Eshel

Noel Freedman

Martin Hengel

Izhar Hirschfield

Jacob Milgrom

Ehud Netzer

Alan Segal

Shemaryahu Talmon

Too many left too soon.

Contents

Contents

Contents

Contributors

MORDECHAI AVIAM is Director of the Institute for Galilean Archaeology at the Kinneret Academic College in Israel.

JAMES H. CHARLESWORTH is the George L. Collard Professor of New Testament Language and Literature at Princeton and Director of the Princeton Dead Sea Scrolls Project.

CLAUDE COHEN-MATLOFSKY received his Ph.D. from the Sorbonne and specializes in the social history of early Roman Palestine.

APRIL D. DECONICK is the Isla Carroll and Percy E. Turner Professor of Biblical Studies and the Director of Graduate Studies in Religion at Rice University.

CASEY D. ELLEDGE is Associate Professor of Religion at Gustavus Adolphus College.

MARK ELLIOTT is the editor of *Bible and Interpretation*.

HOWARD R. FELDMAN is Professor of Biology at Touro College.

JOSEPH A. FITZMYER, S.J., is Professor Emeritus at The Catholic University of America.

CAMIL FUCHS is the head of the Department of Statistics and Operations Research at Tel Aviv University's School of Mathematical Sciences.

SHIMON GIBSON is a Senior Associate Fellow at the W. F. Albright Institute of Archaeological Research and Adjunct Professor of Archaeology at the University of North Carolina at Charlotte.

RACHEL HACHLILI is Professor of Archaeology at the University of Haifa.

ELDAD KEYNAN is a Ph.D. student at the University of Haifa.

KEVIN KILTY is Professor of Mechanical Engineering at the University of Washington.

AMOS KLONER is Associate Professor in the Martin Szusz Department of the Land of Israel Studies at Bar Ilan University.

WOLFGANG E. KRUMBEIN is Professor of the Institute of Philosophy at the University of Oldenburg.

ANDRÉ LEMAIRE is Director of Studies and Chair of Hebrew, Philology, and Epigraphy at the École Pratique des Hautes Études.

LEE MARTIN MCDONALD is President Emeritus and Emeritus Professor of New Testament Studies at Acadia Divinity College.

CHARLES PELLEGRINO is the author of several books relating to science and archaeology.

STEPHEN PFANN is President of the University of the Holy Land.

PETR POKORNÝ is Director for the Centre of Biblical Studies in Prague.

JONATHAN J. PRICE is Professor of Classics at Tel Aviv University.

CHRISTOPHER A. ROLLSTON is Toyozo W. Nakari Professor of Old Testament and Semitic Studies at the Emmanuel School of Religion.

AMNON ROSENFELD is a geologist and micropaleontologist currently working in Jerusalem.

JANE SCHABERG is Professor of Religious Studies and Women's Studies at the University of Detroit Mercy.

ANDREW V. SILLS is Assistant Professor in the Department of Mathematical Sciences at Georgia Southern University.

xii

MARK SPIGELMAN is a visiting professor at the UCL Medical School in the U.K. and the Hadassah Medical School in Israel.

JAMES D. TABOR is Chair of the Department of Religious Studies at the University of North Carolina at Charlotte.

KONSTANTINOS TH. ZARRAS is a Lecturer in Theology at the University of Athens.

Abbreviations

AB	Anchor Bible
ABD	*Anchor Bible Dictionary*
ABRL	Anchor Bible Reference Library
ABS	Anchor Bible Series
AGJU	Arbeiten zur Geschichte des antiken Judentums und des Urchristentums
AGSU	Arbeiten zur Geschichte des Spätjudentums und Urchristentums
ANES	*Ancient Near Eastern Studies*
ANF	*Ante-Nicene Fathers*
ANRW	*Aufstieg und Niedergang der römischen Welt: Geschichte und Kultur Roms im Spiegel der neueren Forschung.* Edited by H. Temporini and W. Haase. Berlin, 1972–
ASOR	American School of Oriental Research
BA	*Biblical Archeologist*
BAR	*Biblical Archeology Review*
BASOR	*Bulletin of the American Schools of Oriental Research*
BBR	*Bulletin for Biblical Research*
BDAG	*Greek-English Lexicon of the New Testament and Other Early Christian Literature.* Edited by F. W. Danker, W. Bauer, W. F. Arndt, and F. W. Gingrich. 3rd ed. Chicago, 1999
BÉ	*Bulletin épigraphique*
BFCT	Beiträge zur Förderung christlicher Theologie
Bib	*Biblica*
BibOr	Biblica et orientalia

BO	*Bibliotheca orientalis*
BR	*Biblical Research*
BSac	*Bibliotheca sacra*
BZNW	Beihefte zur Zeitschrift für die neutestamentliche Wissenschaft
CBQ	*Catholic Bible Quarterly*
CBQMS	Catholic Bible Quarterly Monograph Series
CIJ	*Corpus inscriptionum judaicarum*
CIS	*Corpus inscriptionum semiticarum*
CJAS	Christianity and Judaism in Antiquity Series
CJO	*Catalogue of Jewish Ossuaries in the Collections of the State of Israel*
CRAI	*Comptes rendus de l'Académie des inscriptions et belles-lettres*
CRINT	Compedia Rerum Iudaicarum ad Novum Testamentum
DJD	Discoveries in the Judaean Desert
DMOA	Documenta et Monumenta Orientis Antiqui
DSD	*Dead Sea Discoveries*
EBib	Etudes bibliques
EKK	Evangelisch-katholischer Kommentar
EncyBib	*Encyclopedia Biblica*
EncyDSS	*Encyclopedia of the Dead Sea Scrolls*
ESV	English Standard Version
FC	Fathers of the Church. Washington, DC, 1947–
FRLANT	Forschungen zur Religion und Literatur des Alten und Neuen Testaments
GRBS	*Greek, Roman, and Byzantine Studies*
HadArk	*Hadashot Arkheologiyot*
HO	Handbuch der Orientalistik
HTR	*Harvard Theological Review*
HTS	Harvard Theological Studies
HUCA	*Hebrew Union College Annual*
IDB	*The Interpreter's Dictionary of the Bible.* Edited by G. A. Buttrick. 4 vols. Nashville, 1962
IEJ	*Israel Exploration Journal*
IJCP	*International Journal of Cultural Property*
JAS	*Journal of Archaeological Science*
JBL	*Journal of Biblical Literature*
JFC	*Jewish Funerary Customs*
JJS	*Journal of Jewish Studies*
JQR	*Jewish Quarterly Review*
JSHJ	*Journal for the Study of the Historical Jesus*

JSJ	*Journal for the Study of Judaism*
JSJSup	Journal for the Study of Judaism Supplement
JSNT	*Journal for the Study of the New Testament*
JSNTSup	Journal for the Study of the New Testament Supplement
JSOTSup	Journal for the Study of the Old Testament Supplement
JSP	*Journal for the Study of the Pseudepigrapha*
JSPSup	Journal for the Study of the Pseudepigrapha Supplement
JSS	*Journal of Semitic Studies*
KJV	King James Version
LÄ	*Lexikon der Ägyptologie.* Edited by W. Helck, E. Otto, and W. Westendorf. Wiesbaden, 1972
LASBF	Liber annuus Studii biblici franciscani
LCL	Loeb Classical Library
LHist	*L'information Historique*
MGWJ	*Monatschrift für Geschichte und Wissenschaft des Judentums*
MPAT	A Manual of Palestinian Aramaic Texts
MSBL	Midwestern Society of Biblical Literature
NEA	*Near Eastern Archaeology*
NEB	New English Bible
NIDB	*New International Dictionary of the Bible.* Edited by J. D. Douglas and M. C. Tenney. Grand Rapids, 1987
NIV	New International Version
NJB	New Jerusalem Bible
NKJV	New King James Version
NovT	*Novum Testamentum*
NovTSup	Novum Testamentum Supplements
NRSV	New Revised Standard Version
NRTh	*La nouvelle revue théologique*
NTOA	Novum Testamentum et Orbis Antiquus
NTS	*New Testament Studies*
NTT	*Norsk Teologisk Tidsskrift*
OL	*Orientalia lovaniensia*
OLA	Orientalia lovaniensia analecta
OSB	*Oxford Study Bible*
OTL	Old Testament Library
OTP	*Old Testament Pseudepigrapha*
PEQ	*Palestine Exploration Quarterly*
PJBR	*Polish Journal of Biblical Research*
PL	Patrologia latina. Edited by J.-P. Migne. 217 vols. Paris, 1844-64

RB	*Revue biblique*
REB	Revised English Bible
REJ	*Revue des etudes juives*
RevQ	*Revue de Qumran*
RSV	Revised Standard Version
SBLABib	Society of Biblical Literature Academia Biblica
SBLABS	Society of Biblical Literature Archeology and Biblical Studies
SBLDS	Society of Biblical Literature Dissertation Series
SBLF	*Society for Biblical Literature Forum*
SBLSBS	Society of Biblical Literature Sources for Biblical Study
SBLSP	Society of Biblical Literature Seminar Papers
SBLSymS	Society of Biblical Literature Symposium Series
SBS	Stuttgarter Bibelstudien
SC	Sources chrétiennes. Paris, 1943–
SEG	*Supplementum Epigraphicum Graecum*
SJT	*Scottish Journal of Theology*
SNTSMS	Society for New Testament Studies Monograph Series
SPCK	Society for Promoting Christian Knowledge
STDJ	Studies on the Texts of the Desert of Judah
StPB	Studia post-biblica
SUNT	Studien zur Umwelt des Neuen Testaments
SVF	*Stoicorum veterum fragmenta.* H. von Arnim. 4 vols. Leipzig, 1903–1924
TLG	*Thesaurus linguae graecae: Canon of Greek Authors and Works.* Edited by L. Berkowitz and K. A. Squitier. 3d ed. Oxford, 1990
TSAJ	Texte und Studien zum antiken Judentum
VC	*Vigiliae christianae*
WBC	Word Bible Commentary
WUNT	Wissenschaftliche Untersuchungen zum Neuen Testament
WZKM	*Wiener Zeitschrift für die Kunde des Morgenlandes*
YUP	Yale University Press
ZAW	*Zeitschrift für die alttestamentliche Wissenschaft*
ZDPV	*Zeitschrift des deutschen Palästina-Vereins*
ZNW	*Zeitschrift für die neutestamentliche Wissenschaft und die Kunde der älteren Kirche*

Preface: Contextualizing the Search for Herod's and Jesus' Tomb

James H. Charlesworth

To Mishkenot Sha'ananim, the attractive artists' quarters in Jerusalem, scholars came from many places, including Canada, the USA, Greece, the Czech Republic, and Great Britain, to meet from January 13th to 16th in 2008. Why? We gathered to discuss and debate one topic: "Jewish Views of the After Life and Burial Practices in Second Temple Judaism: Evaluating the Talpiot Tomb in Context."

I had been asked to chair and organize this congress. Why? Earlier, the claim was made on the Discovery Channel that the tomb of Jesus, Mary Magdalene, and their son had been recovered in Talpiot, a district in what is now southeast Jerusalem. I refused to include sensational claims or to focus solely on the Talpiot tomb. I agreed to bring together all specialists who could help us ascertain the facts about pre-70 Jewish burial customs and beliefs. We would, therefore, include reflections on the Talpiot tomb by discussing its importance in light of all other related discoveries. I then agreed to publish the proceedings. The present work contains those proceedings.

This symposium was exceptional for many reasons. Two stand out. First, the media attention before, during, and immediately after spilled into various venues, many of which never considered archaeological or theological issues. As we all know, "The sensational, of course, can distort balanced judgment."[1]

During this emotionally charged symposium I became more aware of

---

1. James H. Charlesworth and Walter P. Weaver, eds., *What Has Archaeology to Do with Faith?* (Harrisburg: Trinity Press International, 1992), p. 2.

the methodologies and agendas that distinguish journalists from scholars. Methodology separates the best journalists from the best scholars. Journalists do not have time for subtleties and qualifications. Scholars sometimes lose their audiences because of too much data and too little focus, failing to clarify which option or answer is most likely. Journalists focus on what is new, and search for ways to tell a story, or "connect the dots." Scholars meticulously examine data in a quest, with colleagues, to reconstruct faithfully an ancient culture. Too often, we scholars tend to focus on one issue or datum, forgetting too often that the past had a story that should be re-presented and not lost.

In my judgment, journalists should be reticent to chase the sensational and rather seek to present a balanced position and engagingly tell "a story" in ways that will be sensitive to those who will hear or read it. Scholars need to communicate — clearly and engagingly — with the masses; that is, we scholars should not allow nonscholars to monopolize the media. What our world culture needs is for scholars to be engaged, again, with the masses and yet "disinterestedly" searching for answers to questions that may be exciting only to "the guild."

The second reason the symposium was exceptional is the inclusion of many diverse disciplines and methodologies. The symposium featured contributions of many specialists who never had appeared together in one auditorium; these included philologians and epigraphers; archaeologists intimately engaged with excavations in Judea and Galilee; biblical scholars; experts in Jewish ornamentation, art, and symbolism; specialists on the Dead Sea Scrolls and on the Jewish apocryphal books; scholars focused on Josephus and rabbinics; statisticians; experts on onomastics and prosopography in Second Temple Judaism; theologians; experts in forensic anthropology, AMS C-$_{14}$, and paleo-DNA; experts on ancient tomb architecture; as well as specialists on the portrayal of Jesus and Mary Magdalene in antiquity. I think most of those who attended the symposium would deem it delusional to presume we could agree on all, or even most, issues. We came together to discuss and debate, not to obtain a consensus on all issues.

Those from considerably disparate disciplines experienced the inestimable value of exchanging ideas and perspectives. Unexpectedly, however, those in attendance amassed data that seemed to converge toward this nearly unanimous conclusion: The Talpiot tomb is neither Jesus of Nazareth's tomb nor Mary of Magdala's tomb. There was some openness for considering that perhaps the Talpiot tomb may be connected, somehow, to Jesus' clan or to the Palestinian Jesus movement. But there was no consensus on this point.

Those discussions that focused on the Talpiot tomb and the archaeological issues pertaining to Jesus' tomb continued during the period that Ehud Netzer (of blessed memory) found Herod's tomb. The search for Herod's tomb absorbed approximately thirty years of scientific excavations in many places, including Jericho, and especially the Herodium. Too often publications and debates devoted to the Talpiot tomb were shaped by unscientific methodologies and emotional assumptions. Without any doubt Netzer's careful methodology in persistently searching for Herod's remains continued within a larger agenda: the study of Herod's monumental achievements and architectural masterpieces. Netzer's devotion to objective and refined methods fortified the claim that Herod's tomb had been discovered from the sensationalism and divisiveness occasioned by the outbursts that marred too many publications and speeches centered on the Talpiot tomb. Sensational discoveries are possible and they can be discussed without being divisive.

The proceedings of the symposium in Mishkenot Sha'ananim, published now, answer many questions; numerous others are seen in a new light. I wish to thank all who participated and made this symposium memorable and a success. None of us can control all the data that is presented, discussed, and edited, selectively, in the present work; but each of us is more informed and perhaps sensitive to many issues. International and interdisciplinary cooperative research is fundamental for advancing research and perceptions, and certainly our re-creation of the past. Sometimes debates become bitter and produce more heat than light; but later they frequently evolve, under favorable conditions, into enlightening vistas for new appreciation and understanding. That is the case with these published proceedings.

JHC
Princeton
January 2011

Introduction: Jerusalem's Tombs During the Time of Jesus

James H. Charlesworth

Sensational Claims and Amateur Responses by Some Professionals

In the winter of 2007 in New York, during the sensational claims and counterclaims regarding the Talpiot tomb, I was on the dais for the international broadcast and then on television to discuss the issues focused on the claim that Jesus' tomb had been located and his ossuary found.[1] Of those involved in this announcement, only Shimon Gibson and I harbored deep doubts about the claim that the ossuaries of Jesus of Nazareth and Mary of Magdala (Magdalene) had been discovered.[2]

1. The event was highlighted by two television features on the Talpiot tomb: Ray Bruce's special for BBC on *The Body in Question* (1996) and S. Jacobovici with J. Cameron's special on the Discovery Channel (2007).

2. I remember sitting with Shimon Gibson, in a coffee shop near the New York Public Library, and pondering what was transpiring. He and I agree that the claims regarding the Talpiot tomb were unpersuasive and emotions were dictating conclusions. E. M. Meyers correctly reported: "Professor Charlesworth and Dr. Gibson were the only scholars in attendance to deny the identification with Jesus." See Meyers, "The Jesus Tomb Controversy: An Overview," *NEA* 69 (2006): 116-18; the quotation is on p. 116.

This publication is a revision of the opening address, on 13 January 2008, in Mishkenot Sha'ananim during the Jerusalem Symposium, "Jewish Views of the After Life and Burial Practices in Second Temple Judaism: Evaluating the Talpiot Tomb in Context." To keep the tone of the opening lecture, I have left some statements anticipatory; others are reflective and represent further reflections and research between January 2008 and January 2011.

I was disappointed by the preprogrammed responses of too many archaeologists and theologians.[3] Many archaeologists who spoke had not studied the evidence but claimed there could be no relation between this first-century tomb and Jesus or his family. Numerous scholars who damned a television special by the Discovery Channel on the Talpiot tomb later admitted they had never seen the film. Such action is hardly professional or responsive to the ever-shifting data archaeologists and biblical scholars depend upon.

While I was being interviewed on television, a gifted and highly ranked theologian played on the emotion and ignorance of those in the audience and those watching at home. He received a good laugh from the audience when he asserted that those who believe in Jesus need no historian and no facts. He implied that new data might confuse believers. Such theologians are often ecclesiastics who tend to claim that they do not need to see the evidence since they know that Jesus rose from the dead and that his bones can never be found. Quite frequently, it is easy to catch a glimpse of a *defensor fidei redivivus*. Dogmatic assertions combined with blindness to archaeological discoveries in Jesus' homeland do not aid Christianity; they usually lead to a growing exodus from institutional religion.

Both archaeologists and Christian theologians misrepresented their positions; they compromised the search for truth within academia and within confessing communities. The respondents claimed to be trustworthy, but many viewers came to distrust those who could interpret data without having examined them. Too often archaeologists and theologians were faced with questions that exposed that they had not pondered many of the questions.

Clearly, many who believe in Jesus have lost patience with scholars. In their opinion, too many scholars since the seventeenth-century Enlightenment have only confused, even undermined, the faith of the church. This opinion is now growing among scholars who are Christians.

In my judgment, the problem lies not only with naïve Christians but also with self-promoting and dogmatic scholars. Quite understandably, many in our culture have simply lost patience with both groups.

By manifestoes and statements of purpose, both archaeologists and theologians claim to search for truth and gather with other learned and respected minds to ask questions and to probe the far too often opaque past. I

---

3. Many who spoke had neither seen the program on the Discovery Channel nor even glanced at Jacobovici and C. Pellegrino's *Jesus Family Tomb* (San Francisco: HarperSanFrancisco, 2007 [in two versions, of which the second is more reliable]).

have helped to organize this symposium since more and more literati and savants are informing me that dialogues have closed and there is a need to restore trust in archaeologists and theologians. The express purpose of this symposium is to clarify the facts about the Talpiot tomb by studying Jewish burial practices, the architecture of tombs, and related beliefs in Judea and Galilee during the Second Temple period. "What do we know and how do we know it" should govern our deliberations. A shared search for truth should override polemics and journalistic spin of ambiguities.

Most distressing to me has been the tendency toward Docetism by some alleged Christians. They implied that Jesus had not been fully human and thus never could have lived "among us" humans. In the attempt to serve as *defensor fide,* too many Christians indicate that the Jesus of history was really an angelic being of celestial substance. The heresy is called "Docetism" because it derives from the Greek word for "seems"; that is, the early heretics believed that Jesus was divine and merely seemed to be human. Before 100 CE, the author of 1 John directs invectives against these false "Christians," calling them antichrists and false prophets who do not confess "that Jesus Christ has come in the flesh" (1 John 4:2). The "heresy" was anathema to the four evangelists. The Fourth Evangelist explicitly announced that the "Word became flesh" (cf. John 1:14); that means that the Word was not poured into flesh — it was flesh. Docetism was the first heresy condemned by the early scholars of the church; and it opens the door to anti-Semitism and anti-Judaism.

A fundamental question brings the debate into focus: "What if Jesus' bones were found?" Christians divide into two camps. Some claim that that would disprove Jesus' resurrection and disprove that his tomb was found empty. Others claim that this discovery would be very good news, proving that Jesus had been a human like us and that the resurrection appearances in the Fourth Gospel indicate that the resurrected Jesus passed through doors or walls and thus could not have bones in his resurrected body. It is obvious that emotions can impede the search for honest answers to the question: Can the Talpiot tomb be related, in any way, to Jesus from Nazareth? The larger question is how and in what ways do Jewish tombs and the discovery of ossuaries in Judea and Galilee before 70 CE help us understand Jewish practices and beliefs within Second Temple Judaism.[4]

---

4. For information regarding the discovery of ossuary in Galilee, see L. Y. Rahmani, *A Catalogue of Jewish Osssuaries in the Collections of the State of Israel* (Jerusalem: Israel Antiquities Authority and Israel Academy of Sciences and Humanities, 1994), p. 22 [B5 and C2, both locally made]; and M. Aviam, "Ossuaries," in *Jews, Pagans and Christians in*

The heart of our questioning in this symposium, however, is not Christology or theology. We will be primarily searching for answers related to archaeological discoveries in Judea and Galilee and at all relevant sites (including Samaria), especially the areas around Jerusalem: Beth Zafafa, Qumran, 'En el-Ghuewir, Jericho, the Herodium, 'En Gedi, Mampsis, and Khirbet Qazone in Jordan.[5] At times the focus will be on the Talpiot tomb; at other times we will be thinking only or primarily of other excavations and the discovery of tombs that help us understand the complex ideologies and cultural dimensions of Second Temple Judaism. All relevant methodologies will be employed and assessed.

The Purpose of This Symposium

This symposium is designed so specialists devoted or experienced in understanding and interpreting Jewish tombs near Jerusalem,[6] and relating them to relevant texts, may discuss in a creative and cordial manner all the data and methods that help us interpret such tombs, including the tomb in Talpiot that some have concluded is related to Jesus, his family, or his clan. Unfortunately, too much misinformation has beclouded the study of the Talpiot tomb; fortunately, Amos Kloner and Shimon Gibson clarify the facts about the archaeological work in their publication contained in the present work.[7]

---

the *Galilee*, Land of Galilee 1 (Rochester: Institute for Galilean Archaeology and University of Rochester Press, 2004), p. 277 (also see fig. 1.9, "Map of the distribution of Priestly Courses, secret hideaways, stone vessels and ossuaries," on p. 19); and Aviam and D. Syon, "Jewish Ossilegium in Galilee," in *What Athens Has to Do with Jerusalem,* ed. L. V. Rutgers, Interdisciplinary Studies in Ancient Culture and Religion 1 (Leuven: Peeters, 2002), pp. 151-87. Ossuaries have been found in Galilee in the following places (from north to south): Gischala, Sasa, Meron, Uza, Yaquq, Kabul, Ibillin, Hittin, Tiberias, et-Taiyiba, Zippori, Kafr Kanna, Tiveon, Mashhad, Beth Shearim, Nazareth, Migdal Ha'Emeq, Dabburiyya, and Kefar Baruch. The term *ossilegium* denotes the process of gathering an individual's disarticulated bones and placing them in a container (usually of stone). See the discussion by Rahmani in *Catalogue,* p. 53.

5. See the earlier work by R. Hachlili, *Jewish Funerary Customs, Practices and Rites in the Second Temple Period,* JSJSup 94 (Leiden: Brill, 2005).

6. For an overview see A. Kloner and B. Zissu, *The Necropolis of Jerusalem in the Second Temple Period* [in Hebrew] (Jerusalem: Yad Izhak Ben-Zvi and Israel Exploration Society, 2003); for "Talpiot," see pp. 208-19.

7. See their contribution in this work: "The Talpiot Tomb Reconsidered: The Archaeological Facts."

Questions will be in central focus; scholars who are dogmatic and cannot learn from discussing issues with renowned specialists are not invited. We are interested in conclusions, but we are more interested in improving our methods and means of asking honest questions so as to obtain reliable insights and approximating a better perception of pre-70 Judaism in Judea and Galilee.

All pertinent data will be included. All conceivable methods for identifying and interpreting ancient tombs will be considered and assessed. We shall seek to learn what is the strength and weakness of a particular method and how it can help in reconstructing the past. Then we shall explore to what extent memory and creative reflection are necessary in interpreting and comprehending the past, and how we might discern when imagination becomes too romantic or separated from solid facts and also when interpretation is left infertile due to the lack of informed imagination.

The focus is broadened to include all Jewish tombs near Jerusalem that date from 40 BCE to 70 CE. The former date is chosen as the *terminus a quo* because it is the year Herod was elected "King of the Jews" by the Roman senate at the nomination of Antony. The year 70 CE is the *terminus ad quem* since in that year Jerusalem was destroyed by Titus, the future emperor of Rome, and worship in the Second Temple ceased. Moreover, ossuaries usually appear in tombs about the time of Herod the Great and cease to appear after 70, when the stone industry in Jerusalem ended and the wealth and population needed for them were destroyed.

Focusing on Interrogatives

Since questions define this gathering, I shall organize some challenging questions that should set the tone for exploring together the wide-ranging options that loom before us. Here are some leading questions:

1. L. Y. Rahmani's *Catalogue of Jewish Ossuaries* is the *vade mecum* for all of us who seek to comprehend how ossuaries may inform us of practices and beliefs in Second Temple Judaism,[8] but there is still much to discuss and ponder. Here are some questions: Why did Jews use ossu-

8. Usually ossuaries are found only in Jewish tombs; exceptions are in the "pagan" burials in nos. 251 and 463 (and perhaps others) in Rahmani, *Catalogue;* see those ossuaries and p. 3 n. 1.

aries? What beliefs do they reflect? How can we date them more precisely?[9] While it is evident that the manufacture of limestone ossuaries ceased following the destruction of Jewish culture in 70 CE, we need to explore what is the importance of the observation that ossuaries, almost always, date from near the end of the reign of Herod the Great to the destruction of 70 CE.[10]

2. Did a coherent system (or theological belief) determine the ornamentation of tombs and ossuaries or their construction?

3. What is definitive, even unique, about Jewish burials during the century before the destruction of 70 CE?

4. Is there any credence in the claim that Jesus "of Nazareth" most likely was buried in a tomb near Nazareth?

5. How do the evangelists describe Jesus' tomb? What did they report about its appearance and location? Was it only a temporary burial?

6. How can DNA analysis help us assess remains? If we do not have a bone or piece of hair from Jesus, how can we compare DNA removed from an ossuary with that person? Has DNA been collected without contamination from those who collect or study it? What are the dangerous repercussions from claiming that the remains of Jesus cannot be examined through DNA, since God does not have DNA, and when can scientists ignore the cultural repercussions of apparently clever use of language?

7. How can patina help us locate the provenience of an ossuary; that is, does a tomb leave a fingerprint on an ossuary? Are all tombs near Jerusalem so similar that no provenience of an ossuary can be ascertained?

8. Does the inscription on an ossuary found in the Talpiot tomb read "Mary, that is, Lord," "Mary and Martha," or "Mary, who is Martha"; and what level of certainty can be claimed for each reading and interpretation?[11]

9. What are the established methodologies developed for deciphering an inscription or graffiti, and how are lapidary inscriptions different from scripts on leather or papyri?

9. As Rahmani states: "As many family tombs had been in use long before ossuaries were introduced, exact dating is difficult" (*Catalogue*, p. 21).

10. See ch. 9: "Chronology and Geographical Distribution," and table 1, "Chronology, Geographical Distribution, Material and Technique of the Ossuaries," in Rahmani, *Catalogue*, p. 22.

11. The issue is settled by the papers in this work by Kloner, Gibson, and Pfann. Also see my following discussion.

10. What are the most common names in first-century CE Judean Palestinian culture?

11. What place do statistics and lists of probabilities play in discerning the relevance of a collage of names in a tomb?

12. How can AMS-C$_{14}$, or carbon dating, help date *realia,* and are the dates precise enough to help adjudicate among competing claims?

13. What can be known archaeologically about the Palestinian Jesus movement, Jewish Christianity, and Jesus' followers in Jerusalem and nearby from 26 to 70 CE?

14. Could the ossuary with the inscription "Jesus, son of Joseph," have belonged to Jesus of Nazareth? Do not two ossuaries[12] contain that same inscription, and, if so, does that not mean we should consider some "Jesus" who is related to some unknown "Joseph"? Is it not incredulous to assume Jesus from Nazareth is to be found in both? On the one hand, do these two ossuaries help prove that "Joseph" and "Jesus" were common names in Palestine (Παλαιστίνη; Herodotus 3.91)[13] before 70 CE? On the other hand, since the remains of a crucified man could have been placed in an ossuary, as we know with the remains of Jehohanan/Yehoḥanan, and if the bones of "Jesus, son of Joseph" (the identification of Jesus according to John), had been placed in an ossuary, what other names would have been put on the ossuary than "Jesus, son of Joseph"? However, if Jesus' bones were removed from a grave and placed in an ossuary, would that not have occurred about one year after his followers were persecuted for claiming God had raised Jesus from the dead? Why would they then place his bones in an undecorated, poor ossuary?

15. Can the tomb have been related in some way to Jesus' clan, the large extended family? Are not all the names in the Talpiot tomb clearly associated with Jesus' larger family? And is it significant that only names connected to Jesus' family have appeared in the Talpiot tomb?

12. As will become clear in these proceedings, E. Sukenik found in a storeroom an ossuary with the inscription "Jesus, son of Joseph." He reported that it was unprovenanced. This ossuary is now on display in the Israel Museum. I had permission to examine it carefully. See Sukenik, "Nochmals: Die Ossuarien in Palästina," *MGWJ* 75 (1931): 462-63; and Rahmani, *Catalogue,* no. 9 (on p. 77 and pl. 2). The name "Yeshua" appears in Rahmani's catalogued ossuaries in 9, 121, 140, 702 (Talpiot), perhaps 704 (the Talpiot tomb).

13. See the important discussion by Y. Elitzur in *Ancient Place Names in the Holy Land: Preservation and History* (Winona Lake, Ind.: Eisenbrauns, 2004), pp. 28-32.

16. What does the proximity of the Talpiot tomb to Caiaphas's tomb indicate, and is the tomb of Caiaphas accurately assessed?

17. How do we know that the ossuary of the high priest Caiaphas has been recovered?

18. Has the tomb of King Herod been located, and how do we know that for certain?

19. What do the crucified bones of Jehohanan/Yehoḥanan tell us about crucifixion and burial customs during the time of Jesus?[14]

20. Has the tomb of Annas the high priest been discovered, and what facts and observations lead to this conclusion?

21. Has the ossuary of Simon of Cyrene been recovered?

22. Is the "open tomb" a fiction invented by Jesus' followers? How can it be proof of Jesus' resurrection when Jesus' followers did not base their resurrection belief on the tomb being empty and when two interpretations of an empty tomb appear in the New Testament?[15]

23. Did Jesus' followers know the precise tomb in which Jesus' corpse had been placed?

24. What archaeological and textual evidence is there for locating Jesus' tomb?

25. Does Mark 16:1-8 mirror a pilgrimage to Jesus' tomb before 70 CE; that is, does "behold the place where they laid him" of Mark 16:6 imply that pilgrims from Galilee venerated the tomb of Jesus when they ascended Jerusalem to fulfill Torah and observe the mandatory festivals?

26. What role did Nicodemus and Joseph of Arimathea play? Are they narrative creations or real persons with functions created by rhetoric or kerygma?

27. Does not Paul refer to a physical body and a resurrected body in 1 Cor

14. See notably J. Zias and J. Charlesworth, "Crucifixion: Archaeology, Jesus, and the Dead Sea Scrolls," in *Jesus and the Dead Sea Scrolls*, ed. Charlesworth, ABRL (New York: Doubleday, 1992), pp. 273-89; M. Hengel, *Crucifixion* (Philadelphia: Fortress, 1989); J. Hewitt, "The Use of Nails in Crucifixion," *HTR* 25 (1932): 29-45; and Zias, "Crucifixion in Antiquity: The Evidence," http://www.centuryone.org/crucifixion2.html (1998). Also see his more recent "Crucifixion in Antiquity: The Anthropological Evidence," www.joezias.com/CrucifixionAntiquity.html [2007].

15. See now D. A. Smith, *Revisiting the Empty Tomb: The Early History of Easter* (Minneapolis: Fortress, 2010). I am not convinced that Mark preserves an early tradition that Jesus was not resurrected but was assumed into heaven. I also cannot separate early Jewish texts that represent or reflect afterlife beliefs into resurrection or assumption. I will have to be convinced that early Jews advocated such distinctions.

15? If so, does this perception imply that Jesus' postmortem body would have been a resurrected body different from a fleshy body?

28. If the resurrected Jesus had bones, how could he have passed through walls and a door as suggested by the author of John 20?

29. Why are Jews and Christians working together on these questions?

30. What discovery could falsify the belief held by most Christians and a few Jews that Jesus was raised from the dead by the Creator?

31. Would the discovery of the tomb of Jesus or the tomb of Jesus' clan add credence to confessional claims about Jesus, or would such a discovery be an embarrassment to Christians?[16]

Perhaps other specialists can add to these questions that are focused on Jewish burial customs and tombs, but they should suffice for setting the tone of this gathering; most likely, not all of the questions will be answered and some of them may be tangential to our present search for answers. What makes a symposium outstanding is not only the gathering of a group of distinguished specialists, who have mastered all the methodologies requisite for a lucid presentation of all pertinent data, but also their willingness and eagerness to explore and debate all issues with a shared respect and a focus on informed interrogatives. I have tried to supply 31 important interrogatives. Not all can be sufficiently discussed in a symposium or in its proceedings. These proceedings therefore not only present solid conclusions but also demarcate the way for further exploration.

16. Clearly, Jesus' family was involved in his movement. His brothers went with him from Nazareth to Capernaum (John 2) and his brother James became head of the Jerusalem "church" and was martyred in the 60s (perhaps in 62). For an attempt to clarify Jesus' clan, see J. Tabor, *The Jesus Dynasty: The Hidden History of Jesus, His Royal Family, and the Birth of Christianity* (New York: Simon & Schuster, 2006). For the conclusion that the early patristic reports (viz. by Hegesippus) about the burial of James are not to be assumed to be historical (and therefore have no bearing on the debates regarding the so-called James ossuary), see R. Bauckham, "Traditions about the Tomb of James, the Brother of Jesus," in *Poussières de christianisme et de judaïsme antiques: Études réunies en l'honneur de Jean-Daniel Kaestli et Éric Junod,* ed. A. Frey and R. Gounelle (Lausanne: Zèbre, 2007), pp. 61-77.

Facts about the Talpiot Tomb

In March 1980 a first-century tomb was exposed during construction work in a southeast section of modern Jerusalem, a district called Talpiot.[17]

This tomb seems to have once preserved the remains of perhaps thirty individuals;[18] eventually J. Gath, an archaeologist, removed ten stone ossuaries.[19]

Only three were intact (but the tomb was not professionally opened, and fragments of ossuaries were observed outside the tomb).[20]

It is conceivable that artifacts were robbed from the tomb before S. Gibson (then a fledgling archaeologist and surveyor) and other archaeologists arrived with a permit and were not, therefore, taken with what was found in the tomb to the IDAM headquarters in the Rockefeller Museum. The ossuaries were received by J. Zias, curator and forensic anthropologist at the Rockefeller, and soon examined by L. Y. Rahmani, chief curator of the Rockefeller storerooms.

The tomb was uncovered inadvertently by men operating heavy equipment; an explosion subsequently destroyed the tomb's external rock-cut courtyard and some of its roofed vestibule. Construction teams were preparing an area for the construction of apartment buildings on (what is now) Dov Gruner Street in East Talpiot, which is considerably south of the purported line of Jerusalem's first-century walls. It is imperative to keep in mind that the archaeologists did not open the tomb, that the tomb lay open during

17. This section of my paper is completely reworked in light of the discussions, the proceedings, and most notably the definitive report by A. Kloner and S. Gibson found in this work: "The Talpiot Tomb Reconsidered: The Archaeological Facts." One needs to recall that Gibson was a young archaeologist who helped to excavate what had been left in the tomb and Kloner was the Jerusalem district archaeologist when the tomb was discovered and a salvage operation was organized.

18. As Kloner and Gibson point out in their chapter in the present work, claiming that the remains of 35 individuals were discovered in the tomb is mere guesswork.

19. Gath died before he could publish an official report. See Kloner and Gibson in the present work, and nn. 11 and 12 above.

20. See the report of Gibson, an archaeologist who saw the tomb after it was exposed, in *NEA* 69 (2006): 118-19. Kloner concluded that the extant shards, found in situ, enable one to date the burial cave "from the end of the first century CE or the beginning of the first century CE, until approximately 70 CE." See Kloner, "A Tomb with Inscribed Ossuaries in East Talpiyot, Jerusalem," *'Atiqot* 29 (1996): 21. The tomb complex may have represented 35 interments; see ibid., 22 n. 2. Also see the definitive publication of the excavation by Kloner and Gibson, "The Talpiot Tomb Reconsidered: The Archaeological Facts," in the present work.

Shabbat, and that the time was one in which many archaeological discoveries, including ossuaries, were pouring into the Rockefeller Museum.[21]

Any discussion of the Talpiot tomb should consider the way the tomb was exposed and the hurried time frame: Shabbat was approaching. The work was simply *a salvage operation.*[22]

Most likely, persons (probably robbers) entered the tomb in antiquity; moreover, Gath's incomplete notes left Kloner and Gibson frustrated. In summation, too much vital information about this Talpiot tomb that is necessary for sustained intense discussion was forever lost.

The archaeologists who first examined the tomb considered it to be rather ordinary. Scientists and archaeologists now conclude that the tomb had bone boxes (ossuaries)[23] with these names:[24]

1, 2 *Yeshua'* (?) *bar Yehoseph*[25] (Aramaic = "Jesus, son of Joseph"). These two names are among the most popular in pre-70 Judaism. [IAA no. 80-503; Kloner no. 4. Rahmani no. 704. Plain]

   3 *Marya* (Aramaic; perhaps "Mary"). The name is common. [IAA no. 80-505. Kloner no. 6. Rahmani no. 706. Plain]

   4 *Matya* as well as *Mata* (in different hands; Aramaic). Both forms are contractions of "Matityahu" or "Matthew." The name "Matthan" appears in Matt 1:15; see also Jesus' genealogy in Luke 3, which includes

---

21. I can vouch for this chaotic time, as I was in the Rockefeller often to study the fragments of the Dead Sea Scrolls and to work with Joe Zias.

22. See Kloner, "Tomb with Inscribed Ossuaries," pp. 15-22. Work on the Akeldama tombs was also a salvage excavation that faced similar problems of security and technical limitations. In distinction to the Talpiot tomb, however, the Akeldama tombs showed foreign influence. Note the evidence of Parthian ware and the foreign-origins ore connections of families (like the Eros family and the Ariston family). See G. Avni and Z. Greenhut, *The Akeldama Tombs* (Jerusalem: Israel Antiquities Authority, 1996).

23. The technical term *ossilegium* (ליקוט עצמות) denotes the act of gathering the disarticulated bones of the deceased into a box, usually of stone.

24. Since the inscriptions and how they should be transcribed has caused a notorious debate, I tend to follow the transcription of my colleague S. Gibson. See Gibson, "Is the Talpiot Tomb Really the Family Tomb of Jesus?" *NEA* 69 (2006): 123; this study reappears in the present work. Also, see S. Pfann's careful research in the present work ("Demythologyzing the Talpiot Tomb: The Tomb of Another Jesus, Mary, and Joseph"). One should not overlook the superb earlier research, notably Kloner, "Tomb with Inscribed Ossuaries."

25. The Hebrew/Aramaic is transliterated in a nontechnical way so those who do not know Hebrew can follow the discussion.

successively from Joseph to Adam: Matthat, Mattathias, Maath, Mattathias, Matthat, and Mattatha. "Matya" is a well-known name. [IAA no. 80-502. Kloner no. 3. Rahmani no. 703. Plain]

5 *Yoseh* (probably Aramaic). This noun seems to be a diminutive form of *Yehoseph*, "Joseph." According to the Greek of Mark 6:3, one of Jesus' brothers is "Joses." In Matt 13:55 this name appears as "Joseph." [IAA no. 80-504. Kloner no. 5. Rahmani no. 705. Plain]

6 *Mariamnē kai Mara* (Greek; probably not *Mariamēnou Mara*). Is this reading accurate, and is the last word a contraction of "Martha"? Are one or two names intended, and if so why? Why would someone imagine that the name could be related to Mary Magdalene? [IAA no. 80-500. Kloner no. 1. Rahmani no. 701. Ornamented]

7 *Yehudah bar Yeshua'* (Aramaic = "Judah, son of Jesus"). Yehudah was a very popular name in pre-70 Palestinian Judaism. [IAA no. 80-501. Kloner no. 2. Rahmani no. 702. Ornamented]

Many of these names are "Hasmonean": Matthew, Judas, and Joseph (cf. 2 Macc 8:22). Is that significant, and if so, why?

While these names were popular in first-century Judaism,[26] the name *Yoseh* seems exceptional, even though it is a contraction of *Yehoseph* or *Yoseph* (Joseph), which was one of the most popular names in early Judaism. Mark reported that one of Jesus' brothers was called *Iōsētos* (Mark 6:3). Does this Greek name represent *Yoseh?*

The sheer number of names that are related directly or indirectly to Jesus — and the absence of "Simon," "Eleazar," and similar names that were very popular in first-century Judaism — arouses this intriguing question: Could the Talpiot tomb be the tomb of Jesus' clan or of some of his followers? I think the cluster of names indicates this possibility should be considered and discussed. Surely, those who violently resist such exploratory thinking reveal less than scientific curiosity.

One ossuary in the Talpiot tomb was catalogued but eventually misplaced (it is IAA no. 80-509 and Kloner no. 10).[27] Some specialists claim that

26. See T. Ilan, *Lexicon of Jewish Names in Late Antiquity*, part 1, *Palestine 330 BCE–200 CE*, TSAJ 91 (Tübingen: Mohr Siebeck, 2002).

27. See Kloner and Gibson's judicious reflections in the present work. Rahmani did not include it in his *Catalogue* but did note it on p. 222 (italics mine): "The Department retained nine ossuaries (Nos. 701-709) recovered from a double-chambered *loculi* and *arcosolia* tomb in 1980; *a plain, broken specimen was also found.* Thanks are due to the late J. Gath, the excavator, for granting permission to publish these ossuaries." This ossuary,

it could be the controversial ossuary that is called "the James ossuary." Here is that inscription:

8 *Ya'aqob bar Yoseph 'aḥui d'Yeshua'* (Aramaic = "James, son of Joseph, brother of Jesus" [or possibly "James, son of Joseph, [who is] the brother of Jesus").[28] [Not in IAA inventory]

Is the full inscription ancient; is any part of it ancient?[29] What is the provenience of this ossuary? Is there any convincing evidence that it was part of the assemblage in the Talpiot tomb? Could it be the ossuary that was not catalogued by the IAA? How could it be the "lost" ossuary when according to the IAA catalogue it was uninscribed? I must confess dubiety with the claim that patina can reveal provenience; and the patina of this ossuary, to some, proves the inscription is not ancient; and to others, it might suggest it was from the Talpiot tomb. Surely, we come together to discuss all these issues.

Is *'aḥui d'Yeshua'* ("and brother of Jesus") a modern addition or part of the original inscription, and do we know that as a fact from the presence of patina, the absence of patina, or a shift in paleography (the study of ancient handwriting) and morphology (the form of consonants)? And does *'aḥui d'Yeshua'* refer to "James" or "Joseph"? If the inscription means that James is the son of Joseph and the latter is the brother of Jesus, then the alleged links to Jesus' family and father dissipate. Joseph Fitzmyer shares his reflections on this option in the present work.

Historical and Theological Questions

Would Jesus have been buried in Nazareth? I was told by some Israeli archaeologists that Jesus must have been buried in the family plot in Nazareth.

---

plain and broken, cannot be the so-called James ossuary, since it is plain; that is, it is uninscribed and cannot thus bear the name "James," unless that name was subsequently added. Kloner and Gibson also point out, in the present work, that the "James ossuary" is complete with a rosette decoration. They speculate that the tenth ossuary "may simply have been thrown away owing to a lack of storage space or it may have lost its labeling." See their definitive work and speculations in the following pages.

28. The scholarly transcription is *Ya'ăqôb bar Yôsēp 'aḥûî děYēšûa'*.

29. See J. A. Fitzmyer's research published in the present work. One should take all that Prof. Fitzmyer reports with deep respect. He is one of the finest Aramaic scholars and specialists on the NT, esp. Luke-Acts, in the world.

They reason that Jesus belongs to Nazareth, since he was known as Jesus of Nazareth. This misunderstanding needs to be corrected. No one who knows the New Testament traditions and the early reliable oral traditions preserved in these writings could imagine that Jesus was buried in Nazareth. Jesus of Nazareth is from Nazareth, but that does not indicate where he was buried. Likewise, Paul was from Tarsus; but he was not buried in Tarsus.

First, the evangelists do not clarify the precise location of Jesus' tomb. One cannot even estimate the tomb's distance from the site of the crucifixion (or Golgotha). Only the author of John adds to the tradition that Jesus' tomb was in a garden near Golgotha; but that scarcely limits and defines the location of Jesus' tomb. Yet all the reports in the New Testament that indicate the place of Jesus' burial or tomb are coherent. They all agree that Jesus' tomb was not in Nazareth; it was outside the walls of Jerusalem.

Second, the phrase "Jesus of Nazareth" is a not a possessive genitive; that is, Jesus is not defined by Nazareth. The noun is a genitive of origin. That is, the genitive "of Nazareth" indicates the origin of Jesus. According to Luke, Jesus was cast out of Nazareth (Luke 4). According to a tradition preserved in John, Jesus' credentials are false since he originates from Nazareth: "Can anything good come out of Nazareth?" (John 1:46). According to both Mathew (4:13) and John (2:12), Jesus leaves the area of Nazareth and begins to live in Capernaum. The genitive of origin is crystal clear in the expression "Jesus from Nazareth," which appears in Mark 1:9 and Matt 21:11. Thus the evangelists are consistent. They report that Jesus is from Nazareth; Jesus left that city. The genitive of origin and the preposition "from" indicate that Jesus would not have been buried in Nazareth. Indeed, all the evangelists state that Jesus was buried somewhere outside Jerusalem.

Could the ossuary of Jesus have been found? In seeking to discern answers to this question it is imperative to keep in focus that an ossuary contained the bones of one who had died, was interred, and whose flesh had decayed. That process took about one year. The rabbinic tractate *Semaḥot* helps us grasp the cultural significance of secondary burial in an ossuary: "Rabbi Eleazar bar Zadok said: 'Thus spoke my father at the time of his death: "My son, bury me at first in a fosse. In the course of time, collect my bones and put them in an ossuary [*gĕlôsqomāʾ*]"'" (12:9, ed. Zlotnick).[30]

---

30. I am indebted to both E. L. Sukenik and M. Aviam with D. Syon for this reference. Sukenik published the first ossuary found near Jerusalem; see his "A Jewish Burial Cave Northwest of Jerusalem" [in Hebrew], *Tarbiz* 12 (1930): 122-24. Also see Aviam and Syon, "Jewish Ossilegium in Galilee," p. 153.

Perhaps that is conceivable, but not all logical options are to be considered conceivable. The letters of the name *Yeshuaʿ* are unclear; if I were publishing this inscription, I would indicate that each letter in the name is uncertain. They look like "a chicken has written them."[31] The name of a "Jesus" may be present on the ossuary; and one should resist the temptation to argue that the appearance of the same name on ossuary 4 helps decipher this name.

Some gifted thinkers have claimed that a poor ossuary of Jesus from Nazareth was chosen by his Palestinian Jewish followers to symbolize his poverty and humbleness. Indeed, this Christology is found in Paul's Philippians and in liturgies that both antedate Paul and most likely stem from the early Palestinian Jesus movement. These early Jews celebrated that Christ Jesus had "emptied himself, taking the form of a servant," and had "humbled himself" (Phil 2:7-8). But if Jesus' bones had been placed in an ossuary, it would have been about a year later. And by then his followers were claiming him to be someone very special. A poor ossuary is not coherent with such high adulation, and the hymn excerpted by Paul in Philippians concludes by saluting Jesus' name as so honorific that it is above all names, so at the name of "Jesus" all knees are to bow.

For centuries, critics assumed that Jesus' bones could not have been placed in an ossuary. They argue that since he was crucified his corpse was probably cast into a mass grave (perhaps in the Hinnom Valley). Any argument that the bones of a crucified man could not have been placed in an ossuary is now fallacious. This long-held claim is now dismissed by the discovery of an ossuary with the remains of Yehoḥanan, who had been crucified about the time of Jesus and near Jerusalem. Quite surprisingly, olive wood is still attached, and the "nail" that anchored him to a cross remains embedded in his heel.[32]

While none of us should ever claim certainty about a debatable issue, each of us should share some thoughts for discussion as we collectively seek to improve our perception and reconstruction of pre-70 Palestinian Judaism. In terms of the issues churned up by the arguments over the Talpiot tomb, perhaps we need to better approximate the mind-set of Jesus' followers after

---

31. I am quoting from the third-century BCE play by Plautus (*Pseudolus* 1.25-30). See the excellent discussion of cursive scripts by R. W. Mathisen in *The Oxford Handbook of Early Christian Studies,* ed. S. A. Harvey and D. G. Hunter (2008; repr. Oxford: Oxford University Press, 2010), p. 151.

32. See Zias and Charlesworth, "Crucifixion," pp. 273-89.

the crucifixion and the interval — perhaps almost a year — demanded for the bones to be disarticulated and placed in an ossuary. By this time (about one year after Jesus' crucifixion), many of his followers were claiming that the resurrected Jesus had appeared to Mary Magdalene, Peter, and other followers, including Thomas. Would they have found Jesus' remains? Would they have placed his bones in an ossuary? If Jesus was resurrected by the Living God, was anything left to bury? What happened to Jesus' bones? Are they somewhere in heaven, as some fundamentalists have told me?

On the one hand, I must confess that I do not know the answers to such questions, and have organized this symposium to learn what answers might be most likely. On the other hand, I cannot comprehend how any believer in Jesus' resurrection by God can claim that there must be a toilet in heaven, since Luke reported that Jesus, after the resurrection, ate a fish; or contend that God had to have taken all of the fleshy Jesus from the tomb.

To reiterate my own position: I find it difficult to imagine that Jesus' followers, who held him in the highest esteem, would about one year after his death have placed his bones in a very poor ossuary and with scribbled letters. Surely the alleged name of "Jesus" on the ossuary appears more like graffiti than a typical inscription.[33]

And by the time Jesus' bones could have been ready for secondary burial, some of his followers acknowledge that "at *the name of Jesus* every knee should bow" (the pre-Pauline hymn found in Phil 2; cf. 2:9 [my italics]).

Why would some of Jesus' followers go to his tomb on the third day? Among the reasons that can be brought forth for discussion is the need to be certain the person is dead. Note the baraita in the rabbinic tractate *Semaḥot* 8:1: "One should go to the cemetery to check the dead within three days, and not fear that such smacks of pagan practices. There was actually one buried man who was visited after three days and lived for twenty-five more years and had sons, and died afterward."[34]

Who is the "Joseph" on the Talpiot ossuary whose name appears as "Jesus, the son of Joseph"? Only one of many possibilities is "Joseph" the father of Jesus from Nazareth. According to the Evangelist Matthew, one of Jesus' broth-

---

33. See Mur 42, "Letter from the Administration of Bet-Mašiko to Yeshua (Jesus) the Son of Galgula." See P. Benoit et al., *Les Grottes de Murabba'ât,* 2 vols., DJD 2 (Oxford: Clarendon, 1961), 1:156-57 (text) and vol. 2, pl. XLV.

34. I am grateful to A. Kloner for this citation and discussions of it. See Kloner, "Reconstruction of the Tomb in the Rotunda of the Holy Sepulchre According to Archaeological Finds and Jewish Burial Customs of the First Century CE," in *The Beginnings of Christianity,* ed. J. Pastor and M. Mor (Jerusalem: Yad Ben-Zvi Press, 2005), pp. 269-78.

ers is named "Joseph" (Ἰωσήφ [var. Ιωσης and Ιωαννης]; Matt 13:55). As should be well known, "Joseph" is a well attested name in pre-70 Judaism. For example, a letter found in a cave in Murabbaʿat mentions a "Joseph" five times, including "Joseph, the son of Joseph (יהוסף בר יהוסף)." Each time it is the form *Yehoseph* (יהוסף),[35] which is a poetic form in the Hebrew Bible but is also the form that appears in papyrological and lapidary scripts.[36] Given Jewish customs, we should expect that this Joseph had sons. One of his sons could well have been named "Jesus," because of the prominence of "Jesus from Nazareth" and the popularity of the name Jesus at that time.[37] For example, note that a letter found in a cave in Murabbaʿat was "from Jesus" (מן ישוע) "to Jesus" (לישוע).[38]

This suggestion is not mere unfounded speculation if 35 people had been placed in the Talpiot tomb. Is it not conceivable, perhaps probable in light of ancient prosopography,[39] that a Joseph was one of the numerous unnamed persons placed in the Talpiot tomb? If this tomb is related in any way to Jesus from Nazareth, then it might have been attractive before 70 CE for a Joseph to name his son after the popular Galilean. Thus "Jesus, son of Joseph," would not be the famous "Jesus from Nazareth." This scenario is conceivable, and one must not spring from "Jesus, son of Joseph," to Jesus from Nazareth. Virtually all attending the symposium would fully agree, but that does not preclude careful examination of all data and reflection.

Did this ossuary preserve the bones of Jesus from Nazareth? If so, in addition to what has been indicated, I would find it odd in contrast to other ossuaries (viz. nos. 1 and 2). One should keep in mind that the name "Jesus" is not obvious; it is a scholarly conjecture.

35. This form appears in the Hebrew Bible only in Ps 81:6 (Eng. 5). I was surprised to find it in the so-called *Genesis Apocryphon* found on Masada (see my forthcoming edition). It is also found on the Talpiot tomb that contains the inscription: "Jesus [?], son of Joseph [*YHWSP*]."

36. See Ilan, *Lexicon*, pp. 152-57, nos. 86-227 (sometimes without the *waw* and sometimes with the *pe* in medial form though in final position).

37. See Ilan, *Lexicon*, pp. 126-29; she lists 103 occurrences. The name "Jesus" in Greek and Hebrew characters appears on many ossuaries and is the name of priests, even a high priest (see Josephus, *War* 6.114; *Ant.* 12.237; 15.322; 17.341; *Life* 193).

38. See Benoit et al., *Grottes de Murabbaʿât*, 1:156 and vol. 2, pl. XLV.

39. The *Oxford English Dictionary*, 2nd ed. (1989) supplies two meanings of this word. I use it in the second sense; that is, to denote a study of individuals in history, including all relations whether familiar or political. See the discussion by T. D. Barnes in *Early Christian Hagiography and Roman History*, Tria Corda 5 (Tübingen: Mohr Siebeck, 2010), p. vii.

A similar question confronts ossuary 6. If it contained the bones of Mary, Jesus' mother, why is it also without ornamentation? Is it not certain that she would have received more honor than indicated by a common ossuary? She was clearly early revered within the Palestinian Jesus movement, especially in light of her prominence in the early group of believers in Jerusalem. Note Acts 1:14, "All these with one accord devoted themselves to prayer, together with the women and Mary the mother of Jesus, and with his brothers." Does Acts 1:14 represent reliable historical memories or is it creative narrative? These are two mutually exclusive options. Which is more likely and how do we make such judgments? In any case, there is no doubt Jesus' mother was highly honored before 70 CE; that is the period during which the concept of the Virgin Birth would have begun to develop, since shortly after it appears in Matthew, Luke, and the *Odes of Solomon.*

Two possible caveats seem wise as we ponder these ossuaries and what they may inform us of. On the ossuaries, "Jesus" is not identified as "Jesus from Nazareth," and Mara and "Mary" are not related to Magdala (if the inscription is linked to Mary Magdalene). This observation needs to be evaluated in the light of the fact that ossuaries do not usually contain geographical specifications.

Emotional Presuppositions That Undermine Research

Now our reflections shift to the too emotional matters of theological presuppositions and claims. On the one hand, it would be wise not to venture into the quicksand of resurrection faith and the blind opposition to it, by Jews and Christians. It is easy to offend many, including Christian fundamentalists and secular archaeologists (both Jews and Christians). On the other hand, one should not shy away from explosively charged areas of our common work. Let us now ponder how agnosticism as well as resurrection confessionalism cause distortions in interpretations. This inclusion of theology is demanded because theological presuppositions — by atheists, agnostics, and Christian dogmatists — have undermined critical historical research and questioning.

If Jesus' ossuary has been found, does that shatter or hinder Christian faith? Some conservative Christians will say yes. While all Christians, by creed and confession, believe that Jesus was "bodily" resurrected by God, some Christians assume that Jesus was resurrected with all his flesh and bones. Some Christians contend that Jesus is now in heaven with his bones and the marks of crucifixion; I have been told this by esteemed theologians at Princeton. Faith statements, as all should recognize, should not be creatively individualistic; they should be grounded in a confessional community that is informed and shaped by the earliest witnesses. All these, despite claims to the contrary, are preserved in what is now labeled "the New Testament." We may now rephrase and focus our question, in the attempt to avoid personal bias or uninformed or unexamined presuppositions.

What was the composition of Jesus' resurrection body, according to those who composed documents preserved in the New Testament? Only three New Testament authors supply definitive answers: the Evangelist Luke, the Evangelist John, and the Apostle Paul. The Fourth Evangelist claims to be an eyewitness (or his Gospel is the edited work of an eyewitness). Luke and Paul contend their report is based on eyewitness accounts. Paul also claims a resurrection appearance by Jesus.

The Evangelist Luke. Let us begin with Luke. Who was he? Many New Testament scholars today follow the ancient report that the author of Luke and Acts was a companion of Paul; others dispute the historical accuracy of the report and point out how it served the emerging church. Luke and Acts (written by the same author) are where conservative Christians (and fundamentalists) would focus our attention. They have scriptural texts that help them in their thoughts; note especially Luke 24. According to this text, when the resurrected Jesus stood among the disciples, they thought he was "a spirit." What was the composition of Jesus' resurrected body? It becomes clear: "See my hands and feet, that it is I myself. Touch me and see; for a spirit has not flesh and bones as you see that I have" (ἴδετε τὰς χεῖράς μου καὶ τοὺς πόδας μου ὅτι ἐγώ εἰμι αὐτόςz ψηλαφήσατέ με καὶ ἴδετε, ὅτι πνεῦμα σάρκα καὶ ὀστέα οὐκ ἔχει καθὼς ἐμὲ θεωρεῖτε ἔχοντα; Luke 24:39). According to this verse, Jesus' resurrected body has flesh (σάρκα) and bones (ὀστέα).

Luke 24:39 evokes two paradigmatically distinct interpretations. Some Christians (informed as well as fundamentalist) believe this passage suffices and one does not need any other textual evidence. Luke reported accurately: Jesus' resurrected body was "flesh and bones." They would add that according to Luke, Jesus, after his resurrection, ate a "broiled fish" (Luke 24:41-43). They could all add that Razis threw parts of his body at his enemies, claiming he would receive them back in the resurrection (2 Macc 14:37-46). They would ask us to note 2 Macc 14:46: "with his blood now completely drained from him, he tore out his entrails, took them in both hands and hurled them at the crowd, calling upon the Lord of life and spirit to give them back to him again. This was the manner of his death" (NRSV). Some Christians would ask us to remember Ezekiel's valley of dry bones and resurrection beliefs in Second Temple Judaism.

Other Christians contend that Luke intended to prove that Jesus' resurrected body was not "a spirit" (ὅτι πνεῦμα). Luke indicates that he was not an eyewitness (see Luke 1:1-4) and may have endeavored to make one point in 24:39: Jesus was not an apparition or a ghost. The disciples were wrong again; Jesus was not a "spirit." Perhaps Luke sought to correct reflections by non-Jews and those who were shaping myths about Jesus. Likely Luke misrepresented himself when he added additional words to prove that point. Luke elsewhere reports that Paul's experience of the resurrected Jesus was by way of a light and a sound (Acts 9:1-9). They would insist that one should not interpret the resurrection appearances of Jesus only according to Luke. Luke 24:39 must not be isolated and allowed to dominate reflections on the nature of Jesus' resurrected body.

In seeking honest and trustworthy answers to a focused question, scholars know that all pertinent data must be included and that all relevant methods must be judiciously employed. Thus we must examine all texts that report Jesus' resurrected appearances. These may lead to another perspective.

According to a widespread exegesis of these texts, Jesus was not resuscitated, like Lazarus (John 13). He was raised by the Creator with an imperishable spiritual body. The two most important witnesses are John and Paul.

The Evangelist John. According to the Evangelist John, those who saw the resurrected Jesus reported that he walked through walls or doors. That implies that Jesus' resurrected body did not have flesh or bones. Note these excerpts from the Gospel of John:

> On the evening of that day, the first day of the week, the doors being shut where the disciples were, for fear of the Judean leaders, Jesus came and stood among them and said to them: "Peace be with you." When he had said this, he showed them his hands and his side. Then the disciples were pleased when they saw the Lord. (20:19-20)

> Eight days later, his disciples were again in the house, and Thomas was with them. The doors were shut, but Jesus came and stood among them, and said: "Peace be with you." Then he said to Thomas: "Put your finger here, and see my hands; and put out your hand, and place it in my side; do not be faithless, but believing." Thomas answered him: "My Lord and my God." (20:26-28)

Twice the Evangelist John states that the resurrected Jesus could pass through doors or walls. Thus he frames conceptions of what is meant by seeing Jesus' hands and side. No bones are mentioned; no flesh seems to be present. The body is one that is spiritual, yet identifiable as that of Jesus from Nazareth. At this point I am reminded of the pervasive ancient Jewish tradition that the righteous shall arise and become stars. Such celestial bodies do not have flesh and bones.

Now that we have looked at the Gospel of John, it seems prudent to ask again about Luke. Is a similar perception evident in some other passages in Luke? Yes; the Evangelist Luke states that after the resurrected Jesus reveals himself to Cleopas in his home, he vanishes from sight: "And their eyes were opened and they recognized him; and he vanished out of their sight" (24:31). Some exegetes would point out that bones and flesh do not normally vanish from sight.

Also according to Luke, the resurrected Jesus takes his disciples to Bethany, which is east of the walled city of Jerusalem. Note what is reported: "And lifting up his hands he blessed them. While he blessed them, he parted from them, and was carried up into heaven" (24:50-51). Bones and flesh do not float into thin air; the exegetes who plead for us to imagine a fleshly Jesus rising into the sky may be guilty of special pleading or missing other possibilities for exegesis and hermeneutics. According to these passages in the Gospels of John and Luke, we are urged to contemplate a resurrected body that is similar to but not identical with the fleshly body.

If these accounts in John and Luke are trustworthy, the resurrected Jesus has a body. Most of us wish to ask: What kind of resurrected body is imagined or reported?

According to the earliest reports by Jews, the resurrected Jesus is not at first recognizable to Mary Magdalene (John 20) and Cleopas (Luke 24). Only later, and not gradually but instantaneously, Mary and Cleopas perceive that the one before them and with them is Jesus from Nazareth. The implication is given that this man is human but a stranger; then, with a word (John) or a gesture (Luke) the supposed stranger reveals himself as Jesus. There is some difference and yet some continuity between the appearance of the resurrected Jesus and the precrucifixion Jesus.

In face of these reports, would it not be wise to resist rushing to claim that Jesus' body after the resurrection must have had flesh and bones? Perhaps Paul can supply some reflections worth pondering.

The Apostle Paul. In 1 Cor 15 Paul contends that God raised Jesus from the dead. He adds: "If Christ has not been raised, your faith is futile" (15:17).

He continues by pondering; "How are the dead raised?" He claims that there are "heavenly bodies and earthly bodies" (15:40); that is, the perspicacious person knows to contemplate not only "a physical body" but also "a spiritual body" (15:44). Many exegetes conclude, rightly in my perception, that Paul intends to stress that the dead once had "a physical body" and are raised with "a spiritual body" (σπείρεται σῶμα ψυχικόν, ἐγείρεται σῶμα πνευματικόν. Εἰ ἔστιν σῶμα ψυχικόν, ἔστιν καὶ πνευματικόν; 15:44).

Did not Paul emphasize that all who believe in Jesus "will be changed"? Did not Paul believe: "For this perishable body must put on imperishability, and this mortal body must put on immortality" (15:53)? Did not Paul contrast Adam, "the man of dust," with Jesus, "the man of heaven" (15:48)? Did not Paul imagine that as those who believe in Jesus "have borne the image of the man of dust," they "will also bear the image of the man of heaven" (15:49)? While one must focus only on Paul, one should include his reflections. Paul's thoughts focused on the resurrected body are apparently harmonious with what the Evangelist John, and sometimes Luke, tell us about the body of the resurrected Jesus.

Do archaeological discoveries hinder authentic Christian faith? According to most archaeologists and theologians, archaeological discoveries ground belief in the reality of a life lived in Second Temple Judaism. If the tomb of Jesus' clan has been recovered at Talpiot, then the incarnation becomes more real for those who doubt Jesus ever existed. These archaeological discoveries help us ponder how Jesus was human like each of us.

What relevance does archaeology have for faith? Archaeologists can recover data that become foundational in imagining and reconstructing the past. Archaeological research can clarify what seems unlikely not only historically but also theologically; but archaeology is not the handmaiden of biblical research and study. Archaeology and theology are two distinct and separate means the human employs to obtain answers; and the questions raised are often unrelated. What we have found in the ground are not "time capsules" left by those who lived long ago for us to comprehend. Excavations of archaeological sites in "the Holy Land" (*Eretz Israel* in Mishnah and Talmudim)[40] are not to be related too quickly, and perhaps not at all, with texts selected and heavily edited that preserve some of the mythologically shaped celebrations, or recitals, of God's activity on earth by those who lived in Eretz Israel.

40. See the very informative work published by Y. Tsafrir with L. Di Segni and J. Green, *Tabula Imperii Romani: IudaeazPalaestina* (Jerusalem: Israel Academy of Sciences and Humanities, 1994).

In my opinion, archaeology cannot form faith. It may, however, serve to *inform* faith.[41] My own faith is enlightened and deepened by the discoveries discussed in the following work. I am convinced that no one can prove that the Talpiot tomb belonged to Jesus' extended family. With others, I have learned that faith should be living and challenged; it should not be blind allegiance.

Jewish thought and Christian theology, as well as the relation between Jews and Christians today, may be deepened as Jews and Christians convene to discuss Jewish tombs near Jerusalem prior to 70 CE.[42] Living in an open universe with black holes and recognizing that the string theory seems impoverished, we may draw closer to those who lived here in Jerusalem before 70 CE and believed in a cosmos with "laws" known only to the Creator. Some of those Jews claimed to have experienced something astonishingly unexpected, yet believed to be a future possibility by many types of Jews.[43] We can better approximate such faith or belief by studying the tombs, ossuaries,[44] and burial means they left for us to study together.[45]

41. See Charlesworth with W. P. Weaver, eds., *What Has Archaeology to Do with Faith?* (Philadelphia: Trinity Press International, 1992).

42. See Hachlili, *Jewish Funerary Customs.* The heated debates during the symposium, especially when I left to help Geza Vermes, were between Jews. Even when I was present, I observed deep respect by Jews of Christians, and by Christians of Jews, but far too often polemical barbs from some Jews to another Jew or Jews. I can understand such hatred only in terms of fears based on perceptions of another's motives. For example, see Zias, "Deliberate Misrepresentation?" in *Biblical Archaeology Review* newsletter; available at www.bib-arch.org/tomb/bswbTombZias.asp. of 1/25/2008.

43. For general data and perspectives on resurrection and archaeological work related to Jesus, see J. H. Charlesworth et al., *Resurrection: The Origin and Future of a Biblical Doctrine* (London: T&T Clark, 2006); Charlesworth, ed., *Jesus and Archaeology* (Grand Rapids: Eerdmans, 2006).

44. Ossuaries do not indicate a belief in some form of resurrection. A study of Annas's and Caiaphas's tombs indicates that Sadducees probably put disarticulated bones into ossuaries and Sadducees did not believe in any resurrection. Moreover, some ossuaries have the remains of over ten persons and not all bones were gathered together. Surely, no mature Jew would believe putting bones in ossuaries was necessary to help God raise the dead. Resurrection belief is clear only in texts, like a few Dead Sea Scrolls, the Apocrypha, the Pseudepigrapha, the NT, and in liturgy (like the Amidah). Obviously, I thus disagree with Rahmani, who concludes: "The concept of *ossilegium* was apparently based on the ideas of personal and individual physical resurrection propagated by the Ḥassidim in the second century BCE" (*Catalogue,* p. 53). Also see Rahmani, "Ancient Jerusalem's Funerary Customs and Tombs," *BA* 44 (1981): 171-77, 229-35; 45 (1982): 43-53, 109-19.

45. Of special importance is S. Gibson, *The Final Days of Jesus: The Archaeological*

Scholars devoted to biblical research obviously must not allow a philosophy or theological position to dictate dogmatic conclusions that masquerade as scholarship. Over the past two hundred years, at least, scholars have developed a scientific methodology for studying the Bible, its complex traditions and historical contexts, and the continuing editing of remembered events and sacred traditions. To nurture young students who yearn to become scholars takes as many years and skill as to train a neurosurgeon. Established biblical scholars thus have a right to become upset when their advanced research, supported by peer reviews and debates cultured in symposia like the present one, is confused with the unhistorical nonsense that made so popular Kazantzakis's *Last Temptation of Christ* and Dan Brown's *Da Vinci Code*.

Postscript

The symposium was a major success because it brought together more disciplines and methodologies than any other international symposium and advanced significantly our interpretations of the facts regarding many ancient Jewish burials and tombs, including the Talpiot tomb. This tomb provides primary data for understanding Jewish burials before 70 (and during the time of Jesus from Nazareth); but one must emphasize that its interpretation must be informed by the study of other pre-70 tombs, such as the "Herod family tomb" in the Hinnom Valley, the Tomb of the Kings near the American Colony, the tombs in the Kidron Valley, the "Shroud Tomb" in the Hinnom Valley, Jason's Tomb (far west of Jerusalem's walls), Nicanor's Tomb, Annas's Tomb, Caiaphas's tomb,[46] as well as the excavations elsewhere, including Galilee.[47] The study of Jesus from Nazareth must be pur-

---

Evidence (New York: HarperOne, 2009). Clearly, what is shown as the "so-called Tomb of Joseph of Arimathea" (between pp. 144 and 145) is a first-century Jewish tomb; it is near where Jesus was most likely buried. In my judgment, the tomb of Herod's family in the Hinnom Valley is much more like the descriptions of Jesus' tomb in the Gospels than the Talpiot tomb.

46. Notably, see Z. Greenhut, "The 'Caiaphas' Tomb in North Talpiyot, Jerusalem" [in Hebrew], *'Atiqot* 21 (1992): 63-72; idem, "Where the High Priest Caiaphas Was Buried," in *Where Christianity Was Born,* ed. H. Shanks (Washington, D.C.: Biblical Archaeology Society, 2006), pp. 146-55.

47. *NEA* 65/2 (2002) was devoted to "The Archaeology of Death." See esp. A. M. Berlin, "Power and Its Afterlife: Tombs in Hellenistic Palestine," pp. 138-48.

sued within Judaism and not in isolation from the study of Jews contemporaneous with him.[48]

We are learning a lot about tomb architecture and burial customs, and at times improving our perception of Jewish beliefs of life and the afterlife. We have advanced significantly in understanding how archaeological discoveries can be related, if at all, to pre-70 texts now collected into categories, including the Jewish apocryphal works and the Dead Sea Scrolls (defined broadly).

I personally continue to have serious doubts about many claims. In my judgment, Jesus' tomb has not been found anywhere.[49] I have always concluded it was located not far from "Golgotha" within the Church of the Holy Sepulchre and was smashed to pieces during the Persian conquest of 614 (Antiochus Strategos).[50] The discussions during the symposium helped me to appreciate more fully that Jesus' burial, according to the Gospels, was hasty and temporary. We have no historical information that will guide us in contemplating what happened to Jesus' bones. Some Christians believe they are in heaven; some professors imagine they were thrown into a pit for executed thieves. Many of those in attendance at the symposium would judge both statements to be speculative and subjective pronouncements.

No official consensus was brought to a vote in the concluding sessions of the symposium. Nevertheless, I could observe a consensus. As I was quoted in many places after the symposium: "There was broad consensus among the vast majority of scholars in attendance, as Professor Charlesworth, the chairperson and chief organizer of the symposium, pointedly ob-

---

48. This was my thesis in *Jesus Within Judaism: New Light from Exciting Archaeological Discoveries,* ABRL (New York: Doubleday, 1988).

49. J. Tabor wisely warns against "an out of hand dismissal of the tomb as possibly, or even likely, associated with Jesus of Nazareth" ("Testing a Hypothesis," *NEA* 69 [2006]: 135). Note Tabor's judgment: "I find it striking that five of the six inscriptions correspond so closely to a hypothetical pre-70 CE family tomb of Jesus in Jerusalem as we might imagine it based on textual evidence" (ibid.).

50. See F. C. Conybeare, "Antiochus Strategos: The Capture of Jerusalem by the Persians in 614 AD," *English Historical Review* 25 (1910): 502-17. The text is available on the Web (thanks to R. Pearse of Ipswich, 25 October 2002). This is Conybeare's translation of N. Marr's Old Georgian version of this eyewitness report. Only a fragment of the original Greek survives. Antiochus Strategos describes how the Persians, like irritated and ferocious snakes, demolished altars and burned churches. For our purposes this comment must suffice: "In Jerusalem there was a certain one by name Thomas. He, blessed one, was armed with the might of Christ. He resembled Nicodemus who buried the body of the Lord, and his wife Mary Magdalene."

serves: 'Most archeologists, epigraphers and other scientists argued persua-
sively that there is no reason to conclude that the Talpiot Tomb was Jesus'
tomb.'[51]

Is the Talpiot tomb related in some ways to Jesus' clan or followers? I
am open to pondering this hypothesis and would urge those who continue
the discussion to distinguish between "Jesus' tomb" and "a tomb perhaps related to his movement or extended clan."[52] While I conclude that the former
option is unlikely (even impossible), I am open to considering, and debating
openly and with respect, the latter possibility. The proceedings of symposia
rarely close debates; this one supplied the requisite data on the Talpiot tomb,
clarified many issues related to numerous tombs, and provided paradigms
for continuing reflection on pre-70 Jewish burial customs and beliefs.

51. N. Norlen, "Princeton Theologian Challenges Latest 'Tomb of Christ' Cover-
age," *Princeton Packet* (February 1, 2008).

52. As J. F. Strange states: "For example, although names like Jesus, Jude (Judas,
etc.), Joseph, Mary, Martha, Lazarus, and so on occur in the New Testament, there is
nothing in the names recorded on ossuaries that makes them unambiguously the same
people as the New Testament personages." That does not disprove a claim; it means: "we
are left with working hypotheses more than developed theories, at least in part because of
the *failure of our methods in interpreting the evidence*" ("Archaeological Evidence of Jewish
Believers?" in *Jewish Believers in Jesus: The Early Centuries,* ed. O. Skarsaune and
R. Hvalvik [Peabody, Mass.: Hendrickson, 2007], p. 741, my italics, to bring out Strange's
major point). The symposium helped us all appreciate more methodologies than those in
which we have received formal training, and we all recognize the need to improve our
methods (including the collecting of DNA so that it is not contaminated) and appreciate
their limitations. From present perspectives, humans will always have questions that extend beyond controlled methodologies. Humility and cooperation help us better grasp
how we belong to the past and are related to the future.

OSSUARIES AND JEWISH BURIAL CUSTOMS IN JUDEA AND GALILEE

The Talpiot Tomb Reconsidered:
The Archaeological Facts

Amos Kloner and Shimon Gibson

In 1980 a burial cave was accidentally unearthed during construction work in the new neighborhood of Talpiot that is on the southeastern outskirts of modern Jerusalem. In appearance this burial cave resembled many others discovered during the building activities that accompanied the expansion of the city in the 1970s and 1980s.[1] Shortly after its discovery, a salvage excavation was conducted in the burial cave by an archaeologist from the Israel Department of Antiquities and Museums (IDAM). Human remains and ten stone ossuaries, some inscribed, were subsequently recovered and transported to the IDAM headquarters at the Rockefeller Museum for safekeeping. A scientific report on the results of the excavation was eventually written and published in 1996 in the archaeological journal *'Atiqot* of the Israel Antiquities Authority (IAA).[2]

This burial cave and its ossuaries would have not merited further scholarly attention aside from rarified scholarly discussions if it were not for the extensive amount of media attention it received (first in 1996 and then again in 2007).[3] This excessive media interest was generated because some of

---

1. A. Kloner and B. Zissu, *The Necropolis of Jerusalem in the Second Temple Period*, Interdisciplinary Studies in Ancient Culture and Religion 8 (Leuven: Peeters, 2007).

2. A. Kloner, "A Tomb with Inscribed Ossuaries in East Talpiyot, Jerusalem," *'Atiqot* 29 (1996): 15-22.

3. A lecture on the topic of this article entitled "Interpretation in Archaeology and the Talpiot Tomb" was given by Shimon Gibson on January 15, 2008, at a conference entitled "Jewish Views of the After Life and Burial Practices in Second Temple Judaism: Evaluating the Talpiot Tomb in Context." The conference was held at Mishkenot Sha'ananim

the ossuaries found in the burial cave were inscribed with personal names familiar from the canonical Gospels: "Jesus," "Mary," and "Joseph." While this general similarity of names was noted by members of the archaeological team working at the burial cave in 1980, it was not deemed a controversial issue since such names were believed to be fairly common among Jews in the first century CE. However, the media thought otherwise. A film airing on the Discovery Channel in 2007 with the rather presumptuous title *The Lost Tomb of Jesus,* really kicked the circus off and resulted in the burial cave being called the "Jesus Family Tomb." News about the tomb appeared in a great many international media outlets.[4] To date, much has been written about the tomb, particularly on the Internet, as well as in articles and books.[5] It has

in Jerusalem. Amos Kloner also lectured at this conference on January 14 on "The Characteristics of the Necropolis of Jerusalem in the Late Hellenistic and Early Roman Periods." We are grateful to Professor James Charlesworth for inviting us to lecture at this event and to write this chapter.

4. The 1996 BBC television documentary that mentioned the Talpiot ossuaries, entitled *The Body in Question,* was produced by Ray Bruce. This documentary served as a catalyst for further thoughts on the significance of the Talpiot tomb made by James Tabor in *The Jesus Dynasty* (New York: Simon & Schuster, 2006), pp. 22-33. The Discovery Channel film was directed by S. Jacobovici in collaboration with the movie director James Cameron. A book was also published at the time the film was aired: S. Jacobovici, and C. Pellegrino, *The Jesus Family Tomb: The Discovery, the Investigation, and the Evidence That Could Change History* (New York: HarperCollins, 2007). This version of the book contains conversations that purportedly took place between the archaeologists who dug at the burial cave (Kloner, Gath, and Gibson), but they are imaginary, though the reader would not know this from the book. A revised and updated version was published later the same year with a slightly different title: idem, *The Jesus Family Tomb: The Evidence Behind the Discovery No One Wanted to Find* (New York: HarperCollins, 2007). This revised edition still contains much incorrect information, although some of the imaginary conversations have now been deleted.

5. For example, three articles appeared in *NEA* 69 (2006): E. M. Meyers, "The Jesus Tomb Controversy: An Overview," pp. 116-18; S. Gibson, "Is the Talpiot Tomb Really the Family Tomb of Jesus?" pp. 118-24; J. D. Tabor, "Testing a Hypothesis," pp. 132-37. It should be noted that this issue of *NEA* was actually published in 2007 *after* the showing of Jacobovici's film. We would also like to mention important commentaries by J. E. Taylor, "The Lost Tomb of Jesus?"; and S. Freyne, "An Easter Story: 'The Lost Tomb of Jesus'" (unpublished manuscripts provided by the authors). A number of articles appeared on the Internet, of which the most important are: J. Magness, "Has the Tomb of Jesus Been Discovered?" *Society for Biblical Literature Forum,* 2007: http://sbl-site.org/Article.aspx?ArticleID=640; R. Bauckham, "The Alleged 'Jesus Family Tomb,'" 2007: http://www.christilling.de/blog/2007/03/guest-post-by richard-bauckham.html; C. A. Evans, "The Burial of Jesus," in C. A.

become quite famous, undeservedly we think, since there are many other tombs around Jerusalem, such as the "Caiaphas" family tomb, which includes finds that are likely to be of greater interest to students of early Christianity.[6]

What is particularly annoying to us, who were present at the excavation of the Talpiot tomb in 1980 and have written articles on the subject,[7] is the amount of misinformation about the discoveries disseminated via media outlets that has (insidiously) infiltrated scholarly discourse. We think much of this garbled data will eventually dissipate. Meanwhile, we feel discussion of the "Jesus" connection to this particular burial cave should only occur after all of the facts regarding the discovery of the cave and the research into these are correctly understood. Otherwise, scholarship will only go round in circles.[8] To that end, we have written this article to set the record straight and to present the discerning scholar with *all* the known facts available to us (in 2010) regarding the discovery of the tomb, its finds, their investigation, and the circumstances of its initial publication.

The Situation of the Tomb and the Circumstances of Its Discovery

The tomb was excavated in 1980 on a westward-facing slope of a hill within the area of East Talpiot, a new residential suburb situated about two kilometers due south of ancient Jerusalem.[9] The general layout of the streets had al-

---

Evans and N. T. Wright, *Jesus, the Final Days: What Really Happened?* (Louisville: Westminster John Knox, 2009), pp. 64-68. The following books are also worthy of attention: G. R. Habermas, *The Secret of the Talpiot Tomb: Unravelling the Mystery of the Jesus Family Tomb* (Nashville: Holman, 2007); D. Burroughs, *The Jesus Family Tomb Controversy: How the Evidence Falls Short* (Ann Arbor: Nimble, 2007).

6. Z. Greenhut, "The 'Caiaphas' Tomb in North Talpiyot, Jerusalem," *'Atiqot* 21 (1992): 63-72; idem, "Where the High Priest Caiaphas Was Buried," in *Where Christianity Was Born*, ed. H. Shanks (Washington, D.C.: Biblical Archaeological Society, 2006), pp. 146-55. For a summary of archaeological evidences for Jesus in Jerusalem, see S. Gibson, *The Final Days of Jesus: The Archaeological Evidence* (New York: HarperOne, 2009).

7. Kloner, "Tomb with Inscribed Ossuaries"; Gibson, "Interpretation," pp. 118-24.

8. This was not the first time the media has reported on the supposed finding of the tomb of Jesus in Jerusalem. In 1931 an ossuary was discovered bearing the inscription *Yeshua bar Yehoseph* (Jesus son of Joseph): see C. R. Kraeling, "Christian Burial Urns," *BA* 9/1 (1946): 16-20.

9. Israel Grid Map ref. 17249 12929. For a map showing the location of the tomb see A. Kloner, *Survey of Jerusalem: The Southern Sector* (Jerusalem: Israel Antiquities Author-

ready been roughly demarcated, and they were sufficiently flat to allow vehicular access to most areas under construction. The buildings were only partly built, or not at all. Some completed apartment buildings to the south already had residents living there since 1976. A petrol station was on the corner of this block of apartment buildings.

The cave was in the side of a rocky scarp just above the street (later known as Dov Gruner Street) with the gaping entrance hole visible from a distance (fig. 1. See photos at the end of this chapter). It was hewn from chalky white rock *(nari)*, and the façade had orange stains derived from the soil fills covering it that had been removed by the bulldozers. Above the doorway was a simple raised carving of a circle and a pointed triangle.

The circumstances of the discovery are quite straightforward. A blast at the construction site resulted in the discovery of the tomb as well as in the destruction of its external rock-cut courtyard and part of its roofed vestibule. On Thursday, March 27, 1980, the burial cave was reported separately by two individuals: Kerner Mandil, who was in charge of the supervisory office of the Armon Hanatziv/East Talpiot Project, and Ephraim Shohat, who was an engineer working with the construction company Solel Boneh. An archaeologist, Eliot Braun, was immediately dispatched that same day by IDAM to check on the nature of the discovery, and he reported back to Amos Kloner, the Jerusalem district archaeologist of IDAM. Kloner eventually reached the site himself to check on the situation. Color and black-and-white photographs were taken of the façade (fig. 1), and black-and-white photographs of the interior (figs. 2-6).[10]

Clearly the burial cave needed to be excavated. The square blocking stone that originally sealed the entrance to the cave was missing and the interior of the burial chamber and the *kokhim* had become blocked with approximately half a meter of soil that had been washed in from outside (the soil level in the cave before excavation is clearly marked in the elevations in fig. 15). Judging by the on-site photographs, the tops of the ossuaries were not visible; therefore it is unlikely that there was any clandestine looting of the burial cave in the hours preceding the visit by Braun to the site.[11] How-

---

ity, 2000), p. 136, with map in envelope. For a summary of the findings at the tomb and its vicinity see Kloner and Zissu, *Necropolis*, pp. 342-43, and fig. 237 showing the tomb façade.

10. The black-and-white photographs of the interior of the tomb are listed in the IAA photographic archives with the following accession numbers: 128521-128525, with the façade: 128520.

11. All the ossuaries were found resting on the rock floor of the burial cave under a

ever, a few ossuary fragments were noticed outside the cave entrance, which are mentioned in a report written later by IDAM inspector of antiquities Joseph Gath (fig. 7). It was too late to do any digging so the work was postponed to the following day. Kloner went back to the office to prepare the request for an official digging permit, which was submitted the next day (fig. 8). Braun did not feel inclined to direct the digging at the cave. The permit (IAA permit no. 938) was prepared on the following day and named Gath as the person in charge of the dig. It was issued on March 31 and signed by then director of IDAM Avraham Eitan (fig. 9).

The next day (Friday, March 28), Gath began excavating and by noon had extracted ten ossuaries from the burial cave. They were laid on a special truck and transported back to the safekeeping of the Rockefeller Museum. It must have been tricky getting the ossuaries out of the ground since some of them were broken. It would appear that Gath concentrated his activities in digging the *kokhim* first, leaving the clearance of the central chamber to the following week. This is also clear from the photographs taken by Maoz (see below). On arrival at the museum, the ossuaries were handed over to the curator and anthropologist Joe Zias and placed into temporary storage, in order to be examined by L. Y. Rahmani, chief curator of the archaeological storerooms, at a later time. The work had to be undertaken in a hurry since excavations were not permitted on Saturday and any ossuaries left in the burial cave might be pilfered by greedy antiquity thieves. Alternatively, members of Jerusalem's Ultra-Orthodox Jewish community might demonstrate, creating disturbances that could lead to a cessation of the excavations altogether. Indeed, this is exactly what happened to another Second Temple period tomb nearby, which was situated on the same slope to the northeast of the excavated tomb and was full of ossuaries. Some of these ossuaries were inscribed, but, because of Ultra-Orthodox Jewish objections, it was later sealed and still remains unexcavated (see description of this second Talpiot cave below).

The Saturday break in the digging was unfortunate because it meant that the burial cave could be visited by people who might want to do some illicit digging. Vandalism and clandestine digging is a general problem at ar-

---

0.50 m layer of soil. The tallest ossuary from this burial cave (no. 80-506) has a height of 0.384 m, which means Gath eventually had to dig down at least 10 cm before reaching the top of an ossuary. Attempts to extract an ossuary from the ground clandestinely before Braun reached the burial cave would have been immediately obvious had that been the case.

chaeological sites in Israel. Not long after Gath left the site that Friday, an 11-year-old boy named Ouriel, returning from school, entered the building site and saw the burial cave entrance. This was after he had heard additional blasting at the site. At that time he says there was only one Arab guard at the building site and all the construction workers had gone home. He peered into the burial cave, and then went home to tell his mother, Rivka Maoz. The Maoz family were living in an apartment block they had moved into in 1976 in the older part of the East Talpiot neighborhood, about 100 meters due south of the area of the tomb. His mother tried to contact the archaeological headquarters at the Rockefeller Museum, but without success since everyone had already gone home for the eve of Sabbath. Maoz took a series of photographs in the tomb (fig. 10), two of which show how Gath had removed soil specifically from the *kokhim,* clearly in order to extract the ossuaries, while leaving the fill in the central chamber untouched.[12]

There were no excavations that Saturday, and the guard at the construction site was apparently not very diligent. As a result the burial cave was visited by local children who had heard about it and were drawn to investigate themselves. This resulted in some human bones being taken out of the tomb and removed from the site. Conscientiously, Rivka Maoz, with the help of her son, collected the pilfered bones from the kids and placed them in a plastic bag. When the excavations were resumed on Sunday, the bones were handed over to Gath.

The excavation within the burial cave was conducted in stages with breaks between March 30 and April 11, 1980, and it was supervised by Gath, with the help of three to four workers provided by the Solel Boneh construction company. Two ossuary lids were found on the floor of the main chamber. Measurements and a drawn plan and elevations of the tomb (scale 1:25) were prepared by Shimon Gibson, who was working at that time as an archaeological assistant and surveyor in IDAM. Having completed the excavation, Gath returned to his office (April 15), wrote up a preliminary report on the excavations (figs. 11-12), and prepared a file card for the site (fig. 13), both of which he deposited in the department's archives.[13] Tragically, Gath died

12. We are grateful to Mrs. Rivka Maoz for permission to reproduce these photographs.

13. Gath only published a short report in Hebrew about the discovery of the burial cave in the official IDAM newsletter: Y. Gath, "East Talpiyot," *Hadashot Arkheologiyot* 76 (1981): 24-25. A typed report about the excavation written by Gath, as well as other records about the dig, are in the excavation file in the IAA archives at the Rockefeller Museum in Jerusalem. Among these papers is the offprint or galleys of a two-page article in

before he was able to publish the results of his excavations, and it was eventually left to Kloner to publish a final report on the tomb in 1996.[14] A major difficulty Kloner had in writing this report was that Gath left behind only sparse and incomplete notes about the results of his excavation. An additional examination made by Gibson of Gath's notes in the archives at the Rockefeller Museum confirms that his notes are minimalist in content and that a lot of vital information about the tomb has consequently been lost.[15]

A Description of the Burial Cave

The following is a description of the burial cave based on the notes made by the excavators, photographs, and the drawn plan and elevations of the burial cave (figs. 14-15). In front of the burial cave's vestibule was an open courtyard (approximately 4.3 m wide and 2.3 m deep) but it was badly destroyed during the blasting operations particularly on its eastern side (fig. 10: C). The covered vestibule was better preserved, and its original size may be ascertained with some certainty (2.0 × 2.4 m; 1.85 m in height); the alignment of its side walls was not entirely perpendicular with the front of the tomb.

The façade of the burial cave (figs. 1; 10: D) had a squared doorway (0.5 × 0.55 m) within an indented frame (0.15 m in width and depth). The upper right-hand and lower right-hand corners of the façade had not been completely hewn out, but were left unfinished. Above the doorway were two decorative carvings in raised relief: a round feature (0.28 m in diameter) consisting of a circular band (0.06 m wide) with a sunken central depression (0.05 m deep), and above it a triangular or pyramid-shaped feature (1.1 m wide and 0.80 m high, with arms 0.15 m wide) with an attachment at its top (0.15 m high and 0.10 m wide) extending to the ceiling of the vestibule.

Similar carvings on rock-cut façades and interior doorways of tombs

---

Hebrew by Gath entitled "Archaeological Discoveries in East Talpiot in Jerusalem," pp. 71-72. We were unable to verify where it was published, if at all. For additional written letters and other archival materials relating to the tomb and to another one situated nearby see IAA administrative archives/peh/J-M/bet/8/X. We are grateful to Aryeh Rochman for showing us this material.

14. For the official publication of the tomb see Kloner, "Tomb with Inscribed Ossuaries." A more detailed draft of Kloner's report was submitted for publication, but it had to be shortened by the editor of *'Atiqot* to fit the house style and requirements of that journal. We thank Dr. Rafi Greenberg for his editing at the time.

15. IAA administrative archives/peh/J-M/bet/8/X.

are known from Jerusalem dating from the end of the first century BCE to the first century CE. However, the Talpiot carvings were rendered in a much simplified form. Whether this was intentional or was the result of the façade remaining unfinished by the workmen hewing it is not known. Gath in his notes suggests that the Talpiot carvings represent an attempt to depict a rosette with a gable above it, and that it was left unfinished, perhaps because the local chalky rock *(nari)* was too soft to make carvings in any great detail. The triangular or pyramid-like feature undoubtedly was meant to represent a gable or pediment, since the appendage at the top (possibly a burial urn representation), which links the triangular apex to the ceiling of the vestibule, has many parallels in the gabled door representations of tombs in the Akeldama ("Field of Blood") cemetery south of Mount Zion (figs. 16-18). The round feature, however, most likely represents a circular band with a rope pattern, representing a form of a diadem or crown. Alternatively, it may have been a simple form of a wreath, but we think it unlikely to have been a rosette-decorated roundel. Examples of diadems and wreaths are known from the decoration of tombs around Jerusalem, notably from the ceiling of the inner chamber of the so-called Tomb of Absalom in the Kidron Valley, from the façade of the Tomb of the Kings, from the Tomb of the Grapes, from the lintel of the Tomb of the Apostles at Akeldama, and elsewhere (figs. 19-21).[16]

The interior chamber of the tomb (fig. 14: 1) was intact and luckily was not harmed by the blasting operations. Tool marks left by the original hewer's chisels (with blades 1 cm wide) were evident on the walls and ceiling of the burial cave. A step (0.60 × 0.45m, with a tread 0.50 m deep) led into the single interior chamber, which was square (2.9 × 2.9 m); it did not have the usual central standing pit with benches around its sides. The ceiling was sufficiently high (2 m) to allow for standing room, so that family members could arrange with ease the burial of their kin.

Two burial shelves within arched spaces *(arcosolia)* were cut in the upper northern and western walls of the burial cave (fig. 14: y and x). These are situated 1.2 m above the level of the floor and are both of a similar size: a length of 2 m, a width of 0.6 m, and a height of 0.7 m. At the time of excava-

---

16. For parallels see R. Hachlili. *Jewish Funerary Customs, Practices and Rites in the Second Temple Period,* JSJSup 94 (Leiden: Brill, 2005), pp. 43-54; Kloner and Zissu, *Necropolis,* fig. 9. A new survey of the Akeldama cemetery was undertaken in 2008 by Boaz Zissu and Shimon Gibson (a monograph on the results is in preparation). See also the recent comments on these carvings by Evans, *Jesus,* pp. 66-68.

tion they had a layer of dried brown mud on them (0.05 to 0.10 m thick), beneath which were signs of decayed bones (this is evident in the photographs made at the time: figs. 2, 4). Additional limb bones and skulls found by Gath on the floor immediately beneath the arcosolia were apparently swept off the shelves by intruders who entered the tomb in antiquity. The presence of bones on the shelves suggests that primary burials were made on them in the first century, notwithstanding the view held by some scholars that such shelves were only used as additional spaces for the storage of ossuaries.[17]

Cut into the lower walls of the main chamber at the level of the floor were horizontal tunnel-like recesses *(kokhim),* with two in each of the three walls, to the north, east, and west (fig. 14: 2-7). They had an average length of 2 m, a width of 0.55 m, and a height of 0.85 m; *kokh* 2 was particularly short with a length of only 1.55 m. The interior of some of the *kokhim* was slightly arched (fig. 14: 5, 6). The openings to the *kokhim* were rounded and none of them seem to have had stone doors, or at least none was found in the excavation. An incised round line above the opening to *kokh* 6 was made by the quarrymen (fig. 10: A-B). Except for *kokh* 4, the rest were used as storage spaces for the ten ossuaries containing human bones in secondary burial.

The burial cave had evidently been forced open, entered, and ransacked at some point before the modern era by tomb robbers. At the time of the excavation this disturbance by intruders was clear to Gath on account of the missing blocking stone for the main door of the burial cave. Also a quantity of soil (0.50 m thick) had accumulated within the burial cave having been washed in from outside since that event.[18] The intruders were probably also responsible for sweeping the intact primary inhumations from the arcosolia shelves, for smashing some of the ossuaries (seven were broken, six

---

17. Kloner and Zissu, *Necropolis,* pp. 81-82. Kloner is of the opinion that the use of arcosolia is a late feature of the first century CE.

18. The geologist Aryeh Shimron (personal communication) is currently undertaking research on possible mineral signatures that might be reflected within the actual stone of the Talpiot ossuaries as a result of their having been covered with soil for some 1500 years. In regard to the patina fingerprinting of ossuaries undertaken by Pellegrino in 2007, we suggest that this line of testing is interesting but remains unproven as a method of provenancing ossuaries, at least judging by the published information presented in Jacobovici and Pellegrino, *Jesus Family Tomb,* pp. 175-92. We hope Pellegrino will eventually publish a detailed study of his results in a peer-reviewed scientific journal. See also the comments by S. J. Cox, "A Forensic Science Analysis of 'The Lost Tomb of Jesus' Documentary," in http://www.uhl.ac/Lost_Tomb/ForensicAnalysisOfTLTJ.pdf.

of which were eventually restored), and for chucking two ossuary lids onto the floor of the main chamber.[19]

The Skeletal Material from the Burial Cave

At the time of the excavation in 1980 Gath noticed skulls and a heap of large limb bones at two points on the floor of the main chamber, and it is feasible that these came from the primary burials that were swept off the arcosolia shelves (y, x) by intruders. The positions of these two heaps of bones were marked by skulls on the plan of the site (fig. 14). Only a thin layer of compacted mud superimposed above crushed bones (5-10 cm thick) had survived on the shelves. A third skull was found in the corner of the main chamber, and it may conceivably have been taken out of one of the ossuaries in the adjacent *kokh* 7. Fragmentary human bones and a few Early Roman potsherds were also noted by Gath randomly scattered throughout the main chamber. The number of interments in the burial cave is unknown. Based on data obtained from other tombs that he had studied, Kloner surmised that it might have been about 35 individuals, but this is informed guesswork.[20]

Unfortunately, the anthropological remains from the Talpiot tomb were never examined or quantified.[21] Anthropologists Joe Zias and Patricia Smith, who studied skeletal material from tombs at that time for IDAM, both confirm (via personal communication) that neither of them examined the human bones from this specific burial cave. Moreover, the bones were

19. It is conceivable that some breakage also occurred at the time the ossuaries were extracted from the ground during the excavation.

20. Kloner, "Tomb with Inscribed Ossuaries," p. 22 n. 2. Since so many of the ossuaries were broken, Kloner believes Gath most likely separated the human bones from the ossuaries in separate bags at the time of the excavation.

21. The interpretation that two individuals from the tomb were married as suggested from the mitochondrial DNA analysis of human bone fragments randomly extracted from two Talpiot ossuaries in the Beth Shemesh IAA storerooms is in our opinion dubious; cf. Jacobovici and Pellegrino, *Jesus Family Tomb*, pp. 167-74. For the sample to be meaningful one would have to have bone samples from each and every one of the ossuaries tested, as well as from the bones seen on the arcosolia shelves in the tomb. This is made more complicated by the fact that ossuaries were used for multiple burials. Hence there is no certainty that bones from a given ossuary actually correspond to the individual named on the same ossuary. We also must remember that at the time of the excavation in 1980 DNA methods of profiling were not yet known.

not available to Kloner for his 1996 study since they had already been transferred to the Jewish religious authorities in Jerusalem for reburial, either by
Gath himself not long after the excavation had been completed, or by someone else working for IDAM. Alternatively, they were transferred in order to
fulfill an agreement made in 1994 between the Israeli government and the religious authorities who had objected to the storage of human bones within
the IAA storerooms.[22]

The Ossuaries

Ten ossuaries were recovered from the Talpiot tomb and removed to the
safety of the Rockefeller Museum on Friday, March 28, 1980. In total, three of
the ossuaries were found intact; the rest were broken and had to be restored.
Six or seven ossuary lids were also discovered, one gabled and the rest flat in
appearance. Five of the ossuaries were plain and five were decorated with
double-rosette motifs in panels, surrounded by bands with chip-carved zigzag designs, except for one which also has a decoration of vertical rows of
small circular disks. Maker's marks were detected scratched on three of the
ossuaries.[23] These served to align the lids with their respective ossuaries.

During the drafting of the measured plan of the burial cave that was
made the following week in April, the position of the ossuary find-spots was
added by Gibson according to information provided by Gath (fig. 14: *kokh* 2:
a-b; *kokh* 3: a-b; *kokh* 5: a; *kokh* 6: a-b; and *kokh* 7: a-c). Since Gath did not
subsequently match up the IDAM accession numbers given to the ossuaries
when stored at the Rockefeller Museum (IAA registration numbers 500-509/
1980) with the attribution numbers as they appeared on the plan of the
burial cave, we shall never know for certain where each ossuary came from.
This is unfortunate and represents a major loss of information. In addition,
we have no information about the ossuary fragments that Gath reported

22. T. Einhorn, "Israeli Law, Jewish Law and the Archaeological Excavation of
Tombs," *International Journal of Cultural Property* 6/1 (1997): 47-79. It should be pointed
out that already in 1984 instructions were given by the Israeli attorney general that human
remains should not be treated as antiquities since they are not mentioned in the antiquities laws of Israel.

23. These marks are usually termed "mason's marks" in the literature, but since
there is no evidence that they were made by the craftsmen who made the ossuaries, one
might term them "maker's marks" instead. Indeed, some of the marks may have been
made by family members at the same time they inscribed the names.

picking up *outside* the tomb entrance. These may eventually have been matched up and restored with one of the broken ossuaries inside the burial cave; we simply lack this information, and Gath did not report further on this matter in his notes.

Six of the ossuaries were inscribed (five in Aramaic and one in Greek). The inscriptions were scratched in different hands with a nail or stylus. The location of the inscriptions varies: three were on the front of the ossuary and another on the back, with two on the short end of the ossuary and one on the inside. The inscriptions were originally read by L. Y. Rahmani (assisted by L. Di Segni), and published in a catalogue he prepared on Jewish ossuaries (nos. 701-709). Another catalogue of the ossuaries was published by Kloner (nos. 1-10).[24]

Catalogue of Ossuaries

The following is an updated and revised catalogue of the ossuaries with a discussion relating to the inscriptions. The measurements of the ossuaries are given by length, width, and height. One should also note certain small inconsistencies between the measurements given by Rahmani, by Kloner, and on the IAA finds cards that go with the artifacts in the IAA storerooms at Beth Shemesh. This is due to the fact that the ossuaries were handmade and their side walls often taper.

1. *IAA accession no. 80-500* (**Rahmani no. 701; Kloner no. 1**); 67.7–68.0 × 25.4-26 × 32.5–34.2 cm (figs. 22-26)
This ossuary was found complete. It has low stub feet. The front was decorated with two six-petaled rosettes asymmetrically aligned within panels. Wide, chip-carved, zigzag frames surround the ossuary front on its four sides. Three parallel vertical zigzag bands also decorate the center of the ossuary front, the latter flanked on either side by vertical lines of three small disks. On one of the narrow sides of the ossuary is a flimsy rendering of a six-petaled rosette; presumably it was left unfinished. Two maker's marks

---

24. L. Y. Rahmani, *A Catalogue of Jewish Ossuaries in the Collections of the State of Israel* (Jerusalem: Israel Antiquities Authority, 1994), pp. 222-24, ossuaries nos. 701-9; Kloner, "Tomb with Inscribed Ossuaries," pp. 17-21, ossuaries nos. 1-10. See also the discussion of the Talpiot ossuary names in C. A. Rollston, "Inscribed Ossuaries: Personal Names, Statistics, and Laboratory Tests," *NEA* 69 (2006): 125-29.

appear on the front and side of the ossuary. The size and width of the gabled lid (62.1 × 22.5 cm) does not match the ossuary itself, suggesting that it came from another ossuary, or that it was already a bad match in antiquity.

A Greek inscription was found on the back of the ossuary (figs. 24-25). Rahmani read the Greek inscription as *Mariamenou Mara* ("of Mariamenon, who is [also called] Mara"), with *Mariamenon* being interpreted as a diminutive form of *Mariamene*, a reading he inferred based on comparisons made with Greek inscriptions (of later date) found at the cemetery of Beth Shearim. *Mara* is interpreted as "honorable lady," but the correct form for "honorable lady" should be *Martha*. *Mara* is either the emphatic male form, which sits oddly on a woman, or a colloquial contracted form. (The Virgin Mary and female saints are given the title Martha in the later Syriac church.)[25] After Rahmani, a number of scholars have suggested, independently of one another, that the inscription should be read as *Mariame kai Mara*, that is, that it represents the names of two separate individuals, Mariame and Mara.[26] The first name is a variant of two very common Jewish names in the first century CE: Miriam/Maryam and Marya. The second name, Mara, is generally held to be a shortened version of Martha.

2. *IAA accession no. 80-501* (Rahmani no. 702; Kloner no. 2); 55 × 23 × 27 cm; the IAA finds card has a different measurement: 54 × 22 cm (figs. 27-28)

This ossuary was found complete. It has a flat bottom. The front was decorated with two six-petaled rosettes within panels. Narrow chip-carved zigzag frames surround the ossuary front on its four sides and down the center. It had no apparent lid.

A deeply incised inscription in Jewish script, *Yehudah bar Yeshua*, was rendered near the center of the decorated front of the ossuary. The names *Yehudah* (Judas) and *Yeshua* (Jesus) were very popular names in the first century CE. Rahmani suggested that this person was the son of the "Yeshua (?) son of Yehoseph" who appears in an inscription on another ossuary (see no. 4 below).

---

25. Taylor, "Lost Tomb."

26. S. J. Pfann, "Mary Magdalene Has Left the Room. A Suggested New Reading of Ossuary *CJO* 701," *NEA* 69 (2006): 130-31. Jonathan Price (personal communication) has suggested another interpretation: *Mariam h kai Mara*, "Mariam, who is also known as Mara." In this case, the inscription would refer not to two people but to a single woman.

3. *IAA accession no. 80-502* (Rahmani no. 703; Kloner no. 3); 53.5-55 ×
28.2–28.4 × 31.5–33.4 cm. (figs. 29-31)
A plain ossuary with vertical chisel marks on its four sides and low stub feet.
It was found in fragments and restored. The IAA finds card indicates it had a
lid, but Kloner does not mention it.

It has inscriptions in Jewish script but in different hands: *Matya* and
Mata, on the narrow side and on the inside of the ossuary, respectively. Both
are contractions of the name *Matityahu* (Matthew). Rahmani suggested that
the *yod* of the second name may have been worn away and that it too should
be read as *Matya*.

4. *IAA accession no. 80-503* (Rahmani no. 704; Kloner no. 4); 62.7-65 ×
25.4–26.0 × 30.5-31 cm (figs. 32-33)
A plain complete ossuary with smoothed exterior walls that are badly
scratched. It has low stub feet and a flat lid with two maker's marks on it.

On the narrow side of the ossuary just below the rim is a badly
scrawled inscription in Jewish script: *Yeshua* (?) *bar Yehoseph*, according to
the reading provided by Rahmani and Kloner. However, the first name
Yeshua (Jesus) is not at all clear, owing to various scratches, and it may even
be superimposed over an earlier name *(Hanun)*, as one scholar (Pfann) has
suggested. The first name is preceded by an "X" maker's mark.

5. *IAA accession no. 80-504* (Rahmani no. 705; Kloner no. 5); 54.5 × 26 ×
34.5 cm; the IAA finds card has a different measurement: 54 × 25 cm
(figs. 34-35)
A plain ossuary with vertical chisel marks on its four sides, with low stub feet
and a flat lid. It was found in fragments and restored.

Inscription in Jewish script: *Yoseh* on the front of the ossuary close to
the rim. This is a diminutive version of *Yehoseph* (Joseph) that itself was a
very popular name in the first century CE. This *Yoseh* may possibly have been
the father of the individual (identified as *Yeshua*) who appears in an inscription on another ossuary (see no. 4 above).

6. *IAA accession no. 80-505* (Rahmani no. 706; Kloner no. 6); 52 × 27 × 33
cm; the IAA finds card has a different measurement: 47 × 22 cm (fig. 36)
A plain ossuary with vertical chisel marks on its four sides, with low stub feet
and a flat lid. It was found in fragments and restored.

Inscription in Jewish script: *Marya* in the center of the front of the
ossuary.

7. *IAA accession no. 80-506* (Rahmani no. 707; Kloner no. 7); 67 × 31.5 ×
38.5 cm; the IAA finds card has a different measurement: 47 × 22 cm
(figs. 37-39)
The front of this ossuary was decorated with two six-petaled rosettes within
chip-carved zigzag frames. It has smoothed back and side walls, and very low
stub feet. A very large maker's mark is incised on the back of the ossuary.
One of the side walls has various scratches. The ossuary was found in fragments and restored. Only half of its flat lid has survived.

8. *IAA accession no. 80-507* (Rahmani no. 708; Kloner no. 8); 49.5-51 ×
25.5–26.5 × 31-31.7 cm (fig. 40)
The front of this ossuary was decorated with two six-petaled rosettes within
double chip-carved zigzag frames, and with a single zigzag frame down its
center. It has stub feet. No lid was found. The ossuary was found in fragments and restored.

9. *IAA accession no. 80-508* (Rahmani no. 709; Kloner no. 9); 61 × 25.8–
26.4 × 23.5-28 cm (fig. 41)
The front of this ossuary was decorated with two six-petaled rosettes within
chip-carved zigzag frames: a double frame along the top and with single
frames on the sides and at the bottom. Down the center are two single
frames on either side of an incised star with six arms. It has a flat lid. The ossuary was found in fragments and restored.

10. *IAA accession no. 80-509* (Kloner no. 10); 60 × 26 × 30 cm.
This ossuary was described by Rahmani as "a plain, broken specimen," but
was not included in his catalogue.[27] Since only nine of the ten ossuaries from
the tomb are at present to be found in the IAA storerooms at Beth Shemesh,
this raised questions about its appearance and present location.

Tabor has suggested that the tenth ossuary might be the same as the
"James son of Joseph, brother of Jesus," ossuary, implying that the ossuary
was stolen by persons unknown and that it eventually ended up in the hands
of an antiquities collector and dealer.[28] The legal status of this artifact is still
unclear. The ossuary is undoubtedly authentic, but the inscription (or part
of it) may be a forgery, and the owner is currently in court arguing his case.[29]

27. Rahmani, *Catalogue*, p. 222.

28. Tabor, *Jesus Dynasty*, pp. 31-33. James was killed in Jerusalem in 64 CE and according to early Christian tradition was buried in the lower Kidron Valley.

29. The ossuary comes from the collection of the Israeli antiquities collector and

We do not believe the so-called James ossuary had anything to do with the missing ossuary from Talpiot, for two reasons. First, the Talpiot ossuaries were hidden beneath a layer of soil (0.50 m thick) that obliged Gath to dig down at least 10 cm before he could reach them. Had there been any attempts to extract an ossuary in clandestine fashion, this could only have been done by digging a pit in the ground, and this would immediately have been obvious to Braun, who was the first archaeologist on the scene. Second, the tenth "missing" ossuary is described by Rahmani as "plain" and "broken," which implies that it was undecorated and uninscribed. This description does not fit the "James" ossuary, which is complete and unbroken, with rosette decorations on its front, and with a deeply carved inscription in Jewish script on its other side.

There is, however, a very clear explanation as to how the tenth ossuary might have been mislaid.[30] All decorated or inscribed ossuaries when received in the Rockefeller Museum in the 1980s were immediately placed on shelves in stores within the building, whereas broken plain ossuaries (of which there were many from Jerusalem tombs) were left on wooden shelving in the external courtyard of the museum. This was because of an acute lack of space. When the ossuaries at the Rockefeller Museum were eventually transferred to their new home at the storage facility at Romema and later to

---

dealer Oded Golan and is the subject of an ongoing court case regarding the authenticity of its inscription. For a description of the ossuary and its study see A. Lemaire, "Burial Box of James the Brother of Jesus," *BAR* 28/6 (2002): 24-33, 70; and H. Shanks and B. Witherington, *The Brother of Jesus: The Dramatic Story & Meaning of the First Archaeological Link to Jesus & His Family* (London: Continuum, 2003). The ossuary itself is undoubtedly authentic; see J. Magness, "Ossuaries and the Burials of Jesus and James," *JBL* 124 (2005): 121-54. That the ossuary was bought from an antiquities dealer, however, reduces its historical value to a minimum since it lacks a clear and unequivocal provenance. See S. Gibson, "The James Ossuary: A Lost Cause," *BAR* 30/6 (2004): 55-58. The "cleaning" or "tampering" that was allegedly done to the inscription itself after the ossuary came into Golan's possession, whether by mistake or with intent, means the resulting value of the names on the ossuary is of little importance to scholarship, for authenticity is obviously crucial in such matters. On the scientific examination of the patina within the letters of the inscription that shows that it differs from the original patina on the surface of the ossuary see A. Ayalon, M. Bar-Matthews, and Y. Goren, "Authenticity Examination of the Inscription on the Ossuary Attributed to James, Brother of Jesus," *Journal of Archaeological Science* 31 (2004): 1185-89. On the circumstances of the alleged forgery see N. A. Silberman and Y. Goren, "Faking Biblical History," *Archaeology* 56/5 (2003): 20-30.

30. This is based on the personal knowledge of all those who dealt with the storing of ossuaries at the Rockefeller in those days, namely Kloner, Rahmani, and Zias.

Beth Shemesh, the tenth broken example may simply have been thrown away owing to a lack of storage space, or it may have lost its labeling.[31]

Additional Tombs and Other Archaeological Remains in the Immediate Vicinity

One aspect that has not been dealt with by those assessing the Talpiot tomb is that there were a number of other archaeological remains in its immediate vicinity and further along the slope, namely terraces and stone boundary walls, an oil press in a cave,[32] cisterns,[33] the remains of a plastered installation (perhaps a *miqweh*) (fig. 42),[34] and additional tombs. One of these tombs (Israel Grid Map ref. 17240 12880) consisted of a single chamber with *kokhim* in its walls; it was situated about twenty meters to the north of the Talpiot tomb and according to Gath's notes was in a state of ruin.[35] This tomb was photographed by Kloner (fig. 43). These archaeological remains were unearthed during building operations made by the Hevrat Shikun Ovdim for the purpose of building 94 housing units in the neighborhood.

31. A search was made in the IAA storerooms at Beth Shemesh for the missing ossuary, but it was not found. As with many large collections of antiquities, certain artifacts are apt to go missing or get mislaid as a result of the labels of artifacts falling off, and especially when artifacts are transferred from one place of storage to another. In the case of the Talpiot ossuaries, as with many other artifacts, these were transferred first from the Rockefeller Museum to the Romema storerooms at the end of the 1980s, and then later to the new modernized storerooms at Beth Shemesh, where they are at the present time. The major reorganization of the IAA storerooms that has been done in recent years will undoubtedly prevent this sort of thing happening in the future. Today the Talpiot ossuaries are easily accessible. Indeed, scholars may view all nine ossuaries by appointment.

32. According to Gath's notes, the oil press is from the Byzantine period, ca. 500 CE, and it belonged to a nearby hamlet or farm. See Gath, "Archaeological Discoveries," p. 72. Since the vicinity of the Talpiot tomb was in use for agricultural purposes in the Byzantine period, we would like to suggest that this might have been the occasion when the tomb was opened and ransacked.

33. In his notes, Gath mentions "two water cisterns close to the cave [Talpiot tomb] which appear to be later [in date]." Elsewhere, he wrote that they were probably from the Byzantine period.

34. According to Kloner and Zissu, *Necropolis,* p. 343, a plastered rock-cut installation possibly identified as a "ritual immersion bath" was seen near the Talpiot tomb, but it was damaged by bulldozers.

35. Kloner and Zissu, *Necropolis,* p. 340; cf. Cave 12-31.

Another tomb was discovered slightly further up the slope to the east, just below the level of the Olei ha-Gardom street.[36] The discovery was made by the construction company Solel Boneh, and their engineer, Ephraim Shohat, informed IDAM of the find on April 15, 1981. Subsequently, that same day, Zion Shabtai, an inspector of antiquities working for the Judea and Samaria Civil Archaeological Unit, was sent by the district archaeologist of Jerusalem, Kloner, to check on the circumstances of the discovery. Upon his return to the IDAM offices, Shabtai reported that he had managed to enter the burial chamber through its ceiling, but with some difficulty. He noticed that the stone doors of several of the *kokhim* had been removed by laborers of Solel Boneh prior to his arrival at the scene. They had also lifted off several of the ossuary lids. Owing to the lateness of the day, it was decided to suspend archaeological recording operations.

On the morning of April 16, Kloner and IDAM staff, which included archaeological inspector Shlomo Gudovitz, visited the tomb (figs. 44-45).[37] Owing to a heavy fall of rain earlier that morning, it took a while to gain access to the burial cave with a rope ladder that dangled through the ceiling and down to the floor of the cave, a drop of about 4 meters. The IDAM team began investigating the burial cave at about 8 a.m. Measurements of the central tomb chamber immediately commenced, but the main entrance was seen to be blocked (fig. 46). A photographic dossier was prepared with pictures taken of individual *kokhim* and ossuaries (figs. 47-49). Kloner's personal records include a list of ossuaries with their dimensions and position, specific noticeable decorations, and a preliminary transcription of the visible Greek inscriptions.[38] The intention of the archaeologists was to transport the ossuaries to the Rockefeller Museum so that the ossuaries and inscriptions might be cleaned and examined with ease. One small child's ossuary (ossuary no. 8 in *kokh* 7) was successfully extracted from the tomb on April 16, or perhaps by Shabtai during his visit on the previous day. The rest of the seven ossuaries were shifted on April 16 from the *kokhim* to the

36. Kloner and Zissu, *Necropolis*, p. 342; cf. Cave 12-45, fig. 236, Israel Grid Map ref. 17240 12880. The distance from Cave 12-45 to the previous Cave 12-31 is unknown. Since they have the same map reference number, according to Kloner this indicates that the maximum distance between the two would have been some 19 meters or so.

37. The IDAM permit issued for work in this tomb is permit no. 1050/1981. It was incorrectly given as 1053/1981 in Kloner's report: IAA administrative archives, peh/J-M/bet/8/X (fig. 45).

38. A separate report is in preparation on the ossuaries, their decorations and inscriptions.

central chamber to prepare them for transportation to the Rockefeller Museum. It was at this point that the ossuaries were numbered with chalk. Following this, measurements were made of each and every *kokh* and these were added to the plan. The resulting plan was schematic (fig. 46) and the record made of the ossuaries was partial.

The recording procedures were halted when, at 10:30 a.m., the burial cave was visited by Rabbi Shimon Enshin, who was active as a monitor on archaeological excavations for the Ultra-Orthodox Jewish Atra Kadisha burial society. Enshin was accompanied by some ten zealous yeshiva students of the Toldot Aharon Yeshiva from Mea Shearim. They demanded that the work stop, and made clear that they would physically prevent the removal of ossuaries. In an attempt to reach a compromise, IDAM representatives expressed their willingness to leave the human bones inside the burial cave so long as they might be able to extract the ossuaries. This compromise, however, was turned down by the religious authorities, represented by Rabbi David Shmidel, who was at that time in charge of the Atra Kadisha burial society. Meanwhile, the religious demonstrations continued outside the burial cave. Eventually, Rabbi Enshin returned from his meeting with Rabbi Shmidel, together with a senior representative of the Religious Affairs Ministry, Zelig Braverman. Braverman informed the archaeologists that they would not be permitted to remove ossuaries from the tomb and that a decision regarding continued work at the site could only be made on a ministerial level at a meeting with the participation of the IDAM director, Avraham Eitan. But this meeting was never convened and no decision was ever made about resuming the work. By that time, more Ultra-Orthodox demonstrators had appeared at the scene, making any further scientific work within the burial cave impossible. Finally, Kloner entered the burial cave alone for a last visit and to collect his equipment and notes, under threat from the demonstrators. The rope ladder was then removed and the burial cave opening was covered over with wooden planks on which a fill of soil and stones was dumped using mechanical equipment. On April 17 Kloner prepared a detailed report on the burial cave and its contents based on the partial results obtained the previous day.

At some point in mid-July 1981 building operations commenced at the site. While preparations were being made for the construction activities, the cave appears to have been entered once more, probably by workers or more likely by members of one of the Ultra-Orthodox religious authorities, resulting in the ossuaries being pushed back into the *kokhim* but not in the original order as observed on April 16. Hence, the present position of the ossuaries in the burial cave does not in any way represent the position of the ossuaries as they were originally discovered (as shown in fig. 46). The burial cave is now buried beneath a residential building and the religious authorities inserted a rounded cemented pier encased in a metal frame and containing a green plastic pipe, extending up from the standing pit in the floor of the tomb to the present level of the building in order to reduce levels of impurity — according to the understanding of the religious authorities — that might emanate from the dead in the burial chamber (as shown in Kloner's memorandum of August 2: fig. 45).

The tomb has a square central chamber with a standing pit (not visible) surrounded by benches on three sides, and a flat ceiling (fig. 46). The rectangular stone door (seen from the inside) is still in situ, indicating that the tomb had not been entered until the time of discovery. There were three *kokhim* in each of its three walls; they have pointed openings within squared frames to accommodate stone doors.[39] The nine stone doors were in situ at the time of the discovery of the tomb in 1981. *Kokhim* 7 and 8 had single primary burials within them (fig. 50), whereas *kokh* 3 had primary burials of an adult and child side by side. The inhumations were positioned with their heads toward the back of the *kokhim*. Scattered skeletal material was observed in *kokhim* 4, 5, and 9; the *kokhim* with the ossuaries also contained skeletal material on their floors. Clearly the earlier skeletal material must have been only haphazardly collected when the ossuaries were inserted into the *kokhim*.

The tomb contained eight ossuaries: three in *kokh* 1, two in *kokh* 2, two in *kokh* 6, and one in *kokh* 7. Seven of these ossuaries had decorations (yellow-brown washes, one with a painted diamond pattern on its side, one with chip-carved rosettes within zigzag frames, and one with a depiction of an amphora and another motif), and two had Greek inscriptions.[40] The small ossuary no. 8 (42.5 × 21 cm; 25.5 cm high), taken out of *kokh* 7, evidently served for the burial of the bones of a child (fig. 51).[41] The front of the ossuary was decorated with two six-petaled rosettes separated by a palm floral branch, and with chip-carved zigzag frames. The ossuary had a yellow-

39. See Kloner and Zissu, *Necropolis*, p. 342; we will later share some unpublished data.

40. Kloner reported seven ossuaries (nos. 1-7) that were left in the tomb in his letter of August 2, 1981, to IDAM (IAA administrative archives/peh/J-M/bet/8/X), but did not include the small child's ossuary (no. 8) that had already been taken out. The full eight ossuaries are mentioned in Kloner and Zissu, *Necropolis*, p. 342.

41. IAA accession no. 81-505; Rahmani, *Catalogue*, p. 229, no. 741, pl. 106.

brown wash of paint, and low stub feet. Kloner also reported finding cook-ing pots in three of the corners of the main chamber of the burial cave.[42] The tomb is dated to the first century CE, with its earliest use possibly going back to the late first century BCE.

Conclusions

Unlike many tombs uncovered in salvage digging operations in Jerusalem that have to be destroyed to allow for modern development to proceed, the Talpiot tomb luckily came to be preserved in a terraced garden situated be-tween two levels of apartment buildings, between the Dov Gruner and Olei ha-Gardom streets in the East Talpiot neighborhood. The place of the tomb is fairly nondescript in appearance, and to get into the tomb one has to de-scend a couple of meters down a cemented square shaft with iron rungs on one side to allow ease of access (fig. 48).[43] Today the shaft is capped by a ce-ment slab to prevent children from falling in, and it cannot be visited with-out permission from the neighbors (fig. 49).

The archaeological evidence from the Talpiot tomb indicates it was undoubtedly in use during the first century CE, perhaps for three or more generations, based on the ossuary inscriptional evidence. We believe it went out of use during the latter part of the first century owing to the "mature" appearance of the tomb and its features. It probably ceased to be used as a Jewish family tomb with the destruction of Jerusalem in 70 CE, though it may also have continued to serve the family in the suburbs of Jerusalem un-til 132 CE.[44] The situation of the ossuaries placed as they are within five of the

---

42. These cooking pots are of a type dating from the first century CE. An intact ves-sel was found in the corner between *kokhim* 3 and 4; two handles and body sherds came from the corner between *kokhim* 6 and 7. Also, a concentration of 25 body sherds was found in the corner next to *kokh* 9.

43. At some point in the 1990s and before the cement slab was put into the place, the tomb was converted into a Jewish *genizah* for holy books and writings by members of the Ultra-Orthodox Jewish community.

44. See Kloner and Zissu, *Necropolis,* pp. 144-48, for a discussion of Jewish tombs that postdate 70 CE. In addition, Kloner summarized the archaeological evidences for Jewish settlement in the hinterland of Jerusalem between the two revolts, i.e., between 70 and 132 CE; see A. Kloner, *Survey of Jerusalem: The Northwestern Sector. Introduction and Indices* (Jerusalem: IAA, 2003), pp. 47-49. Work in recent years in the vicinity of Jerusalem shows the continued presence of Jews in the hinterland of Jerusalem post–70 CE, notably

six *kokhim* in the burial cave, together with clear evidence for primary burials on the arcosolia shelves, reflects the final stage in the use of the burial
cave. How the burial cave was used during its earlier stage is unknown.

There has been a lot of controversy worldwide about the suggestion
that the Talpiot tomb might be the family tomb of Jesus.[45] Beyond the general recognition of the similarity between certain names on the Talpiot ossuaries with that of names known from the Gospels (Jesus, Mary, and Joseph),
the main thrust of this argument has been that the *Mariamene* named on
one of the ossuaries is a form of Mariamne that should be identified as that
of Mary Magdalene, and that the *Yoseh* name on another ossuary should be
identified as that of Joses the brother of Jesus (Mark 6:3). The clustering of
names, when examined statistically in terms of the appearance of Jewish
names of the period, is taken to represent strong evidence in support of the
Jesus family tomb hypothesis.[46]

---

to the north of the city in the area of Tel el-Ful (in the excavations of S. Gibson and
Z. Greenhut, unpublished) and at Shu'fat (R. Bar Nathan and D. A. Sklar-Parnes, "A Jewish Settlement in Orine Between the Two Revolts," in *New Studies in the Archaeology of Jerusalem and Its Region: Collected Papers* [in Hebrew], ed. J. Patrich and D. Amit [Jerusa-
lem: IAA, 2007], pp. 57-64). Hence we cannot discount the possibility that this was also
the case south of the city with the Ramat Rahel site, close to Talpiot of today, surviving
until 135 CE, with tombs in its vicinity still being used by Jewish rural families.

45. Tabor, *Jesus Dynasty,* pp. 22-33; Jacobovici and Pellegrino, *Jesus Family Tomb,*
esp. pp. 193-212.

46. A. Feuerverger, "Statistical Analysis of an Archaeological Find," *Annals of Applied Statistics* 2 (2008): 3-54. This statistical study by Feuerverger is excellent and com-
mendable since the author presents his case with integrity. It is faulty only in so far as the
actual archaeological data he relies upon is extremely limited and incomplete. This requires him to incorporate unproven assumptions into his work regarding the names appearing on the ossuaries, such as the improbable *Mariamne* and Mary Magdalene equation, or that the Joseph and *Yoseh* names represent two individuals, not one, and so forth.
A statistical study is only as good as the data on which it is based, and on this we are sure
Feuerverger would concur. See also S. Scham, "Trial by Statistics," *NEA* 69 (2006): 124-25;
C. Mims, "Special Report: Has James Cameron Found Jesus's Tomb or Is It Just a Statisti-
cal Error?" *Scientific American* 296 (2007): http://www.sciam.com/article.cfm?id=jesus-
talpiot-tomb-or-statistical-error; W. A. Dembski and R. J. Marks II, "The Jesus Tomb
Math," in *Buried Hope or Risen Savior: The Search for the Jesus Tomb,* ed. C. L. Quarles
(Nashville: B&H, 2008). Online: http://www.designinference.com/documents/2007.07
.Jesus_Tomb_Math.pdf. For a critique of Feueverger's results see R. Ingermanson, "Discussion of: Statistical Analysis of an Archaeological Find," *Annals of Applied Statistics* 2
(2008): 84-90. A statistical study has also been published in regard to the so-called James
ossuary (see above, n. 29): C. Fuchs, "Demography, Literacy and Names Distribution in

So what should we make of this? The suggestion that *Mariamne* is Mary Magdalene is based on an assumed association between the two, as reflected in the *Acts of Philip*.[47] However, since this text dates from the late fourth (or early fifth) century, and since the only other possible references to Mary Magdalene as Mariamne are in the gnostic writings of Hippolytus from the early third century CE, one must express extreme caution in the suggestion that Mariamne was Mary Magdalene's real name.[48]

However, as mentioned above, we believe the proper reading for the so-called Mariamne inscription may very well be *Mariame kai Mara,* as a number of scholars have concluded.[49] This would imply that the skeletal remains of the two female individuals placed in the ossuary were a mother and daughter, or perhaps two sisters. If one accepts this reading, then the entire argument about *Mariamene* being Mariamne, and Mariamne being Mary Magdalene, evaporates. Moreover, the name *Yoseh* on one of the other ossuaries could actually be a shortened form of *Yehoseph,* and, in our opinion, this is probably the same Yehoseph who is the father of Yeshua on another ossuary in the tomb, who, in turn, was the father of Yehudah. Hence, if we discount the Mariamne–Mary Magdalene and Yoseh–brother of Jesus connections, then we are simply left with a group of ossuaries bearing common Jewish names of the first century CE.[50]

As a result, there is nothing to commend the Talpiot tomb as the family tomb of Jesus. At best, the names of the ossuaries are suggestive. The authors of this article are both convinced that the actual tomb of Jesus is situated beneath the Edicule within the Church of the Holy Sepulchre, as tradition dictates and on archaeological grounds.[51]

Ancient Jerusalem — How Many James/Jacob Son of Joseph Brother of Jesus Were There?" *Polish Journal of Biblical Research* 4/1 (2004): 3-30.

47. F. Bovon, "Mary Magdalene in the Acts of Philip," in *Which Mary? The Marys of Early Christian Tradition,* ed. F. Stanley Jones (Atlanta: Society of Biblical Literature, 2002), pp. 75-89. It should be noted that Bovon in a statement made to the press about the Talpiot tomb has insisted that this portrayal in the *Acts of Philip* of Mariamne, presumed to be that of Mary Magdalene, is of literary, not historical, significance.

48. Bauckham, "Alleged Jesus Family Tomb," p. 3.

49. Pfann, "Mary Magdalene," pp. 130-31.

50. Tal Ilan, *Lexicon of Jewish Names in Late Antiquity,* Part 1, *Palestine 330 BCE–200 CE,* TSAJ 91 (Tübingen: Mohr Siebeck, 2002).

51. S. Gibson and J. E. Taylor, *Beneath the Church of the Holy Sepulchre, Jerusalem: The Archaeology and Early History of Traditional Golgotha* (London: PEF, 1994); A. Kloner, "Reconstruction of the Tomb in the Rotunda of the Holy Sepulchre According to Archae-

Acknowledgments

We are grateful to Professor James Charlesworth for inviting us to contribute this chapter to the publication. It is dedicated to the memory of the late Yoseph Gath. We thank Miki Sebanne, head of the IAA Beth Shemesh Storage and Research Facility, for allowing us to re-examine the Talpioth ossuaries stored there, and Aryeh Rochman of the IAA archives for giving us access to the documents and photographs relating to the Talpioth excavation. We also wish to thank the following scholars for their help and information: Dr. Sean Freyne; Dr. Joan Taylor; Joe Zias; Dr. Rafael Greenberg; Dr. Boaz Zissu; Dr. Aryeh Shimron; L. Y. Rachmani; and Dr. Stephen Pfann. The illustrations used in this chapter belong to the authors or are the property of the IAA, whom we thank. In particular, we thank Rivka Maoz for allowing us to use her personal photographs of the tomb. We are also grateful to the staff of Eerdmans publishing house for their dedicated work.

---

ological Finds and Jewish Burial Customs of the First Century CE," in *The Beginnings of Christianity: A Collection of Articles,* ed. J. Pastor and M. Mor (Jerusalem: Yad Ben-Zvi, 2005), pp. 269-78. See also Gibson, *Final Days of Jesus,* p. 154, where he suggests that the nearby "Tomb of Joseph of Arimathea" might actually have been the burial place for the immediate or extended family members, owing to its very close proximity to the tomb of Jesus.

Figure 1. The façade of the Talpiot Tomb with the vestibule in front *(Photo: A. Kloner, IAA)*

Figure 2. The northern wall of the Talpiot Tomb main chamber with a*rcosolium y;* note the cracked mud on the shelf of the *arcosolium,* beneath the scale *(Photo: A. Kloner, IAA)*

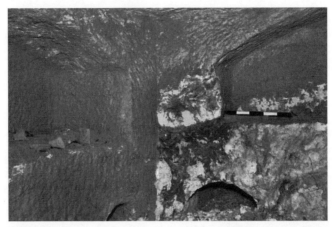

Figure 3. The northwestern corner of the Talpiot Tomb main chamber with *arcosolium x* on the left and a*rcosolium y* on the right *(Photo: A. Kloner, IAA)*

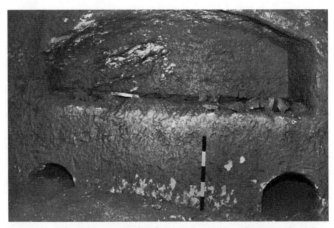

Figure 4. The western wall of the Talpiot Tomb main chamber with *arcosolium x;* note the height of the fills inside the lower *kokhim* *(Photo: A. Kloner, IAA)*

Figure 5. The southwestern corner of the Talpiot Tomb main chamber with *arcosolium x* on the right *(Photo: A. Kloner, IAA)*

Figure 6. The late Yoseph Gath *(Photo: S. Gibson)*

Figure 7. Letter of A. Kloner
of 28 March 1980 to IDAM,
reporting on the discovery of
the Talpiot Tomb *(Photo: IAA)*

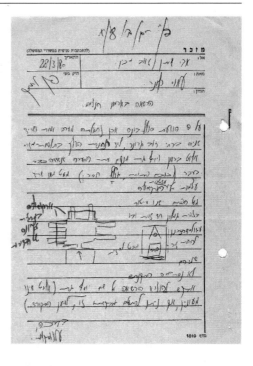

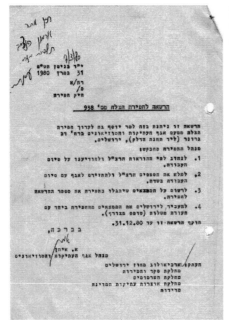

Figure 8. License No. 938 issued
to Yoseph Gath to excavate the
Talpiot Tomb *(Photo: IAA)*

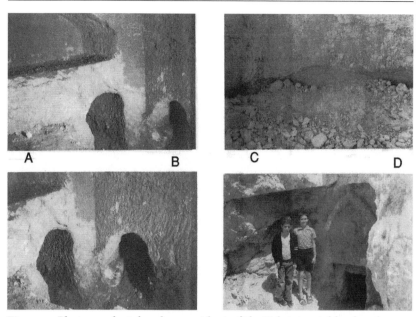

Figure 9. Photographs taken by a resident of the Talpiot neighborhood on 29 March 1980, showing: (a) the northeastern corner of the Talpiot Tomb main chamber with *arcosolium y* on the left; (b) the same – compare with Figure 6, which was taken before the dig began; (c) the eastern wall of the external courtyard of the tomb, which was badly destroyed by the blasting; (d) the façade of the tomb with two boys – Ouriel Maoz is on the right *(Photos: R. Maoz)*

Figure 10. Typed report by Gath from 15 April 1980 on the results of the excavations at the Talpiot Tomb
(Photo: IAA)

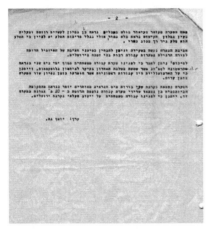

Figure 11. Second page of Gath's report from 15 April 1980 *(Photo: IAA)*

Figure 12. File card prepared by Gath on the Talpiot Tomb from 15 April 1980 *(Photo: IAA)*

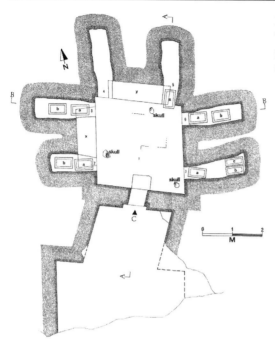

Figure 13. Plan of the
Talpiot Tomb made
in April 1980
(Drawing: S. Gibson)

Figure 14. Elevations A-A,
B-B of the Talpiot Tomb
and the façade drawing C
(Drawing: S. Gibson)

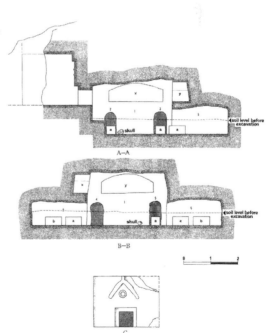

Figure 15. Interior door with carved gable above it from a tomb in the Akeldama Cemetery; note the appendage at the top, which the authors think might be a schematic burial urn representation *(Photo: S. Gibson)*

Figure 16. Interior door with carved gable above it from a tomb in the Akeldama Cemetery
(Drawing: S. Gibson)

Figure 17. Interior door with carved gable above it from a tomb in the Akeldama Cemetery
(Drawing: S. Gibson)

Figure 18. A diadem from the decorated façade of the "Tomb of the Kings"
(Photo: S. Gibson)

Figure 19. A diadem from the
decorated façade of the "Tomb
of the Grapes" *(Photo: S. Gibson)*

Figure 20. The front of Ossuary No. 1 carved with rosettes *(Photo: S. Gibson)*

Figure 21. The front of Ossuary No. 1 carved with rosettes *(Photo: IAA)*

Figure 22. The back of Ossuary No. 1 with inscription "Mariamenou Mara" or "Mariame kai Mara" *(Photo: S. Gibson)*

Figure 23. The back of Ossuary No. 1 with inscription "Mariamenou Mara" or "Mariame kai Mara" *(Photo: IAA)*

Figure 24. One of the short sides of Ossuary No. 1 with unfinished decorations *(Photo: IAA)*

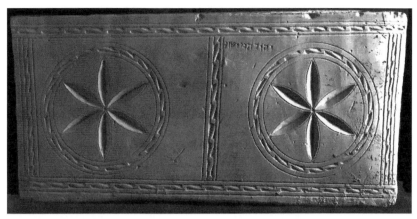

Figure 25. The front of Ossuary No. 2 carved with rosettes and inscribed "Yehuda bar Yeshua" *(Photo: IAA)*

Figure 26. A close-up of the inscription "Yehuda bar Yeshua" on the front of Ossuary No. 2 *(Photo: IAA)*

Figure 27. The front of Ossuary No. 3 showing broad vertical chisel marks *(Photo: IAA)*

Figure 28. The short side of Ossuary No. 3 with inscription "Matya" *(Photo: S. Gibson)*

Figure 29. The short side of Ossuary No. 3 with inscription "Matya" *(Photo: IAA)*

Figure 30. The plain (and scratched) front of Ossuary No. 4 *(Photo: IAA)*

Figure 31. The lightly scratched inscription "Yeshua (?) bar Yehosef" on the short side of Ossuary No. 4 *(Photo: IAA)*

Figure 32. Ossuary No. 5 with an inscription "Yosé" on its front *(Photo: S. Gibson)*

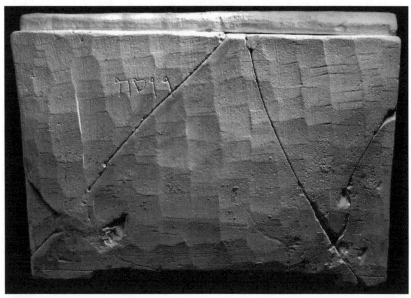

Figure 33. The plain front of Ossuary No. 5 showing broad vertical chisel marks and inscription "Yosé" *(Photo: IAA)*

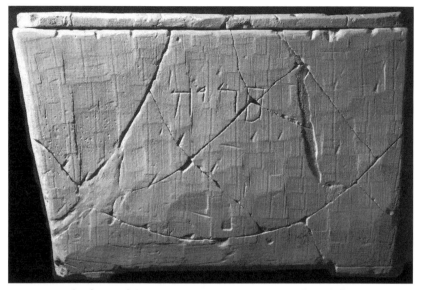

Figure 34. The front of Ossuary No. 6 with inscription "Marya" *(Photo: IAA)*

Figure 35. The front of Ossuary No. 7 carved with rosettes *(Photo: IAA)*

Figure 36. The back of Ossuary No. 7 with scratched maker's mark *(Photo: IAA)*

Figure 37. One of the
short ends of Ossuary
No. 7 with numerous
scratches and marks
(Photo: IAA)

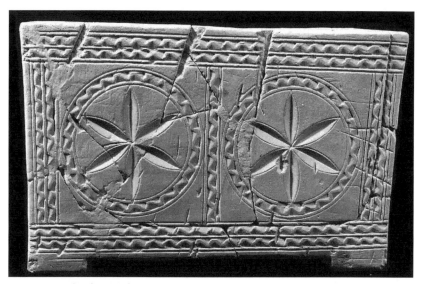

Figure 38. The front of Ossuary No. 8 carved with rosettes *(Photo: IAA)*

Figure 39. The front of Ossuary No. 9 carved with rosettes *(Photo: IAA)*

Figure 40. Remains of plastered installation near the Talpiot Tomb
(Photo: A. Kloner)

Figure 41. Remains of ruined Tomb 12-13 with the ends of a few
***kokhim* still visible** *(Photo: A. Kloner)*

Figure 42. License No. 1050 issued to A. Kloner to excavate the second Talpiot Tomb *(Photo: IAA)*

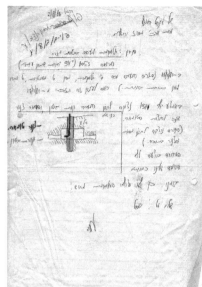

Figure 43. Letter of A. Kloner of 2 August 1981 to IDAM, reporting on the blocking up of the second Talpiot Tomb by the Ultra-Orthodox *(Photo: IAA)*

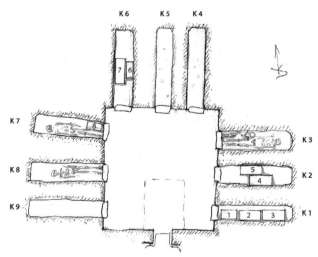

Figure 44. Plan of the second Talpiot Tomb (Israel Grid 172 12880) prepared by A. Kloner in 1981 *(Drawing: A. Kloner / S. Gibson)*

Figure 45. Ossuaries *in situ* in *kokh* No 1
of the second Talpiot Tomb *(Photo: A. Kloner)*

Figure 46. Ossuaries *in situ* in *kokh* No 2
of the second Talpiot Tomb *(Photo: A. Kloner)*

Figure 47. Ossuaries *in situ* in *kokh* No 6
of the second Talpiot Tomb *(Photo: A. Kloner)*

Figure 48. Skeletal remains in *kokh*
No. 4 of the second Talpiot Tomb
(Photo: A. Kloner)

Figure 49. A child's ossuary (No. 8 from *kokh* 7 [see Fig. 44]) from the second
Talpiot Tomb *(Photo: IAA)*

The Imperfect "Tomb of Jesus and Family"

Claude Cohen-Matlofsky

Recently in Jerusalem, at the Third Princeton Symposium on Judaism and Christian Origins, I contributed my thoughts in two panel discussions: one on prosopography, the other on epigraphy, examining the evidence from the Talpiot tomb.

I published my doctoral dissertation in 2001, a prosopographic study of early Roman Palestine that deals in large measure with ossuaries and burial practices of the Jews in the Herodian and post-Herodian periods up to the end of the Bar Kokhba Revolt.[1] Prior to that, I tried to establish the possible relation between secondary burials in ossuaries and the concept of resurrection.[2]

It is true that over the centuries many times evidence of the existence of Jesus of/from Nazareth had been put forward to the public in a rather sensationalistic way, and this includes the so-called James ossuary. It is not the case for the Talpiot tomb. Indeed, we might be dealing with the most tangible evidence ever of the existence of Jesus and his family, and I am afraid I have to say that the negativist scholars might have put themselves in a Peter and the Wolf type of scenario.

I was among the first to question the authenticity of the so-called James ossuary,[3] prior to its exhibit at the Royal Ontario Museum in 2002. I

---

1. C. Cohen-Matlofsky, *Les Laics en Palestine d'Auguste à Hadrien: Étude prosopographique* (Paris: Honoré Champion, 2001).

2. Idem, "Controverse sur les coutumes funéraires des Juifs en Palestine aux deux premiers siècles de l'Empire romain," *L'information historique* 53 (1991): 21-26.

3. Idem, "Was It Jesus Brother's," *Globe and Mail,* November 6, 2002.

judged that the inscription was at least partially fraudulent while the box was authentic. My main concern was the lack of provenance for the ossuary, and I am not prepared to reintegrate it in the Talpiot tomb either, although I shall not discuss the matter in this paper.

In the case of the Talpiot tomb there is no question of provenance, not even of the nature of the findings. The only problem is that the archaeologists could not take proper notes on the spot. So we are left with secondary sources in a sense, since the bones, for instance, had to be reburied by the modern Orthodox Jews of Israel before they could be recorded or properly examined.

This tomb, although typical in many ways, is imperfect for a number of reasons. But how many of the hundreds of tombs of this type excavated in Jerusalem and vicinity presented an archetypal model, like the one of the Goliath family in Jericho? Rachel Hachlili, a leading Israeli archaeologist in the field of funerary customs and burial practices in early Roman Palestine, was very lucky when excavating the Goliath family tomb in Jericho. This was an archetypal tomb. Every member of the family was there, over four generations; the inscriptions, very clearly carved, matched the bones found intact in the ossuaries. That allowed her to draw a family tree.[4] However, there is no mention so far of this perfect Goliath family in the literary sources of the time. Could it have been the tomb of the biblical Goliath? No one has come up with this suggestion even jokingly — at least not yet.

As a social historian, a prosopographist of the Jews in early Roman Palestine, I am inclined to reconstruct Jesus — the man, the Jew — and his family in the proper historical context. One cannot believe in the historical Jesus and deny him a historical context, and this context has to be found in the formative Hellenistic Judaism of ancient Palestine and more specifically in rabbinic roots.

What do we know for sure?

1. A large group of Jews in Roman Palestine had their family tomb hewn in the rock, according to archaeological and literary sources.
2. Some of these tombs were more architecturally elaborate than others. Some contained ossuaries, some of these ossuaries bore inscriptions, some bore decorations, some had both.

---

4. See R. Hachlili, "The Goliath Family in Jericho: Funerary Inscriptions from a First Century A.D. Jewish Monumental Tomb," *BASOR* 235 (1979): 31-63, and the family tree on p. 66. See as well R. Hachlili and P. Smith, "The Genealogy of the Goliath Family," *BASOR* 235 (1979): 67-70. Hachlili supposes that the Goliath family was a sacerdotal family settled in Jericho. However, nothing supports this statement.

3. These family tombs were of a patriarchal type over three or four generations. That means that once a daughter was married she most likely would have been buried in her husband's tomb, unless she was an adulteress.

4. The practice of a secondary burial among probably the largest group of Jews of Roman Palestine is widely attested from the Herodian period up to the Byzantine era.

5. This practice, which consists of the gathering of bones *(ossilegium)*, must have remained in use among the first Christians since burial practices and funerary customs are the last that a people would give up on, due to the sensitivity of the matter, including rites of a superstitious nature, like some borrowings from pagan surrounding religions.[5] The practice of burial in ossuaries was also in use among the Christian monks living in the caves of Cappadocia in Turkey in the Byzantine era.

6. Jesus' corpse was temporarily (referring most likely to a primary burial) placed in a rock-cut tomb in Jerusalem, according to the New Testament sources.

7. A large group of Jews in early Roman Palestine were preoccupied with the afterlife, including immortality of the soul and/or resurrection, at least according to sources such as Flavius Josephus and rabbinic literature.

Is the Talpiot tomb the family tomb of Jesus? The evidence is worth scholarly examination. By paying attention to the matter in a scientific way one could only advance the research on the historical Jesus and his movement, as well as on the social history of early Roman Palestine as a whole with an emphasis on burial practices and funerary customs. The careful review of the evidence could also help reestablish sound methodologies for further discussions in this field.

One cannot pretend to assess the Talpiot tomb without reading the book of Amos Kloner and Boaz Zissu[6] as well as that by Rachel Hachlili,[7] be-

---

5. See R. Hachlili, *Jewish Funerary Customs, Practices and Rites in the Second Temple Period,* JSJSup 94 (Leiden: Brill, 2005), pp. 514-15, where she discusses borrowings from surrounding cultures in Jewish burial practices, including the coin in the mouth or on the eye (pp. 441-43).

6. A. Kloner and B. Zissu, *The Necropolis of Jerusalem in the Second Temple Period,* Interdisciplinary Studies in Ancient Culture and Religion 8 (Leuven: Peeters, 2007).

7. See Hachlili, *Jewish Funerary Customs.*

cause they contain thorough information on burial practices and funerary customs of the time of Jesus, while compiling all the data at our disposal thus far in the field. I am grateful to Kloner and Zissu for completing a catalogue of the tombs in Second Temple Jerusalem. I had myself expressed the need for such an important work. Moreover, Kloner and Zissu carefully added in their list the corresponding number in L. Y. Rahmani's *Catalogue* for each ossuary found in the tomb. Kloner and Zissu's *Necropolis in Jerusalem* is an invaluable source for further research in the field of burial practices in early Roman Palestine. Hachlili's *Jewish Funerary Customs* is an exhaustive reflection on the field that comprises archaeology, funerary art, and beliefs related to the afterlife in early Roman Palestine. It belongs to both archaeology and art and social history, while Kloner and Zissu's is pure old-school archaeology. Both books are very useful for a social historian of the period like myself.

The methodology I intend to follow in this paper consists in going from the general to the particular. I propose to assess the Talpiot tomb according to: (1) historically accepted data based on archaeology and literary sources; (2) examination of the prosopography/epigraphy; (3) statistics.

One should try to find a consensus on the historical Jesus and his family members from the literary sources as a methodological point of departure and then examine the data from the tomb and be thrilled if enough evidence (because one never has *all* the evidence in ancient history) could match. I am not a specialist of the literature of nascent Christianity. Therefore I shall focus my historical analysis on attempting to re-create the Jewish context, based on archaeological and literary sources, in which the Talpiot tomb should be apprehended.

The Talpiot tomb is nothing but a family rock-cut tomb. Eric Meyers and Jodi Magness, two participants at the symposium, were incorrect when questioning the familial character of the Jerusalem rock-cut tombs of the early Roman period. These rock-cut tombs were familial, of a patriarchal type over three or four generations; experts such as Kloner, Zissu, and Hachlili (especially *Jewish Funerary Customs*, ch. 6) all agree on that. The archaeological evidence attesting to this consensus is found in a number of ossuary inscriptions mentioning the filiation of the deceased as *ben* (in Hebrew) or *bar* (in Aramaic) for a son and *bat* (in Hebrew) or *barat* (in Aramaic) for a daughter, and the father's name. The father's ossuary was usually found in the tomb to help us clarify this filiation. Prosopographists like myself were able to identify the custom of patronymy, the naming of a son according to his father's name, and papponymy, the naming of a son according to his grandfather's name. Metronymy, the naming of a daughter after her grandmother, was also, to a certain extent, attested as a practice of the time.[8] I shall come back to this practice later in this paper. In the meantime, it is indeed interesting to note that this very practice of patronymy/ papponymy/metronymy, by its repetitive nature, leaves the sample of names quite narrow and refutes by essence the argument of "very common names" put forward by scholars who deny that the Talpiot tomb could be the one of Jesus' family.

Burials in shafts or trenches were very scarce at the time in and around Jerusalem, except perhaps those of the Essenes. I agree with Hachlili, Kloner, and Zissu on that (Kloner and Zissu, *Necropolis of Jerusalem,* pp. 96-97; Hachlili, *Jewish Funerary Customs,* pp. 478-79). Hachlili strengthens this point by adding that the graves found in Beth Zafafa were similar to Qumran graves; therefore the Qumran people may very well have been Essenes.

In the Second Temple period, 900 family tombs were rock-cut and 60 individual graves were hewn in a ring of about 4 km around the city of Jerusalem. Burials were prohibited inside towns, with an emphasis for this prohibition on Jerusalem because of the laws of purity and impurity that applied more strictly to this city. The spatial distribution of the necropolis was: northern, 309 tombs; eastern, 124 tombs; southern, 237 tombs; western, 123.[9] The tombs are laid out in clusters around the city where plots of land were available and in places where the rock was appropriate for hewing.

The tombs were hewn within families' agricultural estates; each family took care of its own tomb. The landownership of these tombs was presumably the responsibility of the family. Most residents of Jerusalem, however, belonged to urban families that did not own land. Therefore, they would purchase a plot of land for family burial purposes. The owner of the area and his family probably buried their dead there first and they could sell the rest of the land as the necropolis grew (cf. *m. B. Bat.* 6:8). Also described in detail in this passage of the Mishnah is the process of hewing tombs by experienced professionals. This text also gives a detailed description of a plan of a tomb with *kokhim* (in Hebrew) or *loculi* (in Latin), niches carved in the walls

---

8. T. Ilan, *Jewish Women in Greco-Roman Palestine: An Inquiry with Image and Status* (1995; repr. Peabody, Mass.: Hendrickson, 1996), p. 53; Cohen-Matlofsky, *Laics,* p. 17; Hachlili, *Jewish Funerary Customs,* p. 195.

9. See B. Zissu, "The Necropolis of Jerusalem in the Second Temple Period: New Discoveries 1980-1995" (MA thesis, Hebrew University, Jerusalem, 1995), p. 149, fig. 5.

of the tomb. Relatively few burial complexes in the necropolis show evidence of meticulous planning.[10]

The Gospel of John mentions a garden at the site of the crucifixion surrounding the unused tomb in which Jesus was temporarily laid (John 19:41-42). The archaeological record as well as literary sources such as Josephus (*War* 5.54; 6.106) and the Mishnah (*Ta'an.* 4:8; *'Ohal.* 8:2; *Naz.* 7:3) support this picture. It is well known that ornamental gardens surrounded cemeteries in the Greco-Roman world,[11] and in particular around Jerusalem, together with orchards and vegetable gardens.

The above constitutes a good context for the instance described in the Gospels in which Joseph of Arimathea would have "loaned a burial space for Jesus in his freshly hewn tomb." James Tabor does not believe that this new, or more appropriately, unused, tomb belonged to Joseph of Arimathea: "What are the chances that he would just happen to have his own new family tomb conveniently located near the Place of the Skull, or Golgotha, where the Romans regularly crucified their victims?"[12] This statement has been strengthened by one participant at the symposium, Eldad Keynan, who elaborated on the thesis that Jesus was temporarily buried in one of the Sanhedrin's court-owned tombs that *m. Sanh.* 6:5-6 mentions. These two courts were probably close to each other and to the execution ground that appears to be the area known as Golgotha today.

Let's look at *m. Sanh.* 6:5-6 (Danby's trans.): "They used not to bury him in the burying-place of his fathers, but two burying-places were kept in readiness by the court, one for them that were beheaded or strangled, and one for them that were stoned or burnt. When the flesh had wasted away they gathered together the bones and buried them in their own place."

This rabbinic source does not mention the fate of crucified criminals (crucifixion was a Roman mode of execution). However, Jesus was sentenced by the Sanhedrin even though he was executed by the Romans. Therefore one can assume that he was to be buried temporarily in one of the court tombs. In this case, how come this tomb was unused as the Gospels describe it? From 63 BCE to around 30 CE the Sanhedrin had legally lost its authority

---

10. For plans of rock-cut tombs cf. Kloner and Zissu, *Necropolis of Jerusalem,* nos. 538-820.

11. J. Toynbee, *Death and Burial in the Roman World* (London: Thames and Hudson, 1971).

12. See the discussion in J. Tabor, "Testing a Hypothesis," *NEA* 69 (2006): 132-33 and n. 2; quotation from p. 133.

to execute death penalties in Roman-ruled Jerusalem. Therefore at least one of its court tombs had never been used. In my judgment, it was in this new and unused tomb that Jesus was laid, one of the two Sanhedrin tombs meant for temporary burials of criminals, and that would be the primary burial, since after a year their bones were gathered and transferred for a secondary burial in their family tombs. After a year the family gathered Jesus' bones and put them in an ossuary in his family tomb, the Talpiot tomb, as *m. Sanh.* 6:6 prescribes.[13]

Was Jesus' family wealthy enough to possess a rock-cut tomb in Jerusalem? Moreover, one with ossuaries, and even inscribed and/or decorated ossuaries? Jodi Magness contends that if Jesus were reburied, it would likely be in a trench grave, not a rock-cut tomb, trench graves being used by poor people, or people like the Essenes committed to abstaining from private property.

But several points argue against this. First, social status seems to have had little to do with rock-cut tombs. Apparently it took only a few hours to carve a tomb in the Jerusalem limestone, and the various grades of the thousands of tombs show that different social classes could afford it. Second, regarding the social status of Jesus' family, they were apparently not that poor. A carpenter at the time seems to have made a good living.[14] Therefore the

13. For more on the legal analysis of the circumstances surrounding Jesus' death and burial see R. Carrier, "The Burial of Jesus in Light of Jewish Law," in *The Empty Tomb: Jesus Beyond the Grave*, ed. R. Price and J. J. Lowder (Amherst: Prometheus, 2005), pp. 369-92. See also Kloner and Zissu, *Necropolis of Jerusalem*, p. 70: "f. Kokh burial makes it possible to check on the state of the body after about three days"; n. 24: "See the accounts in the Gospels (Matt 27:62-66, 28:1-15; Mark 16:1-5; Luke 24:1-2; John 20:1). In Safrai's opinion (Safrai 1976: 784-85), the date stated in *Semahot* 8:1 for visiting the tomb should be read as three days and not thirty. He thus disagrees with Higger (1931: 148) and Zlotnick (1966: 19), the reason for paying a visit within three days after death and burial was to determine the condition of the corpse (see Safrai 1976: 784 n. 6 and references; Kloner 1999: 29, 76). *Semahot* 8:1 makes more sense if we read it as saying three rather than thirty days: 'One may go out to the cemetery for three [thirty?] days to inspect the dead for a sign of life, without fear that this smacks of heathen practice. For it happened that a man was inspected after three [thirty?] days, and he went on to live twenty-five years; still another went on to have five children and died later.' Jesus' disciples may have visited the tomb on the third day to conform to this Jewish custom."

14. Jesus could even have hewn his own tomb himself. On Jesus' vocation Tabor writes: "Everyone knows he was a carpenter. . . . The Greek word *tekton* is a more generic term referring to a 'builder.' It can include one who works with wood, but in its 1st-century Galilean context it more likely refers to a stoneworker" (*The Jesus Dynasty: The*

mention of poverty linked to Jesus and his family in the Scriptures has to do with later theological views and relates to an early Judeo-Christian ideology of helping the poor and protesting the waste at the temple. Moreover, it looks like the use of ossuaries is attested among Pharisees, mostly with a link to their belief in resurrection, and among Sadducees (if Absalom, the Bene Hezir, Caiaphas, etc., were indeed Sadducees) as a "signe extérieur de richesse."[15]

The distribution of cemeteries around Jerusalem seems to indicate that burial was handled by the family and not by the community. The most common type in the Jerusalem necropolis of the Second Temple period is the rock-cut *kokhim* tomb. This method replaced the ledge or bench tomb, which was common in the Iron Age. *Kokh* burial has a foreign influence for economical and convenience purposes. The origin of the loculi tombs is to be found in Egypt, in Leontopolis, from the Hasmonean times (cf. Hachlili, *Jewish Funerary Customs*, p. 10). The rock-hewn loculi tomb had a rectangular entrance that led to a single square burial chamber with a rectangular standing pit that was lined on all but the entrance side by benches or ledges, very similar to those found in the Iron Age tombs. Recesses such as *kokhim* and arcosolia were carved into the chamber walls for primary and secondary burials. The Talpiot tomb fits this description.[16]

As more space was needed in the tombs, additional *kokhim* and other types of niches were carved into the walls. In more elaborate tombs, room after room might be added, extending the tomb in various directions, thus creating a multichambered burial system. The *golel* (in Hebrew) is a rectangular stone slab, sometimes a round, "rolling stone" that closes the tomb. The round "rolling stone" is extremely rare in the Jerusalem necropolis — only four instances are known so far where it was used to seal the tomb: Herod's family tomb, the Tombs of the Kings, and tombs 7 and 3 in the Kidron Valley. Kloner and Zissu (*Necropolis of Jerusalem*, p. 55): "The use of caves sealed with round stones can be dated to the 1st century CE, chiefly in the middle of the century." I think that Kloner and Zissu's use of the term *cave* throughout their work is inappropriate; I would rather use the term *tomb*. In any case, Hachlili (*Jewish Funerary Customs*, p. 64) agrees with this

---

Hidden History of Jesus, His Royal Family, and the Birth of Christianity [New York: Simon & Schuster, 2006], p. 89).

15. See Cohen-Matlofsky, "Controverse," p. 26.

16. See the inside of the Talpiot tomb looking north, photo courtesy of Tabor, "Testing a Hypothesis," p. 132.

dating of the "rolling stone," one more bit of chronological evidence going in the direction of the Talpiot tomb being Jesus' family's. Since all four canonical Gospels indicate a "rolling stone" (Mark 15:45; 16:3-4; Matt 27:60; 28:2; Luke 24:2; John 20:1, which mentions only a stone), we now assume that they are talking about the criminals' tomb, and therefore the Talpiot tomb would have been Jesus' family tomb. There is no recorded evidence of the kind of stone that sealed the Talpiot tomb.

Archaeological evidence indicates that rock-cut tombs were still in use between 70 and 135 CE. Kloner and Zissu (*Necropolis of Jerusalem*, pp. 147-48): "In our opinion, during the period 70-132 CE Jews were allowed to live in the city's immediate surroundings, and they continued to bury their dead in the ancestral tombs." This corresponds to the assumption that I made in *Laics*, where I adopted a chronological window from the Herodian period to the end of the Bar Kokhba Revolt for every funerary inscription on ossuaries in and around Jerusalem.[17]

In Jerusalem and vicinity, in these rock-cut tombs and from the Herodian period up to the end of the Bar Kokhba Revolt, Jews performed a primary burial; then, after about a year,[18] they did a secondary burial by

17. See Kloner and Zissu, *Necropolis of Jerusalem*, pp. 142 n. 2, 143: "figures given by Cassius Dio (*Historia Romana*, 69, 14:1) who recounts that 985 important Judean villages and 50 outposts were destroyed in the Bar Kokhba Revolt, accurately reflect the dense settlement pattern of rural Judea in the period preceding the revolt. The residents of farmsteads, estates and villages continued to bury their dead in the family burial caves, located near their respective settlements . . . the assemblages of tombs in the Benjamin area . . . in the Judean Shephelah . . . , and elsewhere, indicates that burial in caves [please read 'rock-cut tombs'] continued until the Bar Kokhba Revolt (see discussion and tables in Zissu 2001:302-306). . . . We have no unequivocal evidence of Jewish burial in Jerusalem in the second half of the 2nd century."

18. I believe that the one-year period of wait between primary and secondary burials, the time needed for the decomposing of the flesh (a natural purification of the corpse, since, according to some interpretations, the flesh was considered a receptacle of impurity), has to do with body fluids, and this is corroborated by both literary and archaeological sources. Indeed, the impurity in question was associated with the body fluids that are identified as a source of impurity for both men and women and come out in abundance from the dead body. See *m. Mo'ed Qat.* 3:2, as well as the numerous mikvaot excavated in the vicinity of rock-cut tombs in that period, all evidence of the concern for purification from the body fluids of the corpses. Thus one year was the period safely needed to obtain these "purified dried bones," ready for resurrection. Moreover, Hachlili, *Jewish Funerary Customs*, p. 486, writes: "Several examples of perforation in the bottom of sarcophagi and ossuaries were noted." However, I shall contend that, while the holes were functional for

gathering the bones, a process called *liqut 'atsamot* (in Hebrew) or *ossilegium* (in Latin), sometimes in a stone box called an ossuary. (The terms used for "ossuary" in that period were Greek *ostophagos* [lit. "bone-eater"], Hebrew *'aron,* and Aramaic *halat/halta'.*) The gathering of the bones was performed by close relatives of the deceased. After 135 CE the practice moved to Galilee along with the population.

More than three thousand ossuaries have been found, mostly in the Second Temple Jerusalem necropolis, of which about twelve hundred were ornamented or plain with inscriptions and are in collections in Israel. These collections include the ossuary of a crucified man.[19] Had the bones of the Talpiot tomb been scientifically examined and recorded at the time of discovery in 1980, one could speculate that there were traces of crucifixion on Jesus' bones found in ossuary no. 704 of Rahmani's *Catalogue.*[20] Hachlili (*Jewish Funerary Customs,* p. 96, fig. III-13) provides us with a drawing of tools used to produce ossuaries. Also Hachlili (ibid., pp. 97-100, figs. III-14, 15, 16, 17) has drawings of four types of decorated ossuaries. After the destruction of Jerusalem the ossuaries were undecorated. Clay ossuaries were used as well from 135 CE to the mid-third century CE; most of them were found in southern Judea and Galilee, locally manufactured and purchased. A Roman influence was designated by the introduction of a small funerary chest, suitable for cremation.[21]

Ossuaries from Talpiot tomb 9 were catalogued.[22] Although I am not going to enter the controversy in this paper, it is interesting to notice that in his report of the Talpiot tomb, Kloner catalogues 9 ossuaries while recording 10 in two other references.[23] Rahmani (*Catalogue,* no. 701, *Comm.* 1) also

---

the purpose of fluid drainage in sarcophagi, it is understood that in ossuaries they were just symbolic since it was dried bones that were gathered after about a year in these stone boxes.

19. See N. Haas, "Anthropological Observations on the Skeletal Remains from Giv'at Hamivtar, Jerusalem," *IEJ* 20 (1970): 38-59; and J. Zias and E. Sekeles, "The Crucified Man from Giv'at Hamivtar, Jerusalem," *IEJ* 35 (1985): 22-27.

20. See L. Y. Rahmani, *A Catalogue of Jewish Ossuaries in the Collections of the State of Israel* (Jerusalem: Israel Antiquities Authority and Israel Academy of Sciences and Humanities, 1994), p. 223.

21. See Hachlili, *Jewish Funerary Customs,* ch. 11, which contains a scholarly debate on the causes and origin of ossuaries. See as well ch. 12, which contains the chronology and geographic distribution of ossuaries.

22. See Rahmani, *Catalogue,* nos. 701-9. See also A. Kloner, "A Tomb with Inscribed Ossuaries in East Talpiyot, Jerusalem," *'Atiqot* 29 (1996): 15-22.

23. See Kloner, "Tomb with Inscribed Ossuaries": cf. p. 22, where he estimates the total number of interments in the Talpiot tomb; p. 17, table 3, and p. 10 n. 2.

mentions a tenth plain and broken ossuary. Where is the missing ossuary? I shall leave the investigation to others. Nevertheless, Kloner does mention: "The ossuaries . . . are typical Jewish ossuaries of the first century CE. The number of ornamented ossuaries equals the number of plain ones (Table 3), a ratio common in burial complexes of the period (Kloner 1993: 104).[24] Six ossuaries are inscribed (60%), which is a higher ratio than normally found. Five ossuaries are inscribed in Hebrew and only one in Greek: normally the proportion of Hebrew to Greek is 4:3 (Kloner 1993: 105)."[25]

The exceptional character in the Talpiot tomb in regard to the number of inscribed ossuaries (more than usual) and the languages used (Hebrew script and evidence of an Aramaic-speaking family; only one ossuary inscribed in Greek, the one that may be Mary Magdalene's) contribute to identifying this tomb with Jesus' family.

Moreover, there is every circumstantial reason to believe that Jesus and his followers/family members were practicing burial rites the Jewish way. In fact, among the funerary goods, the unguentaria were the most functional because they contained oil and perfumes used in funerary rituals to anoint body and bones. This corroborates the mention of spices to be used for the burial of Jesus as found in the various passages of the Gospels.[26] Hachlili (*Jewish Funerary Customs*, 444): "Unguentaria vessels served several functions in the burial stages: they contained oil and perfumes brought into the tomb for funerary rituals. The body was cleaned, purified and anointed with water and oil, and sprinkled with perfume in preparation for burial before being wrapped in shrouds. Funerary spices and perfume could add a pleasant scent and prevent the bad odor in the tomb; for fear of contamination, the vessels were left in the tomb or placed next to the bones. The liquid contained in the unguentaria could perhaps help decompose the body."

The use of the *ossilegium* in the Second Temple period is widely attested in the rabbinic literature.[27] In Israel the substantial number of ossuaries dating from the Second Temple period and containing carefully gathered bones corroborates this. In the Scriptures the earliest references to an

---

24. A. Kloner, "Burial Caves and Ossuaries from the Second Temple Period on Mount Scopus" [in Hebrew], in *Jews and Judaism in the Second Temple, Mishnaic, and Talmudic Periods: Essays in Honor of Shmuel Safrai*, ed. I. Gafni, A. Oppenheimer, and M. Stern (Jerusalem: Yad Itzhak Ben-Zvi, 1993), pp. 75-106.

25. Kloner, "Tomb with Inscribed Ossuaries," pp. 16-17.

26. Mark 16:1; Luke 23:56; 24:1; John 19:40.

27. *m. Moʻed Qat.* 1:5; *Sanh.* 6:6; *Pesaḥ.* 8:8; *y. Moʻed Qat.* 1:8, 74; tractate *Semaḥot* 12:4, 6-9; *t. Sanh.* 9:8.

ossilegium and transfer of bones are in the Old Testament, Gen 50:1-14: Joseph sends Jacob's remains to Canaan. Also in Gen 50:25: Joseph commands his brothers to transfer his remains to the familial tomb in Machpelah (Canaan). First Samuel 31:13 says: "They burned Saul and his sons' corpses and then gathered their bones." Archaeology confirms the practice of the *ossilegium* in the Levant as early as the Chalcolithic Age. Gal, Smithline, and Shalem write: "Below these bones there were additional groups of bones intentionally laid in ordered fashion, similar to the fashion of reentering bones in ossuaries. This suggests an earlier stage of secondary burial."[28] Archaeology again confirms the practice of the transfer of bones to be buried in Jerusalem in an inscription on an ossuary.[29]

I disagree with Hachlili's chronology regarding the *ossilegium* in Jerusalem and Jericho (see Hachlili, *Jewish Funerary Customs,* pp. 450-64). I see a contemporaneity of gathering of bones either in pits or in ossuaries both in Jerusalem and Jericho all through the Second Temple period. In my judgment, the introduction of ossuaries in Herodian times did not preclude the *ossilegium* in a pit in the tomb, for purposes of space, economics, and time in the turmoil of wars against the Romans. I therefore even see a possibility of a tertiary burial: transfer of bones from ossuaries to pits sometimes, especially in light of the fact that ossuaries were reused.[30]

As I attempted above to place the Talpiot rock-hewn loculi tomb with its ossuaries within the context of Jewish burial practices and funerary customs of Second Temple Jerusalem, I am now going to re-create the context for Jesus' resurrection.

Jesus and his family were originally from Nazareth in Galilee. Then why would there be a Jesus family tomb in Jerusalem? For two reasons, one practical: they had moved to the capital of Judea; the other has to do with the belief in resurrection, though not in the later Christian sense of the concept but rather in the early rabbinic one: *tehiat hammetim* (vivification of the dead).

Alan Segal argues that the rabbis could have chosen the technical, more explicit term *tequmat hannebelot* (in Hebrew: raising of the corpses) rather than *tehiat hammetim* when dealing with resurrection in their texts.[31]

---

28. Z. Gal, H. Smithline, and D. Shalem, "A Chalcolithic Burial Cave in Peqi'in, Upper Galilee," *IEJ* 47 (1997): 145-54.

29. See E. Puech, "Ossuaires inscrits d'une tombe du Mont des Oliviers," *LASBF* 32 (1982): 355-58.

30. See Cohen-Matlofsky, "Controverse," p. 23.

31. A. Segal, *Life after Death: A History of the Afterlife in the Religions of the West* (New York: Doubleday, 2004), pp. 606-7.

But both terms are taken from Isa 26:19. Therefore in my judgment it really does not matter which one the rabbis chose since the concept of vivification of the dead, *tehiat hammetim,* along with raising of the corpses (more precisely, "dressed again dried bones"), *tequmat hannebelot,* is very well developed in Ezek 37:4-10, and I do not see why the rabbis would have based their discussions on resurrection only on one part of Isa 26:19.

Segal states as well that the rabbis were only dealing with matters of resurrection because pressured to do so by the intellectual environment in a context of acculturation. It was not at the center of their preoccupations, since they were lawmakers. I agree that rabbis were not theologians. However, weren't they first and foremost discussing the written Law? Therefore one has to take into consideration the following:

1. In the written Law itself there is no such a thing as a homogeneous concept of afterlife, since this literary source contains also multiple borrowings from neighboring cultures.
2. While it is true that there is no such a thing as a complete tractate of the Mishnah related to issues of resurrection, it does not allow one to say that the concept itself was not at the center of the layperson's daily life's preoccupations in early Roman Palestine.
3. Moreover, a similar situation is to be seen with regard to messianism. There is no complete tractate of the Mishnah dedicated to messianism either, and for the same reasons. Therefore to say that it was not at the center of the rabbis' preoccupations and not a reflection of the laypeople's belief at the time would be just another big assumption.

In fact, at a time of formative Judaism when rabbis, an elite by intellect (as I like to call them) and not by blood, were democratizing religious observance, it is easy to imagine that the concept of resurrection became the perfect tool for their pedagogical endeavors, even though they could not devote a significant place to such a subject in the framework of their legal documents. Therefore, the rabbis could not legally frame concepts related to the afterlife because they were more preoccupied with the "now-life" (if I may say) issues, but the laypeople were very much preoccupied by these concepts in early Roman Palestine.

Ezekiel 37:12-14 states that tombs would be opened and resurrection should happen in the land of Israel, with an implicit idea of transfer of bones to the land of Israel. I maintain that the concept of resurrection is a parameter not to be neglected in the custom of *ossilegium,* along with others: the concern for space and the continuation of an old practice, as seen above. Rahmani was among the first, if not the first, to relate the practice of *ossilegium* to the concept of resurrection,[32] and I agree with him, adding to the theory that the manner or order in which the bones were gathered in the ossuaries constitutes another evidence of the link between this practice and the concept of resurrection. Legs were placed at the bottom, then spine and arms, then skull on top, a deceased ready to rise.[33]

Hachlili seems to agree with Rahmani on the link between *ossilegium* and resurrection (*Jewish Funerary Customs*, p. 114, quoting Rahmani):

> Although Hellenistic individualistic concepts left their mark on Judaism, the "actual concept of a physical, personal and individual resurrection as found in late first century BCE Jerusalem is clearly Jewish . . ." (Rahmani 1986: 99; 1994: 53-55).[34] Furthermore, the custom of *ossilegium*, as well as the ornamentation of the ossuaries, is distinctly indigenous, and should be considered as "fundamentally Jerusalemite, being conceived without any direct foreign influence." Jerusalem probably strongly influenced the customs and practices of the Jews of Jericho and Judea as a whole.

Hachlili (*Jewish Funerary Customs*, p. 302) on resurrection again:

> The perception of individual burial for the entire population and not just for the upper classes, as in the Israelite period, is probably related to the increasing importance placed on individual resurrection of the body. The concept of individual resurrection is reflected in sources as early as the second century BCE (Dan. 12:2; 2 Macc. 7:9-23; 12:38-45, 14:46; Jos. *Against Apion* II, 218; Finkelstein 1940: 145-159; Rahmani 1961: 117-118, n. 6, 1978: 102-103; 1981, I; 1982, III).[35] L. Y. Rahmani, "Ossuaries and Bone Gathering in the Late Second Temple Period" [in Hebrew], *Qadmoniot* 11 (1978): 102-12; idem, "Ancient Jerusalem's Funerary Cus-

32. L. Y. Rahmani, "Ancient Jerusalem Funerary Customs and Tombs," *BA* 45 (1982): 43-52.

33. See Cohen-Matlofsky, "Controverse," p. 24.

34. See Rahmani, "Some Remarks on R. Hachlili's and A. Killebrew's 'Jewish Funerary Customs,'" *PEQ* 118 (1986): 96-100; also idem, *Catalogue*, pp. 53-55.

35. L. Finkelstein, *The Pharisees: The Sociological Background of Their Faith* (Philadelphia: Jewish Publication Society of America, 1940); L. Y. Rahmani, "Jewish Rock-Cut Tombs in Jerusalem," *'Atiqot* 3 (1961): 93-120.

toms and Tombs," I, II, BA, 44, 1981, pp. 171-77; 229-35. III, IV, BA, 45, 1982, pp. 43-53; 109-19.

Hachlili (*Jewish Funerary Customs*, p. 522) comes back to the link between *ossilegium* and resurrection:

> The belief of individual physical resurrection, of the return from death, is reflected in Daniel (12:2) and later acknowledged in II Macc. 7 and 14:46; this idea might have developed following the Maccabean revolt and the influence of Hellenistic concepts pertaining to the individual. Some scholars maintain that this belief was adopted by the Pharisees and denied by the Sadducees (based on the writings of Josephus) and regard it as the basis for *ossilegium*, the new practice of the late Second Temple period.

Moreover, Hachlili (*Jewish Funerary Customs*, pp. 112-13) says that ossuary ornamentation corresponds to the idea of death and resurrection at that time. She also lists (pp. 494-506) inscriptions with special formulae, including one mentioning resurrection (p. 502 no. 14). Another later ossuary inscription from Beth Shearim mentions resurrection and is listed in Schwabe and Lifshitz as no. 194.[36]

In my judgment, individualization of the deceased became an essential factor in burial practices of Herodian Palestine and is thus to be related to the concept of resurrection, well rooted in the Jewish thought of the time, and especially in the period between the two wars against the Romans. This concept is based on Ezek 37, as well as Isa 26:19.[37]

In Ezek 37 the bones are used as material for creating new bodies and a new community. Their role is to express the continuity of the hope. In the turmoil of early Roman Palestine this concept corresponded well with the democratization of religious practices suggested by the rabbis and with the

---

36. See M. Schwabe and B. Lifshitz, *Beth She'arim*, vol. 2, *The Greek Inscriptions* (New Brunswick, N.J.: Rutgers University Press, 1974).

37. Following the end of the Babylonian exile in the late sixth century BCE, Jews in Palestine expressed mutually exclusive perceptions regarding the afterlife. According to the Sadducees, death ended human existence, while the concept of the resurrection of all or only the righteous became widely popular after 200 BCE as attested in the various sources such as *1 Enoch*, Daniel, 2 Maccabees, *Testaments of the 12 Patriarchs*, *On Resurrection* (4Q521), *Psalms of Solomon*, *Life of Adam and Eve*, *Lives of the Prophets*, the NT, Amidah, 4 Ezra, 2 Baruch, and Josephus.

open tomb theme in early Christian writings. In this context one may understand that the belief in bodily resurrection among the Pharisaic community as well as the Jewish Christians got its influence from the metaphor of dry bones from the Old Testament passage.

Moreover, every Jew should be buried in Jerusalem and vicinity, as stated in Ezek 37. To Kloner and Zissu (*Necropolis of Jerusalem*, pp. 121-22), the "transfer of bones to Jerusalem [is] for family reunification purposes." I say, not only for that, and Gafni corroborates: "Those buried in the land of Israel were conceived as the first to be resurrected with the arrival of the messiah."[38] Therefore Jews believed in resurrection even though they were still aware that someone was in a grave.

This belief in resurrection that could only occur in the land of Israel could partially explain the presence of geographical origin other than Palestinian in some ossuary inscriptions found in tombs excavated around Jerusalem. Such is the case for the Akeldama tombs with people originally from Seleucia in Syria.[39] In other tombs some came from Capoua[40] and from Chalcis.[41] It could mean either that they emigrated to Jerusalem or that they were nonresidents who were only buried (most likely for most of them, in a secondary burial, following the ancestral custom of bones transfer to the land of Israel, attested in the literary sources, as mentioned above) in rock-cut tombs in Jerusalem and vicinity for resurrection purposes.

Moreover, there is no trace of rock-hewn tombs containing ossuaries in Galilee between Herod the Great's rule and the end of the Bar Kokhba Revolt, after which the center of Judaism moved from Jerusalem to Galilee in a forced internal diaspora movement. There is no trace of ossuaries in Galilee until the much later necropolis of Beth Shearim, dating to the third century CE.

It seems that in the Second Temple period the Jerusalem necropolis was quite large compared to other contemporary neighboring necropolises, and that means that it probably included tombs of Diaspora Jews in substantial numbers, and this for the purpose of resurrection in Jerusalem.

In light of the above, rather than dismiss the Talpiot tomb by retroactively imposing Christian theology on a first-century Jewish messiah figure,

---

38. See Gafni, *Land, Center and Diaspora: Jewish Constructs in Late Antiquity*, JSPSup 21 (Sheffield: Sheffield Academic Press, 1997), pp. 79-95.

39. See Cohen-Matlofsky, *Laics*, no. 351.

40. See ibid., no. 381.

41. See ibid., no. 334.

I once again propose to apprehend the Jesus movement in its rightful Jewish context. It is therefore conceivable that Jesus had a secondary burial in an ossuary in a family tomb in the area of Jerusalem for resurrection purposes.

It is now time to enter the Talpiot tomb. Who was buried in it?

One cannot identify the members of this family tomb without bearing in mind the theories developed in the books of Van Aarde,[42] who expands upon the consequences of Jesus growing up fatherless; of Schaberg,[43] who describes Mary's illegitimate pregnancy and Jesus' *mamzerut* (illegitimacy); of Tabor *(Jesus Dynasty),* who elaborates on the idea that Mary was pregnant with Jesus before marrying Joseph. Worth mentioning as well is Barrie Wilson's most interesting thesis, which he calls the "Jesus Cover-Up Thesis": Jesus, a Jew, a rabbi, and a revered teacher, obeyed the Jewish law and encouraged his followers to do so.[44] He did not proclaim himself to be a "Christ." After he was slain by the Romans in about 30 CE, his brother James took over the Jesus movement. When James died in 62 CE, Jesus followers suffered a leadership crisis; and they were eventually, in Wilson's words, "upstaged" and "hijacked" by the Christ movement launched by Paul of Tarsus, a hellenized Jew living in the Jewish Diaspora. The two movements should have remained separate religious sects. Paul, without knowing Jesus, linked him to his Christ movement and in the process tore him from his Jewish roots. Paulinity was indeed a Hellenized religion about a Gentile Christ, a cosmic redeemer rather than the Jewish inspired religion of Jesus. The New Testament is not a neutral document. The Gospels and other writings are arranged in a particular order to give weight to Paul's interpretation of the link between Jesus and the Christ. This thesis is what most reliable historians had sensed. However, it is valuable to have a documented book dealing precisely with this concept, and it becomes very helpful when, in examining the Talpiot tomb in context, we are trying to restore the Jewish roots of Jesus and his family/followers.[45]

Jesus had four half brothers and two half sisters: James, Simon, Jude, Jose(p)h, Salome, and Maria(me).[46]

There were 6 *kokhim* in this Talpiot tomb, typical of the tombs of the

42. A. Van Aarde, *Fatherless in Galilee* (Harrisburg: Trinity Press International, 2001).

43. J. Schaberg, *The Illegitimacy of Jesus: A Feminist Theological Interpretation of the Infancy Narratives* (San Francisco: Harper & Row, 1987).

44. B. Wilson, *How Jesus Became Christian* (Toronto: Random House Canada, 2008).

45. This thesis is corroborated by Tabor, *Jesus Dynasty,* pp. 259-70.

46. Matt 12:46; 13:55; 27:56; Mark 3:31; 6:3; 15:40; 16:1; John 2:12; 7:3-5; Acts 1:14; Gal 1:19; *Gos. Phil.* 36.

time, therefore burial space for twelve ossuaries, if we assume the usual two ossuaries per *kokh*. There were two arcosolia carved in the walls of this tomb. The arcosolia were originally intended to accommodate ossuaries, two each. Therefore the intended burial space was to accommodate 16 ossuaries.[47] Based on the fact that 10 ossuaries were found even though only 9 were recorded, Kloner says ("Tomb with Inscribed Ossuaries," n. 2): "The number of interments may be estimated at 35: 17 in the ossuaries (based on an average of 1.7 individuals per ossuary), and 18 outside the ossuaries. These figures are based on demographic data compiled by the author (see Kloner 1993:105)." One could therefore speculate, according to the above, that 55 (16 × 1.7) people could have been buried in ossuaries in this tomb.

In any case this leaves enough room to believe that Jesus, his wife and child, all four of his brothers, and their alleged wives and children may very well have been interred in this Talpiot tomb whether in ossuaries with or without a recording inscription, or in the tomb, outside the ossuaries. If we exclude Joseph the "father" of Jesus, the burial space was meant for Mary, the mother; Jesus; his wife, Mary Magdalene; his sons Judah, Simon, Jude, James, Jose(p)h, and their respective wives and children. There is every circumstantial reason to believe that Jesus' sisters,[48] Salome and Maria(me), were married and therefore not buried in this tomb but rather in their husbands', as the custom prescribed and as attested in the archaeological data (cf. Kloner and Zissu, *Necropolis of Jerusalem;* and Hachlili, *Jewish Funerary Customs*).

Among the 9 (or 10?) ossuaries found in the Talpiot tomb, 6 bore inscriptions, among them one belonging to Mathia, not a direct relative of Jesus. Five of these inscribed ossuaries are relevant to Jesus' direct relatives. The three remaining plain ossuaries could very well indeed have belonged to Jesus' three other brothers, James, Jude, and Simon. So according to the funerary inscriptions, this tomb included the ossuaries of:

1. YESHUA' BAR YEHOSEPH (Jesus son of Joseph).
2. MARIAH, Greek rendition of the Semitic name Miryam (Jesus' mother).

47. See measurements of *kokhim*, arcosolia, and ossuaries in Kloner, "Tomb with Inscribed Ossuaries."
48. Indeed, the age of marriage for women seems to have been around twelve. To judge from the rabbinic sources, *'erusin* or *qiddushin* (betrothal or engagement) in ancient Judaism took place at a very early age, usually at twelve to twelve and a half years (*b. Yebam.* 62b). Their status as "engaged" would make them pass from their father's authority to their husband's, and that included burial in their husband's tomb.

3. MATHIAH, hypocoristic of the Semitic name Mattityahu (a follower).

4. YOSEH, hypocoristic of the Semitic name Yehoseph (brother of Jesus).

5. YEHUDAH BAR YESHUAʿ (Judah son of Jesus).[49]

6. MARIAM H KAI MARA ("Mariam [Greek rendition of the Semitic name Miryam], also known as Mara" [hypocoristic of the Greek rendition *Maria* of the Semitic name Miryam]) (Jesus' wife, Mary Magdalene).

The use of Aramaic *bar,* as opposed to Hebrew *ben,* for "son (of)," here confirms that Jesus' family did indeed speak Aramaic.[50]

According to the ossuary inscriptions, the Talpiot tomb is a fatherless tomb because Joseph, who married Mary in Nazareth, died there prematurely, while Mary died in Jerusalem. It is worth taking some time here to reflect on J. Tabor's thesis regarding Mary's "husbands": "There is good reason to suppose that Joseph died early, whether because he was substantially older than Mary or for some unknown cause. . . . According to the Torah, or Law of Moses, the oldest surviving unmarried brother was obligated to marry his deceased brother's widow and bear a child in his name so that his dead brother's 'name' or lineage would not perish. This is called a 'levirate marriage' or *yibbum* in Hebrew, and it is required in the Torah (Deuteronomy 25:5-10)" (*Jesus Dynasty,* p. 76).

A few questions come to my mind when reading this: Was not Mary of Clopas the sister of Mary, mother of Jesus (cf. John 19:25)? To what extent was the *yibbum* (along with other aspects of the Jewish law), applied among the Jews of Galilee at that time?[51] In terms of naming a son after the deceased brother, is the form Yoseh sufficient in this case? Tabor (*Jesus Dynasty,* p. 80) elaborates: "Given this information, a rather different but historically consistent picture begins to emerge. Jesus was born of an unknown father, but was not the son of Joseph. Joseph died without children, so according to Jewish Law 'Clophas' or 'Alphaeus' became his 'replacer,' and married his widow, Mary, mother of Jesus." In this case, and since Tabor is a supporter of

49. Judah was the name of one of Jesus' ancestors (Luke 3:30).

50. In fact, ossuary inscriptions are also a good indicator of languages spoken in Roman Palestine since the inscriptions had to be executed in a language understandable by the family members. See Cohen-Matlofsky, *Laics,* p. 195, chart for languages spoken in early Roman Palestine.

51. Cf. S. D. Cohen, *The Beginnings of Jewishness. Boundaries, Varieties, Uncertainties* (Berkeley: University of California Press, 1999).

the Jesus family Talpiot tomb, I shall contend: Why do we not have either an inscribed ossuary of Clophas/Alphaeus as the patriarch in the Jesus family Talpiot tomb or at least an ossuary inscription such as YOSEH BAR CLOPAS (or any other rendition/transliteration of the name)? Nevertheless, I am inclined to agree with the more attractive thesis of Tabor (*Jesus Dynasty,* pp. 59-72)[52] according to which Jesus would be the son of a Roman soldier named Panthera, by whom Mary, mother of Jesus, would have been raped. This does not contradict the Jesus ossuary inscription either since Jesus was in any case adopted by Joseph.

Jesus moved to Jerusalem with his mother and followers. On the other hand, one could have logically expected that Joseph's bones/remains would have been transferred to the family tomb in Jerusalem, a practice very well rooted in the Old Testament era, as seen earlier in this paper. But apparently the father's remains were not transferred to this tomb because he would not (or could not, according to the more strict Jerusalemite halakah regarding adultery and burial practices)[53] be buried with his adulteress wife, and Mary who died after Jesus found proper burial in his tomb, as well as the rest of his family. A fatherless tomb because it was the tomb of Jesus himself, the firstborn of Mary,[54] the *mamzer* (Hebrew for "illegitimate

52. See also J. Tabor's blog, *The Jesus Dynasty,* "The 'Jesus son of Panthera' Traditions," July 13, 2006.

53. Even though Joseph had not repudiated Mary in Nazareth while knowing that she was pregnant by another. The underlying question here indeed is: how much Jewishness was there in Galilee? As opposed to Schaberg, *Illegitimacy of Jesus,* rather than analyzing Mary's rape/adultery and Jesus' illegitimacy from the Christian theological angle, I propose to develop the research in trying to reconstruct what in the Jewish halakah applied in Galilee at the time.

54. Matt 1:24-25 states that Joseph and Mary did not have a sexual union until Mary gave birth to Jesus, her firstborn son. From this we learn: (1) according to Jewish law (although one has to verify if it applied in Galilee at that time) Joseph could have but did not repudiate Mary even though she was an adulteress pregnant with another man's son; (2) Jesus was the firstborn of Mary's children; (3) Mary had other children, probably with Joseph. Here is more relevant information on adultery: about a year typically passed before the woman moved from her parents' house to her husband's house (*m. Ket.* 5:2; *Ned.* 10:5; *b. Ket.* 57b). During that time, although marriage was not yet consummated, the woman was "wife" (Deut 20:7; 28:30; Judg 14:15; 15:1; 2 Sam 3:14), and she could become a widow (*m. Yebam.* 4:10; 6:4; *Ket.* 1:2) or be punished for adultery (Deut 22:23-24; 11QTemple 61). Thus betrothal was the legal equivalent of marriage, and its cancellation, divorce (*m. Ket.* 1:2; 4:2; *Yebam.* 2:6; *Git.* 6:2). Following courtship and the completion of the marriage contract (Tob 7:14), the marriage was considered established: the woman

child"),[55] as the patriarch of the family. His adulteress mother Mary was buried in it along with at least his half brother Yoseh, who likely died before 70 CE, his wife Mary Magdalene (Mariam), his son Yehudah, and one of his followers, Mathiah.[56]

If this tomb is the one of Jesus as the patriarch, then this explains the filiation only on his ossuary (bar Yehoseph)[57] and on his son's ossuary (bar Yeshua'). It explains the absence of filiation on the Yoseh ossuary. Moreover, there is also circumstantial evidence to believe that Jesus was married when he died at age 30.[58] If Paul could have given Jesus' name as an example for the celibate lifestyle, he surely would have. But in the end, the only example Paul had to share was himself. Moreover, unless Jesus, or whoever his wife was, was infertile, there is every circumstantial reason to believe that Jesus had a child — a question of age at marriage and purpose of marriage at the time. Josephus had five sons by age 35 approximately (cf. *Life* 426-27).

---

had passed from her father's authority to that of her husband. Again the question is how much of this legal content was applied in Galilee of the time.

55. This is well expressed in *m. Qidd.* 3:12: "And in any situation in which a woman has no right to enter betrothal with this man but has the right to enter into betrothal with others, the offspring is a *mamzer*." A considerable literature on the subject of Jesus the illegitimate child has emerged. See, e.g., J. Meier, *A Marginal Jew: Rethinking the Historical Jesus*, vol. 1, ABRL (New York: Doubleday, 1991); B. Chilton, *Rabbi Jesus: An Intimate Biography* (New York: Doubleday, 2000); M. Bar Ilan, "The Attitude toward *mamzerim* in Jewish Society in Late Antiquity," *Jewish History* 14 (2000): 125-70; S. D. Cohen, "Some Thoughts on 'The Attitude toward *mamzerim* in Jewish Society in Late Antiquity,'" *Jewish History* 14 (2000): 171-74; B. Chilton, "Jésus, le mamzer (Mt 1.18)," *NTS* 46 (2001): 222-27; S. McKnight, "Calling Jesus *Mamzer*," *JSHJ* 1 (2003): 73-103; C. Quarles, "Jesus as *Mamzer*: A Response to Bruce Chilton's Reconstruction of the Circumstances Surrounding Jesus' Birth in *Rabbi Jesus*," *BBR* 14 (2004): 243-55.

56. There are a number of possibilities for identifying this Mathiah with one of Jesus' followers, but I am not going to enter the discussion in this paper. Nevertheless, for exceptional burials of not-immediate relatives buried in these familial rock-cut tombs, Eric Meyers, a participant at the symposium, mentioned the example of Yehudah Hanassi's disciple buried in his master's tomb.

57. Even though Joseph was not his biological father, since his mother had not been repudiated, he was to be identified as "bar Yehoseph" on his epitaph.

58. *m. 'Abot* 5:21 sets the age of marriage at 18 for men. Moreover, for instance the funerary inscriptions along with the archaeological material found in the rock-cut tomb of Jericho, especially the anthropological analysis lead me to think that Yeho'ezer, son of 'El'azar Goliath, was a grandfather of ten if not of fourteen at the age of 35 when he died in 10 CE. See Cohen-Matlofsky, *Laics,* no. 633. It seems that Josephus had been married four times already when he was in his thirties; cf. Cohen-Matlofsky, *Laics,* no. 312.

An atypical fatherless tomb. It is the tomb of Jesus the eldest son, who became the patriarch, "replacing" the "husband" of his adulteress mother. In this case Jesus would have to have his wife buried there as well as his unmarried sons and daughters, his married sons, daughters-in-law, and grandchildren. As well, he would have to have his adulteress mother and his brothers with their immediate relatives according to the model described above.

Does this match the findings in the Talpiot tomb? It does indeed in the sense that the findings according to ossuary inscriptions do not contradict this theory. So we are dealing with a fatherless Jewish family tomb. How many of this type of tomb do we know of from the same period? More research needs to be done in this field along with Jewish halakah, dealing with burial practices and many other aspects of social life, as applied in Jerusalem versus other parts of early Roman Palestine, especially Galilee in this case.

What are the alternatives for identification of the Talpiot tomb? First, this tomb, not at all Jesus' family tomb, would have been the one of YOSEH (Rahmani, *Catalogue*, no. 705) as the patriarch, especially because there is no filiation in his ossuary inscription, his wife MARIA (no. 706), their children MATHIAH (no. 703) and YESHUA' (no. 704), their grandchild YEHUDAH (no. 702).

Although appealing, and I agree with Rahmani's comments regarding the epigraphical similitude between the ossuaries of YOSEH, MARIA, and MATHIAH, the problems I see with this theory are as follow:

1. Rahmani fails to notice the epigraphical disparity between the ossuaries of YESHUA' BAR YEHOSEPH, YEHUDAH BAR YESHUA', and the above mentioned ones.
2. What do we do with the MARIAM H KAI MARA (Rahmani, *Catalogue*, no. 701) ossuary, the only one inscribed in Greek?
3. Whether a hypocoristic of the name YEHOSEPH or a nickname, the form YOSEH should have been used consistently in the inscriptions of the tomb; the latter name, we must bear in mind, has a familial character. We cannot have two ossuaries referring to the same person with two different names/forms of the name in the same family tomb (cf. especially the Goliath family tomb in Jericho). Therefore if YOSEH and YEHOSEPH are the same individual, then inscription no. 704 of Rahmani's catalogue should have been YESHUA' BAR YOSEH instead of YESHUA' BAR YEHOSEPH. Thus when Kilty and Elliot suggest

identifying YOSEH with YEHOSEPH in a non-Jesus family tomb scenario, they are incorrect.[59]

A second alternative would assume that the Talpiot tomb was the one of YOSEH, Jesus' brother. Yoseh could have named his son, Yeshua', after his slain brother (Jesus). However this was not a common practice at the time. In fact, as mentioned earlier, the naming followed the pattern of papponymy, patronymy, and metronymy, although Jesus apparently did himself name his son, YEHUDAH (after his brother Jude?). In any case the inconsistency in the use of the name forms of YOSEH/YEHOSEPH in the same family tomb applies here again, as explained in alternative number one.

In light of the above, one has to accept the very likely probability that Jesus was married and had a child, and that they all had a secondary burial in a family rock-cut tomb in Jerusalem in the first century CE.

A close examination of the epigraphic material will now elaborate on the prosopography analysis.

First let's take a close look at the YESHUA' BAR YEHOSEPH inscription. Given the circumstances in which Jesus was executed and buried, one can understand the graffiti style of his ossuary inscription. The ossuary was manufactured and inscribed either rapidly after his death or a year after, when it was time to gather his bones and while the Christian movement was still apprehended as a subversive one in Jerusalem. Moreover, a funerary inscription was meant to be read only by intimate family members anyway.

For 27 years, this "Jesus, son of Joseph" inscription stood. Rahmani (*Catalogue*, no. 704, *Comm.* 2) says: "The reading Yeshua' is corroborated by the inscription on No. 702 from the same tomb, referring to Yeshua', the father of Yehudah." The full form of the name would be YEHOSHUA'.[60] There is also a shorter rendition of the name, YESHU, as found in the only other ossuary inscription that says: YESHU BAR YEHOSEPH in Hebrew letters and that combines the two names Yeshu(a') and Yehoseph (cf. Rahmani,

---

59. See K. Kilty and M. Elliot, "Probability, Statistics and the Talpiot Tomb," www.lccc.wy.edu, June 10, 2007, p. 8, fig. 1. In this same figure Kilty and Elliot envisage the theory of this tomb being Jesus' family tomb without the father, Joseph, with Jesus and his son Judas, and Yoseh, Jesus' brother. They consider that Matthew would have been Yoseh's son. But then we would at least have had MATIAH BAR YOSEH, especially because there is no filiation on Yoseh's ossuary inscription.

60. On contemporaneous full and contracted forms of names cf. *m. Shabb.* 12:3.

Catalogue, no. 9). As for the name YEHOSEPH, it seems that it only appears in its full form on ossuaries.[61]

As for the MARIAH inscription, the other renditions of the name in the various sources include: Maria, Mariam, Mariame, Mariamme, and Miryam (cf. Cohen-Matlofsky, *Laics,* p. 194). I believe that we should as well include Mara as a hypocoristic.[62]

As for the YOSEH inscription, on ossuaries there is only one other occurrence of the form YOSEH in Hebrew letters (cf. *CIJ* no. 1249 and Cohen-Matlofsky, *Laics,* no. 703), while on papyri there is only one occurrence of it.[63] According to Tal Ilan's corpus,[64] there are 16 pre-135 CE YOSEYs[65] mentioned in the rabbinic sources, of which 7 are pre-70 CE; as for the Greek renditions of the name, Ilan records one IOSH (= Yoseh) in the Gospel of Matthew; two IOSHS (= Yoses) on ossuary inscriptions (cf. *CIJ* II, no. 1283; and *CJO,* no. 56), and two IOSE on ossuary inscriptions (cf. *CJO,* nos. 444 and 576). This gives us a good picture of the rarity of the name in the period we are dealing with, and it also contradicts S. Pfann's erroneous treatment of the sources for purposes of onomastics.[66] The Greek version of the Gospel of Mark (Mark 6:3; 15:40; 15:47), our earliest literary source for the history of nascent Christianity, mentions Jesus' brother consistently as IOSHS. Moreover, if Yoseh is indeed considered as a hypocoristic of the full name Yehoseph, then the custom of patronymy was indeed respected in Jesus' family.

All of the above contributes to identify the YOSEH of the Talpiot tomb inscription with Jesus' brother.

61. For further examples see J. B. Frey, ed., *Corpus Inscriptionum Judaicarum* (Rome: Pontificio Instituto di archaeologia christiana, 1952), II, no. 1343a; B. Bagatti and J. T. Milik, *Gli Scavi del "Dominus Flevit,"* part 1, *La Necropoli del Periodo Romano,* Pubblicazioni dello Studium Biblicum Franciscanum 13 (Jerusalem: Franciscan Printing Press, 1958), pp. 89 and 96.

62. For the detail of the Greek transliterations and the Hebrew inscriptions of the different renditions of this name see Cohen-Matlofsky, *Laics,* nos. 380-402.

63. In a Murabba'at document, Mur 46; see P. Benoit, J. T. Milik, and R. de Vaux, *Les grottes de Murabba'ât,* DJD 2 (Oxford: Clarendon, 1961).

64. See T. Ilan, *Lexicon of Jewish Names in Late Antiquity,* part 1, *Palestine 330 BCE–200 CE,* TSAJ 91 (Tübingen: Mohr Siebeck, 2002), pp. 151-55.

65. As per the Kaufmann Mishnah manuscript of the thirteenth century, it seems that in early rabbinic literature the form YOSEY was used as opposed to YOSEH in later rabbinic literature.

66. See S. Pfann's UHL Blog, "Yoseh can you see? 'Checking the sources (updated),'" February 5, 2008; "Jose (or is it Jehoseph?) and his amazing dream coat," February 10, 2008.

A detailed analysis of the MARIAM H KAI MARA inscription in the following lines is crucial in order to elaborate on the thesis that the Talpiot tomb is the tomb of Jesus' family.

The first relevant question would be: who are the three women mentioned in the context of Jesus' burial about to perform the Jewish funerary custom of anointing his corpse? The social context of Mary Magdalene's role in Jesus' burial, including the Jewish legal aspect, is relevant here. One would expect the male followers (including the brothers) of Jesus to have gone underground after the crucifixion, since their leader had just been crucified for insurrection. So it was left to three women to "anoint" his body. No stranger would perform this rite unless she was related to Jesus by blood or marriage. So who are the women? Mary the mother, Salome the sister, and Mary Magdalene — the wife. Let us take a closer look at the literary sources.

The earliest spelling of Mary Magdalene's name in the literary sources is MARIA/MARIAM. The one time Jesus addresses Mary Magdalene in our canonical records, he uses MARIAM. As for the chronology of the spelling of Mary Magdalene's name in the Gospels, it is as follows: in Mark, Mary Magdalene is four times called MARIA (Mark 15:40, 47; 16:1, 9). In this earliest source, three of the four times Mary Magdalene is mentioned she is at the side of Jesus' mother and sister at the time of his death and burial, buys the spices to anoint his corpse, and enters his tomb. Who else other than a spouse or a closest relative should it be in these circumstances?

Matthew, using the passages from Mark as his source, twice changes the name to MARIAM (Matt 27:61; 28:1). In any case scholars agree that the name MARIAM is indeed used for Mary Magdalene in the Gospels.

I assumed in the above that the "other Mary" in these particular passages is indeed Jesus' mother (who is also mother of James and Jose[p]h), and that Salome is Jesus' sister.

According to Christian tradition, Mary Magdalene spoke both languages, Aramaic and Greek, common in the north. Indeed, she and her family could very well have been descendants of Galilean pagans converted to Judaism during the Hasmonean conquest of the area, and perhaps Mary Magdalene's first language was Greek. Therefore, her relatives would have inscribed her ossuary in her mother tongue, also because relatives would visit the tomb in the years after the burial and would need to be able to read the inscriptions or at least recognize the characters on the ossuaries of their beloved ones.

The incorrect reading of the Mary Magdalene ossuary inscription by Rahmani (*Catalogue*, no. 701), followed by Ilan (*Lexicon*, p. 244, no. 52), the latter even recording the name erroneously in its genitive (or caritative/diminutive as some participants at the symposium contended) form, Mariamēnou, misled the whole discussion about the identification of the ossuary in question with Mary Magdalene. My reading, MARIAM H KAI MARA, along with Pfann's and Jonathan Price's, does feed the theory that *CJO* 701 indeed belonged to Mary Magdalene.

First let's eliminate the other alternatives:

1. The literal (letter by letter) reading would be: MARIAMHKAIIMARA. I cannot read Mariamēnou from the Greek letters. Rahmani's reading *-nou* is not acceptable. There is no letter *nu* in this inscription. And there is no *omicron* or *upsilon* either. Moreover, other than this occurrence in Rahmani's catalogue, recorded as well in Ilan's corpus, there is no other Mariamēnou in the sources.

2. MARIAMH KAI MARA (Mariame and Mara). This would mean that either two sisters or a mother and an unmarried daughter were buried in this ossuary, according to all compiled data on burial practices. First, considering that Mara is a hypocoristic of Maria, and the latter, along with Mariam, is a variation of the original Miryam, it would be odd that two sisters bore almost the same name. Moreover, according to the metronymy practice only a grandmother and a granddaughter could bear the same name. Yet there is no example of such double burial in our records.

I read: MARIAM H KAI MARA, "Mariam also known as Mara." I choose to ignore the third *iota* before MARA as a slip of the nail likely to have been used by the inscriber. One has to bear in mind that the family members who usually carved the inscriptions on ossuaries made spelling mistakes and/or omissions in the carving of the letters, and it was too late to add and certainly not possible to erase/hide a letter. Therefore one could definitely ignore the third *iota*, as well as imagine that it was meant to be added between the *rho* and the last *alpha* of MARA to make MARIA.

I do not know what the warrant is for Rahmani to believe that MARA is short for MARTA'. More likely is that MARA is short for MARIA (cf. the interpretation of the name in *SEG* 33, no. 1281),[67] with omission of the *iota*. The same phenomenon is found in the name KYRA/KYRIA. In this case we would have MARIAM H KAI MAR(I)A (Mariam also known as Mar[i]a) on

67. See *SEG* XXXIII.

this Talpiot tomb inscription. In any case, I do not see why the inscriber could not have omitted either the *theta* or the *iota* in his carving of the inscription in Greek characters.

The Akeldama tombs are my source for the KYRIA question (see Cohen-Matlofsky, *Laics*, no. 351). KYRIA is indeed the equivalent of the Aramaic MARTA' and of the Latin DOMNA. It means "lady," the feminine form for "master/teacher." KYRIA, MARTA', its hypocoristic MAR(I)A, and DOMNA are all used as proper names in these three languages. KYRIA in its Hebrew transliteration is known in the Jewish onomastic of Second Temple period Jerusalem.[68] Moreover, in the course of time certain names lose their historical significance and a different pronunciation eventually changes their rendition. It was the case for the Semitic name MIRYAM, which became MARIAM with the influence of the Aramaic, and then hellenized and latinized into MARIA and DOMNA, respectively.

Nevertheless, another Greek "Mara" is inscribed on an ossuary of the Dominus Flevit Necropolis (see Cohen-Matlofsky, *Laics*, no. 380). So even though the theory of "MARA/MARTA/MARTA'/MARTAH" or "KYRA/ KYRIA/KYROS/KYRIOS" and "MARA/MARIA/MARIAH" — all meaning "lady/master/teacher" either in Aramaic or Greek — is very appealing, one should remain careful and perhaps translate: "Mariam also known as Mara" (her nickname), if we consider that they were all renditions of the first original name MIRYAM and that the various other examples of a contemporaneous appearance of the full and short forms of the same name on the same ossuary corroborates this (cf. Rahmani, *Catalogue*, nos. 9, 42, 270, 370, 468, 829). This being said, one does not preclude the other, as MARA could be apprehended as a nickname or the title (master/teacher) with my reading of the inscription.[69]

Christian tradition presents Mary Magdalene as a preacher/teacher; therefore the Aramaic hypocoristic MAR(T)(I)A on this inscription could have very well referred to her preaching/teaching ability, as some participants at the symposium contended.

68. See A. Kloner, "A Burial Cave of the Second Temple Period at Givat Ha-Mivtar, Jerusalem," in *Jerusalem in the Second Temple Period: Abraham Schalit Memorial Volume*, ed. A. Oppenheimer, U. Rappaport, and M. Stern (Jerusalem: Yad Itzhak Ben-Zvi, 1980), pp. 198-211.

69. Hachlili (*Jewish Funerary Customs*, pp. 207-33) classifies the nickname types and nicknames as: (a) place of origin, (b) title, (c) occupation, (d) physical characteristics and defects, (e) honorific and age-related titles, (f) disabilities, (g) positive and negative qualities, (h) endearments.

Hachlili (*Jewish Funerary Customs*, p. 224) notes: "*Mar, Mara'* and the Greek equivalent *Kyrios* indicating the title 'master' occur, on ossuary inscriptions (Rahmani 1994: Nos. 327, 560). They also appear at Beth she'arim (Schwabe & Lifshitz, 1974: No. 130). From the third century they became the usual honorific title for father, superior or teacher." (Hachlili misses Rahmani, *Catalogue*, no. 8.)

However, it does not seem that there was a Semitic feminine form of this title. Whether written with an *aleph* (Aramaic ending) or with a *he* (Hebrew ending), the MARA referred to a male in all sources.[70] Therefore in our case the reading of the masculine form Mara, in its Greek transliteration, as a title, would be acceptable only if it referred to Mary Magdalene's "ability" as a preacher. From readings of the New Testament Gospels and the apocryphal *Gospel of Mary*, it is probable that some first-century people regarded her as a "mara/master."

Stephen Pfann argues that when a signum formula such as H KAI is used on an inscription it always links two names but not a name and a title.[71] This may very well be. However, I can still read this inscription: MARIAM H KAI MAR(TH)(I)A. Both MARIAM and MAR(TH)(I)A (the significance of the second being "lady/master/teacher," a title of distinction in any case, or possibly used as her nickname referring to her particular ability) could have identified Mary Magdalene.

I can see two hands in the inscription as well: before and after H KAI. The *alpha*s, the *mu*s, and the *rho*s are different. Therefore I am not ruling out the possibility that the second part of the inscription was added later in antiquity (not too much later), in order to further identify this particular ossuary.

This inscription would be bilingual in its essence if read MARIAM H KAI MARA, with MARA being a title. The Aramaic MARA would have been transliterated in Greek characters on this ossuary inscription, along with MARIAM, a Greek version of the Semitic name MIRYAM. The inscription would be monolingual if read MARIAM H KAI MARA, with MARA being a hypocoristic of the first name. In both cases it corresponds to the languages spoken in Mary Magdalene's family.

---

70. Could we consider "Marah" (with a *he* Hebrew ending) as the feminine form of "Mar," as *Kyria* in Greek is the feminine of *Kyrios*? See Rahmani's discussion in his comments (*Catalogue*, no. 560). Do we know of any other feminine Jewish "Mara" (masteress/teacher) in the sources?

71. See S. Pfann's UHL blog, "An eye for form," the comments section, February 8, 2008.

Unless the negative evidence outweighs the positive evidence for the identification of the Talpiot tomb with the family tomb of Jesus, I see no reason, in light of the above, to exclude the possibility that this particular ossuary might have been the one of Mary Magdalene.

As for the statistical analysis of the Talpiot tomb, in my judgment, one has to follow a strict methodology. First, in order to make a relevant statistical analysis based on the prosopography of early Roman Palestine, one has to establish a sample based on the whole spectrum of contemporary sources at our disposal. In my book *(Laics)* I carefully did so.

A sample based exclusively on ossuary inscriptions would be erroneous by nature for at least two reasons: (1) not all Jewish residents of early Roman Palestine practiced the secondary burial in an ossuary, let alone with an inscription; (2) it seems that at least some Diaspora Jews buried their dead in and around Jerusalem for resurrection purposes as recommended in the Old Testament. Therefore it would be impossible and erroneous to draw conclusions of a statistical nature from deceased people's names found in funerary inscriptions of early Roman Palestine about the living population at the time in this country.

In my research I drew names from the writings of Josephus and other ancient authors; biblical and rabbinical sources, including the New Testament; the documents of Qumran, Murabba'at, and other caves of the Judean desert; and finally the archaeological material, especially funerary inscriptions mostly found in rock-cut tombs excavated in and around Jerusalem. In terms of chronology my window is: 63 BCE to 138 CE. Therefore my sample for the distribution of names in early Roman Palestine is indeed broader than just ossuary inscriptions and is more reliable than Ilan's *Lexicon* since the latter comprises data from 330 BCE to 200 CE, as noted by Andrey Feuerverger.[72] Therefore to be really scientific for the purpose of the statistical analysis of the Talpiot tomb, one should carefully use in Ilan's *Lexicon* exclusively the names found in Roman Palestine sources of people known to have lived between 63 BCE and 70 CE. As if this was not a big enough challenge, Rahmani's *Catalogue* of ossuaries has to be completed with the Israel Antiquities Authority's collection, which should have compiled all the ossuaries found after 1994, the second edition of Rahmani's *Catalogue*.

However, following my reasoning above, my sample is the most rele-

72. See A. Feuerverger, "Statistical Analysis of an Archaeological Find," *Annals of Applied Statistics* 2 (2008): 3-54, esp. 15.

vant for statistical analysis since the spectrum of my sources is exhaustive and my chronological window is the closest to the Talpiot tomb's.

Moreover, Ilan and I sometimes disagree on renditions of names. This explains why in my results Yohanan (and variables) is the second most common name after Shimon, while Yeshua' (with Ya'aqob) is the least common male name in my list. As well, I come up with many more variables of the name Shlomsion (or Shelamsiyon) than Ilan does; therefore in my chart it is the most common female name, ahead of Maria (and variables).

In order to use statistics in a historical perspective one does not necessarily require an exhaustive list but rather a chronologically correct sample.

I propose a revised chart of name distribution in early Roman Palestine (based on Cohen-Matlofsky, *Laics*, p. 194), as follows, on a sample of 549 Jewish names taken in Hebrew, Aramaic, or Greek from the various sources:

Table 1: Name distribution in early Roman Palestine

Among the male names:

43 Shimon and variables (Simai, Simewn [Simeōn], Simwn [Simōn])

41 Yehohanan and variables (Ananias, Ananos, Hanan, Hananah, Hananyah, Hanin, Hanina, Honi, Iwanhs [Iōanēs], Iwanna [Iōanna], Iwannes [Iōannes], Yehoni, Yohanan)

37 'El'azar and variables (Elazaros, Eleazar, Eleazaros)

31 Yehoseph and variables (Iwshph [Iōsēph], Iwshphos [Iōsēphos], Iwshpos [Iōsēpos], Yoseh, Yoseph)

27 Yehudah and variables (Iouda, Ioudas, Ioudhs [Ioudēs])

13 Yehonatan and variables (Iwnathhs [Iōnathēs])

10 Ya'aqob and variables (Iakkwbos [Iakkōbos], Iakwbos [Iakōbos])

10 Yehoshua' and variables (Ihsous [Iēsous], Yeshua')

Among the female names:

26 Shlomsion and variables (Salamsi, Salampsiw [Salampsiō], Salwmh [Salōmē], Selampsin, Shalom, Shlomsi, Shlomsin)

24 Miryam and variables (Mara, Maria, Mariah, Mariam, Mariamh [Mariamē], Mariammh [Mariammē])

As for the names of the Talpiot tomb in light of this chart, Yeshua' is the least common; Yehudah is the fifth least common; Mathiah is not even listed among the top 8 most common male names; I already treated Yoseh as a rare rendition of the name Yehoseph earlier in this paper; and Mariam/

Mar(i)a is not the most common female name in early Roman Palestine. Concerning the "cluster of names" as found in the Talpiot tomb, I wish statisticians could revisit it in light of the above.

In conclusion, Jesus was married, he had a child, and he was buried in an ossuary in a rock-cut tomb outside the walls of Jerusalem around 30 CE. Whether the Talpiot tomb is the tomb of Jesus and family we do not know for sure. However, in my judgment, unless a better configuration emerges, there is enough evidence to believe that it is. By better configuration is implied: the discovery of Jesus' bones with traces of crucifixion in a rock-cut tomb ossuary inscribed "Jesus son of Joseph," along with the inscribed ossuaries of at least his brothers.

A few questions remain after the examination of the Talpiot tomb. Who is Mathiah exactly? Why did he have an ossuary, while, except for Yoseh, the other brothers of Jesus did not? Is it because, like James, they died between 60 and 70 CE, therefore in times of turmoil, and because of the special situation of the Jesus movement it was not easy for them to get an ossuary manufactured?

Indeed, the lost civilization of Jesus and his followers as Judeo-Christians has misled humanity in many ways. It is our duty to restore it with burial practices and other evidence of the socioeconomical background of the family of Jesus. Some of the evidence should be found in the Mount of Olives, particularly in the Dominus Flevit Necropolis, which apparently belonged to the earliest followers of Jesus. It is in this light that scholars should revisit this burial complex.

The research should also be given a genuine "halakic" orientation in order to reconstruct the legal roots in which Judeo-Christianity developed. Especially one has to elaborate on Joseph and Mary's relationship and on Jesus' illegitimacy in light of the halakah and put burial practices and funerary customs in the context of the Jewish legal system of the time with careful comparison between Jerusalem, Galilee, and Qumran. Should Jesus be apprehended beside Hillel and Shammai as the founder of a new school?

Ultimately, only pure historical analysis will solve the problem of Jesus and his family. What is extraordinary is that a scientific methodology for accomplishing this task will challenge the historians to question sources considered so far as ahistorical: early Christian and rabbinic literature, and more closely the Mishnah and the New Testament. Social historians like myself already appreciate the wealth of information one can extract from such documents about the daily life of early Roman Palestine. It will be extremely beneficial in order to advance the research in this field to very carefully and systematically question the halakah in context. More research needs to be done as well in onomastics and prosopography. The frame of this paper did not allow me to do so to the extent I wish I could.

Burial Customs in Judea and Galilee in the Late Second Temple Period: An Important Component in the Discussion about "Jesus' Family Tomb"

Mordechai Aviam

The size and distribution of Jewish cemeteries around Jerusalem in the Judean Shephelah, dated to the last decades of the Second Temple period, were widely studied during the last fifty years and in special focus during the last twenty years (Kloner and Zissu). The most common type discovered in these cemeteries is the *kokhim* tomb, which contains a courtyard, an entrance closed with a door, a central room, and *kokhim* around its three walls. More than a thousand tombs of this type were identified in the cemeteries around Jerusalem (Kloner and Zissu 2007), a couple of hundred in the cemeteries of the Shephelah, and more than a hundred in the cemeteries at Jericho (Hachlili and Killebrew 1999:4). Most of those that were scientifically excavated contained ossuaries or shards of them. The ossuaries were found in the *kokhim,* on the shelves around the central room, or on the floor of the room itself.

In some cases, the remains of wooden coffins were identified, especially in the tombs dated to the late Hasmonean period. It is important to note that the tombs in the Jerusalem region look very similar to those of the Judean Shephelah.

From this period there is evidence of at least 1,500 ossuaries, most of which come from the region of Jerusalem. The sample is very large. The great published collection shows that Jews in Judea used highly decorated ossuaries as well as plain ones; some were inscribed with well-made engraved letters while others were scratched with just a little attention. They used Hebrew, Aramaic, and Greek in their inscriptions, usually carrying individual names and rarely some titles.

Great attention was put into the decoration, which included a lot of different designs of rosettes. Much of the work was based on compass work and architectural elements such as a monument or mausoleum *(nefesh)*.

Other elements found in the tombs are some oil lamps, glass bottles, and few cooking pots. Very few coins were discovered.

It is quite clear that these rock-cut tombs belonged to the upper half of Judaic society. Poor people were buried in different types of tombs, of which not too many have been found, probably as a result of these being cut into soil and not into rock.

In any case, it seems very clear that a common custom and important burial practice of the upper levels of Jewish society at the end of the Second Temple period was secondary burial by gathering bones into stone ossuaries. Of all the inscribed ossuaries published until today, only two were identified as people from another city (Beth Shean), the exception that proves the rule. That no places of origin are inscribed on the ossuaries and their distribution around Jerusalem, Judea, and Jericho support the point that they contain the remains of local Jewish families.

With the destruction of Jerusalem and its surroundings in 70 CE by the Roman troops, the entire industry of making and decorating ossuaries collapsed at once. Only in the Shephelah and Hebron mountains was it slightly preserved. Rahmani, based on archaeological evidence from the excavators and typological aspects, dated this small group to the second-third centuries CE (Rahmani 1994).

About 75 stone ossuaries have so far been discovered at about 25 sites in Galilee, all located within the accepted borders of Jewish Galilee known from Josephus and well supported by abundant archaeological remains. Although the basic manufacturing technology of ossuaries in Galilee is similar to that practiced in Judea, as most of them are made of chalk and clearly bear flat chisel marks, they form a different typological group, more similar to second-century CE ossuaries originating from the Judean Shephelah and Hebron mountains.

Most of the Galilean ossuaries are not decorated, and the exceptional few have a different type of decoration than the customary Judean ones. Even fewer are inscribed (one in Hebrew and one in Greek), and most of them are crudely made.

There is one common denominator among the decorated Galilean ossuaries, the origins of which might be looked for in some of Jerusalem decorated ossuaries. Ossuaries from Kabul, Daburyah, Sepphoris, and Mashhad are decorated with a schematic wreath on one of their short sides and an architectural façade on the other, the latter presumably representing the *nefesh*, or mausoleum. Both of those symbols are known to be part of the funerary artistic fashion common in Judea. The two long sides of the ossuary from Sepphoris were decorated by an architectural complex — three columns carrying an architrave — presumably representing the *nefesh*. A small ossuary from Kfar Kana is also decorated by the same column motif.

All the Galilean ossuaries were discovered in rock-cut tombs, which are similar to the Judean ones but not identical. One should point out that so far no tomb containing stone ossuaries was dated only to the first century CE, the Second Temple period. Ossuaries in Galilee do appear in tombs that contained pottery that can easily be dated to the last part of the first century and mainly to the second century CE.

Researching ossuary tombs in Galilee confirms, in my opinion, the assumption that the *ossilegium* custom spread into Galilee only after the destruction of the temple. Not only do we have no first-century CE dated tombs with ossuaries in Galilee, they are clearly lacking from the Golan and are extremely rare in Perea — a distribution that shows, in my opinion, that *ossilegium* in the Second Temple period was strictly a Judean custom.

In rural Galilee of ancient times, as in the villages of Judea, people were customarily buried in burial fields. An exceptional custom can be observed in the Jewish tradition of reburial of Diaspora Jews in the land of Israel, as the Tosefta says: "whoever is buried in Eretz Israel it as if he were buried underneath the altar" (*t. 'Abod. Zar.* 4:3). On the other hand one should recall the well-known tradition related to Rabbi Judah the Patriarch that although residing for many years at Sepphoris (the Jewish capital of Galilee), he was not buried there. His funeral left Sepphoris on Shabbat evening in the direction of Beth Shearim (his place of origin): "Rabbi lies in Sepphoris but a place is prepared for him at Beth Shearim" (*b. Ketub.* 103b).

The large and unusual Jewish public cemetery of Beth Shearim is also an example (although slightly later, third century CE) to prove that Galilean Jews preferred to be buried in their homeland rocks rather then to be buried in another Galilean town or village cemetery. Out of the dozens of inscriptions in Beth Shearim of places of origin of the deceased, only one is suggested to be from a Galilean village.

If Galilean villagers did not practice *ossilegium* in the Second Temple period, as clearly reflected from archaeological evidence, and if family tradition along generations was to bury the dead in their family burial yard or tomb, it would certainly be hard to accept the unusual assimilation of Jesus of Galilee, as well as his entire family, to an unknown and unfamiliar burial custom of *ossilegium*, far away from home. Funerary traditions are known to be quite strong and important in family tradition, and therefore I would assume that most of the Galilean pilgrims who died en route to and from Jerusalem were most certainly brought back by their families to find their last resting place among all the past members of the family. The fact that until today, aside from two Beth Shean natives (who easily moved their location to Jerusalem and still were identified by their place of origin, as probably the case with the ossuary and the pottery bowl of Simon son of Plataya from Jerusalem that was discovered in Jericho [Hachlili and Killebrew 1999:155-57]), there are no ossuaries with names of people from the Jewish territories of the land of Israel, strengthen the hypothesis that pilgrims who died during their journey were brought home to be buried. Even if this was not practiced in every single case, it would be hard to accept that in those rare and exceptional cases of pilgrims who were buried in Jerusalem, they would switch into an unfamiliar burial custom in which their bones were gathered after a year or so into an ossuary. It is even much harder to assume that the entire family, whose members probably died over the next thirty or forty years after Jesus, would also adopt the Judean practice of *ossilegium* and be brought to Jerusalem to be buried with Jesus.

I do believe that this archaeological evidence of differentiation between Galilean and Judean burial customs should be taken into serious consideration in the ongoing debate about the "Jesus tomb" in Talpiot, Jerusalem.

BIBLIOGRAPHY

Hachlili, Rachel, and Ann Killebrew. *Jericho: The Jewish Cemetery of the Second Temple Period.* IAA Reports 7. Jerusalem: Israel Antiquities Authority, 1999.
Kloner, A., and B. Zissu. *The Necropolis of Jerusalem in the Second Temple Period.* Interdisciplinary Studies in Ancient Culture and Religion 8. Leuven: Peeters, 2007.
Rahmani, L. Y. *A Catalogue of Jewish Ossuaries in the Collection of the State of Israel.* Jerusalem: Israel Antiquities Authority and the Israel Academy of Sciences and Humanities, 1994.

The Ossuary of Simon and Alexander

André Lemaire

An ossuary inscribed with the names Alexandros and Simon has often been, more or less likely,[1] identified as the ossuary of Simon and his son

1. Cf. J. T. Milik, in B. Bagatti and J. T. Milik, *Gli Scavi del "Dominus Flevit,"* part 1, *La Necropoli del Periodo Romano,* Pubblicazioni dello Studium Biblicum Franciscanum 13 (Jerusalem: Franciscan Printing Press, 1958), p. 81: "possibilità"; N. Avigad, "A Depository of Inscribed Ossuaries in the Kidron Valley," *IEJ* 12 (1962): 1-12, esp. 12: "perplexing similarity"; J. P. Kane, "The Ossuary Inscriptions of Jerusalem," *JSS* 23 (1978): 268-82, esp. 278-79: "possible"; K. Beyer, *Die aramäische Texte vom Toten Meer* (Göttingen, 1984), p. 344: "vielleicht"; D. Lührmann, *Das Markusevangelium,* Handbuch zum Neuen Testament (Tübingen: Mohr, 1987), p. 259 (negative); M. Hengel, *The 'Hellenization' of Judaea in the First Century after Christ* (Philadelphia: Trinity Press International, 1989), pp. 11 and 67 n. 39: "possibly"; P. van der Horst, *Ancient Jewish Epitaphs: An Introductory Survey of a Millennium of Jewish Funerary Epigraphy (300 BCE–700 CE)* (Kampen, 1991), pp. 140-41: "at least a good chance"; N. Avigad, "Jerusalem," *New Encyclopedia of Archaeological Excavations in the Holy Land,* ed. E. Stern, 4 vols. (Jerusalem: Israel Exploration Society and Carta, 1993), 2:753; R. E. Brown, *The Death of the Messiah,* 2 vols., ABRL (New York: Doubleday, 1994), 2:916 n. 12: (speculation); A. Millard, *Reading and Writing in the Time of Jesus,* Biblical Seminar 69 (Sheffield: Sheffield Academic Press, 2000), p. 114: "a burial which may reasonably be identified as that of one of the sons of Simon of Cyrene"; C. A. Evans, *Jesus and the Ossuaries* (Waco: Baylor University Press, 2003), pp. 94-96, esp. 96: "we may actually have the ossuary of the Alexander, son of Simon, the man mentioned in Mark's Gospel"; T. Powers, "Treasures in the Storeroom. Family Tomb of Simon of Cyrene," *BAR* 29/4 (2003): 46-51, esp. 51: "very likely"; idem, "A Second Look at the 'Alexander Son of Simon' Ossuary: Did It Hold Father and Son?" www.biblicalarchaeology.org (September 26, 2006): "very likely"; A. Kloner and B. Zissu, *The Necropolis of Jerusalem in*

Alexandros mentioned in Mark's Gospel (Mark 15:21). Before appreciating this problem of identification, it is necessary to better understand what we know from the archaeological and epigraphical data and what we learn from the literary tradition.

Archaeological and Epigraphical Data

The inscribed ossuary with "Alexandros" and "Simon" was found in a tomb discovered on 10 November 1941, "south of Silwan village at a site named Karm esh-Sheikh on the south-western slope of the Kidron Valley."[2] The tomb was dug under the direction of E. L. Sukenik[3] and published twenty years later by his assistant, N. Avigad.[4] The tomb itself could well have been a reused Iron Age tomb. It contained first-century CE pottery and eleven ossuaries. Nine of them were inscribed: seven in Greek, one in Jewish script, and one bilingual (no. 9 below). Several names were new on ossuaries but already attested in Cyrenaica *(Philiskos, Sabatis, Damōn, Thaliarchos, Mnasō).* Thus after N. Avigad and T. Ilan,[5] they can "all" be "considered Cyrenian."

One notes especially:

No. 7: in Greek
Sara Simōnos
Ptylemaikē
"Sara (daughter) of Simon,
of Ptolemais."
Here *Ptylemaikē* probably refers to Ptolemais in Cyrenaica.

No. 9
a. On front, written in green chalk(?) in very thin lines in Greek (and now practically invisible):

---

the Second Temple Period, Interdisciplinary Studies in Ancient Culture and Religion 8 (Leuven: Peeters, 2007), pp. 256-57.

2. N. Avigad, "A Depository of Inscribed Ossuaries in the Kidron Valley," *IEJ* 12 (1962): 1.

3. E. L. Sukenik, "Extracts from a Report of Archaeological Progress in Palestine," *BASOR* 88 (1942): 36-38, esp. 38; idem, *Qedem* 1 (1942): 104 [in Hebrew].

4. Avigad, "Depository of Inscribed Ossuaries," pp. 1-12.

5. T. Ilan, *Lexicon of Jewish Names in Late Antiquity,* part 1, *Palestine 330 BCE–200 CE,* TSAJ 91 (Tübingen: Mohr Siebeck, 2002), p. 49.

Alexandros
Simōn
"Alexander
(son of) Simon"
b. On back, scratched in Greek (*Simōn* is incised deeper and clearer than the following letters):
SimōnAle
Alexandros
Simōnos
"Simon Ale
Alexander
(son of) Simon"
c. On lid, incised in Greek and Jewish script:
Alexandrou
'LKŠ/SNDRWS QRNYT

The first name in Jewish script seems to have been written first with *KŠ*, corrected later on to *KS*.

The last letter of this inscription is "the crux of the Alexander epitaph."[6] According to N. Avigad, "the tracing is undoubtedly correct and has been rechecked on the original. The *T* is very clear, as can be seen from the photograph (Pl. 4A)." He only hesitates about the meaning of this word: either mishnaic *qōrānît*, a kind of medicinal plant, or a connection with Cyrene, already suggested by J. T. Milik, who proposed to read *QRNYH*, "the Cyrenian," "(copia inesatta? errore dell'incisore?)."[7] Unfortunately today this lid is broken, and the break destroyed most of the last letter so that it is impossible to decide on the ossuary itself between *T* and *H* (pl. 1). However, the printed photograph published by Avigad is confirmed by an old photograph kept in the Institute of Archaeology of the Hebrew University (Jerusalem) (pl. 2).[8] Paleographically it is a clear *T*; but this *T*, indicating eventually the feminine or the language spoken, is probably a mistake from the engraver (see already *Ale* and *Š/S* above), who may have confused

6. Avigad, "Depository of Inscribed Ossuaries," p. 10.

7. Milik, *Gli Scavi*, p. 81. Cf. also Y. Yadin and J. Naveh, "The Aramaic and Hebrew Ostraca and Jar Inscriptions," in *Masada I: The Yigael Yadin Excavations 1963-1965 Final Reports* (Jerusalem: Israel Exploration Society and Hebrew University, 1989), pp. 1-68, esp. 26, no. 424.

8. I wish to thank Anat Mendel and the staff of the Institute of Archaeology Collections, Hebrew University, Jerusalem, for their kind assistance.

H and *T* on his model, or else he did not know Aramaic well. From the general context of the other inscriptions in the tomb, such a correction seems justified.

Another problem of this ossuary refers to the number of persons mentioned on it. Avigad thought that the inscriptions "testify to only one buried person" (p. 12) while, for Milik (p. 81), "La teca conteneva, dunque ossa di due persone: cioè di Alessandro figlio di Simone il Cireneo e di Simone suo padre o piuttosto suo figlio"; and more recently, for Tom Powers the ossuary probably contained the bones of the father *(Simōn)* and of the son *(Alexandros)*.[9] Unfortunately we cannot get any information from the bones themselves — whether they belonged to one or two persons — in Avigad's report and apparently in the files of the Institute of Archaeology of the Hebrew University.

If we judge from the inscriptions, it seems that Powers is right:

- *Simōn* was incised first on the side that will become finally the back.
- Later on, the bones of his son were added and *Alexandros (son of) Simōn* was scratched after *Simōn* on the side (with a false beginning *Ale-*) and, carefully enough, *"of Alexandros"* in Greek and *"Alexandros the Cyrenian"* in Jewish script on the lid.
- Finally, when the ossuary was put into the back of the cave, *Alexandros* and *Simōn* were written with chalk on the visible side (= front side).

We have apparently, therefore, in this ossuary the bones of two "Cyrenians": *Simōn*, the father, and *Alexandros*, his son.

It is important to note that the ethnic *QRNY* might also appear on two Hebrew ostraca from Masada, where *HQRNY* might also refer to a village in Judah.[10] Furthermore *BN QRNY* might appear on the Bethphage lid (I, 12).[11] The Greek ethnic *kyrēnaios* appears also on another ossuary with the name

---

9. "Second Look."

10. Cf. Yadin and Naveh, "Aramaic and Hebrew Ostracon," p. 26, no. 424 and perhaps 41, no. 473 (very uncertain).

11. Read *BN QRNW* by J. T. Milik, "Le couvercle de Bethphagé," in *Hommages à André Dupont-Sommer*, ed. A. Caquot and M. Philonenko (Paris: Maisonneuve, 1971), pp. 75-94; esp. 78; but *QRNY* by Yadin and Naveh, "Aramaic and Hebrew Ostracon," p. 26; A. Yardeni, *Textbook of Aramaic, Hebrew and Nabataean Documentary Texts from the Judaean Desert and Related Material*, 2 vols. (Jerusalem: Hebrew University, 2000), 1:221; 2:[78].

Philōn,[12] and on a fragmentary account on leather from Wadi Murabba'at with the name Hillel.[13]

Literary Data

The main text to compare with the inscriptions of ossuary no. 9 is a verse from Mark's Gospel: "A man called Simon Cyrenian, the father of Alexander and Rufus, was passing by on his way in from the country, and they pressed him into service to carry his cross" (Mark 15:21). Two parallel Synoptic texts mention only Simon: "On their way out they met a Cyrenian man, Simon by name, and pressed him into service to carry his cross" (Matt 27:32); "They seized upon a man called Simon Cyrenian, on his way from the country, put the cross on his back, and made him walk behind Jesus carrying it" (Luke 23:26).

Mark's indication has been and is still discussed. Some commentators propose to see Simon here as "a fictional character," while most think he is "a historical figure."[14] Actually there is no clear indication that he should be "a fictional character" and there is no reason to doubt that he is "a historical figure": in fact, he does not play any important role, except that his sons "Alexander and Rufus" may have been known to the readers/audience;[15] as noted by V. Taylor, "Simon appears only to disappear, and we hear no more of him."[16] Even though R. Bauckham's comment that "[t]he reference to Alexander and Rufus certainly does presuppose that Mark expects many of his readers to know them, in person or by reputation, *as almost all commentators have agreed,*"[17] might seem a little too pos-

12. Cf. Milik, *Gli Scavi*, p. 81: ossuary 10, inscription 74.

13. Cf. P. Benoit, in P. Benoit, J. T. Milik, and R. de Vaux, *Les Grottes de Murabba'ât,* DJD 2 (Oxford: Clarendon, 1961), pp. 218-20. (To be compared to the very uncertain but earlier "Hillel HQRNY" *in Masada I,* no. 473.)

14. Cf. more recently W. J. Lyons, "The Hermeneutics of Fictional Black and *Factual Red:* The Markan Simon of Cyrene and the Quest for the Historical Jesus," *JSHJ* 4 (2006): 139-54. One notes that, after explaining in detail both positions, his "own preference" "is for the *factual red* Simon" (p. 153).

15. V. Taylor, *The Gospel According to St. Mark,* 2nd ed. (London: MacMillan, 1966), p. 588: "The fact that Simon is described, without further explanation, as the father of Alexander and Rufus, or at least the sons, [was] known to Mark and his readers."

16. Ibid., p. 587.

17. R. Bauckham, "The Eyewitnesses and the Gospel Traditions," *JSHJ* 1 (2003): 28-

itive,[18] the "historical" interpretation is the most obvious one, "for there is no point in identifying someone by referring to others that are unknown."[19]

However, even if "the incident is undoubtedly historical,"[20] this verse does not go into details and many points are not specified. For instance, it is not specified that Simon became a disciple of Jesus or was still living at the time this verse has been written.[21] The verse seems only to imply that Alexander and Rufus are known at least to part of the audience. Although it is not absolutely necessary, that part of the audience is supposed to know Alexander and Rufus suggests that they joined the Christian movement.

The main problem that remains is to specify the audience of this verse and of Mark's Gospel in general. Here we confront at least two main working hypotheses.[22]

1. Mark's Gospel was written in Rome in the 60s[23] or the beginning of the 70s[24] and, in this context, Rufus might be the Rufus mentioned in Rom 16:13;[25] but the addressees of the numerous greetings of Rom 16 are problematic and the identification of these two Rufuses would be very conjectural.[26] The main problem for an identification in the context of this hypothesis is that, if Alexan-

---

60, esp. 55 = idem, *Jesus and the Eyewitnesses: The Gospels as Eyewitness Testimony* (Grand Rapids: Eerdmans, 2006), p. 52 (emphasis added).

18. Cf. Lyons, "Hermeneutics," p. 141 n. 13.

19. H. N. Roskam, *The Purpose of the Gospel of Mark in Its Historical and Social Context*, NovTSup 114 (Leiden: Brill, 2004), p. 15. Cf. already J. Gnilka, *Das Evangelium nach Markus (Mk 8,27–16,20)*, EKK II/2 (Zurich: Benzinger, 1979), p. 315: "Die Nennung der Namen ist nur sinnvoll, wenn sie der Gemeinde bekannt waren."

20. Taylor, *Mark*, p. 588.

21. Cf. already Bauckham, *Jesus and the Eyewitnesses*, p. 52: "Perhaps Simon himself did not, like his sons, join the movement, or perhaps he died in the early years, while his sons remained well-known figures."

22. Cf., e.g., E.-M. Becker, *Das Markus-Evangelium im Rahmen antiker Historiographie*, WUNT 194 (Tübingen: Mohr Siebeck, 2006), pp. 99-102; A. Yarbro Collins, *Mark: A Commentary*, Hermeneia (Minneapolis: Fortress, 2007), pp. 7-10, 96-102. Of course, there are many other working hypotheses.

23. See, e.g., Taylor, *Mark*, pp. 31-32.

24. Cf., e.g., Gnilka, *Markus*, p. 34.

25. Cf. Taylor, *Mark*, p. 588; M.-E. Boismard, *Synopse des quatre évangiles en français*, 2 vols. (Paris: Cerf, 1971-1972), 2:422; Bauckham, *Jesus and the Eyewitnesses*, p. 52 n. 49.

26. Cf., e.g., S. Légasse, *Le procès de Jésus: L'histoire*, Lectio Divina 156 (Paris: Cerf, 1994), p. 127 n. 25; C. A. Evans, *Mark 8:27–16:20*, WBC 34B (Nashville: Nelson, 2001), p. 500; Yarbro Collins, *Mark*, p. 736.

der and Rufus are known in Rome in the 60s or the beginning of the 70s, it is difficult to suggest that their bones, or at least the bones of Alexander, were put into an ossuary in Jerusalem. Although it would not be completely impossible, it seems unlikely, unless Alexander spent his last years in Jerusalem before 70.

2. Mark's Gospel was written in Syria-Palestine in the 40s[27] or later.[28] A dating in the 40s seems difficult for the final redaction but might be accepted for an earlier Passion Narrative.[29] In this case, the first audience of the Passion narrative would have been the Jerusalem Judeo-Hellenistic community.[30] Such a working hypothesis would be economical since Alexander and Rufus would have stayed in Jerusalem, like their father, and the fact that this Cyrenian family had a tomb in Jerusalem would not be surprising. However, in the hypothesis of a Passion narrative written in Jerusalem in the 40s, one has to suggest that the final redactor kept this mention as it was in his source while Matthew's and Luke's Gospels probably suppressed the mention of Alexander and Rufus, not known at all by their audience.

We must provisionally conclude that there is much uncertainty about the life of Simon, Alexander, and Rufus, especially about their final destiny in Jerusalem, Rome, or elsewhere.

In a more general way, in the first-century literary tradition, one may emphasize the role played by Cyrenians in Acts 6:9 (Jerusalem); 11:20 (Antioch); 13:1 (Antioch); and the mention of "Lybia around Cyrene" already in Acts 2:10, to be compared to the existence of an important Jewish community in Cyrenaica from Strabo of Amaseia (ca. 64 BCE till 23 CE; from Josephus, *Ant.* 14.114-18)[31] and Josephus (*War* 2.381; 6.114; 7.437-50; *Ant.* 16.160, 169-70; *Ag. Ap.* 2.44, 51; *Life* 15.424).[32]

---

27. For instance, J. G. Crossley, *The Date of Mark's Gospel: Insight from the Law in Earliest Christianity,* JSNTSup 266 (London: T&T Clark, 2004), p. 208.

28. Cf., e.g., "in Galilee some time after the destruction of the Jerusalem temple in 70 AD" (Roskam, *Purpose of Mark,* p. 237).

29. It was already Bultmann's interpretation: cf. also lately Yarbro Collins, *Mark,* pp. 732, 819.

30. See, e.g., J. Schreiber, *Die Markuspassion,* BZNW 68 (Berlin: de Gruyter, 1993), p. 60 n. 16.

31. Cf., e.g., M. Stern, *Greek and Latin Authors on Jews and Judaism,* 3 vols. (Jerusalem: Israel Academy of Sciences and Humanities, 1974-1984), 1:277-80. Cf. also G. Lüderitz, "What Is the Politeuma?" in *Studies in Early Jewish Epigraphy,* ed. J. W. van Henten and P. W. van der Horst, AGJU 21 (Leiden: Brill, 1994), pp. 183-225.

32. C. Claussen, *Versammlung, Gemeinde, Synagogue,* SUNT 27 (Göttingen: Vandenhoeck & Ruprecht, 1999), pp. 234-36.

The importance of the Jewish community in Cyrenaica is confirmed by several tens of inscriptions[33] and has been studied by S. Applebaum.[34] We may note that Josephus counted at least "three thousand well-to-do [Cyrenian] Jews" (*War* 7.445) as well as apparently "two thousand" other ones (*Life* 424), both groups being killed during Jonathan's revolt (73 CE).

Identification?

The three inscriptions of ossuary no. 9 do not contain much information, apparently only names:

- two personal names in a relation father-son: Simōn and Alexandros
- Alexandros is probably called "the Cyrenian"

None of these indications seems precise enough that, a priori, only two persons could fit them. Their identification can only be calculated in terms of probability.

What are the arguments in favor of the identification? One may propose:

- The identity of the names of the father and of the son.
- The fact that, on the ossuary as well as in Mark's Gospel, Simon and Alexander apparently belonged, at least for a while, to the Cyrenian Jewish community in Jerusalem.
- The approximate date of the ossuaries and of the inscription (1st century, before 70) could fit.

There is apparently no strong objection against the identification, but one may note many uncertainties:

- In the Gospels Simon is qualified as "Cyrenian," while on the ossuary it is Alexandros who is probably called "Cyrenian."

33. Cf. G. Lüderitz, *Corpus jüdischer Zeugnisse aus Cyrenaika*, Beihefte zum Tübinger Atlas des Vorderen Orients, B 53 (Wiesbaden: Reichert, 1983).

34. *Jews and Greeks in Ancient Cyrene*, Studies in Judaism in Late Antiquity 28 (Leiden: Brill, 1979). Cf. also E. Schürer, *The History of the Jewish People in the Age of Jesus Christ* (*175 B.C.–A.D. 135*), rev. and ed. G. Vermes, F. Millar, and M. Goodman, III/1 (Edinburgh: T&T Clark, 1986), pp. 60-62.

- Mark mentions "Rufus" as another son of Simon, but in the tomb we have apparently only a daughter, "Sara" (unless the bones of Rufus would have been put in one of the two uninscribed ossuaries).
- We have no indication about the place and date of the death of Simōn and Alexandros. We do not know whether "Simon the Cyrenian" and his son "Alexander" (and eventually Rufus?) of Mark 15: 21 died before 70 and were buried in Jerusalem.

This third uncertainty is clearly the main obstacle to the probability of identification. However, even if we could accept the probability of the death of Simon and Alexander in Jerusalem before 70, there would still be the problem of the frequency of the names Simōn and Alexander and of the number of Cyrenians in Jerusalem. Let us elaborate a little on these two points:

- One may suggest that the "Cyrenian" community in Jerusalem, which probably had its own synagogue (Acts 6:9), could have counted several hundreds of persons; however, if it is a hundred or a thousand, it is not at all the same thing for an estimation of probability.
- The estimations of the onomastic data vary according to the sources. For instance, according to the general data collected by Ilan, Simōn is the commonest Jewish male name from about 330 BCE to 200 CE (some 257/1110 [or 23%] according to Ilan[35] but 22% according to R. Hachlili)[36] and, though not so frequent (only about 31/2505 or 1.23%), Alexandros is already well attested in the onomastics of this period (with at least two other attestations on ossuaries, without taking into account several abbreviated forms).[37] It is attested for three or four persons in Acts (4:6; 19:33) and in the New Testament Letters (1 Tim 1:20; 2 Tim 4:14). It is apparently the most popular Greek name among the Jews.[38]
- The situation seems a little different in the Cyrenian community of Cyrenaica with more Greek names: *Simōn* appears 11 times and *Alexandros* 4 times (+ once Alexas) among about five hundred names.[39]

35. Ilan, *Lexicon*, p. 56.

36. R. Hachlili, "Names and Nicknames of Jews in Second Temple Times" [in Hebrew], in *A. J. Brawer Memorial Volume, ErIsr* 17 (1984): 188-211, esp. 189.

37. Cf. Ilan, *Lexicon*, pp. 258-60.

38. Ibid., pp. 56, 259.

39. Lüderitz, *Corpus jüdischer Zeugnisse*, pp. 217, 226; W. Horbury and David Noy,

Just to give a rough example: if Cyrenians were about 1 percent of the Jerusalem population (about 80,000), with about 400 males, using the general data of Ilan, there was probably one "Cyrenian" Simōn having a son called Alexandros in the two generations of the pre-70 period. If this was the case, the identification could be considered as likely.

Finally, especially because of the uncertainties around the death of Simon and Alexander mentioned in Mark's Gospel, it is practically impossible to appreciate the probability of an eventual identification with the names on the ossuary. We may only conclude that, in the present state of our knowledge, nothing clearly contradicts it. It may only be considered as possible.

Jewish Inscriptions of Graeco-Roman Egypt, with an Index of the Jewish Inscriptions of Egypt and Cyrenaica (Cambridge: Cambridge University Press, 1992), pp. 322-31.

INSCRIPTIONS AND PROSOPOGRAPHY

What's in a Name?

Rachel Hachlili

The article will examine Jewish names in the Second Temple period, in particular focusing on the names inscribed on ossuaries discovered in an East Talpiot tomb in Jerusalem.[1] The following discussion will scrutinize and evaluate the claim presented by the film *The Lost Tomb of Jesus* produced by Simcha Jacobovici and James Cameron[2] and supported by some scholars[3] that the East Talpiot tomb in Jerusalem was the tomb of Jesus and his family. The other theme to be discussed is the identification of names with known historical figures.

Choosing or Giving a Name

The choice of names in the Second Temple period was determined by different customs from those in the First Temple period.[4] The practice of names

1. Amos Kloner, "A Tomb with Inscribed Ossuaries in East Talpiyot, Jerusalem," *'Atiqot* 29 (1996): 15-22; Amos Kloner and Boaz Zissu, *The Necropolis of Jerusalem in the Second Temple Period,* Interdisciplinary Studies in Ancient Culture and Religion 8 (Leuven: Peeters, 2007), pp. 342-43, tomb no. 12-46, fig. 237. For the ossuaries' inscriptions see L. Y. Rahmani, *A Catalogue of Jewish Ossuaries in the Collection of the State of Israel* (Jerusalem: Israel Antiquities Authority and the Israel Academy of Sciences and Humanities, 1994), nos. 701-9.

2. 2007, AP Tomb Productions Ltd.

3. James D. Tabor, "Testing a Hypothesis," *NEA* 69 (2006): 132-36.

4. Rachel Hachlili, *Jewish Funerary Customs, Practices and Rites in the Second Temple Period,* JSJSup 94 (Leiden: Brill, 2005), pp. 194-95.

given during the biblical period was frequently in honor of special events that befell the family or the nation, sometimes based on wordplay. The father, the mother, God, or another third party gave the names.[5] Examples of names given by God or his messenger include Isaac: "But God replied, 'No; your wife Sarah will bear you a son and you are to call him יצחק (Isaac)'" (Gen 17:19), which means "he who laughs" (18:12; 21:6);[6] the sons of Jacob, the name of each has its reason. Examples of names given by the mother: Leah said, "The Lord hearing that I am unloved . . . and she called him Shimeon, that is 'hearing' in Hebrew" (29:33); another son: "Now I shall praise the Lord; therefore she named him Judah," that is, "praise" in Hebrew (29:35); Rachel gave birth to a son, "she named him Joseph, saying, 'may the Lord add another son to me'" (30:24). And names given by the father: Noah (5:28-29), the names given by Joseph to his sons Manasseh and Ephraim (41:50-52). Symbolic names appear in Isaiah (7:14; 8:3-4; 10:21-22).

By contrast, during the Second Temple period, naming children after an ancestor was prevalent. Most common was papponymy, that is, naming a son after his grandfather.[7] This custom was common in the Egyptian, Phoenician, and Greek world. The Elephantine and Assuan Aramaic papyri indicate that the custom first arose among the Jews in fifth-century BCE Egypt.[8]

The custom of papponymy was common for both sons and daughters in prominent families such as the Hasmonean dynasty and of the family of the sage Hillel.[9] One of the few literary sources for the custom of papponymy indicates that a child is named Abram after his dead grandfather (*Jub.* 11.14-15).

However, it seems that the most common custom in the land of Israel

---

5. B. Porten, "Name," in *Encyclopedia Biblica* (Jerusalem: Bialik Institute, 1982), 8:35-38.

6. All biblical and NT citations are from *The Oxford Study Bible, Revised English Bible with the Apocrypha,* ed. M. Jack Suggs, Katharine Doob Sakenfeld, and James R. Mueller (New York: Oxford University Press, 1992).

7. Rachel Hachlili, "Names and Nicknames of Jews in Second Temple Times" [in Hebrew], *ErIsr* 17 (1984): 192; idem, "Hebrew Names, Personal Names, Family Names, and Nicknames of Jews in the Second Temple Period," in *Families and Family Relations as Represented in Judaisms and Early Christianities: Texts and Fictions,* ed. J. W. van Henten and A. Brenner (Leiden: Brill, 2000), pp. 83-115; idem, *Jewish Funerary Customs;* Tal Ilan, *Lexicon of Jewish Names in Late Antiquity,* part 1, *Palestine 330 BCE–200 CE,* TSAJ 91 (Tübingen: Mohr Siebeck, 2002).

8. G. Buchanan Gray, "Children Named after Ancestors in the Aramaic Papyri from Elephantine and Assuan," in *Wellhausen Festschrift* (Giessen: 1914), pp. 163-64, 172.

9. Hachlili, "Names and Nicknames," p. 192, fig. 2.

in the Second Temple period was patronymy, that is, naming a son after his father. The custom of patronymy was apparently widespread among the royal Hellenistic dynasties. From the first century BCE on, the practice became increasingly prevalent among prominent Jewish families, resulting in a small number of personal names appearing for several generations in a single family: in families of high priests such as Hanan (Anan) and Onias. An excellent example is the recurring names of Simon and Matthias in Joseph ben Matthias (Josephus) family's genealogy; he himself had a brother named Matthias ben Matthias (*Life* 3-8).

In ossuary tombs in Jerusalem and Jericho many recurring names are inscribed on ossuaries recording the naming of son after father; see the Goliath family inscribed names and other instances.[10]

A well-known example is the naming of John the Baptist (the first record of a name given on the day of circumcision):

> On the eighth day they came to circumcise the child; and they were going to name him Zechariah after his father, but his mother spoke up: "No!" she said. "He is to be called Yohanan [John]." "But," they said, "there is nobody in your family who has that name." They inquired of his father by signs what he would like him to be called. He asked for a writing tablet and to everybody's astonishment wrote, "His name is Yohanan [John]." (Luke 1:59-64)

Often during the Second Temple period nicknames were added to personal names and were an organic part of a person's name. Nicknames were given because of the frequency of some of the personal names and to distinguish individuals bearing the same name, especially in a single family. Another reason was the need of a family to have the same identifying nickname, sometimes for several generations. Quite often a nickname was given describing the place of origin, a title, a profession, or a physical aspect of the individual, occasionally as an endearment or a pet name, or to disgrace a person; and in some cases the nickname became a family name.[11]

---

10. Rachel Hachlili, "The Goliath Family in Jericho: Funerary Inscriptions from a First Century AD Jewish Monumental Tomb," *BASOR* 235 (1979): 53, fig. 49; idem, "Names and Nicknames," pp. 192-94; idem, *Jewish Funerary Customs,* pp. 178-88; 200, 235, 239, 252, 259, 272, 294; table V-2.

11. Hachlili, "Names and Nicknames," pp. 195-204, table 1; idem, *Jewish Funerary Customs,* pp. 205-31.

An example of the variety of nicknames used during the period are the names of the apostles (Matt 10:2-4; Mark 3:14-19; Luke 6:13-16; Acts 1:13):

These are the names of the twelve apostles; first Simon (שמעון), also called Peter and his brother Andrew [see also John 1:41-42], James son of Zebedee (יעקב בן זבדי) and his brother John (יוחנן); Philip and Bartholomew (פילפוס ובר תלמי), Thomas (תומא) and Matthew the tax collector (מתתיהו המוכס), James son of Alphaeus (יעקב בן חלפי), Thaddaeus (תדי), Simon the Zealot (שמעון [הכנעני] הקנאי), Judas Iscariot (יהודה איש קריות), the man who betrayed him [in Acts 1:13 he is named "Judas son of James" (יהודה בן יעקב)].

This list of the names of the apostles presents the various types of names of the period: single proper names, names with patronomy, and names with added nicknames of assorted types.

Burial Practices

The typical underground tomb in the Jerusalem and Jericho cemeteries was hewn into the hillside and consisted of a square chamber, often with a square rock-cut pit in the floor. The height of the chamber was usually less than that of a person, and a pit was cut only when the ceiling was not high enough to permit a person to stand upright (some tombs are without a pit).[12] In tombs with standing pits, benches were left along three sides of the chamber, and the loculi were hewn level with the tops of the benches.

The loculi had roughly vaulted ceilings and were cut into the walls, with the exception of the entrance wall. Usually there were one to three loculi in each wall. Some of the tombs have rock-cut courtyards in front of the entrance.

The small square opening was usually sealed with a blocking stone. In cases where the entrance was at a higher level than the chamber floor, one or more steps facilitated descent from the entrance down into the chamber.

Burial practice in these loculi tombs in the late Second Temple period (first century CE) consisted of burial in wooden coffins in the first century BCE followed by second burial of collected bones in stone ossuaries. The ossuaries were carved from a single limestone block, with a separate gabled,

12. Hachlili, *Jewish Funerary Customs,* pp. 55-56.

vaulted, or flat limestone lid, and were sometimes decorated with incised or chip-carved geometric, architectural, or floral designs.[13]

The ossuaries were placed in the loculi, on the benches, or on the floor. The occupants of ossuaries placed in the same loculus were usually related, as can be deduced from the inscriptions.[14] The bones were placed in the ossuary in a certain order: the long bones lay lengthwise at the bottom, with the bones of the arms and hands on one side and those of the legs and feet on the other. The remaining bones of the body were placed on top, with the skull on top of all the bones at one end.[15] Usually, each ossuary contained the bones of one individual, but in some tombs there were several instances of more than one individual in an ossuary.[16] Care was taken to place the bones in the correct ossuary.[17]

Occasionally inscriptions were carved on the ossuaries found in the Jerusalem and Jericho cemeteries. Quite often the inscription was repeated on the ossuary, and several were bilingual. Such inscriptions usually give the name and the family relationship of the deceased whose bones rested in the ossuary, making it possible to construct family trees, each usually consisting of three generations.[18]

The Names Inscribed on the East Talpiot Tomb

In the East Talpiot tomb (fig. 1) ten ossuaries were found, six of them inscribed with names, five in Hebrew and one in Greek.[19] These inscriptions

13. Ibid., pp. 461-63.

14. Ibid., pp. 235-310.

15. Rachel Hachlili and Ann Killebrew, *Jericho: The Jewish Cemetery of the Second Temple Period,* IAA Reports 7 (Jerusalem: Israel Antiquities Authority, 1999), p. 170, fig. VIII.2.

16. Rachel Hachlili and Particia Smith, "The Genealogy of the Goliath Family," *BASOR* 235 (1979): 68-69.

17. In Jericho the inscriptions in the Goliath Tomb mentioning the name and occasionally the age of the deceased correspond to the sex and age of the individual found in the ossuary: Hachlili, "Goliath Family," table 1; Hachlili and Smith, "Genealogy"; Hachlili and Killebrew, *Jericho,* table IV.1, and Anthropological Table, appendix 1.

18. Hachlili, *Jewish Funerary Customs,* pp. 170-310.

19. Kloner, "Tomb with Inscribed Ossuaries," pp. 16-17; Rahmani, *Catalogue,* nos. 701-9; see also Christopher A. Rollston, "Inscribed Ossuary: Personal Names, Statistics, and Laboratory Tests," *NEA* 69 (2006): 127-29; Shimon Gibson, "Is the Talpiot Tomb Really the Family Tomb of Jesus?" *NEA* 69 (2006): 118-24.

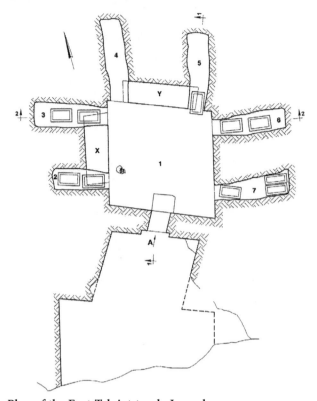

Figure 1. Plan of the East Talpiot tomb, Jerusalem *(A. Kloner)*

will be discussed below and the names will be compared to the onomasticon of the Second Temple period and to the names of members of Jesus' family mentioned in the New Testament.

ישוע בר יהוסף, *Yeshuaʿ son of Yehoseph*

Plain ossuary 4[20] shows on its narrow side a badly engraved and difficult to read inscription ישוע בר יהוסף, "Yeshuaʿ son of Yehoseph" (fig. 2; first read and published by Rahmani).[21] This inscription is one of the main reasons for the claim that the East Talpiot tomb is the tomb of Jesus.

20. Kloner, "Tomb with Inscribed Ossuaries," p. 18.
21. Rahmani, *Catalogue,* no. 704.

Figure 2. Yeshua, Hebrew inscription on ossuary 4, East Talpiot tomb
(A. Kloner)

יֵשׁוּעַ, *Yeshuaʿ*

The name יֵשׁוּעַ, Yeshuaʿ, in Hebrew means "he will save" or "salvation"; it is a contraction of the Hebrew name *Yehoshuaʿ* (יְהוֹשׁוּעַ, Joshua), which means "rescued/saved by YHWH." It was quite a popular name in the Second Temple period.[22]

The Hebrew/Aramaic proper first name יֵשׁוּעַ, Yeshuaʿ (Jesus), appears throughout the four canonical Gospels of the New Testament. The name יֵשׁוּעַ, Yeshuaʿ, was given to him by his parents, and that was the name he was known by during his life, though he had also several nicknames and titles.[23] In Greek the name was written Ἰησοῦς *(Iēsous)*, which was probably the transliteration source, as well as the Latin *(Iesus)*, for the English version "Jesus," which has no intrinsic meaning.

The episode of the naming of Yeshuaʿ (Jesus) as recorded in the New Testament is significant; the angel appeared to Joseph in a dream and said:

> She will bear a son; and you shall give him the name Yeshuaʿ (Jesus), for he will save his people from their sins. All this happened in order to ful-

22. Hachlili, "Names and Nicknames," p. 188, table 1; idem, *Jewish Funerary Customs,* pp. 196-97, table V-2.

23. Geza Vermes, *Jesus the Jew: A Historian's Reading of the Gospels* (1973; repr. Philadelphia: Fortress, 1981). See J. J. Parsons, "Hebrew Names of God" — http://www.hebrew4christians.com/Names_of_G-d/Yeshua/Yeshua.html. Parsons records that the name Yeshuaʿ appears in the NT 973 times.

fill what the Lord declared through the prophet: "A virgin will conceive and bear a son, and he shall be called Emmanuel," a name which means "God is with us.". . . And he named the child Yeshua' (Jesus)." (Matt 1:21-23)

The angel said to Mariam (Mary): "You will conceive and give birth to a son, and you are to give him the name Yeshua' (Jesus)" (Luke 1:31). "Eight days later the time came to circumcise him, and he was given the name Yeshua' (Jesus), the name given by the angel before he was conceived" (Luke 2:21). This narrative not only evoked purposely Isaiah's (7:14) prophecy (Matt 1:23) but was also meant to call to mind the custom during the biblical period in which names were given in honor of special events that happened to the family or the nation.

The genealogy of Jesus presents his descent from King David in Matt 1:1-16 (which is considered Joseph's genealogy),[24] while Luke 3:23-38 is deemed to be Miriam's genealogy, which also has an ancestor by the name Yeshua' (Joshua) in the family (Luke 3:29).

The name Yeshua' possibly appears in the earliest source on Jesus outside the New Testament, Josephus's *Antiquities of the Jews,* the only non-Christian writing of the first century CE in which two paragraphs refer to Jesus (*Ant.* 18.63-64), including: "Now there was about this time Jesus [Yeshua'], a wise man." This has come to be known as *Testimonium Flavianum,* and it is in a controversy that will probably never be resolved. Most scholars agree that some of the phrases in *Ant.* 18.63-64 were interpolations, obvious additions by Christian copyists in the surviving Greek text, in an effort to gain the support of Josephus in Jesus as the Christ.[25]

---

24. Notes for Jesus' genealogy in Matt 1:1-17: M. Jack Suggs, in *Oxford Study Bible,* p. 1267, "These names are drawn from Ruth 4.18-22; 1 Chr. 2.1–3.19. [Verse 17] *Fourteen generations:* perhaps reflecting the numerical value of *David* in Heb.; $d(4) + v(6) + d(4) = 14$."

25. John Meier, *A Marginal Jew: Rethinking the Historical Jesus,* 4 vols., ABRL (New York: Doubleday, 1991-2009), 1:57-88. Eusebius (ca. 324) quotes the *Testimonium Flavianum* in full, in the form that survives today in all manuscripts. See James D. Tabor, "The Jewish Roman World of Jesus; Josephus' Testimony to Jesus." Online: http://www.religiousstudies.uncc.edu/jdtabor/josephus-jesus.html; Steve Mason, "Josephus and Luke-Acts," in *Josephus and the New Testament* (Peabody, Mass.: Hendrickson, 1992), pp. 185-229. Some discussion of authenticity of this passage include: http://members.aol.com/FLJOSEPHUS/testimonium.htm; http://members.aol.com/FLJOSEPHUS/testimoniumBibliography.htm; see full bibliography of the debate; G. J. Goldberg, "The Coincidences of the Testimonium of Josephus and the Emmaus Narrative of Luke," *JSP* 13

The other passage is recorded in *Ant.* 20.200-203: "James [Yaʿakov], the brother of Jesus [Yeshuaʿ] the one called the Christ [Messiah]." This sentence is considered authentic by the majority of scholars,[26] though some writers have suggested that the original may have recorded "and brought before them [a good man] whose name was James, and some others."[27] A minority of writers dismiss the passage entirely because of contradictions between the passages in *Antiquities* and *Jewish War.*[28]

A remarkable episode recorded in Acts 9:1-7 and 26:12-16 (see also 22:6-8) describes Jesus appearing in spirit form in a vision to Saul on the road to Damascus; Saul heard a voice and asked:

> "Tell me, Lord, who you are." The voice answered, "I am Jesus (Yeshuaʿ), whom you are persecuting." (Acts 9:4-5)

(1995): 59-77. See also Richard Carrier, "Luke and Josephus (2000)." Online: http://www.infidels.org/library/modern/richard_carrier/lukeandjosephus.html; A. Whealy, "The Testimonium Flavianum controversy from antiquity to the Present." Online: http://josephus.yorku.ca/pdf/whealey2000.pdf; Christopher Price, "A Thorough Review of the Testimonium Flavianum." Online: http://www.bede.org.uk/Josephus.htm. See also critiques of the authenticity of the *Testimonium Flavianum:* Kenneth Humphreys, "A strong critique of the Testimonium Flavianum." Online: http://www.jesusneverexisted.com/josephus-etal.html; Bernard D. Muller, "The Testimonium Flavianum." Online: http://www.geocities.com/b_d_muller/appe.html; John Dominic Crossan, *The Historical Jesus: The Life of a Mediterranean Jewish Peasant* (San Francisco: HarperSanFrancisco, 1991).

26. Louis H. Feldman, "Josephus," *ABD* 3:990-91. The Christian writer Origen (ca. 230-250) cites Josephus's section *Ant.* 20 on the death of James "the brother of Jesus"; but states twice that Josephus "did not believe in Jesus as the Christ," and he does not cite the *Testimonium Flavianum* passage in book 18. See Peter Kirby, "Testimonium Flavianum." Online: http://www.earlychristianwritings.com/testimonium.html. Kirby regards the shorter reference in *Ant.* 20.200 as authentic. "If Josephus referred to James as the brother of Jesus in the *Antiquities,* in all likelihood the historical James identified himself as the brother of Jesus, and this identification would secure the place of Jesus as a figure in history." He also defends the essential reliability of Josephus as a witness to the historical Jesus (versus Doherty).

27. Earl Doherty, "The Jesus Puzzle, Was There No Historical Jesus?" Online: http://pages.ca.inter.net/~oblio/supp10.htm. Doherty claims: "The authenticity of the reconstructed Testimonium Flavianum in *Antiquities* 18.3.3 is untenable. . . . At the very least, it must be acknowledged that Josephus collapses as reliable evidence for the existence of an historical Jesus. . . . Destroying the credibility of the Josephus references inevitably places a very strong nail in the coffin of the historical Jesus."

28. Frank R. Zindler, *The Jesus the Jews Never Knew: Sepher Toldoth Yeshu and the Quest of the Historical Jesus in Jewish Sources* (Cranford, N.J.: American Atheist Press, 2003).

> We all fell to the ground, and I heard a voice saying to me, in the Jewish [Hebrew] language, "Saul, Saul, why do you persecute me? It hurts to kick like this against the goad." I said "Tell me, Lord, who you are," and the Lord replied, "I am Jesus (Yeshua'), whom you are persecuting." (Acts 26:14-15)

This episode proves that Jesus was known by his Hebrew name Yeshua'.[29]

In the events around Jesus' death (described only in the four Gospels), Jesus is referred to only by his proper personal name, Yeshua' (Matt 27:45-54; Mark 15:33-39; Luke 23:44-47; John 19:28-30). The same is evidenced in the narrative of Jesus' resurrection (Matt 28:1-10; Luke 24:13-32, 36-51; John 20:13-22).

ישוע הנצרי, *Yeshua' of Nazareth*

On some occasions Jesus was identified as "Yeshua' of Nazareth." The family of Jesus settled in Nazareth in Galilee once Joseph took mother and child: "Directed by a dream, he withdrew to the region of Galilee, where he settled in a town called Nazareth. This was to fulfil the words spoken through the prophets: 'He shall be called a Nazarene'" (Matt 2:22-23).[30] In the event of Jesus' arrival at the Jerusalem temple he was identified by the crowds, "This is prophet Jesus (Yeshua'), from Nazareth in Galilee" (Matt 21:10-11). Another account describes: "It was at this time that Jesus (Yeshua') came from Nazareth in Galilee and was baptized in the Jordan by John" (Mark 1:9).[31]

The following examples record Jesus identified quite a number of times as ישוע הנצרי, "Yeshua' of Nazareth," his personal name with the added nickname. When Jesus came to the Capernaum synagogue (Mark 1:24; Luke 4:34) and Jericho, he was approached by a blind beggar, who also called him "Son of David" (Mark 10:47; Luke 18:37).

At the end of his life Jesus was often named ישוע הנצרי, "Yeshua' of Nazareth": during his trial a girl identified Peter as: "He was with Yeshua' of Nazareth" (Matt 26:71; Mark 14:67). Jesus identified himself to temple police in Jerusalem as Yeshua' of Nazareth (John 18:5, 7). When Mary of Magdala, Mary the mother of James, and Salome came to Jesus' tomb, a young man

---

29. Lee Warren, "How Did the Name Jesus Originate?" Ed. Michelle Huff. Online: http://www.plim.org/JesusOrigin.htm.

30. Suggs, *Oxford Study Bible,* p. 1269, note to Matt 2:23: "Probably Isa.11.1 (which contains a Heb. word, *nezer,* translated 'branch,' similar to *Nazareth*) is the intended reference."

31. See ibid., p. 1304, note to Mark 1:9-11, on the baptism of Jesus.

said: "you are looking for Yeshua' of Nazareth, who was crucified. He has been raised; he is not here" (Mark 16:6; Luke 24:19).

John 19:19 describes an interesting episode: "Pilate had an inscription written and fastened to the cross; it read, 'Yeshua' of Nazareth, King of the Jews.' . . . in Hebrew, Latin, and Greek." Peter and others are cited as preaching about Yeshua' of Nazareth (Acts 2:22; 6:14; 10:38; 26:9). In a similar episode recorded in Acts 9:1-7 and 26:12-16, Jesus appears in a vision, speaks to Saul, and identifies himself as Yeshua' of Nazareth (22:8).

Yeshua' the Messiah (Jesus Christ)

Yeshua' was also known as the Messiah (the "anointed one" in Hebrew), which corresponds to the Greek Χριστός *(Christos)* (in English "Jesus Christ"). Yeshua' the Messiah (Jesus Christ) or "called the Messiah" (Matt 1:1,[32] 16, 18; Mark 1:1; John 1:17) appears in the Gospels in relation to the ancestry and birth of Yeshua'. The title occurs more than five hundred times in the New Testament, repeatedly in the theological letters of Paul, James, Peter, John, and in sermonic tracts. ישוע המשיח הנצרי, "Yeshua' the Messiah of Nazareth," appears with both title and nickname in Acts 3:6; 4:10.

בר יהוסף, *"Son of Yoseph"*

The patronymic name on ossuary 4 is יהוסף, Yehoseph (Joseph), which in Hebrew means "may he add" and was the second most common name in the Second Temple period.[33] In the New Testament, Joseph is the husband of Mariam (Mary), whom he marries after the birth of Jesus; thus he is the adopted father of Jesus (Matt 1:18-25; Luke 2:4-7; 3:23). Joseph is last mentioned (not by name) when Jesus was twelve years old and came with his parents to the temple in Jerusalem for the Passover festival (Luke 2:41-52). Joseph was apparently dead by the time of Jesus' trial and crucifixion, since Jesus at the cross entrusts his mother to his disciple (John 19:25-27).

---

32. Ibid., p. 1267, note to Matt 1:1: "Literally *Christ* (or *Messiah*, v. 17) means 'anointed one' and was frequently used of the royal figure whose rule would bring about the final age of righteousness and justice. The genealogy [Matt 1:2-16] presents Jesus as this ruler, descended from *King David*."

33. Hachlili, "Names and Nicknames," pp. 195-204, table 1; idem, *Jewish Funerary Customs*, p. 196, table V-2; Ilan, *Lexicon*, pp. 4-8, table 7.

Yeshua˙ as the "son of Yoseph" appears several times in the New Testament in episodes in his familiar environment, in Galilee and in his hometown of Nazareth by people who know him and his family and were astonished by his words and deeds: "When Jesus began his work he was about thirty years old, the son as people thought of Joseph son of Heli"; the paragraph continues with the description of Joseph's genealogy (Luke 3:23). Jesus addresses the crowd on the Sabbath in the Nazareth synagogue who "were astonished that words of such grace should fall from his lips. Is not this Joseph's son [ben Yoseph]? they asked" (Luke 4:22).

Philip tells Nathanael (in Galilee): "'We have found the man of whom Moses wrote in the law, the man foretold by the prophets: it is Yeshua˙ son of Joseph, from Nazareth.' 'Nazareth'! Nathanael exclaimed. 'Can anything good come from Nazareth?'" (John 1:45).

In Capernaum, in response to Jesus' answer to the crowd, "At this the Jews began to grumble because he said, 'I am the bread, which came down from heaven.' They [the Jews] said, 'Surely this is Yeshua˙, Joseph's son! We know his father and mother. How can he say, "I have come down from heaven"?'" (John 6:42).

In his hometown, in the Nazareth synagogue, the people who know him ask in wonder of the wisdom and powers he shows, "Is he not the carpenter's son?" and mention also the names of his mother and brothers (Matt 13:55-56; Mark 6:3).

The "son of Joseph" in these verses indicates Jesus' relationship with his family and his origin but was in no way his proper name.

In light of the above evidence, it seems that if Jesus had been buried in a tomb in Jerusalem, in an ossuary (which means he was first buried in another place, with his inscribed name beside the burial to be identified for his second interment in an ossuary), the name engraved on his ossuary would have been either ישוע, Yeshua˙, or ישוע הנצרי, Yeshua˙ of Nazareth, emphasizing and confirming his origin.

Names recording a person's origin are quite common in the Second Temple onomasticon. For instance, the names inscribed on three ossuaries found in a Jerusalem tomb, אמיה הבשנית, חנין הבשני, פפיס הבשני, "Ammia the Betshanite, Hanin the Betshanite, and Papias the Betshanite" (fig. 3), record the interred as originating from Beth Shean.[34]

The patronymic of Yeshua˙ as the "son of Joseph," the name of his

---

34. Hachlili, "Names and Nicknames," pp. 199-200; idem, *Jewish Funerary Customs*, pp. 210-13, 255-57.

Figure 3. Hebrew and Greek inscriptions on ossuaries from a family tomb in Jerusalem: "Ammia, Hanin, and Papias the Betshanite/Scythopolitan" *(R. Hachlili)*

adopted father, probably would not have been mentioned on the ossuary, as apparently Joseph was out of Jesus' life already by an early age; moreover, Jesus as "son of Joseph" is referred to by people who know him and his family merely in episodes in his intimate surroundings, in Nazareth, Capernaum, and Galilee. Jesus' proper name was not "Yeshua' bar Yehoseph" in the same manner that יוסף בן מתתיהו, "Yoseph ben Matityahu (Matthias)," was the proper name of Josephus, or the proper names of the apostles were יעקב בן זבדי, "James son of Zebedee," and יעקב בן חלפי, "James son of Alphaeus."

מריה, *Mariah, Marya*

On the front of plain ossuary 6 the name מריה (Mariah/Marya) was inscribed in Hebrew (fig. 4a).[35] מריה, Mariah, and מרים, Mariame, together with שלום, Shalom/Salome, and שלמציון, Shelamsiyon, in several variations were the most common female names in the Second Temple period; about 50 percent of the entire female population bore these names; their popularity is probably due to their being typical names of the Hasmonean dynasty.[36]

35. Kloner, "Tomb with Inscribed Ossuaries," p. 20; Rahmani, *Catalogue,* no. 706.
36. Hachlili, "Names and Nicknames," p. 191; idem, *Jewish Funerary Customs,* pp.

Figure 4. Three ossuaries with
Hebrew inscriptions, East Talpiot tomb: (a) ossuary 6 -
Mariah; (b) ossuary 5b - Yose;
(c) ossuary 3 - Matya (A. Kloner)

Scholars maintain that Maryam and Maria might have been the same name, Maria a diminutive or a contracted or a Greek form of Maryam; however, it is also possible that these were two different names. A number of ossuaries discovered in Jerusalem tombs are inscribed with the names מריה, Mariah,[37] and מרים in Hebrew and Greek;[38] the two names appear also in the Goliath family tomb in Jericho.[39]

Mary the mother of Jesus appears in the Hebrew translation of the New Testament[40] as מרים, Maryam, while in the Greek she is named in both forms: in the narrative of Jesus' birth she is called Μαρίας (Matt 1:16, 18; 2:11; Luke 1:41), and Μαριάμ (Matt 1:20; Luke 1:27, 30, 34, 38, 46, 56; 2:5-7, 16, 19, 34).

Note the episode when Jesus returned to Nazareth: "he came to his home town, where he taught the people in their synagogue. In amazement they asked, 'Where does he get this wisdom from, and these miraculous powers? Is he not the carpenter's (τέκτονος) son? Is not his mother called

198-99; Tal Ilan, "The Names of the Hasmoneans in the Second Temple Period" [in Hebrew], *ErIsr* 19 (1987): 240; idem, *Jewish Women in Greco-Roman Palestine: An Inquiry into Image and Status*, TSAJ 44 (Tübingen: Mohr Siebeck, 1995), p. 55; idem, *Lexicon*, p. 9.

37. Rahmani, *Catalogue*, no. 152, and in Greek no. 405.

38. Ibid., nos. 31, 243, 351, 502, 559 (in both languages), 821; in Greek in some variations: nos. 64, 108, 233, 333, 552.

39. Hachlili, "Goliath Family," p. 49; figs. 3, 14-17; tables 2, 3.

40. Yizhak Salkinson and David Ginsburg, *The Hebrew New Testament* (London, 1999).

Mary [Μαριάμ in Matt 13:55; and Μαρίας in Mark: 6:3], his brothers James [Ya'akov], Joseph [or Joses in Mark], Simon, and Judas? And are not all his sisters here with us?'" (Matt 13:54-56; Mark 6:3).

In other narratives during the life of Jesus, Mary is not mentioned by name but is usually called "his mother" (see Matt 12:46-49; Luke 2:41-52; John 2:5, 12). At the crucifixion, Mary appears as "his mother," not by her name (John 19:25-27); beside her are her sister Mary of Clopas (Μαρία, which some scholars identify with the mother of James the younger and Joseph mentioned in Matt 27:55 and Mark 15:40; 16:1), Mary Magdalene (John 19:25-27), and "the mother of the sons of Zebedee" (Matt 27:56, who might be identified with Salome, mentioned in Mark 15:40).

Mary is mentioned again only after the ascension: "Mary mother of Jesus and his brothers" (Μαρία τή μητρί τοῦ Ἰησοῦ καί σύν τοῖς ἀδελφοῖς αὐτοῦ; Acts 1:14). After that Mary's life and the time and manner of death are not recorded; with no indication that she was buried in Jerusalem, it is possible that she died and was buried in Nazareth, where she lived most of her life and where her husband Joseph was probably buried in their family tomb.

It would have been much more in character that once Mary died and if she was interred in an ossuary in a Jerusalem tomb her inscription would have said: מרים אמה ישוע הנצרי, "Maryam/Mariah mother of Yeshua' of Nazareth," comparable to the inscription of "Shelamsiyon mother of Yeho'ezer Goliath" on ossuary 20 in the Goliath Tomb at Jericho (fig. 5).[41]

יוסה, *Yose*

On plain ossuary 5 the name יוסה, Yose (Joses), is inscribed on the front (fig. 4b).[42] Yose is apparently a contraction of the name Yehoseph (Joseph). Rahmani suggests that the similarities between the ossuaries and the inscriptions of Yose and Marya may designate that these are the ossuaries of the parents of Yeshua' and grandparents of Yehuda; thus the "Yehoseph father of Yeshua'" inscribed on ossuary 4 is identified with Yose of this ossuary. The Yose (Joses/Joseph) ossuary is claimed by some to be that of Jesus' brother noted in Mark 6:3.

41. Hachlili, "Goliath Family," pp. 56-57, inscription 11b, fig. 32; idem, *Jewish Funerary Customs,* pp. 180-83, fig. V-10b.

42. Rahmani, *Catalogue,* no. 705; Kloner, "Tomb with Inscribed Ossuaries," pp. 18-19.

CEΛAMCIOYC MHTPOC IWEZPOY ΓOΛIAΘOY

שלמשיון אמה די יהועזר גלית

CEΛAMCIOYC MHTPOC IOEZPOY ΓOΛIAΘOY

Figure 5. "Shelamsiyon mother of Yehoezer Goliath," inscription 11 on ossuary 20, Goliath Tomb at Jericho *(R. Hachlili)*

מתיה, *Matya*

On plain ossuary 3 the name מתיה, Matya, is engraved on the narrow side and scratched inside (fig. 4c). The name is a contraction of מתתיהו (Matityahu, Matthias).[43] Matya is not related to Jesus' family.

יהודה בר ישוע, *Yehuda son of Yeshuaʿ*

The inscription on the ornamented ossuary 2 reads: יהודה בר ישוע, "Yehuda son of Yeshuaʿ"; the inscription is very well engraved on the left upper side of the ossuary front (fig. 6).[44] The name is inscribed in a different hand than all the other inscribed names in the East Talpiot tomb.

Yehuda is the third most common name in the onomasticon of Jewish male names in the Second Temple period.[45]

This inscription is articulating that Yehuda was the son of Yeshuaʿ, which means that if Yeshuaʿ is Jesus of Nazareth he must have had a son by

43. Rahmani, *Catalogue*, p. 223, no. 703; Kloner, "Tomb with Inscribed Ossuaries," p. 18.

44. Rahmani, *Catalogue*, no. 702; Kloner, "Tomb with Inscribed Ossuaries," p. 18.

45. Hachlili, "Names and Nicknames," table 2; idem, *Jewish Funerary Customs*, p. 200, table V-2; Ilan, *Lexicon*, table 7.

 יהודה הבר ישוע

Figure 6. "Yehuda son of Yeshuʿa," Hebrew inscription on ossuary 2, East Talpiot tomb *(A. Kloner)*

the name Yehuda, which has not been proved. No data is known indicating that Yeshuaʿ was married let alone had a son named Yehuda.

Mariamne/Mara

The last to be discussed is the Greek inscription on ossuary 1:[46] Μαριαμήνου (ἡ) Μάρα, "Mariamne who is (also called) Mara" (fig. 7).[47] Rahmani maintains that the first name is a variant of the name Mariame or Maryam, while "Mara" is a contraction of "Martha." Pfann suggests another reading, Μαριάμη καί Μάρα, "Mariame and Mara"; he claims that two scribes were involved in the writing on separate occasions.[48]

The assumption that this is the ossuary of Mary Magdalene is without any justification as "Magdalene" is not inscribed, no reference is made to Magdala, and no relation of Mary Magdalene to Jesus' family is established; even if she was a family intimate, she would not necessarily be buried in the family tomb.[49]

It seems that the inscription mentions a double name rather than interment of two separate women. Double names appear chiefly among Hebrew-Greek names, but there are also double Hebrew names inscribed on ossuaries from tombs in Jerusalem and Jericho.[50]

---

46. Kloner, "Tomb with Inscribed Ossuaries," p. 17.

47. Rahmani, *Catalogue*, pp. 222-23, no. 701.

48. Stephen J. Pfann, "Mary Magdalene Has Left the Room: A Suggested New Reading of Ossuary *CJO* 701," *NEA* 69 (2006): 130-31.

49. But see the discussion by Tabor, "Testing," p. 135.

50. Rahmani, *Catalogue,* p. 14, ossuaries nos. 31, 95, 477, 552, 868; Hachlili, "Goliath Family," p. 53, inscriptions 8 and 13, figs. 18-26; idem, *Jewish Funerary Customs,* pp. 186-87, fig. V-15.

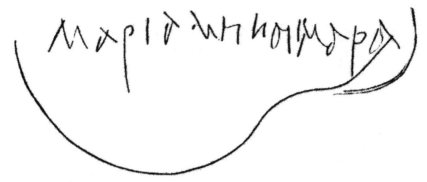

Figure 7. "Mariamne/ Mara," Greek inscription on ossuary 1, East Talpiot tomb
(A. Kloner)

Conclusions

The noticeable features of the East Talpiot tomb names are:

- The inscription ישוע בר יהוסף, "Yeshua' son of Yehoseph," on ossuary 4: in the New Testament "Yeshua'" is Jesus' proper personal name, and sometimes he is called "Yeshua' of Nazareth." Only in his hometown surroundings is Jesus referred as "bar Yehoseph" (the son of Joseph), which refers to his family relation and origin but is not his proper name. Yeshua' (Jesus) was not known as the son of Joseph outside Nazareth and environs; this implies that if he was interred in an ossuary in a tomb in Jerusalem (which is in profound doubt)[51] his inscription would have been engraved either with his single proper personal name ישוע, "Yeshua'," or possibly ישוע הנצרי, "Yeshua' of Nazareth."
- The distinctive similarities between the three plain ossuaries (nos. 3, 5, and 6) in their size (about 54 × 27 × 34) and especially the form of their Hebrew inscriptions: מתיה, יוסה, מריה, Marya, Yose, and Matya (fig. 4a-c), indicate that the inscribed names were possibly executed by the same hand, probably at the same time, and are quite different from the other three inscriptions. These three ossuaries were most likely placed together in loculus no. 7 (fig. 1).[52]
- Family relationship in the East Talpiot tomb is revealed only in two os-

51. But see Tabor, "Testing," pp. 132-33.
52. Kloner, "Tomb with Inscribed Ossuaries," plan 1.

suary inscriptions: the almost unreadable inscription of "Yeshua' bar Yehoseph" (ossuary 4) and the well-inscribed name of his son, "Yehuda bar Yeshua'" (ossuary 2), whereas the other inscriptions disclose no relationships whatsoever. Moreover, the Yehuda inscription actually determined the reading of the Yeshua' inscription by Rahmani.[53]

Thus the East Talpiot tomb was a Jewish family tomb with a father and son each interred in his own inscribed ossuary and three other members of the family who were interred in similar plain ossuaries each inscribed with her or his personal name executed by the same hand, possibly at the same time, and most likely placed in the same loculus. It is interesting to note that all three members of this family (מריה, יוסה, מתיה, Marya, Yose, and Matya) have a four-letter personal Hebrew name, which in each case is a contraction of a fuller name. Is it a coincidence? Or perhaps it is a characteristic feature of this family?

Unless compelling evidence is established that "Yeshua' bar Yehoseph" as identified by some with Jesus had a son by the name of Judas "Yehuda bar Yeshua'," this tomb could not be related to Jesus and is *not* "the lost tomb of Jesus."

If Mary, Jesus' mother, was interred in an ossuary in her son's tomb in Jerusalem (and not in Nazareth where her husband was ostensibly buried, thus it was their family tomb), her inscription could have read "Mariame/Maria mother of Yeshua'" rather than plain "Maria."

The cluster of names associated with Jesus' family, as promoted by the film, consists actually of only three names: Yeshua', Maria, and perhaps Yose, which is far from enough to suggest relation to the family of Jesus, while Yehuda, Matya, and Mariamne/Mara seem a problem for the issue of the Jesus family.

In light of all the above the East Talpiot tomb is a Jewish family tomb with no connection to the historical Jesus family; it is not the family tomb of Jesus; and most of the presented facts for the identification are speculation and guesswork.

---

53. Rahmani, *Catalogue,* p. 223, no. 704: "The reading ישוע is corroborated by the inscription on no. 702 referring to Yeshua', the father of Yehuda."

Matching Inscriptional Names with Known Historical Figures

Inscriptions on some tombs, sarcophagi, and ossuaries provide evidence of eminent individuals who were buried in Jerusalem and Jericho and are known as well from ancient sources. Matching inscriptional names with known historical figures is appropriate when specifically stated or in some cases when identified with figures referred to in contemporary literature.

The Goliath family tomb at Jericho reveals two unique examples of the association of names to known historical figures: (1) A name of a known historical figure is used for a specific reason; (2) the inscriptions mention a recognized historical figure.

1. Among the thirty-two inscriptions engraved on fourteen ossuaries found in the Goliath Tomb at Jericho the name גלית/Γολιάθ/Goliath is inscribed in Jewish and Greek scripts on nine inscriptions carved on four ossuaries (fig. 8).[54] In these inscriptions Goliath is added to the personal name and family relation of the interred individual. It is an amazing phenomenon that a Jewish family in Jericho in the first century CE is adopting the name of an archenemy of ancient Israel, a symbolic historical enemy. The references to this name in the Bible and rabbinical sources all emphasize Goliath's stature, his most outstanding physical characteristic. The examination of the skeletal remains of four male members of this family indicated they were exceptionally tall. The height of Yeho'ezer son of Ele'azar, mentioned in inscription 12a, is estimated at 1.885 m, close to Goliath's height in the LXX[55] (the average stature for males at the time was about 159-168 cm). In antiquity Yeho'ezer bar Ele'azar, possibly the first of the line to be nicknamed Goliath, might have been considered a giant in stature.

The name Goliath is utilized in this Jewish family for the sole purpose of emphasizing the physical stature and was obviously not the tomb of the biblical figure of Goliath.

2. A Greek inscription written twice in ink on the upper corners of the ossuary back reads (fig. 9): ΘΕΌΔΟΤΟΥ ἈΠΕΛΕΥ/ΘΈΡΟΥ ΒΑϹΙΛΊϹϹΗϹ/ ΑΓΡΙΠΠΕΊΝΗϹ — COPÓS, "The ossuary of Theodotos, freedman of Queen

---

54. Hachlili, "Goliath Family," pp. 52-53, table 1, inscriptions 2, 9, 10, 11b; idem, *Jewish Funerary Customs*, pp. 292-95, table V-1, fig. VI-40; idem, "Funerary Practices in Judaea during the Times of the Herods: The Goliath Family Tomb at Jericho," in *International Conference: The World of the Herods and the Nabataeans*, vol. 1, *The World of the Herods*, ed. Nikos Kokkinos, Oriens et Occident 14 (Stuttgart: Franz Steiner, 2007), pp. 268-70.

55. Hachlili and Smith, "Genealogy," p. 69, table 1; Hachlili, "Goliath Family," p. 52.

Figure 8. "Yeho'ezer son of Yeho'ezer Goliath," inscription 10 on ossuary 19, Goliath Tomb at Jericho *(R. Hachlili)*

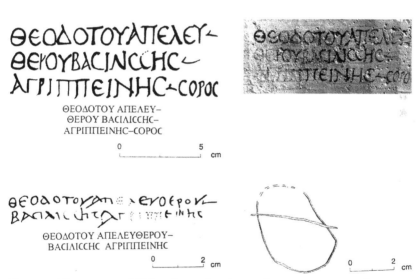

Figure 9. The ossuary of "Theodotos, freedman of Queen Agrippina," inscription 3 on ossuary 8, Goliath Tomb at Jericho *(R. Hachlili)*

Agrippina." The inscription contains the personal, servile name of Theodotos, followed by the status indication (his manumission) and his patron's name, Queen Agrippina.[56] This inscription designates the legal fact of Theodotos's manumission by Queen Agrippina and that he was an "imperial freedman"; it also confirms that the events recorded in this inscription were considered by the family to be important, indicating Theodotos's special status as a Roman citizen.

Queen Agrippina in this inscription should be identified with Agrippina the Younger (15-59 CE), daughter of Agrippina the Elder and Germanicus, who in 49 CE married Emperor Claudius, her uncle. During Agrippina's reign (51-55 CE), Theodotos gained manumission, perhaps due to Agrippina's close relations with the king of Judea, Agrippa II, and his family. After his release Theodotos returned to his home in Jericho, where he died and was placed in the family tomb. Inscriptions on another ossuary in the same tomb inscribed with the name Mariah[57] established his position in the family, that is, Theodotos/Nat[an]el, the freedman of Queen Agrippina, is the son of Shelamsiyon and father of Mariah.

This inscription, which refers to a well-known historical figure, is unique among Jewish burial inscriptions of the Second Temple period.

Some inscriptions from Jerusalem tombs relate to priestly families, in which the inscriptions specify the link of the deceased to the priestly courses serving in the temple, possibly to commemorate and keep eternally the genealogy of the family; several inscriptions mention the name of the interred with the addition of the title priest or high priest:[58]

1. The three-generation family of priests of "sons of Hezir," בני חזיר (the 17th priestly course), is inscribed on the lintel of a tomb in the Kidron Valley (1 Chr 24:15; Neh 10:21).[59]
2. Inscriptions on ossuaries found in the "Kallon" family tomb indicate that the interred family in this tomb belonged to a priestly family of the house of Yeshb'ab (Jeshebeab), the head of the 14th course of the

56. Hachlili, "Goliath Family," pp. 33, 46-47, inscription 3, figs. 40-42; idem, *Jewish Funerary Customs,* pp. 183-85, fig. V-12.

57. Hachlili, "Goliath Family," p. 57, inscription 7, figs. 15-17; idem, *Jewish Funerary Customs,* p. 294, table V-1, fig. VI-40.

58. Hachlili, *Jewish Funerary Customs,* pp. 299-301.

59. Nahman Avigad, *Ancient Monuments in the Kidron Valley* [in Hebrew] (Jerusalem: Bialik Institute, 1954), pp. 37-59; Hachlili, *Jewish Funerary Customs,* pp. 167-68, 262-63, family tomb XII.

temple priests in the period of David (1 Chr 24:13). These family members were buried in this tomb and related their family pedigree.[60] The inscription of "Shelamsiyon daughter of Gamla wife of Yeho'ezer son of Kallon," who belongs to the Kallon family, is identified as the sister of Yehushu'a son of Gamla, the high priest in the reign of Agrippa II (Josephus, *War* 20.213).

3. "Menahem of the sons of Yachim the priest," inscribed on an ossuary from a tomb on the Mount of Olives,[61] belonged to a priestly family of the house of Yachin (Jachin), the head of the 21st course of the temple priests (1 Chr 24:17).

4. "Shim'on of (the family of) Boethos," inscribed on an ossuary from a tomb on Mt. Scopus, was probably linked to the priestly family of Sim'on ben Boethos of Alexandria (Josephus, *Ant.* 15.320).[62]

5. Inscriptions on ossuaries discovered in a North Talpiot tomb may have recorded the family of the high priest Caiaphas.[63]

6. "Yehohanah daughter of Yehohanan son of Theophilus the high priest" is inscribed on an ossuary of unknown provenance.[64]

Other examples of inscriptions engraved on Jerusalem ossuaries cite prominent figures, who were identified with figures mentioned in ancient sources:

7. "Ariston of Apamea," inscribed on an ossuary from the Akeldama tomb, may be identified with the person noted in the Mishnah (*Halla* 4:11) who bears gifts to the Jerusalem temple from abroad.[65]

60. Hachlili, *Jewish Funerary Customs,* pp. 268-73, family tomb XV.

61. B. Bagatti and J. T. Milik, *Gli Scavi del "Dominus Flevit,"* part 1, *La Necropoli del Periodo Romano,* Pubblicazioni dello Studium Biblicum Franciscanum 13 (Jerusalem: Franciscan Printing Press, 1958), pp. 89-92, ossuary 83, inscription no. 22, pl. 81; Hachlili, *Jewish Funerary Customs,* p. 214.

62. E. L. Sukenik, "A Jewish Tomb-Cave on the Slope of Mt. Scopus" [in Hebrew], *Qovetz* 3, *Journal of the Jewish Palestine Exploration Society (dedicated to the Memory of Dr. A. Mazie)* (1934): 67; Hachlili, *Jewish Funerary Customs,* pp. 263-64, family tomb XIII.

63. Hachlili, *Jewish Funerary Customs,* pp. 264-68, family tomb XIV.

64. Dan Barag and David Flusser, "The Ossuary of Yehohanah Granddaughter of the High Priest Theophilus," *IEJ* 36 (1986): 39-44; Rahmani, *Catalogue,* no. 871; Hachlili, *Jewish Funerary Customs,* pp. 215, 315, 320.

65. Tal Ilan, "The Ossuaries and Sarcophagus Inscriptions," in *Akeldama Tombs: Three Burial Caves in the Kidron Valley, Jerusalem,* ed. Gideon Avni and Zvi Greenhut, IAA Reports 1 (Jerusalem, 1996), p. 66, inscription no. 19, ossuary 31; Hachlili, *Jewish Funerary Customs,* p. 212.

8. "Alexander son of Simon Qarnit," inscribed on an ossuary from a Kidron Valley tomb, might be identified with Alexander son of "Simon of Cyrene, father of Alexaner and Rofus," mentioned in the New Testament (Mark 15:21).[66]

9. The Nicanor bilingual inscription engraved on an ossuary found in a tomb on Mt. Scopus (now in the British Museum) records: "The bones of the [sons or descendants?] of Nicanor the Alexandrian who made the doors." The inscription most likely refers to Nicanor of Alexandria, who donated the famous door of Herod's Temple known as the "Gate of Nicanor" (*m. Mid.* 2:3; *Yoma* 3:6; *b. Yoma* 38a; *y. Yoma* 41a). The ossuary apparently contained the bones of some family members of Nicanor the Alexandrian, and he himself might have been interred in the family tomb.[67]

10. The front of a sarcophagus from the tomb of Queen Helene of Adiabene was inscribed in Aramaic and Syriac, "Sadan [or Saran] Malkta," who is identified as Queen Helene (Josephus, *Ant.* 20.95).[68]

Burial in a family tomb as well as the importance of individual interment is evident in Jewish burial practices of the late Second Temple period. This is noticeably attested by the inscriptions found on ossuaries, sarcophagi, and tombs, as well as being represented in the plan of the loculi tomb, which provides for individual burial in the loculi as well as in coffins, or ossuaries placed in loculi, and at the same time allows family members to be buried in the same tomb. The perception of individual burial for the entire population and not just for the upper classes, as in the Israelite period, is probably related to the increasing importance placed on the individual in contemporary Hellenistic society as a whole[69] and to the Jewish belief in the individual resurrection of the body. The concept of individual resurrection is reflected in sources as early as the second century BCE (Dan 12:2; 2 Macc 7:9-23; 12:38-45; 14:46; Josephus, *Ag. Ap.* 2.218).[70] The importance of the family, combined with that of the individual in his family and society, is evident in the Jewish funerary practices of the period.

66. Nahman Avigad, "A Depository of Inscribed Ossuaries in the Kidron Valley," *IEJ* 12 (1962): 10-11; Hachlili, *Jewish Funerary Customs*, p. 214.

67. Hachlili, *Jewish Funerary Customs*, pp. 172-73, 286.

68. Ibid., pp. 121, 168.

69. Donna C. Kurtz and John Boardman, *Greek Burial Customs* (London: Thames & Hudson, 1971), p. 273.

70. Rahmani, *Catalogue*, pp. 53-55.

The evidence of burial inscriptions related to or identifying historian figures is quite meager; only a few of the inscriptions cite their title or relationship to a priestly course; other inscriptions enable scholars to deduce from the name the historical figure's identity. However, the majority of the ossuaries discovered in Jerusalem lack inscriptions, and those that contain inscriptions usually consist of a single personal name or names with patronymics yet with no data that could help identify the interred and establish their family relations.[71]

The number of inscriptions in some of the family tombs indicates that the families were Jewish, literate, bilingual, and in some cases prominent. Those interred in these family tombs apparently constituted extended families of parents, sons, and their families. The inscriptions evidently designate an act of commemoration, indicating the social relationship between the deceased; it seem that family members have been the ones who engraved the inscriptions, implying affection, love, and a sense of duty, as well as the aspiration to preserve some memory of oneself after death. These include commemoration of the elderly, of children, and of members of the nuclear family. The prevailing impression from the data is the centrality of the family as the fundamental social unit, with the father-mother-children triad as the main focus of family duty.

71. For some examples of inscribed ossuaries from the same excavated tomb but for which no family relations could be established see Rahmani, *Catalogue:* (1) nos. 121-22; (2) nos. 217-18, 220, 222; (3) nos. 330, 332, 333; (4) nos. 559-61; (5) nos. 570-73, 576, 579, 582.

Identifying Inscriptional Names in the Century Before 70: Problems and Methodology

André Lemaire

The title of this contribution is somewhat parallel to the title of the book of Lawrence J. Mykytiuk: *Identifying Biblical Persons in Northwest Semitic Inscriptions of 1200-539 B.C.E.*, dealing with First Temple inscriptions, mainly seals.[1] However, one may note that, besides the later and shorter period of time, there are two main differences: there is no direct reference to the Bible, and the problem is seen from the point of view of inscriptions, that is, from the point of view of an epigrapher.

First we shall deal with the main groups of inscriptions of this period and their problems, and second with the main characteristics of the onomastics of this period, before studying in detail various aspects of the identification problems.

Epigraphy

Thus far there is no published general corpus of Palestinian inscriptions of this period, often called the Herodian period. However, numerous inscriptions are included in the more general *Corpus inscriptionum iudaicarum (CII)* by Jean-Baptiste Frey.[2] One hopes that it will be soon completed and

---

1. SBLABib 12 (Atlanta: Society of Biblical Literature, 2004).

2. The subtitle is: *Recueil des inscriptions juives qui vont du IIIe siècle avant Jésus-Christ au VIIe siècle de notre ère*, vol. 2, *Asie-Afrique* (Rome: Pontificio istituto di archeologia cristiana, 1952).

updated with the *Corpus inscriptionum Iudaeae/Palaestinae (CIIP)*.[3] However this last one will not include coins, papyri, leather and copper scrolls and will concern a much larger period. Actually for coins, it is possible to refer partly to the work of Y. Meshorer, and for manuscripts to the Discoveries in the Judaean Desert series.[4]

A general look at this corpus reveals that "personal names are almost nonexistent in the Qumran literature."[5] Some are present in the brief inscriptions from Khirbet Qumrân, from the Herodium, and more from the Masada excavations.[6] Some are also found in occasional inscriptions here and there, especially in the Jerusalem excavations.[7] However, by far the main

---

3. For this project see provisionally "Corpus Inscriptionum Iudaeae/Palaestinae," *Scripta Classica Israelitica* 18 (1999): 175-76. See also P. van der Horst, "Greek in Jewish Palestine in Light of Jewish Epigraphy," in *Hellenism in the Land of Israel,* ed. J. J. Collins and G. E. Sterling, Christianity and Judaism in Antiquity Series 13 (Notre Dame, Ind.: University of Notre Dame Press, 2001), pp. 154-74, esp. p. 155 *(CIIP):* "The estimate is that there will be between 6,000 and 7,000 texts in the corpus"; J. J. Price and H. Misgav, "Jewish Inscriptions and Their Use," in *The Literature of the Sages, Second Part: Midrash and Targum . . . ,* ed. S. Safrai et al., CRINT 2/3b (Minneapolis: Fortress, 2006), pp. 461-83, esp. 462: "approximately 4000 Jewish inscriptions, dating from the end of the fourth century BCE to the sixth or seventh century CE (from Alexander to Muhammad), have been identified."

4. Meshorer, *A Treasury of Jewish Coins from the Persian Period to Bar Kokhba* (Jerusalem: Yad Ben-Zvi Press, 2001). See also, for the Copper Scroll: D. Brizemeure, N. Lacoudre, and E. Puech, *Le Rouleau de cuivre de la grotte 3 de Qumrân (3Q15). Expertise — Restauration — Épigraphie,* STDJ 55/1-2 (Leiden: Brill, 2006).

5. T. Ilan, "Names and Naming," in *Encyclopaedia of the Dead Sea Scrolls,* ed. L. H. Schiffman and J. C. VanderKam, 2 vols. (Oxford: Oxford University Press, 2000), 2:596. See also E. Eshel, "Personal Names in the Qumran Sect," in *These Are the Names: Studies in Jewish Onomastics,* ed. A. Demsky, J. A. Reif, and J. Tabory, 5 vols. (Ramat Gan: Bar-Ilan University Press, 1997-2011), 1:39-52.

6. See A. Lemaire, "Inscriptions du khirbeh, des grottes et de ʿAïn Feshkha," in *Khirbet Qumrân et ʿAïn Feshkha II,* ed. J.-B. Humbert and J. Gunneweg, NTOA Series Archaeologica 3 (Fribourg: Academic Press, 2003), pp. 341-88; E. Testa, *Herodion and I graffiti e gli ostraka* (Jerusalem, 1972); Y. Yadin and J. Naveh, *Masada I* (Jerusalem: Israel Exploration Society and Hebrew University, 1989), pp. 1-68; cf. also H. Cotton and J. Geifer, *Masada 2: The Latin and Greek Documents* (Jerusalem, 1989).

7. See lately, unprovenanced, A. Yardeni and B. Elitzur, "Prophetic Text on Stone from the First Century CE," *Cathedra* 123 (2007): 155-66; for Jerusalem see, e.g., J. Naveh, "Hebrew and Aramaic Inscriptions," in *Excavations at the City of David 1978-1985 Directed by Yigal Shiloh,* ed. D. T. Ariel, Qedem 41 (Jerusalem: Hebrew University, 2000), pp. 1-14, esp. 13.

epigraphic source for Jerusalem names during the Herodian period are the inscriptions on ossuaries. Unfortunately the generally good book of L. Y. Rahmani remains limited and left out many inscribed ossuaries in other collections; furthermore it should be updated by new ossuaries published during the last fifteen years.[8]

This last kind of document may be problematic in several ways: they are generally graffiti, their reading is sometimes uncertain, and paleographically they lack precise dating.[9] Furthermore the inscriptions are generally very short and give us mainly names and patronymics. A few of them mention an ethnicity or a function, but longer inscriptions are rare. The pre-70 ossuaries come generally from Jerusalem and its environs, eventually as far as Jericho, where some Jerusalemites had their secondary residency. In and around Jerusalem, the ossuaries practically ceased to be used with the fall of the city in 70.

The beginning of their use is more difficult to pin down precisely: Rahmani proposed 20-15 BCE, but Rachel Hachlili specified that, at least in Jericho, their beginning is to be dated only in the early first century CE (ca. 6-10?),[10] so that they probably started seriously to be used around the turn of

---

8. *A Catalogue of Jewish Ossuaries in the Collections of the State of Israel* (Jerusalem: Israel Antiquities Authority and Israel Academy of Sciences and Humanities, 1994).

9. For the paleography of the Jewish script of this period, cf. A. Yardeni, *Textbook of Aramaic, Hebrew and Nabataean Documentary Texts from the Judaean Desert and Related Material,* vol. B: *Translation, Palaeography, Concordance* (Jerusalem: Hebrew University, 2000), pp. 145-218. This period corresponds to "the Herodian script" (see esp. pp. 155-56: "A significant increase in ornamental elements in letters is the most prominent feature of the Herodian book-hand"). For the uncertainties of the paleographical dating of the cursive script at this time, see R. Hachlili, "Jewish Funerary Customs During the Second Temple Period, in the Light of the Excavations at the Jericho Necropolis," *PEQ* 115 (1983): 109-39, esp. 130 n. 17: "it should be stressed that palaeography during the Second Temple period is not a good indicator of date as the differences in the cursive script are due to differences in the individual's handwriting and not to the development of the script."

10. Rahmani, *Catalogue,* p. 21; R. Hachlili, "A Second Temple Period Jewish Necropolis in Jericho," *BA* 43 (1980): 235-40, esp. 239; R. Hachlili and A. E. Killebrew, *Jericho: The Jewish Cemetery of the Second Temple Period,* IAA Reports 7 (Jerusalem, 1999), pp. 174-75; R. Hachlili, *Jewish Funerary Customs, Practices and Rites in the Second Temple Period,* JSJSup 94 (Leiden: Brill, 2005), pp. 518-22; idem, "Funerary Practices in Judaea During the Time of the Herods: The Goliath Family Tomb at Jericho," in *International Conference: The World of the Herods and the Nabataeans,* held at the British Museum, 17-19 April 2001, vol. 1, *The World of the Herods,* ed. N. Kokkinos, Oriens et Occidens 14 (Stuttgart: Franz Steiner, 2007), pp. 251-78, esp. 274-75, 277.

the era. Actually the use of ossuaries is connected with the development of the use of stone vessels;[11] and, in my view, this development was probably somehow connected with the "reconversion" of the stonecutters working for the Herodian temple.

This dating has to be taken into account for the problems of probability of identification.

Onomastics

The Jewish onomastics around the turn of the era has been the subject of several studies, especially from Hachlili, T. Ilan, and others.[12] In the *Lexicon of Jewish Names in Late Antiquity,* Ilan considers a larger period but contains most of the data concerning the Herodian period from the inscriptions as well as from the literary tradition.[13] Thus the characteristics that she found for this longer period are very useful for the shorter period, for which they sometimes appear even more clearly:

1. "The pool of names in use was very limited and, as a result, an enormous portion of the population used only a few specific names" (p. 2).
2. Among the most popular ones were "the biblical-Hasmonean names" (p. 2): "31.5% of the male population (792, out of 2509) bore the six names of the Hasmoneans."

11. See Y. Magen, *The Stone Vessel Industry in the Second Temple Period* (Jerusalem: Israel Exploration Society and Israel Antiquities Authority, 2002), pp. 132-37.

12. R. Hachlili, "Names and Nicknames of Jews in Second Temple Times," in *A. J. Brawer Memorial Volume, ErIsr* 17 (1984): 188-211, 9*-10*; idem, "Names and Nicknames at Masada," in *Frank Moore Cross Volume,* ed. B. A. Levine et al., *ErIsr* 26 (1999): 229*, 49-54; idem, *Jewish Funerary Customs,* esp. pp. 193-233; T. Ilan, "Names of the Hasmoneans during the Second Temple Period" [in Hebrew], in *Michael Avi-Yonah Volume,* ed. D. Barag et al., *ErIsr* 19 (1987): 238-41; idem, "Notes on the Spelling of Names in the Second Temple Period" [in Hebrew], *Leshonenu* 52 (1988): 1-7; idem, "Notes on the Distribution of Jewish Women's Names in Palestine in the Second Temple and Mishnaic Period," *JJS* 40 (1989): 186-200; idem, "'Man Born of Woman . . .' (Job 14:1): The Phenomenon of Men Bearing Metronymes [*sic*] at the Time of Jesus," *NovT* 34 (1992): 23-45; idem, "Names and Naming," in *Encyclopedia of the Dead Sea Scrolls,* 2:596-600. See also G. Mussies, "Jewish Personal Names in Some Non-Literary Sources," in *Studies in Early Jewish Epigraphy,* ed. J. W. van Henten and P. W. ven der Horst, AGJU 21 (Leiden: Brill, 1994), pp. 242-76; cf. also H. Misgav, "Nomenclature in Ossuary Inscriptions," *Tarbiz* 66 (1996): 123-30 and p. VIII.

13. Part 1, *Palestine 330 BCE–200 CE,* TSAJ 91 (Tübingen: Mohr Siebeck, 2002).

3. "*Paponymy:* One of the most common naming procedures of the time was after the grandfather" (p. 32).
4. "*Patronymy:* . . . a son bearing the same name as the father is not unheard of among the Jews in Greco-Roman Palestine" (p. 33).
5. However, "it does not appear that they named two siblings by the same name" (p. 33).

These characteristics reveal some of the difficulties in trying to identify inscriptional names in the last century before 70. We shall have especially to take into account the big problem of the frequency of homonymy.

Identification

Because of this frequency of homonymy, it seems clear that, unless it is a very rare name, finding the same name in two inscriptions or in one inscription and in the literary tradition is not enough to speak of a problem of identification. Furthermore, it seems also that finding the same popular names for the son and for the father (or the mother) alone is generally not enough to speak of a likely identification and that we have to be very cautious in the appreciation of the various possible or proposed identifications.[14] What is the methodology to apply?[15] To clarify the problem, it is necessary to distinguish the cases when the identification could be certain because of unique characteristics from the cases when it can only be a problem of probability.

Possible Identifications Because of Unique Characteristics

There are a few cases when the identification could be certain because both presentations of the person are *identical and unique.* It is especially the case when the name is connected with a very high function: king, prefect, high priest, and so on. Let us review a few cases:
 1. A fragmentary Latin stone inscription found in Caesarea mentions

14. See, e.g., J. Schwartz, "Once More on the Nicanor Gate," *HUCA* 62 (1991): 245-83, esp. 249 n. 16: "Extreme care must also be exercised when trying to establish a connection between persons mentioned in literary traditions and names found in inscriptions."
15. Ilan, *Lexicon,* pp. 35-36, "Verifying Identifications," does not deal much in detail with this problem.

Po]ntius Pilatus/[praef]ectus Iuda[ea]e, who is clearly identified with the Roman prefect of Judea mentioned in Josephus,[16] Tacitus,[17] Philo,[18] and the New Testament.[19] We know the names of all the Roman governors of Judea, and only one is called "Pontius Pilate." Furthermore, the discovery of the inscription in the Roman capital of Judea at this time, the use of Latin, and the monumental character of the inscription (with the mention of a *Tiberieum*) fit a Roman prefect at this time. The only element of doubt could come from the fragmentary character of the inscription, but what is left is enough to ascertain the name and the title.[20]

2. As well noted by R. Hachlili, one of the Jericho ossuaries belonged "To Theodotos, freedman of Queen Agrippina."[21] Although the beginning of line 3 is a little blurred, the reading of this well-written ink inscription is certain. The Greek title *basilissēs* clearly indicates that this Agrippina can only be Agrippina the Younger (15-59 CE), who in 49 CE married Emperor Claudius, her uncle (Tacitus, *Ann.* 12.1-8).[22]

3. On coins, the title "king" *(basileōs)* often follows the personal name (cf. Herod [the Great], Agrippa I, Agrippa II), or eventually *ethnarchou* (Herod Archelaus) or *tetrarchou* (Herod Antipas, Philip). The titles can be abbreviated but the context helps to distinguish between two kings bearing the same name as is the case for Agrippa I and Agrippa II.

4. The famous so-called Tomb of the Kings discovered by F. de Saulcy and situated north of the so-called Third Wall is generally identified as the tomb of Helena, queen of Adiabene.[23] This seems to be confirmed by the double (cur-

---

16. *War* 2.169-77; *Ant.* 18.35-89, 177.

17. *Ann.* 15.44.

18. *Leg.* 299-305.

19. Matt 27:2; Luke 3:1; Acts 4:27; 1 Tim 6:13.

20. For the historical figure of Pontius Pilate, cf., e.g., J.-P. Lémonon, *Pilate et le gouvernement de la Judée: Textes et monuments,* EBib (Paris: Gabalda, 1981); H. K. Bond, *Pontius Pilate in History and Interpretation* (Cambridge, 1998); C. A. Evans, "Excavating Caiaphas, Pilate and Simon of Cyrene," in *Jesus and Archaeology,* ed. J. Charlesworth (Grand Rapids: Eerdmans, 2006), pp. 323-40, esp. 330-38.

21. R. Hachlili, *Jericho,* pp. 142-45; cf. also idem, "The Goliath Family in Jericho: Funerary Inscriptions from a First Century A.D. Jewish monumental Tomb," *BASOR* 235 (1979): 31-66, esp. 33-47.

22. Hachlili, *Jericho,* pp. 142-45, esp. 44; idem, *Jewish Funerary Customs,* pp. 183-85. See also Tacitus, *Ann.* 12.64; 13.1-21; 14.1-9; Josephus, *War* 2.249; *Ant.* 20.148, 151.

23. See Ch. Clermont-Ganneau, *Recueil d'archéologie orientale* 1 (1886): 107-8; *CIS* II, 156 (pl. XXII,156); M. Lidzbarski, *Handbuch der nordsemitischen Epigraphik* (Weimar, 1898), p. 117: "die syrisch-hebräische Bilinguis auf dem Sarkophage der Königin Sadda, die

sive Mesopotamian and Jewish) inscription on the sarcophagus: ṢDN MLKT'/ ṢDH MLKTH (*CIJ*, no. 1388). This identification was rejected by S. Klein[24] and doubted by others. Actually one must distinguish the general problem of the identification of the Tomb of Helena of Adiabene, a landmark monument with three pyramids[25] north of the walls of Jerusalem, mentioned several times in by Josephus (*War* 5.55, 119, 147; *Ant.* 20.95), and the identification of the person buried in the sarcophagus with the double inscription. Although there is a small problem with the mention by Josephus of the distance of "three furlongs" (*stadia: Ant.* 20.95) from the city of Jerusalem, most archaeologists place these pyramids at the truly monumental "Tomb of the Kings" dug by F. de Saulcy.[26] The identification with the person buried in the inscribed sarcophagus is a different problem. The cursive Mesopotamian and Jewish Aramaic inscription fits well a queen (MLKT'/H) of Adiabene, but her name is "Saddan" or "Saddah" (or eventually "Sara/Saran")[27] and not "Helena." Thus there are two possibilities: either this sarcophagus refers to another queen of Adiabene, named Saddah/Saddan but not mentioned by Josephus (cf. already Renan),[28] or Saddah/Saddan is another name, eventually the Semitic name of Queen Helena. This last interpretation has been favored by many famous commentators (Ch. Clermont-Ganneau, M. Lidzbarski, R. Dussaud, L. H. Vincent)[29] but is not certain as long as we have no other clear indication of this double name.[30] As indicated by *CIS II*, p. 180: "Rem tamen in dubio linquimus."

---

mit Recht mit der Königin Helena von Adiabene identifiziert wird"; R. Dussaud, *Musée du Louvre, Département des Antiquités Orientales. Les Monuments palestiniens et judaïques* (Paris, 1912), pp. 43-44.

24. *Jüdisch-Palästinisches Corpus Inscriptionum* (Vienna: Löwit, 1920), p. 26.

25. These three pyramids could be represented on a decorated ossuary: cf. S. Fine, "Another View of Jerusalem's Necropolis during the First Century: A Decorated Ossuary from the Nelson and Helen Glueck Collection of the Cincinnati Art Museum," *JJS* 54 (2003): 233-41.

26. See lately Hachlili, *Jewish Funerary Customs*, pp. 36-37; A. Kloner and B. Zissu, *The Necropolis of Jerusalem in the Second Temple Period*, Interdisciplinary Studies in Ancient Culture and Religion 8 (Leuven: Peeters, 2007), pp. 231-34.

27. See W. F. Albright, *JBL* 56 (1937): 159 n. 41.

28. *Journal Asiatique* 2 (1865): 550; *CRAI* (1866): 113-17 and 133 n. 1.

29. L.-H. Vincent and A.-M. Steve, *Jérusalem de l'Ancien Testament*, 3 vols. in 2 (Paris: Gabalda, 1954-1956), 1:355; see more recently M. H. Williams, "The Use of Alternative Names by Diaspora Jews in Graeco-Roman Antiquity," *JSJ* 38 (2007): 307-27, esp. 322.

30. This is emphasized by J. Pirenne, "Aux origines de la graphie syriaque," *Syria* 40 (1963): 101-37, esp. 102-9, although her provisory dating in the third century CE (p. 106) is not compelling.

5. An unprovenanced ossuary bears the Aramaic inscriptions:[31]

YHWḤNH
YHWḤNH BRT YHWḤNN
BR TPLWS HKHN HGDL

"Yehohanah
Yehohanah daughter of Yehohanan
Son of Theophilus, the high priest."

As explained in the editio princeps, "The inscription does not explicitly state who was the high priest, Yehoḥanan or Theophilus. This question, however, may be settled without difficulty. Josephus records that Theophilus was appointed high priest by Vitellius during the three days before he received the news of the death of Tiberius (*Ant.* XVIII, 123-124). One may also add that none of the high priests named Yehoḥanan had a father called Theophilus. This is apparently the first known mention of a high priest in an ossuary inscription. It is noteworthy that although the inscription is in Aramaic, the title HKHN HGDL appears in Hebrew."[32]

6. Another high priest is apparently mentioned in an ink inscription on a jar from Masada with the reading: Ḥ[NNY]H KHN' RB' 'QBY' BRYH, "A[nani]as the high priest, 'Aqabia his son."[33] As stated by the editio princeps, "the partly reconstructed reading Ḥ[NNY]H KHN' RB' 'QBY' BRYH is almost certain. Presumably, before 'the High Priest,' a person who bore this title and served in that office should be mentioned. The most suitable identification of this high priest is Ananias son of Nedebaus, who is mentioned several times by Josephus."[34] As one can see, here some uncertainty comes from the reading that is partly reconstructed, even though it is "almost certain." Furthermore, the proposed explanation of the presence of the son besides the name of his father remains tentative (p. 38). Thus it is permitted here to somewhat hesitate.

7. Without any official title, it is very rare to be able to identify some-

---

31. D. Barag and D. Flusser, "The Ossuary of Yehohanah Granddaughter of the High Priest Theophilus," *IEJ* 36 (1986): 39-44; Rahmani, *Catalogue,* no. 871; C. A. Evans, *Jesus and the Ossuaries* (Waco: Baylor University Press, 2003), pp. 108-9.

32. Barag and Flusser, *IEJ* 36 (1986): 40-41.

33. Ibid., 41 n. 8; Y. Yadin and J. Naveh, *Masada I* (Jerusalem, 1989), pp. 37-38, no. 461.

34. Yadin and Naveh, *Masada I*, p. 37.

body with some certainty. The best case, and maybe the only one so far, could be the famous Greek inscription mentioning "Nicanor of Alexandria who made the doors"[35] on an ossuary discovered in 1902 on the Mount of Olives and now in the British Museum.[36] However, this identification has been doubted by several commentators,[37] and it is useful to check the arguments.

The name *Neicanor* and the ethnic *Alexandreus* are clear and classical but the reference to the making of the doors is more original and curious. With Clermont-Ganneau, but against J. B. Frey, it would be strange to understand the doors as referring to the "doors of the tomb," first because there is generally only one "door," and second because anyone making a tomb had to make a door. The general mention without any precision probably means that these doors were famous and known to every inhabitant of Jerusalem. This would be the case with the doors of the temple. Actually the Mishnah (*Yoma* 3:10) says: "Nicanor: miracles have befallen his doors (DLTWTYW) and his memory is kept in honour" (cf. also *Sheqal.* 6:3: "to the east was the gate (SH'R) of Nicanor"; *Sotah* 1:5: "the Eastern Gate which is over against the entrance of the Nicanor Gate"; *Mid.* 1:4: "There were seven gates to the Temple Court. . . . That to the east was the Nicanor Gate" (cf. also 2:6); 2:3 "All the gates that were there had been overlaid with gold, save only the doors of the Nicanor Gate, for with them a miracle had happened, and some say, because their bronze shone like gold"; *Neg.* 14:8: "and the leper . . . stood at the Nicanor Gate"; *t. Yoma (Kippurim)* 2:4: "What is the miracle that has happened to them: they said that Nicanor had them brought from Alexandria and there was a tempest in the sea: they took one of them and threw it

---

35. I shall not discuss here the problem of the interpretation of the first or of the first two words of the inscription understood as "The bones of the [sons] of" (eventually named NQNR and 'LKS'); cf. M. Lidzbarski, *Ephemeris für semitische Epigraphik* (Giessen, 1908), 2:198; or, less likely, "the bone receptacle of" (cf. E. M. Meyers, *Jewish Ossuaries: Reburial and Rebirth,* BibOr 24 [Rome: Biblical Institute Press, 1971], p. 52).

36. See mainly Ch. Clermont-Ganneau, "La 'Porte de Nicanor' du Temple de Jérusalem," *Recueil d'archéologie orientale* 5 (1903): 334-40; Lidzbarski, *Ephemeris für semitische Epigraphik,* 2:197-98; *CIJ* no. 1256; R. Dussaud, *Syria* 6 (1925): 99-100; N. Avigad, "Jewish Rock-Cut Tombs in Jerusalem and in the Judaean Hill-Country," in *E. L. Sukenik Memorial Volume, ErIsr* 8 (1967): 119-25; J.-P. Kane, "The Ossuary Inscriptions of Jerusalem," *JSS* 23 (1971): 268-82, esp. 279-82; Evans, *Jesus and the Ossuaries,* pp. 91-92. See also Y. Shapiro, "The Nicanor Tomb Cave on Mount Scopus: A Precedent for Mount Herzl," in *Teddy Kollek Volume,* ed. J. Aviram et al., *ErIsr* 28 (2007): 23*-24* and 454-62 [in Hebrew].

37. P. Roussel, "Nicanor d'Alexandrie et la porte du temple de Jérusalem," *Revue des études grecques* 37 (1924): 79-82; apparently *CIJ* no. 1256: "De quelles portes d'agit-il? Sans doute de celles du sépulchre"; Schwartz, "Once More on the Nicanor Gate."

into the sea. They wished to throw the second one, but he [Nicanor] did not allow them. He said: if you cast that one into the sea, then throw me along with it. He was more and more depressed until they reached the port of Joppa and it (the gate) was brought upon dry land."[38]

From all these passages it seems clear that there was a Nicanor Gate in the temple, that this gate was located in the east, that its doors were made of bronze, and that they were brought by an Alexandrian named Nicanor. This Nicanor was apparently a rich man, and the quality of the tomb would fit very well this social position.[39] This personage is not mentioned in Josephus, although Josephus gives a description of the temple gates in *War* 5.201-6: "Of the gates nine were completely overlaid with gold and silver, as were their door-posts and lintels; but one, that outside the sanctuary, was of Corinthian bronze, and far exceeded in value those plated with silver and set in gold. . . . The dimensions of the other gates were all alike, but the one beyond the Corinthian gate, opening from the Women's Court on the east, opposite the gate of the sanctuary, was far larger, having an altitude of fifty cubits, with doors of forty, and richer decoration, being overlaid with massive plates of silver and gold. The nine gates were thus plated by Alexander the father of Tiberius."[40] From the comparison of all these texts,[41] it seems clear that the "Corinthian gate" of Josephus is the "Nicanor Gate" of the Talmud,[42] and that Nicanor is the name of the Alexandrian Jew who gave the doors. In this

38. See also *y. Yoma* 3, 41a; *b. Yoma* 38a.

39. See Avigad, "Jewish Rock-Cut Tombs," pp. 119-42 and 72*; Hachlili, *Jewish Funerary Customs,* pp. 42-43; Kloner and Zissu, *Necropolis of Jerusalem,* pp. 179-81.

40. This Alexander was the alabarch of Alexandria and brother of the philosopher Philo (Josephus, *Ant.* 18.259). His son Tiberius renounced Judaism to take service under the Romans as procurator of Judaea (ca. 46?-48), as prefect of Egypt (*War* 2.309), and as chief of the general staff of Titus at the siege of Jerusalem (*War* 6.237). Josephus very probably met him personally and knew him well. About Tiberius, cf., e.g., K. G. Evans, "Alexander the Alabarch: Roman and Jew," *Society of Biblical Literature 1995 Seminar Papers,* SBLSP 34 (Atlanta: Scholars Press, 1995), pp. 576-94; M. Hadas-Lebel, *Philon d'Alexandrie: Un penseur en diaspora* (Paris, 2003), pp. 53-55, 80-82, 168, 283, 356.

41. See also *War* 6.293-94: "the eastern gate of the inner court and it was of brass and very massive, and, when closed towards evening, could scarcely be moved by twenty men; fastened with iron-bound bars, it had bolts which were sunk to a great depth into a threshold consisting of solid block of stone and this gate was observed at the sixth hour of the night to have opened of its own accord. The watchmen of the temple ran and reported the matter to the captain, and he came up and with difficulty succeeded in shutting it."

42. It is also probably called the "Beautiful Gate" in Acts 3:2, 10.

case, with Ch. Clermont-Ganneau, one can conclude: "Je ne crois pas me tromper en concluant que le Nicanor de notre inscriptions n'est autre que ce personage historique: il s'appelle *Nicanor,* il est d'*Alexandrie* et il est dit *avoir fait les portes* (*tas thuras* = DLTWT) — aucun Juif de l'époque, en presence de ce texte ainsi libellé, ne pouvait se méprendre sur sa signification et méconnaître le donateur dont le nom était sur toutes les lèvres."[43]

Now, the arguments of those who deny this identification are based on an *argumentum e silentio:* Josephus does not use the phrase "Nicanor's gate."[44] For them, "the doors" of the inscription refer to the tomb itself[45] and "the sources are often contradictory."[46] Furthermore, J. Schwartz[47] quotes commentators from the Middle Ages, R. Asher b. Yehiel (1250-1327) and R. Shelomo Sirillo (died ca. 1558), to argue that Nicanor refers "to the Greek general and not to the later donor of the same name."[48] This does not seem a serious historical argument. Furthermore, it would be open to the same objection that he raised against the majority's interpretation; this would not explain why Josephus does not use the name "Nicanor's gate," and this interpretation would be anachronistic for a gate of the temple built by Herod.

These objections do not hold in front of the convergent and coherent mishnaic and talmudic tradition about Nicanor's gate. After Clermont-Ganneau, R. Dussaud, N. Avigad, and many others,[49] in my view the identification of the Nicanor of the ossuary with the donor of the temple Corinthian gate is practically certain.

43. Ch. Clermont-Ganneau, "La 'Porte de Nicanor' du Temple de Jérusalem," *Recueil d'archéologie orientale* 5 (1903): 339; cf. also lately C. A. Rollston, "Inscribed Ossuaries: Perrsonal Names, Statistics, and Laboratory Test," *NEA* 69 (2006): 125-29, esp. 126.

44. See Schwartz, "Once More on the Nicanor Gate," 252-53, 256.

45. Ibid., 248-49, 280 (with some nuance: "perhaps"!).

46. Ibid., 246.

47. Ibid., 263ff.

48. Ibid., 265.

49. See also A. R. Millard, *Reading and Writing in the Time of Jesus,* Biblical Seminar 69 (Sheffield: Sheffield Academic Press, 2000), p. 114: "In one case a reason for fame is noted: 'Bones of the sons of Nicanor the Alexandrian who made the doors' in Greek, the names Nicanor and Alexas being written also in Hebrew script. The reference is almost certainly to the magnificent doors embellished with Corinthian bronze which the Mishnah reports Nicanor of Alexandria presented to the Temple"; Evans, *Jesus and the Ossuaries,* p. 92.

Possible Identifications as a Probability Problem

If there is no unique indication connecting the name with a function or activity of the deceased, the identification can only be proposed as a probability problem. The same is true, for instance, for the inscribed ossuary of "Jacob/James son of Joseph, brother of Jesus." Since I have already extensively explained with nuances my argument about this identification,[50] I shall prefer here dealing with two other cases that have also been much discussed: the "Caiaphas" and the "Mary (Magdalene)" ossuaries.

The "Caiaphas" ossuary was found in a tomb of North Talpiot in 1990 and published by Z. Greenhut.[51] The argument in favor of the identification was well explained by R. Reich.[52] The problem of identification concerns two inscribed ossuaries in Jewish cursive script: ossuary 3, inscribed QP'; and ossuary 6, inscribed YHWSP BR QP' on the narrow side and YHWSP BR QYP' on the long rear side. "**Qaifa or Qofa** is an Aramaic name here encountered for the first time on an inscription."[53] According to Reich, the Aramaic name or rather nickname Qaifa/Qofa is the equivalent of the Greek name *Kaiaphas* mentioned in the New Testament (Matt 26:3, 57; Luke 3:2;

50. A. Lemaire, "Burial Box of James the Brother of Jesus," *BAR* 28/6 (2002): 24-33, 70; idem, "L'ossuaire de 'Jacques fils de Joseph, le frère de Jésus': Une brève réponse," *Polish Journal of Biblical Research* 2/1 (2003): 138-64; idem, "Critical Evaluation of the IAA Committee Reports Regarding the Ossuary Inscription," *Polish Journal of Biblical Research* 2/2 (2003): 29-60; idem, "Israel Antiquities Authority's Report on the James Ossuary Deeply Flawed," *BAR* 29/6 (2003): 50-59, 67, 70; idem, "The 'James Ossuary on Trial': A Short Rejoinder," *Bulletin of the Anglo-Israel Archeological Society* 22 (2004): 35-36; idem, "Trois inscriptions araméennes sur ossuaire et leur intérêt," *CRAI* (2003): 301-17. See also, e.g., Evans, *Jesus and the Ossuaries,* pp. 112-18; idem, "A Fishing Boat, a House, and an Ossuary: What Can We Learn from the Artifacts?" in *The Missions of James, Peter, and Paul,* ed. B. Chilton and C. Evans, NovTSup 115 (Leiden: Brill, 2005), pp. 223-31. After six years of inquiries and the so-called forgery trial still going on, no serious argument has been raised against the authenticity of this inscription (see also H. Shanks, "Help Me! I'm Desperate," *BAR* 34/4 [2008]: 6-8).

51. Z. Greenhut, "Burial Cave of the Caiaphas Family," *BAR* 18/5 (1992): 40-42; idem, "The 'Caiaphas' Tomb in North Talpiyot, Jerusalem," *'Atiqot* 21 (1992): 63-71; idem, "The Caiaphas Tomb in North Talpiyot," in *Ancient Jerusalem Revealed,* ed. H. Geva (Jerusalem; Israel Exploration Society, 1994), pp. 219-22.

52. R. Reich, "'Caiaphas Name Inscribed on Bone Boxes," *BAR* 18/5 (1992): 38-44, 76; idem, "Ossuary Inscriptions of the Caiaphas Family from Jerusalem," in *Ancient Jerusalem Revealed,* ed. Geva, pp. 223-25.

53. Reich, "Ossuary Inscriptions," p. 224.

John 11:49; 18:13-14, 24, 28; Acts 4:6) and Josephus (*Ant.* 18.35, 95: "Joseph who was called Caiaphas"), as well as of the Hebrew name HQWP/HQYYP in *m. Parah* 3:5. He also proposed that it is the equivalent of QNTRS, "Qantheras," but this problem is different and we can leave it aside here.[54] The main argument in favor of this identification is the rarity of the name Qaif/Qofa/Caiaphas/Haqqof/Haqayyaf. However, it is apparently attested as a nickname for an Amora (*y. Ma'aserot* 5:7, 52a) and can be compared to Nabatean QYPW.[55] Actually this identification has been put in doubt by W. Horbury,[56] E. Puech,[57] and C. A. Evans.[58] There are several problems:

1. Nothing indicates that the deceased were high priests or even priests. The inscriptions, even those of the other deceased in the tomb, are completely silent about this function; and the quality of the tomb — especially its outside appearance — and of the cursive inscriptions do not indicate a prestigious family.

2. The reading of the first letters of the name YHWSP is not completely clear.

3. The reading of ossuary 5 indicates that Yehoseph would be the son of Caiaphas and so could not be identified with Josephus's "Joseph who was called Caiaphas." There is a difference between a nickname and a patronym.

4. The reading QP' on ossuary 2 supposes that the Y in QYP' is a *mater lectionis* and not the indication of a diphthong.

54. See R. Brody, "Caiaphas and Cantheras," in D. R. Schwartz, *Agrippa I: The Last King of Judaea,* TSAJ 23 (Tübingen: Mohr Siebeck, 1990), appendix 4, pp. 190-95; B.-Z. Rosenfeld, "The Settlement of Two Families of High Priests During the Second Temple Period" [in Hebrew], in *Historical-Geographical Studies in the Settlement of Eretz-Israel II,* ed. Y. Katz et al. (Jerusalem, 1991), pp. 206-18.

55. See A. Negev, *Personal Names in the Nabatean Realm,* Qedem 32 (Jerusalem: Hebrew University, 1991), p. 58, no. 1030.

56. W. Horbury, "The 'Caiaphas' Ossuaries and Joseph Caiaphas," *PEQ* 126 (1994): 32-48.

57. E. Puech, "A-t-on redécouvert le tombeau du grand-prêtre Caïphe," *Le Monde de la Bible* 80 (1993): 42-47; idem, *La croyance des Esséniens en la vie future: Immortalité, résurrection, vie éternelle,* EBib n.s. 21 (Paris: Gabalda, 1993), pp. 193-95 (however, the argument that Sadducees did not use ossuaries is not convincing: cf. already Horbury, "Caiaphas," p. 46).

58. Evans, *Jesus and the Ossuaries,* pp. 104-8; idem, "Excavating Caiaphas, Pilate, and Simon of Cyrene: Assessing the Literary and Archaeological Evidence," in *Jesus and Archaeology,* pp. 323-29.

Finally, one may conclude with W. Horbury: "*q(y/w)p'* in the ossuary inscriptions cannot be said to correspond directly to the name Caiaphas, and Inscriptions 5 and 6 do not, therefore, clearly attest the Joseph surnamed Caiaphas of Josephus and the New Testament."[59] Although one may hesitate to reject completely the possibility of identification, it does not seem likely in the present state of our knowledge.[60]

The identification of one of the inscribed ossuaries from the Talpiot tomb[61] as belonging to "Mary (Magdalene)" has been proposed lately because the name *Mariamnē* would correspond to the name of "Mary Magdalene" in the *Acta Philippi,* a fourth-century New Testament pseudapocryphon.[62] The historical value of such a late pseudapocryphon seems a priori very dubious, as does the precise meaning of such a variant name; but, from the viewpoint of an epigrapher, the main problem is the reading of the name on the ossuary. As clearly shown by S. J. Pfann,[63] the reading *Mariamnē* on Rahmani ossuary 701 should be corrected. One may only hesitate between two interpretations: *Mariamē kai Mara* or *Mariam ē kai Mara.* The first interpretation would indicate that the ossuary contained the bones of two persons, "Mary and Mara," while the second interpretation would mention only one woman with her nickname: "Mary who is also (called) Mara." Both interpretations are philologically possible. However, in my view, because of the frequent use of *(h)o/(h)ē kai* to indicate a nickname,[64] and the good parallel of the inscription *Kyria ē kai Kyrilē* on an ossuary from Akeldama (burial cave 2),[65] the second interpretation seems somewhat more likely, *Mara* being probably an abbreviation/nickname of *Mariam.* If this is

---

59. Horbury, "Caiaphas," p. 46.

60. J. C. VanderKam, *From Joshua to Caiaphas: High Priests after the Exile* (Minneapolis: Fortress, 2004), p. 436, seems a little more positive ("a decent chance").

61. See A. Kloner, "A Tomb with Inscribed Ossuaries in East Talpiot, Jerusalem," *'Atiqot* 29 (1996): 15-22, esp. 17.

62. About this pseudapocryphon see F. Bovon et al., *Acta Philippi, Textus,* Corpus Christianorum, Series Apocryphorum (Turnhout: Brepols, 1999), pp. 240-41, 312-17.

63. "Mary Magdalene Has Left the Room: A Suggested New Reading of Ossuary *CJO* 701," *NEA* 69 (2006): 130-31.

64. See G. H. R. Horsley, "Names, Double," *ABD* 4:1011-17, esp. 1012; M. H. Williams, "The Use of Alternative Names by Diaspora Jews in Greco-Roman Antiquity," *JSJ* 38 (2007): 307-27, esp. 308 n. 6.

65. See T. Ilan, "The Ossuary and Sarcophagus Inscriptions," in *The Akeldama Tombs: Three Burial Caves in the Kidron Valley, Jerusalem,* ed. G. Avni and Z. Greenhut, IAA Reports 1 (Jerusalem, 1996), pp. 57-72, esp. 57.

the case, not only would the identification of the owner of the ossuary with "Mary (Magdalene)" be a simple possibility because *Mariam*/Mary was a very common name, but actually this interpretation would be unlikely since this *Mariam*/Mary would have already a nickname, different from the nickname "Magdalene."

Furthermore it is very unlikely that the ossuary of "James son of Joseph, brother of Jesus" came from the Talpiot tomb since the missing tenth ossuary was registered as broken and "plain" (i.e., without any inscription!), and a picture of the owner's room appears to reveal that the James ossuary was already in his possession in the 1970s. In these conditions, one may be very skeptical about the hypothesis that the Talpiot tomb would be Jesus' family tomb.

These limited remarks about possible identifications are just one aspect of the research on inscriptions of this period, especially ossuary inscriptions. Actually these small documents can teach us much more about the culture and history of the Jewish people at this time, but this would be the subject of another study.

Demythologizing the Talpiot Tomb:
The Tomb of Another Jesus, Mary, and Joseph

Stephen Pfann

The first time they have been lying side by side in 2000 years.

Simcha Jacobovici

The film *The Lost Face of Jesus* superimposes the faces of the actors playing Mary Magdalene, Jesus, and Mary over ossuaries belonging to another family — not that of Jesus of Nazareth but, perhaps, of a Jesus of Talpiot. As we watch the film, we witness a form of identity theft, an identification to which the original family of this tomb would almost certainly and strongly object if they could speak up today.

But what about this original family? What story would they tell? This story lies silently in the tomb, its bones and its ossuaries. I would like to explore here the tantalizing story that only the Talpiot tomb itself can tell.

Contrary to Simcha Jacobovici's assumption, the names found in the ossuaries are not rare. In fact, they are among the most common names known from first-century inscriptional evidence. Below I present basic data from the current corpus of inscriptions that allows us to frame the discovery in the Talpiot tomb within its proper epigraphical context.

In order to create a statistical probability with which to assess the Talpiot tomb names, one must first create a working database. This can be done by making a general census of inscribed ossuaries based primarily upon the *Catalogue of Jewish Ossuaries.* Such a survey of the entire corpus of inscribed ossuaries brings to light the proportions of names and the ethnic character of those in first-century CE Judea able to afford burial in ossuaries and tombs. Remarkably, only 72 different Jewish names are represented among the 286 personal names found on the 233 inscribed ossuaries. There are more names than ossuaries because some ossuaries contain two or three names using the formula "X son of Y." These 72 personal names include their shortened forms and their Greek or Latin equivalents.

What are the implications for establishing a statistical probability of occurrence? The names in the Talpiot tomb were apparently not just "common" but "extremely common."[1]

Part 1: The Typology of the Ossuaries from the Talpiot Tomb

Ossuary Subgroups

Ten ossuaries were found in the Talpiot tomb, nine of which were catalogued in the Israel Antiquities Authority archives (IAA 80.500–80.508). They were first published by L. Y. Rahmani in the *Catalogue of Jewish Ossuaries in the Collection of the State of Israel* (*CJO* 701-709, respectively).[2] The standard for inclusion in the catalogue was based upon the presence of distinctive features such as decoration or inscriptions. The tenth ossuary, described by the excavator as found in a broken state and neither decorated nor inscribed, was not catalogued.

Of the nine that were catalogued and could be accessed for this study, all were made of the local Jerusalem soft limestone (chalk), were slightly to moderately tapered, and were furnished with four low feet. Table 1 summarizes this information, while specifying a few distinguishing features that could also be ascertained among the ossuaries.

---

1. In fact, statistically speaking, one in every ten tombs from the first century should have a "Jesus son of Joseph," including those whose names were not inscribed. This was confirmed independently by Prof. Feuerverger in a private conversation during the course of the conference. For a statistical breakdown of personal names see Appendix C at www.uhl.ac/en/resources/uhl-articles/demythologyzing-talpiot-tomb.

2. Subsequently, the tomb and its ossuaries were officially published by Amos Kloner in the journal of the Israel Antiquities Authority: A. Kloner, "A Tomb with Inscribed Ossuaries in East Talpiyot, Jerusalem," *'Atiqot* 29 (1996): 15-22. The description of the ossuaries and their inscriptions largely followed that found in Rahmani, *Catalogue*, pp. 222-24, pl. 101.

Table 1: Stylistic features of the Talpiot tomb ossuaries

Ossuary	Cat. No.	IAA No.	Limestone	Low Feet	Decorated	Inscribed
1	701	80.500	semi-hard	X	X	X
2	702	80.501	soft	X	X	X
3	703	80.502	soft	X	—	X
4	704	80.503	soft	X	—	X
5	705	80.504	semi-hard	X	—	X
6	706	80.505	soft	X	—	X
7	707	80.506	soft	X	X	—
8	708	80.507	soft	X	X	—
9	709	80.508	soft	X	X	—
10	—	—	—	—	—	—

Six of the ossuaries were inscribed (*CJO* 701-706) and two ossuaries were both inscribed and decorated (*CJO* 701, 702). Only ossuary #10 was neither inscribed nor decorated.

Decorated Ossuaries

Five of the ten ossuaries were decorated (*CJO* 701, 702, 707-709). *CJO* 701 was polished, surface-sealed, and chip-carved, while *CJO* 702, 707, 708, and 709 have a semi-smooth finish and are chip-carved.

Undecorated Ossuaries

Five of the ten ossuaries were not decorated (*CJO* 703, 704, 705, 706, and the tenth, uncatalogued ossuary). *CJO* 703, 705, and 706 featured rough-adze or chisel-finished surfaces. *CJO* 704, on the other hand, has a smooth finish.

Ossuaries Grouped by Form

Polished, surface-sealed, chip-carved, decorated ossuary with gabled lid: CJO 701

Based on Rahmani's reading of the name on this ossuary, the filmmakers contend that it once contained the bones of none other than Mary Magdalene, inscribed here as "(Little) Mary, the Master." Subsequent study has

Plate 1. Photo of *CJO* 701

shown, however, that the inscription on the side of ossuary *CJO* 701 was mis-read in the original publication, a fact that has been supported independently by numerous scholars.[3] In fact, the inscription preserves names of not one but two individuals: Mariame and Mara, written in two distinct scribal hands, as I demonstrate below.

The filmmakers further assert that, because the mitochondrial DNA found in the ossuary was from a single individual and did not match that taken from ossuary *CJO* 704 (the "Jesus[?] son of Joseph" ossuary), the two individuals must have been married. However, mitochondrial DNA, as opposed to nuclear DNA, can only distinguish children of one mother from those of another. If two sisters were interred in *CJO* 701, their mitochondrial DNA would be indistinguishable. Thus the mitochondrial DNA evidence alone is not able to affirm or deny the number of individuals interred in *CJO* 701, if they are siblings born of the same mother. Furthermore, tombs frequently contained members of extended patriarchal (and not matriarchal) families and occasionally even included the remains of dear friends or guests from outside the clan.[4] Thus mitochondrial DNA should not be expected to be the unifying factor of a single tomb.

3. Some of the most experienced epigraphers in the world, including the editors of *Supplementum Epigraphicum Graecum (SEG)* 46 (1996), J. J. E. Hondius, A. Salac, M. N. Todd, and E. Ziebarth, as well as Phillippe Gauthier of *Bulletin épigraphique* (BÉ) 14 (1998) in *Revue des études grecques,* in addition to epigraphers Tal Ilan, Emile Puech, and Jonathan Price, all agree that the inscription as published by Rahmani represents a misreading.

4. As is the case depicted in the Gospels when Jesus is interred in the tomb of Joseph of Arimathea.

The relatively large size of ossuary *CJO* 701 indicates that it was not manufactured in order to hold the bones of only one person but was intended to contain two or more individuals.[5] The contrast is apparent when a comparison is made with the other personalized ossuaries, all of which name only a single individual and are significantly smaller than *CJO* 701. Only *CJO* 707 is larger. It too would likely have held the remains of several individuals.[6] The number of individuals, their names, and the sizes of the ossuaries are summarized in table 2.

Table 2: Measurements of the Talpiot tomb ossuaries

Ossuary Number	Number of Named Individuals	Measurements in centimeters	Volume in liters
CJO 701 "Mariame and Mara"	2	68.5 × 26 × 32.5	57.9
CJO 702 "Yehudah"	1	55 × 23 × 27	34.2
CJO 703 "Matiah"	1	55 × 28 × 34	52.4
CJO 704 "Yeshua(?)"	1	65 × 26 × 30	50.7
CJO 705 "Yoseh"	1	54.5 × 26 × 34.5	48.9

5. It is possible that *CJO* 701 was designed to contain the bones of one very large person, but then, it would likely not have been a woman (in particular, not a diminutive "Little Mary," as the earlier reading of the inscription might suggest).

6. At Jericho, multiple burials in ossuaries were the exception rather than the rule, especially in the case of the 32 ossuaries inscribed with personal names. Twenty-four (75%) contained one individual each. The remaining eight ossuaries (25%), which contained multiple burials, primarily included single adults with children (5 ossuaries), children (2 ossuaries), or a woman and a man (1 ossuary; likely a married couple); see Hachlili, *Jericho,* pp. 93-111. This apparently gives evidence for actual practice of the mishnaic ruling that prohibits two individuals who were forbidden to sleep together in the same bed from being entombed together on the same bench (or in this case, in the same box). The inscriptions on the ossuaries (sixteen inscriptions in all) tended to conform, by both age and gender, with the contents of each ossuary, item for item, with the exception of ossuary 19, where the bones of a woman and one child were found while the inscription notes a mother and her two sons; Hachlili, *Jericho,* p. 108. Ossuary 13 was inscribed with two names, MANHMOS and SIMWN; the first name, however, may actually be a patronym.

In Jerusalem, at the Akeldama tombs, single adults (and notable pairs or couples) were often buried with children and infants. There are, however, a number of examples bearing Greek inscriptions where only a single name, presumably of the father or the mother, was inscribed; cf. G. Avni and Z. Greenhut, *The Akeldama Tombs: Three Burial Caves in the Kidron Valley, Jerusalem,* IAA Reports 1 (Jerusalem: Israel Antiquities Authority, 1996), pp. 51-53, table 2.1a.

CJO 706 "Mariah"	1	52 × 27 × 33	46.3
CJO 707	uninscribed	67 × 31.5 × 38.5	81.3
CJO 708	uninscribed	51 × 27 × 31.5	43.4
CJO 709	uninscribed	61 × 26.5 × 31.5	50.9

Thus the large size of *CJO 701* and the number of named individuals strongly indicate that the ossuary was not designed to contain the bones of only one individual.[7]

Semi-smooth finished, chip-carved, decorated ossuaries: CJO 702, 707, 708, and 709

This form has a façade bearing two chip-carved metopes, each composed of a simple carved border framing two large rosettes. It is among the most common forms of decorated ossuaries.[8] Each of these four ossuaries has smoothed sides and surfaces that were neither polished nor sealed. Although simple in form, the craftsmanship indicates that special care was taken in cutting the decoration. In all four cases, each of the rosettes stands erect (except for a slight clockwise turn on the right rosette of ossuary *CJO 709*).

Many uninscribed ossuaries were similar in style to one of the inscribed personalized ossuaries (*CJO 702*, Judah bar Jesus), which has a paleographic date of the first century CE; on this basis we can conclude that most of the uninscribed ossuaries were also from the first century CE. These were nicely cut and ornamented with relatively large rosettes but of a medium-quality limestone that tended to break after the sealed surface eroded.[9] The personalized *CJO 702*, the Judah bar Jesus ossuary, was the smallest ossuary in the tomb, which again might indicate that the deceased may have been a youth. However, in this case, the decorative motifs would indicate that the family by then was better off, providing the youth with a more ornately decorated ossuary.

The inscription itself was carefully carved to emulate the appearance of a formal handwritten script, using both the serifs and shading that are typical of handwritten ink inscriptions by a highly skilled formal scribal hand. The first name, Yehudah, was inscribed in larger rectilinear letters

7. Nor does the mitochondrial DNA analysis prevent this from being the case.

8. This form is called "Type I" by Rachel Hachlili, *Jewish Funerary Customs, Practices and Rites in the Second Temple Period*, JSJSup 94 (Leiden: Brill, 2005), e.g., p. 97.

9. For a statistical breakdown of personal names, see Appendix C at www.uhl.ac/resources/uhl-articles/demythologyzing-talpiot-tomb.

Plate 2. Photo of *CJO* 702, 707, 708, 709 (top, left to right; bottom, left to right)

with comfortable spacing between the letters. The lettering in the remainder of the inscription was relatively smaller and more cramped, evidently due to a misjudgment of the scribe, who did not leave enough room to finish the inscription with the same generosity of letter size and spacing. In fact, various letters have been slightly, even substantially, rotated (cf. especially the final letter *ayin*, next to the left border) to provide room to squeeze in the entire patronym.

> *Roughly dressed, chisel- or adze-finished, undecorated ossuaries:* CJO
> *703, 705, and 706*

A number of distinctive features indicate that *CJO* 703, 705, and 706 should be viewed as a special subgroup within the tomb. The surfaces of these three ossuaries were roughly dressed with an adze or chisel. Dissimilarities in the scoring patterns left by the hack marks indicate that a different blade was used for carving each ossuary. This relatively common type of ossuary surface (found on about ¼ to ⅓ of all ossuaries) seems likely to be mimicking the shaved appearance of simple, otherwise undecorated, wooden coffin and wooden ossuary prototypes.[10]

10. Woodcarving tools were commonly utilized in the stone-carving industry in Jerusalem; cf. Hachlili, *Jewish Funerary Customs.*

Far more numerous among the necropolises of Jerusalem and Jericho is a class of ossuaries that uses this same type of surface treatment as the base for additional decoration, including pairs of rosettes set within frames that normally contain zigzag lines (in place of the common uniform beading on other ossuaries). This texturing, along with red ochre surface staining, again appears to convey the appearance of somewhat earlier wooden prototypes found at sites such as Jericho, 'En Gedi, and Qumran.[11]

In addition to their unornamented, chiseled surface texturing, *CJO* 703, 705, and 706 share the following features:

1. They were all in a similar broken state when found in situ.
2. They are nearly identical in size (cf. table 2, where the measurements are no more than 1.5 cm in any direction); *CJO* 703 "Matyah" (52.4 liters); *CJO* 705 "Yoseh" (48.9 liters); *CJO* 706 "Maryah" (46.3 liters)
3. On these ossuaries the standard low feet of contemporary ossuaries are separated from the body by an unusual horizontal line.
4. The openings were not grooved to secure a lid. The two lids that survived were of similar manufacture, with cushion-like, nonsquared profiles, and were carved to sit over the opening without a groove.

Furthermore, with respect to viewing these three ossuaries as a special group:

5. All three were inscribed with personal names.
6. Each inscription is an informal form of a personal name (i.e., a shortened form or a nickname) as opposed to the formal name (thus: Matiah vs. Mattityahu; Yoseh vs. Yehoseph; Maria vs. Mariam).[12]

11. For examples of wooden coffins from Jericho see Rachel Hachlili and Ann Killebrew, *Jericho: The Jewish Cemetery of the Second Temple Period,* IAA Reports 7 (Jerusalem, 1999), p. vii, color plates III 1 and III 2. For those from 'En Gedi, see N. Avigad, "Expedition A — Naḥal David," *IEJ* 12 (1962): 169-83, esp. pl. 22. Also see G. Hadas, *Nine Tombs of the Second Temple Period at 'En Gedi, 'Atiqot* 24 [in Hebrew] (1994): 1-75 (Eng. abstract, pp. 1*-8*); also see idem, "Wood Industry in the Second Temple Period as Reflected in the 'En Gedi Finds" [in Hebrew], *Michmanim* 16 (2002): 23-35 (Eng. abstract, pp. 40*-41*).

12. It was quite common in antiquity, as today, to use informal names in familiar settings among friends and family, especially in the case of children. In more formal, less familiar or professional settings, the formal name would be used (in this case Mariam, Mattityahu, and Yehoseph). Cf. ossuaries which have both name types: Mattiya/Mattai,

Plate 3. *CJO* 703, 705, and 706

7. The inscriptions are deeply inscribed with a similar tool in a relatively large lapidary script with hollow triangular serifs. This is a style that is typical of less than 5 percent of all inscribed ossuaries.
8. All the inscriptions have only a personal name without a patronym (i.e., "son/daughter of so and so" is lacking).

The Story of a Family Tragedy?

The traits enumerated above, held in common by these three ossuaries, appear to unite them as a group. The similar form, the decoration and the size of the ossuaries, along with the peculiar script style and the informal personal names of the inscriptions, make these a unique set among the known ossuaries of Jerusalem's necropolis. These stylistic features suggest that the three were the product of a single workshop and likely contained the remains of individuals who died at the same event or very close to the same time. Indeed, the use of the informal names of the deceased along with the relatively small size of these ossuaries might suggest that those interred were children or youths and were part of an immediate or extended family. Without the bones, it is impossible to determine the actual cause of their deaths. Whatever the case, these factors could well imply that a profound family tragedy had occurred, calling for the commissioning of the three ossuaries at one time.

CJO 42; Martha/Mara, *CJO* 468. Also, in literary texts, individuals can commonly be referred to by either form of their name, depending upon the context. For example, in the NT, Mary the mother of Jesus is called both Mariam (27x) and Maria (27x); Mary Magdalene is called Mariam (4x) and Maria (10x). Jesus' brother is called Joseph (1x) and Jose (1x). For more details see my blog "How Do You Solve a Problem like Maria?" (http://www.uhl.ac/en/resources/blog/how-do-you-solve-problem-maria/) and "Jose, Can You See?" (http://www.uhl.ac/en/resources/blog/yoseh-can-you-see-checking -sources-updated/). Cf. Hachlili, *Jewish Funerary Customs,* pp. 194, 205-33.

Plate 4. Inscribed names of *CJO* 703, 705, and 706

Undecorated Ossuaries

Two smooth-finished, undecorated ossuaries were recovered, *CJO* 704 (inscribed side shown below) and uncatalogued ossuary no. 10. The inner rim of the long sides of the opening of *CJO* 704 were grooved to secure a lid.

Part 2: Four Key Ossuaries for the Evaluation of the Talpiot Tomb

The following detailed sections are devoted to the four inscribed ossuaries that were featured in *The Lost Tomb of Jesus* and in subsequent documentaries and discussions about the tomb. Two ossuaries, *CJO* 704 and 701, were recovered from the tomb itself. The filmmakers also treated two other ossuaries as keys to the interpretation of the Talpiot tomb. They hypothesize the existence of a Jewish Christian necropolis in which Jesus' followers were normally buried in Jerusalem. In each case, the reading of the inscriptions on these ossuaries has been influential in the building of the film's dramatic conclusions. However, in each case the published reading of these inscriptions has proven to be erroneous. A revised reading of these ossuary inscriptions and their implications follows.

Ossuary CJO 704 "Jesus, Son of Joseph"?

Almost universally, epigraphers, including myself, have managed with some difficulty to make out the names "Yeshua (?) bar/ben Yehoseph" ("Jesus [?] son of Joseph") on *CJO* 704. The reading was first published by L. Y. Rahmani, aided by Joseph Naveh, in *Catalogue of Jewish Ossuaries*. At that time, Rahmani transcribed it with a question mark (?) after the name "Yeshua." Two years later Amos Kloner, who had excavated the ossuary, followed the reading in his excavation report.

  The first word, "Yeshua (?)," is embedded among numerous scratches on the surface of the ossuary. The name was not inscribed carefully. Both extra and missing features must be explained. This is not to say that the name "Yeshua" cannot be imagined among the initial lines of the inscription. I first saw the ossuary at an initial viewing in the warehouse in Beth Shemesh, when the producer suggested the name might be present on the ossuary. While looking at the ossuary itself, illuminated with the play of light from a small flashlight, I too could discern the name. However, upon subsequent examination of the excellent pictures taken by veteran photographer Ze'ev Radovan, a much more complex inscriptional picture began to emerge among the scratches, based upon line width and depth, and patina variations.

A close study of Radovan's pictures indicates that two distinct instruments were utilized in inscribing this ossuary.[13] The main inscription is characterized by rather wide, shallow lines made by a dull, pointed object. This inscription appears to have been subsequently interrupted by secondary deep scratches that were made by a sharp, pointed object. Moreover, this side of the ossuary also contains numerous inadvertent scratches. The challenge for the epigrapher is to distinguish which scratches in the inscriptions are intentional and which are accidental.

The Various Instruments Used to Create the Scratches

The first instrument: A dull-tipped knife created troughs with a shallow U shape. The instrument was generally held horizontally, creating an appearance of artificial shading, with broad vertical lines (except in the letter *heh*) and thin horizontal lines. This tool was utilized to inscribe both the private name and the patronym of the first individual whose bones were interred in this ossuary. The private name was effaced and largely scraped away, presumably when the first bones were removed and then replaced with the bones of another individual.

The second instrument: A blade was utilized in an effort to scrape away or obfuscate the strokes of the original personal name. However, this was not done thoroughly, leaving vestiges of the original name still on the surface.

The third instrument: A sharp-tipped instrument (a nail or a knife?) created troughs with a deeper, more V-shaped section. There is little evidence of shading, although there is some variation in the depth of the grooves. This tool was utilized primarily to inscribe over the first private name that of the second individual. Although largely erased, some strokes

---

13. For an account of the examination of the inscriptions on this ossuary, cf. Appendix 4 at www.uhl.ac/resources/uhl-articles/demythologyzing-talpiot-tomb.

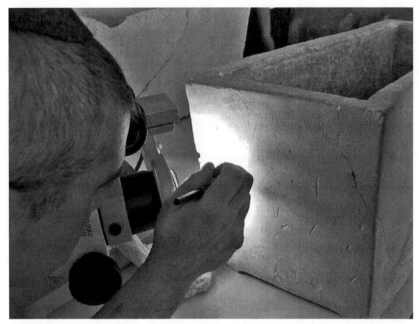

Plate 5. *CJO* 704 **from three sides, inscribed side in the foreground, examined with water pick**

from the original name remained and were apparently incorporated into the strokes of letters of the subsequent name.

Patina inside and outside the Letters

Our patina analysis involved the use of a microscope with careful examination with various light sources. However, even on the basis of a close examination of Radovan's photographs, some preliminary observations can be made with regard to patina variations on the ossuary inscriptions. Of first importance is the fact that the grooves of the last two words *(bar/ben Yehoseph)* share uniform color and texture of the patina, and their patina matches that of the uninscribed surfaces around them.

The area of the first word contains scratches made by two or three different instruments. First, a dull instrument was used to inscribe the private name. A sharp instrument was used by a subsequent hand to inscribe letter strokes. The color and texture of the patina in the scratches made with the dull knife match the surface around them. However, the scratches made with

Plate 6. Photo and drawing of the remnants of the letters of the personal name of the first inscription of *CJO* 704. Erasure marks and scratches are represented in black.

a sharp, pointed instrument by the final hand appear fresher and cut through the lines of the first inscription. Their patina appears to be slightly lighter and smoother than that of the surrounding surfaces, which normally indicates a later set of scratches. The variations in line depth and width and in patina texture and color likely indicate inscriptional activity on at least two occasions by two hands using two different instruments.

How can an epigrapher work to distinguish the underlying original inscription from the secondary activity? If one could "remove" the scratches of the second instrument from the picture, which of the remaining lines would make up the original name? As an exercise in epigraphic methodology, by utilizing the features of Adobe Photoshop, we can examine levels of inscriptional activity on the ossuary that may help to answer these questions. First of all, the superfluous "X" on the far right in itself could be judged to be made up of two separate inadvertent scratches since they appear to have been produced by two separate instruments.

Stages in the Inscription

The picture below (p. 179) shows how the earlier level of inscriptional activity appears with the secondary writing removed. In it, we see a series of letters of shallow scratches made by a dull-tipped knife. The underlying, barely legible vertical and horizontal strokes could form the letters of a relatively short name. Because this name was overwritten subsequently by a more deeply inscribed name, which also apparently incorporated some of the earlier strokes, only a few strokes remain clear.

Reading the inscription is further hampered by the fact that virtually all strokes of the inscription are at least partially filled with hardened mud. This eliminates the possibility of examining irregularities in the bottom of the trough of each stroke throughout much of the inscription. In an area elsewhere on the ossuary, an experiment was made to remove the mud with instruments, including a water pick. In each case, the fragile patina disintegrated along with the hardened mud. For the time being, this leaves observations of the irregularities in the edges of the inscribed lines as the main means of distinguishing early and later strokes.[14] For example, an apparent single line of בר/ב‍ן actually comprises two distinct, subsequent strokes.

Although the surviving strokes may, with some imagination, derive from a certain limited number of possible names, my tentative choice would be ‏ידן/ידן‎ ‏יי‎. *Yudan* is an informal form of the name יהודה *Yehudah* and is found written in both forms on another Jerusalem ossuary (*CJO* 370) pictured below (Plate 8). On this ossuary, the name "Yudan" was overinscribed on a clumsily smoothed (or erased?) surface that had been irregularly shaved with the blade of a knife. Whether it is actually an erasure of a third, earlier name, a mistake made by the scribe himself, or an imperfection on the surface of the ossuary is difficult to discern.

Coming back to *CJO* 704, the letters of ‏ידן בן יהוסף‎ are written in a form of square script similar to the rest of the inscription and with a similar dull-tipped instrument. However, the strokes of ‏ידן‎ are larger and less uniform. This may support either the idea that: (1) ‏ידן‎ was written subsequent to the final two

14. This experiment was carried out by Dr. Ari Greenspan, 21 June 2007; see pl. 5 above.

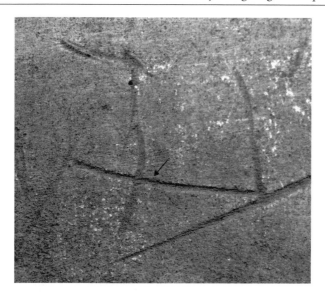

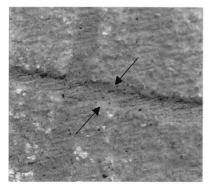 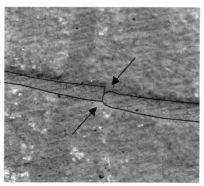

Plate 7. Arrows indicate where the division of the earlier cross stroke of the *beth* (left of the arrows) is met by the later line of the last hand, which connected the *nun* of Yudan with the *beth* of *ben* (to produce *bar*).

words of the inscription בן יהוסף, which originally followed the undecipherable name of another son; or (2) יהוסף at first stood alone, centered on the side of this ossuary that once contained only the remains of the patriarch whose bones were finally removed in order to make room for his son's.[15]

15. Although the consistency of the mitochondrial DNA readings in the ossuary would appear to argue against Joseph's bones ever being in the ossuary. In other words, mitochondrial DNA readings of remains of Joseph's sons and daughters should match

Plate 8. Yeshua ben Yehoseph outlined

Evaluation of Each Name

The personal name written by the final hand is not immediately easy to ascertain. Frank Moore Cross classified it as "a jumble of lines and scratches." The original publication provided a question mark after the name "Yeshua" and dots above the first two of the four letters יֵשׁׁעו of the Hebrew transcription, signifying in that volume that the identification of those letters remained uncertain.

Ben/Bar "the son of" (Hebrew and Aramaic, respectively) is not as easy to discern as one would expect. In the case of both readings, בן or בר, there is at least one extra stroke that does not fit the drawing. The actual strokes used for this word may well have changed from one scribe to the other.

Yehoseph. The letters are clear, though certain of them were apparently retouched by the final hand.

Since there is real difficulty in establishing the reading of the personal name, the following is an analysis of each individual letter.

Yod, as in many ossuary inscriptions, is formed by a simple vertical line, sans serif, and is hardly distinguishable from the *waw. Heh* is typical of noncursive, perhaps semi-formal, hands of the period. The top line of this letter is suspected of having been retouched by the final hand. For *waw,* see *yod* above. *Samekh* appears semi-formal in style and is relatively "squat" in its proportions. *Pe* is a final form.

---

those of the mother and not him. If his remains had been in the ossuary (leaving behind sufficient DNA on the bottom of the box), even after his bones would theoretically be removed to be replaced by a son, there should be a second mitochondrial DNA reading that differed from that of his son.

Plate 9. Photo of Yehoseph

Changes Made by the Final Hand

Sometime after the original inscription had been made on the ossuary, a second inscription was added. This involved writing over the original first name with the name יֵשׁוּעַ. The final hand executed this by adding certain elements to the lines of the original inscription with a sharp, pointed instrument to form the name יֵשׁוּעַ, and eliminating certain strokes from the previous inscription.

Yod: There are two potential candidates for this letter. First the *yod* of the underlying word may have served also for this one. However, it is shallow and has not been retouched to make it more visible, as one would have expected, and as had been done to some of the other letters. Second, it seems more likely that the short stroke descending from the lower stroke of the V of the cursive *shin* was intended to represent the cursive *yod* of יֵשׁוּעַ. This is similar to at least one other example in *CJO* 3, read as either יששבה YISHSHABA? (or perhaps better [ו]יששכר YISSACHAR[W]).[16] Another example of a small diagonal stroke for *yod* is found in the YEHOSEPH BAR KEFAʿ inscription.

Shin: Consisting of three strokes instead of one full stroke (cf. Dominus Flevit, ossuary 29, below), or the more common two-stroke form, which consists of a vertical stroke and a rotated V (cf. the second *shin* in *CJO* 3). The V of our *shin* is broken into two separate strokes and the vertical tail drops to an extraordinary depth. This stroke may be left from the underlying *waw* from *Yudan*, in which case it was recut to make it more pronounced.

---

16. Cf. T. Ilan, *Lexicon of Jewish Names in Late Antiquity,* part 1, *Palestine 330 BCE–200 CE*, TSAJ 91 (Tübingen: Mohr Siebeck, 2002), p. 181.

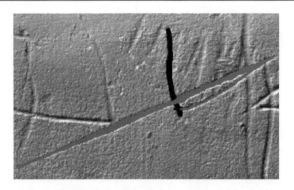

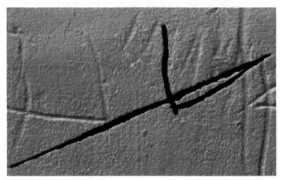

Plate 10. Close-up of "Yeshua(?)" written over erasure

Waw: If this letter actually exists, the engraver seems to be incorporating part of a letter (the leg of the *dalet,* see *Yudan* below) from the previous inscription, adding some retouching.

Ayin: The *ayin* was formed by adding a long diagonal stroke to existing elements from the previous word. Apparently a short tick was added to the upper end, again to emulate an ink trail. The trail ends at, and intersects with, a stroke from the earlier inscription. The final form of this composite letter is composed to emulate the typical single-stroke cursive *ayin* of the period.

Evidence for the Practice of Erasing and Overwriting

The suggestion that this ossuary bears an instance of overwriting is strengthened by the fact that such a practice can be shown to have occurred elsewhere. One potential example comes from the same corpus of ossuaries:

Plate 11. Ossuary *CJO* 428; photo and line drawing

CJO 428. On this ossuary the inscription presents one deceased occupant, שמעון *Shim'on,* written in cursive script, which is then scratched out and re-placed to the right by מריה *Maria* written in a formal script with some lapi-dary overtones. A double groove left on various strokes on both names may indicate that a similar or identical tool was used to inscribe both names, even though the styles are clearly different. The scratches that were used to strike through SHM'WN are not double-grooved and so appear to have been made by a separate tool (possibly on a later occasion).[17]

In the above analysis, I have shown that (1) several different tools were used on this ossuary; (2) there are two different scribal hands (likely at two dif-ferent times); and (3) as a result, we can conclude that at least two individuals, if not more, were interred in this ossuary. This additional epigraphical informa-tion raises real problems for the "Jesus Family Tomb" hypothesis. Was Jesus of Nazareth really buried in a reused bone box? This does not agree with the Syn-optic Gospels and John, which specify that he was placed in a new tomb that had never been used. From a historical perspective, does it seem likely that the devoted followers of Jesus placed him in a reused ossuary, first scratching out the name of a brother, in order to scratch in his informal name with a messy scribal hand? Is this messy inscription that can only be read with great difficulty the only trace left of Jesus? The epigraphical information from this ossuary does not cohere with the information we have from the New Testament that Jesus was laid where none had been laid before; nor does it cohere with what we know on historical grounds about Jesus' high status among early Christians.

In conclusion, the contention that this ossuary bearing the name "Yeshua bar Yehoseph" is the ossuary of Jesus of Nazareth is hampered by the following factors.

---

17. This inscription was transcribed QRYH SHM'WN in the *CJO* catalogue. How-ever, the first word should almost certainly be read MRYH, the scribe having used a final *mem* at the beginning of the word, as in MRYH of *CJO* 706 above.

Plate 12. "Jesus son of Joseph" from *CJO* 9

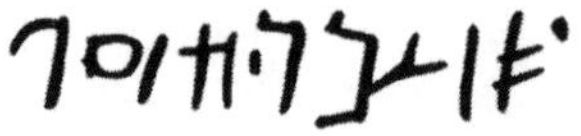

ישוע בן יהוסף

1. This is not the only ossuary that has survived from the Jerusalem necropolis with the name "Jesus son of Joseph" (cf. *CJO* 9).
2. In fact, statistically, one in every ten tombs in the Jerusalem necropolis would contain the remains of one "Jesus son of Joseph" (whether indicated by an inscribed ossuary or not).
3. The Jesus of the Gospels was the first to be buried in the tomb (John 19:41). Based upon the above evidence, the "Jesus son of Joseph" of *CJO* 704 was only one in a sequence of individuals who were interred in the ossuary, even aside from the fact that he was not the first to be buried in the ossuary and thus in the tomb as well.
4. The name "Yeshua" on this ossuary is one of the most carelessly scrawled names found in the Jerusalem necropolis and certainly the most inelegant found on this ossuary and in this tomb. Added to the fact that the name was written on an otherwise plain, undecorated ossuary makes this a very unlikely candidate to be the ossuary of a highly honored member of this family, let alone the revered leader of a popular movement.

Ossuary CJO 701 "Marimēnou (ē) Mara"?

Ossuaries CJO 701 and CJO 108*

The filmmakers assert that the two Marys are critical pieces of evidence for their hypothesis. In response, a clear and thorough analysis of the two ossuary inscriptions must be made to evaluate their claims. The analysis presented here shows that the names "Mariamene" (*CJO* 701) and "Mariamne" (*CJO* 108) are not actually on those ossuaries. In both cases the inscriptions have been misread by Rahmani in the *Catalogue of Jewish Ossuaries*, and in consequence by the filmmakers. In both cases "Mariame," the most common form of the name "Mary" among the ossuaries, should be read instead. The filmmakers make clear that their case rests upon these names, and the apparent rarity of the name "Mariamene." If the reading is instead "Mariame," the most common form of the most common female name, there is no reason to be surprised at finding it. It does not surprise us even in a tomb with a Jesus son of Joseph (found on two ossuaries), given that "Mariame" has the highest occurrence of any name in the inscriptional corpus; 32 percent of all women in the inscriptional corpus bear this name. Thus the epigraphical evidence brought here removes the central pillar of the Jesus tomb hypothesis.[18]

The filmmakers make it abundantly clear that their hypothesis stands or falls based on the reading "Mariamene" for *CJO* 701. The inspiration for the hypothesis, Simcha Jacobovici writes, is that "other than the Jesus, son of Joseph ossuary, to use Feuerverger's term, the most 'surprising' of all the ossuaries in the Talpiot tomb is the one inscribed '[the ossuary] of Mariamne also known as Mara.' From the beginning, we focused on this particular ossuary because it seemed to be the key to the whole story. Everything depended on this unique artifact."[19] At the press conference he stated, "Mariamne was kind of the linchpin of the cluster."[20] Feuerverger gives a very low probability that the Talpiot tomb is not Jesus' family tomb, *if and only "if*Mariamne can be linked to Mary Magdalene."[21] Yet this crucial linkage cannot be made using accepted historical methodology.

The moviemakers make an elementary error regarding the name of Mary Magdalene. Following Prof. François Bovon of Harvard University, the filmmakers and their advisors have accepted Mary Magdalene's name in the apocryphal *Acts of Philip* as being "Mariamne." James Cameron states, "according to certain Christian texts, of the early Christian texts such as the Acts of Phillip and the Gospel of Mary Magdalene, Mariamne is the name of Mary Magdalene. So that's the missing piece, that's the Ringo, and that's what set this whole investigation in motion."[22] However, the filmmakers do not rely exclusively on the estimable work of Bovon, but go on to make highly tenuous assumptions that fly in the face of the earliest sources. Yet it is only on the basis of such tenuous assumptions that their thesis holds to-

18. Concerning the relative frequencies of these names, see Appendix C, "The Significance of Formal and Informal Personal Names and Their Frequency in Archaeology and Literature," at www.uhl.ac/resources/uhl-articles/demythologyzing-talpiot-tomb.

19. *Jesus Family Tomb: The Discovery, the Investigation and the Evidence That Could Change History*, 204.

20. Jennifer Viegas (2007-02-25). "Jesus Family Tomb Believed Found." Discovery Channel. http://dsc.discovery.com/news/2007/02/25/tomb_arc.html?category=archaeology&guid=20070225073000. Retrieved 2007-02-28.

21. *Lost Tomb of Jesus* Documentary. See also A. Feuerverger, "Statistical Analysis of an Archaeological Find," *Annals of Applied Statistics* 2 (2008): 1-112.

22. Viegas (2007-02-25). "Jesus Family Tomb Believed Found."

gether. They make the unsupported assumption that "Mariamne" was also the current and accurate name for the actual historical figure Mary Magdalene of the first century. Yet Prof. Bovon nowhere claims that the name "Mariamne" of the *Acts of Philip* should be linked to the historical figure of the first century. Rather he said that this character is presented as the sister of both Philip of Bethsaida and Martha of Bethany, whose persona evolved over time to become the fictitious gnostic sage and evangelist. This fictitious character is more closely linked to Mary of Magdala in the *Manichean Psalms,* the *Gospel of Mary,* and the *Pistis Sofia.* In order to correct their mistake, Bovon has publicly stated, "I do not believe that Mariamne is the real name of Mary of Magdalene."[23]

These later gnostic stories also speak of a close relationship between Mary Magdalene and Jesus, and give a high prominence to her in the early church. The filmmakers have gone further than the gnostic sources upon which they base the idea, and surmise that Jesus and Mary were married and produced a family. Yet, in response to their film, Bovon has publically stated: "the reconstructions of Jesus' marriage with Mary Magdalene and the birth of a child belong for me to science fiction."[24] Of these assumptions — (1) that the name of Mary Magdalene was not Maria or Mariam, as recorded in the Gospels, but rather Mariamne; (2) that the Mariamne of the *Acts of Philip* is to be identified with Mary Magdalene, though the *Acts of Philip* never says so explicitly; and (3) that Jesus was married and fathered a child — none is supported by any of the earliest records dealing with these individuals, namely the Synoptic Gospels, the Gospel of John, and Josephus.[25] When the filmmakers form their view of history based on apocryphal stories rather than our earliest sources, they exercise creativity quite beyond that warranted by artistic license. Historians can consider it little more than a hack job at revisionist history. It is, in fact, an issue of poor methodology. What follows shows that the hypothesis is also built on an error in epigraphy.

23. François Bovon, "The Tomb of Jesus," *SBL Forum,* n.p. [cited March 2007]. Online: http://sbl-site.org/Article.aspx?ArticleID=656.

24. Ibid.

25. He published this clarification in the Society of Biblical Literature Forum, March 2007.

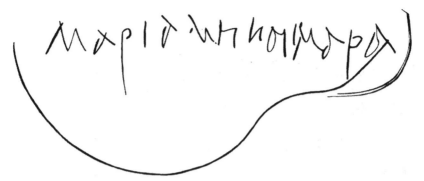

Figure 1. "MARIAMENOU MARA" from *CJO* 701

The Original Reading of Ossuary CJO 701

The original publication of the ossuary by archaeologist L. Y. Rahmani (with L. Di Segni; followed by A. Kloner) interpreted this inscription as reading: MARIAMENOU-MARA, "of Mariamene (a.k.a.) Mara."

Problems with the Published Reading

A panoply of problems is inherent in the original reading of *CJO* 701 by Rahmani and Di Segni. These problems fall into several categories: lexical difficulties, the "signum" formula, use of appositives, and epigraphic issues.

The lexical problems

1. The name MARIAMNH is unattested before the third century CE (aside from *CJO* 108 and 701, which are in question here).
2. MARIAMHNH is nowhere else attested for MARIAMNH.
3. The retrograde reading of *nu* is nowhere else attested in legible inscriptions of the late Second Temple period.
4. According to Rahmani, an unattested lexical form MARIAMHNH is here expressed in a diminutive form MARIAMHNON.[26] He suggests

26. James Tabor quotes Leah Di Segni on this issue in his blog: "I well remember that, while here and there I had some suggestions about interpretation of a particular form (for instance, Mariamenon being an hypochoristic [*sic*] form of Mariam), I could not but confirm all his readings." However, if the name were actually a hypocorism of the name (i.e., MARIAMHNH) there would be no need to change to the neuter endings.

that this would explain the otherwise unattested neuter genitive MARIAMHNOU. However, the diminutive endings, as a rule, should be for masculine nouns -*iskos/iskou;* feminine -*iska/iskas;* and neuter -*ion/iou.*[27] In this case,[28] hypothetically, a neuter diminutive form in the genitive should produce MARIAMHNIOU (not MARIAMHNOU). The problem is compounded by the fact that none of these irregular forms are attested elsewhere.

5. A ligature for OU is epigraphically problematic since it begins to appear regionally (and only sparingly) during the early second century (and even then does not resemble this form at all; cf. especially P. Yadin mss. 12 and 14).

Problems associated with the Suggested Elements of the *Signum* Formula

A *signum* is a term used for an added second personal name, like a middle name or alias. According to M. Schwabe and B. Lifshitz, if it is introduced by the formula *hē kai* or *ho kai,* "who is also called," flanked by two personal names, the names are typically foreign to one another.[29] Thus ethnically Jewish names are paired with Greek names, Greek names with Jewish names.[30]

There are several immediate problems, however, in applying the above profile or definition of this term to the inscription of *CJO* 701:

1. Mariamne and Mara are both Jewish names, thus falling outside the profile for the suggested H KAI + *signum* formula in use here.
2. If MARA is taken to be translated by the title "Master" (so Tabor and Pellegrino), then it is not a personal name, again placing it outside the *signum* profile.
3. In Greek inscriptions of the Second Temple period, no inadvertent scratch (and there are 47 in this area in and around the inscription), stroke, or "clear diacritical mark" is ever substituted for a letter, word, or phrase (including H or H KAI). The vertical stroke that Rahmani suggests "probably represents an *eta*" is unattested elsewhere. In the

27. Herbert Weir Smyth, *Greek Grammar,* rev. Gordon M. Messing (Cambridge: Harvard University Press, 1956), §852.

28. Given that Rachmani/Di Segni's proposed reading is built off of the *neuter* adjective instead of the feminine.

29. *Beth She'arim,* vol. 2, *The Greek Inscriptions* (New Brunswick, N.J.: Rutgers Univeristy Press, 1974), p. 64.

30. For example, Schwabe cites *Saulos de ho kai Paulos,* "Saul who is also called Paul," Acts 13:9.

parallel inscription suggested by Rahmani, Beth Shearim 101, SARA H MAXIMA, the *eta* is written in full. On the basis of Beth Shearim 101, Rahmani suggests that the presumed *eta* would represent the full formula, *h kai*.

4. The earliest inscriptional use of *signa* comes from the beginning of the second century (Schwabe) or from the end of the first century (Tabor, quoting Di Segni).

A Basic Grammatical Problem with the Proposed Reading

In a *signum*, the two names must be in the same grammatical (especially inflectional case) form. In *CJO* 701 they are not. Names in apposition to one another cannot be a mixture of genitive and nominative forms, as has been proposed for this inscription. This would be a jarring violation of basic grammatical rules. Since the first name, according to Rahmani's reading, is in the genitive case, standard Greek grammar would dictate that both the noun MARIAMHNON and its appositive/*signum* H MARA should agree with respect to the inflectional form.[31] In this case, both should be in the genitive, that is, MARIAMHNOU THS KAI MARAS.[32] Or, if a relative pronoun were used, then MARIAMHNOU OU KAI MARAS[33] would be the expected reading, with the relative pronoun agreeing with the preceding noun in both inflection and the neuter gender. The example from *CJO* 868, ALEXAS MARA MHTHR IOUDAS SIMON UIOS AUTHS, does not provide a parallel.[34]

Epigraphic observations concerning the two parts of the inscription must be taken into consideration

1. The inscription bears two writing styles, documentary and cursive, each being characteristically clear, distinct, and consistent for each of the two parts of the inscription (bringing into question the proposed unity of the inscription). Both of the scribal hands preserved on the ossuary betray writers who are both practiced and comfortable in writing Greek.

31. Smyth, *Greek Grammar*, §§976ff.
32. See Schwabe, *Beth She'arim*, 2:185, no. 199: *Topos Theodosias tēs kai Saras Tyrias*.
33. See F.-M. Abel, "Tombeau et ossuares Juifs récemment découverts," *RB* 23 (1913): 276, no. 13.
34. There the anarthrous MARA, rather than carrying the genitive inflection of ALEXAS that precedes it, is grammatically bound to agree with the nominative inflection of MHTHR (this parenthetical string of nominatives ultimately gain their inflections from UIOS AUTHS, which presents a type of *casus pendens* at the end of the inscription).

2. The second part of the inscription, KAI MARA, was written with an instrument similar to that of the first, but with a sharper point.[35]

A Note on Irregularities in Ossuary Inscriptions

The reading proposed by Rahmani and Di Segni for *CJO* 701 requires that the inscriber made at least ten errors or anomalies in Greek grammar and spelling. Such a reading is based on the assumption that irregularities in ossuary inscriptions are commonplace. However, the frequency of variants and errors among the corpus of ossuaries is quantifiable. On the corpus of ossuaries from Beth Shearim, for example, a certain number of orthographic variants are relatively common, especially iotacisms (about 1 in every 5 inscriptions). Actual spelling errors are few (about 1 in 25 inscriptions). Grammatical/syntactic errors are relatively rare among these inscriptions (no more than 1 in every 45 inscriptions). The count of variants and errors is somewhat less among the published ossuaries of the Second Temple period. The odds that ten or more anomalies should be found in an inscription on a single ossuary are extremely low and indicate that such a suggestion is not an acceptable reading of the inscription, given the normal rubrics of epigraphic methodology.[36] *In fact, it is difficult to imagine that an apparently literate Hellenistic Jew of first-century Jerusalem could produce such an extraordinary list of anomalies, lapses in basic Greek grammar, and writing errors, all within the space of two words.*

In the light of this, we really need to look for a better alternative for the transcription. According to normal epigraphic methodology, the reading to be preferred is the one that accounts for the greatest amount of elements with the least number of difficulties.

A New Reading of CJO 701

In place of this problematic reading suggested by Rahmani, the following reading presents no such problems: MARIAMH KAI MARA ("Mariam and

---

35. For a more in-depth evaluation of the two scribal hands, cf. Appendices A, B, and C at www.uhl.ac/resources/uhl-articles/demythologyzing-talpiot-tomb.

36. It does not take an epigrapher to see the inherent problems here. Sadly, the errors are basic enough that anyone who has had even a very basic education in Greek, and has done their homework, should have been able to avoid these pitfalls. It is unfortunate that such sloppy homework by the film's advisors has led to such a needless waste of scholarly time and energy.

Mara"). MARIAMH is the preferred Greek word used among the ossuaries for "Mary" (in Rahmani, *CJO:* MARIAMH 5x, MARAIAMH 1x, MARIEAMH 1x, MARIAM 1x, MARIA 1x; from Dominus Flevit: MARIAMH 1x, MARA 1x).

The First Name and the First Scribe

The first name on the ossuary was written in the contemporary Greek documentary style of the first century. Four letters of the first name are clear and erect: M, A, R, I. The next two letters are written a bit more askew (apparently due to the scribe's avoidance of a scratch or imperfection between the two letters) but are certainly recognizable and in the same style: A, M. This is followed by a proper documentary H of this period, in the same style as the previous letters. So far, the word as it stands forms "MARIAMH," which is the normal Greek form of the Hebrew name "Mariam." ("Mariame" appears seven times in the *Catalogue of Jewish Ossuaries.*)

Of particular note are the *M (mu)*, the *A (alpha)*, and the *P (rho)* of the inscription. The shallow lines on both parts of the inscription were inscribed with a dull, pointed metal object. This instrument may have been a metal stylus, which was commonly used for taking notes on wax tablets and which makes similar marks.

The *M* is formed by a number of separate but intersecting strokes. The separate strokes are indicated by the nonalignment, and the scissor-like appearance of the ends of the various strokes where they intersect.

The *A* is formed by two strokes instead of three, comprising a right-tilted V followed by a left-tilted diagonal line. This reflects a semi-cursive tendency in this letter that appears in nonliterary documents as well as on the ostraca and *tituli picti* in the first century CE at Masada and elsewhere. (*Tituli picti* are inscriptions on wine jars.)

The *P* is inscribed with two strokes. The vertical stroke descends well below the baseline. This feature is common among the ossuaries and is also typical of nonliterary documents of the period as well as on the ostraca and *tituli picti* of Masada.

The *H* here, lacking the upper right arm, is formed with three strokes, although the scribe is endeavoring to mimic the form of the letter as it would be written in ink according to the semi-cursive tradition. This form stands in stark contrast to the contemporary cursive *ēta,* which is formed in a single looping stroke, without lifting the pen from the writing surface and which stands behind the formation of the lower-case *h* (as can be seen in the ossuary *CJO* 108 below).

Figure 2. "Mariame" from *CJO* 701

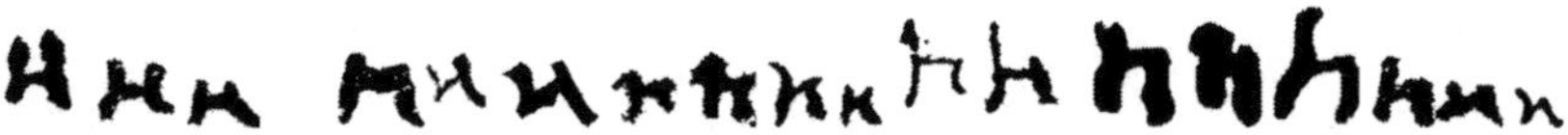

Figure 3. The *H (ēta)* from Masada inscriptions, first century CE: (1) formal; (2) semi-formal; (3) semi-cursive; (4) cursive

This name is followed by a gap that is sufficiently wide to signify a space between distinct words. After this series of letters, the irregularities begin. Rahmani suggested that the next letter was an *N (nu)*. However, it can only be read so if it is taken to be retrograde (i.e., written backward). The suggestion that it should be read as a retrograde *N* raises the question of whether it is truly an *N* at all. Among all of the Greek-inscribed ossuaries listed in Rahmani's *Catalogue* and the numerous ossuaries from Dominus Flevit (on the west slope of the Mount of Olives), there are no other cases in which it has been suggested that an *N* has been written in this way. Furthermore, the following two letters do not resemble the combination *OU*, as proposed in Rahmani's original publication. This combination would form a ligature that does not exist on the ossuaries or at Masada. An *OU* ligature does appear later in early-second-century manuscripts from Nahal Hever and Wadi Murabba'at, but the resulting ligature, in all cases, combines the *O* with a true Y- or V-shaped *upsilon*, which in no way resembles the combination on this ossuary.

As we shall see, this is not because the scribe suddenly introduced anomalous letterforms, or even changed his handwriting style in mid-sentence. Rather, it is because a second scribe subsequently added the last two words of the inscription in a different handwriting style. Upon closer examination, it appears that the three letters Rahmani read as NOU are al-

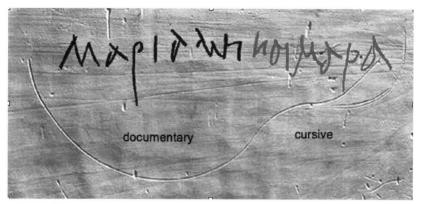

Plate 13. The contrasting styles of the two Greek names on *CJO* 701

most certainly to be transcribed by the common word KAI ("and"), written in the Greek cursive form of the word.[37]

Cursive Tendencies and the Second Scribe

Cursive tendencies among various scribes led to varying degrees of cursive letterforms. These cursive forms often appear in official documents that normally would be written in the formal Greek documentary script. These forms may be termed as cursive or semi-cursive depending upon the extent to which these tendencies were exhibited. The most common cursive tendency was to execute individual letterforms without lifting the tip of the pen from the writing surface. Another tendency was to connect consecutive letters without lifting the pen, thereby creating ligatures. This tendency is known as "connected writing," when the interconnection of letters is more prevalent. The overall appearance of cursive writing is a graceful sequence of looping strokes, as can be seen in KAI MARA. This stands in contrast to the triangular, squared, and rather jagged succession of strokes in the more formal script used by the first scribe while inscribing MARIAME. Also, from the standpoint of horizontal line space, although each scribe inscribed a total of seven letters, the cursive style of the second scribe allowed him to write his seven letters in three-quarters of the space of the first.

37. The KAI reading was independently confirmed by E. Puech and T. Ilan. It was also made by others earlier: in *BÉ* 1998 and *SEG* 46 (1996). Thanks to Prof. Jonathan Price for these latter references.

Figure 4. KAI in cursive writing from *CJO* 701

As usual for both the semi-cursive and cursive K, its left vertical stroke ascends above the rest of the letter (cf. P. Yadin 12 [*olim* 5/6Hev12] and P. Yadin 16 [*olim* 5/6Hev16] below). A *kappa* that is written with only two separate strokes rather than three might be termed "semi-cursive" (as in the case of P. Yadin 12). The *kappa* on this ossuary exhibits the full cursive form of this letter, which requires that the letter's three strokes be executed without lifting the tip of the pen (cf. Masada *tituli picti* 858 and P. Yadin 16 below).

This is also true concerning the cursive form of the remaining letters A and I, which, as in this case, were commonly written together as a ligature, that is, without lifting the tip of the pen (cf. both P. Yadin 12 and 16 below). At times the entire word is written without lifting the pen, as is clearest in P. Hever 63 (*olim* XHever/Seiyal63) and 69 and P. Yadin 16. (The cursive form of the A appears also in the second name "MARA.")

Following normal scribal practice of the period, the scribe engraved the words of his inscription in *scripta continua:* with no space between the words, writing KAIMARA. He, or someone else, subsequently provided a stroke, a word divider, to separate the KAI from the name, apparently to distinguish the two words, resulting in KAI'MARA. (On the other hand, the stroke might defensibly be judged to be a mere accidental scratch, since this area of the ossuary's surface is plagued with other superfluous and accidental scratches both among the letters of this inscription as well as on the uninscribed surfaces.) The proposal that the scratch serves as a so-called *signum* (representing "that is" or "also called") is untenable since it does not resemble such a stroke and such punctuation is not used in contexts where cursive scripts are used.

The scribe also continued in the cursive style with respect to the word MARA. The *M* of the second name "Mara" is written with two strokes, including one continuous looping gesture. The first leg of the letter is initiated

Plate 14. "KALON KERAMION," Masada *tituli picti* 858

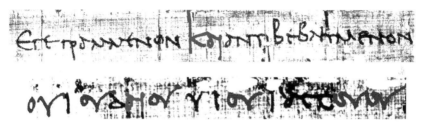

Plate 15. P. Yadin 12 exhibiting KAI with a semi-cursive *kappa* followed by the cursive ligature AI

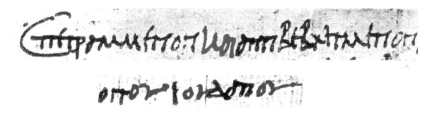

Plate 16. P. Yadin 16 exhibiting KAI with a cursive *kappa*, ligature AI and connected writing, and ligature OU

below the baseline upon which the body of each letter sits, with the center of the letter sitting higher and formed like the letter U, and the right leg curving toward the next letter. This is typical of Greek cursive and minuscule forms of the letter (e.g., see Masada *tituli picti* 858 and both P. Yadin 12 and 16 above). This stands in contrast to the practice illustrated in the first name of this inscription, where the entire letter M remains above the baseline and the middle forms a pronounced V.

The *A* in both cases appears to have been written with one continuous looping stroke. The first form exhibits a counterclockwise rotation, with its final stroke finishing high near the letter's ceiling line. This is common among medial forms of the letter (i.e., a letter appearing before another letter in the same word) where the letter ends in a place near to where the ini-

**Figure 5. The second name
"MARA" written in cursive style**

tial stroke of next letter *rho* will begin (not dissimilar to the formation of the *alpha* of the ligature *AI* in the previous word *KAI*). The second example is a typical final form of the *alpha* (the last letter of a word or line) where the final diagonal stroke of the enlarged letter descends and ends, almost emphatically, at its baseline.

The letter *P* (Greek *rho*) is drawn with two strokes as is generally the case in most contemporary, locally inscribed papyrus documents, with the crescent-shaped head written first, followed by the downstroke, which descends well below the baseline.

Do We Have Another Signum MARIAM H KAI MARA?

Several scholars have suggested reading *CJO* 701 as: MARIAM H KAI MARA "Mariam who is also Mara," as an alternative to MARIAMH KAI MARA "Mariame and Mara." In light of the clear change of scribal hands between MARIAMH and KAI, this suggestion should be rejected. Such a reading is beset with the following inherent problems.

1. The *H* is not detached from MARIAM.
2. The *H* is in the same square/triangular, semi-formal/semi-cursive, documentary writing style of the first name, MARIAM, and not in the rounded/looping, cursive writing style of the words KAI MARA.
3. MARIAMH is the normal formal name for "Mary" among the ossuaries, not MARIAM.
4. According to Schwabe and Lifschitz, the extant examples of the *signum* formula introduced by H KAI provide a second personal name that is nationalistically different from the first, for example, *PN* (Jewish/Semitic) H KAI *PN* (Gentile/Greek) or vice versa. On the

contrary, the two names MARIAM and MARA are both Semitic/Jewish names.

5. No *signum* formulae appear in the inscriptions before the end of the first century (according to Di Segni; the beginning of the second century according to Schwabe and Lifschitz).

Natural and Inadvertent Scratches on the Ossuary's Surface

Ossuaries are notorious for nicks, scratches, and tool marks, which may occur anywhere on the object's surface. In the photographs of *CJO* 701 there appears to be a small line between the last two letters of MARA. Upon close examination, it is clearly a small natural pit that must have preceded the inscription. This is similar to natural pitting found in various places elsewhere on the ossuary.

Another MARIAM — Not MARIAMNOU — Inscription? Ossuary CJO 108

Ossuary *CJO* 108 has been suggested as an attestation of the name "Mariamnou." This ossuary contained the remains of a single, named individual. The name MARIAMH was initially written on the top and bottom of the ossuary's lid. Both original inscriptions were likely inscribed in low-lit to unlit circumstances, since many of the strokes of the inscription were misaligned, providing nearly illegible results. On the top of the lid, the name was reinscribed above the original inscription. On the bottom of the lid, the name was reinscribed below the original inscription, which had been canceled with a line cut through the middle letters (see fig. 6, p. 198 below).

It seems likely that the first line on the lid's bottom did not read MARIAMNOU, but rather MARIAMH, as it does in the other three occurrences on this lid. The line to the left of the *ēta* appears to be an accidental scratch. See the restoration of the *ēta* below. If this reconstruction is correct, then there is no certifiable example of the name Mariamne until the third century CE.

B. *Lid* Across:

Μαριάμη/Μαριάμη Mariame/Mariame

C. *Lid* Across underside:

Μαριάμνου/Μαριά/μη of Mariamne/Maria/me

Figure 6. Ossuary *CJO* 108, top and bottom of lid

Figure 7. Ossuary *CJO* 108, lid bottom with *ēta* in former name restored

Yet Another Mary and Martha?

This revised reading of the inscription on *CJO* 701, based on contemporary inscriptions and documents, would leave the words MARIAME KAI MARA "Mariam and Mara." Mara, as noted by Tal Ilan among other scholars, was a common shortened form of the Aramaic name "Martha."

Because an ossuary would often contain the bones of more than one individual, and because these two names are among the most common female personal names of the first century, the combination of these two names together on an ossuary is not surprising. In fact, an ossuary was discovered at Dominus Flevit (DF 7) on the west slope of the Mount of Olives that has the Hebrew equivalent of the two names as a pair written three times on the same ossuary (however, with the order reversed: "Martha and Maria").

Multiple Burial and DNA

The fact that two individuals were named on the side of an ossuary does not limit the remains within to be only from those two individuals. There may have been others inside whose names were not inscribed. To give us an idea of how many individuals might have been interred in a single ossuary, one should consider Ossuary 37, also from the Dominus Flevit tomb complex, which bears the names of five individuals, indicating that the ossuary contained at least five distinct burials. The named individuals buried in the ossuary were Zechariah, Mariame, Eleazar, Simon, and Sheniit(?). The variety of scripts and character of the cuts indicate that the inscriptions were written by different individuals with distinct instruments. There may be the skeletal and DNA remains from at least five individuals in this box (and perhaps more from others whose names were not inscribed on the ossuary).

In addition to numerous other ossuaries that name more than one individual, there are others in which names are connected by KAI "and," which more often than not indicates family relationships. This type includes several that were apparently written on a single occasion by a single scribe (which may indicate that the bones of those individuals were interred simultaneously; e.g., *CJO* 560, 800, and 139, representing two brothers, a mother and her two sons, and apparently a husband and wife, respectively).

Furthermore, on inscribed ossuary *CJO* 490, KAI is used to connect two individuals. Two distinct scribal hands, and thus two different inscribers, are evident in the two parts of the inscription. The initial name FASAHLOU "of

Pasael," was deeply inscribed in a rounded lapidary script. This is followed by a squared lapidary hand whose inscribed letters had been merely draft-outlined and left unfinished: KAIEIFIGENEIAS "and of Iphigenia."[38]

Conclusion Regarding CJO 701

The so-called Mariamene ossuary contained the names and remains of two distinct individuals. The first name on the ossuary, "MARIAME," was written in the common Greek documentary script of the period when the bones of this woman were interred. The words "KAI MARA" were added sometime later by a second scribe, when the bones of the second woman, Mara, were added to the ossuary. This scribe's handwriting includes numerous cursive elements not exhibited by the first scribe who wrote "Mariame." In view of all these factors, there is no longer any reason to be tempted to link this ossuary (nor the ambiguous traces of DNA inside) to Mary Magdalene or any other person in biblical, nonbiblical, or church tradition.

Conclusion: If Not Jesus of Nazareth, Then Who Was This Jesus of Talpiot? And Who Were His Family? An Alternative Scenario

To have so many inscribed names and ossuary styles in this tomb allows us to say a certain amount about the family or families buried there, but the paucity of material and bone remains that have been preserved limits us from saying too much. With that in mind, the following scenario can be advanced with some caution.

In Jerusalem, the possession of a rock-cut tomb, especially one with an ornamented façade, would speak of a family of some wealth. Like most of Jerusalem's tombs it was equipped with loculi, narrow benches cut perpendicular to the cave walls, into which bodies were inserted head- or foot-first through a narrow opening. Unlike most tombs, it was also furnished with two elevated benches called arcosolia, where members of the family could be laid parallel to the walls of the tomb. This allowed visitors to pay respect to the deceased while viewing the entire body. Like lying in state, this form of display was normally reserved for prominent members of the family or community.

---

38. Cf. Appendix A in www.uhl.ac/resources/uhl-articles/demythologyzing-talpiot-tomb.

Figure 8. *CJO* 490

A wreath ornament above the door of a house or a tomb normally indicated the presence of a patriarch or other renowned family member. The laurel or olive wreath was awarded to accomplished men of letters, statesmen, military heroes, and champion athletes. The first two occupations seem a more likely match for this tomb, since scribes, rulers, and priests figured prominently in Jerusalem tomb inscriptions.

A significant majority of the ossuaries found in this tomb were inscribed with names, some more significantly in lapidary scripts (*CJO* 702, 705, 706, 707), or most significantly in practiced scribal hands (*CJO* 701). Since names were normally inscribed by family members, these inscriptions, along with the tomb's wreath façade, may indicate a number of literate professionals in the family, perhaps even scribes.

The family can be subdivided by the following distinctive features:

Subgroup 1: CJO *704 (early first century* BCE *to mid first century* CE*)*

The names of two or three individuals appear on this undecorated semi-hard limestone ossuary in the most basic unornamented design. Its rather sloppy common cursive Aramaic inscription was overwritten on square stick Hebrew script.

This subgroup represents the first two generations buried in the tomb: a father and two or more sons in succession. It is likely that Joseph or his children were contemporaries with the tragic story of subgroup 2 below, but predated the professional success stories of subgroup 3.

Subgroup 2: CJO *703, 705, and 706 (early first century* BCE *to early first century* CE*)*

These three ossuaries are roughly dressed, chisel- or adze-finished, undecorated soft limestone. The inscriptions "Mariah," "Mattiah," "Yoseh," and "Yehudah bar Yeshua" were written in clear, deeply engraved lapidary scripts.[39] The

39. Based upon the ceramics found in the tomb, A. Kloner states: "This burial cave

beauty and regularity of the script on these four ossuaries suggests the work of a professional engraver. While handwritten scripts are pervasive on inscribed ossuaries, the lapidary script which unites these ossuaries was generally reserved for signs and monuments. That this form was also used throughout this tomb's history indicates that certain family members were skilled enough to write in lapidary script, if in fact the cultural norm was upheld where family members inscribed the names of the deceased on ossuaries.

It appears that early in the family's use of this tomb, approximately in the late first century BCE, a tragedy took the lives of three young family members: Maria, Mattiah, and Jose. The informal form of all three names is utilized, conveying a sense of youth. Each ossuary is relatively small, which may confirm the youth of the individuals inside, while the fact that each received his or her own personal ossuary would indicate that the three had already arrived at puberty, when restrictions on joint burial were enforced.

Subgroup 3: CJO *702, 707, 708, and 709*

These four ossuaries are semi-smooth finished, chip-carved, and decorated with large rosettes. Based upon the style, this set of ossuaries reflects a successful, more professional family. With the exception of *CJO* 702, which is deeply inscribed with shaded script, the ossuaries of this large sector were designed for multiple burials and thus went nameless. The volume of the ossuaries indicates that this sector of the family was the majority of the extended family, and the one inscription indicates that they were local Hebrew or Aramaic speakers.

Subgroup 4: CJO *701 (first century* CE*)*

This polished, surface-sealed, chip-carved, relatively large shared ossuary is decorated with small rosettes and has a gabled lid. The two Greek inscriptions, "Mariame" and "and Mara," were both beautifully inscribed, the first in documentary scribal hand and the second in cursive hand. This Greek-inscribed ossuary may bear witness to two Hellenistic Jews who immigrated from the Diaspora. Interestingly, their bones were not buried in a more ex-

---

was probably used for three or four generations. The finds which included a small quantity of sherds allow for a Second Temple period dating, i.e., from the end of the first century BCE or the beginning of the first century CE, until approximately 70 CE." Cf. A. Kloner, "A Tomb with Inscribed Ossuaries in East Talpiyot, Jerusalem," *Atiquot* 29 (1996): 21.

clusive Hellenistic Jewish family tomb as has been found in several other locations.[40] The fact that they were placed in this tomb may indicate that they were part of the extended family, or perhaps they were close friends of the local family, while the rest of their own immediate family still resided abroad. Whatever the case, the Greek presence in this tomb was seemingly very limited.

Who was Mariam? Perhaps she was an adult, since her formal name was used. Since a husband's name was not inscribed along with hers, she was probably unmarried or widowed. Since all mitochondrial DNA found within was of a single matriarchal line, she must have been buried with a kinswoman, either a daughter or an unmarried sister named Mara (that is, Martha). Since she had a Greek form of a Jewish name, she might have been a Greek-speaker who had come from the Diaspora to Jerusalem. Her immediate family was well-to-do since the ossuary she was laid in was well crafted. Some family members may have been scribes, or well educated, who could write quite skillfully in both standard and cursive Greek script.

Working with the limited data provided by the names on the inscribed ossuaries and the mitochondrial DNA samples, the following family tree can be suggested.

Yehoseph appears to be the first-generation patriarch of the family tomb, who was married to the unnamed matriarch who provided the mitochondrial DNA of the two second-generation sons "Yudan?"[41] and "Yeshua" (of ossuary *CJO* 704).

Yehoseph + mDNA1
/   \
Yudan?   Yeshua

Based upon considerations of paleography and ossuary style which would place *CJO* 703, 705, and 706 in the late first century BCE to the very be-

40. As in the case of the Greek-inscribed ossuaries of the "Simon of Cyrene" tomb from the slopes of the Mount of Olives. It is well known that it was the primary use of Greek language, the adoption of certain aspects of Greek culture, and the continued use of Greek names that separated the Hellenists from the Hebrews in the Jewish world both abroad and in Jerusalem. Acts 5 provides an example of the separation and tensions between these two groups in Jerusalem.

41. The speculative name Yudan? is used here only for comparison's sake to indicate the first person interred in *CJO* 704. The reading is far from certain due to the poor state of preservation of the lines of the first inscription.

ginning of the first century CE, the ossuary cluster containing Mariah, Yoseh, and Mattiah could also be part of the second generation.[42]

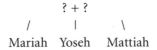

```
              ? + ?
        /       |       \
    Mariah   Yoseh    Mattiah
```

Paleographically, the Yehudah bar Yeshua ossuary is situated well into the first century CE. It is feasible that Yehudah could be the son of Yeshua bar Yehoseph. Such a suggestion could be strengthened if matching mDNA1 would be obtained from Yehudah's ossuary, *CJO* 702. Otherwise, he could simply be the son of another "Yeshua," bearing in mind the frequency of this name among the Judean population of the Late Second Temple period. It is quite possible that the remaining uninscribed ossuaries, decorated in similar style, were also from the second and third generations, but this suggestion is based upon stylistic considerations alone.

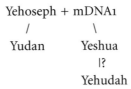

```
        Yehoseph + mDNA1
        /                \
     Yudan            Yeshua
                        |?
                      Yehudah
```

In the light of the Greek language, different ossuary style, and different mDNA, *CJO* 701 stands apart from the other ossuaries. The two individuals who were placed inside, Mariame and Mara, were related by matriarchal mitochondrial DNA since the lab results attested to only one mDNA sequence. Since this sequence did not match the mDNA of ossuary *CJO* 704 (mDNA1), one can infer that the family relationship was vertical, spanning two or more generations, i.e., mother-daughter (or grandmother-granddaughter).

```
        Mariame (=mDNA2)
              |
             Mara
```

---

42. The relatively small sizes of these three ossuaries fit well with those in the southwest niche in Gibson's drawing.

Alternatively, this could also mean that Mariame and Mara were sisters or cousins, descended from the same matriarch.

$$mDNA2 + ?$$
$$/ \qquad \backslash$$
$$\text{Mariame} \quad \text{Mara}$$

Acknowledgments

I thank the Israel Antiquities Authority and Miki Sabenne for assisting me to gain access to the ossuaries and to examine them at the Israel Antiquities Authority in Beth Shemesh, and also for their permission to record and photograph the ossuaries. I would also like to voice my deep appreciation to forensic scientist Steven Cox for his participation in the detailed photography of the inscriptions. In this regard, we are grateful to Charles Greenblatt and the Hebrew University lab at Hadassah Hospital, Ein Kerem, for the use of their high-resolution camera. I would also like to acknowledge and thank L. Y. Rahmani, editor of the *Catalogue of Jewish Ossuaries,* for his generosity and the wisdom he has shared with me in providing numerous parallels concerning the ossuaries included in this paper. This paper is dedicated to him in honor of his arduous work in compiling such a valuable resource for the use of all.

Similarly I thank the Franciscan Museum of the Flagellation in Jerusalem, and especially the museum's director, Father Eugenio Alliata, O.F.M., for allowing me to view and photograph the ossuaries of their collection from Dominus Flevit. I would also like to thank James Charlesworth, along with Eerdmans, for their invitation and encouragement to include this paper in the proceedings from the conference. The illustrations used in this chapter, unless otherwise noted, belong to the author or are the property of the Israel Antiquities Authority or of the Franciscan Museum of the Flagellation, whom I again thank for their generosity.

Prosopography, Mitochondrial DNA, Statistics, and the "Yeshua' Family Tomb": Pensées of an Epigrapher

Christopher A. Rollston

The Study of Names and Identities: Standard Methods and Models

The term "prosopography" derives from two Greek words: *prosōpon*, "face," and *graphē*, "writing." After being coined, this word could be used (e.g., during the Renaissance) of an attempt to pen a physical description of someone. Within more recent scholarship, prosopography has become a technical term for attempts to reconstruct and describe data revolving around the subjects of genealogy, onomastics, and demographics.[1] Within the field of prosopography of antiquity, there is often a predominant focus on the status, vocations, and kinship of elites (because a substantial portion of the

---

1. Lawrence Stone, "Prosopography," *Daedalus* 100 (1971): 46-79; and Thomas F. Carney, "Prosopography: Payoffs and Pitfalls," *Phoenix* 27 (1973): 156-79.

I am pleased to thank James Charlesworth for inviting me to present my research in Jerusalem and I am grateful to Eric Meyers for bringing my prosopographic work to Prof. Charlesworth's attention. I am also grateful to Hava Katz of the Israel Antiquities Authority for permission to collate a number of the inscriptions referred to in this article, including various ossuaries in IAA storage at Beth Shemesh. Iron Age Curator Michal Dayagi-Mendels of the Israel Museum has my gratitude, as always, for allowing me to collate a number of the Iron Age inscriptions referred to in this article. My research assistants, Stephen Paul and Shaun Brown, assisted me with some of the bibliographic work. Also, my thanks to Lindsay Hunter and Ryan Jackson for discussing the DNA evidence with me. A brief version of my article was published under the title: "Inscribed Ossuaries: Personal Names, Statistics, and Laboratory Tests," *NEA* 69 (2006): 125-29.

epigraphic data derived from elite circles).[2] For certain fields of ancient prosopography (e.g., biblical studies), analyses will also sometimes include attempts to argue for (or against) the identification of a person attested in a literary corpus (e.g., Hebrew Bible, Greek NT) with someone attested in the epigraphic corpus.[3] Although certitude is the desideratum, it is often difficult to achieve. Before turning to the Talpiot (Talpiyot) tomb in particular, some discussion of the standard methods should be instructive.

The most reliable prosopographies are those based on a convergence of epigraphic, archaeological, and (when available) literary data. However, *certain minimal controls are mandatory for such analyses to be convincing or even tenable.* Patronymics and matronymics are the most fundamental components of prosopographic analyses. For the ancients, this was a means of differentiating (to some degree) people with the same name; therefore, they are very common in the epigraphic corpus. For example, the Samaria Papyri refer to a slave named "Yehohanan bar She'ilah."[4] Within the corpus of Aramaic and Hebrew inscriptions from Masada, there is reference to "Shimeon bar Yehoseph" and "Shimeon ben Yo'ezer."[5] Although rare, matronymics also occur. For example, a Jerusalem ossuary is inscribed in Greek: "Alexas Mara, mother of Judas Simon, her son."[6] However, because complementary data are not present, nothing more substantive can be said about any of these people and they cannot be identified with anyone in the literary corpus.

Nevertheless, sometimes there are sufficient data to posit that a figure attested in the epigraphic corpus and a figure attested in a literary corpus are

---

2. Karen Radner, ed., *The Prosopography of the Neo-Assyrian Empire*, vol. 1, part 1, *A* (Helsinki: Neo-Assyrian Text Corpus Project, 1998); idem, ed., *The Prosopography of the Neo-Assyrian Empire*, vol. 1, part 2, *B-G* (Helsinki: Neo-Assyrian Text Corpus Project, 1999).

3. E.g., Nahman Avigad, "On the Identification of Persons Mentioned in Hebrew Epigraphic Sources" [in Hebrew], *ErIsr* 19 (1987): 235-37 (English summary, p. 79); and Lawrence J. Mykytiuk, *Identifying Biblical Persons in Northwest Semitic Inscriptions of 1200-539 BCE*, SBLABS 12 (Atlanta: Society of Biblical Literature, 2004). Cf. R. Zadok, *The Pre-Hellenistic Israelite Anthroponymy and Prosopography*, OLA 28 (Leuven: Peters, 1989).

4. Douglas M. Gropp, "The Samaria Papyri from Wadi Daliyeh," in *Wadi Daliyeh II: The Samaria Papyri from Wadi Daliyeh*, and Moshe Bernstein et al., *Qumran Cave 4: Miscellanea, Part 2*, DJD 28 (Oxford: Clarendon, 2001), pp. 33-44, no. 1, line 2.

5. Yigael Yadin and Joseph Naveh, *Masada I: The Aramaic and Hebrew Ostraca and Jar Inscriptions* (Jerusalem: Israel Exploration Society, 1989), p. 40, nos. 463, 466.

6. L. Y. Rahmani, *A Catalogue of Jewish Ossuaries in the Collections of the State of Israel* (Jerusalem: Israel Antiquities Authority and Israel Academy of Sciences and Humanities, 1994), p. 258, no. 868.

probably the same. This can be very useful for prosopographic analysis. For example, during Shiloh's excavations at the City of David, a number of bullae were discovered in stratum X, a stratum that was destroyed by the Babylonians around 587 BCE. Bulla 2 reads: "Belonging to Gemaryahu ben Shaphan." Shiloh posited that the Gemaryahu of this bulla is to be identified with "the scribe Gemaryahu son of Shaphan" who is mentioned in Jer 36:10.[7] However, within the editio princeps of this corpus, Shoham reiterated Shiloh's declaration, but noted a caveat: "It should be borne in mind, however, that the names found on the bullae were popular in ancient times and it is equally possible that there is no connection between the names found on the bullae and the person mentioned in the Bible."[8] Similarly, the Babatha Archive (from the chronological horizon preceding the Second Jewish Revolt of 132-135 CE) refers to a certain elite woman named "Julia Crispina."[9] An Egyptian document refers to a propertied woman of the same horizon and Levantine activities.[10] Ilan has marshaled a substantial amount of evidence and argued that they can probably be identified, but she does not state this definitively.[11]

During the early history of the field, such methodological caution was not the norm. However, it soon became evident that there had been some misidentifications. For example, Albright had argued that the stamped jar handle he found at Tell Beit Mirsim inscribed, "Belonging to Eliakim, the steward of Yokan," was to be associated with King Jehoiachin.[12] After all, the title "steward" (*'bd*) was one that could be associated with the throne, and "Yokan" was arguably a variant of the throne name Jehoiachin. Ultimately,

---

7. Yigal Shiloh, "A Group of Hebrew Bullae from the City of David," *IEJ* 36 (1986): 16-18.

8. Yair Shoham, "Hebrew Bullae," in *Excavations at the City of David 1978-1985, Directed by Yigal Shiloh*, vol. 6, *Inscriptions,* ed. Donald T. Ariel, Qedem 41 (Jerusalem: Hebrew University of Jerusalem, 2000), p. 33.

9. N. Lewis, ed., *The Documents from the Bar Kokhba Period in the Cave of Letters: Greek Papyri* (Jerusalem: Israel Exploration Society, 1989), nos. 20, 24.

10. Yigael Yadin, *Bar Kokhba: The Rediscovery of the Legendary Hero of the Second Jewish Revolt against Rome* (New York: Random House, 1971), pp. 247-48.

11. Tal Ilan, "Julia Crispina, Daughter of Berenicanus, a Herodian Princess in the Babatha Archive: A Case Study in Historical Identification," *JQR* 82 (1992): 361-81.

12. William F. Albright, "The Seal of Eliakim and the Latest Preëxilic History of Judah, with Some Observations on Ezekiel," *JBL* 51 (1932): 77-106. Compare my critique of Marjo Korpel's recent attempt to argue that a putative Iron Age seal with the letters *yzbl* (and no patronymic or title) was Queen Jezebel's: Christopher A. Rollston, "Prosopography and the Yzbl (Jezebel) Seal," *IEJ* 59, no. 1 (2009).

however, it became apparent that the Eliakim jar handles were not to be associated with the same chronological horizon as the Judean monarch. Albright's identification had seemed rational, but it had been wrong.

Although quite rare, there are occasions when someone attested in the epigraphic record can be identified, with enormous certitude, with someone known from literature. This requires substantial corroborating evidence. For example, the Moabite Stone was commissioned by "Mesha, King of Moab." In this inscription, there is also reference to the Moabite site of Dibon and to the fact that Moab was under the hegemony of Israel during the reign of Omri of Israel. Then Mesha states that he was able to secure Moab's independence during the reign of Omri's "son."[13] Because of the correspondences of the personal names, the title "king of Moab," and the basic harmony of the historical data, it is convincing to argue that the Mesha of the Moabite Stone is the Mesha named in the Hebrew Bible (2 Kgs 3:4-5).

Similarly, a number of literary sources refer to the leader of the Second Jewish Revolt (132-135 CE) as a certain Simon "Bar Kokhba" (Dio Cassius, Eusebius). Within the Mishnah and Talmud, he is sometimes referred to as "Bar Koziba."[14] For some time, scholars have stated that Simon's patronymic "Bar Kokhba" ("son of the star") was a messianic appellation rather than an actual patronymic. Of course, the Mishnah and Talmud's "Bar Koziba" ("son of the lie") was understood to be a pejorative. With the publication of the Bar Kokhba Letters, the actual patronymic of Simon became known with certainty: "Bar Kosiba."[15] Ultimately, because of the convergence of the name, the precise chronological horizon, and historical context, we can state confidently that the figure of literature and the epigraphic figure can be identified.

Sometimes ancient inscriptions will contain a personal name and a title. Data such as these would have been useful in antiquity for a number of reasons. A bulla from the City of David contains reference to "[Tobšillem] son of Zakar, the physician."[16] From the Aramaic Persepolis corpus, there is reference to "Data-Mithra the treasurer."[17] Within the corpus of Ammonite

13. Cf. Andrew Dearman, ed., *Studies in the Mesha Inscription and Moab* (Atlanta: Scholars Press, 1989).

14. Yadin, *Bar Kokhba,* 255-59.

15. Yigael Yadin et al., *The Documents from the Bar Kokhba Period in the Cave of Letters (Hebrew, Aramaic, and Nabatean Documents)* (Jerusalem: Israel Exploration Society, 2002).

16. Shoham, "Hebrew Bullae," p. 35, no. 6.

17. Raymond A. Bowman, *Aramaic Ritual Texts from Persepolis,* University of Chi-

inscriptions, a magnificent seal refers to "Palatya ben Ma'aš, the recorder."[18] A beautiful ossuary from Mount Scopus is inscribed with the words "Yehoseph, son of Hananya, the scribe."[19] Of course, these sort of data can be very useful for a modern scholar attempting to do prosopography, and sometimes such data can be the basis for a probable identification. For example, literary sources referred to "Gallio" as a "proconsul of Achaia" (e.g., Tacitus, *Ann.* 16.17.3; Pliny, *Nat.* 31.62; Acts 18:12). During the twentieth century, some nine fragments of a Greek inscription from Delphi referring to "Proconsul Gallio" were published. Based on a convergence of data (including the personal name and title), it has been argued convincingly that the Gallio of the literary sources and the Gallio of the Delphic Inscription are one and the same.[20] Similarly, the Mishnah refers to a temple gate that was known as the "Gate of Nicanor," with Nicanor as someone hailing from Alexandria. During the early twentieth century, an ossuary was discovered in Jerusalem, inscribed in Greek "the "ossuary of Nicanor the Alexandrian, who made the doors," and then in Semitic script: "Nikanor Alexa."[21] It is cogent to argue that this ossuary is the ossuary of the maker of the "Gate of Nicanor" mentioned in the Mishnah.[22] Of course, sometimes even with a title, the most that can be affirmed is that an identification is probable, not certain. For example, an Iron Age Hebrew seal from Mispah refers to "Ya'azanyahu servant of the king," and the book of Jeremiah refers to a prominent figure in the court of the Judean King Zedekiah named "Ya'azanyahu son of the Maacathite."[23] Although this identification is reasonable, it is not certain.

---

cago Oriental Institute Publications 91 (Chicago: University of Chicago Press, 1970), pp. 71-74, no. 1.

18. Mahmud Abu Taleb, "The Seal of *plṭy bn m'š* the Mazkīr," *ZDPV* 101 (1985): 21-29. Note that some consider this seal to be Moabite. For the purposes of this paper, this is not a relevant point. I am grateful to the Department of Antiquities of Jordan and Director Fawwaz al-Khrayshah for permission to collate this seal.

19. Rahmani, *Catalogue*, p. 262, no. 893.

20. Colin J. Hemer, "Observations on Pauline Chronology," in *Pauline Studies: Essays Presented to Professor F. F. Bruce*, ed. Donald A. Hagner and Murray J. Harris (Grand Rapids: Eerdmans, 1980), pp. 3-18.

21. Jack Finegan, *The Archaeology of the New Testament: The Life of Jesus and the Beginning of the Early Church*, rev. ed. (Princeton: Princeton University Press, 1992), pp. 357-59. Cf. J. P. Kane, "The Ossuary Inscriptions of Jerusalem," *JSS* 23 (1978): 279-82.

22. Ilan, "Julia Crispina," p. 367.

23. Cf. W. F. Badè, "The Seal of Jaazaniah," *ZAW* 51 (1933): 150-56. Cf. 2 Kgs 25:23; Jer 40:8; and orthography.

Significantly, Nahman Avigad argued for more rigorous methodologies for attempts to affirm that a personal name attested in the epigraphic corpus and a figure attested in the Hebrew Bible can be identified. First, the name and the patronymic must be the same in the epigraphic corpus and the Hebrew Bible. Furthermore, he affirms that both must hail from the same chronological horizon (i.e., the archaeological context for the inscription and the putative historical context for the biblical personage must be the same). Finally, he affirms that the presence of a distinctive title in the epigraphic and biblical corpus fortifies the identification. Nevertheless, Avigad was not satisfied even with this, for he also stated that because of the preponderance of certain names the presence of the same personal name and patronymic cannot be understood as demonstrating the certainty of an identification.[24]

The Talpiot Tomb

Joseph Gath conducted a salvage excavation at a tomb in the Jerusalem neighborhood of East Talpiot in 1980. The tomb has been described in some detail.[25] Within the tomb complex, ten ossuaries were found, six of which were inscribed.[26] One of the four uninscribed ossuaries was quite damaged.[27] Based on the totality of finds in the tomb, Kloner states that the tomb can be dated to the late Second Temple period. Furthermore, he estimated that the bones of around thirty-five people were interred there.[28] Rahmani read the personal names on the ossuaries as follows: (1) Mariamēnou [ē] Mara ("Mariamne who is also called Mara");[29] (2) Yhwdh br Yšw' ("Yehudah bar Yeshua'"); (3) Mtyh ("Mattiyah"); (4) Yšw' br Yhwsp ("Yeshua' bar Yehoseph"); (5) Ywsh ("Yoseh"); (6) Mryh ("Maryah"). Pfann has now argued that the reading Mariamēnou [ē] Mara is erroneous and has proposed Mariame kai Mara (i.e., Miriam and

24. Avigad, "On the Identification," pp. 235-37.

25. Amos Kloner, "A Tomb with Inscribed Ossuaries in East Talpiyot, Jerusalem," *'Atiqot* 29 (1996): 15-22.

26. Rahmani, *Catalogue*, pp. 222-24, nos. 701-9.

27. Ibid., p. 222 [comment 1]; cf. p. 94, no. 70.

28. Kloner, "Tomb," pp. 21-22.

29. Rahmani states that he believes the name Mara is a short form of the name Martha and that this is the case of a double name (*Catalogue*, p. 222, no. 701; cf. pp. 181-82, no. 468, for Mara and Martha on the same ossuary, arguably referring to the same woman).

Mara).[30] The *kai* ligature is well attested on various media, and I completely concur with Pfann that this is the reading on this ossuary.[31]

The names Yehoseph, Yoseh, Yeshuaʿ, Yehudah, Mattiyah, Maryah, Mariame, Miryam, and Martha (or the variants thereof) all have multiple attestations in the multilingual corpus of ossuaries and some are very common.[32] Note that Sukenik even published an ossuary inscribed "Yeshuaʿ son of Yehoseph" and that the names Yeshuaʿ and Yehoseph are predominant in the family of Babatha's first husband and her first husband's grandfather was named "Yeshuaʿ bar Yehoseph."[33] That is, even with the small corpus of epigraphic attestations of personal names, the Talpiot tomb occurrence of "Yeshuaʿ bar Yehoseph" is not unique.

The Proposal to Identify the Talpiot Tomb with Jesus of Nazareth

Nevertheless, Pellegrino, Jacobovici, and Tabor have argued that the ossuaries of the Talpiot tomb can be identified with Jesus of Nazareth and his family.[34] To be precise, they have argued that it is convincing to affirm that the ossuary of Yeshuaʿ bar Yehoseph is that of Jesus of Nazareth, the ossuary inscribed "Maryah" is that of the mother of Jesus of Nazareth, the ossuary inscribed "Mariam(n)e" (according to their reading, following Rahmani) is that of Mary Magdalene of the Gospels, the ossuary inscribed "Yoseh" is that of Jesus' brother Jose(s), that of "Yehudah bar Yeshua" is that of a son born

30. Stephen J. Pfann, "Mary Magdalene Is Now Missing," Society of Biblical Literature Forum (March 2007). This article was republished as Pfann, "Mary Magdalene Has Left the Room: A Suggested New Reading of Ossuary *CJO* 701," *NEA* 69 (2006): 130-36.

31. In addition to the bibliography cited in Pfann, see also various plates with this ligature in Bruce M. Metzger, *Manuscripts of the Greek Bible: An Introduction to Greek Palaeography* (New York: Oxford University Press, 1981), passim.

32. Rahmani, *Catalogue,* pp. 292-97; and Tal Ilan, *Lexicon of Jewish Names in Late Antiquity,* part 1, *Palestine 330 BCE–200 CE,* TSAJ 91 (Tübingen: Mohr Siebeck, 2002).

33. E. L. Sukenik, "Nochmals: Die Ossuarien in Palätina," *Monatsschrift für Geschichte und Wissenschaft des Judentums* 75 (1931): 462-63; and Lewis, *Documents,* pp. 35-40. Cf. Yadin, *Bar Kokhba,* pp. 233-34; and Carl H. Kraeling, "Christian Burial Urns," *BA* 9 (1946): 18-19.

34. Simcha Jacobovici and Charles Pellegrino, *The Jesus Family Tomb: The Discovery, the Investigation, and the Evidence That Could Change History* (New York: HarperCollins, 2007). Cf. James D. Tabor, *The Jesus Dynasty: The Hidden History of Jesus, His Royal Family, and the Birth of Christianity* (New York: Simon & Schuster, 2006); and Tabor's *Jesus Dynasty Blog.*

to Jesus and Mary Magdalene, and the ossuary inscribed "Mattiyah" is also that of a relative of Jesus of Nazareth. It is also affirmed that the persons buried in the ossuary inscribed "Yeshua' bar Yehoseph" and that inscribed "Mariam(n)e [ē] Mara" (according to their reading) were married. Finally, it has even been argued in the media that the ossuary with the inscription "Ya'akov bar Yehoseph 'aḥui d'Yeshua" (i.e., the "James ossuary") was stolen from the Talpiot tomb decades ago (and it is assumed that the entire inscription is ancient).

However, the problems with this proposal are legion. Note that for these six inscribed ossuaries from the Talpiot tomb, there are just two personal names with patronymics: (1) "Yehudah bar Yeshua'" and (2) "Yeshua' bar Yehoseph." Moreover, there are no matronymics, no references to marital status, no references to fraternal or sororal relationships. These are pivotal issues, because without such data it is not possible for someone in the modern period to ascertain the precise kinship relationships of antiquity. Such tombs were "family tombs," but to assume that a tomb represents some sort of nuclear family *and* to assume that one can discern without empirical evidence the nature of the relationships within that family is problematic.

For example, regarding the Maryah ossuary, there is no empirical reason to assume that she is the mother of Yeshua' bar Yehoseph. She might have been the wife of Yehudah, or the wife of Yoseh, or the wife of Mattiyah, or the wife of Yeshua'. Sometimes we have complementary information that makes an affirmation about marital status. For example, an ossuary from the Kidron Valley is inscribed with the words: "Shalom, wife of Yehudah."[35] An ossuary from Jerusalem's French Hill reads in both Semitic and Greek: "Miryam, wife of Mattiyah."[36] However, on the Maryah ossuary, there is no reference to marital status. Maryah might even have been the daughter of one of the men in the tomb. Sometimes such data are present. For example, an ossuary from Jerusalem's Mount Scopus is inscribed "Judith, daughter of Nadab."[37] An ossuary from Ramat Eshkol, Jerusalem, reads: "Ossuary of Shalom, daughter of Sha'ul, who failed to give birth. Peace, daughter!"[38] However, for the Maryah ossuary, no such data are present; therefore, to as-

---

35. Rahmani, *Catalogue,* p. 81, no. 24.
36. Ibid., p. 197, no. 559.
37. Ibid., p. 201, no. 572.
38. Ibid., p. 132, no. 226. Striking is the fact that an ossuary inscribed "Sha'ul" was found in the same place. It seems that this daughter had been married, but had no children, and was interred in a tomb with her father, rather than in a tomb with her husband.

sume that a modern scholar can discern and make an affirmation about the nature of some relationship is risible.

Similarly, the assumption that the Yoseh of the Yoseh ossuary was the brother of Yeshua' is problematic: the Yoseh ossuary has no fratronymic. Rarely an ossuary will mention the name of a brother of the deceased. For example, an ossuary from Mount Scopus is inscribed "Shimi, son of 'Asiya, brother of Ḥanin."[39] However, there is neither fratronymic nor patronynmic on this ossuary; thus it is not possible to make affirmations about paternity or fraternity. Ultimately, Yoseh could be the son of Mattiyah, or the son of Yehudah, or the son of Yeshua'. Perhaps he was the father of Maryah, or of Mariame, or of Mattiyah. Maybe he is the uncle of one of these (after all, because there is rarely a reference to fraternal relationships, the potential is present for an "uncle" to be buried in a tomb). Perhaps Yoseh was the son or father or brother or uncle of someone who was buried in one of the uninscribed ossuaries. It is possible to suggest that he was a cousin of someone in the tomb. Furthermore, the Yehoseph of the patronymic and the Yoseh of the ossuary could be the same person. After all, these ossuaries were inscribed at two different times and in neither case is there a patronymic for "Yehoseph" or "Yoseh." Sometimes the same ossuary will have the long form and the short form of a name. For example, an ossuary from the western slope of Mount Scopus has "Asous" and "Asoubos," the long form and the short form of the same name, arguably for the same person.[40] The possibilities detailed here are not all mutually exclusive, but ultimately, because there is no patronymic, statement of fraternity, or title, any suggestion about the relationship of Yoseh to those interred there remains conjecture and speculation.

Of course, it has also been suggested that the Mariame ossuary inscription is to be identified with the Mary Magdalene of the Gospels. The problem is that Mariame is hardly a unique name; moreover, the ossuary inscription does *not* contain the word "Magdalene." Sometimes we do have data about the region from which the deceased hailed. For example, an ossuary from the Kidron Valley contains a Greek inscription with the words "Sara (daughter of) Simon of Ptolemais."[41] However, the Mariame ossuary does not contain such a reference (i.e., no "Magdala"). Therefore, for someone to assume that the Mariame of the ossuary must be the Mary Magdalene

39. Ibid., p. 200, no. 570.
40. Ibid., p. 164, no. 383.
41. Ibid., p. 102, no. 99.

of the Gospels is without justification.[42] She could be the wife of Mattiyah, Yoseh, Yehudah, or Yeshua', or she could be the sister of any person in the tomb (even of someone interred in an uninscribed ossuary). Again, not all of these are mutually exclusive, but the point is that to assume that one can state confidently the nature of the relationship of the Mariame of this ossuary to the Yeshua' of the Yeshua' ossuary is rather naïve.

Comparative Analysis of Prosopographic Data from Second Temple Tombs

It is instructive to consider some similar tomb complexes so as to demonstrate that prosopography on the basis of a dearth of data is tenuous at best (i.e., this is a common problem and not something confined to the so-called Yeshua' family tomb). Thus, for example, a (different) tomb from East Talpiot contained five inscribed ossuaries (and nineteen without inscriptions).[43] The personal names on these ossuaries are as follows: "Sha'ul" (no. 716), "Antigona" (no. 717), "Yehoqim" (no. 718), "Alexa" (no. 725), "Yehoseph, son of Sha'ul" (no. 730).

The situation is similar to the so-called Yeshua' family tomb, in which four ossuaries do not contain patronymics. Two of the ossuaries are of women. Just one of these ossuaries, however, has a patronymic. It is possible to suggest a number of different potential relationships for the individuals whose names are inscribed on these ossuaries. For example, it is possible that Antigona was the wife of Yehoqim. It is possible that she was the wife of Sha'ul (no. 716). It is possible that she was the wife of Yehoseph bar Sha'ul (no. 730). Of course, it is possible to argue that Antigona was an unmarried daughter or sister of someone in the tomb. Moreover, someone could suggest that she was the mother of Yehoseph bar Sha'ul (no. 730), or the mother of Yehoqim, or the mother of Sha'ul (no. 716). Conversely, it could be suggested that Alexa married Yehoqim and that Antigona was the daughter of Alexa. Or maybe Yehoqim married Antigona, and Alexa was the daughter of Antigona. It is even possible that Alexa is a shortened form of the personal name Alexander, and so this may be a man, not a woman. These are all possible relational scenarios, but it may be that none of them is correct. It could

---

42. Cf. Joseph A. Fitzmyer, "Review of *The Jesus Family Tomb*," *America: The National Catholic Weekly* 196/13 (2007): 36-37.

43. Rahmani, *Catalogue*, pp. 224-28, nos. 712-35.

be that Antigona and Alexa were the maternal aunts of Yehoqim. It could be that these two were the daughters of Sha'ul (no. 716). It could be, however, that the people buried within the ossuaries without inscriptions were the closest relatives.

Here is the point: All of this is sheer speculation. Therefore, it would be irresponsible to postulate relationships and suggest that they can be understood as probable or cogent. Rather, the most that can be said is that this was arguably a family tomb and those interred there are related in some fashion. Someone might retort that it is plausible to argue that at least one relationship can be posited with some certitude, namely, that Sha'ul (no. 716) was the father of Yehoseph bar Sha'ul (no. 730). I can affirm that this is a reasonable proposal, but I am compelled to state that this too could be wrong. After all, Sha'ul (no. 716) could be the son of Yehoseph bar Sha'ul (no. 730). And there are more possibilities. It could be that there are collateral lines in the tomb. For example, it could be that Yehoseph (no. 730) and Yehoqim were both the sons of a certain Sha'ul and for this reason both Yehoseph and Yehoqim named sons after their father. After all, the practice of papponymy was quite common and there would have been no confusing these two grandsons with the same first name, as their patronymics would be different. That is, one would be known as Sha'ul bar Yehoqim and the other as Sha'ul bar Yehoseph. In sum, even with something as seemingly helpful as a patronymic, absolute certitude is elusive. That is, the data that are not known dwarf many times over the data that are known.

Similarly, in a single-chambered loculi tomb excavated in the Kidron Valley (near Silwan), twelve ossuaries were found.[44] The department retained nine of these, seven of which were inscribed. The personal names on these ossuaries are as follows: "Shimon son of Yannai" (no. 61),[45] "Hagadum" (no. 62), "Yehoshua'" (no. 63), "Mariam" (no. 64),[46] "Shallum" (no. 66), "Martha, daughter of Hananyah" (no. 67), "Yehonatan" (no. 68). Within this corpus are two patronymics, one for a certain Shimon and one for a certain Martha. Obviously, from the perspective of an epigrapher, it is very nice to see inscriptions on ossuaries. Nevertheless, attempting to posit relationships on the ba-

44. Ibid., pp. 91-94, nos. 61-69.

45. This ossuary also contains the word *št*. This could be the Aramaic word for "six," but it could also be the name of an additional person, namely, "Seth." See the discussion in Rahmani, *Catalogue*, p. 92.

46. Note that the name is written on the ossuary twice. Once it is spelled Mariam and once it is spelled Mairam. The spelling Mairam can reasonably be considered to be a mistake.

sis of seven inscribed ossuaries, with just two patronymics, is precarious. After all, five of the inscribed ossuaries have no patronymics. Furthermore, none of these ossuaries contains a title. Also, none of these ossuaries contains a statement such as "wife of," or "husband of," or "daughter of." Obviously, one could engage in endless speculation about the possible nexus of relationships, but this would not be a productive academic venture.

Sometimes, however, more epigraphic data are present in a tomb complex. For example, another tomb in the Kidron Valley was excavated and a total of nineteen ossuaries were discovered. Of these the department considered sixteen to be of sufficient importance to retain (i.e., three plain, uninscribed ossuaries were deacquisitioned).[47] Thirteen of the ossuaries were inscribed. The personal names on the ossuaries are as follows: "Our father, Shim'on (the) Elder, Yehoseph his son" (no. 12), "Shalom, wife of Eleazar" (no. 13), "Yo'ezer [son of Ye]hoseph" (no. 15), "Yehoseph son of Shim'on" (16),[48] "Hel'azar son of Shet" (no. 17), "Shim'on son of Alexa" (no. 18), "Eleazar" (no. 20), "Mother" (no. 21), "Yehoseph" (no. 22), "Salome" (no. 23),[49] "Shalom, wife of Yehudah" (no. 24),[50] "Shelamsiyon, daughter of Shimon" (no. 26), "Shalon, daughter of Li'azar" (no. 27). Obviously, this tomb provides a substantial amount of prosopographic data that are very helpful, for example, patronymics for a number of males and patronymics for two of the women. Also of import is that for two of the women the names of their husbands are provided. This sort of information is rare and particularly welcome. Another useful datum is that one of the women is referred to as "mother." Furthermore, there is a reference to Shim'on the Elder (no. 12), and this nomenclature would suggest that there was a Shim'on the Younger. To be sure, based on the prosopographic data provided by the inscriptions, it would be possible to plot out a number of the relationships.

Nevertheless, to be quite honest, even with all of these data, a large number of questions would still remain. For example, the inscription "Simon'on the Elder, Yehoseph his son" (no. 12), could be understood to mean that both of these individuals were buried in the same ossuary (thus ac-

47. Rahmani, *Catalogue*, pp. 77-82, nos. 12-27.

48. The name Yehoseph is also written on this ossuary (but without a patronymic), in a different place. Both of these could be referring to the same person, although it is possible that this is not the case.

59. The letters *šlm* are also inscribed on this ossuary. This could be the word "peace," but, of course, it could also simply be the Semitic spelling of the personal name Salome.

50. This name is written in full twice (once in Aramaic, once in Hebrew).

counting for the presence of both names on the same ossuary). This would mean that "Yehoseph son of Shim'on" (no. 16) was a different person from the previous Yehoseph (of no. 12). However, the inscription could also be read as "Simon'on the Elder, Yehoseph [was] his son" (no. 12). In this case, the person interred in the ossuary inscribed "Yehoseph son of Shim'on" (no. 16) could indeed be the same Yehoseph named in inscription no. 12. Of course, then the question arises about the kinship ties of the person interred in the ossuary labeled simply "Yehoseph" (no. 22). It could be that he (no. 22) was the father of Shim'on the Elder.[51] Perhaps, though, this Yehoseph (no. 22) was the son of Yehoseph son of Shim'on (no. 16).[52] Furthermore, that one of the interred women was known affectionately as "mother" (no. 21) is priceless, but whose mother was she and who was her husband? Was her husband interred in one of the inscribed ossuaries, or in one of the uninscribed ossuaries? Also, it is useful to know that Shalom was the wife of Yehudah (no. 24), but there is no ossuary inscribed with the name "Yehudah."[53] Was her husband interred in one of the uninscribed ossuaries? Was he buried in an inscribed ossuary, but one with someone else's name on it (e.g., because they predeceased him and no one subsequently added his name)? Conversely, was he buried in a different tomb altogether? If so, why? Also, is the Eleazar named on the ossuary inscribed "Shalom, wife of Eleazar" (no. 13), to be identified with the individual interred in the ossuary inscribed "Eleazar" (no. 20)? Perhaps so, but perhaps she is the mother or grandmother of the Eleazar of ossuary no. 20.[54] Obviously, therefore, even with a fair amount of prosopographic data, an attempt to reconstruct the precise nexus of relationships for those interred in a tomb will be most difficult, and ultimately speculative. Similarly, with regard to the so-called Yeshua' family tomb, any attempt to delineate the nexus of relationships must be considered sheer speculation. We simply do not have the data to delineate these relationships with any degree of certitude.

51. That is, because of the practice of papponymy the father of Shimon the Elder might very well have been named Yehoseph.

52. After all, patronymy was also an established practice.

53. Note that it is entirely possible that this woman's name was not Shalom or Shallum and that she is unnamed. That is, it could be that the letters *šlm* should simply be understood as the word "peace" and so the inscription should be understood as meaning "Peace, O wife of Yehudah."

54. The mother or grandmother argument becomes possible because of the practices of papponymy and patronymy.

The Yeshua' Family Tomb, DNA, and Statistics:
The (Mis)Use of Data

Naturally, some might retort that there are DNA data from the Talpiot Yeshua' family tomb and use these data to argue that a more secure statement of relationships can be made. There have indeed been some attempts to appeal to DNA evidence, but the DNA evidence simply cannot carry the freight that has been placed on it. For example, Jacobovici and Pellegrino have stated that the laboratory was able to recover sufficient bone material from the Yeshua' ossuary and the Mariame ossuary for mitochondrial DNA analysis (but not enough for nuclear DNA analysis). Because the mitochondrial DNA (which reveals data about maternal ancestry) did not "match," they have *assumed* that Yeshua' and Mariame were married. Nevertheless, a number of potential relationships can be posited that would account for the DNA evidence. For example, perhaps they were father-in-law and daughter-in-law, or perhaps they were brother-in-law and sister-in-law. In fact, they could have been brother and sister (with different mothers, but the same father)! Of course, it could even be that Mariame and Yeshua' were paternal aunt and nephew. Numerous options present themselves. Jacobovici and Pellegrino state that the DNA does not "negate [their] conclusion,"[55] but this is much different from *proving* their conclusion. Of course, there is also no means of determining with certainty that the bones analyzed are those of the person whose name is inscribed on the ossuary.[56]

Furthermore, with regard to the analyses of the patinas on the Talpiot ossuaries and those of the Ya'akov ossuary, certain things should be stated. (1) The origin and chain of custody for the Ya'akov ossuary are not known, and it is not possible to reconstruct it with any certitude (nor is it even possible to establish the authenticity of the entire inscription). (2) Several laboratories (including the GSI) have actually *authenticated modern forgeries* during recent years; therefore, the field of epigraphy should be very cautious about credulously accepting a laboratory analysis. There is, after all, a human component to laboratory tests as well. (3) There has been no indication that the laboratory tests were double-blind (a standard practice within the hard sciences). (4) Furthermore, I would suggest that (a) ossuaries made from the same basic Jerusalem limestone and stored in rock-hewn tombs of

55. Jacobovici and Pellegrino, *Jesus Family Tomb*, p. 173.
56. Eric M. Meyers, "The Jesus Tomb Controversy: An Overview," *NEA* 69 (2006): 117.

the same city can have similar patinas, and that (b) the control group must be very large for decisive statements to be made about the differences between the patinas on ossuaries in Jerusalem tombs of the same chronological horizon. Therefore, any attempt to use these patina analyses as corroborating evidence is most precarious indeed.[57] Ultimately, it is readily apparent that the DNA tests performed are not sufficient to permit the positing of a complete nexus of relationships in the face of a dearth of the necessary prosopographic data, nor are the patina tests sufficient for demonstrating that the Ya'akov ossuary hailed from the Talpiot tomb.

Feuerverger has argued that his statistical analysis of the data strongly supports the contention that this tomb is that of Jesus of Nazareth and certain members of his family. Feuerverger posted an open letter describing his basic premises and assumptions.[58] The contents of this letter are telling and reveal a number of problematic presuppositions that formed the basis for his statistical analysis. For example, he wrote: "we assume that 'Mariamēnou ē Mara' is a singularly highly appropriate appellation for Mary Magdalene." However, he concedes that "this assumption is contentious and furthermore that this assumption drives the outcome of the computations substantially." However, I contend that although Mary Magdalene could be referred to as Mariame (or Mariamne), the fact remains that there is no topographicon ("Magdalene") inscribed on this ossuary. Moreover, there were many people in the Late Second Temple period with the name Mary, Mariam, Mariame, Mariamne. Therefore, there is absolutely no reason for Feuerverger to "assume" that the name Mariame (or even Mariamne) on the ossuary should be considered a "highly appropriate appellation for Mary Magdalene." Also, regarding the presence of the name Mar(th)a(h), there is no reason to assume that this must be a title on the ossuary (meaning something along the lines of "lordess"). After all, this is a perfectly acceptable personal name and it is attested in the onomasticon of the Late Second Temple period. Could it be a title? Yes, but there is no reason to assume that it must be. Also, Feuerverger states that "it is assumed that Yose/Yosa is not the same person as the father

57. For a discussion of some of the problems with the laboratory tests on the Ya'akov ossuary, reference to protocols for laboratory tests, and discussion of erroneous results from labs, see Christopher A. Rollston, "Non-Provenanced Epigraphs I: Pillaged Antiquities, Northwest Semitic Forgeries, and Protocols for Laboratory Tests," *Maarav* 10 (2003): 182-91.

58. The citations here are from Andrey Feuerverger's open letter. The formal publication of his statistical analysis is "Statistical Analysis of an Archaeological Find," *Annals of Applied Statistics* 2 (2008): 3-54.

Yosef who is referred to on the ossuary of Yeshua." However, I have noted that this assumption may be erroneous: they may be the same person, and so to assume that they are not the same person and allow that to be factored into a statistical analysis is an Achilles' heel for Feuerverger. In addition, Feuerverger states that "the presence of Matya does not invalidate the find" and that "we also assume that the Yehuda son of Yeshua ossuary does not invalidate the find, but we ignore it in the computations." He then goes on to concede that "this last assumption is contentious." Obviously, Feuerverger's decision *not* to factor in (as negative evidence) the *presence* of names such as Yehudah bar Yeshua' and Mattiyah is particularly problematic. After all, there is no ancient evidence that Jesus of Nazareth fathered a child named Yehudah and the closest known relative of Jesus of Nazareth with the name Matthew was a great-grandfather (Matt 1:14-16)! It seems reasonable to state that Feuerverger's decision to avoid including data that militated against his hypothesis is a critical flaw in his statistical analysis, as is his decision to weigh certain aspects of the (limited) evidence very heavily. I am confident that statisticians will be critiquing Feuerverger's data in some detail, but I would simply state that generating statistics on the basis of a constellation of problematic assumptions is bemusing. That is, I would have *assumed* that a statistician would have been much more methodologically savvy.

Thomas Lambdin's famous dictum is that within the field we often "work with no data." This is a hyperbole, but the fact remains that we do work with partial data, and sometimes the data we have are just plain opaque. With the Talpiot tomb, there is a dearth of prosopographic data and this is a fact. There are no titles inscribed on the ossuaries, and this is a fact. There are no geographica, and this is a fact. Also, there are no associated epigraphic materials in the tomb (e.g., an associated document with some historical data). Based on the dearth of epigraphic evidence, it is simply not possible to make assumptions about the relationships of those buried therein, and it is certainly not tenable to suggest that the data are sufficient to posit that this is the family tomb of Jesus of Nazareth. Finally, it should be stated that at this juncture there is nothing in the statistical or laboratory data that can sufficiently clarify the situation.

DNA AND PATINA:
IMPROVING METHODOLOGIES

A Review of the Significance of the DNA Findings from the Talpiot Tomb

Mark Spigelman

Introduction

The video *The Lost Tomb of Jesus* contained excerpts that allege that the ossuaries with relevant inscriptions may contain ancient DNA (aDNA) of the interred individuals who may be a *"husband and wife,"* and that this allegedly gave credence and even provided evidence to the theory that this tomb may be the tomb of the Galilean Jesus Christ and his family. This paper will focus on the evidence as presented and discuss how factual the claims could be.

Disclaimers/Comments

I am forced to focus my assessment purely on the images from the video since the results of any experiments have never been published in any acceptable refereed journal nor have they been independently verified. The video evidence lacked many aspects of methodology and a time line; I will further discuss this weakness in my conclusion. It is difficult to accept findings that may help change the basic beliefs of billions of people that have never been presented for critical review in a proper forum of peers.

However, the Lakehead laboratory where the work was performed and the chief researcher, Dr. Carney Matheson, are well known to me. Indeed, Carney worked in our laboratory in Jerusalem for a lengthy period of time prior to getting his doctorate; I was also one of his referees in his application for his post at Lakehead. I wish to state that from a technical point the laboratory work would have been done at a very high standard by an extremely capable researcher who can be regarded as one of the pioneers in aDNA research.

Background

The discovery of the chemical structure of the double-stranded helix of deoxyribonucleic acid (DNA) by Crick and Watson opened this new world in medical research in the same manner as the voyage of Columbus.[1] DNA can be found in all organic matter.

DNA is found in the 23 pairs of chromosomes within the nucleus of each cell of the human body, made up in the varied patterns of some thirty thousand genes that constitute the blueprints that make each of us unique. Half of the chromosomes come from each parent, with 22 matched pairs plus one X chromosome from the mother and a corresponding X or Y from the father. If the father contributes an X, the baby will be female; if he contributes a Y, the baby will be male.

The use of DNA to help in understanding the past commenced with the first extraction and cloning of "ancient" DNA from preserved biological material from the skin of an extinct zebra species in 1984, followed shortly after by the extraction and cloning of the DNA from an Egyptian mummy from 500 BCE, soon after the same group extracted mitochondrial DNA (mtDNA) from a 7,000-year-old Egyptian mummy.[2]

The development of the polymerase chain reaction (PCR) by Mullis and Faloona may be one of the major technical advances in molecular genetics.[3] Its importance lies in the ability to amplify traces of DNA either fragmented or intact by a simple technique. The PCR is the method by which a single portion of DNA or RNA can be enzymatically reproduced indefinitely. This permits study from a miniscule sample of tissue. By its use we

1. James D. Watson and Francis Crick, "The Molecular Structure of Nucleic Acids: A Structure for Deoxyribose Nucleic Acid," *Nature* 171 (1953): 737-38.

2. See, respectively, R. Higuchi, B. Bowman, M. Freiberger, O. Ryder, and A. Wilson, "DNA Sequences from a Quagga, an Extinct Member of the Horse Family," *Nature* 312 (1984): 282-84; S. Paabo, J. A. Gifford, and A. Wilson, "Mitochondrial DNA Sequences from a 7000 Year Old Brain," *Nucleic Acids Research* 16/20 (1988): 9775-87; S. Paabo, "Preservation of DNA in Ancient Egyptian Mummies," *Journal of Archaeological Science* 12 (1985): 411-17.

3. K. Mullis and F. Faloona, "Specific Synthesis of DNA in Vitro via a Polymerase Catalysed Chain Reaction," *Methods Enzymology* 155 (1987): 335-50.

can amplify in a few hours over a million copies of a piece of DNA of 50-2,000 or more base pairs (bp) or the letters of the genetic code. In theory a single target molecule in a complex mixture can be thus amplified. The important reagents are a pair of single-strand oligonucleotides (primers) synthesized to be complementary to known sequences of the DNA of the organism being sought.

This became the basis of the study of aDNA in humans, since with the death of the individual the decomposers quickly act to degrade and destroy the DNA so that within a period of a few days the DNA is broken down into small segments mostly below 150 bp.

From ancient remains one of the most important substances that can be recovered is DNA. This appears to survive well though it does break down into fragments. Hagelberg and Sykes reported recovery of 5-10 micrograms of DNA from 2 grams of powdered cortical bone.[4] Their initial experiment suggested "preservation of DNA in a bone depends less on the age of the specimen than on the burial condition of the skeleton." The bones they studied had carbon 14 dates ranging from the seventeenth-century English civil war period to a cave burial at Wadi Makuq in the Judean Desert 5,450 years before the present.

Early on in this work it was recognized that contamination with modern-day DNA was a major problem, and strict precautions had to be taken to avoid this; further the title of aDNA could mistakenly apply to recent contaminants as young as a few weeks or months depending on conditions in the environment surrounding any specimen.

From any archaeological specimen we are now aware that there can be at least four sources of aDNA that may be amplified by the PCR reaction.

1. Nuclear DNA. The DNA of the 23 chromosomes found in the nucleus of every cell in the body.
2. Mitochondrial DNA. Mitochondria are the energy factories of all living cells. They are membrane-enclosed organelles. All living cells have mitochondria; their number varies in different cells, but there can be up to several thousand such organelles in a cell. The human mitochondrial genome is a circular DNA molecule of about 16 kilobases.[5] It en-

4. E. Hagelberg and B. Sykes, "Ancient Bone DNA Amplified," *Nature* 342 (1989): 485.

5. D. C. Chan, "Mitochondria: Dynamic Organelles in Disease, Aging, and Development," *Cell* 125 (2006): 1241-52.

codes 37 genes. As sperm cells have only chromosomal DNA, we acquire mtDNA from the cytoplasm of the mother's egg; hence its use in identifying family relationships. Research on aDNA has concentrated on the analysis of mtDNA fragments because the complete sequence of the 16,569-bp human mitochondrial genome is known. The high number of mitochondria in mammalian cells favors the survival of some mtDNA even in highly degraded samples. The unique maternal mode of inheritance of mtDNA is useful for some evolutionary and phylogenetic studies.

3. Any pathogenic microbe that may be present particularly in the blood at time of death. This was first reported in 1992, but as it has no relationship to the main topic, I will not comment on it further in this paper.[6]

4. Contaminant DNA from environmental bacteria and any animal or human contacts. This is the greatest threat to all work in this field, particularly in figures 1 and 2. As an anecdotal example of how easy it is to contaminate a sample, I recall many years ago I gave a student some sterile urine jars as he was going to Tel Qadash in Syria to excavate the site. I asked him to carefully open the jars (with full precautions, such as be quick, downwind, no talking), plunge them into a newly opened level from the Middle Bronze Age, close the jar, and without exposing them to direct sun bring them back for bacterial analysis. He did, and we cultured the surface of the sample only, as it was the least exposed. We grew an exuberant *Staph. capitis,* the major bacterium of dandruff. When I examined the student he had dandruff, and we grew the same bacteria from his scalp; thus a one- or two-second exposure allowed enough skin scales to float onto a specimen to contaminate it after being isolated for about 3,500 years.

Ancient DNA can provide us with different kinds of information about the human past. What are the questions we could pose if suitable DNA can be recovered?

1. Primary genetic markers might allow us to build a profile for identification and characterization (e.g., gender of remains).

6. M. Spigelman and E. Lemma, "The Use of the Polymerase Chain Reaction to Detect Mycobacterium Tuberculosis in Ancient Skeletons," *International Journal of Osteoarchaeology* 3 (1992): 137-43.

2. Given certain mutations such as found in thalassemia and in the mito-chondrial genome, it may be possible to pinpoint specific origins of the subjects.
3. Certain polymorphisms may give evidence of population affinities.
4. DNA fingerprinting techniques, highly developed in forensic medi-cine, can be brought into play to determine kinship.

As the science of aDNA progressed, certain rules were laid down and have become standard practice for all workers and laboratories in the field. These require stringent precautions not only in the laboratory but also in the field when collecting specimens. We became aware of the dangers of con-tamination with modern DNA, which if present would be better preserved and thus likely to be overrepresented in any extraction, leading to false posi-tive results.

In the field it is important to avoid contamination; in a paper on this topic I stressed the need to avoid direct contact with the collected specimen and the handling of the specimens by fieldworkers and how to prevent con-tamination as well as how to store and transport any collected specimen.[7] The need to check the DNA of all possible contacts with the specimens is also important. The problems concerning this point in relation to the film will be discussed below.

In the laboratory stringent rules have been laid down for handling and working with these fragile specimens.[8] Most are technical, and as I am famil-iar with the high standards at the Lakehead laboratory, I will assume they have met most of the criteria. But three points raised in this paper will need further discussion as they relate to the *Lost Tomb of Jesus:*

a. Repeat of the experiment with positive results.
b. Independent verification.
c. Cloning. (The process of moving a gene or the DNA sequence-of-interest you have found from one DNA molecule to another DNA molecule is called *cloning*.) In the cloning process a fragment of DNA containing a gene- or sequence-of-interest is cloned (moved) into a vector where it can subsequently be grown (copied) and selected in

7. M. Spigelman, "The Archaeologist and Ancient Bio-molecules: Field Sampling Strategies to Enhance Recovery," *Papers from the Institute of Archaeology* 7 (1996): 69-74.

8. A. Cooper and H. N. Poinar, "Ancient DNA: Do It Right or Not at All," *Science* 289 (2000): 530-31.

large quantities and manipulated in a variety of ways. The most common vectors are bacterial plasmids, but viruses and self-replicating units in eukaryotic cells are also employed as vectors.

The Evidence Seen on Video

The Site

Ten ossuaries, or receptacles for the reburial of skeletal remains of the dead, were found during an excavation of a tomb in 1980 in a southern suburb of Jerusalem known as East Talpiot. The tomb was dated between the late first century BCE and 70 CE.[9] We know that Kloner in his report noted ten ossuaries and 35 skeletons in what was a disturbed tomb, though we know that the bones were never studied (J. Zias, personal communication).

The ossuaries were initially taken to the Rockefeller Museum in East Jerusalem and sometime later transferred to Beth Shemesh. Only nine of the ten ossuaries from the tomb are at present in the Israel Antiquities Authority storerooms in Beth Shemesh (nos. 501-508/1980). We do not know who may have looked inside any of the ossuaries during the twenty-five years of storage or if at any time the lids were removed for any period of time.

Sampling

The sampling as seen on the video is done on one ossuary with three people in attendance at the time, Prof. S. Pfann, Dr. S. Cox, and S. Jocobovici, and all three appear to put their arms in part at least into the box. I have been informed that the sampling was done using unsterile containers and a single spatula (figs. 1-3). Further I was informed that at the time of sampling no thought was given to DNA work and thus (as is obvious) no precautions were taken against contamination (Pfann and Cox, personal communication). Looking at the video I could not see any evidence of bones in the main sample shown. The material looked like sand and perhaps flakes of plaster from the ossuary.

9. A. Kloner, "A Tomb with Inscribed Ossuaries in East Talpiyot, Jerusalem," 'Atiqot 29 (1996): 15-22.

Laboratory

The items are then transferred to the Lakehead laboratory, where the DNA work is performed by Dr. Carney Matheson, who is not aware of where the samples came from and is allegedly asked to look for any DNA in the samples (C. Matheson, personal communication). We are not given any idea of the mode of transport, the way the samples are packaged, how they are stored, or the time period for the transfer. The laboratory was apparently able to recover sufficient bone material from the Yeshuaʿ ossuary and the Mariam(n)e ossuary for mtDNA analysis (but could not find any nuclear DNA). However, we are not informed how the bone was recovered from the sand or if just a sample of the sand was taken for analysis. Further we know that in this tomb there were far more bodies then ossuaries, so multiple bodies were placed in each ossuary. To check for such a possibility the base of the ossuary should have been divided by a grid into segments and a sample taken from each segment for comparison.

The discussion of the results confirms that no nuclear DNA can be found, only mtDNA, though they do not mention from which part of the mitochondrial genome the sample came or the size of the DNA chain amplified. Further we are told that the mitochondrial evidence suggests that the two different sequences from the mitochondria confirm that they are not the same person and thus must have had two different mothers (though not necessarily different fathers). In the absence of nuclear DNA the gender of the two individuals cannot be determined; thus to say these two people could be husband and wife is scientifically unsustainable.

Conclusion

The finding of two segments of mtDNA from two individuals by a respected laboratory is not in dispute. What is in great doubt is where these bits of DNA came from. The findings do not in any way support the theory that this could be the DNA of Jesus and Mary Magdalene as appears to be implied.

1. The sampling as seen would have ensured that there was contamination with contemporaneous DNA, so the first step would have been to take samples from the three people seen to have their hands in and around the ossuary.
2. We actually have no idea what material was sampled.

3. We have no idea how many people have looked inside the ossuaries since the burial; they may include robbers in antiquity and anybody who entered the tomb when it was first excavated. Thus the DNA of the archaeologists Kloner (deceased), Gibson, and Zias should be checked, as well as the three people seen in figure 3. Not finding a match to the mtDNA of these people would not remove doubt about authenticity but would take away some of the most recent suspects.

4. From the video we cannot be sure if the mtDNA found belongs to a human or a rodent.

Further Work

There may be more information gained if a proper further excavation is made of the tomb. My experience in this is that when skeletons are removed from a tomb small bones and bone chips may still remain in the dust on the floor; if we can find these and collect them scientifically this may give us the information needed to help determine if this was indeed a family tomb. But it will never tell us whose family, and the information will not be of value in determining if this was the tomb of the family of Joseph and Mary.

The Potential Role of Patina History in Discerning the Removal of Specific Artifacts from Specific Tombs

Charles Pellegrino

Introduction and Development of Methods

Based on the hypothesis that every burial site, in every cavity in the earth, develops its own distinctive and easily identifiable chemical history, recorded in its patina, we viewed the 2005 rediscovery of (and access to) the Talpiot tomb as an opportunity to test this premise against freshly collected patina samples from the walls and ceiling of the tomb, and against ossuaries separated from this same tomb environment and stored in the Israel Antiquities Authority (IAA) warehouse since 1980, for comparison against patina evidence from other local tombs.

During the initial tests (Jan. 30, Feb. 7, and March 20, 2006) six Talpiot tomb wall patina samples were separated from their Jerusalem chalk matrix using nonmetallic tools. The elemental spectra of the samples were compared using S.E.M. and X-ray diffraction. Each sample was "pinged" in a minimum of three locations, standardized with the Calcium Beta peak calibrated to a height of approximately 50%.

This initial series was aimed at standardizing methods and probing the

Sincerest thanks to Robert Genna and Linda Parise (Suffolk Crime Lab), to fiber expert Clyde Wells, to Amnon Rosenfeld and Areh E. Shimron (Israel Geological Survey), Prof. Vertolli (Royal Ontario Museum), to Shimon Gibson — and for some of the most fascinating discussions and analyses relevant to this study, Simcha Jacobovici, James Cameron, and Jesuit scholar "Fr. John MacQuitty." Special thanks also to Andrey Feueverger, James Tabor, James Charlesworth, Doug McClean, Billy Schutt, and Fr. Mervyn Fernando.

233

possibility that the individual chemistry of multiple microenvironments within the Talpiot tomb (and by implication within other tombs) might prove so variable that the patina on the tomb wall was distinct from the patina on every ossuary; and that each ossuary patina might in its own turn be different from others in this same tomb — falsifying, at once, the premise of identifying any object as originating from a specific tomb on the basis of "patina fingerprinting."

The outermost patina layers (as revealed by elemental spectra) were dominated by condensates from *terra rosa* soil — which had begun flowing into the tomb following an ancient breach of the antechamber's seal stone (Shimon Gibson, personal communication). The elemental spectrum of the Talpiot tomb's outer (younger) patina layers were as follows. The tomb's *terra rosa* phase (fig. 1, fig. 2) was characterized by dominant carbon and oxygen peaks (contributed by leaching from the Jerusalem chalk bedrock); followed by what was later diagnosed as an atypical depletion (to extinction) of the sodium peak; followed by *"trace"* amounts of magnesium (defined as 5%-20% height of Ca Beta peak); followed by *"enriched"* levels of aluminum and silicon (defined as approximately equal to or above Ca Beta peak); followed by a phosphorous-dominant ratio of phosphorous-to-sulfur; followed by trace levels of chlorine and potassium; followed by calcium enrichment (from Jerusalem chalk); followed by trace levels of titanium (5%-20% of Ca Beta peak); followed by a *"strong trace"* of iron (defined as 25%-35% of Ca Beta peak).

Variation among all Talpiot tomb wall and ceiling samples was less than 5%.

The tomb patina remained consistent with the elemental spectra of four isolated patina samples from Talpiot ossuary no. 80-500 ("Mariamene"), three isolated patina samples from ossuary no. 80-502 ("Matthew"), and five isolated patina samples from ossuary no. 80-503 ("Jesus, son of Joseph").

Variation within this same tomb environment for patina samples from ossuaries and walls was again within 5% for each given element.

Significantly, for the artifacts tested, we determined that the method was reasonably noninvasive (requiring samples no larger than 1 sq. mm.).

Having demonstrated that microenvironments within an individual tomb did not appear to vary widely, a second series of tests was designed to probe the alterative possibility that every corner of every tomb in the same local geology of the Jerusalem hills might have experienced essentially the same chemical history as the Talpiot tomb. Instead of extreme intratomb variation rendering the method invalid, it could have been rendered equally invalid by the possibility that exceedingly small intertomb variations had

Patina Source	Carbon	Oxygen	Na	Mg	Al	Si	P	S	Cl	K	Ca	Ti	Fe	Cu	Other + Notes
Talpiot Tomb Wall	*	*		✓	*	*	O		✓	✓	*	✓	✓+		
"Jesus"	*	*		✓	*	*	O		✓	✓	*	✓	✓+		
"Mariamene"	*	*		✓	*	*	O		✓	✓	*	✓	✓+		
"Matthew"	*	*		✓	*	*	O	O	✓	✓	*	✓	✓+	?	Cu: Questionable Trace
"James"	*	*	?	✓	*	*	O		✓	✓	*	✓	✓+	?	Na, Cu: Questionable Trace
# 19,20,23	*	*	✓	✓	*	*		*		✓	*	✓	✓+		Patina Layers Variable with sulfer Enrichment
#2H8	*	(-)		✓	*						*	*			
#29	(-)	(-)		✓	✓	✓		O			(-)	✓			
#P3,P6	*	*		✓	✓	*	*		?	✓	*		✓		
#P7	*	*		✓	✓	*	O			?	*		?		K,Fe Questionable or Barely detectable trace
#P2	*	(-)		✓	✓	✓	O				*				
#15	*	*			✓		O				*				
#14	*	(-)	✓	✓	✓		*	*			*				
#30	*	(-)	✓	✓	✓	✓	*		*	✓	*				
#26	(-)	(-)	✓	✓	✓	✓	*		✓+	?	*		?		Fe: Questionalbe Trace
#P5	*	*		✓	✓		*				*				
#P8	*	*		✓	✓	✓+	O	(-)			*				
Shroud Tomb	*	*		✓	✓	*	O	O			*				Variable Distint Patina Layers, Including 1mm depth Si dominant

Fig. 1.
Patina signatures of 14 variable trace elements of 14 tombs (not counted among the 14 tombs: the "James" ossuary, of unknown origin).This series represents the surface (youngest) patina layer only. Elemental signatures are grouped together in order of closest similarity. Electron micro-probe scale standardized with Ca Beta peak at 50% height of Ca peak.
Key:
"O" indicates sulfur dominant vs. phosphorus dominant.
(-): Depleted (defined as anomalously low levels, compared to other Tomb Patinas, and in particular to calcium carbonate matrix).
"?": Barely detectable or questionable trace (against background noise).
"✓": Trace (5% - 20% height of Ca Beta peak).
"✓+" Strong trace (up to or above 30% Ca Beta peak).
"*": Enriched (approximately equal to or above Ca Beta peak).

covered every object in every tomb from Talpiot to the Mount of Olives with the same elemental spectrum — in which case the Talpiot tomb ossuary and wall patinas would have looked alike because all tombs from this region displayed essentially the same elemental spectrum.

Therefore, multiple ossuary patinas, covering objects carved from the same Jerusalem chalk matrix and representing a minimum of fourteen tombs from the Jerusalem region were investigated using this same method.

As a further preliminary test, the patina of a fifteenth object (the controversial "James" ossuary) was compared with the results, to determine whether it could be definitively excluded from any or all of the fourteen test tombs, or whether it might remain provisionally consistent with the patina fingerprints of one or more tombs.

Results

The elemental spectra presented in figure 1 were derived from a minimum of two pings of each tomb ossuary sample (generally with a minimum of two samples from each ossuary and/or tomb). The initial six tomb patinas are represented by up to ten sample zones, the subsequent five by up to four pings. Figure 2 shows representative samples of four elemental spectra. For later samples, after verification that different tomb patina signatures were immediately apparent with repeatable results, a minimum of two pings (and generally three) were judged sufficient.

The results suggest that individual burial sites, even when located in the same geologic matrix, tend to be chemically distinct; and any object removed from a given burial site should also echo the same, private chemical history of magnesium, titanium, and other trace elements.

Of the thirteen additional tombs whose patinas were examined and compared, only one (designated by samples 19, 20, and 23) came close to resembling the Talpiot tomb's elemental spectrum. However, even here a major difference was immediately apparent: though both tombs' patina signatures were consistent with ancient intrusions of the local, titanium- and iron-rich agricultural soil known as *terra rosa,* this closest similarity to the Talpiot tomb's elemental spectrum was significantly enriched with sulfur (one of 15 elemental variables within a patina fingerprint) — to such an extent that the sulfur content within the second tomb exceeded the *terra rosa* signature's already high ("strong trace," up to or above 50% of the Ca Beta peak) iron content. By contrast, except for a barely detectable trace in the "Matthew" ossuary's patina, there was no sulfur at all in the Talpiot tomb samples. Sodium in the absence of chlorine was also noted for the second tomb (samples 19, 20, 23).

The data in figure 1 are presented in descending order of similarity to the Talpiot tomb's patina fingerprint (or elemental spectrum). Although no other tomb in the sample was consistent with the Talpiot patina, from a forensic archaeological perspective, the after-the-fact probability (after having picked a specific tomb or artifact for comparison to, say, the Talpiot tomb) is

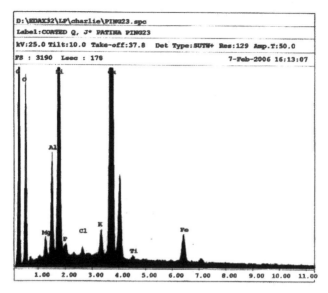

Ping 23 illustrates the typical elemental spectrum of the Talpiot Tomb's wall
and ossuary patina. This particular patina sample is from the Jesus ossuary.

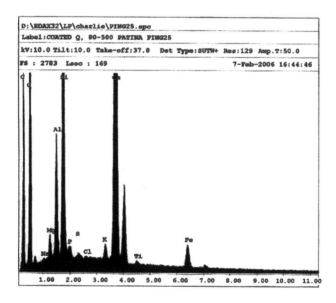

Ping 25 probed the "Mariamene" patina, verifying that it was, in all essentials,
an echo of the elemental spectrum revealed everywhere else in this same tomb.

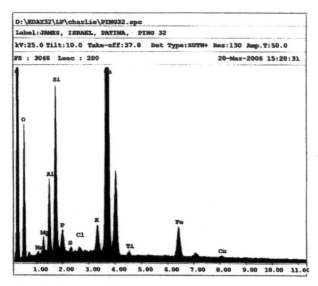

Ping 32 probed the elemental spectrum (or patina fingerprint) of the James ossuary.

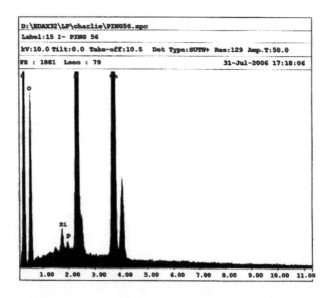

Ping 56 is an average, representative patina fingerprint from another ossuary tomb. There are no iron, titanium, or potassium peaks typical of *terra rosa* soil. Other differences were also immediately apparent.

not nearly so important or instructive as the probability of any two tombs in the sample base randomly "echoing" each other. This has not occurred in the samples studied, and does not appear to be a likely event.

During this study, fifteen elemental markers (C, O, Na, Mg, Al, Si, [P/S ratio], Cl, K, Ca, Ti, Fe, Cu, possible miscellaneous traces) appeared sufficiently variable for identification merely by pinging the surface layer of a patina sample (that is, the most recent layer of chemical history). A second observed variable (fig. 3), rendering the principle of "patina fingerprinting" even more potentially useful, involves determining whether a tomb's chemistry changes through time.

If a tomb has not been breached, then unless long-term droughts or floods affect the flow of groundwater, or unless the soil content through which groundwater percolates has changed throughout time, a closed tomb's patina should remain relatively constant through the centuries.

Two breached tombs were included in the sample: the Talpiot tomb (breached by *terra rosa* mud, centuries in the past) and the Tomb of the Shroud (breached centuries ago by silica-, sulfur-, and calcium-rich water, and about two decades ago by inflows of *terra rosa* mud). The Shroud Tomb's patina (fig. 3) produced two distinct layers: an older layer of oxygen- and calcium-depleted material, succeeded by a layer significantly enriched with oxygen, silicon, and calcium (by greater than 75%). The second layer also enclosed dark carbon granules (fig. 3). The *terra rosa* inflow, though filling the tomb a meter deep (just like the Talpiot tomb), did not, over the course of two decades, produce a detectable *terra rosa* patina layer (with its distinctive Ti and Fe signature) inside the Shroud Tomb, suggesting that at least several decades are required for the *terra rosa* signature to be recorded (and implying the possibility of a general, corroborative dating method). This finding was consistent with the Talpiot tomb patina's basal layer of apatite dominated patina — $Ca_5(PO_4)_3(OH)$ — which (fig. 3) formed during the (approximately) one thousand years preceding the *terra rosa* intrusion. The Talpiot tomb's younger, *terra rosa*–dominated patina layer was at least several orders of magnitude deeper than the apatite layer, consistent with at least several centuries of *terra rosa* phase patina formation.

A tomb partly open to the surface environment, in addition to variable patina layers, would also be expected to receive water inflows during different months (such inflows occurring at different temperatures) — which would (among other effects) deposit varying, temperature-dependent oxygen isotope ratios in the patina layers. Under this circumstance of partial exposure to the outside, limestone walls and limestone ossuaries should undergo more

Source	Carbon	Oxygen	Na	Mg	Al	Si	P	S	Cl	K	Ca	Ti	Fe	Other + Notes
Talpiot Tomb Stone Matrix	✱	✱	?	✓	✓	O					✱			
Jerusalem Chalk Stone Matrix	✱	✱	?	✓	✓	O					✱			
Talpiot Tomb Basal Patina Layer (Pre-Terra Rossa)	✱	✱	✓	✓	✓+	O					✱		✓	Eg: Ceiling (ping 8); "Jesus" (ping 9), Apatite Base.
"James" Ossuary Basal Patina Layer	✱	✱	✓	✓	✓+	O					✱		✓	Ping 42: Section free of P,Cl - contminated fibers
Talpiot Tomb Outer Patina Layer	✱	✱	✓	✱	✱	O		✓	✓		✱	✓	✓+	
"James" Ossuary Outer Patina Layer	✱	✱	?	✓	✱	✱	O	✓	✓		✱	✓	✓+	
Shroud Tomb Basal Patina Layer	✱	(-)	✓	✓	✓	✓	✱		✓		(-)			Brown Layer
Shroud Tomb Carbon Inclusion Patina Layer	✱	✱								✓	✓			
Shroud Tomb Outer Patina Layer	✱	✱	✓	✓	✱	O	O	✓			✱			Ca - Si Dominated

Fig. 3 Elemental signatures at different layers of patina, representing the Talpiot Tomb and the Shroud Tomb, compared against basal layer and upper layer of the "James" ossuary (of unknown provenance). Election micro-probe scale standardized with Ca Beta peak at 50% height of Ca peak.
Key:
"O" indicates sulfur dominant vs. phosphorus dominant.
(-): Depleted (defined as anomalously low levels, compared to other Tomb Patinas, and in particular to calcium carbonate matrix).
"?": Barely detectable or questionable trace (against background noise).
"✓": Trace (5% - 20% height of Ca Beta peak).
"✓+": Strong trace (up to or above 30% Ca Beta peak).
"✱": Enriched (approximately equal to or above Ca Beta peak).

extensive evaporative pitting and water-borne mineralization than in a sealed tomb — and this effect is evident in ossuary samples from both the Shroud Tomb and the Talpiot tomb — as, for example, in the extensive pitting around the letters and through all the ancient chisel marks, near the upper rim of Talpiot's "Matthew" ossuary. Similar weathering and redeposition effects are evident on Talpiot's "large cross mark" ossuary (where an inscription appears to have been obliterated by erosion), and on the "Jesus" ossuary's surface (most notably to the left of the "Yeshua" inscription).

Avner Ayalon, Miryam Bar-Matthews, and Yuval Goren have noted variable oxygen isotope ratios in patina samples from the "James" ossuary.[1]

1. "Authenticity Examination of the Inscription on the Ossuary Attributed to James, Brother of Jesus," *Journal of Archaeological Science* 31 (2004): 1185-89.

James Tabor had pointed out (personal communication) that the "James" ossuary's (prebreakage and repair) dimensions were consistent with a tenth ossuary that "went missing" during the 1980 excavation of the Talpiot tomb. While the consistent measurements appeared significant on first hearing, actual comparison with cross-matches between one hundred randomly selected, measured ossuaries (whose dimensions are largely determined by the length of the longest adult human bone, the femur) revealed that the "James" ossuary and the Talpiot tomb's "missing tenth" ossuary both represented a common size, and that cross-matches of ossuaries in this size range could occur with a frequency of almost 10%. Therefore, the "match," while not truly indicative of a relationship between the "James" ossuary and the "missing tenth," had nonetheless failed (as a major inconsistency would have succeeded) to definitively eliminate a Talpiot tomb origin for the "James" ossuary. For the purposes of this study, aside from failing to exclude the "James" ossuary, we did not consider the Tabor data to be significantly inclusive, because common size cross-matches of only three ossuary dimensions are significantly more likely to occur than, say, fifteen variable trace elements in a single patina layer.

At the Israel Geological Survey, Amnon Rosenfeld and Shimon Ilani performed independent electron microprobe analysis of patina samples from the "James" ossuary and sent us their results, along with the requisite microscopic sample. A second "James" ossuary sample was provided by Prof. Vertolli of the Royal Ontario Museum. Figure 1 and figure 3 illustrate how the elemental spectra of the Talpiot tomb's walls, ceiling, and ossuary patinas were exactly (and so far uniquely) consistent with the "James" patina, and with Rosenfeld and Ilani's electron microprobe results, using SEMs in different laboratories to examine the same patina.

We also noted (in the case of the "James" samples) extensive contamination by microshreds of paper-and-"rag"-based fibers overlaying the patina. The paper yielded high phosphorus and chlorine peaks, consistent with phosphate-based detergents of the late 1970s and early 1980s (and suggestive of an amateurish cleaning of the ossuary about that time, with detergent-soaked towels, presumably in preparation for the antiquities market).

The elemental spectra of the fourteen tombs whose patinas were tested proved distinct from the Talpiot tomb and, most significantly, from one another. A result of this is that patina analysis begins to look like a promising method, even for discerning differences between tombs carved out of the same bedrock and exposed to groundwater percolating down through soils of similar composition.

The results also proved useful in testing Tabor and Gibson's hypothesis (personal communication) that the former owner of the "James" ossuary had not been at all forthright about when he had acquired the artifact (allegedly sometime between 1977 and 1980). They suspected that he had actually purchased it much more recently than claimed, as plunder from the Tomb of the Shroud — which Tabor and Gibson had discovered, already extensively looted and vandalized, only a few months before the "James" ossuary's existence was announced in 2002.

Tabor reasoned that "of course" the man who purchased the "James" ossuary from the antiquities market would be required to claim that he acquired it sometime around 1977, because under Israeli law any antiquities purchased and linked to a tomb that could be demonstrated to have been discovered and excavated after January 1978 immediately became the property of the IAA. Because the Shroud Tomb, like the Talpiot tomb, had been filled to an approximately 1-meter depth by *terra rosa* soil (through a construction breach dated to about 1982), it became a very good candidate for a tomb patina most likely to resemble the Talpiot tomb. Simultaneously, it was an opportunity to see whether patina testing was sufficiently precise to definitively eliminate (in the case of a Shroud Tomb patina very different from the Talpiot tomb and "James" patinas) a possible candidate for tomb origin.

Figure 3 demonstrates how the Shroud Tomb's patina clearly eliminated it as a possible site of origin for the "James" ossuary. The results were also instructive in terms of estimating possible rates of patina formation. After approximately two decades of *terra rosa* inflow, the Shroud Tomb's patina did not record a detectable trace of the *terra rosa* signature, suggesting that at least several decades are necessary for its formation. The *terra rosa* phase dominates at least half of the Talpiot tomb's patina — which appears consistent with its first *terra rosa* inflows having occurred in antiquity. A second phase consistent with the Talpiot tomb's *terra rosa* phase also dominates the "James" patina to the same depth as the Talpiot patina.

Discussion and Conclusions

Certainly, more tombs and sites must be added to the data base (a task that is probably worthy of graduate theses for years to come — a task simplified by the wide accessibility of the equipment used for the patina testing method, and in the case of Israel's antiquities, by the fact that the IAA already warehouses more than one thousand ossuaries, each catalogued in accordance with location, specific tomb origin, and year of discovery).

242

Of particular interest, in terms of broadening the data base, is development of a clearer resolution of the probability with which any two objects buried in the same geologic matrix (for example, two objects from the Jerusalem hills, or the Valley of the Kings, or the buried city of Herculaneum) will produce, by chance, either the same or a very similar "patina fingerprint."

Against a background in which the elemental spectra from any two of fourteen tombs in the Jerusalem hills failed to yield the same signature, the method appears to be valid (or in the very least, quite promising). In terms of probability, the finding that none of the fourteen tombs whose patina signatures are known "match up" with each other is more significant than the fact that none of them echoes the Talpiot tomb patina. The number of variables is sufficiently large to have definitively excluded the "James" ossuary from an origin in the Shroud Tomb, or in any of the other tombs except one: the Talpiot tomb — with which both patina phases of the "James" ossuary (a basal apatite layer and a relatively younger *terra rosa* phase, as in fig. 3) were entirely consistent.

These findings do not address the question of whether individuals fraudulently enhanced the "James son of Joseph" inscription by adding the "brother of Jesus" portion (although personal communication from Amnon Rosenfeld regarding two sections of original, ancient patina in the *shin* or "brother of" portion of the inscription suggest that the controversy will continue to defy resolution). Regardless of the final verdict on the inscription (if such is possible), the likelihood that the "James" ossuary patina should randomly prove consistent with only the Talpiot tomb (and in particular with both patina phases) appears to be a low probability event.

The trifold "James" ossuary/Talpiot tomb congruence of thermal environment (in a partly open tomb, with inflows of the same rare, agricultural soil — *terra rosa* — at different temperatures, at different months, during a period of at least several decades, and likely centuries), a similar erosive environment (which had, for example, produced unusual, distinctive pitting in both the "James" ossuary and the "Matthew" ossuary), and a parallel patina environment point toward, rather than away from, the possibility (indeed, now a probability) that the "James" ossuary is the missing tenth ossuary, misappropriated from the Talpiot excavation about March 1980.

Even with a data base originally intended as a test of concept and method, these data point compellingly toward the conclusion that the current owner of the "James" ossuary did not purchase the object prior to the legal date of January 1978 (but, rather, in the aftermath of the 1980 Talpiot excavation), and that the object should be returned permanently to the IAA.

TALPIOT, A JESUS FAMILY, AND MARY MAGDALENE

The Talpiot "Jesus" Tomb: A Historical Analysis

James D. Tabor

This paper poses a simple question: Is there sufficient historical evidence to identify a modest first-century CE Jewish rock-hewn tomb, accidentally opened by a construction crew in 1980 in East Talpiot, just south of the Old City of Jerusalem, as the probable burial tomb of Jesus of Nazareth and his intimate family?

The first time this Talpiot "Jesus" tomb received any public attention was sixteen years after its excavation when a BBC-produced documentary titled *The Body in Question* aired in the United Kingdom on Easter 1996. The *London Sunday Times* ran a feature story titled "The Tomb that Dare Not Speak Its Name," based on that documentary.[1] Both the documentary and the newspaper article called attention to the interesting cluster of names inscribed on six ossuaries found in the tomb: Jesus son of Joseph, two Marys, a Joseph, a Matthew, and a Jude son of Jesus. A flurry of wire stories followed with headlines that the "tomb of Jesus" had perhaps been found. Archaeologists, officials from the Israel Antiquities Authority (IAA), and biblical scholars quickly weighed in, assuring the public that "the names were common." One lone voice, Joe Zias, an anthropologist with the IAA at the Rockefeller Museum in Jerusalem, demurred, stating that the *cluster* of names considered together was so significant that had he not known they were from a provenanced IAA excavation he would have been certain they were forged.[2]

---

1. *London Sunday Times,* March 31, 1996, p. 1.
2. Zias commented: "Had it not been found in a tomb I would have said 100 percent of what we are looking at are forgeries. But this came from a very good, undisturbed

Zias called for further investigation. Within a short time the press dropped the story, and no one in the academy other than Zias saw any reason for more to be done. It was in response to that 1996 story, and the attention that it drew, that Amir Drori, then director of the IAA, asked Amos Kloner to write up an official report on the tomb, published later that year in the IAA journal *'Atiquot*.[3]

The media attention quickly subsided, and other than Kloner's article no further academic evaluations of the tomb were published. That all changed in March 2007 with the broadcast of the Discovery Channel TV documentary *The Lost Tomb of Jesus* and the publication of the book, *The Jesus Family Tomb*, both of which argued that the Talpiot tomb was indeed the tomb of Jesus of Nazareth and his family — including Mary Magdalene his wife, and an otherwise unknown "Judah, son of Jesus," their son.[4] Both the film and the book have generated a massive worldwide reaction, characterized by passion, emotion, and heated debate. The academic world, the traditional media, and the Internet have all been abuzz with discussion. One might have expected strong opposition to the thesis of the book and film from more traditional Christian circles, but the negative assessment by a cadre of scholars, equally passionate in their denunciation of its hypotheses, has played a significant role in highlighting many of the important issues relevant to a proper scientific evaluation of the tomb and its contents. Unfortunately, more heat than light is often generated when the media serve as the primary forum for discussions involving such emotionally charged issues.

---

archaeological context. It is not something that was invented" (ibid.). Zias has since changed his mind and joined those scholars who hold that the names are so common in the period that their occurrence together is of no special significance.

3. Amos Kloner, "A Tomb with Inscribed Ossuaries in East Talpiot, Jerusalem," *'Atiquot* 29 (1996): 15-22. Two years earlier nine of the ossuaries were included in the catalogue description in L. Y. Rahmani, *A Catalogue of Jewish Ossuaries in the Collections of the State of Israel* (Jerusalem: Israel Antiquities Authority and Israel Academy of Sciences and Humanities, 1994), pp. 222-24. The late excavator Joseph Gath had published a short preliminary report in 1981, but before the ossuary inscriptions had been deciphered (*Hadashot Arkheologiyot* 76 [1981]: 24-26).

4. The Discovery Channel film was produced by Simcha Jacobovici and James Cameron, and the book was coauthored by Jacobovici and Charles Pellegrino, *The Jesus Family Tomb: The Discovery, the Investigation, and the Evidence That Could Change History* (San Francisco: HarperSanFrancisco, 2007). A revised and expanded paperback edition was published in 2008 with an updated title: *The Jesus Family Tomb: The Evidence Behind the Discovery No One Wanted to Find* (New York: HarperOne, 2008).

In January 2008 an international group of scholars gathered in Jerusalem, convened by Prof. James H. Charlesworth of Princeton Theological Seminary, in an attempt to generate the proper kind of academic and scholarly debate on what we know of the Talpiot "Jesus" tomb and how it might be responsibly evaluated.[5] I thank Prof. Charlesworth and his colleagues for the opportunity to publish my own analysis of these questions from the perspective of a biblical scholar and historian of early Christianity and Late Second Temple Judaism.

I am convinced that there is a surprisingly close fit between what we might postulate as a *hypothetical* pre-70 CE Jesus family tomb based on our textual records, correlated with this particular tomb in Talpiot and its contents. Rather than starting with the tomb and its six inscribed ossuaries, and exploring all the alternative possibilities (which, given the scarcity of data, are endless), I take a different approach.

It is true, for example, that a nickname like Yoseh — short for Joseph (or *Yehoseph* in Hebrew or Aramaic) — appearing alone without further identification could be any male of a Jewish clan of the time, whether father, brother, son, nephew, or uncle. In fact Joseph is the most common male Jewish name of the period. But if we begin with our historical records asking a different set of questions — who was the "Yoseh" in Jesus' life and is there any reason we might expect him to be in a hypothetical pre-70 CE Jesus tomb? — the answers are specific and singular. Jesus did have a brother who bore this precise and rare nickname — Yoseh (Greek *Iōsē*), according to Mark 6:3 (RSV Joses). What one needs to ask then is whether we have any evidence to think that Jesus' brother Yoseh might have died before 70 CE, and thus be an appropriate "candidate" for inclusion in a Jesus family tomb.

Rather than starting with an endlessly open and undetermined set of unknowns, my approach, in terms of method, is to begin with the specific "knowns." Essentially what I want to do is test a hypothesis, something we constantly do when we seek to correlate the material evidence of archaeology within our known textual and chronological horizons. It is obvious, no matter what one's theory might be, that one can always posit other possibili-

5. The Third Princeton Symposium on Judaism and Christian Origins: "Jewish Views of the After Life and Burial Practices in Second Temple Judaism: Evaluating the Talpiot Tomb in Context," was held January 13-16, 2008, at the Mishkenot Sha'ananim Conference Center in Jerusalem, with 54 scholars participating. On the press controversies following the conference and the various dispute and positions of the participants see James D. Tabor, "The Meyers/Magness Talpiot Tomb Statement: Some Observations," SBL Forum, n.p. [cited Jan. 2008]. Online:http://sbl-site.org/Article.aspx?ArticleID=749.

ties and alternatives. In terms of method I think what I suggest here can turn out to be quite enlightening, and I hope it will contribute to the discussion in a positive way.

What I want to explore first is what one might imagine for a hypothetical, pre-70 CE, Jerusalem tomb of Jesus and his family. Given our textual evidence, what might we reasonably construct in terms of likelihood? Toward the end of the article I will then briefly deal with the two main objections to my hypothesis — that the names are common and that Jesus and his followers were too poor to have a family burial cave — as well as a few closing theological observations.

The Second Burial of Jesus

I begin with what we know about the burial of Jesus of Nazareth from our earliest sources — the New Testament Gospels. Although the Apostle Paul knows the tradition that Jesus was "buried," he provides no narrative details that we might analyze historically (1 Cor 15:4). It is often assumed that the Gospels report that Joseph of Arimathea took the corpse of Jesus and laid it in *his own new tomb* late Friday night. The problem with this assumption is that a careful reading of our Gospel accounts indicates that this tomb, into which Jesus was *temporarily* placed, did *not* belong to Joseph of Arimathea. Mark, our earliest account, says the following:

> And when evening had come, since it was the day of Preparation, that is, the day before the Sabbath, Joseph of Arimathea . . . bought a linen shroud, and taking him down, wrapped him in the linen shroud, and laid him in a tomb that had been hewn out of the rock; and he rolled a stone against the door of the tomb. (Mark 15:42-46)[6]

John's Gospel, reflecting an independent tradition, offers a further explanation:

> Now in the place where he was crucified there was a garden, and in the garden a new tomb where no one had ever been laid. So *because of the Jewish day of Preparation, as the tomb was close at hand,* they laid Jesus there. (John 19:41-42, emphasis mine)

6. Quotations from the NT are from the RSV.

Mark implies that it was the pressing necessity of a quick temporary burial brought on by the nearness of the Sabbath that prompted Joseph of Arimathea to act in haste and approach the Roman governor Pontius Pilate for permission to bury Jesus' corpse. The Gospel of John makes this specifically clear. This *initial* burial of Jesus by Joseph of Arimathea was a temporary, emergency measure, with the Passover Sabbath hours away. It was a burial of necessity and opportunity. This particular tomb was chosen because it was unused and happened to be near the place of crucifixion. The idea that this tomb belonged to Joseph of Arimathea makes no sense. What are the chances that Joseph of Arimathea would just happen to have his own new family tomb conveniently located near the Place of the Skull, or Golgotha, where the Romans regularly crucified their victims?[7] Kloner offers the following analysis, with which I wholly agree:

> I would go one step further and suggest that Jesus' tomb was what the sages refer to as a "borrowed (or temporary) tomb." During the Second Temple period and later, Jews often practiced temporary burial. . . . A borrowed or temporary cave was used for a limited time, and the occupation of the cave by the corpse conferred no rights of ownership upon the family. . . . Jesus' interment was probably of this nature.[8]

Mark indicates that the intention of Joseph was to complete the full and proper rites of Jewish burial after Passover. Given these circumstances, one would expect the body of Jesus to be placed in a second tomb as a permanent resting place. This second tomb would presumably be one that either belonged to, or was provided by, Joseph of Arimathea, who had the means and had taken on the formal responsibility to honor Jesus and his family in this way. Accordingly, one would not expect the permanent tomb of Jesus, and subsequently his family, to be near Golgotha, just outside the

---

7. The assumption that Joseph owned this tomb is based on a theological interpolation of Matthew, where he adds two words to his source Mark, "he laid it in *his own* new tomb" (Matt 27:60), to make Jesus' burial fit the prophecy of Isa 53:9, that the grave of Yahweh's "Servant" would be "with a rich man."

8. Amos Kloner, "Did a Rolling Stone Close Jesus' Tomb?" *BAR* 22/5 (1999): 26. Kloner cites several rabbinic texts to support his assertion. Compare his fuller academic treatment, "Reconstruction of the Tomb in the Rotunda of the Holy Sepulchre According to Archaeological Finds and Jewish Burial Customs of the First Century CE," in *The Beginnings of Christianity: A Collection of Articles*, ed. Jack Pastor and Menachem Mor (Jerusalem: Yad Ben-Zvi, 2005), pp. 269-78.

main gate of the city, but in a rock-hewn tomb outside Jerusalem. These circumstances also address the issue that some have raised that the Talpiot tomb could not be that of Jesus since he was poor and from Galilee. James, the brother of Jesus, became leader of the Jesus movement following Jesus' death in 30 CE. Our evidence indicates that the movement was headquartered in Jerusalem until 70 CE. The core group of followers, banded around Jesus' family and the Council of Twelve, took up residence there as well, even though most of them were from Galilee.[9] This evidence points strongly toward the possibility of a Jesus family tomb in Jerusalem, but one different from the temporary burial cave into which Jesus' body was first placed.

A Jesus Family Cluster

Based on our earliest textual sources, I propose the following list of individuals as potential candidates for burial in a *hypothetical* Jesus family tomb:

- Jesus himself
- Joseph his father
- Mary his mother
- His brothers: James, Joses, Simon, and Judas/Jude; and any of their wives or children
- His sisters: Salome and Mary (if unmarried)
- Any wife or children of Jesus

There had to be, of course, many other names we simply do not know, with various connections to the Jesus family, but these names and relationships we can at least consider as hypothetically likely. I realize that the matter of Jesus having a wife and children is usually seen as unlikely, but one has to factor in the nature of our records and the social context in which Jesus lived. None of the wives or children of any apostles or the brothers of Jesus are ever named in the Gospels, yet Mark indicates that Peter was married (Mark 1:30), and Paul mentions that the apostles and brothers of Jesus traveled about with their wives (1 Cor 9:5). Silence regarding women, in late, post-70 CE, theological sources such as our New Testament Gospels, does

9. See Jeffrey Bütz, *The Brother of Jesus and the Lost Teachings of Christianity* (Rochester, Vt.: Inner Traditions, 2005), pp. 95-99, for a survey of a growing scholarly consensus that James, the brother of Jesus, had likely already taken up residence in Jerusalem prior to Jesus' crucifixion.

not imply nonexistence. Also, when Paul strongly recommends celibacy as a superior spiritual lifestyle, he fails to use Jesus as an example even in a context where he is desperate to refer to him for authority (1 Cor 7:8-12).

We next ask which of these individuals might hypothetically be buried in a pre-70 CE Jesus family tomb in Jerusalem, *after* the year 30 CE when Jesus was crucified. In 70 CE the Romans devastated Jerusalem and exiled much of the Jewish population; and normal Jewish life, including the common use of burial caves around the city, diminished. Given this watershed disaster we come up with a more chronologically restricted list of potential candidates, since we would only include those in the family that we can assume might have died before 70 CE:

- Jesus himself
- Mary his mother
- Joseph his brother, and perhaps James
- Any wife and children of Jesus who died before 70 CE

Jesus' father Joseph we would eliminate because he seems to have died decades earlier, probably in Galilee, and we have no record of him in Jerusalem in this period (see Acts 1:14). Jesus' mother Mary, given her age, could well have died before 70 CE, and as a widow, according to Jewish custom, would be put in the tomb of her oldest son. Based on our records, Jesus' brothers Simon and Jude apparently lived past 70 CE, so they should be eliminated from our list.[10] Jesus' brother Joses is a strong candidate since he is the "missing brother" in our historical records. When James is murdered in 62 CE, it is Simon, the third brother, not Joses, the second, who takes over leadership of the movement — indicating that he had most likely died by that time. The New Testament letters of James and Jude testify to their influence, and we even have an account of the death of Simon by crucifixion, but nothing survives whatsoever regarding the brother Joses. Given the culture it is likely that both of Jesus' sisters would be married, and thus buried in the tombs of their husbands, so they are not prime candidates either. Since we have no textual record of a wife or children, we can only say, hypothetically, that if such existed they might be included.

10. For the historical records of what happened to Jesus' brothers and the disastrous impact of the 70 CE Roman destruction of Jerusalem see my *Jesus Dynasty: The Hidden History of Jesus, His Royal Family, and the Birth of Christianity* (New York: Simon & Schuster, 2006), pp. 284-304.

The Talpiot Tomb

There were ten ossuaries in the Talpiot tomb, six of them inscribed. This is an exceptionally high percentage. For example, just taking the sample of ossuaries retained in the Israeli State Collection, only about 20 percent are inscribed, but that percentage is much too high for ossuaries in general, since plain ones are regularly discarded. It is not the case, as has been reported, that the remains of up to 35 additional individuals were found in this tomb. As Kloner makes clear in his article, this is a demographic estimate, not data based on any kind of anthropological study of the Talpiot tomb remains. There were remains of at least two or possibly three individuals — skulls, vertebrae, and limb bones — apparently swept from the arcosolia, perhaps by intruders in antiquity, and found just below on the floor. Cooking pots dating to the Second Temple period were also found in three corners of the main chamber. That the bones of these individuals were never gathered and put in ossuaries seems to indicate that the 70 CE destruction of Jerusalem terminated the family use of the tomb.[11] Although it is possible that the bones of more than one individual were placed in the ossuaries, the mitochondrial DNA (mitDNA) results of the two that could be tested, that of Yeshua and Mariamene, showed clear singular profiles.[12] The Talpiot tomb seems to be a small (2.9 × 2.9 meters), modest, pre-70 CE family burial cave with remains of at least a dozen or so individuals.

The six inscriptions in the Talpiot tomb show a rather remarkable cor-

11. Rahmani writes, "Following the destruction of Jerusalem in 70 CE, the manufacture of both hard limestone and chip-carved soft limestone ossuaries ceased" (*Catalogue,* p. 23). Such is the case with the Akeldama "Tomb of the Shroud," found by Boaz Zissu in 1998 and subsequently examined by Shimon Gibson and me; here the shrouded remains of a skeleton dating before 70 CE were found (see Zissu, Gibson, and Tabor, *Ḥadashot Arkheologiyot* 111 [2000]: 70*-72*). For a discussion of Jewish tombs that postdate 70 CE see Amos Kloner and Boaz Zissu, *The Necropolis of Jerusalem in the Second Temple Period,* Interdisciplinary Studies in Ancient Culture and Religion 8 (Leuven: Peeters, 2007), pp. 144-48. The exceptions are relatively rare, and each tomb must be looked at individually to determine if artifacts or other evidence indicate continued use past 70 CE.

12. Despite claims to the contrary the mitDNA tests carried out on bone samples taken from the Jesus and Mariamne ossuaries were collected and handled with proper scientific rigor and care to avoid any possibility of modern contamination. My university supervised the tests, and samples were shipped to the Paleo-DNA at Lakehead University in Thunder Bay, Ontario. Dr. Carney Matheson, who did the mitDNA work, says more than one individual would have shown up in the sample given the methods of testing that he followed.

respondence to the chronologically restricted hypothetical list of potential candidates one can construct from the textual evidence:[13]

1. Yeshua bar Yehoseph (Aramaic)
2. Maria (Aramaic)
3. Yoseh (Aramaic)
4. Mariamene [also known as] Mara (Greek and decorated)
5. Yehudah bar Yeshua (Aramaic and decorated)
6. Matyah (Aramaic)

Yeshua bar Yehoseph is an appropriate inscription for Jesus of Nazareth. Its messy informal style and the lack of honorific titles ("the Messiah," or "our Lord") fit what I would expect for his burial in 30 CE. I would also not expect the place designator "of Nazareth" since the use of the terms "Nazareth/Nazarene," like the titles, is more reflective of later theology than contemporary informal usage — especially within the family.[14]

The Aramaic form of the nickname *Yoseh* (יוסה), short for *Yehoseph/* Joseph, is rare in the Second Temple period, found only here on an ossuary and in two other inscriptional examples. It is equivalent to the later popular spelling of this nickname as *Yosey/Yosi* (יוסי) found in rabbinic texts from the late second to third centuries CE. However, in the first and second centuries CE it is extremely rare. It corresponds to an equally rare form of the name in Greek, *Yōsēs* or *Yōsē* (Ιωσῆς/Ιωσῆ), which occurs only five times in all our sources, literary and inscriptional. This is the precise form of the

13. Two of the decorated ossuaries had inscriptions (IAA 80.500: *Maramenon [he] Mara* [Greek] and IAA 80.501: *Yehudah bar Yeshua*) and four of the "plain" or undecorated ones (IAA 80.502: *Matyah/Matah*; IAA 80.503: *Yeshua bar Yehoseph*; IAA 80.504: *Yoseh*; and IAA 80.505: *Maria/Maryah*). See Rahmani, *Catalogue*, pp. 222-24.

14. Jesus is legally known as the "son of Joseph" in both the Synoptic tradition and in John (Luke 3:23; 4:22; Matt 13:55; John 1:46; 6:42). One other example of "Yeshua bar Yehoseph" is known on an ossuary (no. 9/pl. 2 in Rahmani). It was "discovered" by Eleazar Sukenik in a basement storage area of the Palestinian Archaeological Museum in Jerusalem in 1926 but unfortunately is unprovenanced. He published a report about the ossuary in January 1931, and the news that such an inscription existed, the only one ever found until the Talpiot tomb in 1980, created no small stir in the world press, particularly in Europe. See L. H. Vincent, "Épitaphe prétendue de N.S. Jésus-Christ," *Atti della pontificia: academia romana di archaeologie: Rendiconti* 7 (1929-1930): 213-39. The nickname Yeshua, a contracted form of Yehoshua/Joshua (which makes up 3.9% of male names in the period), occurs elsewhere on eleven ossuaries.

Figure 1. Close-up of the "Yeshua bar Yehosef" inscription *(Photo: James D. Tabor)*

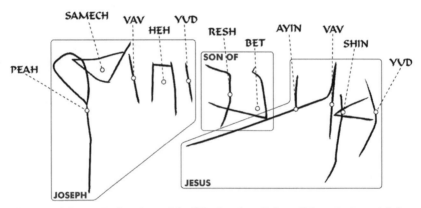

Figure 2. Schematic drawing of the "Yeshua bar Yehosef" inscription with letters traced *(Drawing: Associated Producers, Ltd.)*

nickname by which the Gospel of Mark, our earliest source, knows Jesus' second brother, Joseph/Joses (Mark 6:3).

There are two Marys in this tomb, known by different forms of that name, Maria and Mariamene. The mitDNA test indicates the Mariamene in this tomb is not related to Yeshua as mother or sister on the maternal side. That leaves open the likelihood that Maria could well be the mother, especially if we have two of her sons, Yeshua and Yoseh, in this tomb. It would

Figure 3. The "Yose" inscription *(Photo: James D. Tabor)*

make sense that she would be buried with her children in this intimate, small, family tomb and that her ossuary would be inscribed "Maria."

Given the presence of the named son of Yeshua in this tomb, namely Yehudah/Jude, and based on the mitDNA evidence (that she is neither mother nor sister of Jesus), it seems quite likely that Mariamene is the mother of this son. If this is indeed the tomb of Jesus of Nazareth, the speculation that she might be Mary Magdalene is based on a cluster of later evidence.

There were three intimate Marys in Jesus' life: his mother, his sister, and Mary Magdalene. Indeed, it was Mary Magdalene, his mother, and his other sister Salome who attended to his burial rites (Mark 16:1). Family intimates carried out this important rite of washing and anointing the corpse for burial. If Mariamene is not Jesus' mother or sister, as the mitDNA indicates, it seems a logical possibility that she could be the third Mary, namely Mary Magdalene, his follower and close companion, based on her inclusion as a named intimate in our earliest records. We do not know much about Mary Magdalene in our New Testament sources, but she does seem to be a woman of means and she is associated with several other women of standing from Galilee (Luke 8:1-3). The Mariamene ossuary is decorated and the inscription is in Greek, which surely fits this data, as Migdal, according to the record of Josephus, was a large, thriving, and culturally diverse "Romanized" city with a theater, a hippodrome, and a large aqueduct system.[15]

Some have suggested that this Greek inscription be read as *Mariame kai Mara* — Mary *and* Martha, referring to two individuals.[16] Even though these two names might fit a hypothetical Jesus family tomb, given the two sisters Mary and Martha mentioned in the Gospels, I find this extremely unlikely even beyond the strict epigraphical issues involved.[17] The inscription itself appears to be from one hand, written in a smooth, flowing style, with a decorative flourish around both names — pointing to a single individual who died and was placed in the inscribed ossuary pictured on page 259.

I accept the reading of Rachmani (reaffirmed by Leah Di Segni) that Mariamene is a diminutive or endearing form of the name Mariamne, derived from Mariame.[18] Although Mariame is a common name, the form Mariame*ne* — spelled with the letter *n* *(nu)* — is quite rare. In fact, a check of the *Thesaurus Linguae Graecae,* a comprehensive digital data base of Greek literature from Homer through 1453 CE, finds only *two* ancient works that use Mariamn- as a form of the name Mariame — both referring to Mary Magdalene! One is a quotation from Hippolytus, a third-century Christian writer who records that James, the brother of Jesus, passed on secret teachings of Jesus to "Mariamene," that is, Mary Magdalene.[19] The other is in the fourth-century CE *Acts of Philip,* which regularly refers to Mary Magdalene as *Mariamene.* It seems unlikely to the point of impossibility that Rahmani, who made no association whatsoever between his reading of the ossuary name as *Mariamene* with Mary Magdalene, would have just happened to come up with this exceedingly rare form of the name Mariame as

---

15. See Jane Schaberg, *The Resurrection of Mary Magdalene: Legends, Apocrypha, and the Christian Testament* (New York: Continuum, 2002).

16. See S. J. Pfann, "Mary Magdalene Has Left the Room: A Suggested New Reading of Ossuary *CJO* 701," *NEA* 69 (2006): 130-31. Pfann's reading is accepted by Jonathan Price and others.

17. Luke 10:34-41; John 11–12. It is conceivable that one of Jesus' brothers, or for that matter Jesus himself, might have married one of these sisters, thus accounting for their presence in this tomb.

18. See Rahmani, *Catalogue,* p. 222, as well as his introductory comments, p. 14. The Greek reads Μαριαμήνου, in the genitive case, a diminutive form of Μαριαμήνη. This form of the name is rare and is found also on one other ossuary, Rachmani, no. 108. Di Segni also continues to support Rahmani's reading (as per private email correspondence with me in 2007).

19. Hippolytus, *Refutation of All Heresies* 5.7.1.

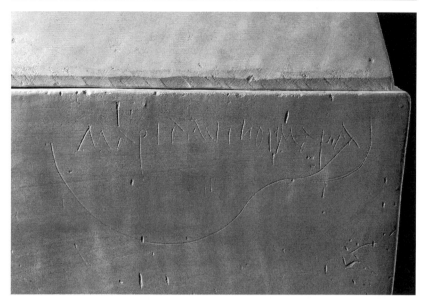

Figure 4. The "Mariamene" inscription *(Photo: James D. Tabor)*

his preferred reading. It seems clear to me that Rahmani's keen eye and years of experience have unwittingly provided us with one of the most important correlations between the names in this tomb and those we might expect, hypothetically, to be included in a Jesus family tomb — a name uniquely appropriate for Mary Magdalene. That this rare form appears in later sources strengthens rather than diminishes the case here since one would not expect such a "later" literary form of a name for Mary Magdalene to appear on a first-century CE ossuary in Jerusalem.

That Mariamene is also known here on the ossuary by the Aramaic designation "Mara" (Μαρα in Greek comes from the Aramaic מרא, meaning "sit" or "matter"; in Greek this form of the name is feminine), which, like "Martha" (the emphatic feminine), means "lordess," seems all the more appropriate.[20] Recent scholarship on Mary Magdalene has gone a long way toward rehabilitating her important place in the earliest history of the Jesus

20. There is another ossuary in the Israeli State Collection, Rachmani, no. 868, that reads in Greek: Αλεξας Μαρα (of Alexa Lordess), which offers a strong parallel to this usage. The name Alexa is also in the genitive case, followed by Mara. See the limited examples of the use of Mar/Mara in Aramaic and Greek in Tal Ilan, *Lexicon of Jewish Names in Late Antiquity*, part 1, *Palestine 330 BCE–200 CE*, TSAJ 91 (Tübingen: Mohr Siebeck, 2002), pp. 422-23.

movement. In a diverse collection of early Christian sources dating from the late first century through the fourth, she is a prominent leader and voice among the apostles and an intimate companion of Jesus, holding her place over against better-known male disciples.[21]

I find it striking that five of the six inscriptions correspond so closely to a hypothetical pre-70 CE family tomb of Jesus in Jerusalem as we might imagine it based on textual evidence. The one inscription we cannot account for in terms of what might be expected in our hypothetical Jesus family tomb is Matya or Matthew. The name is relatively rare (2.4% of males, compared to Joseph at 8.6% and Yeshua at 3.9%). It is worth noting that Matthew is a name known within the family of Jesus (see the genealogies of Matt 1; Luke 3). Also, the only Matthew known to us in the Gospels, also called Levi, is said to be of the Alphaeus family clan (Mark 2:14). In some early Christian traditions this Alphaeus or Clopas is the brother of Joseph, the father of Jesus. Still, just who this particular Matthew was and why he would be in this tomb, if it did belong to Jesus and his family, we simply do not know.

I find this hypothetical fit between the intimate pre-70 CE family of Jesus and Nazareth and the names found in this tomb quite impressive, and it argues strongly against an out-of-hand dismissal of the tomb as possibly, or even likely, associated with Jesus of Nazareth.

How Common Are These Names?

The most common reaction to this interesting cluster of six names found in the Talpiot tomb — a Jesus son of Joseph, two Marys, a Joseph, a Jude son of Jesus, and a Matthew — is that these are common names. That perception is why the tomb was not given any special attention when it was discovered in 1980, nor again in 1996 when it briefly came to public light and was subsequently forgotten. The problem is, statistical probabilities are not intuitive. It is possible to test the oft-stated assertion by scholar and nonspecialist alike that this cluster of names is highly probable/common and thus meaningless. Is it the case that in the time of Jesus there would have been any number of

---

21. Karen L. King, *The Gospel of Mary of Magdala: Jesus and the First Woman Apostle* (Santa Rosa, Calif.: Polebridge, 2003); and Ann Graham Brock, *Mary Magdalene, the First Apostle: The Struggle for Authority,* HTS 51 (Cambridge: Harvard Divinity School, 2003).

other tombs and/or families with these precise names — rendering this cluster meaningless in terms of any historical identification with what we know of Jesus of Nazareth and his family? One needs to clarify what one means by "common."

For example, the name Joshua, from which we get the nickname Yeshua or Jesus, has a frequency percentage of 3.9% among the 2,538 examples of male names of the period surveyed by Tal Ilan.[22] Is 3.9% a high enough number to call it common? I suppose it depends on how one uses the word "common." But remember, that is the percentage of all forms of the name Joshua in Aramaic and Greek, not the specific nickname Yeshua. If we just take the Rahmani catalogue of 231 inscribed ossuaries in the Israeli State collection, there are three examples of Yeshua (nos. 9, 121, 140) plus the two in the Talpiot tomb, for a total of five out of 286 total names.[23] Should one refer to that as "common"? The Rahmani collection does not include all inscribed ossuaries found in the Jerusalem area for the period, but the name frequencies and distributions appear to be fairly representative of our large body of data.[24]

"Joseph" was certainly a relatively common name (14%), but then the specific form Yoseh, in Aramaic, occurs only one other time on an ossuary, and two additional times in other sources. One would surely not call the name Yoseh common.

Still, in the end, it is not merely the frequency of the names but the cluster that one has to consider. If we are considering a hypothetical "Jesus family tomb" with these names we would then ask: What are the probabilities of a Jesus son of Joseph, with a brother named Yoseh, and a mother named Mary being found in a first-century Jewish family tomb? That is actually something a statistician can work with and the results can be correlated with what a historian might then postulate as the likelihood of these particular names being in a pre-70 CE Jesus tomb. The fact is that of the hundreds of tombs in the Jerusalem area that have been opened in a random way over the past two hundred years, *no other tomb* so far has been found with even this limited cluster of names: Jesus son of Joseph, Maria, and Yoseh. So

22. The percentages of the most common male and female names and their variants based on data from Ilan and Rahmani are conveniently tabulated by Andrey Feuerverger, "Statistical Analysis of an Archaeological Find," *Annals of Applied Statistics* 2 (2008): 3-54.

23. Rahmani, *Catalogue,* p. 11.

24. Rahmani's catalogue, though published in 1994, only covers ossuaries in the Israeli State collection up through August 1989; see Rahmani, *Catalogue,* p. 1.

it is not the case that most family tombs in the period are likely to have a person named Yeshua, and certainly not a Yeshua son of Joseph. If the Talpiot tomb had contained other names, such as Eleazar, Menahem, or Daniel, for instance, or names of women such as Sarah, Martha, or Joanna — all common Jewish names of the period, but with no connection to the family of Jesus — then identifying the ossuaries in this tomb with the family of Jesus would be more problematic.

In examining the Talpiot tomb a first step is to run the statistics on the six names and their specified relationships in the Talpiot tomb itself without any reference to Jesus of Nazareth or his associates or family. One has to decide whether to handle the names generically (count a special form Yoseh as just another "Joseph," Mariamenon as just another "Mary," etc.), or include the aspect of "rarity." It is always best to take a more conservative approach at the outset, so taking the names generically — that is, a Jesus son of Joseph, two Marys, a Jude son of Jesus, a Matthew, and a Joseph — is a good beginning. The question then becomes what is the probability of this cluster of names and the specified relationships based on frequency ratios? The latest statistical studies indicate that the chances of the combination of this cluster of names, in these relationships, are exceedingly rare.[25] This addresses the question of whether the cluster is common (i.e., probable), but leaves the matter of whether these names might fit with a hypothetical tomb of Jesus of Nazareth to the historians.

I want to make one final point about the argument over how common the names are and how significant the cluster in this particular tomb might be. As it turns out, my hypothetical "family tomb of Jesus" is not all that hypothetical. Approximately 600 inscribed ossuaries, out of 2,000 or more found in the Jerusalem area, have been documented. They come from an estimated 900

25. The primary and most fundamental statistical study is that of Feuerverger, "Statistical Analysis," followed by six discussion papers in response and a final rejoinder by Feuerverger, pp. 66-73, 99-112. Since that publication the statistical discussion and its variables have been considerably advanced by Kevin Kilty and Mark Elliott, "Probability, Statistics, and the Talpiot Tomb" [cited June 2007]. Online: http://www.lccc.wy.edu/Media/ Website%20Resources/documents/Education%20Natural%20and %20Social%20Sciences/ tomb.pdf; and "Inside the Numbers on the Talpiot Tombs" [cited March 2008]. Online: http://www.lccc.wy.edu/Media/Website%20Resources/documents/Education%20Natural %20and%20Social%20Sciences/tombNumbers.pdf. A comprehensive overview of the various statistical proposals with their strengths, weaknesses, and varied assumptions is provided by Jerry Lutgen in his most enlightening paper, "The Talpiot Tomb: What Are the Odds?" [cited Oct. 2009]. Online: http://www.bibleinterp .com/articles/tomb357926.shtml.

tombs. Of these 600 only 21 ossuaries have the name "Jesus," whether in Hebrew/Aramaic (13) or in Greek (8).[26] If you take out the Talpiot tomb, which has two, that leaves us with only 19 ossuaries total with the name Jesus. Keep in mind these are not 19 individuals named Jesus, since the name can occur more than once in a given tomb, on more than one ossuary, but still refer to the same single individual. What is clearly the case, however, is that there is not another tomb that contained a Jesus ossuary that one could even hypothetically argue might be connected to Jesus of Nazareth and his family. Unfortunately, the provenance of a few of the "Jesus" ossuaries is unknown, but most can be studied in the context of the tombs in which they were found. Invariably, they are surrounded with names like Shelamsiyon, Chananiya, Shapira, Dositheos, or Sara that have no known association with Jesus of Nazareth in our texts. This means that the Talpiot tomb, with its inscription "Jesus son of Joseph," surrounded by other names, including the special forms of the names *Yoseh* and *Mariamne,* that we can trace to the Jesus family, is the only one known to us for which one could even argue its possibility or probability. This does not prove that the Talpiot tomb is the family tomb of Jesus, but it goes a long way toward addressing the oft-made but invalid point that we have lots of tombs with Jesus inscriptions, as if to say that this one is like all the others. Such is simply not the case, so this objection, considered by some to be the weightiest, simply fails.

Was the Jesus Movement Too Poor to Have a Burial Cave?

Some scholars have suggested that Jesus and his family, as well as his movement as a whole, was too small, insignificant, and poor to have a family burial cave in Jerusalem.[27] The argument is that whoever took the body from the initial cave burial would have buried him in a simple trench grave with no marker since the family was too poor to afford a rock-hewn tomb. This objection overlooks that at least one follower of influence and means,

---

26. See Hannah M. Cotton et al., eds., *Corpus Inscriptionum Iudaeae/Palaestinae,* vol. 1, *Jerusalem,* part 1 (Berlin: de Gruyter, 2010), pp. 8-9. The 21 "Jesus" inscribed ossuaries in this latest catalogue are the following: nos. 36, 109, 139, 195, 206, 239, 247, 267, 295, 320, 425, 456, 473, 474, 479, 480, 489, 546, 547, 548, 583.

27. See Jodi Magness, "Has the Tomb of Jesus Been Discovered?" SBL Forum, n.p. [cited Feb. 2007]. Online: http://sbl-site.org/Article.aspx?ArticleID=640; as well as my response: James D. Tabor, "Two Burials of Jesus of Nazareth and the Talpiot Yeshua Tomb," SBL Forum, n.p. [cited March 2007]. Online:http://sbl-site.org/Article.aspx?ArticleID=651.

Joseph of Arimathea, did see to the initial burial in a rock-hewn tomb. Why would one assume that either Joseph or other followers of means who were devoted to Jesus' messianic program would not be able to provide a permanent tomb? We also have evidence that a group of wealthy and influential women, including Mary Magdalene, were supporting Jesus' movement financially, had followed him from Galilee, and were involved in the preparation of spices and ointments for his proper burial. The descriptions and circumstances all fit well with the idea of a body prepared for burial in a rock-hewn tomb with ossuaries.[28]

The Jesus movement, led by James the brother of Jesus following his crucifixion, was headquartered in Jerusalem for the next forty years, and their numbers and influence were significant enough to be noted by Josephus.[29] The family of Mary, Martha, and Lazarus, who lived in Bethany and with whom Jesus was intimately connected, could afford to bury their dead in a rock-hewn tomb. It has also been argued that some of the rock-tomb burials with inscribed ossuaries elsewhere in Talpiot, at Dominus Flevit, and on the Mount of Offense are connected to the early followers of Jesus.[30]

On more general grounds what this objection overlooks is the extraordinary devotion that followers exhibit toward their spiritual/messianic leaders. Mark tells us that the followers of John the Baptizer went to collect his body and that they placed him in a tomb (Mark 6:29). The Syriac *Ascents of James,* for example, recounts how devout followers of James buried another murdered leader, known in some traditions as Stephen, in a tomb to which they made an annual pilgrimage close to Jericho.[31] I have studied apocalyptic and messianic movements, both ancient and modern, and it is universally

28. See Luke 8:2-3; 23:55-56.

29. *Ant.* 20.200-201.

30. See Jack Finegan, *The Archaeology of the New Testament,* rev. ed. (Princeton: Princeton University Press, 1992), pp. 359-74, for a summary of the positive case. Not all scholars agree. James Strange offers an assessment of the evidence for and against in "Archaeological Evidence of Jewish Believers," in *Jewish Believers in Jesus: The Early Centuries,* ed. Oskar Skarsaune and Reidar Hvalvik (Peabody, Mass.: Hendrickson, 2007), pp. 710-41. For other dissenting views see Joan Taylor, *Christians and the Holy Places* (New York: Oxford University Press, 1993), as well as Gideon Avni and Shimon Gibson, "The 'Jewish-Christian' Tomb from the Mount of Offense *(Batn Al-Hawa')* in Jerusalem Reconsidered," *RB* 115 (1998):161-75.

31. See the Syriac *Recognitions* 1.43.3 as reconstructed by Robert E. Van Voorst, *The Ascents of James: History and Theology of a Jewish-Christian Community,* SBLDS 112 (Atlanta: Scholars Press, 1989).

the case that devoted groups have the collective means to support their leaders. It is an open and debated question in the field of Christian origins as to whether Jesus was poor and without means of any sort, but even if that were granted, to rule out the likelihood that devoted followers of means would have provided him and his family with a place of burial is unwarranted.

The Talpiot tomb is quite modest in size and arrangement, measuring under 3 × 3 meters and less than 2 meters high. It is nothing like the more monumental decorated tombs closer to the city. Also, of the six inscribed ossuaries, four are "plain," and only two are "decorated" (Mariamene Mara and Yehudah bar Yeshua). I am not convinced that the mere existence of a modest rock-hewn tomb of this type indicates high status and wealth. Indeed, the comprehensive Kloner and Zissu survey of Jewish burial in and around Jerusalem in the period indicates little evidence of trench burials. Instead, rock-hewn burial tombs were the norm for most of the population. As one moves away from the "front row" seat near the Old City, the tombs south of Akeldama, around the Mount of Offense, and south into Talpiot are often more modest in form and size.[32]

A Final Theological Note

I want to note here that I do not consider the investigation of this tomb as an attack on the Christian faith. Any scientific or academic investigation of an archaeological site related to biblical history, by definition, cannot be an "attack" on faith. I often tell my students, "Good history can never be an enemy of proper faith." Historians neither disallow nor preclude evidence, and the methods and tasks of history cross all lines of faith. Proper historical investigation involves posing hypotheses and testing them in order to determine what we can know, what we might suppose, and what we might responsibly assume to be the case. In the case of the Talpiot tomb, which is in fact a tomb of a first-century Jew named "Jesus son of Joseph," it is entirely proper to investigate in an objective manner upon what grounds this particular Jesus might be identified with Jesus of Nazareth.

In terms of the Christian faith I would also maintain that belief in the resurrection of Jesus does not have to be understood as a literal flesh-and-bones event, with Jesus ascending to heaven as a physical being. Jesus himself, when asked about resurrection of the dead, indicated that those so

32. Kloner and Zissu, *Necropolis of Jerusalem.*

raised would have spiritual bodies undifferentiated as male and female (Luke 20:34-36). The book of Revelation speaks of the "sea" giving up the dead that is in it — indicating the former physical body is completely lost and destroyed (Rev 20:13). The earliest testimony to the resurrection of Jesus comes from Paul writing in the 50s CE (1 Cor 15). He writes that Christ "appeared" to him, but he distinguishes between a "natural" or physical *(psychikos)* body and what he calls a "spiritual" *(pneumatikos)* body, which he attributes to Christ, whom he says was raised as a "life-giving spirit." When Paul describes death in general, he speaks of "putting off" the body like a tent or garment, and "putting on a heavenly dwelling" or new body (2 Cor 5). When he describes the future resurrection of the "dead in Christ," he says they will be raised with incorruptible bodies, and there is no implication that the physical components of their physical bodies, now turned to dust, will be literally raised.

Mark, the earliest Gospel, has no "appearances" of Jesus, while the account in Matthew takes place in Galilee and has a "visionary" quality to it. Although it is true that Luke and John, as our latest Gospel records, written in the 90s CE, picture Jesus eating food after his resurrection, that view does not necessarily imply a physical body. Angels in the Bible are often portrayed as eating with physical mortals, but remaining nonetheless in a spiritual form (e.g., Gen 18). When Jesus speaks of the future resurrection of Abraham, Isaac, and Jacob, he pictures them as "sitting at table" in the kingdom of God, but clearly they are in a new and transformed state — not a physical body of flesh and bones (Matt 8:11).

One might even see the discovery of the tomb of Jesus as a boon to faith in that it serves to ground his life and death in the very real history of the times. Such tangible evidence of Jesus and his family, buried together in death as in life according to the common Jewish custom of the times, provides a real "time-space" context for the Gospel stories that some might otherwise take as mythological.

The Memorial Mary Meets the Historical Mary:
The Many Faces of the Magdalene in
Ancient Christianity

April D. DeConick

Introduction

Mary of Magdala: Who was she, memorialized for us in the Bible as the woman who stood at Jesus' cross and visited his tomb, the woman who saw Jesus shortly after his resurrection? From the pulpit, we might hear of her as the sinful woman who anointed Jesus' feet with her tears and wiped them away with her hair, the repentant prostitute and exemplar of the reformed sinner. Feminist voices today laud her as a prophet and visionary, a woman leader among equals, a beloved disciple, the Apostle to the Apostles. Her pop image has been cultivated as the outspoken demon-possessed whore. Who can forget that provocative scene of the Magdalene from Cecille B. DeMille's famous film, *King of Kings,* when Jesus stares at her haughty figure and the seven deadly sins emerge from her body as ghostly apparitions? Or Martin Scorsese's tattooed temptress, naked behind the gauzy veil, hurling insults at Jesus for his voyeurism? Then there is the Magdalene as wife of Jesus and mother of his dynasty, most recently popularized by Dan Brown in the bestseller, *The Da Vinci Code.*

What is difficult to distinguish among all these faces of Mary is the his-

---

I wish to extend my gratitude to several scholars for reading various versions of this paper, giving me helpful feedback and criticism, and generously offering me their time and wisdom. Thanks to Holly Hearon, Alan Kirk, Barry Schwartz, Tom Thatcher, and Yael Zerbuvabel.

torical from the rest, especially when we are operating in the realm of pop culture, where references in ancient manuscripts are so easily mistaken to be historical facts about Mary. This common mistake arises from an uncritical attitude about the written word, likely derived from Christian conviction in the givenness of the factuality of the biblical narratives. As scholars, we approach both the subject and literature much more skeptically and critically. Because an ancient text identifies her as a visionary or Jesus' lover does not mean that she was so. In fact, we know that the old literature that mentions Mary was produced by ancient Christians with their own special interests. They used the Magdalene's image in much the same way as pastors, priests, and pop writers do today — to support and forward their own convictions, platforms, and agendas.

Such a re-creation of her persona, however, need not be considered deliberate falsification on the part of the ancient authors. More often than not, it occurred as the result of the normal operation of communal memory, which inevitably renews and refurbishes older traditions in light of a new generation of people and its needs. Earlier memories and received traditions are reframed to coincide with contemporary experiences and attitudes of the group. The result is the safekeeping and preservation of traditions that might otherwise fade into oblivion, but in a new remodeled format that is pleasing and relevant to the fashions of the community involved.[1]

In the case of Mary Magdalene, we find in the early Christian literature the emergence of several memorial Marys from the bones of older collective memories. Building communal memory, like individual memory, is a reconstructive process, resulting in an ideal memory of the past, not a simple retrieval of what actually happened. So the connection between the memorial Marys in the ancient literature and the "historical" Mary Magdalene may be impossible to determine. It is more apparent why a particular community memorialized her in a chosen manner than whether its memory of her was "historical."

Recognizing this, however, does not mean that communal memories

1. Seminal studies on social memory include Maurice Halbwachs, *On Collective Memory,* trans. and ed. Lewis A. Coser (Chicago: University of Chicago Press, 1992); Jan Assmann, *Das kulturelle Gedächtnis: Schrift, Erinnerung und politische Identität in frühen Hochkulturen* (Munich: Beck, 1992); idem, "Ancient Egyptian Antijudaism: A Case of Distorted Memory," in *Memory Distortion,* ed. Daniel L. Schachter (Cambridge: Harvard University Press, 1995), pp. 365-78; Yael Zerubavel, *Recovered Roots: Collective Memory and the Making of Israeli National Tradition* (Chicago: University of Chicago Press, 1995); Barry Schwartz, *Abraham Lincoln and the Forge of National Memory* (Chicago: University of Chicago Press, 2000).

are simple fabrications with no connection to what actually happened. We do not construct our models from nothing but our imagination. Rather we tend to idealize certain people because they already were our models, and they were our models because of real, not imaginary, traits and accomplishments.[2] Indeed, Barry Schwartz argues, "Given the constraints of a recorded history, the past cannot be literally constructed; it can only be selectively exploited."[3] Yael Zerubavel points out that communal memory "continuously negotiates between available historical records and current social and political agendas." It is in this process of "referring back to history" that our collective memory "shifts its interpretation, selectively emphasizing, suppressing, and elaborating different aspects of those records."[4]

Like our own personal memories, the communal memories we hold in common with others are built from bits and pieces of our past, from our collective remembrances of what actually happened. Yet they do not recount what actually happened, but what we think happened, what we heard happened, even what we would like to have had happen. So there is an uneasy tension between the actual past and how we remember it. There are fragments of history there, but the history is subservient to the processes of human recall and its tendency to memorialize, explicate, and contemporize.

In some societies, multiple, even contrasting, collective memories can exist side by side without dispute.[5] But often this process of adjusting our memories within the social frames of each new generation is a political process, and such was the case in pre-Constantinian Christianity, where countermemories competed on common ground. Countermemories do not usually emerge out of "new" data. In order for the countermemories to be acceptable, they need to be considered legitimate. They cannot diverge wildly from the older traditional memories. The creation of countermemories is done by reconfiguring the older received memories, focusing on less prominent features of those memories, while rekeying them with new reference points and reframing them into new contexts.

---

2. Barry Schwartz, "Memory as a Cultural System: Abraham Lincoln in World War II," *American Sociological Review* 61 (1996): 922-23.

3. Barry Schwartz, "The Social Context of Commemoration: A Study in Collective Memory," *Social Forces* 61 (1982): 393.

4. Yael Zerubavel, "The Death of Memory and the Memory of Death: Masada and the Holocaust as Historical Metaphors," *Representations* 45 (1994): 73.

5. Doron Mendels, "Societies of Memory in the Graeco-Roman World," in *Memory in the Bible and Antiquity,* ed. Loren T. Stuckenbruck, Stephen C. Barton, and Benjamin G. Wold (WUNT 212; Tübingen: Mohr Siebeck, 2007), pp. 143-62.

Eventually a master collective memory emerges, reflecting the stance of the dominant group and marginalizing the competing memories. Groups in power tend to use their collective memories to support the maintenance of their own hegemony.[6] But it is also a fact that certain memory reconstructions by communities are countermemories, serving to subvert the official memories of the dominant group. In the case of collective memories of religious traditions, the counternarratives often will introduce deliberate inversions into the official commemorative narratives, a move that violates their previously sacred character, as Zerubavel has shown was done with the subversive narratives about Masada that arose in the 1970s and 1980s.[7] These countermemories sometimes are put into place by intellectuals and scholars who return to the ancient texts and archaeology, attempting to reintroduce "history" alongside memory, challenging the master commemorative narrative that has dominated the communal landscape.[8]

The Talpiot tomb has been a lightning rod for such memorial activity. It evokes not only the dominant commemorative narrative of Mary Magdalene, but a subversive narrative too. The image of the Magdalene as Jesus' wife has been enjoying a historicization of sorts. The focus of attention has been three inscriptions found on different Talpiot ossuaries said to read, "Jesus, son of Joseph," "Judah, son of Jesus," and "Mariamene, who is Mara." From this reexamination of the tomb's ossuaries, a counternarrative has emerged in the media and in scholarship that Jesus indeed was married to Mary of Magdala and fathered a son named Judah. This narrative has inverted the official communal memory of Jesus. Because it violates the sacred master narrative that knows Jesus of Nazareth as a celibate single man, the backlash from the public and scholars alike has been severe.

The object of this paper, however, is not to examine this contemporary backlash, but to consider whether ossuary 701 may have contained the bones of Jesus' wife, Mary Magdalene. My charge is to determine from the ancient literary evidence, with special attention to the extracanonical, whether Mary Magdalene may have been married to Jesus. In order to meet this challenge, Mary Magdalene's story must be explored as a "site of memory."[9] What of

6. Schwartz, "Memory as a Cultural System," p. 909.

7. Zerubavel, "Death of Memory," pp. 89-91.

8. Ibid., pp. 83-84.

9. On the coinage of this phrase, see Pierre Nora, *Les Lieux de mémoire*, 3 vols. (Paris: Gallimard, 1984-1986); English translation, *Realms of Memory: Rethinking the French Past*, ed. Lawrence D. Kritzman, trans. Arthur Goldhammer, 3 vols. (New York: Columbia University Press, 1996-1998).

her history, if anything, can be recovered from the writings of early Christian communities who memorialized her?

Foundational Memories of Mary

It is not an easy task to be true to the historical developments of early Christianity, because these developments have been framed for centuries in anachronistic terms as a fight between the "orthodox" or apostolic catholic church and the "heretics" who broke away to form deviant cults. The heretics were responsible for writing the literature that was not accepted into the New Testament canon, and therefore their testimonies are late and fabricated. What they say has no theological, let alone historical, value.

This anachronistic frame has deteriorated under the pressure of information that we have gleaned from newly found texts from the Dead Sea, Nag Hammadi, and El Minya. The difficulty we face is that we, as an academy, have yet to put into place a new historical paradigm with better language that grants noncanonical texts the same respect as canonical ones. If we did so, we would have to say that the development of early Christianity was not linear and dependent on an orthodox perspective from an early date. The catholic perspective, which was grown in the apostolic churches, came to dominate as the "orthodox" perspective by the fourth century when it thrived under the auspices of Constantine. But prior to this, many Christian traditions competed for supremacy and framed their own perspectives as "orthodox" and their detractors' as "heretical."

The real historical situation is very complex, but one in which we can say with certainty that various Christian churches in the second century inherited cycles of oral and written stories from the Christian communities in the late first century. I call these stories the foundational memories. Some have been lost because they only remained in oral circulation. Some are recoverable because we have written versions of them. The foundational memories in the Gospels were not written down until at least forty years after the historical events. So even the foundational written stories are communal adaptations of older received oral stories.

Holly Hearon has explained that Mary Magdalene's story can be found in at least three different independent written versions preserved in the canonical Gospels. Although there are shifts in the details and special interests, all three versions are aware that Mary was Jesus' disciple and primary witness to his resurrection. Hearon explains that the written versions of her story were adapted by three authors from a larger complex of oral stories about Mary that circulated in the Christian communities and continued to circulate even after the Gospel versions were recorded. The authors reframed elements from the oral Magdalene cycles. In all cases, the reframing of Mary's story by the evangelists limited or subordinated her discipleship by shifting elements of her story to men who are clearly delineated as "disciples." Hearon concludes that this reframing was done to engage the evangelists' own special interests about their named leaders, who were competing in particular congregations with charismatic prophets and teachers, some of whom were women.[10]

Sociologically this mirrors a shift. Paul, who is writing at least twenty years before the evangelists, tells us that women were both praying and prophesying in the church at Corinth, a practice he is concerned about and attempts to limit.[11] He also is aware that Phoebe was a leader of the church of Cenchraea.[12] We know from Acts that Philip the evangelist had four daughters who were prophets.[13] So what we are seeing in the reframing of the story of Mary Magdalene in the Gospels is a swing in policy and politics, from an early unconventional movement where leadership was not limited by gender, to a later development in some churches that were beginning to authorize that only the twelve male disciples, the apostles, could be authentic bearers of the Christian traditions.[14]

10. For a detailed analysis of these three stories, see Holly E. Hearon, *The Mary Magdalene Tradition: Witness and Counter-Witness in Early Christian Communities* (Collegeville, Minn.: Liturgical Press, 2004).

11. 1 Cor 11 and 14.

12. 1 Cor 11:4; Rom 16:7.

13. Acts 21:9.

14. In addition to Hearon, *Mary Magdalene Tradition*, discussions of various aspects of this swing can be found in Elisabeth Schüssler Fiorenza, "Mary Magdalene: Apostle to the Apostles," *Union Theological Seminary Journal* (April 1975): 22-24; idem, "Word, Spirit, and Power: Women in the Early Christian Communities," in *Women of Spirit*, ed. Rosemary R. Ruether and Eleanor McLaughlin (New York: Simon & Schuster, 1979), pp. 51-56; idem, *In Memory of Her* (New York: Crossroad, 1984), pp. 304-9, 332-34; François Bovon, "Le privilege pascal de Marie-Madeleine," *NTS* 30 (1984): 51-52; Mary Catherine Carson, "And They Said Nothing to Anyone: A Redaction-Critical Study of the Role and Status of Women in the Crucifixion, Burial and Resurrection Stories of the Canonical and Apocryphal Gospels" (Ph.D. diss.; University of Newcastle upon Tyne, 1990); Susanne Heine, "Eine Person von Rang und Namen: Historische Konturen der Magdalenerin," in *Jesu Rede von Gott und ihre Nachgeschichte im frühen Christentum*, ed. Dietrich-Alex Koch, Gerhard Sellin, and Andreas Lindemann (Gütersloh: Gerd Mohn,

By the end of the first century, Christian churches were split on the question of gender and leadership. The "proto-orthodox" or apostolic churches were closing down the old prerogative of Christian women to be prophets and teachers. They began simultaneously to close women out of these leadership roles while also insisting on their marriage. In fact, the early-second-century author of one of the Pastoral Letters in the New Testament claims that, because a woman (Eve) was a secondary creation and the one who transgressed in the garden, women must be subordinate to men, and unconditionally refrain from teaching men. The author of the letter commands, "Let a woman learn in silence with all submissiveness. I permit no woman to teach or to have authority over men. She is to keep silent. For Adam was formed first, then Eve. And Adam was not deceived, but the woman was deceived and became a transgressor."[15] Women's salvation, according to this author, can only be attained through marriage and bearing children from that union. So he writes, "Yet woman will be saved through bearing children, if she continues in faith and love and holiness, with modesty."[16]

But not all churches at this time held this perspective. Indeed, some churches argued voraciously against this position, wanting instead to maintain the old ways of the early charismatic unconventional movement. In order for these second-century churches to keep their clergies open to women, they developed countermemories about Mary to support their view.

Countermemories of the Encratic Mary

Countermemories of Mary Magdalene as Jesus' "male" disciple emerge in a set of texts that scholars call "encratic" (from *encrateia*, "self-control") because the heroes are radical renunciates. In the past, encratic Christianity has been confused with gnostic Christianity because it was thought that both encratites and gnostics degraded the world and spurned marriage. This opinion is no longer au courant since we have now realized after studying

---

1989), pp. 187-91; Claudia Setzer, "Excellent Women: Female Witnesses to the Resurrection," *JBL* 116 (1997): 260-71; Ann Graham Brock, *Mary Magdalene, the First Apostle: The Struggle for Authority* (Harvard Theological Studies 51; Cambridge: Harvard University Press, 2003); Jane Schaberg, *The Resurrection of Mary Magdalene: Legends, Apocrypha, and the Christian Testament* (New York: Continuum, 2002).

15. 1 Tim 2:11-14.
16. 1 Tim 2:15.

the Nag Hammadi texts that not all gnostics degraded the world or spurned marriage. In fact, we will meet pro-marriage gnostics in the next section.

The cluster of encratic texts I will be referring to in this section were written in east Syria in the second century, and reflect normative ideals and practices in early Syrian Christianity. To be baptized into the east Syrian church meant that the convert had vowed to forsake the matrimonial bed. It is not until the fourth century that Syrian Christianity begins to conform to the beliefs and practices of the Roman West, when the Syrian churches begin to allow baptized members to marry.

The most famous reference to Mary is found in the encratic text, the *Gospel of Thomas:* "Simon Peter said to them, 'Mary should leave us because women do not deserve life.' Jesus said, 'Look, in order to make her male, I myself will guide her, so that she too may become a living spirit — male, resembling you. For every woman who will make herself male will enter the Kingdom of Heaven.'"[17] The meaning of this saying reflects the view of early Syrian Christianity that marriage must be renounced in favor of a single life once the convert became a full member of the church following baptism.

The reason that this sort of lifestyle was expected of Christians was tied to the metanarrative that the Syrian Christians had developed to explain salvation. Their understanding of the meaning of the Genesis story was key. They were careful exegetes and noted that the reference to the simultaneous creation of the human being in Gen 1:27 as "male and female" beings differed substantially from that in Gen 2:22, where Eve is created out of Adam as God's afterthought. In order to harmonize these two stories, they argued that, in chapter 1, the primordial human being was an androgynous "man," a "him" consisting of male and female aspects: "So God created man in his own image, in the image of God he created him; male and female he created them."[18] Then, in Gen 2:22, this primordial androgynous "man" fell asleep and God cut into his side and took the rib out and made woman.

These encratic exegetes concluded from their study of these verses that the ideal state that all humans beings should strive to attain is the primordial androgynous one described in Gen 1. It was the state of "man" before he sinned, when Adam was created in God's image with the female, Eve, concealed inside him. This was a paradisiacal time when the first "man" was "a living spirit."[19] This theology in practice meant that the encratic Christians

17. *Gospel of Thomas* 114 (my trans.).
18. Gen 1:27.
19. Gen 2:7 LXX.

strove to recreate a sexless Eden within their churches, to live their lives in imitation of the primordial Adam. To imitate this androgynous "male" ideal, both male and female members of the churches renounced marriage, became single, and lived as celibates. This ideal state the encratites described as becoming "neither male nor female" as well as "male."[20] It is an interpretation of the Genesis story that appears quite old, known also to Paul: "For as many of you as have been baptized into Christ have put on Christ. There is neither Jew nor Greek, there is neither slave nor free, there is neither male nor female. For you are all one in Christ Jesus."[21]

Stories like those found in the *Acts of Paul and Thecla* suggest that some women took this metaphor quite literally. They chopped off their hair and donned pants, and then headed out on the road with the men as missionaries. Detailed studies of this corpus of literature have suggested that its encratic message was particularly appealing to women because they were given an opportunity in encratic communities to be something other than wives and mothers. Once women converts refused marriage, they were baptized and became honored as "virgins" and "brides" of Christ. By refusing the sexual advances of their betrothed and their husbands, these women ceased childbearing. In this capacity, they shed "femaleness" and became "male," which allowed them to take on leadership roles.

As we learned in the last section, this openness to women as leaders and celibates was not universally accepted among Christians even at an early date. Many apostolic churches were shutting women out of leadership roles while also insisting that women marry based on their reading of the Genesis story in which woman is a secondary creation responsible for sin. Her only salvation is acceptance of her perpetual punishment — to submit to the totalitarian rule of her husband and to painful childbearing. In no case should she be permitted to teach men. Following this line of interpretation, Simon Peter in the *Gospel of Thomas* insists that Mary should leave the company of the male disciples, the male leadership, because women are not worthy of salvation. This Genesis-inspired teaching appears to have been a well-known

20. April D. DeConick, *Recovering the Original Gospel of Thomas: A History of the Gospel and Its Growth* (London: T&T Clark, 2005), pp. 187-88. Cf. K. Vogt, "'Becoming Male': A Gnostic and Early Christian Metaphor," in *The Image of God: Gender Models in Judaeo-Christian Tradition,* ed. K. E. Børresen (Minneapolis: Fortress, 1995), pp. 170-86. For androgyny language see *Gos. Thom.* 22; *2 Clem.* 12.2; *Gospel according to the Egyptians,* according to Clement of Alexandria, *Strom.* 3.13.93. For "male" language see *Strom.* 6.12.100; Hermas, *Vis.* 3.8.4; *Acts of Paul and Thecla* 40; *Acts Phil.* 44.

21. Gal 3:27-28.

appeal by authorities in churches wanting to discredit and invalidate women's leadership roles.

The encratic community wholeheartedly disagreed with this interpretation of Genesis, understanding it to be an abuse of the text. In the *Gospel of Thomas,* the encratic author cleverly brings forward his own appeal to Genesis, a saying of the "living" Jesus to counter the apostolic position voiced by Peter. According to the encratic position, women are worthy of life. Women too can become "living spirits" like the original Adam. How? To become the primordial Adam, the first man, they believed that women had to reject "femaleness," which they understood to be marriage and procreation, just as they thought Mary had been able to do as Jesus' "male" disciple.

This memorial Magdalene is the celibate disciple Mary, a student Jesus favors for her chastity. She stands up in encratic texts to combat apostolic teachings that were being used by some church leaders to subordinate and silence women by reducing them to temptresses, tricksters, and transgressors. This combat over the worth of women is nowhere more visible than in the *Dialogue of the Savior,* an encratic Syrian Christian text from the early second century. The text quotes a sexist saying, which it attributes to Jesus: "Pray where there is no woman."[22] This saying is in line with the words of Peter in the *Gospel of Thomas,* "Mary should leave us because women do not deserve life," and the words of the author of 1 Timothy, "I permit no woman to teach or to have authority over men. She is to keep silent." The Christians who were touting this sexist saying as Jesus' must have been using it as leverage to deny women access to their traditional roles as Christian leaders.

The authenticity of this saying in the ancient world appears to have been undisputed since the author of the *Dialogue of the Savior* assumes its veracity. He knows the saying as one that has been brandied about as Jesus' own, and he does not like how other churches are using it to subjugate women. So to defuse it, he does not address the authenticity of the saying itself, only its meaning. Immediately he offers a corrected interpretation of it. "Pray where there is no woman," he says, means that we must "destroy the works of femaleness," that is, women "should stop [giving birth]."[23] So the author reframes the saying by inverting its meaning. The erasure of "woman" should not be understood as the rejection of women from the churches' body of clergy. Rather, he says, it refers only to the cessation of female activity. The saying is rekeyed to promote encratic ideals rather than

22. *Dial. Sav.* 144.15-16 (my trans.).
23. *Dial. Sav.* 144.19-21 (my trans.).

church sexism. A troublesome teaching about women's subjugation in the apostolic churches becomes a commandment from Jesus to stop having sex and children in the encratic churches.

In this context, Mary asks Jesus if procreation will ever be destroyed. Jesus tells her that she knows that this will be so. His statement assumes that Mary herself is an exemplar of the celibate woman.[24] Her responsibilities do not include traditional marriage, procreation, and childrearing. In her capacity as the woman who has put off the "female," Mary is the ideal disciple who says to Jesus, "I want to understand everything [as] it is." Jesus responds by telling her to seek "life" rather than the wealth of the world.[25]

She is granted a vision of the future along with the male disciples Matthew and Judas (Thomas), who was the apostolic hero of Syrian Christianity.[26] She is described by the encratic author as the "woman who understood everything," and consequently is confident to teach Jesus' words to others.[27] So, in the course of the dialogue between Jesus and his inner circle of disciples, it is the disciple Mary who orates three sayings of Jesus: "'The wickedness of each day.' And 'laborers deserve their food.' And 'the disciple resembles the teacher.'"[28] When she speaks, she does so with the authority of a teacher, and Jesus responds by telling her that her remarks show "the greatness of the revealer."[29]

What inspired encratic communities to form this particular memorial Magdalene? They linked their knowledge of Mary from the old oral memories of her as a disciple and leader with their interpretation of the written foundational stories about her preserved in the canonical Gospels. The written narratives present her as a woman alone, far away from her home in Magdala. In these stories, she is the woman without a husband or children. Unlike Joanna the wife of Herod's steward Chuza or Mary the mother of James and Joseph who appear beside her, Mary's name does not connect her to a husband, or suggest any other familial associations.[30] The encratic Christian may have wondered whether it was her willingness to renounce her traditional female roles that earned her Jesus' favor. Had she given up her home in order to become Jesus' favored student?[31]

24. *Dial. Sav.* 144.22–145.2.
25. *Dial. Sav.* 141.12-19 (my trans.).
26. *Dial. Sav.* 134.24–137.3.
27. *Dial. Sav.* 139.8-13 (my trans.).
28. *Dial. Sav.* 139.8-13 (my trans.); cf. Matt 6:34; 10:10, 35; Luke 10:7; 1 Tim 5:18.
29. *Dial. Sav.* 140.17-19 (my trans.).
30. Luke 8:3; Matt 27:56.
31. John 20:18.

Such an understanding of the foundational written stories about Mary would easily result in memorializing this woman as the encratic Magdalene who had renounced her traditional roles as wife and mother to attend to the teachings of Jesus, and carry them on after his death as an apostle herself. Mary's "maleness" in fact derived from her refusal to marry and take on the traditional roles of the female, including procreation. This is a subversive memory, undermining the conventional picture of women in the ancient world. Because the women have become "men," however, it is a powerful argument that allowed women to continue to operate as public Christian leaders.

Countermemories of the Gnostic Mary

Gnostic Christian churches in the second century were diverse, and not all were interested in Mary Magdalene. The type of gnostic Christianity that was interested in her story we call by convention "Valentinianism," although they called themselves "Christian." They were esoteric Christians who attended apostolic churches while also attending gnostic lodge meetings where they were instructed and initiated into the mysteries of God. The Valentinians developed a mythology with a creator god who was not evil but inferior. So the cosmos was not a dark evil place that opposed the divine world, but an inferior one that shadowed it.

The memorial Magdalene in the Valentinian gnostic literature is quite different from the Magdalene found in the encratic literature. One might even say that the countermemories developed by the Valentinians rendered her into her doppelganger. She is memorialized in the *Gospel of Philip* as Jesus' partner: "And the partner of the [Savior] is Mary Magdalene. The [Savior loved] her more than all of the disciples, and often he kissed her on her [mouth]. The other [disciples . . .] said to him, 'Why do you love her more than all of us?' The Savior answered and said to them, 'Why do I not love you all like her?'"[32] The English translation "partner" for the noun *koinōnos* is a bit deceptive, since its verbal form, *koinoō*, can mean "to have intercourse with." In this sort of context, the noun *koinōnos* can refer to "spousal partner." Their spousal partnership is quite clearly indicated in another passage from the *Gospel of Philip*, which reflects on three women in Jesus' life: "There were three walking with the Lord all the time. Mary his mother and her sister

32. *Gos. Phil.* 63.30–64.6 (my trans.).

and Magdalene, the woman who was called his partner. For 'Mary' was his sister and his mother and his partner."[33]

Jesus married, and to the Magdalene nonetheless? Where does this idea originate? It reflects Valentinian theology thoroughly.[34] In Valentinianism, God is not just a Father in heaven. He is a Father-Mother, a god with male and female complements that function like a married couple, what they call a *syzygy*. The Godhead or Pleroma consists of thirty Aeons who were perceived to be similar to glorified angels. Like the Father-Mother, the Aeons are wedded couples, male-female syzygies. The sole purpose of their marriages is a type of procreation that resulted from mutual reflection upon the Father. Even though there is a contemplative component to their intercourse, an active eroticism is not missing. Each new syzygy is created through an act of lovemaking when the male Aeon deposits seed in the womb of the female Aeon, a process begun by the unknown Father himself.[35] The Godhead falls apart when a single Aeon, the female Sophia, decides to procreate passionately and independently.

Aeonic marriage is the ideal that humans are to strive for. The Valentinians considered human marriage a sacrament deriving from the divine Aeons above.[36] Even the Valentinian vision of eternity focused on the matrimonial bed. The saved would marry guardian angels at the end of time when a communal wedding would occur. The Pleroma would open its doors to the newlyweds as their bridal chamber.

The Valentinians, however, are careful to distinguish between two types of human marriage. There is a lower form of marriage that they call the "marriage of impurity." It is characterized by carnal desire, what is called in their texts *epithymia* or lust. The Valentinians taught that people generally are involved in impure marriages, because they treat lovemaking and procreation as an orgy of flesh, as a fulfillment of their lust. This passion, the Valentinians said, impacted the conception of the child negatively, resulting

33. *Gos. Phil.* 59.6-11 (my trans.).

34. This following description of Valentinian marriage and the sacraments is based on a series of articles that I have written and published elsewhere: "The True Mysteries: Sacramentalism in the Gospel of Philip," *VC* 55 (2001): 225-61; "The Great Mystery of Marriage: Sex and Conception in Ancient Valentinian Traditions," *VC* 57 (2003): 307-42; "Conceiving Spirits: The Mystery of Valentinian Sex," in *Hidden Intercourse: Essays on Eros and Sexuality in the History of Western Esotericism,* ed. Wouter J. Hanegraaff and Jeffrey J. Kripal (Leiden: Brill, 2008), pp. 23-48.

35. Irenaeus, *Haer.* 1.1.1.

36. *Gos. Phil.* 64.31; Clement of Alexandria, *Misc.* 3.1.

in a child with a weakened "female" spirit, which would have trouble thwarting the passions of his or her soul. If the spirit was so weak that the person was not able to overcome the passions, the child would be doomed. If the spirit could gain enough fortitude to rule the emotive self, and if it chose to be baptized in the Christian church, it could become "male" and be worthy of salvation.

The ideal marriage, however, has nothing to do with *epithymia*. Pure marriages, which the Valentinians trained themselves to enjoy, were believed to reflect the ideal Aeonic marriages. Instead of a lustful focus, the partners were supposed to include in their lovemaking contemplation of God and prayer, raising the sex act from a hedonistic affair to an intellectual and spiritual orgasm in harmony with the physical. This resulted in the conception of children with strong "male" or "elect" spirits, which would be able to easily strengthen their souls and be saved without a moment's hesitation.

The only Aeon who comes into being outside a syzygy or a marriage is the Aeon Jesus. He comes into being after Sophia falls and her negative aspect is expelled from the Pleroma as Achamoth. All of the Aeons pray to the Father to save her. The result of their union is the production of the Aeon Jesus. His job is to descend out of the Pleroma, redeem Achamoth, and restore to God our spirits, which had become trapped in matter. Since it is Achamoth's independent procreative activity outside marriage that resulted in sin, her salvation is her marriage. Jesus is single. Achamoth is single. What could be more convenient than their marriage? So they become betrothed, awaiting matrimonial consummation at the end of time when the Pleromic bridal chamber will receive the newlyweds. The Aeon Jesus descends to earth to redeem our spirits. He is born as the human being, Jesus of Nazareth. There was no doubt in the mind of the Valentinians that this Jesus was married too. And the wife they betrothed to him was Mary Magdalene.

But she was remembered by the Valentinians not only as Jesus' wife. Mary was also his favorite disciple who carried on Jesus' esoteric teaching after his death as a leader among the apostles. This iconic portrayal of her is very prominent in the *Gospel of Mary*, a Gospel that is a Valentinian "midrash" on John 20:18: "Mary Magdalene went and announced to the disciples, 'I have seen the Lord.' And she told them that he had said these things to her." The *Gospel of Mary* reveals her teaching to the male disciples, a teaching that the Valentinians believed she had received earlier from Jesus in the garden. What did the Valentinians think this esoteric teaching was? It was a Valentinian homily on the Eucharist delivered by Mary Magdalene.

To set up her delivery of this homily, the Gospel opens with a discussion between Jesus and the disciples about the nature of sin. Mary is present as one of his disciples. Jesus explains that sin has arisen because the soul has become embedded in matter. When the soul descended into the material body, it descended into a condition of disturbance and temptation. This disturbed condition of the soul leads us to commit sins like adultery. The only way that this situation can be resolved, he says, is with the descent of the Savior, when he unites with our souls. So Jesus exclaims: "Watch out that no one leads you astray, saying, 'Lo here!' or 'Lo there!' For the Son of Man is within you. Follow him!"[37] When he finishes speaking, Jesus leaves the disciples, who begin to grieve.

Mary steps forward and consoles them, reminding them that Jesus' "grace" is with them. She tells the other disciples not to despair, but to "praise his greatness, for he has made us ready. He has made us men."[38] And with this, she turns the hearts of the disciples to God. This language resonates liturgy. The word normally translated as "praise" in Coptic is *cmou*, which means "to give thanks." In many cases, it can mean "to take" or "give a sacrament." The "thanksgiving" sacrament is the Eucharist, and this is what is referred to here. Mary is leading the disciples in a Eucharist ceremony, beginning by lifting their hearts to God just as is done in the modern-day Catholic mass. What does the ceremony do according to the *Gospel of Mary*? It is a ritual that brings about the descent of the Son of Man within the person, or as Levi says at the end of the Gospel, it enables the person to "put on the Perfected Man and have him for ourselves."[39]

This is technical language. Like many other Valentinian texts, "putting on the Perfected Man" refers to receiving the body of Christ by participating in the Eucharist ceremony.[40] According to the Valentinians, Jesus the Perfected Man is the reflection of the primordial Man, who is the androgynous Man before Adam's sin. It is this body that we acquire in the Eucharist. They believed that, when the faithful ate the divine man Jesus, his body would work internally like medicine, healing our brokenness. By eating and drinking the Perfected Man, our fallen bodies are rebuilt or resurrected into glorious bodies. This is a reference not to a new fleshly body, but to a spiritual or angelic one that will be able to ascend through the spheres of heavens undetected by the vicious celestial guardians, a topic that Mary

37. *Gos. Mary* 8.15-20 (my trans.).
38. *Gos. Mary* 9.19-20 (my trans.).
39. *Gos. Mary* 18.15-18 (my trans.).
40. *Gos. Philip* 55.11-14; 73.27.

preaches about throughout the rest of the extant *Gospel of Mary.*[41] So redemption by participation in the Eucharist is characterized as the recovery and transformation of the woman Eve into the primordial man, Adam. As Mary says to the male disciples in the *Gospel of Mary,* in this way Jesus "made us into men."

But that is not all. The transformation into the primordial man is also connected to marriage. Twice referencing Eve's movement back into Adam, the author of the *Gospel of Philip* teaches that the return to the prelapsarian unity is the joining of husband and wife in marriage.[42] So what we have in the Valentinian gnostic community is the argument that through marriage, women are able to achieve the primal androgyny of the first "man," thus becoming "male." This "male" conversion allowed the women gnostics to stand up as church leaders alongside the men, giving sacraments and delivering homilies like the "male" Mary Magdalene.

Given this interpretation of the Genesis story, we should not be surprised that in the *Gospel of Mary* Mary's leadership role is threatening to Peter and Andrew, who represent the opinion of the apostolic church. Mary is in direct conflict with Peter and Andrew, who challenge her opinions as "some other ideas."[43] They question whether Jesus taught esoteric things to a woman, while leaving themselves, the male disciples, out of the conversation. Didn't he speak openly to us? Does he want us to listen to her? Did he prefer her to us? These are all social questions that have arisen as a result of the gender debate that gripped Christianity.

Mary responds by asking whether Peter thinks that she is lying. Levi, an advocate for the gnostic position, jumps in and tells Peter to be quiet. "If the Savior made her worthy, who are you to cast her out?" Levi says. "Certainly the Savior knows her very well. This is why he loved her more than us. Let us be ashamed, put on the Perfected Man, and have him for ourselves as he commanded us. Let us preach the gospel, and stop laying down rules that are beyond what the Savior said."[44] These words are telling, revealing a social situation in which the Valentinians, like the Syrian encratites, are arguing that some of the apostolic churches are institutionalizing rules that exclude women from pulpit activities when Jesus never meant or said any such thing. Instead, the Valentinians argue that women, like Mary Magdalene, do have a

---

41. Cf. *Gos. Phil.* 76.23-30; 86.6-11.
42. *Gos. Phil.* 70.10-22; 68.23-26; cf. *Interp. Know.* 10.24-36.
43. *Gos. Mary* 17.15 (my trans.).
44. *Gos. Mary* 18.10-21 (my trans.).

route to "maleness." It is achieved sacramentally, mainly through their participation in the Eucharist and marriage.

Why did the Valentinians choose Mary Magdalene as Jesus' *koinōnos?* Like the encratic Christians, the Valentinians based their countermemories on universal givens about Mary, elements such as her discipleship and leadership that transcended the written narratives but were generally accepted by Christians as genuine. They also appear to have been very familiar with the canonical narratives, favoring the version of Mary's story found in the Gospel of John because of the intimacy featured between Jesus and Mary. From these narratives, the Valentinians also seem to have recognized her as a single woman. This, however, did not mean that she had renounced marriage and procreation as the encratic Christians claimed. This meant that she was available for marriage. Jesus is single. Mary Magdalene is single. What could be more convenient than their marriage?

The countermemories of the Valentinians are not so much subversive as they are adaptive. Socially, the Valentinians considered themselves to be members of the apostolic church until the mid-third century. So they accepted the apostolic pro-marriage argument, but they refocused it. They agreed with the other apostolic Christians that the marriage of the female to the male is salvific, but they disagreed about what type of relationship it should be. They argued that it is not a relationship of subordination, but one of harmonious cooperation between partners mirroring the Aeonic syzygies. Marriage is a unification of the divided primal androgyny, before Eve became separated from Adam. This primal Adam, the androgynous "male," was their redemptive goal, and had to be achieved sacramentally through the Eucharist and marriage. Because women could recreate this primal androgyny by participating in the Eucharist and marrying, they could return to the garden as the prelapsarian Man. They could become "men" as Mary Magdalene did. On this basis, they concluded, women should be allowed to stay in the clergy.

Master Narratives of the Apostolic Mary

The apostolic church emerged as the orthodox tradition by the fourth century, and when this happened women definitively were locked out of the clergy. Mary's memory as a powerful leader could not survive within the apostolic environment. In order to control her memory, two different master narratives about Mary Magdalene arose in the Western and Eastern apostolic churches.

Western theologians realigned her with the stories of Mary of Bethany and the prostitute from Luke's Gospel who wept on Jesus' feet and wiped them with her hair. This new counternarrative transformed the foundational stories of Mary by confusing them with stories of other Marys and women, casting Mary as a prostitute.[45] This countermemory appears to have been fairly well known already in the mid-second century, since the pagan philosopher Celsus refers to it when he insinuates that Jesus and his disciples were supported by certain women whom Jesus healed, and that this support was garnered through "a disgraceful and importunate way."[46] Tertullian calls Mary Magdalene "the woman who was a sinner," a clear reference to her conflation with the sinner woman in Luke.[47] In a sermon once attributed to Hippolytus, Mary and Martha, Lazarus's sisters, seek Christ in the garden. Martha's sister is confused with Mary Magdalene. Hippolytus considers her a second Eve whose obedience to Jesus compensates for the sin of the first Eve.[48]

Mary as the repentant whore becomes the official master narrative of the Roman Church by the sixth century. In a sermon delivered on September 14, 591, Pope Gregory the Great seals her fate. He definitively transposed the story of the Magdalene into the stories of Mary of Bethany and Luke's sinful woman who used her flesh "in forbidden acts."[49] In so doing, Gregory was able to successfully suppress the earlier contrasting memories of Mary as a powerful woman leader, memories that had the potential to continue to threaten the hegemony of the patriarchal order. What is most disturbing about this recreation was that Gregory did not just lock women out of the clergy. He cemented a memorial bridge that would connect all women with Mary the repentant whore.[50] As the redeemed whore, she became the character model for women, a manageable and controllable woman whose "new" story would be used as propaganda to subjugate women on divine writ for hundreds of years.

45. For a good overview of this process, see Susan Haskins, *Mary Magdalen: Myth and Metaphor* (New York: Harcourt Brace, 1993), pp. 3-97; Schaberg, *Resurrection of Mary Magdalene*, pp. 65-120.

46. Origen, *c. Cels.* 1.65.

47. Tertullian, *Against Marcion* 4.18.9, 16-17.

48. Hippolytus, *Comm. Cant.* 8.2; 24.60.

49. Gregory the Great, *Hom.* 33.

50. On the types of bridges, see Yael Zerubavel, "Antiquity and the Renewal Paradigm: Strategies of Representation and Mnemonic Practices in Israeli Culture," in *On Memory: An Interdisciplinary Approach*, ed. Doron Mendels (Bern: Peter Lang, 2007), pp. 331-48.

Interestingly, the apostolic churches in the West were silent when it came to memories of Mary's discipleship and her leadership. When the Western apostolic churches created their countermemories of Mary the prostitute, they did not invoke memories of either her discipleship or her leadership. They did not dispute them nor agree with them. Their silence is telling. If these two memories were universally accepted givens about Mary, to deny them would sabotage the countermemory that the apostolic community is producing because it would be openly defying accepted knowledge about Mary. So to subdue these threatening but accepted memories of Mary, the Western apostolic churches overwhelmed them by confusing Mary Magdalene's story with the story of other women found in the Gospels. Furthermore, they focused on her singleness at the expense of all other memories of her. In the ancient world, where unmarried public women were stereotyped as prostitutes, Mary's public singleness was her greatest liability and the Western apostolic churches used it against her. Once her name was linked with the image of the Lukan prostitute, her good reputation was irrevocably damaged. Mary Magdalene was brought to her knees along with all women leaders in the West who emulated her.

In the Eastern apostolic tradition, a different memory shift takes place. By the fourth century the hierarchies in the Syrian churches had become male-dominated and, under pressure from Rome, the Syrian churches had begun to accommodate married members into its congregations. When this happened, the memory of the "male" Magdalene became less and less necessary. Memories of Mary in the fourth-century Syrian literature become eclectic and confused. Her image erodes when she is superimposed with other characters, oftentimes male, but most prominently the Virgin Mary. This further exaggerated the suppression of women's leadership, because women were faced with a paradox, a woman model who was both a virgin and a mother, a Mary they could never emulate. The result of this shift in communal memory is a Syrian tradition that the resurrected Jesus appeared to Mary his mother first. Other than her name "Mary," the memory of the Magdalene all but disappeared from the garden.[51]

In other Eastern traditions, she is neither confused with the Virgin Mary nor amalgamated to Luke's prostitute or with Mary of Bethany, as she is in the West. Rather, in later Eastern Orthodoxy she remains her own

---

51. Brock, *Mary Magdalene,* pp. 123-42; Robert Murray, *Symbols of the Church and Kingdom: A Study in Early Syriac Tradition* (Cambridge: Cambridge University Press, 1975), pp. 144-50, 329-35.

woman. She is depicted in late legends as so chaste that the devil sends seven demons into her because he mistakes her for the Virgin Mary and wants to hinder the incarnation. She is given the honorable title "Apostle to the Apostles" and is considered an "Equal to the Apostles." Although this might seem like an acknowledgment of her old apostolic prominence, it does not work that way in the Eastern Orthodox tradition itself. The title "Equal to the Apostles" is given to Mary because she was the first messenger commissioned by Jesus to announce his resurrection.[52] "Apostle to the Apostles" is her title because she proclaimed the resurrection to the apostles, who then proclaimed his resurrection to the whole world.[53]

What happened to Mary when this master narrative formed in Eastern Orthodoxy? The later Eastern traditions may be aware of Mary's prominent reputation in the early church as a single woman who was commissioned by Jesus as an apostle. Yet in their official master narrative there is a reliance on the canonical Gospels to restate her narrative as it is told by the evangelists, where earlier memories of her prominence are recontextualized in a hermeneutic that subordinates her to the male apostles whom she entrusts with her vision and its dissemination. The male apostles are reconfirmed as the official bearers of the Christian traditions in the east, and apostle Mary is effectively silenced.

The Historical Mary

In the ancient Christian literature, many faces of Mary Magdalene emerge, all of them countermemories formed by early communities. These contrasting memories of Mary emerge at a time when the demotion of women was the norm in many apostolic churches. When apostolic churches began to restrict access to the clergy to men and teach women that their salvation is to be found in their matrimonial submission and fecundity, both the encratites and the Valentinians challenged them with memorial Marys who were "male." In the second-century West, the apostolic churches had begun to spin their own countermemory of Mary Magdalene as a whore, albeit a repentant one. In Syria she is eventually amalgamated with the Virgin Mary,

52. *Holy Myrrh-Bearer Mary Magdalene: Equal of the Apostles: Life, Liturgical Service, & Akathist Hymn*, trans. Isaac E. Lambertsen (Liberty, Tenn.: The Saint John of Kronstadt Press, 1999), p. 14.
53. Ibid., p. 15.

while in Eastern Orthodox traditions she is made subordinate to the male apostles by returning to her canonical story and underlining the Johannine interpretation of her apostleship as a commission to Jesus' male disciples only.

With so many competing memories, how can we ever determine which pieces of these memories reveal information about the historical Mary Magdalene? There is no definitive answer to this question. But we can draw some conclusions about her that are more likely than others. What premises might aid our reasoning?

First, we must recognize that the creation and maintenance of communal memory is complicated. It is both a creative process *and* a retentive process, although always a distortive one.[54] Jan Assmann notes that the past is never preserved "in a pure, complete, and authentic form" but is always reconstructed from the viewpoint of the present.[55] However, Yael Zerubavel reminds us that when the past is updated, in order for the updates to be credible, the present version requires a close resemblance to the older version; otherwise society will reject it.[56] Creative adaptations of our past are successful only to the extent that we can accept them as legitimate based on what we already know to be true.

So this suggests that historical reality may limit what any given generation can say about Mary Magdalene. The memories that survive depend on their acceptability, on how well they support what we already know to be true. It is therefore more likely than not that the earliest memory formations of a historical person or event are not wholly fabrications with no root in reality. It is equally likely that those memories that have passed through fewer interfaces and interest groups are those that have retained a better connection with the historical reality itself, even though this reality is distorted and constructed. Furthermore, since successive memory formations survive because they rely on linking to accepted aspects of memories already in circulation, some of these links may be relying on creative memory adaptations that had become mainstream, rather than the retention of historical information.

54. Anthony Le Donne, "Theological Memory Distortion in the Jesus Tradition," in *Memory and the Bible in Antiquity,* ed. Loren T. Stuckenbruck, Stephen C. Barton, and Benjamin G. Wold; WUNT 212 (Tübingen: Mohr Siebeck, 2007), p. 166.

55. Jan Assmann, "Ancient Egyptian Antijudaism: A Case of Distorted Memory," in *Memory Distortion,* ed. Schachter, p. 366.

56. Yael Zerubavel, "The Historical, the Legendary and the Incredible: Invented Tradition and Collective Memory in Israel," in *Commemorations: The Politics of National Identity,* ed. John R. Gillis (Princeton: Princeton University Press, 1994), p. 106.

A good contemporary example of this tension between the retention of historical realities and their distortion can be seen in the memories that circulated a decade ago about Elian Gonzalez, the five-year-old boy who survived a sea journey on a homemade raft from Cuba to Florida. By the second day of reporting, it was being repeated that Elian was in perfect physical condition because a school of dolphins had protected the child from sharks. We may never be able to determine whether dolphins swam around him during the ordeal, although while being interviewed by Diane Sawyer, he did draw a picture of himself on the ocean with a dolphin swimming next to him. His physical condition was better than the other two survivors, although it was by no means perfect. He was treated for minor exposure to the elements. His better physical condition can be attributed to his mother's actions. She wrapped him in her coat before lashing him to an inner tube and giving him a bottle of water. As the days passed, stories about Elian became more and more complicated, yet each one linked to some aspect of the older stories about him that were already in circulation. Quickly his story took on religious meaning as it passed through various interest groups. Santerian priests linked Elian to a prophecy that Castro would be overthrown by a child who had been saved by "angels at sea." How could they make this link work? In earlier reports, Elian is said to have remembered that an angel kept him company at night. Very rapidly he became labeled *El Niño Milagro*, "The Miracle Child," and his story was keyed to the biblical one by a Catholic priest. Castro became Herod, Clinton became Pilate, and Elian became the Messiah.[57]

This process of memory formation suggests that the memories about Mary Magdalene contain aspects of her history, although it may be difficult to tease them out. To do so, we may find it helpful to start by eliminating the least likely aspects. What are these? They are the biases that reframe the material to support the special interests of the new community or generation that has received the earlier information as well as any hermeneutical associations. In the case of the Elian story, the Santerian association of the child with the prophecy would represent the reframing of earlier reports that Elian said that an angel appeared to him.

What are the special interests in the case of Mary Magdalene? The canonical authors want her to be subordinate to the twelve male disciples, a special interest that later Eastern Orthodoxy reaffirms. The encratites and later Eastern Orthodox Christians want her to be celibate. The Valentinians

57. For information about Elian, I relied on Jeff Elliott, "Debunking Elian," *Albion Monitor* (issue 74), www.monitor.net/monitor/0004a/elian.html.

want her to be married. The apostolic Christians in the West want her to be a prostitute. All of these aspects are biases that reframe her story to support the special interests of each individual community. In all cases, the communities do this to engage the gender debate that was tearing apart the early Christian churches. Does this mean that Mary was not subordinate, not celibate, not married, or not a prostitute? Not necessarily. But what it means is that because these memories support the special interests of these groups, they cannot be trusted without further evidence that would allow us to preference one memory over the others. So we are justified to bracket them and set them aside.

What about hermeneutical connections that make her "male" by keying her story to the early Christian interpretation of the Genesis story? Although the hermeneutic itself should be discarded — Mary was no man — the hermeneutic is being linked to explain something that was known to be true about her. What is that? I suggest that the encratic and gnostic communities know that she was an unusual woman for her time, with a public persona and authority that the ancient people usually associated only with men. The Western apostolic churches seem to know this too, since they link to the fact that she was a public woman, but degrade this by confusing her hermeneutically with Luke's prostitute. Unmarried public women were often stereotyped as whores in the ancient world, so this hermeneutical link was easily forged and sustained.

Once we have adjusted for the generational effects of memory by removing the biases, special interests, and hermeneutics from Mary's story, we are able to identify which memories are the older memories that the communities have adapted to formulate their special interest Marys. Three older memories emerge, forming a triangulation of information: Mary was a single woman; Mary was one of Jesus' disciples; Mary was a prominent public woman leader in the beginning years of Christianity. What makes this triangulation particularly interesting is that knowledge of this information was shared by all of our constituents. These three pieces of information appear to be commonly accepted knowledge that the communities knew to be true.

Does this triangulation represent genuine independent knowledge about Mary, or is it dependent on a common interface that all these communities shared, like the canonical stories about Mary? While knowledge of Mary's singleness may have been inferred by each community from the scriptural interface, it is much less likely that her discipleship and prominence as a leader were too, because the canonical stories exclude her from Jesus' disciples and subordinate her leadership to theirs.

So the oldest recoverable memories of Mary Magdalene know her to be an important woman disciple in Jesus' movement who was a public Christian leader after his death. The public nature of her mission and the authority that she commanded as a woman disciple of Jesus became a real liability for her memory in a movement that was initially unconventional and that gradually conformed to the norms of its society, norms that often stereotyped public women as prostitutes and closed public offices to women. We know that the shift to limit the roles of women and their access to positions of authority within the churches began within the first twenty years of the movement because Paul faced it in his Corinthian correspondence.

Twenty or thirty years later, the pressure to conform to societal norms increased as the movement became predominantly a Gentile movement. In this environment, the Gospel evangelists provide our first three testimonies about Mary. But they are testimonies that downplay her discipleship and prominence by placing her story into a context that allows her to remain important while also being subordinated and controlled by the men in the movement. Although the three evangelists never explicitly say that Mary was single, they all independently assume it when they attach other women to husbands and sons, while leaving Mary with none. This appears to be a detail that is older than their independent written accounts, and generally accepted knowledge about her at the time they wrote their accounts. So her singleness is a detail that we can return, with a good deal of certainty, to our list of her oldest memories.

So I have little doubt that the oldest memories of Mary recognized her as a single woman who was among Jesus' disciples. This connection to Jesus gave her the authority to go on after his death as a prominent public Christian leader. Are these old memories historical facts about her? They are the closest we are going to get. So if the Talpiot tomb turns out to be an early Christian clan tomb (rather than the Jesus family tomb), and the reading of the ossuary inscription turns out to be "Mariamē and Martha" (rather than "of Mariamēne, who is [also called] Mara"), it may be that we, like Hippolytus and Gregory, have confused the Magdalene with Mary of Bethany whose sister was Martha.

Mary Magdalene as Mara, Honorable Teacher

Jane Schaberg

My contribution to this discussion comes from the field of historical-critical, literary-critical biblical studies, which subject the text to series of questions designed — in this case — to help reconstruct aspects of history, aspects of the biblical writers' perspectives, and use of earlier sources. My interpretive framework and my presuppositions are feminist. In this framework, it is possible to place women as agents at the center of historiography,[1] and to understand them as makers as well as bearers of meaning — a point that is extremely important for analysis of the role of Mary Magdalene. Feminist analysis is grounded in wo/men's[2] experience of oppression and historical agency, that is, in wo/men's participation in and contribution to struggles for justice. Our educated assumption is that androcentric recounting and stereotypes and centuries of androcentric interpretation have garbled and diminished and all but erased the presence of wo/men[3] and silenced their voices, a process that continues to occur (as at this Jerusalem conference, in my opinion, and that of Simcha Jacobovici in his summary statement at the last meeting). This directs us to read gaps and slippages in the texts, to map out ancient and contemporary strategies of suppression and resistance in an attempt to uncover wo/men's history, making for a fuller hu-

1. See E. Schüssler Fiorenza, *Jesus and the Politics of Interpretation* (New York: Continuum, 2000), pp. 35, 51-55.

2. Schüssler Fiorenza's term for all women and nonelite men is widely used.

3. Tal Ilan, *Integrating Women into Second Temple History* (Tübingen: Mohr Siebeck, 1999), p. 5.

man history. We are rightly suspicious of the received records, and trained in the use of historically grounded imagination. Feminist studies (of literature, law, psychology, politics, medicine, domestic violence, and any other subject) are part of our phase of the women's movement. This is work done to empower social change and liberation.

The massive scholarship on the search for the historical Jesus and Christian origins is over two hundred years old; feminist scholarship on historical women of this period only in its second generation. The latter has not developed different methods but often assesses differently data gleaned from the use of traditional methods. Take the case of Mary Magdalene's sevenfold demonic possession (Luke 8:2).[4] John Meier thinks that the criteria of embarrassment and of coherence suggest that historically Jesus performed an exorcism on her.[5] But whose embarrassment? We can suppose the prominence of a flawed female figure was *less* embarrassing to those who opposed her and her memory than an unflawed female, especially when that flaw, even if healed, connotes madness, deviant behavior, and heresy. I am suspicious of Luke, who may present her exorcism as integration into the patriarchal order and use it as a means of tarnishing her memory.

Unfortunately, in my opinion, feminist scholarship by men and women in biblical studies is still of little or no interest to many male scholars; it is not deemed important or necessary for many of them to know our work and engage in serious discussion with it — yet. Perhaps this is due in part to the largely conservative and patriarchal nature of religion in general. While repeating that the ossuary possibly associated with Mary Magdalene is of great importance, some scholars at this conference with no background in Magdalene studies could call her "an enigma" and hold in error that the significant evidence we have about her is not in the first-century canonical Gospels but is second century and later.

The following is my assessment of the possibilities of what we can know of the historical Mary Magdalene. She was a Jewish woman, from the Galilean town of Magdala (Migdal), known for its salted fish trade. She was a member of the *basileia tou theou* (reign of God) movement associated with Jesus of Nazareth, a movement many feminist scholars have characterized as one of struggling egalitarianism. By egalitarianism I do *not* mean the achieved ideal of a social organization that is without sexism, without structures and ideolo-

---

4. See the Markan appendix, 16:9, a later addition to the Gospel of Mark, drawn from Luke.

5. John Meier, *A Marginal Jew,* 4 vols. (New York: Doubleday, 1991-2009), 2:657-59.

gies of domination, without traditional division of labor at times, or blind spots, or failures. I also do not mean an ideal or a platform of gender equality that is clearly perceived and articulated by leaders or followers, or identical with the feminist ideals taking shape in our own time. But I also do not mean a society or ideology that ignores all issues and implications of what we call gender, or that is compatible with virulent misogyny, sexism, and condescension. I *do* mean, rather, a social reality characterized by the attempts of women and men to live and work together for a common goal or goals as equals, in a variety of changing circumstances, and with a range of understandings and a range of success and lack of success.[6] In a religious sense, what characterizes egalitarianism is the attempt actually and fully to incarnate or embody certain beliefs — to take them seriously enough to act on them — such as the belief that all have equal access to salvation, or that all are created in the image of God. These beliefs are deeply embedded in Judaism, and this egalitarianism is a possibility within Judaism. The movement Mary Magdalene belonged to was one of "shared prophecy,"[7] focused on the *basileia* of God, and not on Jesus.

Mary Magdalene traveled with the group, not in a position of (domestic) service and patronage (we owe this idea again to Luke, who in his Gospel and in Acts highlights women in this role, as he obscures women in prophetic roles).[8] Participation would have involved learning, studying, working together. I judge it likely that she, with other women, was present at Jesus' crucifixion and burial, returned to his tomb, and found it empty.[9] In line with and developing Jewish apocalyptic/wisdom belief and praxis, Elijah traditions, and the earliest teaching within the movement about the Human One's (Son of Man's) suffering and resurrection (a figure I see as at some levels corporate),[10] she believed Jesus resurrected, vindicated. She communicated that belief and others developed it. She was therefore likely a major source of information later about the movement and Jesus' death, and an originator of the Christian resurrection faith.

6. See Mary Ann Beavis, "Christian Origins, Egalitarianism, and Utopia," *Journal of Feminist Studies in Religion* 23 (2007): 27-49.

7. Mary Rose D'Angelo," Reconstructing 'Real' Women," in *Women & Christian Origins*, ed. R. Kraemer and M. R. D'Angelo (New York: Oxford University Press, 1999), pp. 122-25.

8. See J. Schaberg, "Luke," in *Women's Bible Commentary*, ed. C. Newsom and S. Ringe, exp. ed. (Louisville: Westminster John Knox, 1998), pp. 363-80.

9. I am well aware of studies that see nothing historical in the resurrection narratives, and of those which interpret the canonical Gospels as primarily the myths of warring factions.

10. Before it is narrowed to refer only to Jesus.

We know nothing of her education, age, looks, previous occupation. There is no indication at all that she was a prostitute, a legendary result in Western Christianity of the conflation of texts like Luke 7 (an unnamed "woman of the city, a sinner," who weeps at Jesus' feet) and John 8 (the near-stoning of a woman for adultery).[11] We know nothing of her family, her relationship with others, sexual preferences, health, economic status, reasons for joining the movement; there is no narrative of her call, nor that of any other woman. There are no teachings or actions in the ministry period associated with her. She is named, as are some other women, without reference to father, son, or husband. Analysis of canonical materials indicates that her importance was early on blurred, obscured, and probably contested. I give that opposition historical weight. We have only late legends about her life after the resurrection, her travels, her work, her death and burial.

Were the historical Mary Magdalene and Jesus married and/or parents of a son? Married, I think probably not. I have argued that Jesus was possibly a *mamzer* (conceived in the period between betrothal and home-taking, with Joseph not the father)[12] and forbidden marriage within Israel to the tenth generation (Deut 23:3). If the reading on one of the Talpiot tomb ossuaries is Yeshua bar Yehoseph, this does not disprove it being a reference to Jesus of Nazareth, nor does it disprove the illegitimacy reading of the infancy narratives, since Joseph was reputed to be his father (Luke 3:23: he was "the son [as was supposed] of Joseph").[13] Reducing Mary Magdalene to the role of "Mrs. Jesus" (Crossan's term) distracts from her important role in the formation of Christianity and is a good example of using a woman to think about a man (in this case, to present Jesus as a "real" man and a heterosexual male.) Note that her legendary designations whore /lover /wife are all designations with respect to men; they reduce the woman to her biological functions. Virginia Woolf wonders why romantic love is "the only possible interpreter" of a woman of power.[14] There is simply no evidence of a marriage

11. The latter is the story Mel Gibson uses to introduce his Mary Magdalene in *The Passion of the Christ*. See my "Mel Gibson's Mary Magdalene," in *Mel Gibson's Bible*, ed. T. Linafeldt and T. Beale (Chicago: University of Chicago Press, 2006), pp. 69-79.

12. J. Schaberg, *The Illegitimacy of Jesus: A Feminist Theological Interpretation of the New Testament Infancy Narratives*, 2nd ed. (Sheffield: Phoenix, 2006). See also B. Chilton, D. Capps, S. Mitchell, and others who develop this idea.

13. According to Matthew, Joseph completes the home-taking, accepting the child as his own.

14. V. Woolf, *A Room of One's Own* (New York: Harcourt, Brace & World, 1929), p. 87.

between Jesus and Mary Magdalene,[15] and as far as I can see no credible reasons for keeping a marriage secret. "The DaVinci Code syndrome" with regard to Mary Magdalene amounts to the reduction of her to the Holy Grail, a vessel, a womb.[16] Jacobovici does a better job with the erotic element in his DVD's reenactments, showing Jesus caressing the shoulder of Mary Magdalene in one scene, and in others showing her teaching. She is young, beautiful, sexy, *and* intelligent.

The erotic elements in John 20 (which has echoes of the Song of Songs) and in several apocryphal texts (especially the *Gospel of Philip*) do signal love, but they are ambiguous about its nature. Elaine Pagels has argued that these elements have to do with mystical understanding and connection, and if sexual activity also, that aspect is *intentionally* ambiguous.[17] The Valentinian *Gospel of Philip* 63.32–64.9 is a tantalizingly corrupt passage: "And the companion *(koinōnos)* of the [Lord was] Mary Magdalene. [He loved] her more than [all] the disciples [and used to] kiss her [often] on her [mouth]." The rest of the disciples ask Jesus, "Why do you love her more than all of us?" The Savior answers, "Why do I not love you like her?" The implied answer to both questions seems to be that Mary Magdalene is loved because she is not blind but sees the light (64.5-9). That is, the answer has to do with insight and with spiritual worth, undercutting the competitiveness. The Greek term *koinōnos* has a wide range of meanings in the Bible and elsewhere.[18]

The lack of DNA connection between bone residue found in the Yeshua bar Yehoseph ossuary and one attributed by some to Mary Magdalene is no indication of marital status. Personally, I hope that Jesus and Mary Magdalene both had healthy sexual lives — with each other or with others, if they so chose. They could have been parents of a son. But we need to remember that ascetics were known in Judaism of the period: the Therapeutae, some Essenes, John the Baptist, Paul.

In my opinion, the idea that the Talpiot tomb is that of the dynasty of Jesus or the family or clan of Jesus runs counter to understandings of this movement's focus on "family of God" as *not* a biological reality. For exam-

15. See B. A. Pearson, "Did Jesus Marry?" *BR* 21/2 (2005): 32-39, 47.

16. Joe Zias wrote of "the Da Vinci Code syndrome, whereby anthropological and archaeological evidence is deliberately ignored by textual scholars, 'journalists,' and film makers in order to bring fame and fortune" (his notes for conference presentation).

17. E. Pagels, "The 'Mystery of Marriage' in the Gospel of Philip Revisited," in *The Future of Early Christianity*, ed. B. Pearson (Minneapolis: Fortress, 1991), pp. 442-54.

18. See *Resurrection of Mary Magdalene*, 152-55.

ple, Mark 3:31-35: "And his mother and his brothers came; and standing outside they sent to him and called him. And a crowd was sitting about him; and they said to him, 'Your mother and your brothers are outside, asking for you.' And he replied, 'Who are my mother and my brothers?' And looking around on those who sat about him, he said, 'Here are my mother and my brothers! Whoever does the will of God is my brother, and sister, and mother.'" Parallels in Matt 12:46-50 and Luke 8:19-21; John 7:5: "Even his brothers did not believe in him"; cf. Matt 4:9, a saying of John the Baptist: "Do not presume to say to yourselves, 'We have Abraham for our father'; for I tell you, God is able from these stones to raise up children to Abraham."

Even though some members of his family came over into the movement after his death, it would seem a supreme irony for the bones of Jesus to be contained in a tomb whose very nature (dynasty, family) ran counter to a powerful aspect of his message — but, then, of course, stranger things have happened to Jesus in Christian history. If we think of the Talpiot tomb as the tomb of early and important members of the movement, we can put aside (1) the objection that Jesus' family could not afford a rock-hewn tomb (the tomb would have been donated by wealthy member[s] of the movement), (2) the objection that his tomb would more likely have been in Galilee, and (3) DNA analysis. We can also think of the ossuary inscriptions Matya, Marya, and Jose in this broader way. There is a Matthew among the Twelve (Matt 9:9, called Levi in Mark 2:14 and Luke 5:27). Many Marys appear in the Gospels besides the mother of Jesus: Mary of Bethany (John 11, 12; Luke 10:38-42), Mary the wife of Clopas (John 19:25),[19] Mary the mother of James and Joseph (Joses) (Mark 15:40; Matt 27:56; Luke 24:10). The Jose mentioned here is not the same person as the brother of Jesus in Mark 6:3.

I privilege the moment at the empty tomb as a catalyst or trigger of Mary Magdalene's claim that Jesus had been raised.[20] Given the range of contemporary Jewish beliefs, "resurrection" would be ultimately compatible with a mysteriously empty tomb, a corpse removed by followers or stolen by enemies, a mix-up (Jesus' corpse is in another grave), a never-found corpse/ bones. It would be compatible with a body translated/exalted to the heavens. It would be compatible also with a subsequently found corpse/bones, and eventual burial in an ossuary.[21] (Many — perhaps most — Christians are

19. I agree with R. E. Brown (*The Death of the Messiah*, 2 vols. [New York: Doubleday, 1994], 2:1014-15) that John lists four women at the cross.
20. My hope is to work on the empty tomb texts with regard to trauma theory.
21. See A. Segal, *Life after Death: A History of the Afterlife in the Religions of the*

not aware of the range of beliefs about resurrection in Jesus' time; so many hold the belief that resurrection *must* have entailed an empty tomb, that resurrection *must* have entailed the reanimation or standing-up-again of the dead body, à la Gibson's *Passion of the Christ,* in which Jesus with light shining through the holes in his body walks forward. We can speculate that the place revered at the Holy Sepulcher may have been the first burial site, provided by Joseph of Arimathea on behalf of the Sanhedrin; this would be the "empty tomb." Empty, who knows why? It is the site of insight and faith that resurrection has begun. Then there may have been a secondary burial at Talpiot, and then the bones of Jesus put there in an ossuary. So Talpiot would not be the Christian Testament's tomb site.

Many intriguing questions arise from investigation of the Talpiot tomb, such as the following. Were there other tombs that were not family tombs? I am thinking here of Qumran, of the Jewish catacombs in Rome, of the question of how the Therapeutae may have buried their members.[22] Did the early Christians who remained in Jerusalem until the war of 66-70 abandon or lose the memory of this tomb and its location? Or if we look for mention in Jewish Christian materials especially in the Transjordan might we find something of the memory that has been overlooked or misunderstood? Is there any relation to other tombs in the Talpiot region? If the bones become available for study, we would certainly learn much from them, as from the bones of the Jehohanan found at Giv'at ha-Mivtar.

I want to focus now on the most elaborate ossuary, the only one with an inscription in Greek. Its inscription has been read in a variety of ways:

1. *Mariamēnou (ē) Mara:* "of Mariamene who is (also called) Mara." In this case the name is the genitive Mariamenou, a diminutive of Mariamene, one of the many variants of the name Miriam/Mariam/Mariame. The vari-

West (New York: Doubleday, 2004), pp. 701-5; cf. Jon Levenson, *Resurrection and the Restoration of Israel* (New Haven: Yale University Press, 2006). See also Israel Knohl's conference paper, "'By Three Days, Live': Messiahs, Resurrection, and Ascent to Heaven in *Hazon Gabriel*" (dated to the beginning of the CE): You don't have to imagine an empty tomb for resurrection; at least some saw it this way. In this inscription, the body is said to lie like dung, is totally disfigured and disappeared, but resurrected. There is no need to have a complete body to be resurrected; resurrection is not connected to the status of the body. I agree with Knohl that this was the view of some Jews of the time. See also Peter Steinfels, "3 Scholars Agree, Resurrection Is Often Misunderstood, by Christians and Jews," *New York Times,* Saturday March 1, 1008, on books by Magidan, Levenson, and N. T. Wright

22. My thanks to Eldad Keynan for discussion of several possibilities.

ant on this ossuary was further contracted to Mariamne, which was explicitly equated with Mariame.[23]

2. *Mariamē kai Mara:* "Mariame and Mara," two persons (so Pfann; the second name is a shortened form of the Aramaic name Martha).[24]

3. *Mariam ē kai* (or *Mariamē kai*) *Mara:* "Mary who is called Mara [= the Master, a title]." Note that there is really no English equivalent for the feminine of the Aramaic title Mar, a prophetic title (Mar Elijah, Mar Elisha, Maranatha). "Honorable Lady," "Lordess," "Mistress," or "Lady" will not do. "Honorable Teacher" is better. If there are two scribal hands here, the title may have been added later.

Epigraphers may never agree on a correct reading of the inscription (which in *any* reading *can* refer to Mary the Master). Nor may they agree on the significance of the fact that it is in Greek: if this is the ossuary of Mary Magdalene, is the Greek due to the sophistication of her hometown, Magdala, or her own sophistication, or travels, or influence among Greek speakers? Or is it some recognition of the breadth of her influence? The flourish under the name makes some sort of statement, most likely a sign of great respect.

Note also that the name Mary is especially slippery, having many forms: Mariamne was Herod's Hasmonean wife, murdered in the 20s CE; her name was taken by Israelites in honor of her Hasmonean heritage, in sympathy. Josephus calls the prophet Miriam Mariamne. It seems to me that Mary Magdalene could have been known also to some as Mariamne for either of these reasons — opposition to Rome or prophetic stature. In later works, Mary Magdalene is called Mariham in the *Gospel of Thomas* and in *Pistis Sophia* IV. She is called Mariamme in the Greek fragments of the *Gospel of Mary* (earlier than the Coptic). In *Pistis Sophia* I-III she is usually called Maria, sometimes Mariham, and once Mary of Magdala. She is Mary Magdalene in the *Gospel of Peter;* Mariahamme in the *Sophia of Jesus Christ;* in the *Dialogue of the Savior* she is sometimes Marihamme, sometimes Mariham. In the *Manichean Psalm Book* she is called Marihama (the last letter is uncertain) and Marihamme. In the *Acts of Philip* she is Mariamne, Mariamme, or Maria the Magdalene. Hippolytus calls her Mariamme (so also Origen) and Mariamne. As early as the first century CE (traditions in

23. So Rahmani, who understood Mara to be a contraction of Martha, the second name or double name of this person.

24. S. J. Pfann, "Mary Magdalene Has Left the Room: A Suggested New Reading of Ossuary *CJO* 701," *NEA* 69 (2006): 130-31.

the *Gospel of Thomas,* Greek fragments of the *Gospel of Mary,* Josephus), we find variety.

I am interested in exploring the possibility (1) that the Talpiot tomb is not a family or dynastic tomb, and (2) that this ossuary inscription does not refer to two individuals, nor to two personal names of one individual. The ossuary refers rather, I think, to a Mary who is called Mara, understood as a title, Master, Honorable Teacher. The following analysis provides a literary and sociological context for this reading: Mary the Master. A. Feuerverger assumed that this "is a highly appropriate appellation for Mary Magdalene," and I agree. He knows that "the assumption is contentious and drives the outcome of his computations substantially."[25]

If Mary Magdalene were important only for her presence at Jesus' crucifixion, and her claim that she discovered his tomb empty and received revelation about his afterlife (in both the Synoptic and Johannine Gospels) — and I have argued that these elements can be regarded as historical[26] — this would be enough to secure for her in some circles the title Mara. That is, there is good first-century support for this title being appropriate for her. There is reason to consider her the founder of Christianity, if one likes such contentious titles.

Her role, however, in each canonical Gospel is diminished by subsequent and climactic focus on the male disciples, on appearances to them and their commissioning. She and the other women are reduced to, in Crossan's phrases, "a secretarial role" delivering information to the males, who have an "executive role."[27]

We can say more about the historical importance of Mary Magdalene. There are traditions of a first appearance (protophany) of the risen Jesus to her in Matt 28 and John 20, which have at least eighteen points of contact, indicating a pre-Johannine, pre-Matthean tradition. Further, I think John may be using a source which he does not fully use; it has been truncated. Sarah Coakley asks, what was it about Mary Magdalene's testimony that was both formative and yet in need of being downplayed?[28] In

25. A. Feuerverger, "Open Letter to Statistical Colleagues on the Tomb Computation," version of March 12, 2007. Online: http://fisher.utstat/edu/audrey/OfficeHrs.txt. Accessed Feb 7, 2008. Now see his article, "Statistical Analysis of an Archaeological Find," *Annals of Applied Statistics* 2 (2008): 3-54.

26. Schaberg, *Resurrection of Mary Magdalene,* 204-99.

27. J. D. Crossan, *The Birth of Christianity* (San Francisco: HarperColllins, 1995), p. 560.

28. S. Coakley, "Response," to W. P. Alston, "Biblical Criticism and the Resurrec-

John 20 I see fragments of the claim that Mary Magdalene was seen as a successor of Jesus.

I read this story of the appearance of the risen Jesus to Mary at the tomb, as containing a subtext of allusions to 2 Kgs 2: the "taking" of Elijah in a whirlwind and the witnessing of his ascent by Elisha. Elisha knows that his master is going to be taken from him; he refuses to leave Elijah as they travel from Gilgal to the Jordan. Elisha insists: "I will not forsake you." The witnessing of Elijah's ascent is the condition upon which, or assurance, or sign that what Elisha asks his master — to inherit a double share of his spirit — will be granted him by God. "Elijah said to Elisha, 'Tell me what I may do for you before I am taken from you.' Elisha said, 'Let me inherit a double share of your spirit.' He responded, 'You have asked a hard thing; yet if you see me as I am being taken from you, it will be granted you; if not, it will not.' As they continued walking and talking, a chariot of fire and horses of fire separated the two of them, and Elijah ascended in a whirlwind into heaven." Elisha cries out, "My father, my father, the chariots of Israel and their horsemen." He then picks up the mantle of Elijah, crosses the Jordan, and the company of prophets declares, "The spirit of Elijah rests on Elisha." They bow to the ground before him.

The witnessing of ascent is powerful stuff biblically and postbiblically. The witness is the successor of the ascender; Elisha goes on to fulfill the jobs given to Elijah. I see the "do not hold me" (Jesus to Mary Magdalene) as evoking Elisha's attempts to hold on to his master who will be taken from him. Mary Magdalene is told to tell the disciples that Jesus said to her, "I am ascending to my father and your father, to my God and your God." He is, that is, in the process of ascending and she is witnessing this. John 20 is like a palimpsest overwriting 2 Kgs 2 as applied to Jesus and Mary Magdalene. The connections are not so much verbal (except for references to seeing and "I am ascending") as in terms of the action and emotion in the texts.

When I presented something of this reading of John 20 at a Society of Biblical Literature meeting, one of the respondents said, "I can see how I can read the text in the way you're proposing, but I don't see why I should." Well, I think we should at least try — in order possibly to get at more accurate assessments of the gender roles in early Christianities. The history of the interpretation of John 20 is riddled with misogyny: it stresses Mary's ignorance, her carnal mentality, and the strange incompleteness and unimportance of what she is said to experience.

---

tion," in *The Resurrection*, ed. S. T. Davis et al. (Oxford: Oxford University Press, 1998), pp. 189-90.

In the *Testament of Job* Job's three daughters witness their father's ascent in the chariots of the spirit and are themselves empowered to share in the kingdom, ecstatically singing hymns in the language of the angels; see also the *Testament of Adam and Eve*. These are examples of women witnessing ascent in the context of the merkabah (chariot) mysticism tradition, which I think we are discovering was very significant in some of the earliest forms of Christianity (see the work of the Society of Biblical Literature consultation on Early Jewish and Christian Mysticism).[29]

In any work that would have ended with the scene in John 20, Mary Magdalene would be the only guarantor of the vindication of Jesus, and verse 17 his final message. We can imagine the narrative continuing with a series of events consolidating Mary Magdalene's authority (the conferring of the Holy Spirit on her; the recognition and rejoicing of the disciples). But John's narrative does not continue in this way. Instead we have a silence about her that dismantles her authority and makes her report superfluous and abortive. The Elijah-Elisha tradition and its spirit-giving is truncated and distorted: Mary is not said to receive the spirit of Jesus, but instead that spirit is given in the next chapter to the male disciples. She is not said to fulfill the duties of Jesus, and is not seen as his prophetic successor.

There is no response at all to her report to the disciples. Her vision is discounted in chapter 21's numbering of the appearances of Jesus. The Beloved Disciple is said to be the first to believe (at the tomb), and Peter receives commission; she disappears from the story.

But if this tradition was truncated and all but obscured in the canon, it was developed in apocryphal works. In the *Gospel of Mary* (Magdalene), she stands up as comforter, encourager, and replacement for Jesus after he has departed. Her leadership role is accepted until Peter asks her to tell him and the others what she had learned from Jesus, which they have not heard. She tells of a vision she had had of Jesus, and of his description of his ascent — past the adversaries. Her account is met with anger and disbelief — and awareness of its implications on the part of Peter and Andrew: "Would Jesus have spoken secretly to a woman and not to us? Are we to turn around and listen to her? Did he prefer her to us?" They reject her testimony but Levi defends her: "If the Savior considered her to be worthy, who are you [Peter] to disregard her? For he knew her completely and loved her devotedly."[30]

---

29. See April D. DeConick, ed., *Paradise Now: Essays on Early Jewish and Christian Mysticism*, SBLSymS 11 (Atlanta: Society of Biblical Literature, 2006).

30. See the translation and commentary by Karen L. King, *The Gospel of Mary of*

Mary Magdalene appears as a visionary, a favorite disciple, a beloved one, praised for her great understanding in many other works such as the *Pistis Sophia,* the *Gospel of Philip, Dialogue of the Savior, Sophia of Jesus Christ, First Apocalypse of James, Manichean Psalm Book,* as mentioned above.

So my conclusion: Given the central importance of Mary Magdalene in the canonical Gospels, my reading of John 20 as indicating she is a successor of Jesus and inheritor of his Spirit; and given her importance and leadership in so many later apocryphal works — although her leadership is always contested — it is possible, even likely that some — those who could overcome the gender conflict — did honor Mary Magdalene as Mara.

To accept this as a possibility is to recognize that our understanding of movements within the early decades of what became Christianity must be expanded. I have argued that even if we may not be able precisely to locate its center(s), we can — and should — imagine what I call Magdalene Christianity, a movement or set of movements that continued on a trajectory of sorts from the first century to the fourth and beyond, to exist and create on the basis of wo/men's insight, revelation, and leadership. I am using the name of Mary Magdalene, which appears in the canon only in the Gospels (not in Paul, not in Acts) to refer to something that was unnamed,[31] and I am associating it with the testimony of this specific named woman, testimony understood as central to certain understandings of the resurrection and as rooted in Jewish apocalyptic and wisdom traditions. Examination of the opposition to Magdalene Christianity posed by Petrine, Pauline, and Jamesian, and other traditions and versions will eventually give a fuller picture of the origins of Christianity, in particular of its struggles regarding egalitarianism and of specific theological metaphors (Woman Wisdom; a corporate Son of Man or Human One), rites (baptism), and beliefs (resurrection experienced in the present and involving interconnectedness).[32] In my opinion, this may have been a form of Christianity that found no contradiction in proclaiming the resurrection of Jesus while knowing of his burial site and ossuary in Jerusalem.

Magdala (Santa Rosa, Calif.: Polebridge, 2003), pp. 17, 55, 88-89. Note the intriguing differences between the Coptic and earlier Greek fragments.

31. Cf. M. F. Bekenky, L. A. Bond, and J. S. Weinstock, *A Tradition That Has No Name: Nurturing the Development of People, Families, and Communities* (New York: Basic Books, 1997).

32. See J. Schaberg, "Magdalene Christianity," in *On the Cutting Edge: The Study of Women in Biblical Worlds. Essays in Honor of Elisabeth Schüssler Fiorenza,* ed. J. Schaberg et al. (New York: Continuum, 2004), pp. 193-220.

This, then, is what I am imagining: The Talpiot tomb and the ossuary that can be read as "Mary the Master" brings us in touch with physical evidence of this form of earliest Christianity. The bones of the honored woman and the bones of others important in the beginning were gathered by someone or some group in a rock-hewn tomb in Jerusalem. Its existence and location were forgotten or wiped out of historical memory, perhaps in some way connected to the fleeing of some Christians to Pella during the war of 66-70, according to Eusebius. What did remain in memory, however, or resurged was a traditional location of what had been the *empty* tomb, the place of revelation to Mary Magdalene.

What we need is further examination of the possibilities presented here. I would suggest that scholars who have worked on early Magdalene traditions be involved, such as E. DeBoer, H. Hearon, M. R. D'Angelo, K. King, F. Bovon, T. Ilan, E. Schüssler Fiorenza, and A. Brock. And scholars who have worked on the resurrection traditions, such as R. Hamerton-Kelly, C. Rowland, J. D. Crossan, P. Perkins, J. Levenson, K. J. Madigan, N. T. Wright, J. Collins, E. Schüssler Fiorenza, A. Segal, and D. Allison. Systematic theologians as well. The Society of Biblical Literature should devote a major session to this discussion, which I sincerely hope will not just go away.

The Mariam Ossuary in Greek

Jonathan J. Price

Much of the modern controversy about the significance of the first-century Jewish tomb in East Talpiot (Talpiyot),[1] particularly the radical suggestion (purveyed in a popular film) that the tomb's inscriptions reveal that Jesus of Nazareth was buried there together with his wife Mary Magdalene and their son Yehudah, depends on the correct reading of the Greek inscription on the ossuary with the Israel Antiquities Authority (IAA) registration number 1980-500. The claim that this ossuary, the only one bearing a Greek inscription from the burial cave, was that of Mary Magdalene is based first of all on the reading published by L. Y. Rahmani in his authoritative corpus of Jewish ossuaries.[2] The inscription in question is incised on the undecorated back side of the ossuary (the façade is ornamented with two rosette metopes), and appears as a string of letters with no spaces between words, in accordance with the common practice in ossuary inscriptions. Rahmani interpreted the string of letters as follows: Μαριαμήνου (ἡ) Μάρα = "of Mariamene who is (also) called) Mara." This was the reading followed by A. Kloner in his 1996 publication of the tomb, and it has been widely quoted and rarely challenged in subsequent discussions and presentations.[3]

---

1. For a recent summary of the issues, see the articles in *NEA* 69 (2006): 116-37. The film has provoked a flood of discussions and debates on the Internet, continuing to the present day.

2. L. Y. Rahmani, *A Catalogue of Jewish Ossuaries in the Collections of the State of Israel* (Jerusalem: Israel Antiquities Authority and Israel Academy of Sciences and Humanities, 1994).

3. A. Kloner, "A Tomb with Inscribed Ossuaries in East Talpiyot, Jerusalem," *'Atiqot* 29 (1996): 15-22.

The case for identifying this ossuary as that of Mary Magdalene rests, first, on the unusual nickname for Mariam, Mariamene = Mariamne. In later Christian literature (*Acts of Philip*, Origen, Hippolytus, etc.) she is indeed called Mariamne,[4] although those sources were compiled two to three centuries after her time (she does not have this name in the Gospels). Moreover, Μάρα is interpreted as an Aramaic title meaning "lordess," appropriate especially if she was married to Jesus and/or had an elevated role in the early Christian community, as some think. Finally, the language of the inscription, Greek, is seen to reflect Mary Magdalene's place of origin, Migdal (= Taricheae), an urban settlement on the shores of the Sea of Galilee, where it is supposed Greek was spoken more frequently than in the more landlocked, rural Jewish settlements like Nazareth or Bethlehem.

First, some purely epigraphical matters. Rahmani's reading requires certain unusual features in the otherwise clear and competently executed Greek: (a) the *nu* in Μαριαμήνου is written backward; (b) the *omicron* and *upsilon* are in ligature; and (c) the vertical chisel mark between Μαριαμήνου and Μάρα stands for H (ἡ) = ἡ καί. Of these features, only the second, the ligatured OY, is conventional, but as for that, the ligature in the present inscription more closely resembles AI than OY, as Stephen Pfann has shown with numerous parallels, albeit from papyri.[5] This leads us to a better reading of the supposed backward *nu* as a *kappa*. My personal inspection of the box has confirmed that this is undoubtedly the correct reading, and that the sequence of these symbols forms the Greek word καί, "and."

So far we have MAPIAMHKAI (ligature). The last four letters are unambiguously MAPA, as in Rahmani's reading. This leaves the chisel mark, which Rahmani interprets as follows: "The stroke between the *upsilon* of the first and the *mu* of the second name probably represents an *eta*, standing here for the usual ἡ καί . . . used in cases of double names."[6] Yet personal inspection has again persuaded me to question this reading, and to doubt even whether this mark was intended to be part of the inscription. I know of no parallels to such a slight half-line representing *eta*, it does not conform to the epigraphic idiom of ossuary inscriptions, and indeed there is no need for it to represent

4. See J. Tabor, "Testing a Hypothesis," *NEA* 69 (2006): 135.

5. See, e.g., his article "Mary Magdalene Has Left the Room," *NEA* 69 (2006): 130-31, although I do not agree with his theory that the second half of the inscription, from the καί, was written by a different hand. Different letterforms in the second half of the line mean nothing, especially in an informal, nonprofessional context like an ossuary inscription; note the differently formed *mu*s in the first name, especially in the first *hasta* of each.

6. *Catalogue*, 222, no. 701, n. 3.

any letter or letters. There are many flaws and stray chisel marks on the surface of this box, as found often on ossuaries. These many flaws and marks could have been on the box when the family acquired it, before they incised the name Mariam on its back side. The box could have acquired even more gouges and scratches when it was moved about in the cave, first by family members when the cave was in use, and then subsequently by robbers and explorers. For these reasons, flaws and stray marks are quite common on ossuaries, especially on the less expensive boxes made of soft stone, as this one was. Moreover, the small mark in question could also be a false start: the inscriber started to make the *mu* of MAPA, and then realized that the straight stroke he made would suit neither the left leg nor the lefthand middle stroke of the letter; a simple comparison of the three *mus*, all of which are different, makes this quite clear. Reading an ossuary inscription often requires critical selection of which lines and strokes belong to the letters and which are to be disregarded.

The resulting string of letters in the full inscription is thus MAPIAMHKAIMAPA. This string can be parsed in two ways. First, it can be Μαριαμ ἡ καὶ Μαρα, where ἡ is a relative pronoun, thus: "Mariam who is also known as Mara." This Greek form of Mariam imitates the original Hebrew, and is used by the Septuagint, as opposed to Μαριάμη, which is the usual Greek form, used by Josephus and other literary sources, as well as many documentary texts, including ossuaries.[7] The name Mara for a woman is attested on other ossuaries: one from Dominus Flevit,[8] another from an undisclosed location in Jerusalem,[9] and one in Aramaic (מרא) from the Mount of Offense (*CIJ* 1310). On another ossuary from Jerusalem it is clearly a hypocoristic of Martha.[10] There are also two instances of a Greek Mara in the Roman catacombs[11] and one in Cyrene.[12] The word *Mara* in any case

7. See T. Ilan, *Lexicon of Jewish Names in Antiquity*, part 1, *Palestine 330 BCE–200 CE*, TSAJ 91 (Tübingen: Mohr Siebeck, 2002), pp. 242-48. For examples on ossuaries, see Rahmani, *Catalogue*, no. 64; and P. Nahshoni et al., "Ḥorbat Zefiyya" [in Hebrew], *Excavations and Surveys in Israel (Ḥadashot Arkheologiyot)* 109 (1999): 129.

8. B. Bagatti and J. T. Milik, *Gli Scavi del "Dominus Flevit,"* part 1, *La Necropoli del Periodo Romano*, Pubblicazioni dello Studium Biblicum Franciscanum 13 (Jerusalem: Franciscan Printing Press, 1958), p. 99 no. 41.

9. Rahmani, *Catalogue*, no. 868.

10. Ibid., no. 468.

11. D. Noy, *Jewish Inscriptions of Western Europe*, vol. 2, *The City of Rome* (Cambridge: Cambridge University Press, 1995), nos. 190 and 458.

12. G. Lüderitz, *Corpus jüdischer Zeugnisse aus der Cyrenaika* (Wiesbaden, 1983), p. 50d.

cannot be the Aramaic title translated "lordess," for which the correct feminine form is מרתא or מרתת, which of course became the personal name Martha as well. Thus if this parsing is correct, the woman had a Hebrew and an Aramaic name, double names being quite common in Jewish nomenclature of the period.

The second possible interpretation of these letters is Μαριάμη καὶ Μαρα, "Mariame and Mara"; in other words, the box contained the bones of two persons. In this interpretation, Mariame is spelled in the standard manner for Greek, and she was interred in the box along with Mara. This is the reading favored by the two authoritative annual reviews of Greek epigraphy, the *Bulletin Épigraphique* (1998, no. 522) and the Supplementum epigraphicum graecum (46, no. 1996). If this is the correct reading, then it is interesting to note that Mara could be a male name, often appearing in the form Μάρης.[13] Of course, if it is a male name, then there is only one way to read the inscription. Unfortunately, the tomb and ossuaries had been disturbed already in antiquity and were found in a semichaotic state by the original excavators in 1980,[14] and the conditions in which it was quickly excavated guaranteed that we will never know, on the basis of bone analysis, how many people were interred in the box or what their gender was. Moreover, we have no knowledge of the person who made the inscription, a year after Mariam's death, nor of his or her relation to her.

In either case, the correct reading of the ossuary inscription does not allow the name Mariamene/Mariamne, and thus there is no epigraphical or onomastic reason to ascribe it to Mary Magdalene.

The Mariam ossuary, as already indicated, has the only Greek inscription among the six inscribed boxes from the tomb. Is there significance to this fact? There may be, but we cannot know what it is, not only because we do not know whose bones are interred in the box, but more importantly we do not know who wrote the inscription. When dealing with ossuary inscriptions, it is important to remember this principle: *The language of an epitaph does not necessarily reflect the mother tongue or even linguistic knowledge of the deceased.*[15]

13. Rahmani, *Catalogue*, nos. 413, 870; and note Μαρ and Μαρι at Jatt (J. Porath, ʿAtiqot 37 [1999]: 50, 51); Μαρις from Jaffa (J. Price, *Scripta Classica Israelica* 22 [2003]: 22); the Aramaic example in Rahmani, *Catalogue*, no. 327; cf. Ilan, *Lexicon*, p. 392; and see H. Wuthnow, *Die semitischen Menschennamen in griechischen Inschriften und Papyri des vorderen Orients* (Leipzig, 1930), p. 73.

14. See the description by S. Gibson, "Is the Talpiot Tomb Really the Family Tomb of Jesus?" *NEA* 69 (2006): 118-24.

15. See J. J. Price and H. Misgav, "Jewish Inscriptions and Their Use," in *The Litera-*

The language of commemoration and the spoken language(s) of the deceased can never be assumed to be identical, even if they often were. A contemporary example brings the point home: using epitaphs as a sole guide, one would conclude from Jewish cemeteries in the United States that American Jews were much more conversant in Hebrew than they in fact are. The ancient world is even more complex. Many people spoke languages that were not written at all, and in commemoration they had to choose from among the written languages used in epigraphy in the particular area where the epitaph was set up. A person could commission an epitaph in a language other than his or her mother tongue as an expression of cultural or religious identification. Moreover — especially in the case of ossuaries — a person may not have given any thought to his or her inscription at all, and merely relied on family members to take care of it. Thus the language of a funerary inscription very often reflects the choice of the inscriber, not the deceased. The choice of the inscriber *may* reflect what that person thought his dear departed would have wanted, but it also may reflect what the inscriber himself felt more comfortable writing.

The connection between the language of an epitaph and the spoken language of the deceased is least certain in the case of ossuary inscriptions, which were not vehicles of commemoration at all but merely labels to identify who was interred where, that is, to keep family members (who often had identical or similar names) straight in the burial caves. The inscription was made a year after the death of the family member, when the flesh had decayed and the bones were gathered for interment in the ossuary.[16] Most ossuary inscriptions were amateurishly produced, scratched onto a side of the box with a nail, which was often found on the cave floor. These inscriptions were never made for public display; the inscriber most naturally used whatever language he or she could write most comfortably; and many ossuary inscriptions do not reveal a high level of comfort with writing. The content of the inscription as well would not need to be planned ahead of time, since its purpose was primarily to record a name: that was all that was needed for the utilitarian purpose they had to fulfill.

Thus the language of the Mariam inscription is by no means an infalli-

---

ture of the Sages, part 2, *Midrash and Targum . . . ,* ed. S. Safrai et al., CRINT 2/3b (Assen: Van Gorcum, 2006), pp. 466ff.

16. On Jewish funerary practices in general, and especially secondary burial in ossuaries, see now R. Hachlili, *Jewish Funerary Customs, Practices and Rites in the Second Temple Period* (Leiden-Boston, 2005); and A. Kloner and B. Zissu, *The Necropolis of Jerusalem in the Second Temple Period* (Leuven, 2007) (Introduction: pp. 4-135).

ble guide to what language Mariam, and possibly a second person named Mara, spoke in life. The reason why this inscription was written in Greek, while the others from the same cave were in Jewish script, remains unknown to us, just like the identity of the family and its history.

THE JAMES OSSUARY

The James Ossuary and Its Implications

Joseph A. Fitzmyer, S.J.

"Sensation" is the word the Russian newspaper *Pravda Online* used to announce the discovery in 2002 of an ossuary with an inscription said to read, "James, son of Joseph, brother of Jesus." It has also been a sensation because of the way in which books and articles written about it have interpreted it. Perhaps it might be more accurate to say that the interpretation of the inscription has been sensational — more sensational than the ossuary itself. For this reason I consider it important to recall what is really known about the ossuary and what it means, and to reflect on the implications of the inscription on this important ancient object.

An ossuary is a stone box used in ancient Judea in the first centuries BC and AD to store the bones of a person who had died and whose flesh had decomposed. It served as a second burial. Hundreds of them have been recovered in the last century. Many of them are preserved in Israeli museums, for example, the Israel Museum in West Jerusalem or the Rockefeller Museum in East Jerusalem. Ossuaries are often artistically adorned, but some of them are simply plain. Both kinds sometimes bear an inscription, written in Greek, Hebrew, or Aramaic. Usually the inscription is merely the name of the person whose bones are within, sometimes supplied with a patronymic, or father's name. In 1994 an Israeli scholar, L. Y. Rahmani, published *A Catalogue of Jewish Ossuaries in the Collections of the State of Israel,*[1] in which he

---

1. See L. Y. Rahmani, *A Catalogue of Jewish Ossuaries in the Collections of the State of Israel* (Jerusalem: Israel Antiquities Authority and Israel Academy of Sciences and Humanities, 1994). See further E. M. Meyers, *Jewish Ossuaries: Reburial and Rebirth: Second*

described 897 of them, supplying photographs and details about their provenience, artistry, and inscriptions. This mode of second burial was practiced in ancient Judea from about 20 BC to AD 70, when Jerusalem was besieged and sacked by the Romans; after that the use of ossuaries became obsolete. So when this new inscribed ossuary came to light, it joined hundreds of other similar bone boxes from ancient Judea.

Its Aramaic inscription reads: *Yaʿăqôb bar Yôsēp ʾaḥûî dĕYēšûăʿ*, and it has been translated, "James, son of Joseph, brother of Jesus," or more literally, ". . . his brother, of Jesus." The first name *Yaʿăqôb* can be translated either "Jacob" (as in the OT) or "James" (as the name appears in the NT). This ossuary inscription is said to identify Jacob or James not only by his father but also by his brother, which is very rare; only one other instance of the mention of a brother has been found on an ossuary.

My further remarks about the new ossuary will be made under five headings: the authenticity of the ossuary and its inscription; problems in the Aramaic language of the inscription; the three names that occur in the inscription; the meaning of "brother"; and the implications of the discovery.

The Authenticity of the Ossuary and Its Inscription

Is this ossuary a genuinely antique Judean bone box or a modern fake? Is the Aramaic inscription it bears an authentic ancient engraving or a modern forgery? These two questions have to be answered first because the ossuary was bought from an antiquities dealer in East Jerusalem about 35 years ago. The dealer told the Israeli, in whose possession it now is, that it came from Silwan, an Arab village across the Kidron Valley to the east of Jerusalem, on the southern slope of the Mount of Olives or Mount Scopus. The Israeli owner, who at first wanted to remain anonymous, is Oded Golan, an engineer from Tel Aviv, who can no longer remember the Arab dealer's name from whom he bought the ossuary or even where his shop was located. Being an avid collector of ancient artifacts ever since childhood, he has a sizable private collection.

---

ary Burials in Their Ancient Near Eastern Setting, BibOr 34 (Rome: Biblical Institute, 1971); P. Figueras, *Decorated Jewish Ossuaries*, DMOA 20 (Leiden: Brill, 1985); E. Regev, "The Individualistic Meaning of Jewish Ossuaries: A Socio-anthropological Perspective on Burial Practice," *PEQ* 133 (2001): 39-49; Y. Peleg, "Gender and Ossuaries: Ideology and Meaning," *BASOR* 325 (2001): 65-73.

Because the ossuary was not discovered by archaeologists in a controlled excavation, its context or provenience is immediately suspect. Normally no scholar or archaeologist would put any credence in allegedly ancient artifacts that turn up in antiquities dealers' shops. For instance, the Archaeological Institute of America and the American Schools of Oriental Research have the policy of ignoring artifacts coming from antiquities dealers and will not allow articles about such objects to be published in their periodicals. Because of this policy, this new ossuary is suspect. It may be simply another instance of "looted goods."

Consequently, scholars such as Eric M. Meyers, an archaeologist of Duke University and editor of the *Oxford Encyclopedia of Archaeology in the Near East*,[2] has been quoted as having "serious questions about [its] authenticity." Meyers publicly expressed his misgivings about this inscription at the 2002 meeting of the Society of Biblical Literature in Toronto, while the ossuary was on display at the nearby Royal Ontario Museum. Meyers is not alone in such a judgment, even if one can easily dismiss the negative views of some mavericks who have claimed that the inscription is a forgery either because it is just "too pat,"[3] or because one can clearly see that the second part of the inscription ("the brother of Jesus") was added several centuries later.[4] The latter reason, however, is highly questionable in my opinion, because careful study of the entire inscription shows that it has been inscribed by one hand, as established by a comparison of the *'ayin* in the first and last names, even though one or other letter has not been too carefully drawn.[5] Unfortunately,

2. 5 vols. (New York: Oxford University Press, 1997).

3. A verdict attributed in the media to R. Eisenman, author of *James the Brother of Jesus: The Key to Unlocking the Secrets of Early Christianity and the Dead Sea Scrolls* (New York: Viking, 1996).

4. So Rochelle Altman, "Final Report on the James Ossuary" (www.israelinsider.com). Though Ms. Altman claims expertise in paleography, she is unknown to any of the recognized Semitic paleographers. She acquired a Ph.D. in medieval English from Arizona State University and says that she later studied paleography and calligraphy in Europe and Israel; for thirty years she was a printing consultant (see http://ccat.sas.upenn.edu/ioudaios/bio/altman.html). Not only has she maintained that the inscription was written in two different hands and at two different times, but she claims that it was not incised, but rather excised. In the latter view she is clearly wrong, because she apparently made that judgment solely from photographs and had not seen the ossuary itself. When one looks at the ossuary itself, it does not take an educated eye to discern that the inscription has not been excised, but incised.

5. Others who regard the inscription as a forgery are Jeff Chadwick, associate professor of church history at Brigham Young University; and D. Eylon, engineering professor at the University of Dayton. See J. N. Wilford, "Experts Question Authenticity of Bone

because the provenience of the ossuary is unknown, such doubts about it will never be dispelled.

There are, however, many scholars who have seen or examined the ossuary itself and maintain that it is an authentic ancient bone box and that its inscription is very probably not a modern forgery. To begin with, the inscription has been considered authentic by André Lemaire, a well-known and competent French epigrapher from the Sorbonne in Paris, who first learned about the ossuary from its Israeli owner, Oded Golan, who, although he possessed the ossuary for decades, was unacquainted with the New Testament and seems not to have suspected to whom the three names might refer. Lemaire was invited by Golan to look at some objects in his collection, and when he read the inscription, he immediately realized its possible relevance. Lemaire eventually published its text in the November–December 2002 issue of *Biblical Archaeology Review,* "Burial Box of James the Brother of Jesus."

Accompanying Lemaire's article is a report addressed to Hershel Shanks, editor of the *Review,* who had requested scientists of the Geological Survey of Israel to examine the ossuary. Two of them did so, analyzing the limestone of which the ossuary was made. They found that it came from Mount Scopus, the hill to the east of Jerusalem, and concluded that it was to be dated in the first or second century AD. They also reported on the patina, the sheen or surface coating of the limestone, which was produced by aging or the weathering of it over the centuries: "the patina does not contain any modern elements (such as modern pigments) and it adheres firmly to the surface. No signs of the use of a modern tool or instrument was [*sic*] found."[6]

If the inscription were made in recent times on an otherwise ancient ossuary with such a patina, the inscribed marks would differ from the rest of the surface, and the patina of the surface would be disturbed; but, according to these scientists, it has not been disturbed. The patina is clearly evident within the grooves of the inscribed letters, as it is also on the surrounding surface of the letters. The script itself in which the inscription is written certainly resembles that of many other inscriptions dated confidently to the first century AD. Only one letter in the inscription is difficult to read, the

---

Box for 'Brother of Jesus,'" *The New York Times* Science Section, 3 December 2002, D3. For criticism of Eylon's views, see E. J. Keall, "New Tests Bolster Case for Authenticity," *BAR* 29/4 (2003): 54-55.

    6. See A. Lemaire, "Burial Box of James the Brother of Jesus," *BAR* 28/6 (2002): 24-33, 70-71, esp. 29. The geological report was signed by Drs. Amnon Rosenfeld and Shimon Ilani.

dalet ("of") prefixed to the name "Jesus," but there can be no doubt about its meaning. Lemaire ended his discussion, saying, "It seems very probable that this is the ossuary of the James in the New Testament."[7]

The ossuary was brought to Toronto to be displayed in the Royal Ontario Museum especially during the annual meeting of the Society of Biblical Literature, held there 23-26 November 2002. Unfortunately, the ossuary was cracked, and it broke into five pieces during the trip from Israel. Curators of the museum repaired the ossuary, and museum experts were able to examine the bone box in great detail. The Toronto team concluded that the ossuary and its inscription are genuinely ancient and not a modern forgery.[8] When I examined the ossuary in the museum on 24 November along with Professor Lemaire, Frank M. Cross (professor emeritus of Harvard University),[9] and P. K. McCarter (professor at the Johns Hopkins University), all eventually agreed, "nothing in the inscription suggested a modern forgery."[10]

7. Ibid., p. 33.

8. See "News Release of 23 July 2003: Royal Ontario Museum Statement: Oded Golan's Arrest/James Ossuary" (Media@rom.on.ca); also Keall, *BAR* 29/4 (2003): 52-55, 70.

9. An advertising blurb for Hershel Shanks and Ben Witherington III, *The Brother of Jesus: The Dramatic Story & Meaning of the First Archaeological Link to Jesus & His Family* (San Francisco: HarperSanFrancisco, 2003), quotes Cross as follows: "The script is good for late Herodian, say A.D. 30-70. I think it's one piece; it's done beautifully. If it's forged, it's by a genius." However, J. A. Greene, writing in *Semitic Museum News* 6/2 (2003): 5, reports that Cross thinks differently, "While the ossuary is authentic, the inscription is a forgery. . . . The inscription is epigraphically flawless, even that questionable *dalet*. The deciding factor in his mind is the relative freshness of the lettering compared with the very weathered geometric rosette incised on the opposite side. If the inscription were as old as the ossuary itself, the letters would be as worn as the decoration. Very likely, the expertly forged but modern inscription was added to this ancient object in an attempt to increase its value on the antiquities market." It has been reported further that Cross "circulated a letter to colleagues around the world regretting Shanks' 'continued persistence in making claims' for the authenticity of the James ossuary, and declared that he now stood 'wholly and unambiguously with those who believe the ossuary inscription to be a forgery, a good forgery, but a forgery'" (N. A. Silberman and Y. Goren, "Faking Biblical History," *Archaeology* 56/5 [2003]: 20-29, esp. 29).

There may be, however, a way to explain the difference of the two sides: the "relative freshness" of the inscribed side may be owing to the fact that the ossuary lay for centuries on that side, whereas the geometric rosette on the back was exposed to the atmosphere in the burial cave. We shall never know, unfortunately, because the provenience of the ossuary is unknown.

10. See Shanks and Witherington, *Brother of Jesus*, p. 40. Prof. J. C. VanderKam of the University of Notre Dame also has been quoted as saying that "it looks like it is [au-

There is no way that one can be 100 percent sure about the authenticity of any ancient object or text. Consequently, one has to be content with a high degree of probability, and that is what I think we have in this case. Having said that, however, I think it is important to add that many, many of the Dead Sea Scrolls were acquired from Kando, an antiquities dealer in Bethlehem, who was the go-between for the bedouin discoverers of the scrolls and fragments of Qumran Caves 1, 4, and 11, and the scholars who pieced together the giant jigsaw puzzle that came from the 15,000 fragments of Qumran Cave 4. Hence some things that have come from antiquities dealers have proved, indeed, to be authentic. This inscribed ossuary may be too, even if one can never be certain about it.

Having written the above paragraphs, I was surprised to read reports in newspapers on 19 June 2003 that the Israel Antiquities Authority (IAA) had issued a public statement after an investigation of the ossuary that the inscription was "a modern-day forgery."[11] The deputy director of the IAA, Uzi Dahari, was quoted as saying that "microscopic and chemical analyses showed that a forger had cut through two layers of ancient varnish and patina to write the inscription, then had covered the letters with a recently applied mixture of water and ground chalk."[12] The question now is, does that IAA report settle the matter once and for all?

That public statement, issued in June 2003, was based on a report of the two committees set up by the IAA in March 2003, which were given three months to file their verdict. The committees met on 18 June 2003, after which an oral report was given. On 16 July a written summary report, addressed to Dr. Shuka Dorfman, Director General of the IAA, but dated 20 June 2003, was released. Hershel Shanks published this report, announcing: "'Final' Report Released," but he also observes that "*there is no final report —* no document subscribed to by all committee members explaining . . . that . . . the James ossuary . . . [is a] modern forger[y]. Instead, the 'final report' consists only of individual statements by committee members commenting on the inscriptions from the viewpoint of their expertise."[13] Those com-

---

thentic]" (see J. N. Wilford, "'Jesus' Inscription on Stone May Be Earliest Ever Found," *New York Times,* Tuesday October 22, 2002, p. A12).

11. See G. Gugliotta, "Agency: Inscription Citing Jesus Is Fake," *Washington Post,* Thursday, 19 June 2003, p. A6; G. Myre, "Israelis Say Burial Box of Jesus' Brother Is Fake," *New York Times,* Thursday, 19 June 2003, p. A11.

12. *Washington Post,* p. A6, col. 1.

13. See H. S[hanks], "The Storm over the Bone Box: Ossuary Update," *BAR* 29/5 (2003): 26-38, which incorporates the text on pp. 27-31.

ments, however, promise a scientific article or report that two committee members are still to write "in the usual scientific format."[14]

The so-called final report comes from fourteen Israeli scholars, with no contributions from non-Israeli experts and, strikingly, with no mention or recognition of the competence of either Prof. Lemaire or the Israeli scientists of the Geological Survey of Israel. Their work is simply ignored. Moreover, the summary report admits that "the most suitable experts were chosen even if they had, in the past, expressed an opinion on the subject, as well as top scholars who had never been involved with the authenticity question."[15] As far as can be ascertained, those who had expressed an opinion "in the past" had uttered a negative opinion; so this may be a question of parti pris.

From the summary report and the so-called final report, we learn that eight members of the Writing and Content Committee were to study the script, paleography, and content of the ossuary inscription, and six members of the Materials and Patina Committee were to submit the ossuary inscription to petrographic analysis, carbon 14 examination, and patina investigation. They are said to have concluded that "to the best of our scientific judgment . . . the James Ossuary inscription is a forgery" and that "the patina . . . is forged and significantly varies from the original patina."[16]

The reasons for such a conclusion are supplied in the individual statements of the final report. The conclusion just quoted sounds like a unanimous decision of the fourteen members. However, when one reads the individual comments of those members whose judgments are cited — only five of the eight on the Writing and Content Committee,[17] and only four of the six of the Materials and Patina Committee[18] — one finds that several of the statements are strikingly nuanced, despite their negative reaction. Moreover, this reaction sometimes depends on reasons other than the individuals' "own expertise," which was part of the original mandate of the IAA when it set up the committees.

For instance, Writing Committee member Prof. S. Ahituv, "expert on Ancient Hebrew inscriptions," frankly admits, "On palaeographic grounds

14. Ibid., p. 29.

15. Ibid., p. 28.

16. So quoted in ibid., p. 31.

17. One member, S. Ahituv, admitted that he was not "qualified to decide in this area of Second Temple period palaeography."

18. One member, E. Boaretto, a radiocarbon expert, admitted that there was nothing organic in the inscription that could be tested.

alone the authenticity or otherwise of the ossuary inscription cannot be proved. But I do not see myself qualified to decide in this area of Second Temple period palaeography."[19] In other words, although he has disqualified himself, his vote has somehow been part of the "scientific judgment."

Dr. Tal Ilan, another member of the Writing Committee, said to be a "historian, expert on the Hebrew and Aramaic names in the Second Temple period," has admitted that she is not "an expert on . . . carved inscriptions or palaeography" and that she has relied on what "experts have determined," without mentioning who such experts might be. Ilan has published indeed a *Lexicon of Jewish Names in Late Antiquity,* part 1, *Palestine 330* BCE–200 CE, which lists 3,193 names.[20] She notes that "Joseph" is the second most popular name, "Jesus" the sixth most popular, and "James" the eleventh; in all, 379 men bear these names. Moreover, she admits that she studied the ossuary in the summer of 2002, before Lemaire's article was published, and noted that "the letters were clear and their context did not raise in me any special interest. The names were plausible." That would seem to mean that she, an Israeli Jewish scholar, considered the ossuary inscription to be genuine. In the summary report, however, she is quoted as saying, "Even if the ossuary is authentic, there is no reason to assume that the deceased was actually the brother of Jesus. But I am of the opinion that the inscription is a forgery."[21] However, she has given no reason why she opines that the inscription is a forgery. In effect, that is an unsubstantiated negative judgment that has become part of "scientific judgment."

Again, Prof. Roni Reich, another member of the same committee, an "archaeologist, expert on First and Second Temple periods," filed two reports about the ossuary. In the first (27 April 2003), he reveals that he examined the inscription "only by naked eye": "all the letters are clear and easily legible"; with no "difference in engraving between parts of the inscription," which was "written in one continuum." Its writing is "first century CE 'Jewish Script,'" and he concluded that the ossuary bore "an authentic late Second Temple period (mainly first century CE) inscription," because it "does not show any mixture of morphological or textual aspects from different periods that could indicate forgery." In a later report (16 June 2003) he still assumed that the inscription was authentic, "unless I will be convinced by my

19. The text of the individual statements of the final report can be found at www.bib-arch.org.

20. TSAJ 91 (Tübingen: Mohr Siebeck, 2002).

21. *BAR* 29/5 (2003): 30.

own observations, or by those of other scholars"; but he added, "My committee colleagues did not convince me" (i.e., other members of the Writing Committee). When, however, the results of the investigation of the patina inside the letters of the inscription conducted by Drs. Ayalon and Goren, members of the other committee, were presented, Reich admitted, "*I am now convinced* that the patina . . . could not have been produced in nature in ancient times. . . . As a result, I am forced to change my opinion on the matter." In other words, when consulting his own expertise, as he was commissioned by the IAA, he considered the inscription authentic; but when he listened to others in an area where he could not judge, he considered it "a modern forgery," along with others of the Writing Committee, who yielded to the verdict of two scholars of the second committee. Yet both Ilan's and Reich's unsubstantiated negative judgments are counted as negative in the "scientific judgment."

I could quote still other statements of members of the Writing Committee (E. Eshel, A. Kloner) that raise issues that are not always wholly convincing. Although most of the negative statements of the Materials and Patina Committee sound impressive, I am not competent to assess them. Yet even there one has to be careful, for one member of that committee, Prof. Y. Goren, maintains that the ossuary inscription "was inscribed or cleaned in a modern period."[22] That it was "cleaned in a modern period" would mean something quite different from being "inscribed in a modern period." Perhaps the cleaning process has left some modern traces that have influenced this committee's judgment; and it is known that the ossuary has been cleaned in modern times. Since, however, cleaning is not the same thing as inscribing, are traces so produced sufficient to declare the inscription a modern forgery?

The reports that I have cited are sufficient to show that the last word has not yet been uttered on this new ossuary inscription, even by this "flawed" final report of the IAA.[23]

Lastly, two aspects of this problem have to be recalled: (a) The ossuary had been examined by scientists of the Geological Survey of Israel and also by expert curators at the Royal Ontario Museum in Toronto; neither of these teams concluded that the ossuary or its inscription was fake. Indeed, as already mentioned, the Israeli scientists went out of their way to stress that the

22. This ambiguity was noticed by Shanks too (ibid., p. 33).
23. See further the scathing criticism of it written by A. Lemaire, "Israel Antiquities Authority Report on the James Ossuary Deeply Flawed," *BAR* 29/6 (2003): 50-58, 67, 70.

patina does not seem to have been disturbed, and no sign of the use of a modern instrument was found.[24] (b) The reaction of the IAA is simply the same as the attitude of most archaeologists about artifacts obtained from antiquities dealers, as already mentioned. Only now it has become a matter of politicized archaeology, advocated by the highest authority on antiquities in the State of Israel. The IAA even arrested and interrogated (for 30 hours) the owner of the ossuary, Oded Golan, but was unable to charge him or convict him. Is that sort of political archaeology sufficient to undo the judgment of the Israeli geologists and the Toronto curators? In my opinion, *adhuc sub iudice lis est:* the jury is still out!

Problems in the Aramaic Language of the Inscription

The first problem is the way in which almost everyone who has read the Aramaic inscription has translated it, "James, son of Joseph, brother of Jesus," understanding the two phrases to be in apposition to the name "James," that is, that James was a son of Joseph *and* a brother of Jesus.[25] However, since there is no *waw*, the Aramaic copula "and," before the word "brother," one could just as easily take the last phrase to be in apposition to the name "Joseph," that is, "James, son of Joseph, the brother of Jesus." This is, in fact, the way several names are found in the Old Testament that are followed by the name of the person's father and that of his brother. The Aramaic translation of the names in the Targums uses the same formulation as in the new ossuary. Thus "Othniel, son of Kenaz, brother of Caleb" (Josh 15:17; Judg 1:13; 3:9); or "Jonadab, son of Shimeah, brother of David" (2 Sam 13:3, 32).[26] In such in-

---

24. And yet Ms. O. Cohen, another member of the Materials and Patina Committee, asserts that "the first part of the inscription is new, cuts through the original patina and is coated with a granular patina that appears to have been produced from chalk dust mixed with water" (p. 30). "Cuts through the original patina"! Whom is one to believe? Did Ms. Cohen ever read the earlier Geological Survey report?

25. So Witherington unquestioningly translates it (*Brother of Jesus,* p. 98 [line 9]).

26. In *Targum Jonathan* one reads *'tny'l br qnz 'ḥwhy dklb* (Josh 15:17); *ywndb br šm'h 'ḥwhy ddwyd* (2 Sam 13:3, 32). See also *yhwntn br šm'h 'ḥwhy ddwyd,* "Jonathan, son of Shimei, brother of David" (2 Sam 21:21). The same formula is found in *'ḥyh br 'ḥyṭwb 'ḥwhy d'ykbwd,* "Ahijah, son of Ahitub, brother of Ichabod" (1 Sam 14:3), but some interpreters consider the verse spurious (see R. W. Corney, "Eli," *IDB* 2:85). Again, the formula occurs in 2 Sam 23:18, "Abishai, son of Zeruiah, brother of Joab," but *Targum Jonathan* translates it with an inversion of the appositives, *'byšy 'ḥwy dyw'b br ṣrwyh,* "Abishai, brother of Joab, son of Zeruiah."

stances, the last phrase is an appositive to the second name, not to the first. This would mean, then, that Jesus was the brother of Joseph and that James was the nephew of Jesus. That would complicate things even more, because it would still be asserting that someone named Joseph was the brother of Jesus.

Consequently, this alternate way of reading the inscription reveals how much of the discussion of it has been dominated by established or customary ways of interpreting New Testament data. This is the first problem, with which most interpreters of the new ossuary have not reckoned.[27]

The second problem that calls for explanation is the unusual form of the Aramaic word for "brother," *'aḥûî*. Because of it, I supplied above a more literal translation of the last phrase, "his brother, of Jesus." Normally, one would have expected *'ăḥā' dĕYēšûă'*, "the brother of Jesus." Instead one finds a form with a pronominal suffix meaning "his brother," which is then explained by *dalet*, "of," and the following name, "(that is) of Jesus." This combination of a suffixal form of a noun followed by the pronoun *dĕ* is a well-known feature in later stages of the Aramaic language (e.g., in the Targums), but it is rare in first-century Aramaic. Furthermore, such a suffixal form meaning "his brother" would have been written at that time: *'aḥûhî*. A little research, however, has shown that the syncopated form *('ăḥûî)* is attested in an Aramaic text of the Dead Sea Scrolls, *Genesis Apocryphon,* 1QapGen 21:34: *Lôṭ bar 'aḥûî dî 'Abrām,* "Lot, the son of Abram's brother," literally, "the son of his brother, of Abram." It has the same construction. Lemaire too had discovered the same syncopated form on another ossuary in the Rahmani catalogue (no. 570), "Shimi, son of 'Aśiyah, brother of Ḥanin," or literally, "his brother, of Ḥanin."[28] Hence, even though the Aramaic formulation seemed at first unusual, it merely records a contemporary way of pronouncing and writing the patronymic, which heretofore was practically unknown.[29] So even though some hesitated about the inscription at first because of this

27. It has been noted by a reader who wrote to the editor of *BAR* about it; see *BAR* 29/2 (2003): 12; there is a reply by P. K. McCarter, who claims that the usual way of reading the new ossuary inscription follows "the ordinary formula" or "the usual practice in writing names," even though he cites 2 Sam 13:3, 32 as an exception. Yet given the number of instances cited in n. 25, it is hardly the exception, because they are clearly instances in which the third person named is indeed the brother of the second person named.

28. In Aramaic it reads: *šymy br 'śyh 'ḥwy [d]ḥnyn.*

29. As a matter of fact, the same syncopated form has been found in yet another ancient Aramaic inscription, published by J. Naveh, *'l psyps w'bn hktwbwt h'rmywt wh'brywt mbty-hknst h'tyqym* (Jerusalem: Israel Exploration Society, 1978), p. 41 (no. 20.3).

form, it bears the earmarks of genuine contemporary Aramaic writing. The only questionable thing in the inscription is the form of *dalet*, "of," before "Jesus."

The Three Names That Occur in the Inscription

The collocation of the three names in this Aramaic inscription is noteworthy, especially because of their order and the kinship they may express. Let us presume for a moment that the usual way of reading this new inscription were correct, "James, son of Joseph, brother of Jesus," meaning that James was a brother of Jesus. The paternity of James is ascribed in the inscription to "Joseph," which is otherwise unknown about Joseph, the husband of Mary, in the New Testament.

In the case of Jesus, however, fatherhood is ascribed in the New Testament to Joseph. John 1:45 records the words of Philip speaking to Nathanael, "We have found him of whom Moses in the law and also the prophets wrote, Jesus of Nazareth, son of Joseph" (RSV). Again, the same Gospel records the query of Capernaum Jews, "Is not this Jesus, the son of Joseph, whose father and mother we know?" (6:42 RSV). The same query is recorded also in Luke's Gospel, "Is not this Joseph's son?" (4:22). Although the New Testament speaks of a "Jacob" as the father of Joseph in the Matthean genealogy (Matt 1:16), one does not find there the inverse relationship, such as is expressed in the Aramaic inscription of this new ossuary, "James/Jacob, son of Joseph."

Yaʿăqôb was a name commonly used in ancient Judea; it is known from texts among the Dead Sea Scrolls (1QTLevi [1Q21] 4.1; 19.1; 29.1;[30] 4QLevib ar [4Q213a] 2.12; 4QLevic ar [4Q213b] 1.4 ["my father, Jacob"]). Could the "James" mentioned on the new ossuary be one of those mentioned in the New Testament? In the New Testament, the Greek name *Iakōbos* is a grecized transcription of Hebrew *Yaʿăqôb* and is usually translated into English as "James." It is used of at least five different persons: (1) the apostle, son of Zebedee (Matt 10:2); (2) the apostle, son of Alphaeus (Matt 10:3): (3) the son of a Mary (Mark 16:1), who is called "the little" (probably meaning "the younger') in Mark 15:40; (4) the father of the apostle Jude (mentioned only in Luke 6:16; Acts 1:13); and (5) James of Jerusalem, an important figure in the church there (Acts 12:17; 15:13-21; 21:18). Apart from the two apostles,

---

30. In each case, partly but certainly restored.

however, the father of none of the others is named in the New Testament.[31] The two apostles are usually called Saint James, whereas James of Jerusalem is not, unless he is identified wrongly with an apostle.[32]

Of these five, the last named is called by Paul "the brother of the Lord" (Gal 1:19). He is said to have been in Jerusalem, when Paul first visited the city after his conversion (Gal 1:18). So he is often called "James of Jerusalem" to distinguish him from the two apostles, the son of Zebedee and the son of Alphaeus. Paul mentions this James of Jerusalem also in Gal 2:9, 12; 1 Cor 15:7.[33]

The fourth-century historian Eusebius of Caesarea (AD 260-340), in speaking of James of Jerusalem, sometimes repeats the Pauline title, "the brother of the Lord" (*Hist. Eccl.* 2.23.1). He also quotes a second-century writer, Hegesippus, who recounted that James, called "the Just," because of "his excessive righteousness," became the first Christian bishop of Jerusalem (*Hist. Eccl.* 2.23.1, 4, 7), thus building on the meager data of Acts.[34]

Flavius Josephus, the first-century Jewish historian, narrates how the

---

31. Witherington (*Brother of Jesus*, p. 98) claims that Matt 13:55 implies that Joseph is the father of the James of Jerusalem. That, however, depends on how one interprets Matt 13:55, because, whereas the Matthean Gospel speaks there of Jesus as "the carpenter's son," the earlier parallel in Mark 6:3 identifies Jesus himself as "the carpenter," and it is silent about who his father is.

32. So *The Washington Post* ("Stone Box May Be Oldest Link to Jesus," October 22, 2002, pp. A1, A19): "once held the bones of St. James, leader of the Christian church of Jerusalem." The same error occurs in *Archaeology* 56/5 (2003): 22.

The way the Greek text of Gal 1:19 is often translated leads one to think of this James as an apostle (and hence call him Saint James): "I saw none of the other apostles except James, the Lord's brother" (KJV, NKJV, RSV, NRSV, ESV, NEB, REB). That translation, however, is problematic for two reasons: (a) 1 Cor 15:5-7 distinguishes this James not only from the Twelve, but also from "all the apostles." (b) The conjunction *ei mē*, besides meaning "except," can also be the equivalent of *alla*, "but," as *ei mē* is used in Gal 1:7, and cognate *ean mē* in Gal 2:16. See also Matt 5:13; 12:4; 17:8; Luke 4:26; consult BDAG, p. 278 (col. 2, last 5 lines); K. Beyer, *Semitische Syntax im Neuen Testament,* 2nd ed. (Göttingen: Vandenhoeck & Ruprecht, 1968), p. 139; H. Koch, "Zur Jakobusfrage Gal 1,19," *ZNW* 33 (1934): 204-9.

For this reason, NIV rightly translates Gal 1:19 thus: "I saw none of the other apostles — only James, the Lord's brother"; similarly, NAB: "But I did not see any other of the apostles, only James the brother of the Lord"; NJB; NEB (note).

33. See also Jude 1.

34. "James the Just *(dikaios)*" is also mentioned in the third-century Coptic *Gospel of Thomas* saying 12.

high priest Ananos brought "a man named James, the brother of Jesus who was called the Christ" (*Ant.* 20.9.1 §200) before the Sanhedrin, accused him and others of having violated the Mosaic law, and delivered them up to be stoned. This would have been about AD 62-63. Strikingly, the ossuary inscription now preserves the Aramaic equivalent of the first part of the title used by Josephus for James of Jerusalem, "brother of Jesus." Yet there is no evidence, either in the New Testament or in later historical records, that this James of Jerusalem had a father named Joseph.

Moreover, Eusebius gives an extended but similar account of James's death, recording that he was thrown down from the pinnacle of the temple, stoned, clubbed to death, and buried "on the spot," in Jerusalem near the temple (*Hist. Eccl.* 2.23.18).[35] At times, however, Eusebius, in speaking of this James, says, "who is called the brother of the Lord" (*tou kyriou chrēmatizōn adelphos,* 3.7.8); "who was said to be the Lord's brother" (*ho tou kyriou legomenos adelphos ēn,* 4.5.3). In such cases, is Eusebius quoting the terminology of others, or is he affirming such a relationship of James to Jesus on his own? It is hardly the second alternative, because, when he tells of the risen Christ appearing to James (referring to 1 Cor 15:7), he says of him, "who was one of the alleged brothers of the Savior" (*houtos tōn pheromenōn tou sōtēros adelphōn,* 1.12.5). This last passage may give an answer to my query; but Eusebius cites Hegesippus again, "After James the Just had been martyred for the same reason as the Lord, Symeon, the son of Clopas, also related to the Divine One, was appointed bishop [of Jerusalem], whom everybody proposed because he was another [literally, a second] cousin of the Lord" (*onta anepsion tou kyriou deuteron,* 4.22.40). That seems to mean that Eusebius considered James to have the same relationship to Jesus, not as a brother, but as a "cousin." It has often been said that the cousin relationship entered the church tradition because of Jerome's writing *Against Helvidius.*[36]

---

35. See further J. Painter, *Just James: The Brother of Jesus in History and Tradition* (Edinburgh: T&T Clark, 1999); R. J. Bauckham, *James* (London: Routledge, 1999); B. D. Chilton and C. A. Evans, eds., *James the Just and Christian Origins,* NovTSup 98 (Leiden: Brill, 1999).

36. §§15-17; PL 23:208-12; FC 53:33-37 (composed AD 383). So it was argued by J. B. Lightfoot, *Saint Paul's Epistle to the Galatians* (1900; repr. Grand Rapids: Zondervan, 1967), pp. 255-65, esp. 256, "Thus James the Lord's brother was in reality the Lord's cousin. . . . So far St Jerome, who started the theory." In reading the passages in Jerome's treatise *Against Helvidius,* however, I find that he does explain *adelphos* by *cognatio,* "kinship," but I fail to find there any equivalence of *adelphos* and *anepsios.* In his later treatise, *Comm. in Matth.* 12.49; SC 242:262, however, Jerome writes: *fratres Domini non*

In that treatise Jerome was unable to cite any prior tradition affirming such a relationship and depended solely on his own exegetical skill, maintaining that *adelphos* connoted *cognatio,* "kinship," not *natura,* "actual brotherhood." "Cousin," however, is a very questionable meaning of *adelphos,* as has been pointed out many times,[37] since the New Testament has a word for "cousin," *anepsios,* the very term that Eusebius used in the last passage quoted above. So much then for the name "James" and who it might be and how he is related to Jesus. If he is not Jesus' brother, he may be a kinsman, but not specifically a "cousin." To the implications of this we shall return momentarily.

Yôsēp, "Joseph," is also a name that was commonly used in ancient Judea. The Hebrew form occurs at least a dozen times, and the Greek form of it a few times on ossuaries in Rahmani's catalogue. It is found also in Aramaic texts of the early second century from the caves of Murabbaʿat; with the spelling *Yĕhôsēp* it is even more common in those texts.

Similarly, *Yēšûáʿ,* "Jesus," is attested on ossuaries also (six times in Hebrew, and four times in Greek, *Iēsous,* in the Rahmani catalogue); it also occurs in Murabbaʿat texts.[38] Hence theoretically the new Aramaic inscription could refer to any one of these persons, when the names are considered in isolated fashion.

That the three names appear together on this new inscription, however, is significant, but what is the likelihood that the names refer to persons with the same names in the New Testament? It is certainly a possibility, but is it probable? Lemaire concluded that "it seems very probable that this is the ossuary of the James in the New Testament," even though he also admitted earlier on the same page that "nothing in this ossuary inscription clearly confirms the identification."[39]

---

filios Ioseph sed consobrinos Saluatoris Mariae liberos intelligimus materterae Domini, "we understood the brothers of the Lord not to be sons of Joseph, but cousins of the Savior, children of Mary, the Lord's maternal aunt." See also *De viris illustribus* 2; PL 23:639: *Jacobus, qui appellatur frater Domini . . . ut nonnulli existimant, Joseph ex alia uxore, ut autem mihi videtur, Mariae sororis Matris Domini, cujus Joannes in libro suo meminit, filius, post passionem Domini statim ab apostolis Hierosolymorum episcopus ordinates.*

37. Most recently by Witherington, *Brother of Jesus,* p. 204; see also BDAG, p. 18.

38. See further L. Díez Merino, "'Jesús' en la onomástica aramea judía antigua (s. II a. C–s. II d. C.)," *Miscelanea Comillas* 41 (1983): 351-55. Recall too the statistics given by Ilan, quoted above.

39. "Burial Box," p. 33.

Although it is not widely known, this is not the first time that the name "Jesus" has been discovered on an ossuary. In January 1931 the Israeli scholar E. L. Sukenik published an inscription from an ossuary found in 1926 in what was then called the Palestine Archaeological Museum in East Jerusalem. Its provenience was unknown, and no one then called it a fake! It read: *Yēšûaʿ bar Yĕhôsēp*, "Jesus, son of Joseph."[40] If this ossuary were related to the newly published one, it might be the same Joseph, and possibly the same Jesus. Sukenik, however, careful scholar that he was, drew no conclusion from it about any New Testament personages, realizing that "Joseph" and "Jesus" were commonly used names for first-century Judean Jews.

To illustrate how common such names were, I cite yet another ossuary, this one found by archaeologists in a controlled excavation of 1980 in East Talpiot, a section of Jerusalem. It bore the inscription, *Yēšûaʿ bar Yĕhôsēp*, "Jesus, son of Joseph."[41] It was discovered with eight other ossuaries, six of which bore inscriptions; five of them have the names *Mariamēnou Mara* (in Greek!), "of Mariamene (also called) Mara"; *Yĕhûdāh bar Yēšûaʿ* (in Aramaic), "Jude, son of Jesus"; *Matyāh* (in Aramaic?), "Matthias" or "Matthew"; and elsewhere on same ossuary, *Mat[y]āh* (badly preserved); *Yôsēh* (nickname for) "Joseph"; *Maryāh* (contracted grecized form of *Miryam*), "Mary."[42] Because the names Jesus, Mary, and Joseph appeared in this batch of ossuaries, claims were made, especially in Great Britain, that the tomb of the Holy Family had been found. In 1996 the BBC sent a research team to Jerusalem to investigate; *The Sunday Times* (31 March 1996) carried an article entitled, "The Tomb that Dares Not Speak Its Name." Israeli archaeologists and the IAA, however, were much more restrained. A member of the IAA, Prof. Amos Kloner, was quoted, "I would not say that it deserves a special interest other than the chance of the appearance of the names. . . . I can't say a possibility that it is the tomb of the Holy Family does not exist at all, but I

40. Rahmani, *Catalogue*, no. 9. See E. L. Sukenik, *Jüdische Gräber Jerusalems um Christi Geburt (Vortrag gehalten am 6. Januar 1931 in der archäologischen Gesellschaft, Berlin)* (Jerusalem: Azriel Printing Press, 1931): "Ich möchte hier ausdrücklich betonen, dass ich keine Konsequenzen aus der Auffindung dieser Namen ziehen möchte und sie nicht mit irgendwelchen Persönlichkeiten aus jener Zeit, die im Neuen Testament erwähnt sind, zu identifizieren gedenke. Die Namen waren zu jener Zeit ziemlich häufig und für irgendeine Identifikation fehlen uns jegliche Beweise" (pp. 19-20). See also MPAT §106; Figueras, *Decorated Jewish Ossuaries*, pp. 13, 17.

41. Rahmani, *Catalogue*, no. 704. The first name is poorly written, and Rahmani puts a question mark behind it.

42. See Rahmani, *Catalogue*, nos. 701-703, 705-706.

think such a possibility is very close to zero."[43] The whole incident simply points to the fact that names like Jesus and Joseph were in common use, and so they create the very problem of identifying the three persons mentioned on the new ossuary that we are discussing.

The main difficulty in accepting the new ossuary as that of "James, the brother of the Lord," is that James of Jerusalem is never said in the New Testament to have had a father named Joseph. This may be an argument from silence, but even if the ossuary could possibly be his, it still remains probable that it is not.

The Meaning of "Brother"

Another problem in the inscription is the meaning of "brother." For both Aramaic *'aḥ* and Greek *adelphos* denoted in the ancient world of such inscriptions blood brother or sibling, which might be what is meant in this new Aramaic inscription. This meaning is not certain there, however, because the words were used often in a broader sense to denote a "relative" or "kinsman."

A broader sense of *'aḥ* occurs in the Aramaic texts of Tobit from Qumran Cave 4. In 4QToba (4Q196) 6.11, Sarah prays in her grief, "I am my father's only child; he has no other child to be his heir; and he has no close relative or kinsman *(wĕ'aḥ lēh waqĕrîb)*, for whom I should keep myself" (Tob 3:15). See also in 4QTobb (4Q197) 4 iii 2, 4, 5. Sometimes *'aḥ* even means "compatriot" (4QToba 2.12); and it can be used in a more generic sense, when a speaker does not yet comprehend the precise relationship. Thus in 4QTobb 4 iii 5, Edna, the wife of Raguel, asks the young Tobiah and Azariah (the angel in disguise) on their arrival at Raguel's house, "Where are you from, brothers?" *(min'ān 'attûn 'ăḥay* [lit., "my brothers"; = Tob 7:3 NRSV]).[44]

Similarly, in the Greek version of Tobit, *adelphos* means "relative" or "kinsman" in 3:15 (quoted above); 5:6, 13, 14; 6:18; 7:1, 2, 4, 7, 10, 11; it too has the sense of "compatriot" in 1:10, 16; 2:2, 3. In 4QToba 14 ii 5, young Tobiah even addresses the angel Raphael in disguise as "[my] brother, Azariah" (= Tob 7:1 NRSV). This meaning of *adelphos* occurs not only in the translation Greek of the Septuagint, but also in many extrabiblical writings.[45]

---

43. http://orion.mscc.huji.ac.il/orion/archives/1996a/msg00155.html.

44. See further P. Grelot, "Les noms de parenté dans le livre de *Tobie*," *RevQ* 17 (1996-97): 327-37.

45. See BDAG, p. 18: used of members of a religious community, of hermits at the

Consequently, the description of James given by Paul in Gal 1:19, "the brother of the Lord," does not necessarily mean that James was the blood brother of Jesus. If this James of Jerusalem were the same as the James of Mark 6:3, along with siblings Joses, Judas, and Simon (also mentioned in Matt 13:55), there is a further problem. The James of Mark 6:3 might seem to be a sibling of Jesus of Nazareth, but it is not a foregone conclusion. For in the same Gospel, the evangelist depicts a Mary standing at the cross with two other women, Mary Magdalene and Salome (Mark 15:40; cf. 16:1), and calls her "the mother of James the little and of Joses." James and Joses, however, are two of the four said to be *adelphoi* of Jesus in Mark 6:3. The Mary of Mark 15:40 is scarcely the mother of the crucified man, on whom she and the other women are gazing from afar.[46] The evangelist, who has already called Jesus "the son of Mary" (6:3), would never have used such a circumlocution — "the mother of James the little and of Joses" — to identify Mary, the mother of Jesus. Moreover, one cannot use the data of the Johannine Gospel, where the mother of Jesus does stand at the foot of the cross (John 19:25), to identify the "Mary" of Mark 15:40; the Synoptic tradition gives no evidence of the mother of Jesus standing at or near the cross.[47] This means, therefore, that *adelphos* in Mark 6:3 does not necessarily mean blood brother, and that it carries rather the nuance of a relative or kinsman.[48] Thus the problem of the meaning of *adelphos* is created by the data of the New Testament itself, and does not arise simply because of later Christian tradition (about Mary's perpetual virginity). On the contrary, the later Christian tradition has been formed in light of such a New Testament problem.

Serapeum in Memphis, of Essenes (Josephus, *War* 2.122); also of Christians in the NT (Rom 16:23; 1 Cor 1:1, etc.).

46. See K. P. Donfried et al., "Mary in The Gospel of Mark," in *Mary in the New Testament: A Collaborative Assessment by Protestant and Roman Catholic Scholars*, ed. R. E. Brown et al. (Philadelphia: Fortress, 1978), pp. 51-72.

47. Witherington so interprets the passage, apparently seeing no difficulty in such eisegesis (*Brother of Jesus*, p. 200). Indeed, he goes so far as to say that *hē adelphē tēs mētros autou, Maria hē tou Klōpa*, which is part of the same verse and is translated usually as "his mother's sister, Mary the wife of Clopas" (RSV), is more likely "a sister-in-law than a sister" (p. 201). There is a good Greek word for "sister-in-law," *galoōs*, which is not used by the evangelist.

48. See further J. Blinzler, *Die Brüder und Schwestern Jesu*, SBS 21 (Stuttgart: Katholisches Bibelwerk, 1967), pp. 71-93; but cf. J. P. Meier, *A Marginal Jew: Rethinking the Historical Jesus*, 4 vols., ABRL (New York: Doubleday, 1991-2001), 1:220-22; idem, "The Brothers and Sisters of Jesus in Ecumenical Perspective," *CBQ* 54 (1992): 1-28.

When one considers the new ossuary inscription and if one thinks that it refers to James as the "brother" of Jesus of Nazareth, one would have to show, first of all, that the *Yēšûă'* mentioned there is exclusively Jesus of Nazareth. Since there is no way of showing that, it will remain always possible that it refers to another person so named. Second, the appearance of the three names together in this inscription could denote the very persons known from the New Testament, with whom we are all familiar; but how does one exclude sheer coincidence, given the frequency of such names? Third, the final phrase in the inscription, "brother of Jesus," goes beyond the usual identification of the person whose bones are within. That was normally expressed in such ossuary inscriptions only by the use of the father's name. One cannot claim, then, that the last phrase was added to stress that he was the brother of a well-known Jesus, Jesus of Nazareth. The other ossuary mentioned above (§570) has the same sort of final phrase, and no one knows who Ḥanin was.[49] So one cannot say that the final phrase is indubitably a sign of notoriety. The brother may have been simply the one who saw to the second burial of the bones, or who owned the burial cave in which the ossuary was deposited. Since Jesus of Nazareth was crucified in the early 30s of the first century, he could hardly have been caring for the second burial of James, who was put to death about AD 62.

If one has such difficulties with the identification of the three names in the usual way in which the Aramaic inscription has been read and understood, how much more problematic would they become if the second phrase, "brother of Jesus," were in apposition to "Joseph," who is said in this new ossuary inscription to be the father of the James named there! I have already explained that that is a way in which the inscription should be read, if one uses the examples from the Old Testament of persons identified by a father's name and a brother's name, where the latter always denotes the brother of the father. If this mode of understanding the new ossuary inscription were to prove acceptable, the whole issue of this James as "James, the brother of the Lord" (Gal 1:19), would disappear. The issue would then be, who is Joseph, said to be "the brother of Jesus," and what

---

49. There is mention in the sixth-century Babylonian Talmud to a house of ḥanin, a much-feared Sadducean high priestly clan, said to be related to the high priest Annas; but coming from so late a source, it cannot be used for the interpretation of a first-century ossuary. Among the fourth generation of Amoraim in Palestine, there was a Rabbi ḥanin of Sepphoris, again from a very late date with little relevance to the first century; see H. L. Strack and G. Stemberger, *Introduction to the Talmud and Midrash*, trans. M. Bockmuehl (Edinburgh: T&T Clark, 1991), p. 103.

reference would that have to persons in the New Testament with the same names?

The Implications of the Discovery

The discovery of this new ossuary is undoubtedly important because of the Aramaic inscription it bears, and it will long be discussed. From it we have learned something about the Aramaic language that was little known before its discovery (a new instance of the first-century use of the suffixal form of the word for "brother"). Even if one cannot be sure that the three names are meant to be identical with three persons so named in the New Testament, they are important at least because of their similarity.

If one accepts the usual way of reading the inscription, it may affect one's understanding of the doctrine of the continuous or perpetual virginity of Mary. Early church belief in Mary's virginity was formulated by Christians in the postapostolic era, making use of an interpretation of some passages in the New Testament, but passing over others that were problematic, such as those that were quoted above (John 1:45; 6:42; 7:5; Luke 4:22). The result was that that doctrine of Mary's virginity was not universally accepted at first, even though it was formulated in the second-century writing *Protevangelium of James* (8.1; 9.1-2; 13.1–16.2; 17.1-2; 18.1).[50] Eventually, it became crystallized in the long-standing belief about Mary as *aeiparthenos* or *semper virgo*, "ever virgin," in creeds from the fourth century on.[51]

In light of that belief, there grew up two different ways of understanding Paul's phrase, "James, the brother of the Lord." In the church of the East, James was regarded as the son of Joseph, who as a widower married Mary, of whom Jesus was born through conception of the Holy Spirit (see Matt 1:18-20), as in the *Protevangelium of James*. Hence James would have been a half-brother of Jesus. That interpretation of *adelphos* is still used today in Eastern Orthodox churches.

50. In these texts there is not only the assertion of Mary and Joseph about the child conceived "of the Holy Spirit" (14:2), but also the mention of Joseph among the widowers (8:3–9:1) and of his "son" or "sons" (9:2; 17:2). See J. K. Elliott, *The Apocryphal New Testament: A Collection of Apocryphal Christian Literature in an English Translation* (Oxford: Clarendon, 1993), pp. 57-67; also E. de Strycker, *La forme la plus ancienne du Protévangile de Jacques,* Subsidia hagiographica 33 (Brussels: Bollandistes, 1961).

51. See H. Denzinger and P. Hünermann, *Enchiridion symbolorum . . . ,* 37th ed. (Freiburg im B.: Herder, 1991), §§44, 46, 55.

In contrast to that interpretation, the church of the West insisted on the broader sense of *adelphos* as kinsman or relative. Jerome wrongly translated it "cousin," even though the New Testament has a specific word, *anepsios,* which is never used of James or Jesus.[52] This interpretation of *adelphos* persists today in the Roman Catholic Church. In the sixteenth century, the Reformers (Luther and Calvin) still affirmed the tradition of the West that Mary remained ever a virgin, but in time, especially under the influence of the so-called Enlightenment, Protestant belief interpreted *adelphos* to mean blood brother or sibling, so that James came to be understood as Jesus' natural brother in many present-day Protestant churches.

As a result, interpreters of this new Aramaic ossuary inscription undoubtedly will read it in the way they have been interpreting Greek *adelphos* used of James of Jerusalem in Gal 1:19. In other words, as the Orthodox have understood *adelphos* in Gal 1:19 to mean "half-brother," and Protestants have understood it to mean "blood brother," and Catholics have understood it to mean "relative," so they will now interpret *'aḥûî* in the new ossuary inscription accordingly. Such considerations as these have to be recalled when one seeks to evaluate the new Aramaic inscription.

The evangelist Luke, however, offers a practical solution to this problem. At the beginning of the genealogy of Jesus in his Gospel, he wrote, "Jesus, when he began his ministry, was about thirty years of age, being the son (as was supposed) of Joseph" (Luke 3:23 RSV). Luke wrote that statement along with its qualifying clause long before any of the various later church traditions about Mary's virginity emerged, and hence about the ways of explaining "James, the brother of the Lord" (Gal 1:19). The qualifying clause, *hōs enomizeto,* "as was supposed," shows that people in the 80s of the first century were already questioning the relationship of Jesus to Joseph, and the clause was added to set the matter straight. So if it were to emerge that the three names in the inscription of this new ossuary are indeed the names of three well-known persons of the New Testament, then one would have to conclude that the inscription was written by someone like the person whom Luke sought to correct by adding his qualifying clause about Jesus, the son of Joseph, "as was supposed."[53]

---

52. The Greek word *anepsios* occurs in Col 4:10, where Mark is called the "cousin" of Barnabas.

53. See further E. H. Merrill, "'The Burial Box of James the Brother of Jesus,' *BAR* 28/6 (2002): 24-33, 70," *BSac* 160 (2003): 235-36; C. A. Evans, "Jesus and the Ossuaries," *BBR* 13 (2003): 21-46, esp. 39-46 (the rest is irrelevant); N. A. Silberman and Y. Goren, "Faking Biblical History," *Archaeology* 56/6 (2003): 20-29.

On the Authenticity of the James Ossuary and Its Possible Link to "the Jesus Family Tomb"

Amnon Rosenfeld, Howard R. Feldman, and Wolfgang E. Krumbein

Results of an archaeometric analysis of the James ossuary strengthen the contention that the ossuary and its inscription are authentic. Patination consists mainly of the weathering product of the source rock (Early Senonian, Mount Scopus Group) and the in situ accreted variable environmental and anthropogenic components. The stone of the ossuary is enriched in phosphorous due to leaching from the original bones it contained. The composition of the patina is mainly $CaCO_3$ 93% and contains the following elements: Si, Al, Fe, P, and Mg. It contains no modern elements and adheres firmly to the stone. The beige to gray patina and its morphology can be observed on the surface of the ossuary, continuing gradationally into the engraved inscription, despite the fact that the ossuary was cleaned unprofessionally with a sharp implement and with unidentified cleansers. The engraving clearly does not cut the patina. Ultraviolet illumination does not indicate any new engraving marks. Thin striations, over which the patina has accreted, about 0.5 mm wide and several centimeters in length, are found on the outer sides of the walls. Some vertical to diagonal ($\approx 45°$) patinated striations that continuously transect the letters appear to be from the friction of falling roof rocks induced by earthquakes, floods, and landslides during long burial in the cave. Many dissolution pits are superimposed on several of the letters. In addition to calcite and quartz, the patina contains the following minerals: apatite (calcium phosphate), whewellite (hydrated calcium oxide), and weddelite (calcium oxalate). These minerals result from the biogenic activity of microorganisms such as microcolonial fungi, yeasts, lichens, and bacteria that require a period of at least fifty years to form the bio-patina.

Lately, the "James son of Joseph brother of Jesus" ossuary was dismissed as "fake" on grounds of oxygen isotopic investigation (Ayalon et al. 2004), even though there have been no studies of oxygen isotope values of patinas from archaeological artifacts not only in Israel but worldwide. Moreover, due to variable environmental anthropogenic conditions over the centuries, as well as the episodic development of the patina in ancient unprovenanced artifacts, the oxygen fractionation values are an unreliable tool for authentication.

Dust is a significant albeit underrecognized component of patinas that accumulates on exposed surfaces of artifacts and in soil. Storm dusts that contribute up to 50% of the soil are ubiquitous in the Levant; however, often unnoticed key substances such as minerals, microfossils, and pollen can be found within the patina of an artifact, preserving its geological signature. We have identified microfossils (nannofossils and foraminiferans) and quartz grains from sites in the patina that are consistent with what is expected of deposition of wind-blown particles in the Jerusalem area. The exposed rock belongs to the Judea and Mount Scopus groups and contains within the sediments microfossils that are light enough to become airborne. The heterogeneous existence of wind-blown microfossils, quartz, and other airborne minerals that characterize the patina of the ossuary, including the lettering zone, reinforces the authenticity of the ossuary. The chemical fingerprint of the patina and soil of the James ossuary agree well with the surface of the cave walls and with the patina analyses of the ossuaries found in the Talpiot cave, indicating that the James ossuary might originate from the surroundings area of the Talpiot cave complex (see Pellegrino's essay in this volume).

Introduction

An ossuary made of chalk and covered by a beige to gray patina was brought to the Geological Survey of Israel in August 2002 in order to study its archaeometry. The following Aramaic inscription appears on one of the long outer walls of the ossuary (Lemaire 2002, 2003):

יעקב בר יוסף אחוי דישוע

Ya'aqob son of Yoseph brother of Yeshua'

(James son of Joseph brother of Jesus)

Rosenfeld and Ilani (2002) were the first scientific team to investigate the archaeometry of the James ossuary. They concluded that the patina indicates a burial in a cave and that the surficial patina is found also within some of the letters. The inscription was cleaned and the patina covering some of letters is absent. They found a high concentration of phosphorous (P) within both the stone and the patina. This indicates a dissolution process in which the bones (high in phosphorous) that were originally in the ossuary dissolved and the phosphorous was incorporated into the stone of the ossuary as well as into the patina, a process that takes time.

Keall (2003) led a team at the Royal Ontario Museum (ROM) in Toronto that investigated the ossuary and its patina after it was cracked during transportation from Israel to Canada. The team found the following: (1) a high phosphate content in the stone wall of the ossuary as well as in the patina, (2) thin layering in the patina (with phosphate), and (3) prominent veins of calcite crystals (due to differential weathering) running consistently across the surface of the ossuary and through the incised letters of the inscription. Keall's team also refuted the so-called two-hand theory that maintains that the last two words of the ossuary, *'aḥui Yeshua'*, "brother of Jesus," were added by a second hand to an already existing inscription that read "James, son of Joseph." They recognized that the first part of the inscription was vigorously cleaned by a sharp tool but maintained that they could observe signs of natural aging of the inscription. It was clear to them that the inscription is not a modern forgery.

In his report to the Israel Antiquities Authority (IAA) Materials Committee, Goren (2003; see Ayalon 2003 and Ayalon et al. 2004) concluded that the inscription was forged. But he also noted that the ossuary might have been cleaned. He provided no explanation as to why he did not consider that the cleaning process could have been consistent with his observations.

Ayalon (2003) and Ayalon et al. (2004) described a new method using oxygen isotopes to authenticate patinas in archaeological artifacts. They concluded that the forger prepared the patina of the James ossuary artificially by applying powdered chalk immersed in boiling water over the freshly cut inscription. They claimed that microfossils were found only in the inscription, indicating additional evidence that the ossuary was forged.

Harrell (2004) reviewed the work of the IAA Materials Committee and concluded that their evidence did not support their conclusion that the inscription is a forgery. In addition, their interpretation that the James ossuary inscription is a modern fake was biased and based on flawed geochemistry.

We would like to emphasize that the knowledge of patinas on archaeological artifacts is still scarce and needs additional research, especially in Israel, where unprovenanced artifacts are very common. About 80-90% of the archaeological artifacts in Israel come from the antiquities market and are unprovenanced. These artifacts should definitely not be overlooked or discarded by archaeologists. It is evident that authentication of the ossuary requires a wide, interdisciplinary approach. The interaction between rocks, environment (soil, dust, water, climate, etc.), and anthropogenic activity and cleaning processes should always be considered when examining archaeological artifacts.

Methods and Materials

The mineralogic composition of the ossuary and patina was determined by using a petrographic microscope and a Philips X-ray diffractometer. Samples were removed from the ossuary and from the patina by peeling with a sharp steel blade. The samples were studied at the Geological Survey of Israel. A scanning electron microscope (SEM; JEOL-840), equipped with an energy dispersive spectrometer (EDS; Oxford-Link-Isis) was employed for detailed inspection of the physical properties and structural features of the samples as well as for chemical analysis. A Hitachi S-3200N SEM with low vacuum was used for further analyses of microorganism content within the patina layers. In addition, we used the ICBM electron microscopy unit at the Soil Science Department of Carl von Ossietzky Universität Oldenburg as well as the Institute of Crystallography of Würzburg University for microscopy and X-ray diffractometry determination. The stone ossuary and the patina were examined by magnifying lens and binocular (magnification up to X40). The following samples were examined: remnants of the soil attached to the cavities found in the lower part of the outer sides of the ossuary, six samples of the chalk, and six samples of the patina.

The location sampling from the ossuary is as follows: samples 1 and 2 represent chalk of the ossuary, samples 3 and 4 represent brown patina; these 4 samples were taken from the fragment that was broken in the lower right corner of the inscription face; samples 5 and 6 are from the patina near the letters; sample 7 represents soil from the pits from the lower part of the ossuary (zone 1; see below for locations of the zones); sample 8 represents soil from the lower right corner of the inscription face; sample 9 is from the patina above the letter *samek* (of *Yoseph*); and samples 10 and 11 represent the original chalk from inside the ossuary.

Description of the Ossuary

The length of the ossuary is 50.5 cm at the base and flairs out to almost 56 cm at the top. When viewing the inscription, one of the short sides is 100° from the base and the other is slanted at 110°, giving the box a trapezoidal shape. The maximum width of the ossuary is 26 cm and maximum height is 30 cm. Based on its dimensions, it is clear that this ossuary was used to store the bones of an adult. A flat lid, also made of chalk, rests on a small ledge, 0.6 cm wide, running inside the rim of the long sides of the ossuary. A groove forming a frame of about 1.2 cm wide is found along the outer edges. A faded decoration of two rosettes, engraved and encompassed by weak outlines of three circles, is found on the long wall opposite to that of the inscription. A subhorizontal welded crack 12 cm in length on the long wall, crossing the right corner and continuing to the slanted short side of the ossuary, is found about 9 cm beneath the inscription. The lid and the opposite wall of the inscription display faint spots of red iron-oxide paint, a common feature in many ossuaries (see Porat and Ilani 1993).

The long wall with the inscription on it contains dense oval solution cavities, or pits, that form three distinct zones from left to right that dip, or tilt, at an angle of about 20°. Pits are small indentations or depressions on the surface of a rock as a result of some eroding or corrosive process such as differential solution (Jackson 2007), and bio-pitting that takes a long time to form (Krumbein 2005). The lowermost zone (zone 1) extends from the bottom of the ossuary along the left side for about 13 cm in maximum width. Zone 1 consists of large pits up to 10 mm in size and depth. Above is the middle zone (zone 2) that extends for another 12 cm in maximum width along the left side of the ossuary. Zone 2 consists of numerous smaller pits about 2-5 mm in diameter. A third and uppermost zone (zone 3) extends to the top of the left side of the ossuary for 5.5 cm and contains randomly scattered pits about 1-3 mm in diameter.

Thin striations, up to 0.5 mm wide and up to several centimeters in length, are found on the outer sides of the walls. These marks are mostly vertical, but there are also diagonal striations (45°). The striations were probably made by falling stones from the ceilings and walls of the cave due to earthquakes, floods, and landslides. Most of the striations and the pits are coated with the beige patina.

Archaeometric Analysis

Rock

The ossuary is made of chalk and was mined from the Cretaceous (Senonian) Menuah Formation in the lower Mount Scopus Group (see Flexer 1964; Flexer et al. 1990). This rock unit attains a thickness of up to 10 m in the Jerusalem area. The properties of this formation and the microfossil content are well known (e.g., Flexer 1964; Mimran et al. 1996; Reiss et al. 1985). Chalk is a sedimentary deposit composed mainly of marine microorganism skeletons made of calcium carbonate (calcite). The use of this chalk in Jerusalem was extensive during the Second Temple period (2000 years BP) mainly for the manufacture of stone vessels and ossuaries (Magen 1984, 1988, 1994, 2002; Flexer et al. 1990). Ossuaries were used for storing the bones in a cave tomb. The production of chalk vessels and Jewish ossuaries around Jerusalem during the first centuries BCE and CE were related to the Jewish customs of purity. Several chalk stone quarries were discovered from that period in the Jerusalem area (Magen 1984, 1988, 1994, 2002). The destruction of the Second Temple in 70 CE explains the cessation of the production of the stone vessels and the ossuaries in Jerusalem.

The rock of which the ossuary was carved is not homogeneous; it was partially converted to a nari. Nari is a variety of caliche that forms by surface or near-surface alteration of permeable calcareous rocks and that occurs in the drier parts of the Mediterranean region (Jackson 1997). Due to intensive weathering and the narization process the ossuary is extremely fragile. In fact, Keall (2003) reported that the ossuary broke on its way from Israel to Toronto for exhibit at the ROM. It arrived in a cardboard carton encased only in layers of bubble wrap, which, when removed, revealed a soft limestone bone box that had broken into five pieces. The lack of homogeneity of the rock can explain why the letters seems to be engraved at different depths and the "different hands" hypothesis suggested by some epigraphers.

Patina

The patina of an archaeological artifact is the outer weathered layer consisting mainly of the weathered source rock that, due to physical, chemical, and biological (e.g., microorganism) factors, began to disintegrate over the years. Another component of the patina is the accretion of material from the environment and its interaction with soil and dust, including anthropogenic material as well as water that sometimes deposits calcite. Patina rich in phosphate is typical of burial places, where there is an abundant supply of bones. Thus the patina is heterogeneous in its character.

In the James ossuary we observed two layers of patina, a thin (film-like) beige layer above a white-gray layer. A similar double layered (gray below and yellow above) patina is found on the Acropolis monument at Athens, Greece (Krumbein 2003). The patina is up to 1 mm in thickness and discontinuous in places; deposition is episodic. This suggests that the patina on the ossuary was not developed continuously at a constant rate over a two-thousand-year period. It may be that the patina was partially eroded during that time.

The beige patina can be found inside the letters, accreting gradationally into the inscription. The patina can be observed on the surface of the ossuary continuing into the engraving. The engraving clearly does not cut the patina. This phenomenon can be seen in almost every letter of the inscription despite cleaning with a sharp tool. The last letters of the inscription were not cleaned, and the entire patina can be observed in these letters.

There are numerous fine striations crossing almost every letter. These striations were probably caused by falling roof rock in the cave during the past two thousand years. They occur on the surface of the ossuary, moving into the letters, and are aligned in at least three sets dipping from upper left to lower right, upper right to lower left, and vertically. Not only are the letters patinated but so are some of the striations.

The striations can be seen in other letters of the inscription, including the letters *shin* and *'ayin* of the word *Yeshua'* at the end of the inscription. The striations are filled with the same patina that is found within the letters and are another strong proof for authenticity.

Zone 2 contains pits that are also superimposed on the engraved letters. The following letters have superimposed pits: *'ayin, qof,* and *bet* (in *Ya'aqob*), *resh* (in *bar*), *samek* (in *Yoseph*), *'aleph* (in *'ahui*), *dalet* (two pits), *shin,* and *'ayin* (in *Yeshua'*).

That the pit zones and striations are at varying angles suggests that the ossuary shifted from its original horizontal position over the years and was at times partially submerged in water. Thus the top of each pitted zone represents the height at which the water reached. The lowermost zone (zone 1) was immersed for the longest time, evidenced by the larger pits in that zone. Some of the lineaments can also be attributed to plant roots or climbing plants on the lower part of the ossuary.

In addition to calcium carbonate, the patina on the ossuary is also composed of the following minerals in descending order of volume: apatite (calcium phosphate), whewellite (hydrated calcium oxalate), weddelite (calcium oxalate), and quartz (silicon dioxide) (Krumbein 2005). These minerals within the thin layers (films) of beige to gray patina are the product of subaerial biofilm geomicrobiogenic activity that covers all surfaces of the ossuary (Gorbushina 2007). The presence of microcolonial long-living black yeast-like fungi forming pitted embedded circular structures indicates slow growth over many years. Microcolonial fungi (MCF), known to concentrate and deposit manganese and iron, play a key role in the alteration and biological weathering of rocks and minerals (Staley et al. 1982; Gorbushina 2003; Gorbushina and Krumbein 2004). They are microorganisms of high survivability, inhabiting rocks in extreme conditions, and are also known to survive in subsurface and subaerial environments. Long-living, black, yeast-like fungi form pitted embedded circular structures (Krumbein 2003; Krumbein and Jens 1981; Sterflinger and Krumbein 1997). These MCF structures and minerals were found on the surface of the ossuary and, more importantly, within the letters.

The patina on the long wall of the inscription is more condensed and darker to the right side, where the first four words, including the letter *'aleph* of the word *'aḥui,* reflect the intense cleaning. On the opposite long wall (with the rosettes), the patina is darker in the upper half. The same gray to beige patina is also found within some of the letters. The inscription was cleaned (Rosenfeld and Ilani 2002; Keall 2003) and the patina is therefore less prominent in several letters. The patina in several localities, mainly on the upper parts of the external walls, has numerous cauliflower shapes known to develop in a cave environment. The margins of the letters are weathered, sometimes even heavily weathered.

The so-called James Bond patina that was described by Goren (2003; Silberman and Goren 2003) as a "grainy" gray material is actually the same beige patina that covers the rest of the ossuary. This so-called fake James Bond patina actually represents the chipped flakes of the original patina that were exfoliated by a cleaning process. Goren (2003) observed this patina only in a few letters in the middle of the inscription (e.g., half of the *ḥet* in *'aḥui* and the *waw* of *Yoseph*); it was not found at the beginning or the end of the inscription. We believe that the few areas deep within the letters in which the patina is found represent fragmentary remnants of an original "real" patina. If a forger had done this we should have found this patina scattered all over the inscription rather than just in a few recesses of some letters. The

341

forger would have tried to disguise his work by applying the patina more completely. We maintain that the inscription was cleaned, and Goren's (2003) "grainy" patina is the remnant of the genuine cleaned patina that remains in a few letters found in the middle of the inscription and can only be seen with special illumination.

We are unable to observe the "James Bond" patina because of the careless treatment by the IAA and the Israeli police. They extracted the remains of the patina by using a red plastic/silicone waxy (?) mold used to replicate footprints at a crime scene. We maintain that in science when an examination cannot be repeated, the original results are suspect. Thus the oxygen isotope results of Ayalon et al. (2004) are not valid; they cannot be verified since the original surface no longer exists. In other words, their results are not falsifiable.

The ossuary and its inscription were tested at the ROM in 2002 with ultraviolet illumination and showed no suspicious glowing, which, according to Newman (1990), is a strong indication for the authenticity of an inscription.

Geochemistry

Based on energy dispersive spectrometer (EDS) analysis of the scanning electron microscope (SEM) laboratory of X-ray microanalysis, we found that the ossuary is composed mainly of $CaCO_3$ (97%) and contains Si (1.5%), Al (0.7%), Fe (0.4%), P (0.3%), and Mg (0.2%). The accreted patina shows similar composition composed mainly of $CaCO_3$ (93%) and contains Si (5.0%), Al (0.7%), Fe (0.3%), P (0.4%), and Mg (0.2%). The soil is composed mainly of $CaCO_3$ (85%) and contains Si (7.4%), Al (2.5%), Fe (1.7%), P (1.0%), Mg (0.7%), and Ti (1.0%). Note that there is a discrepancy between total amounts in the various samples due to the nature of EDS-SEM analysis.

The patina is enriched with silica (about 5.0%) relative to the original stone (about 1.5%) over the ossuary surface as well as in its inscription. The calculated enriched phosphate in the patina is 1.3% and in the soil is about 3%; all of it probably originated from the dissolution of the bones. The patina does not contain any traces of modern tools and it adheres firmly to the stone. No evidence that might detract from the authenticity of the patina and the inscription was found.

Dust

Dust is an important component in soil and patina formation in the Middle East. Storm dusts that contribute about 50% of material to the soil are ubiquitous in the area; however, often unnoticed key substances such as minerals, microfossils, and pollen can be found within the patina of an artifact, preserving its geological signature. The microfossil and mineral constituents in a patina could serve as a tool to authenticate unprovenanced artifacts (Ganor et al. 2007).

Ayalon et al. (2004) reported that only the "letters patina" from the James ossuary contains microfossils of marine origin. This constituted an indication of forgery according to them (Goren 2003; Ayalon et al. 2004). However, we found microfossils embedded within the entire patina, as well as on and within all other surfaces — not only on the letters. We find it odd that Ayalon et al. (2004) did not observe the presence of these microfossils. Calcareous nannoplankton (about 5-10 microns) and foraminifera (about 100-200 microns) are elements that are commonly found in the dust of the Jerusalem area (Ganor 1975; Ganor et al. 2007). Ayalon et al. (2004) suggest that the microfossils were artificially deposited by grinding marine carbonate sediments (possibly chalk from the same burial box) and dissolving them in warm water.

The microfossils are not recent, but range from the Cretaceous to the Paleogene, similar in age to the marine carbonate rocks that are widely exposed over most of Israel. The obvious source of this dust component is from mechanical erosion of the prevalent outcrops of limestones and chalks. They should be as plentiful in the historical past as they are today. Indeed, their absence within a patina purportedly coming from Jerusalem would be suspicious; the entire city is situated upon marine carbonate exposures of the Judea and Mount Scopus groups (of limestones) containing microfossils.

In addition, the fact that the foraminifera are well preserved and have empty chambers (empty of sediment infilling) precludes the possibility that the patina was artificially deposited by the grinding of marine carbonate sediments as proposed by Ayalon et al. (2004). Grinding the limestone along with its microfossil content would not have enabled the grinder to extract the sediment that infilled the chambers. The sediment could only have been removed by a natural, slow, erosional process.

Oxygen Isotopes

Recently, the oxygen isotopic composition of the carbonate of the patina was analyzed and the results used to suggest that the James ossuary inscription was not authentic (Ayalon 2003; Ayalon et al. 2004). This conclusion was based on the assumption that the presence of oxygen in the carbonate could be explained by precipitation from meteoric groundwater in the Jerusalem area. The data contains seven analyses of the letters patina. Six reported $\delta^{18}O{ff}_{PDB}$ values are depleted relative to the expected stalagmite/stalactite range carbonate formation data (-4 to -6 $\delta^{18}O{ff}_{PDB}$) (Bar-Matthews and Ayalon 1997).

The six letter samples were more negative compared to the samples taken from the surface of the ossuary. However, Rosenfeld and Ilani (2002) reported that the inscription was intensively cleaned chemically as well as by a sharp tool. The lettering was enhanced and contamination of the patina can surely be expected. Thus the comparison between the oxygen isotopes from the letters and the surfaces (Ayalon et al. 2004) is irrelevant because of contamination and definitely cannot indicate a forgery.

Harrell (2004) notes that very negative $\delta^{18}O{ff}_{PDB}$ values for six samples from the letters patina imply that the material within the patina formed at a high temperature, perhaps at 40-50°C as they (Ayalon 2003; Ayalon et al. 2004) suggest. He further states that this is only true if the patina consists of pure calcite, a qualification that the authors fail to make. The authors claim that the patina covering the letters was artificially prepared, most probably by grinding marine sediments, dissolving them in hot water, and depositing them onto the underlying modern engraved letters (Ayalon et al. 2004). As Harrell (2004) states, ground calcite will not dissolve in hot water. There is an inverse ratio of calcite solubility such that solubility increases as water temperature decreases. Thus the contention of Ayalon et al. (2004) that the patina was artificially deposited, after it was made by grinding marine carbonate sediments and dissolving them in warm water, is suspicious and based on flawed geochemistry.

The letter *'ayin* of *Yeshua'* was found by Ayalon et al. (2004) to have values of ($\delta^{13}C{ff}_{PDB} = -5.14$; $\delta^{18}O{ff}_{PDB} = -5.82$). Another letter (*ḥet* from *'aḥui* ["brother of" in Aramaic]) yielded expected oxygen isotope ratios of cave deposition ($\delta^{13}C{ff}_{PDB} = -2.41$; $\delta^{18}O{ff}_{PDB} = -4.65$) and surprisingly was not reported by Ayalon et al. (2004). However, in the Geological Survey of Israel Carbonate Analysis log of April 22, 2003, the data from their analysis (lines 9) are clearly listed. Two samples yielded the expected oxygen composition values according to the examination of Ayalon and were not taken into their consideration of authenticity (Ayalon et al. 2004). We propose that discrepancies in the isotope ratios were caused by the cleaning and enhancing processes, and the small quantity of the so-called James Bond is a mixture of the real patina and the chemical cleaning substance. The two expected values are probably the remains of the calcitic patina that was sampled. In fact, Pellegrino found extensive contamination by microshreds of paper-and-rag–based fibers overlying the patina. He noted that the paper yielded high phosphorous and chlorine peaks consistent with phosphate-based detergents of the late 1970s and early 1980s, and suggestive of amateurish cleaning of the ossuary about that time, with detergent-soaked towels, presumably in preparation for the antiquities market.

The compositions of oxygen isotopes were measured in patinas on several artifacts from officially sanctioned excavations and exhibit a wide range of values (Prof. Aldo Shemesh, Weitzman Institute, personal communication). The values of the oxygen isotopes not only vary between different geographic locations but vary also in the same location as well as in the same artifact. Discrepancies from stalagmite deposition range up to $\delta^{18}Off_{PDB}= -8$. The kinetic processes of the oxygen isotopes clearly indicate that there are more variables than water composition and temperature (as assumed incorrectly by Ayalon et al. 2004). Thus it is clear that oxygen isotopes are not a reliable method for the authentication of any archaeological artifacts.

The various patina layers may have different isotopic compositions both laterally and vertically. Thus, when Ayalon et al. (2004) measured the isotopic values of the patina layer on the James ossuary that resulted in different readings, they concluded that the ossuary was forged. However, the readings may have been correct and the variability of the readings could have been accurate. This is a line of investigation that should be explored.

The development of the patina was compared to the development of a (cave) stalagmite by Ayalon et al. (2004). In a stalagmite cave one can clearly observe the annual growth rings representative of calcium carbonate deposition. This growth is indicative of a constant supply of water over the years. However, the formation of a patina on archaeological artifacts is produced in a few sporadic events. The patina on archaeological artifacts is not comparable to continuous growth of stalagmite rings. Thus it is inaccurate to assume that patina formation is comparable to the formation of stalagmites in a closed system ignoring all interactions with the environment, including anthropogenic ones.

Bar-Matthews and Ayalon (1997) developed a climatic ruler based on

the averages of stable isotopes (oxygen and carbon) from the Beit Shemesh
stalagmite cave measured every 200 years over several millennia. However,
we maintain that patination is not a continuous, average process but forms
under extreme conditions of episodic seasonal events probably in years of
high rainfall and warm temperatures. Thus their climatic ruler determined
by stalagmites and stalactites is not applicable in studying the formation of
archaeological patinas with a restricted water supply. Within the accreted
patina particles of the dust and soil (e.g., microfossils, sand, and clays) were
observed. In addition, one must take into account the effect of micro-
biogenic activity patina formation. Most importantly, since the artifact is
unprovenanced its geographic location is not known, yet the geographic
location is very important in determining the oxygen isotope results. Oxygen isotope as a method of authentication is not used and was not approved
to be an authentication in any lab in the world. There is no archaeological
database for comparison of oxygen isotopes from artifacts found in known
excavated sites.

The Connection of the James Ossuary to the Jesus Family Tomb

In 1980 a burial tomb was unearthed in Talpiot, East Jerusalem, containing
ten ossuaries, six of which bear inscriptions with names such as Yeshua bar
(son of) Yehoseph, Mariya, Mariamne (also known as) Mara, Yose, Yehudah
bar (son of) Yeshua, and Matya (Matthew) — names that match those of the
New Testament but were commonly used during the first century CE (Kloner
1996; Tabor 2006). The Talpiot cave has six niches (Kloner 1996). The *golal*
(rolling stone) that was used to seal the tomb was not found.

The niches (2 eastern, 2 western, and one northeastern; in Hebrew,
kokhim) contained the ten ossuaries. The 2-meter-long northwestern niche
was empty of ossuaries when discovered in 1980. One meter of soil from the
floor of the cave covered the ossuaries when it was first explored and was removed in a salvage excavation.

Pellegrino examined fourteen caves in the Jerusalem area (including
the Talpiot cave) and discovered that each of the patinas bears its own chemical signature. He based his analysis on fourteen separate elements. These
quantitative elemental "fingerprints" match the patina on the ossuaries
found in each cave. In other words, each ossuary can be matched to the cave
in which it was buried. Elemental variability between the ossuary and its
cave ranges up to 5%. Even caves in close proximity to one another, within

the same rock formation, exhibit different elemental fingerprints. This makes it easier to match the ossuaries to the host cave and is a powerful tool for linking unprovenanced artifacts to their cave of origin.

According to Pellegrino, the James ossuary has the same elemental fingerprints as are found in the Talpiot cave (= Jesus family tomb) and its ossuaries; it has equivalent peaks of phosphorous, titanium, iron, and aluminum. The phosphorous peak originates from the dissolution of the bones, whereas the titanium and aluminum peaks can be linked to clay particles, and the silica peak originates from quartz grains that come from atmospheric exposure to dust and soil.

The James ossuary is very similar in size to the missing tenth ossuary (Kloner 1996). The measurements of the width and the height are identical, but the length falls short by 3-4 cm. Based on similar size and the elemental fingerprints it is possible to conclude that the James ossuary from the Talpiot cave is the missing tenth ossuary. However, we suggest that the James ossuary could in fact be a missing *eleventh* ossuary. That the James ossuary was "caliched," intensively weathered, and cracked suggests that this cave was breached a long time ago and another adjacent niche of the Talpiot cave with the same chemical history held an eleventh ossuary. The Talpiot cave could have very well been looted before it was discovered in 1980, because it was exposed to atmospheric conditions by a partial collapse and the penetration of soil and water for at least two hundred years (Krumbein 2005). The massive pitting and striations as well as the intense weathering of the James ossuary are not found in the other nine ossuaries. Only the Matya ossuary exhibits sporadic pitting; the diameters of the pits are 1-3 mm but they are very shallow. No ossuary was affected as much from climatic conditions as the James ossuary, and it could possibly be considered an eleventh ossuary.

That the James ossuary exhibits the same geochemical fingerprints as the Talpiot cave and its ossuaries is a very important observation in regard to the Jesus family tomb. Adding this ossuary with the inscription *Ya'aqob bar Yoseph 'aḥui d'Yeshua'* to the cluster of the names found in this tomb has a great statistical weight. It raises the calculated odds (Feuerverger 2008) in a combined probability equation that it does not belong to the New Testament Jesus family from 1 in 1600 to a compelling level of certitude that it is really the historic holy family tomb. This completes the last piece in the jigsaw puzzle of the holy family.

Conclusions

1. A natural beige patina can be found inside the letters, accreting gradationally into the inscription. The patina can be observed on the surface of the ossuary continuing into the engraving. The engraving clearly does not cut the patina. Deposition of the patina is episodic, suggesting that it was not developed continuously at a constant rate over a two-thousand-year period.

2. Ancient patinated striations probably caused by falling roof rock in the cave transect the letters and the surface of the ossuary in the same direction.

3. Massive pitting developed under atmospheric conditions after the engraving of the inscription on the ossuary is also superimposed on several letters.

4. In addition to calcium carbonate, the patina on the ossuary is also composed of minerals (apatite, whewellite, weddelite) that are the products of geo-microbiogenic activity. The presence of microcolonial long-living black yeast-like fungi forming pitted embedded circular structures indicates slow growth over many years.

5. The so-called James Bond patina that was described by Goren (2003; Silberman and Goren 2003) as a "grainy" gray material is actually the same beige patina that covers the rest of the ossuary.

6. The patina is enriched with silica (about 5.0%) relative to the original stone (about 1.5%) and extends over the ossuary surface as well as in its inscription. The calculated enriched phosphate in the patina is 1.3% and in the soil is about 3%; all probably originated from the dissolution of the bones. The presence of phosphate (from bones) that is incorporated into the patina is another indication of slow growth. This heterogeneous patina does not contain any traces of modern tools and it adheres firmly to the stone.

7. The microfossils in the patina are not recent, but range from the Cretaceous to the Paleogene, similar in age to the marine carbonate rocks that are widely exposed over most of Israel. The obvious source of this dust component is from mechanical erosion of the numerous outcrops of limestones and chalks as well as minor quartz. They should be as plentiful in the historical past as they are today. Indeed, their absence within a patina purportedly coming from Jerusalem would be suspicious; the entire city is situated upon marine carbonate exposures of the Judea and Mount Scopus groups (of limestones) containing microfossils.

8. That the foraminifera are well preserved and have empty chambers precludes the possibility that the patina was artificially deposited by the

grinding of marine carbonate sediments as proposed by Ayalon et al. (2004). Grinding the limestone along with its microfossil content would not have enabled the grinder to extract the sediment that infilled the chambers. The sediment could only have been removed by a natural, slow erosional process.

9. The contention of Ayalon et al. (2004) that the patina was artificially deposited, after it was made by grinding marine carbonate sediments and dissolving them in warm water, is suspicious and based on flawed geochemistry.

10. It is inaccurate to assume that patina formation is comparable to the formation of stalagmites in a closed system ignoring all interactions with the environment, including anthropogenic ones.

11. Oxygen isotopes were not found to be a reliable method for the authentication of archaeological artifacts.

12. That the James ossuary exhibits the same geochemical fingerprints as the Talpiot cave and its ossuaries is a very important observation in regard to the Jesus family tomb. Adding this ossuary with the inscription *Ya'aqob bar Yoseph 'ahui d'Yeshua'* to the cluster of the names found in this tomb has a great statistical weight. It raises the calculated odds (Feuerverger 2008) in a combined probability equation that it does not belong to the New Testament Jesus family from 1 in 1600 to a compelling level of certitude that it is really the historic holy family tomb.

Glossary

Al = aluminum
Ca = calcium
$CaCO_3$ = calcium carbonate; the mineral calcite
$\delta^{18}Off_{PDB}$ = measurement value of oxygen isotopes
$\delta^{13}Cff_{PDB}$ = measurement value of carbon isotopes
Delta value = the difference between the isotope ration in a sample and
     that in a standard, divided by the ration in the standard, and ex-
     pressed as parts per thousand per mil
Fe = iron
Foraminifera= a protozoan characterized by the presence of a test (shell)
     usually composed of calcite or agglutinated particles
Isotope = one of two or more species of the same chemical element
Mg = magnesium
Nannoplankton = passively floating unicellular organisms

P = phosphorous
PDB standard = used as a standard of comparison in determining the isotopic composition of carbon and oxygen
Si = silicon
Ti = titanium

WORKS CITED

Ayalon, A. 2003. "Examination of Authenticity of the James Brother of Jesus Ossuary and Yehoash Inscription: A Report in Israel Antiquities Authority 2003." *Bible and Interpretation,* accessed at http://www.bibleinterp.com/articles/Goren_report.htm.

Ayalon, A., M. Bar-Matthews, and Y. Goren. 2004. "Authenticity Examination of the Inscription on the Ossuary Attributed to James, Brother of Jesus." *Journal of Archaeological Science* 31:1185-89.

Bar-Matthews, M., and A. Ayalon. 1997. "Late Quaternary Paleoclimate in the Mediterranean Region from Stable Isotope Analysis of Speleothems at Soreq Cave, Israel." *Quaternary Research* 47:155-68.

Feuerverger, A. 2008. "Statistical Analysis of an Archaeological Find." *Annals of Applied Statistics* 2:3-54.

Flexer, A. 1964. "Paleogeography of the Senonian and Maestrichtian in Northern Israel." Unpublished Ph.D. diss. (in Hebrew; Eng. abstract), Hebrew University, Jerusalem.

Flexer, A., A. Honigstein, A. Rosenfeld, and B. Polishook. 1990. "Geology, Geotechnical Properties and Exploitation of Chalk in Israel — an Overview." Pp. 63-70 in *Chalk: Proceedings of the International Chalk Symposium Held at Brighton Polytechnic on 4-7 September 1989.* London: Thomas Telford.

Ganor, E. 1975. "Atmospheric Dust in Israel: Sedimentological and Meteorological Analysis of Dust Deposition." Unpublished doctoral diss., Hebrew University, Jerusalem.

Ganor, E., S. Ilani, J. Kronfeld, A. Rosenfeld, and H. R. Feldman. 2007. "Environmental Dust as a Tool to Study the Archaeometry of Patinas on Ancient Artifacts in the Levant." Geological Society of America Annual Meeting, Denver. 39:574.

Gorbushina, A. A. 2003. "Microcolonial Fungi: Survival Potential of Terrestrial Vegetative Structures." *Astrobiology* 3:543-54.

Gorbushina, A. A. 2007. "Life on the Rocks (Mini-Review)." *Environmental Microbiology* 9:1613-31.

Gorbushina, A. A., and W. E. Krumbein. 2004. "Role of Organisms in Wear Down of Rocks and Minerals." Pp. 59-84 in *Microorganisms in Soils: Roles in Genesis and Functions,* ed. F. Buscot and A. Varma. Berlin: Springer.

Goren, Y. 2003. "Examination of Authenticity: James Brother of Jesus Ossuary and Yehoash King of Yehuda Inscription. A Report in Israel Antiquities Authority."

Bible and Interpretation. Accessed at http://www.bibleinterp.com/articles/Goren_report.htm.

Harrell, J. A. 2004. "Flawed Geochemistry Used to Condemn James Inscription." *BAR* 30:38-41.

Jackson, J., ed. 2007. *Glossary of Geology.* Alexandria: American Geological Institute.

Keall, E. J. 2003. "New Tests Bolster Case for Authenticity." *BAR* 26/4:52-55.

Kloner, A. 1996. "A Tomb with Inscribed Ossuaries in East Talpiyot, Jerusalem." *'Atiquot* 29:15-22.

Krumbein, W. E. 2003. "Patina and Cultural Heritage — a Geomicrobiologist's Perspective." Pp. 39-47 in *Proceedings of the 5th European Common Conference "Cultural Heritage Research: A Pan-European Challenge."* Ed. R. Kozlowski. Cracow.

Krumbein, Wolfgang E. 2005. "Preliminary Report: External Expert Opinion on Three Stone Items," n.p. *Biblical Archaeology Review* "Finds or Fakes." Biblical Archaeology Society Web site.

Krumbein, W. E., and K. Jens. 1981. "Biogenic Rock Varnishes of the Negev Desert (Israel): An Ecological Study of Iron and Manganese Transformation by Cyanobacteria and Fungi." *Oecologia* 50:25-38.

Lemaire, A. 2002. "Burial Box of James the Brother of Jesus — Earliest Archaeological Evidence of Jesus Found in Jerusalem." *BAR* 26/6:24-33.

Lemaire, A. 2003. "Ossuaire de Jacob/Jacque fils de Joseph, le frère de Jésus — Trois inscriptions araméennes sur ossuaire et leur intérêt." *CRAI* (Jan.-March): 301-19.

Magen, Y. 1984. "Jerusalem as the Center for Stoneware Production during Herodian Times" [in Hebrew]. *Qadmoniot* 17:124-27.

Magen, Y. 1988. The Stoneware Industry in Jerusalem of the Second Temple Period [in Hebrew]. Society of Nature Conservation.

Magen, Y. 1994. "The Stone Vessel Industry during the Second Temple Period." Pp. 7-27 in *Purity Broke Out in Israel.* Ed. Ofra Rimon. Haifa: Reuven and Edith Hecht Museum, University of Haifa.

Magen, Y. 2002. *The Stone Vessel Industry in the Second Temple Period — Excavations at Hizma and the Jerusalem Temple Mount.* Ed. Levana Tsfania. Jerusalem: Israel Exploration Society.

Mimran, Y., A. Honigstein, Y. Arkin, A. Rosenfeld, L. Michaeli, and Y. Hatzor. 1996. "The Use of Ostracod Biostratigraphy in Geotechnical Evaluation of the Santonian Chalk for the Proposed Mount Scopus Tunnel." *Israel Geological Survey, Current Research* 10:138-42.

Newman, R. 1990. "Weathering Layers and the Authentification of Marble Objects." Pp. 263-82 in *Marble: Art Historical and Scientific Perspectives on Ancient Sculpture.* Ed. M. True and J. Podany. Malibu: J. Paul Getty Museum.

Porat, N., and S. Ilani. 1993. "Pigments Derived from Minerals." Pp. 9-12 (Hebrew text on pp. 16-38) in *Colors from Nature — Natural Colors in Ancient Times.* Ed. C. Sorek and E. Ayalon. Tel Aviv: Eretz Israel Museum.

Reiss, Z., A. Almogi-Rabin, A. Honigstein, Z. Lewy, S. Lipson-Benitah, S. Moshkovitz, and Y. Zaks. 1985. "Late Cretaceous Multiple Stratigraphic Framework of Israel." *Israel Journal of Earth Sciences* 34/4:147-66.

Rosenfeld, A., and S. Ilani. 2002. "SEM-EDS Analyses of Patina Samples from an Ossuary of "Ya'akov [*sic*] son of Yossef brother of Yeshua." *BAR* 28/6:29. (Reprint of a letter to Hershel Shanks.)

Silberman, N. A., and Y. Goren. 2003. "Faking Biblical History." *Archaeology* 56/5:20-29.

Staley, J. T., F. E. Palmer, and J. B. Adams. 1982. "Microcolonial Fungi Common Inhabitants on Desert Rocks." *Science* 215:1093-95.

Sterflinger, K., and W. E. Krumbein. 1997. "Dematiaceous Fungi as the Main Agent of Biopitting on Mediterranean Marbles and Limestones." *Geomicrobiology Journal* 14:219-31.

Tabor, J. 2006. "Testing a Hypothesis." *NEA* 69:132-36.

TALPIOT, STATISTICS, THE HOLY SEPULCHER, AND THE APOSTLES

Who Is in the Talpiot Tomb? A Statistical Approach

Mark Elliott and Kevin Kilty

Among the more controversial questions of the debate swirling around the interpretation of the Talpiot tomb is what role statistics and probability have to play. Statistics and probability serve several useful purposes, but in this essay we concentrate on the role of probability and statistics in providing input about, or in settling, claims.

Claims about the Talpiot Tomb

Among claims that depend on probability or statistics for support, and that we find unreasonable in light of relevant data, are the following:

- The Talpiot tomb is an unsurprising find because it contains a collection of individual names common to the first-century population.
- One should not expect an inscription like "Jesus son of Joseph" on the tomb. One would more likely find an inscription like "Jesus of Nazareth."
- The inscription *Jesus son of Joseph* is so common that one cannot ascribe much weight to having observed it in the Talpiot tomb.
- The extended tomb complex Dominus Flevit is yet another example of a Jesus family tomb. Such tombs must be quite common.
- The only interesting name among the inscriptions at Talpiot is that of *Mariamne*. If this inscription does not refer to Mary Magdalene, then the tomb is actually a rather ordinary find.[1]

1. See, e.g., the statement from the Duke University Religion Department, "The

- While the collection of names is interesting from a probability standpoint, other "evidence" completely discounts the find.

Let us analyze each of these claims in turn, and use statistics and/or probability to argue why they are wrong.

Probability and Name Clusters

It is important to a partial understanding of the controversy surrounding the issue of probability of name clusters that there are no accepted statistical methods for evaluating such at present. Even so, one may list two essentially different approaches.

One approach is that of a classical statistician, who naturally thinks of separating a distribution into a tail (rejection) region, consisting of name groups expected of a Jesus family, and a nominal (acceptance) region, consisting of all others. A "surprising" observation is one that lies within the rejection region. Its surprisingness comes from its limited support from probability. This is the approach that Feuerverger took in his analysis, and it became a major focus of controversy.[2]

In contrast, we take a Bayesian approach because, in our view, it treats observed data as evidence. It uses observations to move probability of identification forward and allows for consistent revision as data accumulates. Surprisingness in our view means a large ratio between prior and posterior probabilities, that is, a large likelihood of identification.

Keep in mind that statistics is already central to many of the scientific and technical analyses such as radioisotope age dating, EDX analysis of patina, and mitochondrial DNA analysis, which have uncertainties arising from sampling or uncertainties that are inherent in the method. In these cases the application of statistics is an accepted and uncontroversial issue. Analysis of name groups is a novel application lacking accepted procedures. This situation will change eventually through practice, argument, and analysis.

Talpiot Tomb Controversy Revisted," http://dukereligion.blogspot.com/2008/01/talpiot-tomb-controversy-revisited.html.

2. Andrey Feuerverger, "Dear Statistical Colleagues," http://Fisher.utstat.toronto.edu/andrey/OfficeHrs.txt.

Inscriptions as Evidence

We propose to start with known facts, or at least with evidence that one can weigh in some manner, and then use Bayes' Theorem to modify our beliefs about the Talpiot tomb in light of the evidence. Our analysis depends on several assumptions that we feel most people have not appreciated fully and that we need to make absolutely clear. These assumptions may turn out to be incorrect in the long run. However, our work will still serve a useful purpose as an example of how to proceed.

- We assume that Jesus and some of his family are, in fact, entombed in the Jerusalem area. Furthermore, the probability of taking any tomb in the area at random and having it turn out to be the Jesus family tomb is one divided by the number of tombs. In this last regard one might think that our analysis depends on the number of tombs, which is an unknown. However, it is the ratio of prior and posterior probabilities that measures evidence in this case, and this is independent of the assumed number of tombs.
- We examine only name inscriptions. In principle one could include other sorts of information in the analysis, but we have no other physical data to guide us at the Talpiot tomb. In particular the number of ossuaries and number of remains within the Talpiot tomb are immaterial.
- We condition all calculations on the actual form of the Talpiot tomb inscriptions — that they consist of four male names, one of which is in the form of *Jesus son of Joseph,* and two female names. If we condition on a collection of six ossuaries without regard to the sex of the name, then we obtain artificially high posterior probabilities simply because of the rarity of female names on ossuaries.
- We assume that all of the possible combinations of names one might expect to find in a "Jesus family tomb" are equally likely to occur.
- We assume that we can calculate the probability of finding combinations of names in the general population by using name frequencies appropriate to first-century Palestine. Table 1 illustrates the name frequencies we use. The data are largely from the total of all sources listed in Bauckham,[3] except that we have made *Yoseh* a separate entry. We

---

3. Richard Bauckham, *Jesus and the Eyewitnesses* (Grand Rapids: Eerdmans, 2006).

have used Feuerverger's number for the occurrences of *Yoseh,* but this agrees also with Ilan.[4]

First we assign an a priori probability *(P(A))*. We know the Jesus family existed; that Jesus died in Jerusalem and by Jewish custom was buried or entombed there; and that Mary and Jesus' brothers, including James, moved to Jerusalem, where James became a leader of the early followers of Jesus. Some portion of this family must have been entombed before 70 CE. Therefore, a Jesus family tomb with ossuaries most probably exists somewhere in the Jerusalem area, *not in Nazareth.*

Table 1: Jewish names and frequency of occurrence in first-century Palestine

Name	Number of Instances/Total	Frequency
Simon	243/2625	0.093
Joseph	218/2625	0.083
Judas	164/2625	0.062
Jesus	99/2625	0.038
Matthew	62/2625	0.024
James	40/2625	0.015
Yoseh	9/2625	0.003
Mary	70/328	0.213
Not Joseph or Judas or Jesus or Matthew	2082/2625	0.793

The last entry helps explain calculations in equations 9 and 10.

The a priori probability of a randomly selected tomb being, in fact, the Jesus family tomb is the inverse of the number of tombs in the area. Feuerverger implies an a priori probability of about 0.001.[5]

Perhaps the actual number is greater or less but not much so.

Let *A* and *B* stand for a proposition and observation, respectively. In this particular case, the proposition of interest is *A = the Talpiot tomb contains the Jesus family* and *B = observation of ossuaries bearing the noted names.* By Bayes' Theorem

4. Tal Ilan, *Lexicon of Jewish Names in Late Antiquity,* part 1, *Palestine 330 BCE–200 CE,* TSAJ 91 (Tübingen: Mohr Siebeck, 2002).

5. Take the inverse of his 1100 trials, for instance.

$$P(A \mid B) = \frac{P(B \mid A)}{P(B)} P(A) \qquad (1)$$

which we read in this instance as $P(A|B)$ = *the conditional probability that the Talpiot tomb contains the Jesus family given our observation of the six inscribed ossuaries in the tomb*. The probability $P(A)$ is the a priori probability of this tomb being that of the Jesus family, which we just placed somewhere near 0.001. $P(B|A)$ is another conditional probability, which we feel is not difficult to calculate in principle, but which requires input from scholars to calculate reasonably. It is the probability that a Jesus family tomb would contain these particular inscriptions on ossuaries.[6] $P(B)$ is a "normalizing" factor that represents the total probability of obtaining the observed names whether the family is the Jesus family. It is easiest to calculate $P(B)$ using the *Law of Total Probability*, $P(B) = P(B|A)P(A) + P(B|A')P(A')$, where A' is the negative of proposition A. In other words, it is the proposition that the tomb *does not* contain the Jesus family, but is instead a family with coincidentally similar names drawn from the general population.

Let us calculate the conditional probability $P(B|A)$ first, because the probability $P(B)$ is much easier to analyze after we explain $P(B|A)$. A reasonable way to proceed is to assume that the names Jesus son of Joseph, Yoseh, and Mary are the only three names within the tomb that pertain to the Jesus family. In two following sections we will also consider adding the name Judah, and also the name Mariamne.

Table 2: A list of all possible combinations of significant names in a Jesus family tomb

Jesus son of Joseph +	Mary + Yoseh
Mary	Simon
Mary + Simon	Simon + James
Mary + Simon + James	Simon + James + Yoseh
Mary + Simon + James + Yoseh	Simon + Yoseh + Judah
Mary + Simon + Yoseh	Simon + Yoseh
Mary + Simon + James + Judah	Simon + Judah
Mary + Simon + Yoseh + Judah	James
Mary + Simon + Judah	James + Yoseh

6. Unreasonable critics are going to set this value to zero, but more realistically it has a finite value, and scholarship would provide it.

Mary + James   James + Yoseh + Judah
Mary + James + Yoseh   James + Judah
Mary + James + Yoseh + Judah   James + Yoseh
Mary + James + Judah   Yoseh
Mary + Judah   Yoseh + Judah
Mary + Judah + Yoseh   Judah

The list uses Mark 6:3 for Jesus' brothers' names, and is conditioned on the requirement that there be no more than four male names and two female names. The + sign following *Jesus son of Joseph* indicates that it must be in all name groups, and the further numbered combinations are added to it. Obviously the fundamental name is *Jesus son of Joseph,* as it is difficult to make a convincing case about a tomb without such an inscription. Not all combinations necessarily are equally probable, and there may be other names suggestive of the Jesus family that would expand the list — Mary Magdalene, or his sisters' names, for example. This table is for purposes of example calculation.

Table 2 lists various possible sets of names one might expect to find in a Jesus family tomb, hence the list of all possible elements involved in *P(B|A)*. Not all possibilities in the list are equally likely to occur,[7] but let us assume each is equally likely for the moment. The actual observed set of names occurs only once in the list as combination number 16 and is then 1/30 of the total probability. Therefore *P(B|A) = 0.0333*.

Let us calculate *P(B)* at this point using the law of total probability. Since *P(A) = 0.001*, it follows that *P(A′) = 0.999*. *P(B|A′)* is just the probability of obtaining the significant names using a random draw from the list of name frequencies. We use multinomial factors to calculate the probability of drawing six inscriptions, with three of them being the three Jesus family names, the second female-name inscription being any female name at all, and the other two male-name inscriptions being any names except Jesus' other brothers Simon, James, and Judah.[8] With Yoseh as a unique form independent of Joseph, we find

$$p = \frac{4!}{2!1!1!}(1-0.17)^2(0.00343)(0.00314)\frac{2!}{1!1!}(0.213)(1) \tag{2}$$

7. For example the combination of "Jesus son of Joseph" with "Mary" is conceivably more likely to occur; and the combination involving Jesus, Mary, and three of Jesus' brothers is less likely.

8. The inclusion of other brothers' names would have us considering a list element different from number 16 in table 2.

which is thirty-eight per one million (0.000038), and using the more common "Joseph," we find this probability to be a little under one per thousand (0.00096). Therefore, using Bayes' Theorem and "Yoseh," rather than "Joseph," we find

$$P(A\mid B) = \frac{P(B\mid A)}{P(B)}P(A) \qquad (3)$$

$$P(A\mid B) = \frac{(0.0333)}{(0.0333\times0.001)+(0.000038\times0.999)}\cdot 0.001 \qquad (4)$$

$$= 0.469 \qquad (5)$$

In other words, if "Yoseh" is not considered a form of "Joseph," this Talpiot tomb represents, by this calculation, a 47% probability of being the Jesus family tomb.[9] On the other hand, if we use a probability appropriate to "Yoseh" being simply another form of "Joseph," then

$$P(A\mid B) = \frac{P(B\mid A)}{P(B)}P(A) \qquad (6)$$

$$P(A\mid B) = \frac{(0.0333)}{(0.0333\times0.001)+(0.00096\times0.999)}\cdot 0.001 \qquad (7)$$

$$= 0.034 \qquad (8)$$

which is to say that the probability is then only a little more than 3%. In an earlier paper[10] we calculated values of 48% and 6%, respectively, for these two figures. We revised these values here to make them entirely consistent with table 2 and with our stated assumptions.

Patronymics or Place of Origin?

Numerous people argue that a tomb containing the Jesus of early Christianity would not contain an ossuary inscription identifying family relationships. Rachel Hachlili from the University of Haifa provides a typical example. She argues that the Talpiot

---

9. By way of comparison, the equivalent probability as Feuerverger calculates it is 599/600. This is the most widely reported and argued-about statistical result in the debate.

10. See Kevin Kilty and Mark Elliott, "Probability, Statistics, and the Talpiot Tomb." http://www.lccc.wy.edu/Index.aspx?page = 547, 24-26.

tomb could not be identified with a tomb of Jesus of Nazareth for a significant reason: In all references in the New Testament Jesus is named only Yeshua with no patronymic (i.e., "son of"). Why then would the name "Yeshua son of Yehosef" be inscribed on an ossuary of a person known only as Yeshua? More likely an inscription on the ossuary of Jesus would have been "Yeshua from Nazareth" or "Yeshua son of Mariame."[11]

What matters is not how Jesus was referred to in the New Testament, but rather what was common practice in ossuary inscription during the relevant time period. On this basis, a study of Rahmani's catalogue of ossuaries does not support a claim that an ossuary holding the remains of Jesus would not be inscribed with *Jesus son of Joseph*.[12] Out of the 227 ossuaries recorded in Rahmani, about half of the inscriptions refer to the deceased and their kinfolk, and there are "seventy-three inscriptions that refer to the father of the deceased."[13] Very few ossuaries are inscribed with the names of the deceased person's birthplace or hometown. Indeed, only six such ossuaries inscribed with origins or birthplace are listed in Judea or its immediate environs.[14] Nearly twice as many inscribed ossuaries refer to women and the names of their husbands than refer to local origins.[15] Statistically, ossuaries are far more likely to refer to the deceased person's nickname than his or her local origin. Nicknames include "the dour," "the amputated," "the mute or strong," "beetle-browed," "the small," "grasshopper," "the fat or stout," and "one-eyed."[16] Of the 43 inscribed ossuaries at the large necroplis uncovered

11. Rachel Hachlili, "The Media and Three Surveys by the Tomb Symposium Participants." http://www.uhl.ac/blog/?cat = 3&paged = 2.

12. L. Y. Rahmani, *A Catalogue of Jewish Ossuaries in the Collections of the State of Israel* (Jerusalem: Israel Antiquities Authority, 1994).

13. Ibid., p. 15.

14. Ibid., p. 17, lists the following ossuaries with birthplaces and/or hometowns: Beth Shan/Scythopolis, no. 139; Sokho, no. 257; Beth Alon, no. 293; Beth Ezob, nos. 797, 803; Jerusalem, no. 777. Rahmani lists Bethel with no ossuary number.

15. Ibid., p. 15. There are only a few locations outside Judah referred to on other ossuaries such as Berenike in Cyrenaica as a possible location, no. 404; Ptolemais, possibly Cyrenaica, no. 99; Hin in Babylonia or near Caesarea, no. 290. A number of ossuaries are inscribed with a name that scholars suspect are common to Egypt or Cyrenaica. These place names are too speculative to be regarded as evidence of origins, and cannot be considered in the same category as inscribed place names.

16. Ibid., p. 14. The IAA ossuaries are numbered 44, 62, 117, 288, 421, 498, 579, and 822, respectively.

at Dominus Flevit, none bears an inscription indicating origins from Judea or its immediate environs, even though two ossuaries inscribed in Greek may mention Crete and Cyrene.[17] A lack of ossuary inscriptions including place names at Dominus Flevit is exactly what we would expect based on Rahmani's work. In effect, place names on ossuaries are so rare among observed inscriptions that "Jesus son of Joseph" occurs some twelve times more often as an inscription than does "Jesus of Nazareth."

Furthermore, several scholars have defended their positions on this question using Rahmani's argument that "the deceased's place of origin was noted when someone from outside Jerusalem and its environs was interred in a local tomb." Magness points out, "If the Talpiyot tomb is indeed the tomb of Jesus and his family, we would expect at least some of the ossuary inscriptions to reflect their Galilean origins, by reading, for example, Jesus [son of Joseph] of Nazareth (or Jesus the Nazarene), Mary of Magdala, and so on."[18] We find very little evidence for this conclusion. In Rahmani's catalogue only three inscribed ossuaries located in Jerusalem tombs refer to origins from Judea or its environs.[19] The paucity of inscribed ossuaries indicating origins uncovered in Jerusalem tombs does not sustain the claim that only Jews living outside Jerusalem inscribed their place of origin. As we have mentioned above, statistically, an inscription like "Jesus of Nazareth" would have been exceedingly rare. "Jesus son of Joseph" matches the archaeological evidence uncovered in the tombs of Jerusalem. More data is needed to support Rahmani's claim concerning the deceased's origins.

These conclusions are confirmed in the larger compilation of ossuary inscriptions of Tal Ilan. We are cognizant that Ilan cautions readers that a number of her entries are doubtful,[20] and that Pfann has also been critical of Ilan's use of sources from the rabbinic period.[21] Ilan records 22 ossuaries inscribed with the name Jesus and its variant spellings. Not one of these in-

17. See B. Bagatti and J. T. Milik, *Gli scavi del "Dominus Flevit,"* part 1, *La Necropoli del Periodo Romano*, Pubblicazioni dello Studium Biblicum Franciscanum 13 (Jerusalem: Franciscan Printing Press, 1958). We thank our colleague, Pat Landy, for these Greek translations.

18. See Jodi Magness, "Has the Tomb of Jesus Been Discovered?" http://sbl-site.org/publications/article.aspx?articleId = 640.

19. Rahmani, *Catalogue*, p. 17. The number may be less. Sokho's provenance no. 257 is listed as "Jerusalem?"

20. Ilan, *Lexicon*, p. 2.

21. Stephan Pfann, "Yoseh Can You See? Checking the Sources (Updated)." http://www.uhl.ac/blog/?p = 448.

scribed ossuaries includes a geographical origin.[22] Ossuaries inscribed with the name Joseph number 44,[23] and of these only two also record a place name.[24] If we expand our analysis to include all recorded instances in written sources of the name Jesus from 330 BCE to 200 CE, the results demonstrate that geographic place names were not a usual form used for identification. Ilan lists 103 instances of the name Jesus located in a variety of literatures from the Greco-Roman period. There are four occurrences of place names among them.[25] Places of origin associated with the name Joseph number only 14 out of 231.[26] In effect, place names on ossuaries and other written sources are unusual, and there is no compelling evidence that would demand an inscription such as "Jesus of Nazareth." We would also point out that Hachlili's insistence that "In all references in the New Testament Jesus is named only Yeshua with no patronymic (i.e., 'son of')" is clearly contradicted by John 6:42: "Is not this Jesus the son of Joseph?"

How Common Is "Jesus son of Joseph"?

A number of scholars have stated that *Yeshua bar Yehoseph* or *Jesus ben Joseph* is not unique in the corpus of names located in Palestine during the first century. Christopher Rollston has argued:

> The names Yehosep, Yoseh, Yeshua', Yehudah, Mattiyah, Maryah, Mariam(n)e, Miryam, and Martha (or the variants thereof) all have multiple attestations in the multilingual corpus of ossuaries and some are very common. For example, Sukenik published an ossuary inscribed "Yeshua' son of Yehosep" more than seventy-five years ago (Sukenik 1931). . . . even with the small corpus of epigraphic attestations of personal names, even the Talpiot tomb occurrence of "Yeshua' bar Yehosep" is not unique.[27]

22. Ilan, *Lexicon,* pp. 127-28.

23. Ibid., pp. 152-54.

24. Ibid., p. 153, no. 103, the Galilean; no. 111, of Hin.

25. Ibid., pp. 126-27. These are: no. 17, Galilean; no. 30, of Gerasa; no. 32, of Ono; and no. 34, of Uza. We did not include no. 4, General in Idumea, and no. 5, General in Tiberias. Both are clearly not places of origin.

26. Ibid., pp. 150-57. We excluded origins that Ilan regarded as fictitious. On these fictitious names see ibid., p. 47. For examples see no. 83 and no. 84, specifically.

27. See Christopher Rollston, "Inscribed Ossuaries: Personal Names, Statistics, and

However, a closer look at the distribution of *Yeshuaʻ* or Jesus and *Yehoseph* or Joseph does not support Rollston's assertions. In the 42 inscribed ossuaries containing the name Joseph listed in Ilan, there are only two combinations of Joseph and Jesus.[28] In effect, in arguing for the commonness of the Talpiot tomb combination of *Yeshua/Jesus and Yehoseph/Joseph,* Rollston points as an example to the only other documented occurrence. When we expand our inquiry to all instances of *Yehoseph*/Joseph in the literary corpus in Ilan, over 231 examples, we find only one more example: "Joseph, Joshua's brother."[29] Considering that Ilan's work records "712 valid persons recorded on ossuaries" and 2,826 in all sources,[30] three occurrences of *Yeshua* with *Yehosep* cannot be considered evidence for a typical or common patronymic.

Are There Many "Jesus Family Tombs"?

The necropolis known as Dominus Flevit contains ossuaries inscribed with many of the Jesus family names. Opponents of the idea that the Talpiot tomb could be the tomb of the Jesus family use this as an example of name groups similar to the Jesus family being common among tombs.[31] This is simply not so. To show why, we apply probability once again to a hypothetical tomb the size of Dominus Flevit.

With due skepticism about the utility of name frequencies for analyzing large groups of names, let us use, nevertheless, a sampling distribution derived from name occurrences and calculate the probability of obtaining a single occurrence of Talpiot tomb names from a random association of names in a hypothetical tomb the size of the tomb complex at Dominus Flevit with 43 inscribed ossuaries. This problem becomes complicated by the assumption of how many such inscriptions should be of female names and how many of male names, since ossuaries bearing male name inscriptions outnumber those bearing female name inscriptions by three to one. Assume,

---

Laboratory Tests," *NEA* 69 (2006): 127. See also idem, "Prosopography and the Talpiyot Yeshua Family Tomb: Pensées of a Palaeographer," http://www.sbl-site.org/publications/article.aspx?articleId = 649.

28. Ilan, *Lexicon,* p. 155, ossuaries nos. 106 and 117.

29. Ibid., p. 155, no. 177, Babatha archive.

30. Ibid., pp. 43, 57, respectively.

31. For example, see a letter circulated by Michael Heiser and quoted in Darrell Bock, "Lectures Wrapping up and the Tomb at Dominus Flevit at the Mount of Olives March 14," http://blog.bible.org/bock/node/129.

for example, that the 43 ossuaries comprise 32 inscriptions of male names and 11 of females. The probability is then the product of two multinomial factors: the probability of two occurrences of Joseph and one occurrence each of Jesus, Judas, and Matthew among the 32 males, and two occurrences of Mary among the 11 females.[32] The actual calculation is then

$$p = \frac{32!}{2!\ldots 27!}(0.083^2)(0.062)(0.039)(0.024)(0.763)^{27}\,\frac{11!}{2!9!}(0.213)^2(1-0.213)^9 \quad (9)$$

which is 2,663 per million (0.002663). The equivalent calculation for the Talpiot tomb is one each of Joseph, Jesus son of Joseph, Judas, and Matthew among the four ossuaries bearing male names, and Mary twice among the two ossuaries bearing female names. The numerical calculation is

$$p = \frac{4!}{1!1!1!1!}(0.083)(0.062)(0.0034)(0.024)\frac{2!}{2!}(0.213)^2 \quad (10)$$

which is under one in a million (0.00000046). The ratio of the two is 5789. In other words, the Dominus Flevit necropolis, mainly by virtue of its size, is thousands of times more likely to contain just one occurrence of these names than is the Talpiot tomb. It is not reasonable to argue that Dominus Flevit is pertinent to an argument against the uniqueness of names in the Talpiot tomb, when an extended tomb complex of its size is a priori several thousand times more likely to contain these names than the Talpiot tomb.[33]

The Significance of Other Names

Several names in the Talpiot tomb beg for explanation, and may even be key to eventually identifying the tomb names with a particular family. Certainly a valid route to identification is through unusual names. Feuerverger's calculation, for example, looks at two names in the Talpiot tomb as being especially relevant, and these two names account for nearly all of his power of identification. More significantly, though, Bauckham alludes to an analo-

32. We use two occurrences of Joseph here because there is no *Yoseh* and no "Jesus son of Joseph" inscription at Dominus Flevit, requiring two Josephs in order to make the two instances roughly equivalent. We treat Mary and *Mariamne* as equivalent to two Marys.

33. Allowing multiple occurrences of some Talpiot names among forty-three inscriptions produces an even larger likelihood ratio.

gous case: "Clopas is a very rare Semitic form of the Greek name Cleopas, so rare that we can be certain this is the Clopas who, according to Hegesippus, was the brother of Jesus' father Joseph and the father of Simon, who succeeded his cousin James as leader of the Jerusalem church."[34] Therefore let us examine how treating names like *Yoseh* as unique, or including names like Judah and *Mariamne* as part of the "Jesus family," modifies our results.

Significance of Yoseh

We believe the most significant name in the tomb is *Yoseh*. Some scholars lump this name with other forms of Joseph,[35] but others, most notably Evans and Feldman,[36] claim the name *Yoseh* has nothing to do with Joseph and is a misrepresentation of Ilan's statement in the Discovery Channel documentary.[37]

The name *Yoseh (YWSH)* located on an ossuary in the Talpiot tomb creates a number of problems. It appears to be a rare name, found in Talpiot, at Jason's Tomb, and in the Murabba'at papyri.[38] *Yoseh* is considered by most scholars a variant spelling of Joseph *(Yoseph, YWSP)* and generally as a contraction of Joseph.[39] However, Evans and Feldman wrote a highly negative article on the Talpiot tomb and the name *Yoseh* on the Biblical Archaeology Society Web site. Here they insist:

> The name YWSH should be pronounced "Yosah" (as Professor Tal Ilan in fact does in the documentary), not "Yoseh," as the documentary consistently does. "Yosah" is not the Hebrew equivalent of the Greek form

34. Bauckham, *Jesus and the Eyewitnesses*, p. 47.

35. Ibid., p. 85. Bauckham tabulates *Yosi* with Joseph, and Ilan, *Lexicon*, p. 159, no. 96, catalogues occurrences of *Yosi* and *Yoseh* with Joseph.

36. Craig Evans and Steven Feldman, "The Tomb of Jesus? Wrong on Every Count," http://bib-arch.org/bswbKCtombevansfeldman.html.

37. Ilan, *Lexicon*, p. 159. Indeed, in no. 96 regarding the name Joseph, Ilan states, "*'Isi, Yosi, Yoseh,* and *Yoseph* seem to be variations on the same name." Therefore it appears that however she pronounces the name in the Discovery Channel documentary, Ilan views *Yoseh* as a variant of Joseph.

38. Ibid., p. 154 for ossuary no. 118, p. 154 for no. 133, and p. 155 for no. 154.

39. Ibid., p. 23, section 2.4.1.1; Rahmani, *Catalogue*, p. 223, ossuary no. 705; Bauckman, *Jesus and the Eyewitnesses*, p. 85, simply lists the Greek form *Joses* with Joseph and does not make a distinction between the two.

Joses, the name of Jesus' brother (as in Mark 6:3 and elsewhere). The Hebrew equivalent is YWSY (and is found on a number of ossuaries in Greek and in Hebrew). The documentary's discussion of this name is very misleading.[40]

Referring to the argument over *Yoseh,* Pfann wrote:

> A cautionary note on the YWSH/YWSY point [YWSY = Yosi, a common form for the contraction of Yoseph]. Once we assess the sources, only YWSH can be attributed to the late Second Temple period [in] Judea and the Galilee (and which is basically true for the late Roman period as well). The only evidence for the pronunciation of vowels that comes from that period is from Greek forms of the name. There we only have "Iose/Ioses" and not "Iosah." Although this published claim is weak, we can, on the other hand, challenge the assertion of the filmmakers that this name is so rare. What comes down to us is in Greek. The Markan passage is unique with respect to providing this shortened Greek name for Jesus' brother. However, in Greek inscriptions, the shortened form "Iose/Ioses" is more popular than "Iosepos."[41]

James Tabor of the University of North Carolina at Charlotte has written that BAS got it wrong and that *Yoseh* is indeed the name found at Talpiot; that it is a very rare name, being found perhaps on only one other ossuary; and that it is most likely the equivalent of *Joses,* the brother of Jesus found in Mark 6:3.[42] Furthermore, Tabor states, "Much of the statistical work on the Talpiot cluster of names has been done using the nickname *Yoseh* as if it was the equivalent to the much more common name Joseph/Yehosef (8.6% of male names), which it plainly is not."

If we consider finding the inscription *Yoseh* as meaning more than merely finding the inscription "Joseph" on an ossuary, how does this change arguments based on probability? Table 1 shows the name *Yoseh* to be more rarely observed than the name Joseph by a factor of about 29. Obviously such a large change in probability means that observing the name *Yoseh* is very much more significant than observing the name Joseph in any tomb

40. Evans and Feldman, "Tomb of Jesus?"

41. Pfann, "Yoseh."

42. See James Tabor, "The Name Yoseh on the Talpiot Tomb Ossuary," http://jesusdynasty.com/blog/2007/09/02/the-name-yoseh-on-the-talpiot-tomb-ossuary/.

suspected of containing remains of Jesus' family members. However, we cannot just use the factor of 29; we should, instead, compare identical calculations with Joseph and *Yoseh* exchanged. For example, our calculation using Bayes' Theorem that we made in equations 2 through 8 using the name *Yoseh* rather than Joseph have a posterior probability ratio of about 14:1 (47%/3.4%). So, we might say that observing the name *Yoseh* is fourteen times more significant as a piece of evidence regarding the Talpiot tomb being the tomb of Jesus' family than is observing the name Joseph in this instance.

Significance of Judah

One ossuary bears the inscription *Judah son of Jesus.* We have no idea who this person is, or what relationship he has to others in the tomb. Depending on how one decides to interpret this inscription, and what one's prior beliefs are, this inscription alone could cause one to discount the Talpiot tomb from being the Jesus family tomb altogether. However, we believe that the existence of an ossuary inscribed with Judah son of Jesus does not negate the possibility that the Talpiot tomb is the tomb of the Jesus family. As we argued in an earlier paper,[43] Jesus' marital status arouses little interest in the Gospels. On whether Jesus had been married previously or had a son, the Gospels are silent. Moreover, the Gospels rarely reveal any information on the marital status of Jesus' apostles. There is a brief mention of Peter's (Simon's) mother-in-law but nothing on his wife or possible children (Mark 1:30). Can we suppose that all the original disciples excluding Peter were not married simply because their marital status remains unmentioned in the Gospels? If not for Paul's brief comment concerning the wives of the other apostles and the brothers of the Lord and Cephas (1 Cor 9:5), we would have no creditable information concerning the wives of the apostles. The Gospel writers scarcely show any interest in the marital status of Jesus or his disciples.[44]

43. Elliott and Kilty, "Inside the Numbers of the Talpiot Tomb," http://www.lccc.wy.edu/Index.aspx?page = 547.

44. We could speculate here in many ways. For example, suppose that the Judah identified by Mark as a brother of Jesus was Jesus' son; or perhaps "Judah son of Jesus" suggests that Jesus had an illegitimate child; and just as occurs often in our own society, his mother, Mary, raised this child as a brother to Jesus, as depicted in Mark 6:3. Another possibility follows a suggestion Rahmani made in his discussion of ossuary 706 from Talpiot; perhaps Mary in this tomb is actually *Yoseh*'s wife and not Jesus' mother, and Matthew is the child of *Yoseh* and Mary — this does not invalidate the tomb as that of the

Significance of Mariamne

The name that has caused the most intense speculation about the Talpiot tomb is one inscribed in Greek, which Ilan lists as Μαριαμηνου, and which scholars working with the Discovery Channel documentary translated as *Mariamne*, "Little Mary." Though *Mariamne* is an appellation given to a Mary Magdalene–like person in *Acts of Philip* (fourth century CE), Pfann considers this point irrelevant, being three centuries too late for legitimate consideration.[45] Evans and Feldman are even more emphatic about the irrelevance of this name.

At the January 2008 conference several scholars took an opposing stance. Schaberg, for example, was a panelist and argued that one could not exclude the possibility that one of the ossuaries contained Mary Magdalene.[46] If this *Mariamne* were proven to be the Mary Magdalene of Christian tradition (and we do not believe there is such evidence at present), then probabilities regarding identification of the Talpiot tomb change dramatically because *Mariamne* occurs so rarely.[47] Rather than try to argue that *Mariamne* equals *Mary Magdalene,* let us assume that we might expect a second, Mary-like name to be found in a Jesus family tomb. Such an expectation adds a second *Mary* into the list of combinations of names in a Jesus family tomb (table 2) and produces 61 possibilities that are consistent with our assumptions. Combining this second Mary with the names Jesus son of Joseph, *Yoseh,* and the other Mary now produces a posterior probability of 89%.[48] Once again, if we substitute Joseph for *Yoseh* we arrive at a posterior probability of 25%.

Jesus family. There are limitless other possibilities, but no facts, making names like Judah and Matthew neutral to the present issue.

45. Stephan Pfann, "The Improper Application of Statistics in 'The Lost Tomb of Jesus'" http://www.uhl.ac/JudeanTombsAndOssuaries.html.

46. See Jane Schaberg, "Response to Charlesworth," http://www.sbl-site.org/publications/article.aspx?articleId = 753.

47. We find a name form similar to *Mariamne* on only three entries in Ilan, for example.

48. Of course, one ought to consider whether we expected beforehand to find Mary Magdalene in a tomb with Jesus or this simply became convenient after finding the inscription *Mariamne.*

Miscellaneous Counterarguments

Many people have now made statistical analyses of the tomb.[49] Several of these are coincidentally similar to ours. For example, Randy Ingermanson[50] independently considered this approach and assembled, sometimes with Jay Cost, several well-written Web articles that analyze the statistics of this issue and discuss the application of Bayes' Theorem to it. Several scholars suggest that these are the most complete statistical works on the subject. For example, Habermas states, "Probably no one has done more work on the statistics of the Talpiot Tomb than Randy Ingermanson."[51] However, we disagree with some of their presuppositions and maintain that their results can be misleading. A problematic feature of Ingermanson and Cost's original work is their failure to acknowledge that the name *Yoseh* can be rare as well as a variant of Joseph. As we have shown, this always lowers the likelihood of identifying the tomb.[52] We have not read anything that convinces us that *Yoseh* must always be interpreted as simply a form of Joseph.

Additionally, we confine our statistical model to an analysis of inscriptions. Yet Ingermanson, in his latest statistical offering, analyzes name fre-

49. See, e.g., *Annals of Applied Statistics* 2 (2008): 1-112, http://projecteuclid.org/DPubS?service = UI&version = 1.0&verb = Display&handle = euclid.aoas.

50. See Randy Ingermanson, "Statistics and the 'Jesus Family Tomb,'" http://www.ingermanson.com/jesus/art/stats.php. See also Ingermanson, "Bayes Theorem and the 'Jesus Family Tomb.'" http://www.ingermanson.com/jesus/art/stats2.php. Jay Cost and Randy Ingermanson, "'He Is Not Here,' or Is He? A Statistical Analysis of the Claims Made in The Lost Tomb of Jesus," http://www.ingermanson.com/jesus/art/tomb/HeIsNotHere.pdf.

51. Gary Habermas, *The Secret of the Talpiot Tomb: Unravelling the Mystery of the Jesus Family Tomb* (Nashville: Holman Reference, 2008), p. 59; or Darrel Bock, http://blog.bible.org/bock/node/146.

52. Ingermanson, "Statistics and Jesus Family Tomb," and Ingermanson, "Bayes' Theorem and Jesus Family Tomb," consistently explore ways to discount the possible interpretation of the Talpiot tomb as bearing the remains of the Jesus family. For example, he states that the Talpiot tomb contains the remains of as many as 35 persons, when we are actually considering only six inscribed ossuaries, no matter what else was in the tomb. This inflation of the number of individuals involved has the effect of suppressing the value of evidence, as one can see from all of Ingermanson's graphs. As another example, he interprets the Matthew and Judah mentioned in the tomb as being disciples of Jesus, and from there assumes that any two disciples would be equivalent. This has the effect of inflating the probability of finding an equivalent tomb because probability in this case is additive and the names of the disciples Simon, Judas, John, Matthew, and James constitute a huge proportion of male names in use.

quencies on the inscribed ossuaries and adds computations regarding the improbability of Jesus' burial in a rock-cut tomb and Jesus' marital status in the context of the ossuary inscribed with "Judas son of Jesus."[53] We have argued elsewhere that these assumptions are unproven.[54] We have no evidence whatsoever regarding the probability of Jesus being buried in a rock-cut tomb relative to that of other men of the period. We have no records from 30-70 CE that indicate whether his tomb is known or unknown. Moreover, we do not agree that the fact that there is an ossuary inscribed with *Judas son of Jesus* that invalidates the tomb or should be considered a negative factor in these calculations. We have no idea who this Judas son of Jesus is. We also know that the Gospel writers show little interest in Jesus' marital status or whether Jesus had a son. On these issues the Gospels are silent. We suggest that the evidence available cannot justify inserting these elements in any form regarding a statistical analysis of the names engraved on the ossuaries at Talpiot. To do so encourages an error of overspecification.

Rather than overspecification, William Demski and Robert J. Marks discount the significance of the tomb through an error of underspecification.[55] They include the entire population of Judea in the analysis, some one million souls, rather than just the population of the Jerusalem area in the first century, without any acknowledgment that practically none of the families from outside Jerusalem would have any significant probability of being entombed there.

Conclusion

In view of how easily people manage to misstate analysis regarding the Talpiot tomb, we conclude this essay by reiterating our analysis of claims in the order we introduced them.

- The Talpiot tomb is a surprising find because while it contains some names that are common to the first-century population, the combination is not at all likely to occur.
- An inscription like "Jesus son of Joseph" is exactly an inscription one

53. Randy Ingermanson, "Analysis of the Talpiot Tomb Using Bayes' Theorem and Random Variables" lib.stat.cmu.edu/aoas/99g/supplement.pdf.

54. Elliott and Kilty, "Inside the Numbers."

55. William Demski and Robert J. Marks, "The Jesus Tomb Math," in *Buried Hope or Risen Savior: The Search for the Jesus Tomb*, ed. Charles Quarles (Nashville: B&H Academic, 2008), pp. 113-51. Footnotes 19 and 20 there discuss the size of the relevant population.

would expect to find on an ossuary containing the remains of "Jesus of Nazareth."

- The inscription *Jesus son of Joseph* is itself quite rare among ossuaries.
- No tomb the size of the Talpiot tomb contains a group of names so like what one would expect of a Jesus family tomb. The only other "tomb" known to contain a comparable collection of names is Dominus Flevit, which is not comparable by virtue of its being a tomb complex of great size.
- While many scholars view the name *Mariamne* as being the significant inscription in terms of identifying this tomb, the names *Yoseh* and *Jesus son of Joseph* are also quite significant.
- There is no other unequivocal physical evidence at the present time to examine at Talpiot except ossuary inscriptions.
- If we consider the name *Yoseh* as meaning more than a variant of Joseph, and considering our underlying assumptions, then the probability that this tomb is that of the Jesus family is 47%. However, if *Yoseh* is to be regarded as simply "Joseph" in all circumstances, then the probability that this tomb is "The Lost Tomb of Jesus" is 3%.

Bibliography

Annals of Applied Statistics. http://projecteuclid.org/DPubS?service = UI version = 1.overb = Displayhandle = euclid.aoas (accessed July 2, 2008).

Bagatti, B., and J. T. Milik. *Gli Scavi del "Dominus Flevit,"* part 1, *La Necropoli del Periodo Romano.* Pubblicazioni dello Studium Biblicum Franciscanum 13. Jerusalem: Franciscan Printing Press, 1958.

Bauckham, Richard. *Jesus and the Eyewitnesses.* Grand Rapids: Eerdmans, 2006.

Bock, Darrell. "Lectures Wrapping up and the Tomb at Dominus Flevit at the Mount of Olives March 14." http://blog.bible.org/bock/node/129 (accessed May 30, 2008).

Cost, Jay, and Randy Ingermanson. "'He Is Not Here,' Or Is He? A Statistical Analysis of the Claims Made in The Lost Tomb of Jesus." http://www.ingermanson.com/jesus/art/tomb/HeIsNotHere.pdf (accessed May 27, 2008).

Demski, William, and Robert J. Marks. "The Jesus Tomb Math." Pp. 113-51 in *Buried Hope or Risen Savior: The Search for the Jesus Tomb,* ed. Charles Quarles. Nashville: B&H Academic, 2008.

Duke University Religion Department. "The Talpiot Tomb Controversy Revisted." http://dukereligion.blogspot.com/2008/01/talpiot-tomb-controversy-revisited.html (accessed May 30, 2008).

Elliott, Mark, and Kevin Kilty. "Inside the Numbers of the Talpiot Tomb." http://www.lccc.wy.edu/Index.aspx?page = 547 (accessed May 30, 2008).

Evans, Craig, and Steven Feldman. "The Tomb of Jesus? Wrong on Every Count." http://bib-arch.org/bswbKCtombevansfeldman.html (accessed May 30, 2008).

Feuerverger, Andrey. "Dear Statistical Colleagues." http://Fisher.utstat.toronto.edu/andrey/OfficeHrs.txt (accessed June 29, 2008).

Finegan, Jack. *The Archeology of the New Testament.* Princeton: Princeton University Press, 1992.

Habermas, Gary. *The Secret of the Talpiot Tomb: Unraveling the Mystery of the Jesus Family Tomb.* Nashville: Holman Reference, 2008.

Hachlili, Rachel. "The Media and Three Surveys by the Tomb Symposium Participants." http://www.uhl.ac/blog/?cat = 3&paged = 2 (accessed July 14, 2008).

Ilan, Tal. *Lexicon of Jewish Names in Late Antiquity, Part 1: Palestine 330 BCE–200 CE.* TSAJ 91. Tübingen: Mohr Siebeck, 2002.

Ingermanson, Randy. "Analysis of the Talpiot Tomb Using Bayes' Theorem and Random Variables." lib.stat.cmu.edu/aoas/99g/supplement.pdf (accessed May 27, 2008).

————. "Bayes' Theorem and the 'Jesus Family Tomb.'" http://www.ingermanson.com/jesus/art/stats2.php (accessed May 27, 2008).

————. "Statistics and the 'Jesus Family Tomb.'" http://www.ingermanson.com/jesus/art/stats.php (accessed May 27, 2008).

Kilty, Kevin, and Mark Elliott. "Probability, Statistics, and the Talpiot Tomb." http://www.lccc.wy.edu/Index.aspx?page = 547 (accessed May 30, 2008).

Levine, Lee I. *Jerusalem: Portrait of the City in the Second Temple Period.* Philadelphia: Jewish Publication Society, 2002.

Magness, Jodi. "Has the Tomb of Jesus Been Discovered?" http://sbl-site.org/publications/article.aspx?articleId = 640 (accessed July 1, 2008).

Pfann, Stephan. "The Improper Application of Statistics in 'The Lost Tomb of Jesus.'" http://www.uhl.ac/JudeanTombsAndOssuaries.html (accessed June 20, 2008).

————. http://ntgateway.com/weblog/2007/05/new-article-on-talpiot-tomb.html (accessed June 20, 2008).

————. "'Yoseh Can You See?' Checking the Sources (Updated)." http://www.uhl.ac/blog/?p = 448 (accessed June 20, 2008).

Rahmani, L. Y. *A Catalogue of Jewish Ossuaries in the Collections of the State of Israel.* Jerusalem: Israel Antiquities Authority, 1994.

Rollston, Christopher. "Inscribed Ossuaries: Personal Names, Statistics, and Laboratory Tests." *NEA* 69 (2006): 125-29.

————. "Prosopography and the Talpiyot Yeshua Family Tomb: Pensées of a Palaeographer." http://www.sbl-site.org/publications/article.aspx?articleId = 649 (accessed June 20, 2008).

Schaberg, Jane. "Response to Charlesworth." http://www.sbl-site.org/publications/article.aspx?articleId = 753 (accessed May 27, 2008).

Tabor, James. "The Name Yoseh on the Talpiot Tomb Ossuary." http://jesusdynasty.com/blog/2007/09/02/the-name-yoseh-on-the-talpiot-tomb-ossuary/ (accessed June 20, 2008).

————. http://sbl-site.org/Article.aspx?ArticleId = 651 (accessed June 20, 2008).

Names, Statistics, and the "Jesus' Family" Tomb Site

Camil Fuchs

The statistical analysis of the cluster of names from the ossuaries in Talpiot played a crucial role in the heated debate related to the possibility that the Talpiot tomb site was the secondary tomb for Jesus' family. Among the various statistical analyses, Feuerverger's research is a prime reference in terms of both the depth of the research as well as in exposure. At the same time, it is also likely that the complexity of assumptions and calculations led many to think about the statistical analyses in term of the phrase attributed by Mark Twain to Disraeli: "There are three kinds of lies: lies, damn lies, and statistics." Mark Twain's semi-ironic phrase succinctly describes how, in some people's opinion, statistics can be used to bolster inaccurate arguments. The opinion is likely to be particularly pervasive among those who were convinced in advance that it is unconceivable that the Talpiot tomb site was Jesus' family's burial tomb.

However, to adopt such an attitude is an easy and unfair way out of the discussion. It is certainly easy since it avoids the complexities involved in the analyzed evidence. And it is unfair since it assumes a priori that some statisticians have deliberately performed a less than optimal analysis of the data.

Let me start with a somewhat surprising statement resulting from the statistical analysis of the cluster of names inscribed on the ossuaries in Talpiot: Today, *none* of the statisticians of whom I am aware who analyzed the data considers that *the Talpiot find is statistically significant in any meaningful way*. And yes, I do include Prof. Feuerverger in this statement. I defer to section 5.1 the evidence to support this contention. At the same time, Feuerverger's research and paper (Feuerverger 2008a) concluded that the odds that the Talpiot tomb site was Jesus' family's burial tomb are very high, and those conclusions are still widely cited and were crucial in the still ongoing debate.

In this paper I address the two separate issues that evolve from the previous and the present analyses: (a) To what extent is Feuerverger's suggested method of analysis (denoted below as "the RR approach," Feuerverger 2008a) reasonable, and can we rely on the computed results and on the stated conclusions? (b) Assuming that there are reasons to criticize the RR approach, is the overall conclusion from the research devoted to the analysis of the data that the Talpiot tomb cannot be the Jesus family tomb? It is important to realize that while Feuerverger's analyses and the resulting figures are a prime reference, there are also several additional studies devoted to the Talpiot find, and their results are discussed together with the results of this research.

An undesirable side effect of the statistical analysis of the Talpiot find and of the published categorical conclusion was that it provoked several scholars to seriously doubt the basic ability of statistical theory to provide satisfying answers to problems evolving from the archaeological research. I address in the final section some of those concerns and present my view in the matter.

Following an illustration of the problematic nature of the RR approach, I present in section 2 the assumptions and reservations presented in the various articles devoted to the Talpiot find. The assumptions of my analysis of the relevant data and the resulting estimates follow in section 3. The detailed calculations can be found in a supplementary paper (Fuchs 2008b). To anticipate the results from section 3, under the set of assumptions from the supplementary paper, the probability that the Talpiot tomb site was the Jesus family burial tomb was assessed to be about 20%. The results of other published analyses are presented in section 4. The bottom line regarding the substantive answer to the research question is presented in section 5, and I conclude in section 6 with a discussion of the important issue mentioned above regarding the role of the statistical theory in archaeological research.

1. The RR Approach

1.1. Two Simple Examples

The basic element in the RR approach is the assessment of the "relevance" and the "rareness" of the cluster of names. The statistical properties of the suggested method of analysis are quite complex. In order to illustrate the contentions with the method, I use two simple hypothetical situations. The examples were also mentioned in my published discussion of Feuerverger's article (Fuchs 2008a).

Let us first pretend that another tomb with five inscribed ossuaries was excavated. The gender configuration of the inscribed ossuaries in that fictitious tomb is assumed to be as in Talpiot: two ossuaries with female names and three ossuaries with male names, including one with generational names. In both tombs, I ignore for the moment the ossuary with the Yehuda bar Yeshuaʿ inscription. (Throughout the paper I generally use the transliteration of the inscriptions and not their English counterparts. In particular, as in the inscriptions, I use the Aramaic *bar* instead of "son of.")

Assume that the inscriptions in the fictitious tomb read: "Mariamenou[η]Mara and Marya," and "Yoseh bar Matya, Yaʿakov, Yehosef," respectively. Note that in the fictitious tomb, Yeshuaʿ does not appear at all and Yoseh is the son of an arbitrary Matya. As a reminder, after discarding the Yehuda bar Yeshuaʿ inscription, the remaining inscriptions in the Talpiot tomb are: "Mariamenou[η]Mara and Marya" and "Yeshuaʿ bar Yehosef, Yoseh, Matya."

Given the two clusters of inscriptions, which tomb would be considered as a more likely candidate for belonging to Jesus' family? The seemingly obvious answer is that the Talpiot tomb is a much more likely candidate. Indeed, the configuration of names in the fictitious tomb is likely to be ignored and considered a noncandidate. Yet if one used the RR approach for comparing the two tombs, the configuration in the fictitious tomb (without Yeshuaʿ and with Yoseh bar Matya) would be more surprising and closer to the Jesus family tomb hypothesis.

Let us now consider a second example that avoids the intricacies of the speculations related to the Mariamenou[η]Mara inscription. Assume that still another tomb with the same basic configuration of ossuaries was excavated. The inscriptions in that tomb read "Mariam, Marya" and "Yehosef bar Yoseh, Yaʿakov, and Yeshuaʿ," respectively. Note that in the second fictitious tomb, Yehosef is the son of Yoseh (and not the other way around) and no ossuary bears a Mariamenou[η]Mara inscription. As before, in the comparison between the Talpiot and the fictitious tombs, the Talpiot tomb seems a much more likely candidate for belonging to Jesus' family. The configuration of names in the fictitious tomb is unlikely to raise any excitement. Yet the use of the RR approach for comparing the two tombs would yield a result similar to that from the previous comparison: the second fictitious tomb (with the Yehosef bar Yoseh inscription) would have been considered as having a more surprising configuration of names than the Talpiot tomb (with Yeshua' bar Yehosef).

1.2. Lack of Monotonicity in the RR Approach

The above examples illustrate the contention that the surprisingness values assigned by the RR approach to the various configurations are not necessarily monotonic with our perceptions. In other words, whenever the RR approach is used to compare two configurations, one cannot assume that the configuration considered by "common knowledge" as closer to the tested hypothesis will also have a higher surprisingness value. Hardly anyone will disagree with the statement that the configuration in the Talpiot tomb with the male inscriptions (Yeshua' bar Yehosef, Yoseh, Matya) is closer to the Jesus family tomb hypothesis than the configuration whose male inscriptions read "Yoseh bar Matya, Ya'akov, Yehosef." That the fictitious configuration has nevertheless a higher surprisingness value is disturbing and casts doubt on the method's ability to reach the correct conclusion.

Why does the configuration with Yoseh bar Matya and Ya'akov have a higher surprisingness value? Simply, the relative frequency of the name Ya'akov is lower than that of the name Yeshua'. The rareness of Ya'akov's name leads to a more surprising configuration of names. The suggested method grants a bonus to the Yeshua' bar Yehosef generational ossuary, but its magnitude does not compensate for the difference in the relative frequencies.

In more general terms, the fundamental issue is the entity with respect to which we define a priori our surprisingness. If the tested hypothesis is that a particular tomb was the Jesus family tomb, the function that assigns a numerical value to the level of surprisingness should ensure that whenever a configuration is closer than another to the tested hypothesis, the measures of surprisingness should reflect the ordering.

Undoubtedly, the assignment of numerical values to perceptions of relative surprisingness is a difficult task. The RR approach suggests the combined use of "relevance" with respect to the a priori list and "rareness" of the cluster of names as a proxy meant to express those perceptions. Unfortunately, the examples presented above seem to indicate that the suggested measure is doing a less than optimal job in this matter.

To anticipate the discussion from the next section, some of the other methods of analysis do consider various criteria and methods that address the *actually* tested hypothesis. The estimates assessed by those methods vary as a function of the underlying assumptions. However, even without the benefit of a single pseudo-exact figure, the results go a considerable way toward a *substantive* answer to the question at hand.

2. The Assumptions and the Estimated Probabilities

Feuerverger's analyses triggered a series of additional statistical studies on the Talpiot data. Their conclusions do not concur either with the originally publicized results from Feuerverger's study or with those published in his recently comprehensive article (Feuerverger 2008a). The various studies differ both in their assumptions as well as in the methods of analysis. The variance in the assumptions is critical in this research. Here I address some of those assumptions and contend that while the numerical results may differ, the statistical analyses provide a solid basis for the substantive answer in this research.

The articles by Ingermanson (2008a, 2008b) and Ingermanson and Cost (2007) present the most comprehensive set of assumptions incorporated in the statistical analysis. Obviously, the agreement with the comprehensiveness and the validity of their set of assumptions does not necessarily imply a similar agreement with the method of analysis. Other questions and resulting assumptions (e.g., Tabor 2007) can also be raised but cannot be easily incorporated in the models. On the other hand, we are not convinced that they should be.

2.1.1. Is there a tomb site in Jerusalem that belonged to Jesus' family?

Contrary to the common belief, the RR approach does not explicitly assume that a tomb site that belonged to Jesus' family existed in Jerusalem. The "tail area" in Feuerverger's article (2008a) is interpreted as the chance that such a tomb site exists. However, the RR analysis is conditioned upon the assumption that with probability 1 (i.e., certainty) there did exist such a tomb (see also Bentley 2008). Bentley asserts that the model cannot assume with certainty the existence of the tomb. Ingermanson (2008a), Höfling and Wasserman (2008), and Mortera and Vicard (2008) also mention that the existence of the tomb cannot be assumed with certainty. Ingermanson (2008a) and Höfling and Wasserman (2008) include in their model a factor that accounts for such uncertainty. However, while Höfling and Wasserman performed their computations under the "optimistic" scenario and assign a value of 1 to that factor (i.e., certainty), Ingermanson includes the uncertainty term in the model.

2.1.2. *The uninscribed ossuaries*

In addition to the six well-known inscriptions, the Talpiot tomb site contained four uninscribed ossuaries. Except for Ingermanson, the analyses performed by all other researchers excluded the uninscribed ossuaries. For some models, the assumption that the uninscribed ossuaries contain no relevant information is justifiable. However, in other models, as those used by Ingermanson and by Ingermanson and Cost, the estimated probability is a function of both the number of inscribed ossuaries and their gender configuration.

2.1.3. *Mariamenou[η]Mara in the RR approach*

Unquestionably, the debate surrounding the Mariamenou[η]Mara inscription surpassed by far the attention received by the other assumptions. The RR approach lists Jesus' sisters Mariam and Salome, Marya (Jesus' mother), and Mary Magdalene as potential female candidates for being in Jesus' family tomb. The addition of Mary Magdalene is explained by her being "present at the burial ritual." Furthermore, the identification of the Mariamenou[η]Mara inscription with Mary Magdalene's is justified by stating that Mariamenou is "the most specific appellation to Mary Magdalene from among those known."

Following the discussants' remarks and criticisms, Feuerverger emphasizes in the rejoinder (Feuerverger 2008b) that Mary Magdalene's inclusion in an a priori list of potential female candidates should be dissociated with Mary Magdalene's identification with Mariamenou[η]Mara. He contends that due to Mary Magdalene's pivotal role in Jesus' life and ministry and the accounts of her presence at the crucifixion, her inclusion in the potential candidates list is clearly warranted. He also readdresses the contention that Mariamene is "the most specific appellation to Mary Magdalene."

The separation of the two issues is so noted. However, the data analysis indicates that the identification of Mariamenou[η]Mara with Mary Magdalene is intertwined with the previous issue. Indeed, although the relevant list records only Mary Magdalene (MM) and not Mariamenou[η]Mara, the analysis was performed as if the potential list of candidates had to include the particular rendition Mariamenou[η]Mara. The Mariamenou[η]Mara inscription is presented as being a unique[1] and relevant rendition of Mariam. Its assigned rareness value has the largest effect on the cluster's measure of surprisingness. As I mentioned elsewhere (Fuchs 2008a), if there is evidence that the ossuary inscribed Mariamenou[η]Mara is indeed Mary Magdalene's ossuary, the finding is sensational by itself. But based only on the evidence at hand, the inclusion in the list of that rendition is at least problematic. If Mariamenou[η]Mara were treated as "Other," the overall measure of surprisingness would have been two hundred times smaller.

In the rejoinder of the main paper (Feuerverger 2008b) Feuerverger mentions that he retracts the statement that Mariamenou[η]Mara is the most appropriate specific appellation to Mary Magdalene. In section 5.1 I return to this topic and discuss the implications of this retraction as well as other issues related to that inscription. I mention parenthetically that the Third Princeton Symposium on Judaism and Early Christianity dedicated a special session to Mary Magdalene. Undoubtedly, several scholarly papers on the issue will find their way to the proceedings, and the findings related to the identification of Mary Magdalene with Mariamne are likely to be properly discussed.

---

1. The inscription from the Talpiot tomb (ossuary 701 in Rahmani's *Catalogue*) is presented as the only instance of the "full and unusual" Μαριαμηνου. However, Rahmani's *Catalogue* lists an additional ossuary with two "Mariamne" inscriptions. The Hebrew inscription on ossuary 108 (108A) is listed by Rahmani as Mariamne, and the Greek inscription on the lid underside (108B) is also listed as Μαριαμηνου. The additional inscription on the lid across (108C) is listed as Mariame. One can wonder why the inscription on ossuary 108 should not be an additional and maybe a better Mariamne candidate to relate to Maria Magdalene. In reply to my inquiry, A. Lemaire (personal communication, 2008) states that "if we take Rahmani's book as a reference, the Greek inscription 108B is clearly a better parallel to *Mariamnē* in the Acts of Philip, and eventually the Hebrew 108A." Lemaire mentions that he concurs with neither of Rahmani's readings of the relevant inscriptions from ossuaries 108 and 701. He assents with Price that in the Talpiot inscription (701) the dilemma is how to separate the words: either *Mariamē kai Mara* (two names: Mariamē and Mara) or *Mariam ē kai Mara* (one name with a surname: Mariam who (is) also (called) Mara). None of those alternatives includes the Mariamne reading. He also claims that there is no chance that *Mariamnē* in the later *Acts of Philip* kept a better historical spelling of the name of Maria Magdalena than the Gospels. According to Lemaire's reading, the inscription on ossuary 701 is thus another Mariam, the most common female name. Alternatively, if one adopts Feuerverger's provisos related to Mariamne, the inscription from ossuary 108 has to be added to the pool.

2.1.4. *The Yoseh and Marya renditions*

In addition to Mariamenou[η]Mara, the RR approach uses the Yoseh and Marya special renditions, identified with Jesus' second brother and with Jesus' mother, respectively. Those renditions are justified similarly as Mariamenou[η]Mara: "Marya is the most appropriate rendition for the mother" and "Yoseh is the most appropriate rendition for the second brother, as in Mark 6:3." In the analysis of name renditions, the relative frequencies of the generic names (Yehosef and Mariam, respectively) are multiplied by factors corresponding to the rareness of the particular renditions within the generic name. The effect is an increase in the overall surprisingness value, that is, more surprisingness.

Feuerverger emphasized several times that the assumptions are not universally accepted. Indeed, it is well known that Matt 13:55 referred to the second brother as Yehosef, and Ingermanson (2008b) quotes Pfann (2007), who found that Jesus' mother was called 13 times by the name of Mariam and only 6 times as Marya. As for Yoseh, Tabor (personal communication, 2008) considers that since Mark is the source for Matthew, the change that Matthew made is secondary and editorial.

Overall, the assumptions regarding the renditions are not shared by the other analysts. The researchers do not consent either with the assumption that Mary Magdalene is an a priori candidate for inclusion in the tomb or with the statement that, a priori, Jesus' mother should be assumed to be inscribed as Marya. Kilty and Elliott and Ingermanson treat the Mariamenou[η]Mara as an "Other," while Höfling and Wasserman consider the rendition in one of the versions, assuming that the name could in some way be interpreted for Jesus' mother (Maria) or sister (Mariam) or Maria Magdalene.

2.1.5. *The Yehuda bar Yeshua' inscription*

The RR approach assumes that the ossuary inscribed Yehuda bar Yeshua' "can be explained and may be discarded from the analysis." Feuerverger mentions candidly that if "an ossuary inscribed 'Yehuda son of Yeshua' may (for whatever reason) not be located in a NT family tombsite, then the Talpiyot site cannot be that of the NT family and the names found there must be purely coincidental" (2008a, 27). However, the implications of this fair statement do not penetrate the original calculations, and the published probabilities rely on the data set that excludes the inscription.

Furthermore, Feuerverger mentions that according to the RR approach, if the grandfather-father-son sequence were allowed, no change in the results would have occurred since Jesus' family's genealogy has no known father-and-son pair both dying in the relevant period of time. In other words, the son Yehuda would have been another "Other" with no implication. But the fact that the inclusion of the quite fascinating additional inscription has no effect under the proposed approach does not necessarily reflect on the insignificance of the added data. It rather reflects on the proposed method of analysis.

Among the researchers who analyzed the data, only Ingermanson and Cost (2007) and Ingermanson (2008a and 2008b) include in their alternative analysis the generational configuration of the Yehuda bar Yeshuaʿ inscription. Kilty and Elliott (2007) also assume that that inscription can be treated as "Other." Höfling and Wasserman present an interesting compromise and "do not consider the generational part" of the inscription (i.e., the "son of Yeshuaʿ"), and assign weights to Yehuda similar to those assigned to Matya (i.e., an "Other" that was found in the tomb, with no known relationship to the family). Following Ingermanson and Cost (2007), Ingermanson (2008a and 2008b) confronts "head on" the Yehuda bar Yeshuaʿ inscription, and considers the possibility that Jesus had a son. He includes in his model a random variable to represent the event that decreases the probability that Yeshuaʿ bar Yehosef from the Talpiot tomb refers to Jesus of Nazareth. Remember that Rahmani (1994) surmised that the similarities between Yoseh and Marya's inscriptions, both coming from the same tomb, may indicate that Yoseh and Marya were the parents of Yeshuaʿ and the grandparents of Yehuda.

2.1.6. Further reservations

The discussants of Feuerverger's paper commend him for undertaking the investigation and for the thoroughness of his analyses. However, they express clear reservations regarding the assumptions and the conclusions. Some of those reservations are briefly summarized below. As a general comment, I believe that a distinction should be made between reservations of general nature and specific assumptions related to the names and their surprisingness. While reservations of a general nature (like the possibility of fraud, the lack of information on the uninscribed ossuaries and on the placement of the ossuaries in the tomb) are relevant, they should not deter the statistician from plunging into the difficult problem and performing the computations even if the assumptions are not universally accepted. Proper reservations should be explicitly formulated, and one has to specify that the results and conclusions are conditioned upon the assumptions made being true, as Feuerverger indeed clearly did in his study. On the other hand, specific assumptions related to the names and their surprisingness have to be carefully considered. If possible, those assumptions should be incorporated in the model that assesses the conditional probability that the Talpiot tomb site was the Jesus family burial tomb.

Stigler (2008) mentions the possibility of fraudulently manufactured evidence, the lack of information on the placement of the different ossuaries among the *kokhim,* and finally reminds us of Galton's caution from 1863 regarding the "plastic" nature of very limited sample sizes "in the hand of men with preconceived ideas." Stigler does not necessarily infer that "preconceived ideas" played a role in this case, but mentions that occasional suppression and slight modification can also be part of sound statistical analysis, and from the context it seems that he does not consider as unlikely the possibility that such perturbations may have occurred in this case.

Bentley (2008) reminds us of Moses' law (that is, Lincoln Moses' law) that "Statistics is the umpire of the sciences," and addresses the basic assumptions of the RR approach. He questions the assumption that with probability 1 (i.e., certainty) Jesus' family had a tomb, then that the tomb has to be in the vicinity of Jerusalem, as well as the assumption that the number of tombs can be deduced from the estimated population size, without accounting for nonresidents during festivals and other non-Jerusalemites who wished to be buried in Jerusalem. He further questions Feuerverger's selective willingness to accept or reject Rahmani's interpretations of the inscriptions as suiting the theory. Feuerverger accepts Rahmani's reading on ossuary 1 leading to "Mariamene [diminutive] also known as Mara" (although Rahmani says that it is "probable") but definitely rejects Rahmani's presumption that "the similarities between ossuaries #5 [Yoseh] and #6 [Marya] may indicate that Yoseh and Marya were the parents of Yeshua and grandparents of Yehuda."

Bird (2008) is skeptical about the trail of events related to the chronology of the tomb discovery and excavation, the reburial of bone material (and the subsequent DNA analysis), as well as the time trail of interpretations of the inscriptions versus the publication of those interpretations. Mortera and Vicard (2008) present reservations about the fact that the analyses fail to account for the uncertainty in the relative frequencies of names used in the computations.

2.2. Models and Estimated Probabilities

The research question related to the possible identification of the Talpiot tomb with the tomb site of Jesus' family can be defined in various ways, which in turn affect the analyses and the estimated results. The most common formulation is: "Given 'the evidence' in Talpiot, what is the probability that this tomb site was Jesus' family's burial tomb?" The research question was so defined by Kilty and Elliott, Höfling and Wasserman (in their Bayesian analysis), Feuerverger (in the aftermath of the RR analysis), as well as in the present analysis from section 3. On the other hand, Ingermanson defines it differently: "Given 'the evidence' in Talpiot, what is the probability that Yeshua bar Yehosef inscribed in the tomb is Jesus of Nazareth?" The relevant evidence differs accordingly. The Yeshua' bar Yehosef inscription is an integral part of "the evidence" in the first formulation but is not part of "the evidence" in the second one. Other aspects of "the evidence" were mentioned above when I discussed the various assumptions.

Both formulations are consistent with the Bayesian analysis that assesses the probability of "an event" given "the evidence." In daily life we are frequently exposed to such assessments. For example, the criminal and the civil courts have to assess (consciously or unconsciously) the chances of guilt or the preponderance of evidence, given "the evidence." Obviously, as illustrated above, agreement on the class of formulations does not necessarily imply agreement either on the definition of the probability that we are trying to assess or on "the evidence."

The data were also analyzed using other statistical methods. I mention first the RR approach that assessed the proportion of relevant clusters of names that are rarer than the cluster in Talpiot. The frequentist approach employed by Höfling and Wasserman expanded the question and assessed the probability of getting some interesting sets of names, rather than the only set found in Talpiot.

3. The Proposed Model and Results

The analysis of the data performed for this paper attempted to assess "the probability that the Talpiot tomb site was the Jesus family burial tomb" under a series of assumptions that consider the reservations presented above. The tested hypothesis is that the Talpiot tomb site was the Jesus family burial tomb, while its alternative, denoted as the null hypothesis, states that this is a random tomb. The model under which we computed the probability has the following characteristics and assumptions:

a. The research question is defined as above, that is, the assessment of the probability that the Talpiot tomb site was the Jesus family burial tomb.

b. The existence of a Jesus family tomb in Jerusalem is not certain and the probability of its existence is assumed to be uniformly distributed between zero and one.

c. All the information from the Talpiot tomb is relevant, that is, there are six inscribed ossuaries with the inscriptions Yeshua' bar Yehosef, Yehuda bar Yeshua', Yoseh, Matya, Mariamenou[η]Mara, and Marya as well as four uninscribed ossuaries with unknown gender distributions.

d. Under the tested hypothesis, there is a significant probability (of 0.5) of finding a Yeshua' bar Yehosef inscription (equal to the probability that the inscription will not contain the father's name).

e. There is a very small probability that Jesus had a son. The probability was set to be 0.0001. However, *if* Talpiot is Jesus' family tomb *and if* Jesus had a son, we assume that there is a significant probability (of 0.5) that the son's ossuary will be found in the tomb and that the inscription will contain both the father's and the son's names. If Jesus did not have a son, the probability of a Yehuda bar Yeshua' inscription in the Jesus family tomb is assumed to be the same as in any other random tomb.

f. Under the tested hypothesis, it is equally probable that all Jesus' brothers are in the family tomb.

g. The Matya and the Mariamenou[η]Mara inscriptions are considered as "Others" both under the null and under the tested hypotheses.

h. Since some ossuaries are uninscribed, I assume under the null hypothesis that each male and female person has a gender-related prior probability of being in an inscribed ossuary. Under the tested hypothesis I assume that the brothers' and mother's probabilities of being in inscribed ossuaries is twice as high as the probabilities under the null hypothesis.

i. Under the tested hypothesis, I consider that whenever an inscription corresponds to one of the brother's or to the mother's name, that ossuary may have contained the remains of that person or of another person with the same name.

j. I address the issue of the probability of finding a son's inscription reading Yoseh in the family in which both the son's and the father's name is Yehosef, and assume that the corresponding coefficient is the same under the null and the tested hypothesis.

k. As usual, I assume independence between the various events in "the evidence."

l. Under the tested hypothesis, the tomb is assumed to contain a number of brothers, which can range from zero to four, and to contain or not contain the name of the mother. The computations were performed under all those configurations.

m. All the computations were performed under two configurations of gender distribution of the four uninscribed ossuaries: either three male and one female or two male and two female ossuaries. The first configuration is more consistent with the distribution of male and female names in the onomasticon.

The models and the calculations are detailed in Fuchs (2008b). The results for the various configurations are presented in table 1 below. I also present the averages over the various configurations of core Jesus' family members (number of Jesus' brothers and mother). The averages are computed for each of the two gender configurations of the four uninscribed ossuaries.

As can be observed from the table, the averages for the two gender configurations in the uninscribed ossuaries are 19% and 21%, respectively. If one is willing to consider that the most likely configuration is that in Jesus' family tomb site rests only one of the four brothers, the averages are 17.5% and 17.3%, respectively.

Table 1

Gender configuration of the uninscribed ossuaries	Configuration of core members of Jesus' family assumed in tomb under the tested hypothesis		Probability that the Talpiot tomb site was the Jesus family burial tomb
	Number of brothers	Mother	
(2 males, 2 females)	0	Assumed	12%
	1		23%
	2		29%

	3		33%
	0	Not assumed	6%
	1		12%
	2		16%
	3		18%
		Average	19%
(3 males, 1 female)	0	Assumed	14%
	1		23%
	2		30%
	3		35%
	4		38%
	0	Not assumed	6%
	1		11%
	2		14%
	3		17%

4. Odds under Various Sets of Assumptions

The effects of some of the assumptions and of the method of analysis can be assessed by comparing the published results of Feuerverger with those yielded by other analyses performed on the same data. As a reminder, the narrator in the movie (Cameron 2007) announced that Feuerverger's model concludes that "there is only one chance in 600 that the Talpiot tomb is not the Jesus family tomb, if Mary Magdalene can be linked to Mariamene," and that figure gained considerable exposure. The "tail area," which is represented in Feuerverger (2008a) as "the proportion of obtaining surprisingness levels as great as at Talpiot," is computed as 1 in 1,655, widely understood as representing the chance that the Talpiot tomb is not the Jesus family tomb. Furthermore, from the odds ratios mentioned by Feuerverger (2008a), it can be deduced that that under his provisos and method of analysis the a posteriori probability that this is indeed the Jesus family tomb is estimated at well above 99.4% and up to 99.94%.

The analyses presented below differ in their assumptions and in the fitted models. The rareness of the various configurations of names is considered by all as one of the factors. However, their additional common feature is that other criteria related to the likelihood of those names to appear in Jesus' family tomb seem to weigh more heavily.

4.1. Höfling and Wasserman's Analyses

Höfling and Wasserman (2008) reanalyze the data and compute under various scenarios the posterior probability that the Talpiot tomb site was the Jesus family burial tomb. They consider the model in which the event that Jesus had a tomb in Jerusalem is a random variable, but their calculations are under the simplistic assumption that the probability of the event is 1 (i.e. certainty). Their "neutral" scenario is presumed to consider no information gathered from the tomb. All the names are considered in their generic form with special weights assigned to names as to how likely it is to find that person in Jesus' family tomb. Under those conditions they assessed the probability that the Talpiot tomb site was the Jesus family burial tomb as 3.4% (as compared to over 99% above). When the Mariamenou[η]Mara is treated as a special rendition which is more likely to appear in Jesus' tomb (which can refer to Mary Magdalene, but also to other Mariams in the family) the probability increases to 22%. Finally, under the "very optimistic" scenario which is admittedly strongly affected by the observed data, the probability increases to 64%.

4.2. Kilty and Elliott's Model

Kilty and Elliott (2007) propose a listing of 32 scenarios of possible combinations of names which, in their opinion, one might expect to find in the Jesus family tomb. Those combinations include all the possible selections of names out of the five names of Jesus' brothers and mother as listed in Mark 6:3. They thus do not accept the provisos that the deaths of Simon and Yehuda did not occur in the relevant period of time. The configurations of names are supplemented by "Others" to complete two female and four male ossuaries. In all the scenarios there are either one or two "Other" female names. The number of "Other" male names ranges from zero to four. In addition, all the scenarios assume that an ossuary inscribed Yeshuaʿ bar Yehosef has to be found in the Jesus family tomb. The scenarios are assumed to be a priori equally probable.

Unlike Feuerverger, Kilty and Elliott consider the name Mariamenou[η]Mara as irrelevant per se and treat it as "Other," similarly to the treatment rendered to the names on the ossuaries inscribed Yehuda bar Yeshuaʿ and Matya. They assume that the female "Other" can be any name except Mariam, while the male "Other" can be any name except Yehosef and Yeshuaʿ. The assumptions are problematic since the female names seem to preclude Mariamenou[η]Mara as a Mariam.

In their main calculation they consider that the name of the second brother of Jesus should be Yoseh (as in Mark 6:3), treated as a special name and not as a rendition of Yehosef. Under those assumptions they estimate the posterior probability that this is indeed the tomb of Jesus' family as 48.7%. However, when they re-calculate the probability using the generic name Yehosef instead of the rendition Yoseh, the probability drops to about 6%. For a more valid comparison with Feuerverger's result, we can use Ilan's name distribution instead of Bauckham's name distribution. The calculated estimates are 40.1% and 4%, depending on whether we use the rendition Yoseh or the generic Yehosef. Furthermore, if one uses the RR approach for the Yoseh rendition, the resulting overall probability is estimated as 17.8%.

4.3. Ingermanson's Analysis

As mentioned, Ingermanson (2008a) differs from the other researchers in the formulation of the research question. Instead of estimating the probability that Talpiot is the Jesus family burial tomb, he assesses the probability that the inscription Yeshuaʿ bar Yehosef from Talpiot refers to Jesus of Nazareth. His model conditions on the findings from Talpiot with the exception of the Yeshuaʿ bar Yehosef inscription. Thus, the findings in Talpiot for which we assessed the probability exclude the very relevant Yeshuaʿ bar Yehosef inscription.

His comprehensive set of parameters considers the likelihoods of various events which were conditioned upon in other analyses. He sets probabilities on the event that Jesus has been buried in a rock-cut tomb. Prior probabilities are also set on the event that Jesus had a son and on the event that a

Yoseh inscription would be found in a tomb site which contains a father's inscription Yehosef.

Following Kilty and Elliott (2007), he tests 32 hypotheses of possible clusters of names which one might expect to find in the Jesus family tomb. The hypotheses contain all the possible combinations of names out of the five names of Jesus' brothers and mother, that is, Mary, James, Yoseh, Yehuda, and Simon. The defined probabilities that Yeshua' bar Yehosef from Talpiot refers to Jesus of Nazareth are assessed by simulations. Under the basic calculation which assumes that there are two male and two female names in the extra four ossuaries, the upper bound of the probability that the inscription Yeshua' bar Yehosef refers to Jesus was estimated as 2.3%. Under a scenario which Ingermanson considers as unlikely, the calculated probability increased to over 5.6%. As mentioned, Ingermanson's model doesn't include the inscription Yeshua' bar Yehosef in the findings of the Talpiot tomb, and thus lowers the level of significance. In my opinion, this formulation of the research question is unwarranted. As detailed in Fuchs (2008b), I also consider that his analysis of the Yehuda bar Yeshua' inscription under the tested hypothesis is problematic.

5. "Statistically Compelling" or "Virtually Nil"? A Substantive Answer

Let us now summarize the data and ask to what extent is the evidence connecting the Talpiot tomb to the Jesus family tomb convincing? The expressed opinions range from "statistically compelling" as stated by the narrator in the movie (Cameron 2007) to "virtually nil if the Mariamene named on one of the ossuaries is not Mary Magdalene" as concluded in a press announcement issued by several scholars who participated in the Third Princeton Symposium on Judaism and Early Christianity. Various aspects of the issue may have played a role in the process in which experts formed their opinions and drew their conclusions. Undoubtedly, the statistical evidence on the cluster of names was cardinal in this respect and triggered the entire investigation.

So, given the data, what is the probability that the Talpiot tomb site was the Jesus family burial tomb? From the review presented so far it is clear that there is no easy answer, and certainly not a universally accepted answer. But in my opinion **we are much closer to a substantive answer** than it might be deduced from the previous sentence.

The issue of the assessed probability can be divided into two distinct but intertwined sub-issues: (a) the assessment of whether the Talpiot find is statistically significant and (b) the assessment of the actual probability.

5.1. Statistical Significance

Despite the variance among the researchers, the results of the alternative analyses clearly indicate that the researchers are unanimous in their conclusion with respect to the statistical significance issue. They all concluded that the cluster of names in the Talpiot tomb site is not statistically significant. Furthermore, they also concluded that the statement that the Talpiot tomb site was the Jesus family burial tomb is not even "more likely than not," which is the standard of proof required in the civil law. This standard of proof is lesser than "beyond reasonable doubt" required in the criminal law, which is sometimes considered comparable to reaching statistical significance.

It seems that Feuerverger (2008b) also agrees now with this statement. He mentions that new evidence to which he was exposed forces him to retract, somewhat obliquely, his previously published conclusions. The reasons for this retraction are relevant and are briefly summarized here. Feuerverger (2008b) mentioned that when he performed the analysis, one of the seven elements on which he constructed a presumably a priori list of name renditions for Mary Magdalene was the information provided to him that Professor Bovon "was on record as having authenticated that Mariamne was most likely the actual name of Mary Magdalene." He mentions that the information provided to him has inadvertently been misinterpreted and conveyed out of context. He candidly quotes from Bovon's statement (2007) to the Society of Biblical Literature: **"I do not believe that Mariamne is the real name of Mary Magdalene."** Feuerverger states that without the benefit of this information, he does not regard the assumption concerning the most the most appropriate name rendition for Mary Magdalene "as being equally justified by the remaining (six) elements. In particular, this means that **we cannot** (on the basis of our RR procedure) **say that the Talpiot find is statistically significant in any meaningful way.**" This conclusion, shared by all the other researchers and to which I concur, takes us a long way towards a substantive answer to the question regarding the cluster of names in the Talpiot tomb site.

As expected, the general agreement on this qualitative finding does not necessarily translate into a similar agreement on the estimate of the actual probability. The computations rely on different sets of assumptions, resulting in non-surprising differences among the estimates. However, I shall suggest that the ranges of all the reasonable estimates lead us again to similar substantive conclusions.

5.2. The Estimated Probability

The estimated probability that the Talpiot tomb site was the Jesus family burial tomb is conditional on the observed data, that is, on the relevant cluster of names inscribed on the ossuaries. In the previous sections we quoted some of the estimated probabilities as computed in this study and by other researchers under various assumptions.

5.2.1. The estimated probability by the RR procedure

The values obtained by Feuerverger (2008a) range from 99.94% to 99.4%, depending on the assumptions presented in section 2 above. Feuerverger (2008a) defines the observed data slightly differently than the other researchers, and instead of considering the specific cluster of names he considers clusters of names at least as surprising as that in Talpiot.

The range of values quoted above was obtained under the original assumptions of the RR approach. We discussed at large the assumption related to the identification of Mariamenou[η]Mara with Mary Magdalene and treatment of the inscription as unique. The retraction in the rejoinder (2008b) obviously affects the computed values. If we now consider Mariamenou[η]Mara as just another Mariam and estimate the probability by the RR procedure, the change in computed probability is substantial but not as dramatic as might have been expected. The other assumptions (including that referring to Yoseh) are kept as in the original article.

The resulting "tail probability" was assessed by dividing the number of configurations which have a more surprising value than the new configuration in Talpiot (with Mariamenou[η]Mara as Mariam) by the overall number of possible configurations. The value obtained is 38.1 times smaller than in the original article. The odds that the Talpiot tomb site was the Jesus family burial tomb decreases accordingly by a factor of 38. The change in the estimated probabilities is, however, much more modest. The previous estimate of 99.94% is replaced by 97.75% while the estimate of 99.4% is replaced by 81.3%.

5.2.2. *Other Estimated Probabilities and the "Virtually Nil" Statement*

The range of values obtained by the various researchers is wide. Furthermore, even the values obtained by the same researcher under various conditions have a wide range. We briefly review the values presented in this paper.

The estimated probabilities calculated in this study and presented in Fuchs (2008b) range from 12% to 38% with averages close to 20%. Höfling and Wasserman's computations yielded (a) a value of 3.4% under the "neutral scenario," (b) a value of 21.8% under the "neutral scenario with special rendition" for Mariamenou[η]Mara as more likely under the hypothesis of Jesus' family tomb site, but not necessarily Mary Magdalene, and (c) a value of 64.1% under a "very optimistic scenario" which assigns weights that effectively require that a Jesus' family tomb site should include for sure an ossuary inscribed "Yeshuaʿ bar Yehosef" for Jesus and another inscribed Marya for the mother. Höfling and Wasserman (2008) mention that that scenario's assumptions were highly influenced by the observed data. The highest value obtained by Ingermanson (2008a) under assumptions considered by him as unlikely was of 5.7%. The estimate obtained by him under his "basic" assumptions has an upper bound of 2.3%. Kilty and Elliott (2007) obtained a value of 48.7% using the rendition Yoseh as a special name and a value of 6% using the generic name Yehosef for the second brother of Jesus (or 40.1% and 4%, respectively if one uses Ilan's instead of Bauckham's name distribution).

Again, the range of values obtained by the various researchers is quite wide. But the substantive conclusion from all the data presented above is that with the exception of Feuerverger's results, all the researchers concluded that the statement that the Talpiot tomb site was the Jesus family burial tomb does not meet the "more likely than not" criterion, and most of them consider the probability as slim.

At the same time, I find myself in disagreement with the statement that the overall conclusion from the statistical analysis of the cluster of names is that the probability is "virtually nil." Let us recall that the inscriptions on three out of the six inscribed ossuaries in the Talpiot tomb read Yeshuaʿ bar Yehosef, Yoseh, and Maria. Now, if you assume a priori that the inscriptions in the tomb can contain both names expected from the New Testament as well as arbitrary additional names (and thus **none** of the other inscriptions cannot disqualify the tomb from belonging to Jesus' family), the Talpiot tomb's probability of being Jesus' family tomb cannot be "virtually nil."

In my opinion, based solely on the cluster of names, and unless disqualifying evidence is presented, we cannot discard the possibility that the

Talpiot tomb site was the Jesus family burial tomb. Quite unlikely, but certainly possible.

6. Statistics and Archaeology

The analysis of the Talpiot tomb and the media buzz which accompanied the event seems to have had a detrimental effect on the scholar's opinion on the applicability of statistics to archaeology. It seems that agreement on this issue crosses the camps. Tabor (2007) who supported the conclusions which identify the Talpiot tomb with that of Jesus' family has nevertheless gloomy thoughts regarding the effectiveness of the statistical analysis in the study of questions of historical prosopography. He mentions that "I am not optimistic that more advanced statistical models can be effectively applied to questions of historical prosopography since the kinds of identifications and subtle correspondences used are not easily quantified. Is Mariamene an appropriate name for [Mary Magdalene]? How could you put a number on it? Is it significant that her ossuary is decorated and her inscription is in informal Greek? How is that quantified? Does it matter that the name Yeshua᾿ bar Yehosef is written in a very messy graffiti style while the others are elegant and block? How do you put a number on that? What of how the ossuaries were placed in the various kokim, and with names grouped in twos and threes? Are there hints of potential relationships implied? I have about 25 other factors of this sort that I am considering in formulating my own prosopographic proposal, including the symbol on the tomb that comes from contemporary temple gate imagery. As far as I can tell many of these factors can not be quantified."

Scham (2007) who vehemently opposes the conclusions related to the Talpiot tomb, nevertheless agrees with Tabor on the dubious role of statistics in archaeology. She states that "At one time we archaeologists loved statistics, happily performing complex regression and cluster analyses on our data and spitting out conclusions from our computers that, likely, *proved the conjectures we had begun with.* In the last two decades, however, we have begun to question these facile *validations of our common sense.* The problem is with the data. The methods may be perfectly suited to a world in which a representative sample, normal distribution or even an idea of what the population in question might be is possible. Archaeological evidence is precisely the opposite. We do not, in point of fact, know any of these things. In the words of one former statistically enthralled antiquarian, 'Even when the odds were good, we knew that the goods were odd.'"

The complexities and the difficulties in the archaeological data were vividly presented by the two scholars. It is interesting to observe that while Tabor and Scham seem to agree on the futility of the statistical analysis, they present diametrically opposite facets of the problem. Tabor focuses on historical prosopography with unique data and subtle clues which may or may not be relevant. On the other hand Scham mentions complex regression and cluster analyses which obviously necessitate large amounts of data. But they do share the doubt on the effectiveness of statistics to their field.

The question of the relevance of statistics to archaeology is certainly relevant and worth a separate discussion. The fact that the issue was raised in the context of the Talpiot tomb is revealing. Some statisticians (e.g. Bentley 2008) share Tabor and Scham's view. But I don't agree that the complexity of the archaeological data should in general preclude the statistical analysis. In some particular cases it may be so. However, whenever the data permits, I believe that good statistics can give insight in the collected data. The problems are certainly complex. As a result, first and foremost the statisticians have to show a great deal of humility. We have to admit that the statistical methodology is unable to address some complex issues with limited data. Moreover, whenever statistical analyses are performed we have to accept the limitations and to clearly specify the reservations.

But the complexity of the problems shouldn't deter the statisticians from developing new methodology. On the contrary, it should encourage them. In this context, although I disagree with Feuerverger's analyses I applaud his initiative and the thoroughness of his study. Whether we use new or old methodology, it is vital for the model and the analysis to be so designed as to avoid as much as possible the error of "solving correctly the wrong problem." Various applications of statistical methodology are susceptible to the hazard of such errors, but the peril may be even larger in the archaeological applications. The effort to avoid such errors has to include a good understanding of the problem and the context, the evaluation of the importance of the various parameters, and the inclusion of the relevant ones in the model even as indicators in a sensitivity analysis. The models presented by Cost and Ingermanson are an example of a concentrated effort to include as much relevant information as possible in the model. In many cases, even if the conclusions are modest and qualified, the statistical analyses and the results are likely to provide some insight and directions to the investigators. After all, in our particular case, after some back and forth, the substantive answer to the Talpiot was yielded by a series of statistical analyses. And the road in between was quite fascinating and challenging.

References

Bentley, D. L. 2008. "Discussion of: Statistical Analysis of an Archeological Find." *Annals of Applied Statistics* 2:66-73.

Bird, S. M. 2008. "Discussion of: Statistical Analysis of an Archeological Find." *Annals of Applied Statistics* 2:74-76.

Bovon, F. 2007. "The Tomb of Jesus." Society of Biblical Literature Web site. Available at: http://sbl-site.org/Article.aspx?ArticleId=656.

Cameron, J. 2007. *The Lost Tomb of Jesus.* Discovery Channel, March 4, 2007.

Cost, J., and R. Ingermanson. 2007. "'He Is Not Here,' or Is He? — A Statistical Analysis of the Claims Made in *The Lost Tomb of Jesus.*" Available at: http://www.inger manson.com/jesus/art/tomb/HeIsNotHere.pdf.

Feuerverger, A. 2007. "Dear Statistical Colleagues." Text page, http://fisher.utstat .toronto.edu/andrey/OfficeHrs.txt.

Feuerverger, A. 2008a. "Statistical Analysis of an Archeological Find." *Annals of Applied Statistics* 2:3-54.

Feuerverger, A. 2008b. "Rejoinder of: Statistical Analysis of an Archeological Find." *Annals of Applied Statistics* 2:99-112.

Fuchs, C. 2008a. "Discussion of: Statistical Analysis of an Archeological Find." *Annals of Applied Statistics* 2:57-65.

Fuchs, C. 2008b. "The Probability That the Talpiot Tomb Site Was Jesus' Family's Burial Tomb." Technical Report, Tel Aviv University.

Höfling, H., and L. Wasserman. 2008. "Discussion of: Statistical Analysis of an Archeological Find." *Annals of Applied Statistics* 2:77-83.

Ilan, T. 2002. *Lexicon of Jewish Names in Late Antiquity,* part 1: *Palestine 330 BCE–200 CE.* TSAJ 91. Tübingen: Mohr Siebeck.

Ingermanson, R. 2008a. "Analysis of the Talpiot Tomb Using Bayes' Theorem and Random Variables. Supplement to 'Discussion of: Statistical Analysis of an Archeological Find.'" DOI: 10.1214/08-AOAS99GSUPP.

Ingermanson, R. 2008b. "Discussion of: Statistical Analysis of an Archeological Find." *Annals of Applied Statistics* 2:84-90.

Jacobovici, S., and C. Pellegrino. 2007. *The Jesus Family Tomb: The Discovery, the Investigation, and the Evidence That Could Change History.* San Francisco: HarperCollins.

Kadane, J. B. 2008. "Discussion of: Statistical Analysis of an Archeological Find." *Annals of Applied Statistics* 2:97-98.

Kilty, K. T., and M. Elliott. 2007. "Probability, Statistics and the Talpiot Tomb." Available at: http://www.lccc.wy.edu/Index.aspx?page=547.

Mims, C. 2007. "Q&A With the Statistician Who Calculated the Odds That This Tomb Belonged to Jesus — an Interview with the Professor Who Estimated the Probability That a Particular Tomb Could Have Been the Final Resting Place of a Family Other Than That of Jesus." *Scientific American* Web site: http://sciam.com/ article.cfm?articleID=13C42878-E7F2-99DF-3B6D16A9656A12FF.

Mortera, J., and P. Vicard. 2008. "Discussion of: Statistical Analysis of an Archeological Find." *Annals of Applied Statistics* 2:91-96.

Pfann, S. 2007. "How Do You Solve Maria?" Available at: http://www.uhl.ac/ HowDoYouSolveMaria.

Rahmani, L. Y. 1994. *A Catalogue of Jewish Ossuaries in the Collections of the State of Israel*. Jerusalem: Israel Antiquities Authority and Israel Academy of Sciences and Humanities.

Scham, S. 2007. "'The Tomb of Jesus' on TV." *Archeology*. Available at: http://www .archeology.org/online/reviews/jesustomb2.html.

Stigler, S. M. 2008. "Discussion of: Statistical Analysis of an Archeological Find." *Annals of Applied Statistics* 2:55-56.

Tabor, J. 2007. "Probabilities, Statistical Theory, and the Talpiot Tomb." Available at: http://jesusdynasty.com/blog/2007/03/19/probabilities-statistical-theory-and-the-talpiot-tomb.

A Critical Evaluation of the Occurrences of Common Names, Rare Names, and Nicknames: The Name *Yose* (יוסה) from the Talpiot Tomb as a Test Case

Eldad Keynan

Understanding Jesus in context, as well as the contextual relevance of the Talpiot tomb, must take into account all available sources, particularly Jewish sources. Counting the frequency of and evaluating the occurrences of Jewish names dated to the Second Temple era has the same requirements. In this paper, I will evaluate the names found in the Talpiot tomb relative to how they appear in rabbinic literature. Although the focus will be on the name *Yose,* the other names in the Talpiot tomb will also be evaluated. Thus the method has two benefits: emphasizing Jesus' Jewish context, and enlarging the available database.

However, the method also has some weaknesses: (1) The earliest rabbinical text that we know of is the Mishnah, compiled around 220 CE, almost two hundred years after the events. (2) As we shall see, some names that were commonly found on ossuaries dated during the Second Temple era were relatively rare in the rabbinic literature's references to people who have lived during the Second Temple era. On the other hand, other names that were rarely found on ossuaries were very common in rabbinic literature, thus questioning the reliability of the rabbinic literature for this purpose. Some phenomena stemming from this problem are not sufficiently explainable by archaeological means and require other methods, data, and tools to be more fully explained.

The next methodological consideration is as follows: scholars can employ two methods to count the frequency of and evaluate names: as generic names or as individual names. Both are sufficient, but it depends on the purpose of the research. The generic method is more suitably applied to the research of wider social questions, such as Greek influence on the Second Temple era and, later, on the Hebrew and Aramaic languages. But when applied to an individual tomb, the generic method is misleading, since an individual name or a cluster of names, in a certain tomb or other site, must be evaluated as they are — as unique individuals. The *Yose* problem exemplifies this mainly because the generic counting and evaluating approach reduces *Yose* (יוסה) to a common name while it was not so intended. The individual method might also show that some of the other names were not as common as initially thought.[1]

The *Yose* Problem as a Methodological Model

The name יוסה *(Yose)* is a contraction of *Yehosef* (Joseph), which is "the second most popular name in the Second Temple period."[2] Is this evaluation correct? If we relate to *Yehosef/Joseph* generically, it is. But a brief survey of Ilan's *Lexicon* reveals totally different results. Based on a variety of inscribed and written names in a number of different languages, she counts 231 variants of the original *Yosef* (יוסף) or *Yehosef* (יהוסף). When it comes to the specific Hebrew version יוסה (found in the Talpiot tomb), the identifications are as follows:

> 1. Wall inscription, Jason's Tomb: "*Honi bar* יוסה."[3] I count this as one occurrence, although the יוסה here is a patronymic occurrence.

---

1. The same critic regards the tendency to "average" all numbers: averaging the number of deceased in one ossuary when we deal with large social issues is a proper method. But the exact number in an ossuary in a certain tomb is highly important in other cases.

2. Amos Kloner, "A Tomb with Inscribed Ossuaries in East Talpiot, Jerusalem," *'Atiqot* 29 (1996) 19. He repeated this statement in the film. C. A. Rollston, "Inscribed Ossuaries: Personal Names, Statistics, and Laboratory Tests," *NEA* 69 (2006) 127, views the names in the Talpiot tomb according to the generic counting method. He mentions "Yeshua' son of Yehosep" (ossuary discussed by Sukenik, 1931) and "Yeshua' bar Yehosep" (Babatha archives) to conclude that this combination is not unique. But the first is not identical with the Talpiot tomb "Yeshua' bar Yehosef": "son of" in the first is Hebrew *ben*, while *bar* is Aramaic, though it means "son of" as well. The find in the Babatha archives is about a century later than Jesus' time. Each of these combinations is unique in terms of a specified context or time.

3. Tal Ilan, *Lexicon of Jewish Names in Late Antiquity*, part 1, *Palestine 330 BCE–200 CE* (TSAJ 91. Tübingen: Mohr Siebeck, 2002) p. 154.

2. Ossuary, Mount of Offense: "יוסה."[4] This is the Talpiot tomb *Yose!*

The Greek versions:

1. *Iwsh* (Greek: *Iōsē*), Mat 27:56, *Mariam's* son.[5]
2. *Iwse* (Greek: *Iōse*), ossuary, Giv'at Hamivtar.[6]

Only two of the occurrences are inscribed as Hebrew יוסה; only one of them is on an ossuary and is not patronymic. This conclusion perfectly matches the results of the Greek versions, of which one is *Mariam's* son (i.e., Jesus' brother). Regardless of the Talpiot tomb, this Hebrew version is extremely rare as an inscription in terms of the Second Temple era.

Can rabbinic literature support this conclusion? For that we have three types of rabbinic literature sources: (1) the Bar-Ilan Responsa Project (BIRP); (2) the Henkind Talmud Text Databank (HTTD); and (3) the Kaufmann Manuscript of the Mishnah (KM).

The table below demonstrates the Talpiot tomb name forms found in the Talpiot tomb and the most common version for comparison. The Talpiot tomb names in table 1 are emphasized. Note the following clarifications:

1. The form *Yose* is for Hebrew יוסה, and *Yosey* is for Hebrew יוסי.
2. The form *Matiah* is for Hebrew מתיה, and *Matia* is for Hebrew מתיא. *Matiah* and *Matia* do not appear in rabbinic literature as single names, but always with a patronymic name or as fathers.
3. The table counts *Yeshu Hanotsri* to show that the Babylonian Talmud is testifying to the historical Jesus and "insulting" him repeatedly, while early Palestinian sources almost totally ignored him.
4. The Talpiot tomb females' names, *Mariah* and *Mariamne*, are not included in the table since they do not occur in the rabbinic literature as names.
5. The table will not count the name *Yehudah* occurrences in the HTTD since its large prevalence is not debated (see below).
6. The KM is not included in the table since it employs the *Nikkud* (or *Niqqud*) vowel system (see explanation below). Owing to this method,

4. Ibid.
5. Ibid., p. 151.
6. Ibid., p. 153.

the names information in the KM regarding *Yose* and *Yosey* will be better analyzed and valuated textually than numerically.

Table 1: The Talpiot tomb male names frequencies in comparison to the same names in rabbinic literature, not including the KM

Total	Midr.	b.	Mas. Qet.	y.	t.	m.		
10126	6296	2145	187	1108	167	223	Yehoshua	BIRP
33	22	6	0	3	2	0	Yeshua	BIRP
23	17	6	0	0	0	0	Yeshu Hanotsri	BIRP
11289	3414	3332	121	3523	473	426	Yosey	BIRP
1212	36	0	0	861	315	0	Yose	BIRP
10	2	0	0	8	0	0	son of Matia	BIRP
39	20	10	0	0	6	3	son of Matia	BIRP
57	29	17	7	0	0	4	Matia son of X	BIRP
12	2	0	2	8	0	0	Matiah son of X	BIRP
20340	9090	7449	234	1552	1252	763	Yehudah	BIRP
20312	20312						Yosey	HTTD
20	20						Yose	HTTD
10374	10374						Yehoshua	HTTD
46	46						Yeshua	HTTD
40	40						X son of Matia	HTTD
13	13						X son of Matiah	HTTD
85	85						Matia son of X	HTTD
24	24						Matiah son of X	HTTD

In addition, rabbinic literature refers to two sages with forms of the name *Yosef* who lived *before* the destruction, probably in the first century BCE: Y. son of *Yoezer* of *Tsreda* and Y. son of *Yohanan* of Jerusalem.

- יוסי בן יועזר (*Yosey* son of *Yoezer*): m.: 5. t.: 0. *Mas. Qet.*: 3. y.: 6. b.: 14. Midrash: 10. Total: 38.
- יוסה בן יועזר (*Yose* son of *Yoezer*): Total: 2. Both in t.
- יוסי בן יוחנן (*Yosey* son of *Yokhanan*): m.: 2. t.: 1. *Mas. Qet.*: 1. y.: 2. b.: 2. Midrash: 2. Total: 10.
- יוסה בן יוחנן (*Yose* son of *Yokanan*): Total: 0.

Clearly the Babylonian in BIRP follows the BIRP Mishnah in this respect. More important if the observation that as the sources are older and closer to the Second Temple era, the יוסה becomes increasingly rare or is simply missing.

KM. Concerning the third source of rabbinic literature, this manuscript of the Mishnah is the only one in which the *Nikkud* vowel system is employed. It was compiled around the thirteenth century CE, and is considered to be the best Mishnah manuscript that we know of. Instead of counting individual forms, we will test the vowels that it uses. In the *Nikkud* system, a *sere* is pronounced *ē* (like *ey* in "they"), while a *segol* is pronounced as a short *e* (as in "bet"). The יוסה and יוסי appear in the KM hundreds of times. In both forms there is a *sere* under the ס *(samek = s)* of the form. If we follow the KM in this respect, we might suggest that both יוסי and יוסה *(Yosey and Yose)* are to be pronounced *yosē*. Therefore, at the very least, one can conclude that though the KM includes the form יוסה *(Yose)*, it is still to be considered rare in the KM, as in other sources.

HTTD. This source includes manuscripts and old printed additions only from the Babylonian Talmud, and was compiled around 500 CE. It cannot directly testify for Palestinian traditions of the Second Temple era. However, it can at least reflect some traditions, and it mentions Jesus by the Hebrew name ישו הנוצרי (Jesus of Nazareth). Another chronological problem is that all the manuscripts in HTTD are dated no earlier than the Middle Ages, and the printed editions are even later, from the sixteenth century CE and later.

- יוסה בר חנינה Vatican 109, *Pesaḥ.* 2a: *Yose bar Khanina.*
- ר' יוסה בר' חנינה :Vatican 113, *Ketub.* 49b: *R. Yose son of R. Khanina.*
- ר' יוסה :Vatican 125, *Pesaḥ.* 87b: *R. Yose.*
- ר' יוסה :Vatican 125, *Pesaḥ.* 93a: *R. Yose.*
- ר' יוסה :British Library HARL. 5508 (400), *Yoma* 47a: *R. Yose.*
- ר' יוסה :R. Herzog Memorial, *Ta'anit* 10b: *R. Yose.*
- ר' יוסה :Munich 95, *Yebam.* 24a: *R. Yose* (mentioned twice).
- יוסה :Munich 95, *Sanh.* 60a: *Yose* (mentioned twice).
- ר' יוס(ה)[ף] :Göttingen 3, *Meg.* 7a: *Rav Yos(e)[f].*
- ר' יוסה :Escorial I-G-3, B. *Mes.* 7a: *R. Yose.*
- יוסה :Florence II I 9-7, *Sanh.* 49b: *Yose* (mentioned twice).
- יוסה :Florence II I 9-7, *Sanh.* 60a: *Yose* (mentioned six times).
  Occurrences of *Yose*: Total: 20 (only in manuscripts).
  Occurrences of the form יוסי in HTTD: Total: 20,312 in manuscripts and printings.

One must bear in mind that the HTTD includes a large number of repeats. That is, certain versions in certain tractates might appear in the count many times.

With regard to the sages' names from the Second Temple era and the immediately following era, it appears that the Babylonian Talmud "copied" the Mishnah attitude and tradition accurately. That is, as much as the Babylonian Talmud can testify, Babylonian sages received the form יוסי *(Yosey)* as greatly prevailing over the form יוסה *(Yose)* from the traditions of their Palestinian colleagues. Interestingly enough, the generic *Yosef* and its forms were not as common among Babylonian sages as among Palestinian sages. This fact may stress the power that Palestinian names traditions had, and thus indirectly testify for the relative rarity of the *Yose* form among Palestinian sages and in rabbinic literature originating from Palestine.

This investigation of the forms יוסה and יוסי not only shows that the form יוסה was rare in the Second Temple era. It also demonstrates my second point: counting and evaluating the prevalence of a certain name in a certain era cannot be done properly using the generic counting method. Further, using generic names for analysis purposes, as it relates to a specific tomb or site, might mislead us even more.

Still, there is a problem that demonstrates a weakness of the methods I employed: rabbinic literature shows clearly that the form יוסי *(Yosey)* was the most common of all the forms stemming from *Yosef*. If so, then why has not a single ossuary inscribed with יוסי been found until recently?

I begin with a general explanation: יוסי occurs several hundreds of times in the *earlier* rabbinic literature sources, Mishnah and Tosefta. That is, the form יוסי was also rare in the Second Temple era, but probably a little more common than יוסה. Still, if so, where is the יוסי ossuary? Here the explanation is social. I assume that both יוסי and יוסה have been used mainly by the lower social classes of Judean Jews. In contrast to their contemporary higher social classes of Judean Jews, they did not have the means to afford ossuaries and rock-cut tombs.[7] Lack of means combined with the rarity of the names explains the "missing יוסי ossuary." Thus a יוסי ossuary must be considered a surprise — if and when found and dated to the Second Temple era.

As for the written sources, although occurring thousands of times across the rabbinic literature, יוסי and יוסה represent a large number of individuals; Margaliot counts about 40 *Yoseys*.[8] The earliest of these are *Yosey* son

---

7. When Ilan refers to the form יוסף and all its versions, the Greek forms are the majority. These forms testify for Greek influence and are related mainly to wealthier Jews, who tended to be hellenized more than other Jews at the time.

8. M. Margaliot, ed., *Encyclopedia of the Sages of the Talmud and the Geonim* [in Hebrew], 2 vols. (Tel Aviv, 1958) 1:521-51.

of *Yoezer,*[9] and *Yosey* son of *Yohanan,*[10] both from the Second Temple era. The latest is *R. Yosey* son of *R. Bon* (= *Abon,* mid to late fourth century CE),[11] the last known leader of the Tiberian *Bet Midrash.* A few nonrabbinical figures might be added to this list. Some *Yoseys* in it are mentioned in the rabbinic literature as *Yose* also, thus creating a total of 1,212 *Yoses.*

A simple conclusion might be drawn from this list: the forms יוסה and יוסי became more common following the Second Temple era, with the form יוסי being preferred. The replacement of the י of יוסי with the ה of יוסה might imply that some Jews, including scribes, tended to be moderately Hellenized, since the Greek *ēta* could be pronounced both as short *e* (as in "bet") and as *ē* (like *ey* in "they"). Even so, *Yosey* is the preferred form.

Still there is a problem: naturally the rabbinic literature primarily mentions the names of sages. How accurately does it represent the prevalence of names in the Jewish society in Palestine in the Second Temple era and later? Most of the rabbis and their students were poor or relatively poor. That is, the main "source" of the rabbinic movement's manpower was the bulk of Jewish society. The right to be a student and then to be ordained as a rabbi was not dependent on blood line or origin, but exclusively on personal skills. The ancestors of the rabbinic movement were the Pharisees. They were probably not a large social movement in the Second Temple era and in the eras immediately following. But both before and after the destruction of Jerusalem the human source was the same: mainly the lower strata of the Jewish society. Combining these elements leads to a highly probable assumption that the rabbinic movement literature is a reliable representation of Jewish society regarding the prevalence of names. One might ask the same question regarding the New Testament: do the names in the New Testament represent the prevalence of names in the Judean Jewish society in the Second Temple era (if not all over Palestine)? Taking into account all written sources and kinds of inscriptions, the answer is positive.

Other Names in the Talpiot Tomb

To evaluate the commonness of other names found in the Talpiot tomb, we employ the methods described above. We start again with BIRP.

9. Ibid., cols. 539-41.
10. Ibid., cols. 536-37.
11. Ibid., cols. 529-30.

1. ישוע = *Yeshua*: TOTAL: 33 (see table 1).

   In *t. Hul.* 2:22: ישוע בן פנטרא = *Yeshua* son of *Pantra* or *Pantera*.

   In *t. Hul.* 2:24: ישוע בן פנטירי = *Yeshua* son of *Panteirei*.

The patronymic *Pantera* or *Panteirei* is meant to dishonor Jesus. The Jerusalem Talmud mentions ישו פנדירא = *Yeshu Pandeira* in *Shabb.* 14:4, 14d; and ישו בן פנדרא = *Yeshu* son of *Pandera* in *ʿAbod. Zar.* 2:2, 40d. This name's uniqueness was the reason for excluding it from table 1.

The Jerusalem Talmud also mentions ישוע twice in reference to *Yehoshua* son of *Nun*, and R. *Yehoshua* son of *Levi* (early to mid-third century CE). The Babylonian Talmud mentions ישוע in reference to *Yehoshua* son of *Nun* or *Yehoshua*, a distinguished Babylonian Jew who emigrated from Babylon to Palestine with *Ezra*. The Midrash mentions ישוע in reference to *Yehoshua* son of *Nun* and a priestly family משמרת ישוע. Other forms in the Babylonian Talmud:

2. יהושע = *Yehoshua*: TOTAL: 10,126 (see table 1).

3. ישו הנוצרי = *Yeshu Hanotsri* (Jesus of Nazareth): TOTAL: 23 (see table 1).

Two linguistic phenomena should be noted here: (a) the vowel ו (*waw*) of the original ישוע (*Yeshua*) was moved from the left side of ש (*shin*) of the original form to the right side of the ש in the form יהושע. (b) The form ישו (*Yeshu*) is clearly meant to dishonor Jesus in the sages' language; it is an abbreviation of the Hebrew phrase: ימח שמו וזכרו, "may his name and memory be wiped out."

HTTD:

ישוע = *Yeshua*. TOTAL: 46, of which ישוע הנצרי, *Yeshua Hanotsri* (Jesus), in R. Herzog Memorial, *b. Sanh.* 43a, 5 times; 103a, once; 107b, twice.

יהושע = *Yehoshua*. TOTAL: 10,374 (see table 1).

Margaliot counted 23 individuals with the name יהושע (*Yehoshua*).[12] This list includes three individuals with the name *Yehoshua* from the Second Temple era: R. *Yehosua* son of *Perahia*, *Yehoshua* of *Gamla* (a high priest) and R. *Yehosua* son of *Hanania*. There is no ישוע (*Yeshua*) in this list.

12. Ibid., cols. 453-76.

The main conclusion drawn from these numbers is that the form יהושע (*Yehoshua*) was much more common than the form ישוע (*Yeshua*). As in the case of יוסה (*Yose*), the earlier that the rabbinic literature sources are, the less frequently does the form ישוע appear. One might also suggest that the sages tended to ignore Jesus for obvious reasons. But this suggestion makes no difference regarding the fact that even when the rabbinic literature mentions sages of the Second Temple era, the form ישוע is rare. Ilan identifies 103 individuals bearing forms of יהושע, including the Greek forms (יהושע being the generic name). Eleven of those are inscribed ישוע on ossuaries, whether as first names or patronymics. Two of them are the ossuaries ישוע בר יהוסף and יהודה בר ישוע (Yehudah son of Yeshua) found in the Talpiot tomb.[13] On the other hand, in Ilan's list the form ישוע constitutes the majority of all *Hebrew* forms that stemmed from the generic יהושע, both before and after the destruction, up to 200 CE. Thirteen of the occurrences are dated before 70 and are inscribed on ossuaries as well as in tomb inscriptions. Taking these numbers into account, we cannot firmly state that ישוע was such a common name: 11 out of 103 is not a number that testifies for commonness. However, that this form is almost totally absent from the Mishanh, Tosefta, and Jerusalem Talmud is probably the result of the sages' tendency to ignore Jesus.

The form מתיה (*Matiah*) in BIRP, מתתיה (*Matatiah*) being the generic name:

As a patronymic name בן מתיה (son of *Matiah*): TOTAL: 10 (see table 1).

The patronymic בן מתיא (pronounced like בן מתיה): TOTAL: 39 (see table 1).

First name: . . . מתיה בן (*Matiah* son of X): TOTAL: 12 (see table 1).

First name: מתיא בן . . . (*Matia* son of X): TOTAL: 57 (see table 1).

The numbers are clear: the Hebrew forms מתיא and מתיה are rare in the rabbinic literature, especially in the earlier sources, closer to the Second Temple era. Of the two, מתיא is more common.

In the Babylonian Talmud, *Sanh.* 43a mentions מתי, one of five of Jesus' disciples.[14] The Babylonian sages demonstrate here a certain knowledge

---

13. Ilan, *Lexicon*, pp. 126-29. Ilan also suggests that those ossuaries are of a father and his son, ibid., p. 131 n. 113.

14. "Our rabbis said: Yeshu Hanotsri had five disciples: Matai, Naqai, Netser and

regarding Jesus and his disciples and the later Jewish view of the meaning of his death and burial. This passage is important as evidence of Jesus' existence and the fact that he had disciples.

When we analyze מתיה in Ilan's *Lexicon*, the results are different. The generic מתתיה *(Matatiah)* occurs 63 times (the ninth most common male name in this list); its derived forms are:

מתיא — 5, all from literary sources.

מתיה — 5, literary sources.

מתיה — 7, ossuaries, one of which is from the Talpiot tomb, מתיה.[15]

As in the case of יוסה, the Babylonian Talmud "copies" the Palestinian sources' approach to the forms מתיא and מתיה. Both were rare in the Second Temple era, while מתיא was a little more common than מתיה. This phenomenon is not paralleled by inscriptions. As we see above, the generic מתתיה was not so common in the Second Temple era, but in this "group" מתיה is the most common of the Hebrew forms. All in all, although מתיה was not extremely rare in the Second Temple era, it was not as common as was claimed; 12 out of 63 is less than 20% of the ninth most common generic name, and this is regardless of patronymic occurrences.

How common was the name יהודה *(Yehudah)*, the fourth male name in the Talpiot tomb? The BIRP counts TOTAL: 20,340 (see table 1). That is an impressive sum. Of course, one must remember that the province יהודה (Judea/Judah) is included in this sum almost a thousand times. Another important factor is the inclusion of R. Yehudah the Patriarch, the most prominent sage and the Mishnah compiler. An additional detail to consider: both R. Yehudah the Patriarch's grandson, and the grandson of this grandson, were patriarchs as well and called R. Yehudah. So naturally this name occurs in the rabbinic literature more than others. However, even if we reduce the total owing to those factors, the list is impressive. יהודה in Ilan's *Lexicon:* 179

Boni and Toda. They brought Mati, he said to them: shall Mati be killed? Since it is written [in the Bible] "when shall I come and see the face of God?" [In Hebrew the word מתי is "when" and similar to מתי, a name. But the "when" is pronounced *matai* and the name is *Mati*. Here it is a sort of letters exegesis.] They told him: Yes! Mati will be killed since it is written, "when he will be killed and his name will be lost." . . . They brought Netser. He asked: Netser will be killed? Since it is written: "and a shoot will stem from his roots"! They told him: Yes, Netser will be killed, since it is written: "and you shall be thrown out of your tomb like a contemptible shoot" (my trans.).

15. Ilan, *Lexicon*, pp. 191-93. On the Talpiot tomb מתיה, see ibid., p. 192 n. 38.

occurrences[16] (third most common name). So by all means יהודה was the most common form of the generic Yehudah and a very common name.

The female name מרים *(Miriam)* was the most common of all female names in the Second Temple era and later. But counting and evaluating it across the rabbinic literature is pointless, since women are so infrequently mentioned in this literature. Of 802 occurrences in the BIRP, the vast majority relate to Moses' sister. Only a few times does it relate to other women. The form מריה *(Maria, Mary)* is totally absent from rabbinic literature as a female name. However, it is an Aramaic word, meaning "his master" or "the landlord of . . ." and pronounced *marē (ey* as in "they").

In Ilan's *Lexicon* מרים is listed 80 times generically, while the form מריה occurs 10 times.[17] Again, these numbers do not support the claim that this form is common.

Nicknames

Could these fluctuations be explained by a possible system of nicknames of any sort? First, there is no reason to dismiss such a possibility altogether. Second, rabbinic literature recognizes a type of nickname system and relates the issue as follows in *Midr. Tannaim* to Deut 25:6: . . . ולא ימחה שמו מישראל אלא שמו יוסף קורין אותו יוסף יוחנן קורין אותו יוחנן יקום על שם . . . אחיו לנחלה, "will be after his brother's name for a property . . . but if his name is *Yosef*, he is to be named *Yosef*; if *Yohanan*, he is to be named *Yohanan* . . . so his name will not be wiped out of Israel" (my trans.). The *Tannaim* dealt here with the problem of *Yibbum*: the younger brother of a married Jew who died childless should, according to Jewish law, marry the widow and also inherit the late brother's property. To leave no doubts, this halakah is quite definitive about a possible problem with the use of a nickname: the property must be under a formal birth name. Clearly it is so important because, according to the ancient Jewish names system, a formal name was regularly represented by a combination of "X son of Y." By this halakah, the law helps the family to keep its property secure.

Such a law implies something else: ancient Jews had nicknames, some of them at least. But when it comes to highly important matters, things are differ-

---

16. Ibid., pp. 112-18.

17. Ibid., pp. 242-48. I skip the form *Mariamne* since it is totally absent from rabbinic literature and a unique form in Ilan's *Lexicon*.

ent. Hachlili excavated a family tomb in Jericho and found an inscription גלית
יועזר (*Yo'ezer Goliath*).[18] Clearly, *Goliath* is a nickname. A nickname with a
formal name included together in the same inscription is a rare phenomenon,
if not unique. Probably *Yo'ezer* also carried his nickname throughout his life,
to the extent that people mainly or only called him *Goliath*. This family had a
few *Yoezers*, so probably the nickname was a means to distinguish one from
another. At any rate, in matters of consequence, a formal name was very important. Burials were of very high importance especially because burials
meant eternity and spiritual rights (connected to afterlife), and symbolized familial property ownership. So important was the formal name that it has been
the first optional name to be inscribed. Since we do not know any other occurrence of inscribed nicknames, the conclusion is that inscribed nicknames were
rare as part of burial inscriptions and as only inscribed names. Thus we cannot
clearly state that the single first names in the Talpiot tomb were nicknames.

While discussing the names in the Talpiot tomb, Rollston suggests: "the
Yehosep of the patronymic and the Yoseh of the ossuary could be the same
person. After all, this is actually the same name."[19] This statement is a result of
a generic method of counting and evaluating, and its degree of conviction
might be revised regarding Jewish burial practices in the Second Temple era.
The form יהוסף (*Yehosef*) was clearly not a nickname but a formal birth name,
so in this case it stands for itself. When we converge the data presented above
as well as the results of the nicknames discussion, יוסה is not a nickname but a
formal birth name, a descendant of יוסף (*Yosef*), but an independent form. If it
was not, one could ask: are the names, יוסה, ישועמריה, and מתיה nicknames?

As we can see, there is a difference between a nickname and a "form" of
a generic name. But in the rabbinic literature, there are some occurrences of
two forms of a name in the same paragraph or version. For instance, *y. Suk.*
1:7, 52c: הא רבי יוסה הא רבי יוסי בשם רבי יוחנן, "(Said) R. *Yose,* (but said)
R. *Yosey* in the name of R. Yohanan."

This phenomenon appears again in *y. Rosh. Hash.* 4:8, 59c: ר' לעזר
בר ר' יוסה בשם ר' יוסי בר קצרתא, "R. La'azar son of R. *Yose* in the name
of R. *Yosey of Qatzarta*" (my trans.). In both cases, the Jerusalem Talmud attests to different people who carried different forms of the generic *Yosef.*
Thus this fairly rare phenomenon does not testify that both forms were
nicknames. But the rabbinic literature even recorded two forms of a generic

18. R. Hachlili, "Beit 'Goliath' — a Family in Jericho in the First Century CE" [in
Hebrew], *Qadmoniot* 14 (1981) 118-22.

19. Rollston, "Ossuaries," p. 128.

name, related to the same sage, in a single phrase! Thus *y. Ta'an.* 4:4, 68b:
אמר רבי אחא דרבי יוסה היא דרבי יוסי אמר . . ., "said R. Aha, this (tradition) is R. *Yose's* since R. *Yosey* said . . ." (my trans.).

How can this be explained? Might it support the "nicknames" claim? It does not, since two lines further: . . . אמר רבי אחא דרבי יוסי היא דרבי יוסי אמר, "said R. Aha, this (tradition) is R. *Yosey's* since R. *Yosey* said . . ." (my trans.). Clearly R. Aha is referring to the same single sage, and assuming he made a mistake is unreasonable. One explanation is that the actual writers (or scribes) committed scribal errors. Another explanation is that different writers or scribes had different accents. Those explanations might well be applied to writers and scribes who lived later than the initial compilation of the Jerusalem Talmud (ca. 370-380 CE). When we disregard the prevalence of these phenomena, we can still confidently say that they cannot testify for or support a "nicknames" claim. In order to support this conclusion, we choose the generic *Yehudah* (יהודה) and its forms in the rabbinic literature: (1) יודה *(Yudah)*, 1,414; (2) יודן *(Yudan)*, 1,751; (3) יודא *(Yuda)*, 114. Might these be nicknames so as to support the "nicknames" claim?

To answer that, a textual test shows as follows: A sage named ר' יודן קפודקיא (R. Yudan of Cappadocia) is mentioned three times, all in the Jerusalem Talmud. This sage's name is not mentioned in the rabbinic literature in any other form. One of these occurrences is in *y. Ber.* 4:1, 7c, and R. Yudan is mentioned here with R. Yudah ben (= son of) Pazi. In this particular case it is easy to conclude that the form *Yudan* is a formal birth name. If so, what is the *Yudah* form? It seems that the Jerusalem Talmud provides an answer here too in *Shabb.* 20:1, 17c: רבי יודה בן פזי בדקון ואשכחון דלאו מדעת רבי יהודה בן פזימדברי, "They checked up what R. *Yudah* ben Pazi said and found that it was not the opinion of R. *Yehudah* ben Pazi" (my trans.). When we compare the last quotes, we may conclude that *Yudan* was a formal birth name in the former, but the only explanation for the replacement of *Yudah* with *Yehudah* in the latter, referring to the same sage and in a single line, is a scribal error. This kind of error was so frequent across the Jerusalem Talmud that it occurred even with patriarchal figures' names, as in *y. Ber.* 3:1, 6a: . . . דחף ר' חייא בר אבא לר' בכנישתא כד דמך רבי יודה נהוראי אחתיה דרבי יהודה נשיאהזעירא נשיאה בר בריה דר' יודה נשיאה דגופנה דציפורין וסאביה כד דמכת, "when R. *Yudah* the Patriarch the grandson of R. *Yudah* the Patriarch died, R. Hiya son of Aba pushed R. Zeira in the synagogue of Gofna of Zippori and caused him corpse defilement. When Nehorai, the sister of R. *Yehudah* the Patriarch, died . . ." (my trans.). The woman, Nehorai, was the sister of the late grandson, R. Yehudah the Patriarch. At any rate, this patriarchal figure is mentioned here by two forms: the generic *Yehudah* and its derived form *Yudah*. Again, as in the case of the forms of *Yosef* (above) and R. *Yudah/Yehudah* son of Pazi, the same person is mentioned by two forms of a name, in a single line. And again, the only reasonable explanation is a scribal error, almost certainly not the result of a nicknames system.

All in all, with reference to rabbinic literature, probably some of the written forms were birth names, while other written forms were the result of scribal errors.

Could יוסה be *Yosa?*

Some scholars have suggested reading יוסה as *Yosa*. We dismiss this reading for the following reasons:

1. Since the ס *(samek)* of both יוסה and יוסי always has the vowel *sere* under it, the only possible Hebrew way to pronounce it is *Yosey*. That is, *Yosa* could not derive from Hebrew roots.
2. Might *Yosa* be an offshoot of Greek influence? Absolutely not. In order to have a *Yosa*, the Greek form must be *Iōsa*. This form is not to be found in Ilan's *Lexicon* or elsewhere. There is simply no *Yosa*.

Conclusions

When evaluating the commonness of the names in the Talpiot tomb, I conclude:

1. The form יוסה *(Yose)* was extremely rare in the Second Temple era. יוסי *(Yosey)* appears to be slightly more common.
2. The form מתיה *(Matia)* was fairly uncommon.
3. The form ישוע *(Yeshua)* was not very common.
4. יהודה *(Yehudah)* was a very common name.
5. The female form מריה *(Maria)* was fairly uncommon.

A Few "Statistical" Notes

Generally, statistics is a means to evaluate the probability of an occurrence before it occurs. The very occurrence itself is a line separating history from statistics. Historians debate the alleged events, their context, and so on. In historical terms, every event is unique, therefore not sufficient as statistical data. As a historian one cannot employ a methodology meant for evaluating events before they occur. In other words, statistics might be enormously misleading when employed in historical research and reconstruction. One example is a statistical calculation that defines the *Mariamne* in the Talpiot tomb as statistically "not existing" — though it is there.

I am a historian. Complex statistics are far beyond my capability. Still one can employ a basic "statistical" calculation. If we disregard the Talpiot tomb, evaluating the prevalence of a name in the Second Temple era (or any other ancient era) might yield a certain result, as we have seen above. But my evaluation was mainly concerned with the prevalence of individual names. Four names in the Talpiot tomb are actually first names: יוסה, מתיה, מריה, and *Mariamne*. The other two are ישוע בר יהוסף and יהודה בר ישוע. The survey shows that ישוע was not such a common name, and יהודה was one of the most common names among Jews in the Second Temple era. We must not evaluate these names as individual names; they are a person's name with his father's name — X son of Y.

Who is מתיה? We can only offer a suggestion, as this ossuary carries no patronymic name. The conclusion that מתיה was not as common as was claimed (in the Second Temple era) does not help to connect this person to a certain family or clan. This is the very reason we cannot connect מתיה to Jesus' or any other family; and, in this case, we might only suggest a possible (or rather, plausible) explanation for this ossuary being in the Talpiot tomb. This suggestion would be based upon textual and contextual considerations, which I will deal with in a subsequent paper.

However, how many of the combinations ישוע בר יהוסף and ישוע בר יהודה have been found? Are they rare, based on archaeological data? Are they rare according to textual data? When we search all available data, the answer is: these combinations are very rare. Sukenik found a ישוע בן יהוסף on an ossuary back in 1931.[20] Further, it is not identical with ישוע בר יהוסף. Though both בן and בר mean "son of," the former is Hebrew while the latter is Aramaic. Thus we do not have the combination ישוע בר יהוסף inscribed

20. Ilan, *Lexicon*, p. 127 n. 43.

on two ossuaries. Can one of them be Jesus Christ? Statistically both might either be or not be. Textually, we know only one ישוע בר יהוסף, so the question remains. But even so, the claim that all the names in the Talpiot tomb were common in the Second Temple era is based neither on archaeological data nor on textual data. When we look at יהודה בר ישוע the data is even more compelling: we do not know this combination from textual sources or archaeological data. Even if both יהודה and ישוע were common names in the Second Temple era, the ossuary יהודה בר ישוע is unique, just like this combination itself.

Four of the six inscriptions in the Talpiot tomb were not really common names in the Second Temple era. In fact, יוסה was extremely rare and unique to the Talpiot tomb, just like יהודה בר ישוע, according to textual sources and archaeological data. ישוע בר יהוסף is found on only two ossuaries.

Do all these prove that the Talpiot tomb is Jesus' and his family's tomb, or at least allow for such a suggestion? Not yet. A significant number of considerations must first be taken into account in order to allow a reasonable suggestion of this sort. Here I have only tried to demonstrate the merits and the problems resulting from certain methods chosen to calculate and evaluate the prevalence and commonness related to the names found in the Talpiot tomb.

The Holy Sepulcher, Court Tombs, and Talpiot Tomb in Light of Jewish Contemporary Law

Eldad Keynan

Introduction

Studying and understanding the historical Jesus must take into account his Jewish background. Jesus was born a Jew, and he lived, acted as, and died a Jew. His death and burial are deeply rooted in a Jewish context. In the Second Temple era (and both before and after), burials symbolized the beginning of the afterlife, thus the very life of the deceased demonstrated the firmness of his or her spiritual rights for eternal afterlife. The custom of primary (for the first year after death) and secondary (eternal) burials was connected to the belief in afterlife, and could almost exclusively be applied to tombs rather than trench graves. However, burials generally symbolized landownership as well. The term נחלת אבות (*naḥalat 'abot,* "ancestors' property") generally pertains to a family-owned tomb. Naturally, wealthy Jews could have rock-cut burial caves (tombs), while other Jews had to be buried in ordinary trench graves.

Who owned the tombs connected to Jesus' burial? The answer might help to reconstruct the events that occurred the day Jesus died, two days later, and perhaps a year later as well. The sources by which we answer this question are the New Testament and rabbinic literature. Both complete each other in this respect, as in others.

Jesus' Death and Primary Burial

Our sources for Jesus' death and burial are Mat 27:57-66; 28:1-8; Mk 15:43-47; 16:1-5; Lk 23:50-56; 24:3-1; Jn 19:38-42; 20:1-12. All give the impression of being pressured by time on Saturday evening, and that the burial site is a tomb, very close to the crucifixion site. All state that Joseph of Arimathea asked Pilate's permission to remove the body off the cross and to bury it, and so he did. All depict Joseph of Arimathea as one of Jesus' followers, and share a depiction of the high socioeconomic status that Joseph of Arimathea enjoyed; he was a man of influence. His influential status is well evidenced by his easy access to Pilate and by the latter accepting his request. Mark and Luke state also that Joseph of Arimathea was a member of the council or a councilor. In Second Temple era Jewish terms, this means that he was a member of the Sanhedrin. Matthew states that the tomb in which Joseph of Arimathea laid the body was his own newly carved tomb, so as to confirm Joseph of Arimathea's socioeconomic status. The others state nothing about this tomb ownership. However, Luke reports that the tomb was not in use before, and John states that the tomb was new and had never been used before.

On the basis of Matthew's account, Joseph of Arimathea could bury the body in this particular tomb since he owned it. This tomb ownership should be evaluated by the rabbinic literature. Bearing in mind the extreme importance that Second Temple era Jews attached to burials, one might ask: how did the Jewish legal code treat felons who were sentenced to death by a Jewish court? Would these felons lose their burial and spiritual rights? The *m. Sanh.* 6:5-6 is very clear: "and they did not bury him in his ancestors' tombs but two grave yards were installed for the court; one for those who were executed by sword or strangulation and one for those who were executed by stoning and burning. And after the flesh was completely decayed they collected the bones and buried them in their proper place."[1]

The Mishnah here is clarifying a few points:

1. Parallels: *y. Sanh.* 6:9, 23b; *b. Sanh.* 46a. See Amos Kloner, "Did a Rolling Stone Close Jesus' Tomb?" in *The Burial of Jesus*, ed. K. E. Miller et al. Online: http://jesustomb.bib-arch.org (2007): 9; and Jodi Magness, "What Did Jesus' Tomb Look Like?" in *Burial of Jesus*, ed. Miller et al. Online: http://jesustomb.bib-arch.org (2007): 2, for the familial nature of tombs in the Second Temple era. For the decaying flesh process see Kloner, "Did a Rolling Stone," p. 10. However, if we read only *m. Sanh.* 6:5, we miss the importance of secondary burial, and the implications this important passage has regarding Jesus' death and burial.

1. The clear distinction between privately owned tombs — "his ancestors' tombs" — and the public nature of the tombs under the court authority: two graveyards were installed for the court. The Mishnah is not dealing with the structure of the court tombs, but rather with their function and authority. The structure is implied by the function: if a felon's body was buried in a trench grave, the act of collecting the bones could not be performed.

2. There is no question of financing these burials. No one is to be charged, naturally. Financing and maintaining the court tombs were the duties of the court.

3. Executed Jewish felons were entitled to every spiritual right conferred on any Jew.

4. The court was responsible for the treatment of the body during the first year after death, the primary burial, and also for the body itself. So even if the relatives performed the burial, they did it under the supervision of the court. Probably only court members could open and close the court tombs.

5. The felon's relatives were responsible for the secondary, eternal, burial.

6. The court tombs were temporary tombs by definition, because the executed felon's relatives had to take his remains after a year to be buried in the "proper place," that is, in the felon's ancestors' tombs. A. Kloner contends that Jesus was buried in the tomb within the Holy Sepulcher, and he is convinced about the size and the function of this tomb. It is a small tomb, for temporary, limited time burial. He continues: "Jesus' interment was probably of this nature,"[2] which is acceptable; only the court tombs could and should be temporary. Probably this is why the rabbinic literature is not dealing with temporary, privately owned tombs. Owning a family tomb was expensive enough, and tombs have been designed to serve family burial needs for generations. No Jew would spend money for another expensive tomb, and there are no other tombs that were meant to be only temporary by nature and function, as far as archaeological data can tell us.

Generally, the practice of collecting bones has undergone a change: "Beginning in about 20-10 B.C.E., the practice of placing bones from the *loculi* in a charnel room or pit changed to placing the bones in stone boxes called ossuaries. Ossuaries remained common in rock-cut tombs in Jerusa-

---

2. Kloner, "Rolling Stone," p. 12.

lem until the destruction of the city by the Romans in 70 c.e."[3] This change could have been applied to executed felons, at least to some of them.

The court tombs issue raises further questions. (a) Could Jewish courts enforce death penalties under Roman rule? The answer is negative. Since Rome conquered Palestine (63 bce), the Jewish legal system lost the authority to enforce death penalties, though it never lost the authority to issue death penalties.[4] (b) What was the location of the court tombs? With regard to Jerusalem, no tombs were permitted inside the city's ancient walls.[5] Another point to notice is the nature of the land that the court had to choose for its tombs. This land could not be private but public, owing to the public nature of the court tombs. The best choice should have been a large public burial ground, outside the ancient wall. This choice had to take into account additional considerations: the prevention of the corpse's defilement and humiliation, relatives' feelings, and simple practicality. These dictated that the execution site must be very close to the court tombs. All relevant New Testament reports depict the tomb as being very close to the execution site, thus providing support for my view.

D. Bahat noted that the area "where the Holy Sepulchre Church was to be built . . . had also been honeycombed with tombs."[6] He identified the crucifixion site as follows: "the adjacent rock of Golgotha where he had been crucified," and noted that though we cannot be certain, it seems likely that the "Constantinian rotunda was actually built over the true site of Jesus' burial." The above suggested connection between the court tombs and the public cemetery is probably confirmed by Bahat as follows: "the site was a turn-of-the-era cemetery. The cemetery, including Jesus' tomb. . . ." He concluded that all these considerations support "the accuracy of the preserved memory that Jesus had been crucified and buried here."[7]

Kloner confirms that the depictions of Jesus' interment are based on, and describe, the first burial and tending of bodies as practiced by first-century Jews.[8] Since the court tombs had a specified function — keeping the

---

3. Magness, "Jesus' Tomb," p. 4.

4. L. I. Levine, "The Face of the Era: *Erets Israel* as a Part of the Roman Empire and the Great Revolt," in *The History of Erets Israel* [in Hebrew], vol. 4, ed. M. Stern (Jerusalem: Keter, 1990) p. 95. See also Jn 18:3; when Pilate told the Jews to judge Jesus by the Torah, they replied: "we have no authority to execute any person."

5. Magness, "Jesus' Tomb," p. 2.

6. Dan Bahat, "Does the Holy Sepulchre Church Mark the Burial of Jesus?" in *Burial of Jesus,* ed. Miller et al. Online: http://jesustomb.bib-arch.org (2007): 18.

7. Ibid., p. 20.

8. A. Kloner, "Reconstruction of the Tomb in the Rotunda of the Holy Sepulchre

felon's body for only one year — they did not have to be as large as private tombs, in which the wealthy owners could perform both the primary and the secondary burials.[9] Kloner suggests that Jesus' tomb was a simple and small one,[10] which is highly plausible. He further connects this tomb structure to a "borrowed tomb," owned by Rabban Gamaliel in Yabneh.[11] This term is unique, and requires explanation: as far as I know, we have no other evidence of a borrowed tomb. Rabban Gamaliel was the head of the Sanhedrin in Yabneh — a fact that explains "his" borrowed tomb. The main interpretation of the term is that laying a body in this kind of tomb conferred no rights of ownership to the deceased's relatives,[12] just as is expected with regard to court tombs of a public nature.

The Mishnah, cited above, relates to two court tombs. Where is the other one? Kloner reports another tomb, a few yards away from the Holy Sepulcher.[13] Bahat also reports a nearby tomb, traditionally related to Joseph of Arimathea and Nicodemus, connected by a passage to the tomb beneath the rotunda.[14] Obviously this tradition stemmed from the story in Matthew, according to which Joseph of Arimathea buried Jesus in his own tomb. But suggesting that Joseph of Arimathea had his own tomb in this site is in sharp

---

According to Archaeological Finds and Jewish Burial Customs of the First Century CE," in *The Beginnings of Christianity: A Collection of Articles*, ed. Jack Pastor and Menachem Mor (Jerusalem: Yad Ben-Zvi, 2005) pp. 277-78.

9. See Kloner, "Rolling Stone," for the differences between simple, small tombs, and the wealthy Jews' tombs. Magness, "Jesus' Tomb," p. 2; and *idem*, "The Burial of Jesus in Light of Archaeology and the Gospels," *ErIsr* 28 (2007): 1, agrees with Kloner. Eric M. Meyers, "The Jesus Tomb Controversy: An Overview," *NEA* 69 (2006): 117, claims by sharp contrast that the practice of reburial in ossuaries "is most often associated with the most pious individuals, namely, the Pharisees." Except for a disagreement with Kloner, "Rolling Stone," and Magness, "Jesus' Tomb," there is a simple fact: hundreds of ossuaries are inscribed in Greek (see Tal Ilan, *Lexicon of Jewish Names in Late Antiquity*, part 1, *Palestine 330 BCE–200 CE*, TSAJ 91 [Tübingen: Mohr Siebeck, 2002]). Were the most pious Pharisees so Hellenized, and rich enough, to have ossuaries? Further, generally, wealthy Jews in the Second Temple era tended to be more Hellenized, which explains the large number of "Greek" ossuaries.

10. Kloner, "Rolling Stone," p. 12.

11. Ibid.

12. Ibid.

13. Ibid., p. 13.

14. Bahat, "Holy Sepulchre," pp. 16-17; note that the connecting passage implies that both tombs were not familial. Families did not connect their own tombs with those of other families, for obvious reasons.

contrast to Joseph of Arimathea's socioeconomic status: a Jew of means and influence would not locate his own tomb in a public burial site, filled with the graves of low-status Jews and in close proximity to an execution site and the felons' primary burial site. His own tomb must have been located elsewhere.

In any case, laying Jesus' body in a court tomb makes other questions unnecessary. It has been claimed that Jesus (and his family) could not afford a rock-cut tomb, since they were relatively poor. If we accept the court tombs concept presented here, it was unnecessary for either Jesus or his family to have the means for his primary burial. Another claim is that Jesus should have been buried in Galilee as a Galilean Jew. This claim is correct only if we are dealing with ordinary Jews, not Jewish felons who were sentenced to death by a Jewish court. When we look at the Mishnah above, nothing is said there regarding the felons' place of origin. Naturally, the court that sentenced him was responsible for his primary burial, and that could be done only in the town or city in which this court performed its duties. So whether or not Jesus and his family moved from Galilee to Jerusalem, his trial before a Jewish court took place in Jerusalem, and thus he must have been buried, for the first year, under this court's local authority, that is, in Jerusalem.

Another problem we have to deal with in this respect is the New Testament reports, according to which the tomb was new or had never been used before. Naturally, the authors of these reports preferred a new or an unused tomb for their master's body. But the court tomb concept sheds some light of reality here too. Rome conquered the land of Israel in 63 BCE and ever since had deprived the Jewish legal system of its authority to enforce death penalties (as noted above). Jesus' trial took place in 30 or 33 CE. That is, the court tombs were not used for almost a hundred years. A later author could easily interpret these conditions as a depiction of a new tomb. So when New Testament sources state that the tomb was new, or had never been used, they are not entirely wrong. Rather, Luke, who states that the tomb was never used before, is right. The court tomb concept solves yet another problem: how could anyone dig, or carve, a tomb under such great time pressure as on Saturday eve? The court had tombs under its authority and control, and naturally would have installed them long before; no tomb had to be prepared under any time pressure.

Now, one can suggest that according to rabbinic literature sources regarding New Testament reports, since Jesus was sentenced to death by a Jewish court, his body had to be deposited in the court tomb, regardless of the executioner's identity. Based on the primary and research sources above, I suggest identifying the court tombs with the tomb beneath the Holy Sepulcher and the tomb nearby.

This suggestion explains another detail: Joseph of Arimathea could approach and open the court tomb because he was a Sanhedrin member, and as such he could take care of Jesus' body, open the tomb, deposit the body, and close it,[15] while at the same time not evoking any suspicions. Then he would have immediately gone home for Shabbat. As a follower (if not a disciple) of Jesus, Joseph of Arimathea could not have been pleased that his master's body rested in the felons' tomb, and under the Sanhedrin's (a prominent symbol of the Jewish establishment) authority and control. This situation alone was in sharp contrast to Jesus' teaching. The solution was at hand: giving his dead master his own tomb by transferring the master's body to Joseph's tomb. But as a Sanhedrin member Joseph of Arimathea must have been well aware of the possibility that returning to the tomb on Sunday, opening it, and taking the body away might be suspicious. This possibility was probably why Joseph of Arimathea returned to the court tomb early on Sunday morning, perhaps before sunrise, and took the body away. Later Mary and Mary Magdalene approached the tomb and found it empty. I believe Joseph of Arimathea took the body to a tomb he owned near Jerusalem, a tomb known today as the Talpiot tomb.[16] A year later, Joseph of Arimathea or Jesus' relatives would have transferred the bones to an ossuary, according to contemporary custom.

Kloner, too, suggests that Jesus' burial in the Holy Sepulcher tomb was temporary by nature, and took place in a temporary tomb.[17] According to Jewish burial custom and the Mishnah mentioned above, Jesus' relatives

---

15. Does it mean Matthew is totally wrong in this respect? Not necessarily. When Matthew was written, a dim memory of a Jew approaching a tomb could well be understood as an act performed by the tomb owner. Meyers, "Jesus Tomb," p. 117, seems to accept Jesus' primary burial in Joseph of Arimathea's tomb. As noted above, Joseph of Arimathea's tomb being located in the public cemetery around the Holy Sepulcher is almost impossible when the concept of court tombs and Joseph of Arimathea's socioeconomic status are considered.

16. Note the quality of the inscription ישוע בר יהוסף; compared to other Talpiot tomb inscriptions, this one is very poor and hardly readable. If the others were made by professionals, this one was not. Might this inscription have been made by Joseph of Arimathea himself or by another unprofessional for Joseph of Arimathea? One cannot dismiss this idea all together. Anyway, it seems Joseph of Arimathea had every reason not to take care of this inscription openly and publicly.

17. Kloner, "Rolling Stone," p. 12.

could not receive the body less than a year later for the secondary burial. Thus assuming they received it after only three days is problematic. Regardless, when Mary and Mary Magdalene visited the tomb on Sunday morning, it was empty. Kloner explains the empty tomb as follows: "Jesus' disciples may have visited the tomb on the third day to conform to this Jewish custom. But by that time, he had risen."[18] Although this is a theological explanation, Kloner clearly accepts that Jesus' primary burial had been performed according to contemporary Jewish burial custom, and that by the third day the tomb was empty. Leaving theology aside, we may look for Jesus' secondary burial site elsewhere.

Jesus' Tomb and Jewish Custom and Law

Who else could or would be buried in a tomb containing Jesus' remains? In the following discussion I will try to answer this question according to rabbinic sources, and determine whether the Talpiot tomb is Jesus' secondary burial. We begin with a short rabbinic passage: "a man is comfortable with his ancestors" (*y. Moʿed Qat.* 2:4, 81b, my trans.). This passage not only confirms the familial nature of tombs. It also questions the reliability of the assumption that Joseph of Arimathea granted his own tomb to Jesus. So the question is: did any Jewish law or custom allow for such a grant? We have no evidence in the rabbinic literature to answer this question. But there is no Jewish custom or law that *prohibits* the transfer of a tomb's ownership! On the contrary, a later rabbinic source states: "Reish Lakish in the name of Bar Kapara, whosoever sells a tomb to another, if the buyer buried a corpse in a niche he gets custody over the entire niche; if he buried three corpses in three niches, he gets custody over the entire tomb" (*y. B. Bat.* 3:4, 13d, my trans.). This source is very late compared to the Second Temple era. But Bar Kapara was one of the last Tannaim (died in the first half of the third century), so he could preserve good testimonies of ancient customs. Though we may dismiss this passage as evidence of a custom in Second Temple era Jerusalem, still we have no evidence that the transfer of a tomb's ownership was prohibited then. Unfortunately, the first scientific report of the Talpiot tomb does not include a detailed, accurate location of each ossuary found in it;[19]

18. Ibid., p. 13.
19. Kloner, "A Tomb with Inscribed Ossuaries in East Talpiot, Jerusalem," *'Atiqot* 29 (1996): 15-22.

therefore we cannot even try to match these locations to Bar Kapara's information.

Following the familial nature of tombs in the Second Temple era, we may accept the ossuaries inscribed ישוע בר יהוסף, מריה, and יוסה (Mariah, Yeshua bar Yehoseph, and Yose) as containing the remains of Jesus' mother Mary, Jesus, and his brother Yose. Should this be the situation, things might have been easier to deal with, textually at least. But three additional ossuaries have been found in the Talpiot tomb, inscribed מתיה, יהודה בר ישוע, and the Greek *Mariamnē* or *Mariamēne* (Yehudah bar Yeshua, Matiah, and Mariamne/Mariamene). How can we connect them to a familial tomb when we have no record of them being Jesus' family members?

Some have claimed that the identification of the Talpiot tomb as Jesus' tomb is extremely doubtful since the inscriptions found there bear no signs of any sort of kinship relationships among the interments, except two: Yehudah bar Yeshua and Yeshua bar Yehoseph.[20] Here we may ask, were kinship signs customary?

Another claim is that since there is no empirical reason to assume Mariah is Yeshua bar Yehoseph's mother, she could be the wife of Yehudah, or Yose, or Matiah, or even Yehoshua. Here Rollston evaluates the prevalence of kinship inscribed signs: "Sometimes we have complementary information that makes an affirmation about marital status."[21] The qualifier "sometimes" is accurate and thus also answers our question above: kinship signs were not customary. Similar argument concerning Mariah is that she might even be the daughter of any of the men in the Talpiot tomb.[22] This is possible, of course, as is the claim that *Yose* could be the son of Matiah, or Yehudah, or Yeshua, or the father or even the uncle of some of the other interments; still, an almost identical argument is raised regarding Mariamne/Mariamene.[23]

Can one confidently reject all these suggestions? The answer is negative. But in this case every answer is possible, since the variety of possible bonds the interments could or could not have does not exclude or rule out the possibility that the Talpiot tomb was Jesus' (and his family's) tomb. The rabbinic literature might explain the kinship relations of some of the inter-

---

20. Christopher A. Rollston, "Inscribed Ossuaries: Personal Names, Statistics, and Laboratory Tests," *NEA* 69 (2006): 127.

21. Ibid., pp. 127-28.

22. Ibid., p. 128.

23. Ibid.

ments in the Talpiot tomb, as it explains another point that Yehudah bar Yeshua cannot be identified as Jesus' son since we do not have any evidence of Jesus being married. True, we have no such evidence. The reason is that Jesus was not married since he was a *mamzer.*

The *Mamzer* Problem

According to Jewish law, a *mamzer* is a child born as a result of unlawful sexual intercourse or matrimony: "Who is a *mamzer?* Any unlawful relative, said R. Aqiba. R. Shimon Hateimany says: Anyone who is to be punished by *Karet* (divine punishment by untimely death or eternal excommunication). . . . Said R. Shimon ben Azai: I have found a genealogical chart in Jerusalem and it is written there: so-and-so is a *mamzer* of a married wife" (*m. Yebam.* 4:13, my trans.).

In Mat 1:18-24 we read that Mary (Miriam) was engaged to Joseph (Yoseph), and before they had sexual intercourse she was expecting the child of the Holy Spirit. Joseph was a righteous man and did not want her to suffer such a major disgrace, so he thought to send her away secretly. But an angel appeared in his dream and told him not to be afraid of having her as a wife, since she is expecting the child of the Holy Spirit, and he should name the child Jesus (Yeshua). All this was to fulfill the prophecy of the pregnant virgin and her child to be named Emmanuel. Then Joseph woke up and did what the angel told him to do, and brought his wife to his home and they had no sexual intercourse until she gave birth to her first child, and he named him Jesus. Luke 1:2 depicts a slightly different story: Mary is a virgin engaged to Joseph and bearing the Holy Spirit's child, and they moved from Galilee to Bethlehem on the occasion of a general census.

In Second Temple era Jewish legal terms, an engaged virgin's status is similar to a married wife's status; she is not allowed to have sexual intercourse with anyone except the man that she is engaged to. We read this in *m. Ned.* 10:6: "an engaged woman is totally her man's" (my trans.). The similarity of a married wife's status and an engaged virgin's status is the base of the following: "an engaged girl who committed adultery is to be stoned close to her father's home entrance, and if she doesn't have a father's home entrance she is to be stoned at the place that she committed the adultery, and if it is a Gentile town she is to be stoned close to the court's entrance" (*t. Sanh.* [Zukermandel ed.] 10:10, my trans.). Here a short clarification is required: as in the Second Temple era, later Jewish courts could issue death penalties, but they could not perform any executions. That is, the rabbinic sources mentioned above are not dealing with actual stoning but with the severe implications, legal and social, of adultery. So any discussion of formal stoning is purely theoretical.

A convergence of the sources above is the base of Jesus' legal status: Mary was engaged to Joseph when she was bearing a child who was not his. She was still not married, yet her legal status was similar to that of a married wife's status. Matthew is right in describing the major disgrace that she was to undergo. This description is in accord with the legal definitions that the rabbinic literature sources provide regarding this issue. So decisive were those definitions that Joseph had to consider sending her away secretly. As an engaged virgin she was pregnant, which in itself was not a felony. But clearly the child was not her man's. Joseph understood the situation as a Second Temple era Jew and thought and acted accordingly, and so did his neighbors — the reason of the disgrace he was so afraid of and the thoughts about sending her away.

Any *mamzer* suffered a great deal, not only owing to his legal status. A *mamzer* was also a social problem, and a serious one, according to Deut 23:3: "A *mamzer* shall not enter the community of God; even his tenth generation will not enter the community of God." Conceptually, the *mamzer's* parents should be punished by God. But the *mamzer* himself is to be excommunicated for ten generations, including almost all kinds of social activities, with an exception: he is allowed to study. This detail explains the importance that the Pharisees and their followers, the rabbinic sages, generally attached to study. Thus *m. Hor.* 3:8 declares: "A learned *(talmid hakam) mamzer* takes precedence over an ignorant high priest." Rabbinic sources imply that Jesus was a rabbinical student: "May we never have a son or a student *(talmid)* who burns his dish publically, like Yeshu Hanotsri" (*b. Ber.* 17b, my trans.). Rabbinic literature even follows with a kind of apology while trying to explain the way that Jesus left the rabbinic system: "Our rabbis said may always your left (hand) push away and your right (hand) bring closer . . . not like Yehoshua ben Perahiah, who pushed Yeshu Hanotsri with both hands." Historically, Yehoshua ben Perahiah preceded Jesus by decades. But rabbinic literature is using the former to exemplify a tough teacher and the latter to exemplify the outcome. In the process we learn that Jesus was educated, partially at least — enough to understand his legal and social status. A *mamzer* has a severe socio-legal problem: there are almost no Jewish women that he can marry.

The only options that a *mamzer* had were a *mamzer* female or a converted Gentile female.[24] Each one of these two combinations is permitted, but the descendants of such a couple will remain *mamzerim* (plural of *mamzer*) for the next nine generations. As a former student, Jesus knew that well enough. But as a student he knew that there are two brilliant solutions. Assuming that he wanted to have a "kosher" Jewish child, just like every Jew of his time, he could meet a Gentile female, impregnate her, and have her give birth. But should she remain a Gentile, the child would remain a Gentile like her, and the woman would not be allowed to be buried in the Jewish father's tomb, according to Jewish law. Jesus would probably reject this option. Yet a Gentile female is the key: if a *mamzer* had sexual intercourse with a Gentile and she gave birth, initially the child would be like her, a Gentile. But if later she decided to convert, the child could independently convert as well. Then they would both be "kosher" Jews and the father's *mamzer* status would not be conferred upon them. Though this solution is good enough, yet there is an even better one: "A converted female whose sons have converted with her . . . even if the pregnancy of the first was not sacred but his birth was sacred and the second one's pregnancy was sacred and his birth was sacred" (*m. Yebam.* 11:2, my trans.). Meaning: when she carried her first child she was still a Gentile ("not sacred"); but since she had converted during the pregnancy, when the child was born he would automatically be a Jew like his mother ("sacred"). This is why the second child was sacred both in pregnancy and in birth.

I cannot be sure whether Jesus had this in mind when he first met Mary Magdalene. Geographical conditions made this meeting possible in the first place: Jesus spent some time in Kephar Nahum (Capernaum) on the north shore of the sea of the Galilee, and Magdala is just a few miles away. Mary was probably a Gentile (which explains the Greek inscription *Mariamnē/Mariamēne*). As their relationship developed, it became more personal and intimate. She was, as a Gentile, a key to his desire to have a Jewish and non-*mamzer* child. He knew that they could have only one child under these conditions, since after her conversion any child she would have with him would definitely be a *mamzer*. Based on these considerations, I believe that Mary Magdalene was initially a Gentile, she carried Jesus' child, and she probably converted before the child was born (as she could convert after he was born and still have the same result). In any case, she became a Jew, and so would her son, allegedly Jesus' son, יהודה בן ישוע.

One might ask: could any Jew in the Second Temple era have a child

24. *m. Qid.* 4:1, 3.

while not being married? Generally the Jewish law and custom did not recommend this situation. But it was not forbidden. The *m. Qidd.* 3:12 tells us: "Wherever *qiddushin* [legal marriage] is permitted and there is no felony, the [status of the] child is after the male . . . wherever *qiddushin* is permitted but there is a felony, the [status of the] child is after the defective one . . . every woman who cannot have *qiddushin* with a certain Jew and with any other Jew, the child is like her [the same status]; what child? Of a female slave and a Gentile" (my trans.). The *m. Ketub.* 3:2 is specific: "those who are not to be fined: the ones who had sexual intercourse with a converted woman, or a former female prisoner or slave, who have been redeemed and freed and converted, provided that their age was more than three years and a day" (my trans.). That is, the Jewish law permits some types of sexual relations with no marriage. These two texts are precisely describing the legal options that Jesus had when he decided to have a child; he could only have a converted Gentile as his child's mother. However, he did not marry her since after the conversion her status would be absolutely Jewish, and a *mamzer* could not legally marry a "kosher" Jewess and have "kosher" children with her.

Jesus' Relatives, His Tomb, and Jewish Custom and Law

Assuming that Jesus did have a certain tomb raises other questions. First, why wouldn't Mary, Jesus' mother, be buried in her husband's tomb, should he have one? And how could she be buried in the same tomb with Jesus, according to Jewish ancient law and custom?

As we have seen above, according to contemporary Jewish law, Mary's pregnancy with Jesus would have been accepted as if she had committed an act of adultery. Thus: "so-and-so preached publically against Jerusalem, R. Eliezer (the Tanna) told him: go and see the abomination of your mother. They investigated him and found that he is a *mamzer*" (*Mas. Qet. Sophrim* 9:12, my trans.). Generally, a woman's abomination is interpreted as the act of a married woman who committed adultery. The problem with the unknown father is well attested and presented as follows: "She was pregnant; they asked her: Who is this child's father? (She said): He is so-and-so and a priest. Rabban Gamaliel and R. Eliezer say: She is to be trusted. R. Yehoshua says: We do not believe her but she is considered to have sexual intercourse with a converted man or a *mamzer* unless she can prove her claim" (*m. Ketub.* 1:9, my trans.). This text casts the burden of proof on the woman's shoulders. Mary and Joseph could claim that the child is the Holy Spirit's child. But legally this claim is totally irrelevant, turning Mary's legal status into an adulteress. Even if we accept Joseph's generous attitude toward her and assume that he had his own tomb in Galilee, Mary could not be buried in his tomb since a Jewess who committed adultery would be forced to divorce, and henceforth was forbidden to her husband and every right conferred by him.

In *Mas. Qet. Semaḥot* 14:6, we read the possible solution to Mary's situation: "her father says, 'Bury her in mine,' and her husband says, 'Bury her in mine,' she is to buried in her father's; and if she has sons, and (while she was alive) she said, 'Bury me in my sons' (tomb), she is to be buried in her sons'" (my trans.). At first glance, this halakah pertains to married wives and gives precedence to the father. But her marital status is unnecessary: what matters is that she has at least one son. Assuming that people moved from one place to another, a Jew could move to another place and his mother could spend her last years in his new place. So this halakah is not meant to solve any adulteress's problem, but to reaffirm a woman's total right to be buried in her son's tomb regardless of her legal status. This right clarifies the obscurity of a woman's burial place, as presented above by the debate between her father and her husband.

Still, what legal right could a *mamzer* have? Surprisingly enough, being a *mamzer* does not mean losing every legal right. In *t. B. Bat* (Lieberman ed.) 7:1, we read: ממזר מוריש את קרוביו. It might be ambiguous, since the verb מוריש could be interpreted here as both "bequeath" and "inherit." If it was מוריש לקרוביו, then it would mean "bequeath" to his relatives. But here we have את קרוביו, meaning "inherit his relatives." Logically both are complementing, not contradicting, since both define a *mamzer*'s legal rights. This halakah may be considered as less important than the former, since the base of Mary's right to be buried in Jesus' tomb is the former. But the latter serves to eliminate all doubts regarding Mary's right to be buried in Jesus' tomb, and explains how his other relatives could legally be buried there.

Are the rabbinic sources above sufficient to support Yose's (Jesus' brother) right to be buried in Jesus' tomb? This question is important since even if Joseph of Arimathea granted his own tomb to Jesus, he would have done it only after his master's death, and a deceased person is not capable of bequeathing anything to anyone. We have seen that Mary, Jesus' mother, could decide and order that she be buried where her son was. But Jewish ancient law conferred another right upon her, as follows: "A woman who inherited a tomb is to be buried in it, she and any offspring she has, so said

R. Meir. Other sages said: She and not any offspring she has. But the other sages said: if she saw them while she was alive, they would be buried next to her when they died, meaning that she had inherited a family tomb and her sons are related to her husband's family, and it is a dishonor to the members of her family [meaning: her father's family] to be buried next to her sons" (*Mas. Qet. Semahot, Mourning Baraitot*, 3:16, my trans.). What seems complex is quite comprehensible: if a Jewish woman inherited her father's tomb, her brothers and their sons would have a problem, because if her sons and their sons were to be buried with her in this tomb, it would dishonor her brothers and their sons. This halakah might explain why Mary would not be buried in her father's tomb, whether or not she was legally defined as an adulteress.

Further, if Jesus had a tomb, since he was not married his preferred heir would be his son. But if the son was still underage when Jesus died (as was probably the case), Jesus' heirs were his mother and brothers. That is, Mary had a total right to be buried where her son was, but she could also inherit his tomb, and so could Yose. In this case, Jesus might, or might not, have been dead when a certain tomb became his tomb. Jewish ancient law defined the rights above regardless of the timings of death, since it dealt with rights that it regarded as natural rights, based upon blood relations. So as much as Jewish laws and customs are under discussion, Mary and Yose could well be buried in Jesus' tomb, whatever its identity was and is.

Still we have another problem: since Jesus and Mary Magdalene were not married, how could she be buried in the same tomb as he was? First, to the extent that we follow Jewish law, the answer to that question is simple: she could not possibly be buried in the same tomb with Jesus because legally they were not husband and wife. Mary Magdalene must have had a legal "link" to Jesus in order to be buried where he was. Here too Jewish burial customs provide a solution. The only legal link that she could have was a child who was Jesus' child as well. Generally, no one doubts a Jew's right to be buried in his ancestors' tomb. So if Jesus had a son, this son would be absolutely entitled to be buried where Jesus was. And just as Mary had a total right to be buried with Jesus, Mary Magdalene had a total right to be buried with her son. This son was entitled to be buried there also since his grandmother could well be considered the owner of this tomb by inheritance, so as to confer her right to any offspring that she had, as we have seen above.

That being said, we may ask: who died first, Mary Magdalene or her son? In terms of burial rights it makes no difference, since a son's right, in this case, stems from his father's burial in a tomb and from his grandmother's right by inheritance. That is, whether or not he died before his mother, his right to be buried next to his father is unquestioned. It appears that he died before his mother, while he was still a boy, probably being a reason for the absence of any written report concerning him.

Up to this point, and according to Jewish ancient law and custom, I may suggest the following: a tomb in which Jesus' secondary burial took place could legally contain the remains of his mother, his brothers, and his son. This tomb could also contain the remains of the mother of his child, though she and Jesus were not married. Her burial right in this tomb stemmed from her son's presence.

The last name in the Talpiot tomb list is problematic: מתיה (Matiah). There is no record of any brother of Jesus by this name. The possibility that Jesus had another child by this name is unacceptable, since for that to be permitted we would have had to assume that Jesus agreed to have his second son legally defined as a *mamzer,* since Mary Magdalene would have converted during her first pregnancy or shortly thereafter. Assuming that Matiah was a relative of Mary's father's side is possible. But Jewish law and customs provide no evidence upon which to establish the suggestion of a relative being allowed to be buried in another remote relative's tomb. Could Matiah be a disciple of Jesus? This possibility is tempting, and Jesus did have an important disciple by this name (Matthew). We also know that some Jews wished and ordered their descendants to bury their remains close to the tombs of important Jews, even in niches close to those important figures' burial niches in certain tombs. However, this custom developed much later, during the first half of the third century.[25] So who could he be?

In the following I will try to offer answers. But I must emphasize that the possibilities are based upon the level of existing knowledge, and might well undergo serious changes if and when the Israel Antiquities Authority (IAA) will permit further excavations and study of the Talpiot tomb and the tomb located a few steps away [see Charlesworth's appendix to this volume].

As demonstrated above, Jewish burial custom allowed a Jewess to inherit a tomb and conferred burial rights in that tomb on every offspring that she had and had seen during her lifetime. So if Mariah had a grandson Matiah, he could well be buried next to her. His father could be any of Mary's sons, except Jesus', of course.

It is plausible that Matiah was a relative of Joseph of Arimathea, prob-

---

25. Yeshayahu Gafni, "Bringing the Dead for Burial in Palestine — the Beginning and Development of the Custom" [in Hebrew], *Qatedra* 4 (July 1977): 113-20.

ably buried in the Talpiot tomb after Jesus died. Joseph of Arimathea understood that granting Jesus a single niche could end up with transferring the entire tomb ownership to Jesus' family, assuming Jesus' close relatives would be buried there as well.[26] If this occurred, then Joseph of Arimathea had to order another tomb[27] for possible deaths among his family members until the new tomb would be ready for use. One should bear in mind that the Talpiot tomb ossuaries numbered 7, 8, and 9 are well ornamented,[28] thus implying the high socioeconomic status of the interments inside them — the same as Joseph of Arimathea had. These ossuaries were presumably in the Talpiot tomb before Jesus' body had been laid there as well. Why, then, is the Matiah inscription plain, and why is this ossuary not decorated? An answer might be that since Matiah died after Jesus' body had been already been laid in the Talpiot tomb, and since Joseph of Arimathea did not want to expose the presence of his master in his own tomb, he was cautious enough not to ask or order a well-known, highly professional scribe to perform the inscription. If this was the case, where is Joseph of Arimathea's new tomb? Possibly the tomb next to the Talpiot tomb is Joseph of Arimathea's new tomb.

Summary

According to New Testament and archaeological reports and evaluations, the tomb within the Holy Sepulcher was by definition and function a temporary tomb, located in the middle of a large public cemetery, close to an execution site known in Second Temple era as *Gulgoltha* (Hebrew or Aramaic for "skull") and today as *Golgotha*. This tomb was, in all likelihood, not Joseph of Arimathea's owned family tomb; his socioeconomic status was high and he was rich enough not to have his own tomb in the middle of a public cemetery, next to an execution site and the felons' primary burial site.

The ownership of this tomb may be clarified only according to rab-

---

26. Ossuaries 7, 8, and 9 were in niches carved into the left Talpiot tomb wall, thus implying mutual kinship.

27. The IAA refuses to allow for an excavation of this tomb. But we do know that at least two very well decorated ossuaries are still in this tomb (filmed by a robot camera and presented in the documentary *The Lost Tomb of Jesus Christ*), meaning the interments were done by or for the rich. See Charlesworth's appendix.

28. Kloner, "Tomb," pp. 20-21. Ossuary 10 is plain ("Tomb," p. 21). During the symposium Gibson said it was broken and later reconstructed by the IAA. Since there is no reconstruction report, I overlook this one here.

binic literature. These sources point to the nature and function of the tombs under the Jewish court authority: keeping a felon's body for the first year after his death, until the flesh is completely decayed. A felon, in this case, is a Jew who was sentenced to death by a Jewish court. His family could retrieve his remains only after the year of primary burial for the purpose of secondary burial in the family tomb or a trench grave. By defining the nature and the function of the court tomb, rabbinic literature is in accord with the New Testament and archaeological reports and evaluations. That is, the tomb in which Joseph of Arimathea initially laid Jesus' body, according to the New Testament, was probably one of the two court tombs mentioned in the Mishnah.

Following the New Testament and rabbinic literature, Jesus' legal and social status was a *mamzer*. This harsh classification did not deprive a *mamzer* of every right. A *mamzer* could have property and he could bequeath his own and inherit his relatives' property. Thus a Jesus tomb could well be the burial site of his mother, his brothers, and his son.

However, a *mamzer* had to face serious problems regarding a candidate for marriage. Legally he could marry a female *mamzer* or slave, or a converted Gentile. But in those cases the descendants would remain *mamzers* for the next nine generations. As a former rabbinical student, Jesus knew that there was a way to have a "kosher" Jewish child: a Gentile could bear his child and convert during the pregnancy or shortly thereafter. If this occurred, the mother would become a complete Jew and so would her son, although Jesus would remain a *mamzer*. Hence the child, as a Jew, could be buried in the same tomb that his father was. As the grandson of Jesus' mother he had the same right through his grandmother by inheritance, as shown above. Since a Jewish woman could choose to be buried where her son was, the mother of Jesus' child could likewise choose to be buried where this child was buried or was to be buried. All in all, a Jesus tomb could legally be the burial site of his mother, his brothers, his son, and the mother of this son.

Was *Mariamne* the formal birth name of Mary Magdalene? Was she the mother of Jesus' son? If, as suggested here, she was initially a Gentile, the name *Mariamne* could support this suggestion, while her past as a Gentile is the only explanation of Jesus' fatherhood.

When we evaluate the possible interments in a Jesus tomb, we must bear in mind that none of the potential interments would be buried in a temporary tomb, but in a secondary, eternal tomb. It seems appropriate to quote here New Testament hints for Jesus' eternal burial. In Mat 26:12, after a woman poured expensive perfume on his head, Jesus told his angry disciples to calm down because she did it "to embalm me." Mark 14:8 is more precise: "she did whatever she could ahead of time to anoint my body for its burial."

The task now is to point to an optional site as the secondary tomb for Jesus' bones. Unfortunately, no Jew ever inscribed on his ossuary: "I am so-and-so." But according to available sources and an elaborate convergence of them, there is some likelihood that the Talpiot tomb is this site. It cannot be totally dismissed as an option — among others.

The Apostles and Brothers of Jesus

Andrew V. Sills

Jesus and Statistics

The Talpiot tomb, excavated outside Jerusalem in 1980 and brought to worldwide public attention in 2007, contained ten ossuaries, six of which were inscribed with names. The English equivalents of the names are Jesus son of Joseph, two Marys, a rare diminutive form of Joseph, a diminutive of Matthew, and a Judah son of Jesus. Because of the similarities between this collection of names and certain names appearing in the Christian New Testament, some are curious as to whether the Talpiot tomb may have once interred the remains of Jesus of Nazareth and some of his relatives. A number of statisticians have weighed in on the issue, and come to drastically different conclusions, admittedly based on different assumptions.[1] The diversity

---

1. See the following essays in *Annals of Applied Statistics* 2 (2008): Andrey Feuerverger, "Statistical Analysis of an Archaeological Find," pp. 3-54; Camil Fuchs, "Discussion of: Statistical Analysis of an Archaeological Find," pp. 57-65; Donald L. Bentley, "Discussion of: Statistical Analysis of an Archaeological Find," pp. 66-73; Sheila M. Bird, "Discussion of: Statistical Analysis of an Archaeological Find — Skeptical Counting Challenges to an Archaeological Find," pp. 74-76; Holger Höfling and Larry Wasserman, "Discussion of: Statistical Analysis of an Archaeological Find," pp. 77-83; Randall Ingermanson, "Discussion of: Statistical Analysis of an Archaeological Find," pp. 84-90; J. Mortera and P. Vicard, "Discussion of: Statistical Analysis of an Archaeological Find," pp. 91-96; Joseph B. Kadane, "Discussion of: Bayesian Views of an Archaeological Find," pp. 97-98; Andrey Feuerverger, "Rejoinder of: Statistical Analysis of an Archaeological Find," pp. 99-112.

of conclusions is at least in part due to the difficulty of modeling the problem for the purpose of statistical analysis.

Here we will consider a question of identity among certain persons in the New Testament that lends itself to a much more straightforward probabilistic analysis.

The Brothers of Jesus and the Apostles

The Gospels refer to Jesus having brothers. Mark 6:3 (NRSV) lists them as James, Joses, Simon, and Judah. Matthew 13:55 parallels Mark 6:3, but lists Judah just before Simon, and has the much more common variant "Joseph" in place of "Joses." Paul makes reference to "James the Lord's brother" in Gal 1:19. Those churches that hold to the doctrine of the perpetual virginity of Mary mother of Jesus assert that either these brothers are actually sons of Joseph by a prior marriage, and thus really adopted half brothers of Jesus (the Eastern Orthodox view), or they were not really brothers but rather cousins of Jesus (the Roman Catholic view). The traditional Protestant view is that Mary and Joseph went on to have normal marital relations after the birth of Jesus, and therefore these are the younger (half) brothers of Jesus. Those that deny the virgin birth, of course, have no problem seeing James, Joses, Simon, and Judah simply as the younger (full) brothers of Jesus. These alternatives will not concern us here. All of the preceding perspectives view James, Joses, Simon, and Judah as close relatives of Jesus of the same generation. I will use the term *brothers* to refer collectively to James, Joses, Simon, and Judas without favoring one viewpoint over the others.

Traditionally, most Christians have believed that the family of Jesus, including his brothers, opposed him during his earthly ministry, and did not become "believers" until after his death and resurrection. Nonetheless, this view appears to be supported by only two verses in the New Testament, Mark 3:21 and John 7:5. A number of modern scholars have come to doubt the historical accuracy of this assertion. Richard Bauckham states that "at least by the time of his last visit to Jerusalem, Jesus' relatives — his mother, brothers, his uncle Clopas and his wife, and probably another aunt — had joined his followers."[2] John Painter argues that Jesus' brothers "are portrayed

---

2. Richard Bauckham, *Jude and the Relatives of Jesus in the Early Church* (Edinburgh: T&T Clark, 1990), p. 56.

as 'fallible followers' rather than outright unbelievers. In this their portrayal does not differ greatly from that of the disciples. . . . The overall effect is to lead the reader to the conclusion that the mother and brothers of Jesus were among his intimate supporters."[3]

John Gunther judged that the Beloved Disciple was one of the twelve apostles, and speculated that he was Jesus' brother Judas.[4] James Charlesworth concludes that the Apostle Thomas was a brother of Jesus, and that Thomas is the best candidate for the Beloved Disciple.[5] James Tabor goes even farther and asserts, "This is perhaps the best-kept secret in the entire New Testament. *Jesus' own brothers were among the so-called twelve apostles.*"[6]

But is this going too far? For Bauckham, "the Gospel tradition several times distinguishes the brothers of Jesus from the Twelve (Mark 6:13-15; John 6:66–7:10; Acts 1:14), which would be tolerable if one of the brothers were a member of the Twelve, but not if more were. We conclude that it is unlikely that any of the Twelve were related to Jesus."[7]

I will attempt to assess the likelihood that the brothers of Jesus were among the twelve apostles based on name frequencies.

But first, let us review the names of the apostles. Matthew 10:2-4, Mark 3:16-19, and Luke 6:14-16 each lists the twelve apostles (see table 1).

Table 1: The lists of the twelve apostles in the Synoptic Gospels

Mark 3:16-19 (NRSV)	*Matt 10:2-4 (NRSV)*	*Luke 6:14-16 (NRSV)*
• Simon (to whom he gave the name Peter); • James son of Zebedee; • and John the brother of James (to whom he gave the name Boanerges, that is, Sons of Thunder); • and Andrew,	• first, Simon, also known as Peter; • and his brother Andrew; • James son of Zebedee, • and his brother John;	• Simon, whom he named Peter, • and his brother Andrew, • and James, • and John,

3. John Painter, *Just James: The Brother of Jesus in History and Tradition* (Minneapolis: Fortress, 1999), pp. 17-18.

4. J. J. Gunther, "The Relation of the Beloved Disciple to the Twelve," *Theologische Zeitschrift* 37 (1981): 127-48.

5. James H. Charlesworth, *The Beloved Disciple: Whose Witness Validates the Gospel of John?* (Valley Forge, Pa.: Trinity Press International, 1995).

6. James D. Tabor, *The Jesus Dynasty: The Hidden History of Jesus, His Royal Family, and the Birth of Christianity* (New York: Simon & Schuster, 2006), p. 165.

7. Bauckham, *Jude*, p. 18.

- and Philip,
- and Bartholomew,
- and Matthew,
- and Thomas,

- and James son of Alphaeus,
- and Thaddaeus,
- and Simon the Cananaean,
- and Judas Iscariot, who betrayed him.

- Philip
- and Bartholomew;
- Thomas
- and Matthew the tax collector;

- James son of Alphaeus,
- and Thaddaeus;
- Simon the Cananaean,
- and Judus Iscariot, the one who betrayed him.

- and Philip,
- and Bartholomew,
- and Matthew,
- and Thomas,

- and James son of Alphaeus,
- and Simon, who was called the Zealot,
- and Judas son of James,
- and Judas Iscariot, who became a traitor.

While the lists are not identical, there is enough consistency that the standard attempts to harmonize them do not seem particularly farfetched.

Luke 6:16 mentions a "Judas brother of James" (presumably this James is the son of Alphaeus), but no Thaddaeus, so this Judas and Thaddaeus are usually taken to be one and the same.

Mark 2:14 mentions a "Levi son of Alphaeus sitting at the receipt of custom" who is called by Jesus. This Levi is usually identified with Matthew the tax collector. Note also that he is a son of Alphaeus, which would make him a brother of James son of Alphaeus, and therefore also a brother of Judas/Thaddaeus.

Some complications arise when one attempts to cross-reference the preceding with the Gospel of John, which is based on sources independent of Matthew, Mark, and Luke. John's Gospel refers several times to "the Twelve" (John 6:67, 70, 71; 20:24) but never provides a full list. A disciple named Nathanael appears in six verses (John 1:45, 46, 47, 48, 49; 21:2), but nowhere outside the Gospel of John. Nathanael is often identified with Bartholomew, because of his interaction with Philip in John 1:46, combined with the consistent pairing of Philip with Bartholomew in the listings of the apostles in the Synoptic Gospels. John also refers to the following apostles by name: Simon Peter, Andrew, the sons of Zebedee, Philip, Thomas, Judas Iscariot, and another Judas called "Judas (not Iscariot)." Presumably, Judas *not Iscariot* is Judas (brother of James)/Thaddaeus. We learn in John 11:16 that Thomas is also called "the Twin" (or Didymus).

Finally, we note that in the noncanonical *Gospel of Thomas*, Thomas is called "Didymus Judas Thomas." Further, *Didymus* (δίδυμος in Greek) and *Toma* (תאומא in Aramaic) both mean "twin" and neither is a proper name. It would appear that the real name of Thomas is therefore Judas, which means that *three* of the twelve apostles had the name Judas.

Jeffrey Bütz argues that the brothers of Jesus were supportive of his earthly ministry, but does not suggest that the brothers were among the twelve apostles.[8] Indeed, "We also have evidence that Jesus' brothers are *not* to be identified with the apostles."[9] Further, Bütz states, "Ιακοβ [Greek for James] was an exceedingly common name in first-century Israel, as witnessed by the fact that eight different people in the New Testament bear the name."[10] The problem is that this assertion *presupposes* that all eight of those called James are in fact different people and *then* concludes that the name was exceedingly common. However, according to Bauckham's[11] compilation of Ilan's[12] data, only 1.5%[13] of Jewish male contemporaries of Jesus were named יעקב (= Ιακοβ = James). I would therefore like to assess the relative likelihood of two alternatives: the brothers of Jesus are among the twelve apostles, or the brothers of Jesus and the twelve apostles are two distinct groups.

James Brother of Jesus and Son of Alphaeus

Eastern Orthodox and Protestant Christian traditions, as well as most modern scholars, take James brother of Jesus and James son of Alphaeus to be different people. On the other hand, Jerome believed them to be the same, and this view is generally supported in Roman Catholic circles.[14]

Tabor provides a line of reasoning based on the uncertain paternity of Jesus, the identification of Alphaeus with Clopas (who is believed to be a brother of Joseph, the husband of Jesus' mother Mary), and levirate mar-

8. Jeffrey Bütz, *The Brother of Jesus and the Lost Teachings of Christianity* (Rochester, Vt.: Inner Traditions, 2005).

9. Ibid., p. 14.

10. Ibid., p. 9.

11. Richard Bauckham, *Jesus and the Eyewitnesses* (Grand Rapids: Eerdmans, 2006), pp. 85-88, table 6. In particular, the total valid occurrences of Jacob/James are 40 out of 2,625 individual males; 40/2,625 is about 1.5%.

12. Tal Ilan, *Lexicon of Jewish Names of Late Antiquity*, part 1, *Palestine 300 BCE–200 CE*, TSAJ 91 (Tübingen: Mohr Siebeck, 2002).

13. While one could question the validity of this estimate based on the fact that we do not have anything approaching complete census records for first-century Jerusalem, Ilan's compilation is the largest and most complete sample of names we have from this location and time period. Using the standard statistical technique of confidence intervals for proportions, we note that based on Ilan's data as compiled by Bauckham, we are 95% certain that the true percentage of men named Jacob/James was between 1.1% and 2.0%.

14. Jerome, *De viris illustribus* 2.

riage law (Deut 25:5-10).[15] Interestingly, Tabor's analysis has the unintended consequence of partially *harmonizing* several traditional understandings of the actual relationship between Jesus and his brothers. They are simultaneously *half brothers* (as sons of Mary by a different father) and *first cousins* (as sons of Joseph's brother Clopas/Alphaeus).

A Probability Calculation Concerning Men Named James

As noted earlier, about 1.5% of Jewish males at the time of Jesus were named Jacob/James. Accordingly, 98.5% of males were named something other than James. (Actually, this is a bit of an oversimplification; as we have seen, some of the apostles seem to have been known by several names each. Accordingly, there may be some individuals who fit into both categories. We shall ignore this complication.)

As a preliminary, let us consider the probability that a randomly selected group of twelve men will contain exactly one James.[16] The probability that the first man is named James is about 1.5% or 0.015. The probability that the second is *not* named James is thus 1 - 0.015 = 0.985; likewise the third, fourth, and so on. Assuming the names are chosen independently of one another, the overall probability is thus

$$0.015 \times \underbrace{0.985 \times 0.985 \times \cdots \times 0.985}_{(11\ times)} = 0.015 \times 0.985^{11} \approx 0.013.$$

But this is not quite the probability we seek. The preceding calculation only considers the possibility that the *first* person is named James and the others are not. We would like to take into account the possibility that the second man is a James (and none of the others are), the third man is a James (and none of the others are), and so on. Accordingly, we must multiply 0.013 by 12 to account for any one of the twelve men to be a James, while the other eleven are not James:

15. Tabor, *Jesus Dynasty*, pp. 73-81.
16. Students of statistics will immediately notice that what we are about to do is equivalent to the following: Let X be a random variable denoting the number of men named James in a randomly selected group of twelve men. The X is a binomial random variable with $n = 12$ Bernoulli trials and probability of success p approximated by

$$\hat{p} = \frac{40}{2625} \approx 0.015.$$

So

$$\Pr(X = 2) = \binom{12}{2}\left(\frac{40}{2625}\right)^2\left(1 - \frac{40}{2625}\right)^{10} \approx 0.0013.$$

$$0.015^2 \times 0.985^{11} \times 12 \approx 0.154$$

In other words, in the time and place of Jesus, if we took a thousand randomly selected groups of twelve men each, we would expect about 154 of those groups of twelve to contain exactly one man named James.

To calculate the probability that there will be exactly two men called James in a group of twelve men, we multiply

$$0.015^2 \times 0.985^{10} \times 66 \approx 0.013,$$

where 66 is the number of different ways two items can be selected from a group of twelve. Students of mathematics will recall that the number of ways to select r objects from a set of n objects is denoted

$$\binom{n}{r},$$

and equals

$$\frac{n \times (n-1) \times (n-2) \times \cdots (n-r+1)}{1 \times 2 \times 3 \times \cdots \times r},$$

so in this case we have

$$\binom{12}{2} = \frac{12 \times 11}{1 \times 2} = 66.$$

Thus we would expect there to be about thirteen groups in which exactly two of the twelve men are named James, out of our hypothetical thousand groups.

Let us now turn our attention to the second possibility, that the brothers of Jesus are *not* among the apostles. Then we have a group of sixteen men, three of whom are named James. The probability that this will occur is[17]

---

17. Note to students of statistics: Let Y be a random variable denoting the number of men named James in a randomly selected group of 16 men. Then Y is a binomial random variable with $n = 16$ Bernoulli trials and probability of success p approximated by

$$\hat{p} = \frac{40}{2625} \approx 0.015.$$

So

$$\Pr(X = 3) = \binom{16}{3}\left(\frac{40}{2625}\right)^3\left(1 - \frac{40}{2625}\right)^{13} \approx 0.0016.$$

$$0.015^3 \times 0.985^{13} \times 560 \approx 0.0016 \approx 0.002,$$

where 560 is the number of ways three objects can be selected from a collection of sixteen objects. Notice that

$$\binom{16}{3} = \frac{16 \times 15 \times 14}{1 \times 2 \times 3} = 560.$$

So only about 2 in 1,000 randomly selected groups of 16 men will contain exactly 3 men named James.

Note that the ratio $0.013 \div 0.0016$ is about 8.1; that is, we are more than *eight times as likely* to encounter a group of twelve men with two named James as we are to encounter a group of sixteen men with three named James.[18]

A Probability Calculation Concerning the Apostles and Brothers of Jesus

We will now perform the analogous calculation taking into account not just James but all four brothers of Jesus.[19] Everyone will presumably agree that Jesus had brothers named James, Joses, Simon, and Judas (provided the term "brothers" is appropriately explained). Furthermore, there is no controversy over the assertion that Jesus had, among his apostles, men named James, Simon, and Judas. Tabor has suggested that Levi/Matthew might be identified with Joses (whom he calls Joseph).[20] While this is intriguing, we would like to keep our assumptions as conservative as possible, and thus we will not assume this identification, nor will we use it in our calculation.

18. This calculation is based on the estimate that the proportion of men named James was 40/2,625, or about 1.5

19. Note to students of statistics: the analogous calculation, of course, uses a multinomial distribution in place of a binomial distribution.

20. Tabor, *Jesus Dynasty,* p. 164.

Table 2: Frequency of selected Jewish male names in late antiquity (based on Bauckham, *Jesus and the Eyewitnesses*, pp. 85-88, table 6)

Name	Transliteration	Translation	Total valid	Relative frequency
שמעון	Shimon	Simon/Simeon	243	0.0926
יהוסף	Yehoseph	Joseph/Joses	218	0.0830
יהודה	Yehudah	Judah/Judas	164	0.0625
יעקוב	Ya'aqov	Jacob/James	40	0.0153
		Total males in Ilan database	2,625	

Suppose a group of n objects is divided into r distinct categories, with n_1 objects in the first category, with n_2 objects in the second category, and so on, and

$$n_1 + n_2 + \cdots + n_r = n.$$

The total number of ways of doing this is

$$\frac{n!}{n_1! \, n_2! \cdots n_r!},$$

where $k!$ ("k factorial") denotes the expression $1 \times 2 \times 3 \cdots \times (k-1) \times k$ and $0!$ is defined to be 1.

The twelve apostles include two men named James, two named Simon, and three named Judas. Bearing in mind the data in table 2, the probability that a randomly selected group of twelve men consists of exactly two named James, two named Simon, three named Judas, and five with other names is

$$\left(\frac{40}{2625}\right)^2 \times \left(\frac{243}{2625}\right)^2 \times \left(\frac{164}{2625}\right)^3 \times \left(1 - \frac{40+243+164}{2625}\right)^5 \times 166{,}320 \approx 0.0000317,$$

where

$$166{,}320 = \frac{12!}{2! \, 2! \, 3! \, 5!}$$

is the number of ways to choose 2 objects of one type, 2 objects of another type, 3 objects of a third type, and 5 objects of a fourth type from a group of size twelve.

On the other hand, if the four brothers are distinct from the twelve apostles, we have a group of sixteen men, in which three are named James, three are named Simon, four are named Judas, and six have names other than these. The probability of a randomly selected group of sixteen having this shape is

$$\left(\frac{40}{2625}\right)^3 \times \left(\frac{243}{2625}\right)^3 \times \left(\frac{164}{2625}\right)^4 \times \left(1-\frac{40+243+164}{2625}\right)^6 \times 33{,}633{,}600 \approx 0.000000469.$$

The ratio of these two probabilities 0.0000317 ÷ 0.000000469 is about 67.6; that is, the scenario that Jesus' brothers James, Simon, and Joses are among the twelve apostles is *more than sixty-seven times as likely* as the traditional scenario that the brothers are separate from the apostles, based on name frequencies.

Conclusion

While unlikely events and coincidences do occur, it is clear that under the preceding analysis, the view that the brothers of Jesus were among the apostles is much more likely than the traditional view. Surely this possibility should be taken seriously and studied further, as we continue our search for the historical Jesus.

BELIEFS IN SECOND TEMPLE JUDAISM
ABOUT BURIAL AND THE AFTERLIFE

The Burial of Jesus in Light of Jewish Burial Practices and Roman Crucifixions

Lee Martin McDonald

Introduction

Almost annually a new interest in the death and resurrection of Jesus moves into the forefront of media attention and scholarly inquiry. Because of the central importance of these traditions in the Christian community (1 Cor 15:12-20), they are likely to continue to receive considerable focus in the future. The renewed interest in the burial of Jesus, an event mentioned in all of the canonical Gospels and Acts, as well as the *Gospel of Peter* (ca. 100-130 CE), may have been spurred by the media hype over the Talpiot tomb and the discovery of the so-called James ossuary. If it could be shown that Jesus was not properly buried and that his remains were left exposed on a cross, or in an indiscriminate burial site for criminals, how would this affect the traditional Christian affirmations about his resurrection, not to mention the empty tomb traditions reported in the Gospels? If it could be shown that Jesus did not actually die of crucifixion, but rather recovered, married Mary Magdalene, and sired a child named Judah; or if it could be proved that Jesus' body decomposed in Jerusalem and within a year it was subsequently buried in an ossuary in the vicinity of Jerusalem; or if it could be shown that Jesus had a family tomb in the vicinity of Jerusalem and that it contained the bones of many of his family — would any of that affect the Christian belief in the resurrection of Jesus or any aspect of the Christian faith?

While the answer is not as obvious to some, clearly the interest in such allegations has sparked considerable media attention and brought reaction from church leaders around the globe. In the first of these allegations that some scholars have argued, the discovery that Jesus did not die of crucifixion and that he was married and sired a child, flies in the face of all early and later Christian beliefs and teachings. Whether his family had a tomb in the vicinity of Jerusalem would not necessarily adversely affect the Christian faith, but to contend that the body of Jesus was later placed in an ossuary after decomposing in Jerusalem clearly does go contrary to Christian teaching about the resurrection of the body, despite many scholarly attempts over the last fifty years or more to argue for a spiritual resurrection that does not need an empty tomb, beginning with Hans Grass. Such arguments contend that what Paul experienced was a spiritual vision.

At present, there is no convincing evidence that demonstrates that Jesus was married to Mary Magdalene or anyone else, or that he fathered a child named Judah, or that his earliest followers misplaced the location of his tomb, or that any family or disciple returned in a year or so to place his bones in an ossuary box, or that his bones were a year later transferred to another family tomb (perhaps in Nazareth) — all of which has been alleged recently. No credible evidence can be shown to say that Jesus' tomb was lost or that he was placed in an open grave and devoured by animals or birds, as John Dominic Crossan contends. If it were possible to discover the body of Jesus or prove that he died a natural death, would it have an adverse effect on the Christian faith? Of course it would! The world's attention to such matters in the months following the publicity about the Talpiot tomb discoveries and the Christian reaction to such comments demonstrate that it would adversely affect Christian faith if these assertions could be proved — and how could it be otherwise, since at the core of Christian teaching Jesus died and was buried and soon after his tomb was found empty.

Even in the New Testament there are three explanations for the empty tomb, but no suggestion that it was lost or continued to contain his body. At the heart of early Christian preaching is the message of his death, burial, and resurrection. The empty tomb was not initially part of the proclamation because the empty tomb by itself was not part of Christian preaching, but it would have been very difficult if not impossible to proclaim the resurrection of Jesus in Jerusalem had anyone been able to produce his body or argue that the tomb continued to contain his body. Jewish notions of resurrection at that time required a bodily resurrection, even if a transformed bodily resurrection as we see in 1 Cor 15:12-20, 35-52. While it is possible to see various notions of life after death among the Jews even in the time of Jesus, those who held to the notion of resurrection also held to a bodily resurrection. Often Paul's comments about resurrection of the body are ignored and an emphasis is placed on a spiritual resurrection based on the supposed requirements of the technical term *ōphthē* (aorist passive indicative of *horaō*, "to appear" or "to see"). The term is not uniformly used of visions in antiquity, but it is used of visions often. Nevertheless, in Paul, resurrection of the body incorporates the old into the new, and this is present in Rom 8:11, 23; 2 Cor 5:4; Phil 3:21; and even in 1 Cor 15:35-52, where what is sown is also raised.

In what follows, I will limit my focus to the burial of Jesus in the New Testament traditions, and I will conclude that the earliest multiple surviving traditions of his burial are in agreement on the basic facts of the matter. Indeed, as I will show below, *seven of the earliest traditions about Jesus' death uniformly agree that he was buried in accordance with Jewish burial traditions.*

In their worship, Christians around the world regularly affirm the burial of Jesus when they cite the Apostles' and Nicene Creeds, but some biblical scholars have questioned whether he was properly buried and whether his body was disposed of in some other way. Gerd Lüdemann contends that we cannot know where Joseph of Arimathea (not clearly a disciple or friend of Jesus in Mark and Luke) buried the body of Jesus and that the two traditions that speak of those responsible for his burial (either Joseph or the enemies of Jesus) are in conflict.[1] Scholarly discussions of typical Jewish burial practices and Roman crucifixions raise the possibility that the body of Jesus may not have been properly buried, but rather was left exposed to the elements and decomposed, or perhaps even that his body was devoured by the birds and wild animals.[2] Those who reject such notions as fanciful often appeal to the Jewish scriptural practice of burying the dead, even the bodies of those who had been executed for crimes (Deut 21:22-23). The essential question I will focus on here is whether the traditional Jewish practices of burying the dead were in conflict with typical Roman crucifixion practices of allowing bodies to rot on crosses or to be left to be eaten by vultures or wild animals, and possibly left exposed in open graves. In other words, when Jewish cus-

---

1. *What Really Happened to Jesus: A Historical Approach to the Resurrection* (Louisville: Westminster John Knox, 1995), pp. 17-24. He is convinced that Jesus' body decomposed in Palestine and denies that the tomb of Jesus was ever empty. He states unambiguously, "I am convinced that the tomb was full and that Jesus' body decayed"; see idem, *The Unholy in Holy Scripture: The Dark Side of the Bible* (Louisville: Westminster John Knox, 1997), p. xvii.

2. This view lies behind J. D. Crossan and J. L. Reed, *Excavating Jesus: Beneath the Stones, Behind the Texts* (San Francisco: HarperSanFrancisco, 2001), pp. 230-70 and 288-97; and in Crossan's *Who Killed Jesus? Exposing the Roots of Anti-Semitism in the Gospel Story of the Death of Jesus* (San Francisco: HarperSanFrancisco, 1995), pp. 160-88, esp. 188.

toms and Roman practices were in conflict, what actions were followed or who took priority? While it is obvious that the preferences of the powerful Roman occupying forces would normally be followed, especially in times of conflict as in the siege of Jerusalem in 66-70 CE, when bodies were left hanging on crosses to discourage the Jews and bring them to submission to Roman authority, it is not so clear, contrary to Crossan, that this took place during times of peace in the land of Israel.[3] As I will show below, both Philo and Josephus refer to peacetime exceptions to Roman practice. What other considerations may have been involved in the death and burial of Jesus?

Questions about the burial of Jesus have been debated for many years,[4] but new attention has been given to the recent discoveries of the supposed tomb of Jesus in the Talpiot tomb burial site (an identification now largely rejected by leading archaeologists in Israel), bringing matters related to the burial of Jesus to the table for discussion once again. Was Jesus properly prepared for burial and placed in a tomb owned by Joseph of Arimathea, as Christian tradition claims, or was his body discarded by the Romans or disposed of in another manner?[5] That is the focus of the following inquiry.

3. *Excavating Jesus,* pp. 289-91.

4. See the discussion of these matters in Rudolf Bultmann, *The History of the Synoptic Traditions,* trans. J. Marsh; rev. ed. (Oxford: Blackwell, 1969); Joseph L. Lilly, "Alleged Discrepancies in the Gospel Accounts of the Resurrection," *CBQ* 2 (1940): 98-111; Willi Marxsen, *The Resurrection of Jesus of Nazareth,* trans. M. Kohl (London: SCM, 1970); Gerald O'Collins, *The Easter Jesus* (London: Dalton, Longman, and Todd, 1973); Reginald H. Fuller, *Formation of the Resurrection Narratives* (London: SCM, 1972); E. L. Bode, *The First Easter Morning: The Gospel Accounts of the Women's Visit to the Tomb of Jesus* (Rome: Biblical Institute Press, 1970); and Raymond E. Brown, *The Death of the Messiah: From Gethsemane to the Grave; A Commentary on the Passion Narratives in the Four Gospels,* 2 vols., ABRL (New York: Doubleday, 1994), 2:1204-1348; see also his helpful bibliography on pp. 1201-4 and his discussion of the relevance of the charge of blasphemy against Jesus and the possible consequences in regard to Jewish burial practices in 1:530-47. Likewise, see J. Zias and J. H. Charlesworth, "Crucifixion: Archaeology, Jesus, and the Dead Sea Scrolls," in *Jesus and the Dead Sea Scrolls,* ed. Charlesworth, ABRL (New York: Doubleday, 1992), pp. 273-89; and S. Fine, "A Note on Ossuary Burial and the Resurrection of the Dead in First-Century Jerusalem," *JJS* (2000): 69-76.

5. A very helpful summary of Jewish burial practice is in Craig A. Evans, "Jewish Burial Traditions and the Resurrection of Jesus," *JSHJ* 3 (2005): 233-48. See also his forthcoming "The East Talpiot Tomb in Context" for other relevant sources related to the topic of this paper. Several of the sources he mentions there have been useful in constructing this paper.

Jewish Burial Practices

Every known society in history has taken special measures to bury its dead with some form of dignity and honor. This is also true in the biblical traditions. For Jews, the appropriate methods of acceptable care for the dead included placing the body in the earth or in a sepulcher. Biblical descriptions of burials are to be found in the formula "he lay with his fathers" (1 Kgs 14:31; 2 Chr 12:16) or "he was gathered to his people" (Gen 25:8; Deut 32:50). For the Jews, the burial of the dead was a religious obligation that extended even to the burial of criminals executed for major crimes (Deut 21:22-23). The reason had to do chiefly with the belief that leaving any corpse on the ground brought impurity to the land (Deut 21:23). Sometimes, especially for the most serious offenses against God, a corpse was left exposed or experienced a dishonorable disposal.[6] While there were occasional exceptions, the usual practice was to bury the dead, even those who had committed crimes or were so accused. Indeed, according to the book of Tobit, burying the dead was considered a special act of kindness demonstrating the most charitable act that one could practice (1:18-20; 2:3-8; 4:3-4; 6:15; 14:10-13), and Tobit himself was the outstanding model of this kind of piety. This is also illustrated in Philo (*Joseph* 22-23).

Before, during, and after the time of Jesus a common form of burial in the land of Israel, especially for the wealthy or those with appropriate means, was the practice of secondary burial called *ossilegium*. Essentially this meant that a body was placed in a tomb, normally a cave, for a year; and after the body had decomposed, the bones were placed in an ossuary (or bone box, hewn out of limestone) and left in the family tomb. These bone boxes were usually around 60 × 35 × 30 cm for adults, and smaller for children. Some of the ossuaries were highly decorated, as in the case of the Caiaphas ossuary, but most were rather plain with simple etchings of the name of the deceased and the family name on them, but sometimes also with the deceased's profession or trade; occasionally other information was inscribed on the ossuary such as place of origin, age, or status, namely whether the person was a "freedman," or related to others generally in the same tomb, or some other things about the person. Secondary burials in this manner took place roughly from 30 BCE to 70 CE and sporadically after that until around 135 CE.[7]

---

6. See Deut 28:25-26; 1 Kgs 14:10-11; and esp. Jer 7:33; 8:2; 14:16; 16:4; 20:6; 22:19; 25:33; Ps 79:2-3; Ezek 29:5. For a discussion of ancient Jewish burial practices, see Elizabeth Bloch-Smith, "Burials," *ABD* 1:785-89.

7. See Rachael Hachlili, "Burials, Ancient Jewish," *ABD* 1:789-94.

This practice of secondary burials may be something like what is pictured in 2 Kgs 22:20, "being gathered to one's ancestors," a practice that may have its roots in the story of Joseph transferring the body (bones?) of Jacob from Egypt to the burial site of his ancestors (Gen 47:29-30; 50:4-14) and subsequently also of Joseph requesting that his bones be carried to the land God had promised Abraham. This was done when the Israelites left Egypt (Gen 50:24-25; cf. Exod 13:19; cf. also Josh 24:32 and 1 Sam 31:12-19). Jesus' word to a man who wanted to be his disciple to "let the dead bury the dead" likely assumes this practice of placing the deceased's bones into an ossuary and in the family tomb (Matt 8:21-22; Luke 9:59-60).[8] The practice of shivah (Heb. שבעה), seven days of mourning, began after the body was interred; it may have roots in the mourning of seven days that Joseph observed for his father (Gen 50:10), or perhaps even in the death of Moses as we see in *y. Ket.* 1. The location of such burial sites was, according to Jewish law, outside the city limits or city wall (*m. B. Bat.* 2:9). In Jerusalem, as well as elsewhere in Jewish communities such as Hierapolis and Antioch on the Orontes, tombs were located outside the city walls. Emile Puech has concluded that the activities practiced at Qumran were based on Deut 32:43, and that the Essenes, like the Pharisees, believed in the resurrection of the body, so care was given to burial procedures.[9]

As a general practice, secondary burials took place outside the city walls of Jerusalem or in other communities in that vicinity from roughly 30 BCE to around 70 CE, and subsequently secondary burials were practiced in other places where Jews resided until around the third century, though it was

---

8. For a fuller discussion of this, see B. R. McCane, *Roll Back the Stone: Death and Burial in the World of Jesus* (Harrisburg: Trinity Press International, 2003); idem, "Burial," *NIDB* 1:509-10; Hachlili, *ABD* 1:789-94; Elizabeth Bloch-Smith, *Judahite Burial Practices and Beliefs about the Dead,* JSOTSup 123 (Sheffield: Sheffield Academic Press, 1992); idem, "Burials, Israelite," *ABD* 1:785-89. A more comprehensive discussion of such practices is R. Hachlili, *Jewish Funerary Customs, Practices, and Rites in the Second Temple Period,* JSJSup 94 (Leiden: Brill, 2005). Similarly, any study of the use of ossuaries is now also heavily dependent on L. Y. Rahmani, *A Catalogue of Jewish Ossuaries in the Collections of the State of Israel* (Jerusalem: Israel Antiquities Authority and Israel Academy of Sciences and Humanities, 1994).

9. Emile Puech, "Resurrection: The Bible and Qumran," in *The Dead Sea Scrolls and the Qumran Community,* ed. J. H. Charlesworth, vol. 2, *The Bible and the Dead Sea Scrolls: The Princeton Symposium on the Dead Sea Scrolls* (Waco: Baylor University Press, 2006), pp. 277-81. See also Joe Zias, "The Cemeteries of Qumran and Celibacy: Confusion Laid to Rest?" *DSD* 7 (2000): 220-53.

never as common as it was in the vicinity of Jerusalem.[10] The majority of Jewish burials would have been in trench graves rather than in hewn-out caves, which were more common among the rich. According to Josephus, the Jewish customs of the day required that all persons who died be buried, whether they were enemies (*War* 3.377; 4.317) or even those condemned by Jewish law to death (*Ant.* 4.264-65). Occasionally one sees an exception to this practice among the Jews that allows the "wicked who rejoice in the death of the righteous" to be left to decompose on the ground, but this was not the usual practice. Josephus mentions that Achar (Achan) was given an "ignominious burial proper to the condemned" (*Ant.* 5.44; cf. 4.264), but this was unusual. More commonly was his reference to activities of pious Jews who "furnish fire, water, food to all who ask for them, point out the road, not leave a corpse unburied, show consideration even to declared enemies" (*Ag. Ap.* 2.211; cf. 2.205). Despised persons would normally not be placed in their family tombs, but rather in a common place for persons of low esteem (criminals), but they would nevertheless be buried, and in time their bones could be placed in the family tombs.[11] This tradition is also found in the Mishnah (*Sanh.* 6:5) and later in the Tosefta (*Sanh.* 9.8). The Mishnah allows that in some cases the body of the deceased criminal could be placed in the family tomb (*Sanh.* 6:6).

Later the rabbis raised the question of whether a good person who was executed by a wicked empire could be buried in a family tomb or given an honorable burial. The answer was that that person could be buried in the family tomb (*b. Sanh.* 47a-b). Brown describes this situation in the circumstance of the Maccabean martyrs receiving honorable burials.[12] Jesus was accused of blasphemy by the Jews, however, and was, according to Jewish tradition, worthy of death. Josephus indicates that blasphemers would be hanged, stoned, and buried "ignominiously and in obscurity" (*Ant.* 4.202). *Mart. Pol.* 17.2 tells the story of the Jews objecting to giving the body of Polycarp to his friends and followers for an honorable burial. When the centurion in charge of the execution "saw the contentiousness caused by the Jews, he put the body [of Polycarp] in the midst, as was their custom, and burned it. Thus we [his followers], at last, took up his bones, more precious than precious stones . . . and put them where it was appropriate" (18.1-2). Brown observes, however, that Jesus was crucified by the Romans not for blasphemy, but for

10. Hachlili, *ABD* 1:790-91.
11. Brown, *Death of the Messiah,* 2:1209-11.
12. Ibid., 2:1210.

claiming to be the king of the Jews. He asks whether this might have opened the possibility for an honorable burial.[13]

More important for our purposes is whether Jesus was placed in a *loculus* tomb (a small chamber or cell in an ancient tomb), or some other kind of interment after his crucifixion. Because he was crucified under Roman rule as a traitor to the empire, would Jewish custom be overridden and his body be allowed to decompose on the cross, or was it placed in an open grave with criminals? Jewish custom is clear that dead bodies were buried, even those of criminals, but what was the Roman practice in such instances? Would they have allowed the burial of crucified victims? That is our next focus.

Roman Crucifixions

The Romans were not the first to practice crucifixion and may have learned of it from the Carthaginians; but unlike those at Carthage, the Romans generally did not use this form of execution on Roman citizens.[14] Such executions were done in daytime and in public places to instill fear in all who observed the execution and to deter similar action that led to the crucifixion of the ones hanged in public places. Torture, humiliations, and beatings were common in both Carthaginian and Roman executions by crucifixion;[15] but the crucifixions were considered more horrible than hangings since hanging a person was quick, while crucifixion took much longer and the person endured longer torment and pain before death. Besides the usual beatings that preceded such executions, those crucified were often hanged naked to add to their humiliation. Martin Hengel has observed the report of Melito of Sardis who, in his *Homily on the Passion*, bemoaned that Jesus was so displayed at his crucifixion: "The Master has been treated in unseemly fashion, his body na-

---

13. Ibid., 2:1211.

14. The standard resource on Roman crucifixions with all of the pertinent data listed is that of Martin Hengel, *Crucifixion in the Ancient World and the Folly of the Message of the Cross* (Philadelphia: Fortress, 1977). See esp. pp. 22-50 for an extensive discussion of Roman crucifixions.

15. See Livy 22.13.9; 28.37.3; Josephus, *Ant.* 19.94; and *Dig.* 48.19.8.3. *Digesta* is a summary of Roman law prior to the time of Emperor Justinian, who instigated this summary begun in 530 and completed in 533. Most of the *Digesta* focuses on Roman law from roughly 100 to 250 CE. It is not always a simple matter to discern between earlier and later Roman law in this document, but it is instructive of the notions that were prevalent within sixty to seventy years after the time of Jesus and beyond.

ked, and not even deemed worthy of a covering, that [his nakedness] might not be seen. Therefore the lights [of heaven] turned away, and the day darkened, that it might hide him who was stripped upon the cross."[16] Also, as we will see below, victims of Roman crucifixion were often not buried, but rather left to decompose on their crosses, or birds and wild animals devoured them. In the land of Israel and during peaceful times, however, considerations were given to the Jews, and they were often allowed to bury their dead.

Again, the relevant question for our purposes is whether Jesus' body received a proper burial according to Jewish standards or whether his body was discarded by the Romans and/or left to decompose on the cross or in an open grave subject to the ravages of birds and wild animals. Both Josephus (*Life* 75.420-21) and Roman law (*Dig.* 48.24.1-3) reflect the Roman practice of allowing bodies to be removed from their crosses and buried. Philo was also aware of this practice, and he complained that Flaccus, Roman governor of Egypt, did not allow for the burial of the bodies of those persons executed by crucifixion on the eve of a holiday (*Flaccus* 10.83).

While the Romans wanted to frighten the Jews into submission during the war of 66-70 CE, and consequently left the bodies of crucified victims on the crosses in clear view of the Jews in the city without the normal burial privileges extended to them (Josephus, *War* 5.450-51), this was not the normal practice in the land of Israel. This is similar to the testimony of Pseudo-Quintilian, who claims that the Romans' practice of crucifixion was intended to terrify. As a result, crucifixions were placed on the most crowded roads so that large numbers of people could see them and be "moved by this terror." He adds: "For penalties relate not so much to retribution as to their exemplary effect" (*Decl.* 274). In the time of Jesus, when there was relative peace in the land and a Passover holy day about to begin with the area crowded with Jewish pilgrims, it is unlikely that given the potential for riots in Jerusalem that the Romans would deny the Jews their sacred duty of burying the dead in accordance with their religious traditions. Both Philo and Josephus claim that in general the Romans honored the Jewish customs (Philo, *Legat.* 300; *Flacc.* 83; Josephus, *Ag. Ap.* 2.73), and this is similar to the Roman law cited in the *Digesta*. The relevant text for exceptions to the usual practice reads as follows:

> The bodies of those who are condemned to death should not be refused [to] their relatives; and the Divine Augustus, in the Tenth Book of his Life, said that this rule has been observed. At present, the bodies of those

---

16. Hengel, *Crucifixion*, p. 21.

who have been punished are only buried when this has been requested and permission granted; and sometimes it is not permitted, especially where persons have been convicted of high treason. . . .

The bodies of persons who have been punished should be given to whoever requests them for the purpose of burial. (48.24.1-3)

It is obvious here that the Roman practice of allowing the burial of the bodies of crucifixion victims was common if the body was requested. The New Testament story of Joseph of Arimathea requesting the body of Jesus for burial following his crucifixion does have precedence in Roman law. As is well known, the skeletal remains of a crucified man by the name of Yehohanan were discovered in his family tomb at Giv'at ha-Mivtar. Because of the difficulty of extracting the spike from his ankle, it was left in him, and some of the wood to which it was attached was also placed in the ossuary with his bones. Crossan claims that this one example shows that this was most exceptional given the large number of crucifixions in the land of Israel in those days and that most of them were left unburied,[17] but this does not take into account that nails were normally extracted from the victims of crucifixion by the Roman soldiers themselves and often sold as amulets. The extraction of the nails is supported by *Gos. Pet.* 6.21, which indicates that the soldiers removed the nails from Jesus' body: "And then the Jews drew the nails from the hands of the Lord and laid him on the earth." Because of the extraction of the nails as a normal practice and because of decay, we simply cannot tell how many persons who were placed in the ossuaries were crucified, and Crossan does not take into account that many of the crucifixions used not nails but ropes.[18] Yehohanan was not a typical case, since the nail could not be removed from his foot.

The Burial of Jesus and the New Testament

There are several inconsistencies in the New Testament burial traditions, and those who reject the notion of Jesus' resurrection from the dead tend to em-

17. Crossan, *Excavating Jesus,* pp. 290-91.
18. Dale C. Allison, *Resurrecting Jesus: The Earliest Christian Tradition and Its Interpreters* (London: T&T Clark, 2005), p. 361. Allison also mentions the reference in the Mishnah to this practice among the heathen, but condemns the practice. The text reads: "Men may go out with a locust's egg, or a jackal's tooth or with a nail of [the gallows of] one that was crucified, as a means of healing. . . . But the Sages say: Even on ordinary days this is forbidden as following in the ways of the Amorite" (*m. Shabb.* 6:10, Danby trans.).

phasize these variants; but likewise those who affirm the traditional Christian beliefs about the death and resurrection of Jesus tend to minimize these differences and occasionally adopt rather fanciful explanations to account for the variants in the stories. There are also several consistencies in the Gospel traditions that reflect both a common origin as well as some level of historical reliability in the Christian affirmations that Jesus received a proper burial in accordance with Jewish practice and law. While Alan Segal is certainly correct in stating that there is nothing in the Christian proclamation about the Easter tradition that can be called "history" in the normal sense of that word,[19] this does not preclude an element of historical reality in the Easter proclamations, namely that Jesus was buried and later that his tomb was found empty.

There are categorical limitations on historians that inhibit historical judgments about such matters, and *as historians* they cannot affirm Christian beliefs about the resurrection of Jesus since such events are beyond the historians' experience, historical probability, and any rational explanation known to them to explain nonnatural activity. The burial and empty tomb traditions, however, are not unique, and both stories are subject to some historical inquiry and rational explanation. Historians often seek for analogies in contemporary literature as a means of explaining remarkable events.[20] As in much of ancient and even modern history, the artifacts of history often do not provide sufficient evidence for adequate historical explanation, but any inquiry into the events of Easter also incur further limitations. Easter faith contends that God acted in history in the life, ministry, and fate of Jesus, and historians are unable to make definitive judgments about such theological

19. Alan F. Segal, "The Resurrection: Faith or History?" in *The Resurrection of Jesus: John Dominic Crossan and N. T. Wright in Dialogue,* ed. Robert B. Stewart (Minneapolis: AugsburgFortress, 2006), pp. 121-38; see esp. 135-38, where he focuses on the "categorical" problems related to historical inquiry and theological affirmations.

20. In a forthcoming article by Adela Yarbro Collins, "Ancient Notions of Transferal and Apotheosis in Relation to the Empty Tomb Story in Mark," Collins cites as an analogy to the empty tomb of Jesus an incident in Plutarch's *Life of Numa* in which Numa's body was not burned but rather placed in a coffin. Later (about 400 years!), "when Publius Cornelius and Marcus Baebius were consuls, heavy rains fell, and the torrent of water tore away the earth and dislodged the coffins. When the lids had fallen off, one coffin was seen to be entirely empty, without any trace whatsoever of the body, but in the other the writings were found" (Plutarch, *Lives, Numa* 22.2). The parallels are not exact, as can be seen, but it promotes among the Romans a view of life after death in a bodily form that follows upon an empty tomb.

affirmations or divine interventions in human activity.[21] The aspect of the Easter traditions that clearly invites historical consideration is whether Jesus was buried appropriately, even if the bigger question in those traditions, namely whether Jesus was actually raised from the dead, cannot be settled through the positivistic historical assumptions that were developed in the late nineteenth and early twentieth centuries.

How do the New Testament's crucifixion and burial of Jesus narratives stand up in light of Jewish burial practices and Roman crucifixions? Although there are a number of variations in New Testament traditions, the writers of the New Testament agree that, following his death, Jesus was buried in a tomb (Mark 15:42-47; 16:1-3; Luke 23:50-56; 24:1-3; Acts 13:28-29; Matt 27:57-66; 28:1; John 19:31, 39-42; 20:1; 1 Cor 15:3-4). The canonical Gospels; *Gos. Pet.* 2.3-4; 6.23-24; and *Acts Pil.* 15.5-6 (perhaps as early as the late second century or even as late as the fourth century CE) agree that Joseph of Arimathea buried the body of Jesus.[22] It is possible that Joseph acted at the behest of the Sanhedrin to keep Jewish law and ensure that the body would not defile the land (Deut 21:22-23; cf. Ezek 39:14-16). This may be implied in John 19:31 and Acts 13:29, namely the Jewish leaders' concern about burial practices and the law led them to request the body of Jesus for burial; but if so, it is strange that John reports that Joseph went to Pilate secretly for *fear* of the Jews (John 19:38). If he went to Pilate as a member of the Sanhedrin

---

21. For a discussion of the limitations of historical inquiry, see Lee Martin McDonald and Stanley Porter, *Early Christianity and Its Sacred Literature* (Peabody, Mass.: Hendrickson, 2000), pp. 1-22.

22. The *Gospel of Peter* (ca. 100-130 CE) has some interesting parallels with the Gospel traditions as well as several differences. Although this Gospel has been accused of containing a docetic heresy (Eusebius, *H.E.* 6.12.3-6), nothing in the surviving fragment of that Gospel indicates this aside from an easily explained "My power, O power, you have forsaken me" (5.19), though something else in the document that has not survived this fragmentary text may have been contrary to the common Christian tradition circulating at the end of the second century. It could be that such traditions were very popular in some churches at the end of the second century, but were later seen by Serapion and others to be contrary to the received traditions found in the canonical Gospels or in oral tradition. As a result, it was excluded from churches. But that is conjecture. This writing has several important parallels with the canonical Gospels as well as some important differences. The similarities could be explained on the basis of shared oral or written traditions in the churches rather than direct dependence. The author of that Gospel is clearly not as familiar with the Jewish traditions, the land, or the circumstances in the land of Israel in the first century, but that does not detract from the fact that the author shows an awareness of some of the important traditions surrounding the death and burial of Jesus.

(Mark 15:43; Luke 23:50) at the behest of the Jews (John 19:31), his discipleship did not have to be declared and there would be no need for a private meeting with Pilate as well as no occasion for fear. On the other hand, if Joseph was a secret disciple of Jesus, or eventually became one, that could account for his name being included in the biblical narratives and in subsequent Christian sources *(Gospel of Peter* and *Acts of Pilate).* The multiplicity of reports about Joseph's participation in the burial of Jesus in both the canonical and noncanonical traditions strongly suggests his involvement in the burial of Jesus.

In what follows, I will assume that Mark 15:42-47 is the earliest account of the burial story, but that 1 Cor 15:3-4 and Acts 13:29 reflect the earliest traditions stating that Jesus' body was buried after his death. The *Gospel of Peter* and the *Acts of Pilate* also reflect the early church's belief that Jesus was buried by Joseph of Arimathea. The *Gospel of Peter* cannot reliably be dated much before 100 CE at the earliest, and it likely depends on the canonical Gospels for much of its material, though clearly not all of it. Crossan calls this the *Cross Gospel* and contends that all other Gospels are dependent upon it, but there are serious objections to his view.[23] Some of the story that it shares is clearly contrary to historical credibility, especially Pilate being submissive to the will of Herod and also the famous speaking cross. This does not mean that its witness can be ignored, but it may be de-

---

23. Crossan's view that this Gospel was the source for all four canonical Gospels (see his *Cross that Spoke: The Origins of the Passion Narrative* [San Francisco: Harper & Row, 1988]) has gained little support from NT scholars, and a careful evaluation of the fragmented Gospel will not support his proposal. See, e.g., the conclusions of Helmut Koester, *Ancient Christian Gospels: Their History and Development* (Philadelphia: Trinity Press International, 1990), pp. 216-20. Koester suggests that this document has independent traditions not found in the canonical Gospels, but he raises three important arguments against Crossan's thesis: (1) the surviving text is not reliable; (2) he presumes major literary activity at a time when it is not present in the early church and also ignores the presence of oral tradition in the churches for many decades after the emergence of the early church; and (3) the variety of traditions in the Easter proclamation of the canonical Gospels cannot be reduced to one common source as Crossan supposes. Further, evaluating the parallels between the canonical Gospels and the *Gospel of Peter* makes much more sense if the author of the *Gospel of Peter* depends on the canonical Gospels. These parallels are conveniently listed in Christian Maurer's translation of the Akmim Fragment of the *Gospel of Peter* in Wilhelm Schneemelcher, ed., *New Testament Apocrypha,* trans. R. McL. Wilson, rev. ed., 2 vols. (Louisville: Westminster John Knox, 1991), 1:226-27. See also Maurer's and Schneemelcher's discussion of the origin and date of this document in ibid., 1:216-22.

pendent in some places on oral or written traditions not found in the canonical Gospels.

N. T. Wright makes eight telling arguments that this document is later and more developed than the canonical Gospels: (1) the sensational appearance of two enormous angels coming out of the tomb is followed by a speaking cross; (2) it is easier to see that the *Gospel of Peter* depends on the canonical Gospels, which have no biblical references, than to explain why, if the canonical Gospels were dependent upon the *Gospel of Peter,* they eliminated biblical exegesis and Scripture references that are present in the *Gospel of Peter;*[24] (3) the strong anti-Jewish bias in the *Gospel of Peter* is more at home with a later development than in the first century; (4) that a large crowd of soldiers and Jewish leaders actually witnesses the resurrection is contrary to all four canonical Gospels; (5) historical details of Herod, instead of Pilate, sending Jesus to his death are historically indefensible; (6) the text speaks of the resurrection on the "Lord's Day," which is a late development and only in the New Testament at Rev 1:10; (7) if all the canonical Gospels used the *Gospel of Peter* it is remarkable that all of them omitted several of the same elements in the story, such as three men coming out of the tomb, two of which had descended from heaven; and it suggests a resuscitation rather than a resurrection; and (8) the meaning of the speaking cross is obscure and reflects later theological thinking in the church.[25] It is more likely that a *largely* independent witness supports the traditional burial stories of Jesus in the canonical Gospels, namely that Jesus was buried following his death and that Joseph of Arimathea was instrumental in that burial. In the following, I assume that Mark 15:42-47 is the earliest story of the burial of Jesus and that all four canonical Gospels, as well as 1 Cor 15:4, Acts 13:29, and *Gos. Pet.* 2.3; 6.23-24, all agree that Jesus was appropriately buried in accordance with Jewish custom. There are a number of variations in the narratives, however, and we will look at those momentarily; but again, all agree that he was buried.

In all four Gospel narratives, Joseph of Arimathea requests and receives permission from Pilate to remove the body of Jesus for burial. John alone claims the removal of the crucified victims from their crosses was ini-

---

24. Allison, *Resurrection Jesus*, p. 356, also makes the important observation that if the early Christians had wanted to make the death of Jesus and his burial fit with Scripture, they would surely have cited Isa 53:9 ("they made his grave with the wicked"), but they did not.

25. N. T. Wright, *Christian Origins and the Question of God*, vol. 3, *The Resurrection of the Son of God* (Minneapolis: Fortress, 2003), pp. 594-95.

tiated by "the Jews" rather than by Joseph (John 19:31), but after that initial request Joseph asks permission from Pilate to take the body of Jesus, and it is granted to him (19:38). According to John, Joseph and Nicodemus prepared the body for burial with spices and by covering it with linen cloths (19:39-40). Nothing is said in John about the women preparing the burial spices. Further, neither Mark nor Luke, unlike Matthew and John (Matt 27:57; John 19:38), claims that Joseph was a disciple of Jesus at the time of his request, though both say that he was a member of the council and waiting expectantly for the kingdom of God (Mark 15:43) or a "good and righteous man" (Luke 23:50). Luke adds that he was a righteous person who did not agree with the council's decision (23:51). This does not preclude that Joseph may have become a disciple later (Matthew and John), or even that he was at the time, but Mark and Luke are silent about it.

Mark says that Joseph placed the body of Jesus in a tomb (Mark 15:46), but Luke and John agree that it was a new tomb "where no one ever had been laid" (Luke 23:53; John 19:41). Matthew is close to Luke and John when he reports that Joseph placed the body in "his own new tomb, which he had hewn in the rock" (Matt 27:60). These stories are not incompatible, but signs of growth in the tradition are discernible. Further, John indicates that Nicodemus helped Joseph with the burial of Jesus. It is interesting that Mark 16:6 reflects that someone must have helped Joseph in the burial process: "Look, there is the place *they* laid him." Does this reflect the tradition used in John 19:39-42? All four Gospels agree that the day of the burial was late on the Day of Preparation prior to the beginning of the Sabbath (Mark 15:42; 16:1; Luke 23:54; Matt 27:62; 28:1; John 19:42).

Mark, Luke, and Matthew claim that the women saw the tomb where Jesus' body was placed, although there is some variation in their names. John and Matthew say nothing about the women preparing or bringing spices for the body. Mark and Matthew (unlike Luke and John) say that Joseph rolled the stone against the entrance of the tomb after the body was placed inside (Mark 15:46; Matt 27:60). Luke and John presume that the tomb was closed since the women found the stone rolled away (Luke 24:2; John 20:21). We may presume that all four evangelists agree that the stone was placed over the tomb entrance. Unlike Matthew (27:62-66 and *Gos. Pet.* 8.28-33; 9.34), Mark, Luke, and John do not say that the tomb was either sealed or had a guard posted at its entrance.

According to John, Joseph was a secret disciple of Jesus who because of fear of the Jews privately asked Pilate for the body of Jesus, and that permission was granted (19:38). Mark, however, says Joseph went "boldly" to Pilate to request the body (15:43). Mark apparently was unaware of the private nature of the request or that Joseph was a secret disciple. In fact, if Joseph were not a secret disciple, he should have no fear of the Jews for trying to bury the body of Jesus since that act was in accord with Jewish tradition (Deut 21:22-23). Mark may have assumed that Joseph was simply concerned with keeping the Jewish laws regarding the purification of the land and did not want to leave the corpses exposed on the ground or on the crosses. Matthew assumes that the Roman guard and Jewish leaders knew the location of the tomb where Jesus' body was placed. John indicates that Mary, a Galilean, also knew where to find the tomb of Jesus, but says nothing about her following Joseph to the tomb or how she knew of its location (20:1). Further, Mark, Luke, and Matthew say nothing about Joseph and Nicodemus adding spices or ointments to Jesus' body during the preparation for burial (John 19:39-42). Unlike Mark, Luke, and Matthew, John says nothing about the women at or near the tomb during the burial of Jesus. All four evangelists do speak of the women (or just Mary) coming to the tomb on the first day of the week. None of the evangelists says that the women saw the preparation of Jesus for burial, and it may be that the women were unaware of the specific preparations already done for Jesus' body by Joseph and Nicodemus (John 19:39-42), so they planned to bring their own spices for the preparation after the Sabbath was over (Mark, Luke). The testimony here is imprecise, and other scenarios are possible.

All four evangelists mention the presence of the women (or just Mary Magdalene as in John 20) at the tomb on the first day of the week, but there is some variation in the names of the women. Mark says that Mary Magdalene and Mary the mother of Joses saw the place where the body was laid. Matthew simply says it was Mary Magdalene and the "other Mary" sitting opposite the tomb where Jesus was placed. Luke says that it was the women who came with Jesus from Galilee who saw "how his body was laid," evidently in the linen cloth (23:53), and went home to prepare spices. John only mentions Mary Magdalene (20:1, 11), but then quotes Mary as saying "they have taken the Lord out of the tomb, and *we* do not know where they have laid him" (20:2), which suggests others; but this may be an attempt to bring John into harmony with the other Gospels.

Both Mark and Luke attribute the obtaining of spices to the women — Mark says they were bought and Luke says that the women prepared them. Mark and Luke agree that the women who came to the tomb on the first day of the week brought spices, but John says that the spices and ointments were brought by Nicodemus before Jesus was placed in the tomb and before the

Sabbath. More importantly, was the careful burial preparation mentioned in John (John 19:40) consistent with the claim that haste had to be made due to the rapidly approaching Sabbath (John 19:42; Luke 23:54)? Three of the four evangelists agree that spices were involved in Jesus' burial.

Bultmann rejects the Markan (16:1) and Lukan (23:50-55; 24:1) accounts of the women coming back after the Sabbath to bring spices for the burial, since after two nights and a day it would be impossible to prepare a body, given the climate of the Middle East.[26] This may not be a serious concern since the time of the Passover in Jerusalem can be unseasonably cool. The elevation of the city is just over 3,000 feet, and a tomb could be quite cool at that time of year; and there would be some shelter from the outside temperatures in a tomb anyway. Likewise, if John's story is correct, the women may not have been aware that Joseph and Nicodemus had already prepared the body of Jesus.

More importantly, if the burial of Jesus was complete and the women were witnesses to it (Mark 15:47), why did they come to the tomb at all on the first day of the week?[27] This problem may be resolved if we see that the women came out of devotion and to deal with their grief over the loss of one who was very special to them and that they came simply to perform a common feature of respect for burials (anointing with spices), not knowing what had already been done. Again, despite several variations in the burial traditions, all evangelists agree that Jesus was buried, and three of them indicate that spices were either applied before the burial or it was the intention of the women to do so after the burial.

The oldest New Testament tradition on the matter, one that precedes Paul, agrees that Jesus was buried (*etaphē*, 1 Cor 15:4).[28] The question here is

---

26. Bultmann, *History of Synoptic Tradition*, p. 285. Marxsen, *Resurrection of Jesus*, p. 45, believes Matthew deliberately altered Mark's text at this point because on reflection he knew it was impossible to undertake the anointing of a body on the third day, "for the process of mortification would have already begun. Consequently Matthew strikes out this feature of his copy [of Mark]." However, it is more probable that Matthew omitted the story about the spices because he already had stated that the tomb was sealed and a guard posted (27:66). For Matthew the women probably came to the tomb out of simple devotion and not necessarily with the purpose of anointing the body of Jesus.

27. Bultmann believes that this inconsistency in Mark points to the secondary nature of the empty tomb tradition in Mark and that 16:1-8 was not constructed with the chronology in mind that controlled Mark. See Bultmann, *History of Synoptic Tradition*, p. 285 n. 1.

28. Allison, *Resurrecting Jesus*, p. 353, correctly argues that had Jesus been discarded

not whether he was buried, but rather how the tomb in which he was placed became empty. An empty tomb by itself, as the evangelists indicate, did not initially mean to the disciples that Jesus was raised from the dead, even if the empty tomb tradition was later used in the church's apology. Mary thought someone had stolen the body (John 20:13), and the puzzled disciples saw the empty tomb but did not perceive its meaning (John 20:9) until the resurrection appearances. The empty tomb without the appearances would not have initiated faith in the risen Lord. Historically the burial of Jesus was not challenged, but only the circumstances that followed the burial, namely the empty tomb and how it got that way (see Matt 28:11-15) — in other words, the resurrection of Jesus.

The important question here is, who was responsible for the burial of Jesus? All of the evangelists and the author of the *Gospel of Peter* and the later *Acts of Pilate (= Gospel of Nicodemus)* agree that Joseph of Arimathea was responsible for the burial of Jesus. Mark adds that he was a respected member of the council or Sanhedrin (15:42), and Luke adds that he was a good and righteous man and a member of the council (23:50). Matthew and John call him a disciple of Jesus (Matt 23:57; John 19:38), but Mark and Luke say only that he was "waiting expectantly for the kingdom of God" (Mark 15:43; Luke 23:52). Matthew and John may well have expanded the tradition to include that he was a disciple based on their understanding of "a good and righteous man" or that he was "expectantly waiting for the kingdom of God," but this is not certain.

What do we make, however, of Acts 13:27-29, which implies that the Jews who condemned Jesus also buried him? John and Acts may not be far apart if we see that "the Jews" ask that those who were crucified be removed from their crosses so that they may be buried and Joseph of Arimathea was designated to perform that duty. Luke adds that Joseph was against the decision of the council to crucify Jesus (23:51). It is possible that all four evangelists were right if the latter two witnesses (Matthew and John) knew that Joseph had eventually become a Christian and inserted that into their texts, but that may be begging the question. If Joseph was not a disciple, it is likely that he was primarily interested in making sure that Jewish laws were upheld and that the land not be polluted on the Sabbath rather than showing his devotion to Jesus. While it is possible that Joseph later became a follower of Jesus, as we see in Matthew and John, that may also be a later tradition de-

---

in an open grave as "dog food" surely another term rather than this would have been used.

signed to enhance the story of Jesus' burial by disciples and not by his enemies, as Acts 13:29 suggests. This may also be the conclusion drawn by Matthew and John based on the statements of Mark and Luke about Joseph. If Joseph did eventually become a disciple, we could hardly expect Matthew and John to hide that fact, even if he played no known role in the developing churches of the first century.

Luke and John have many agreements, including in their empty tomb and resurrection appearance stories. This suggests a common source (oral or written) behind Luke and John. For example, in Luke and John two angels are present at the tomb, but only one ("angel" or "angel of the Lord") in Mark and Matthew; the location of the Easter appearances of Jesus is in Jerusalem in both Luke and John, but they are in Galilee in Matthew and Mark; the ascension of Jesus is mentioned in both Luke-Acts and John, but not in Mark and Matthew. These similarities suggest a common source that Luke and John used in their death and resurrection narratives. Since there are several agreements between Matthew and Mark in their passion and resurrection stories, Matthew's dependence on Mark is also clear (number of angels at the tomb, location of the appearances) as well as an oral or written source about the resurrection stories (M) in Matthew.

Since Luke was written before John, and since John shows little dependence upon Luke in other details of his Gospel, it seems likely that they both had a common source (oral or written) for this part of their narrative. However, apart from the material form of the appearances and their location, John and Luke are quite different. For example, Luke's empty tomb story, the disciples on the road to Emmaus, and Luke's understanding of the ascension of Jesus as a *final* appearance are all foreign to John. Unlike John, Luke has no major emphasis on the Holy Spirit in his Gospel except in the promise of the Spirit in 24:49 and subsequently in Acts 2 and following. John does, like Luke, refer to the giving of the Holy Spirit to the disciples following the ascension that comes earlier in John (between the first and second appearances) than in Luke (as a final appearance). The similarities in Luke and John are due to dependence upon a common written or oral tradition, and the writers made use of that tradition in a way that best suited their individual purposes.

There appears also to be a Markan tradition (Matthew showing dependence upon Mark) and a separate Easter tradition common to both Luke and John. These traditions dominate the resurrection narratives, though each evangelist takes the liberty to add what contributes to his own purposes. Matthew, for example, adds the apologetic story of the guard at the tomb, while Luke includes the story of the disciples on the road to Emmaus. John shows concern for later generations of followers of Jesus, and adds the story of the special appearance of Jesus to Thomas, concluding, "blessed are those who have not seen and yet believe" (John 20:29).

Three of the more significant variants in the burial stories are the following:

1. The spices and who provided them. Is there a discrepancy between John, who says the spices were provided by Nicodemus, and Mark and Luke, on the other hand, who say that the women brought the spices? The answer may lie in the ignorance of the women on how the body was prepared for burial. Having seen only the burial itself and not necessarily the preparation of the body, they might well have considered coming back after the Sabbath to prepare the body adequately for burial. Should anything be made of the silence of John and Matthew about the women (or just Mary in John) bringing spices? Should it be assumed that in all four Gospels the purpose of the coming of the women (or woman, in John) to the tomb on the first day of the week was to anoint the body with spices, or should we simply conclude that they came to pay their customary respects? This is an argument from silence, though not an impossible one. Bultmann's view that Mark 15:46 indicates that the burial of Jesus was complete and needed nothing further does not take into consideration the possible ignorance of the women regarding what had already occurred on Jesus' behalf.[29] Also, his view does not allow that this act was simply one of devotion on the part of the women. Because of the lateness of the day when Jesus was buried, the women may well have had no time to pay their final respects of devotion and honor to their fallen Master. On the Day of Preparation *(paraskeuē)*, or Friday, there was only enough time to perform the most necessary of burial obligations, and further acts of devotion were postponed until after the Sabbath.

2. The elaborate burial procedures. The evangelists indicate that, because of the impending approach of the Sabbath, Jesus' body was wrapped in a linen cloth (a normal practice) and placed in a tomb somewhat hastily (see Matt 27:57-60; Mark 15:42, 46; Luke 23:52-54; John 19:42). John indicates that this preparation included the spices, according to customs of the Jews (19:39-40). Interestingly, the rabbis gave proper burial of the dead a higher priority than the study of the law, circumcision of one's son, or the offering of the Passover lamb (*b. Meg.* 3b). The Jews permitted all necessary steps to be taken for a decent burial on the Sabbath, and the duty of burying the dead

---

29. Bultmann, *History of Synoptic Tradition*, p. 274.

took precedence over other laws whenever there was a conflict. It is likely that what obtained priority in later Judaism was also true in the time of Jesus. Since Deut 21:23 expressly states that the body of a condemned man could not hang upon a tree all night but had to be buried on the same day as his death, there seems to be no contradiction between Jewish practice and the burial story of Jesus, which took place on Friday afternoon as the Sabbath was approaching. Also, the burial given to Jesus (Mark 15:46; John 19:39-41) is not necessarily in conflict with the lateness of the Day of Preparation as the Sabbath was approaching. According to the Mishnah, preparing the body even late on the Day of Preparation is in keeping with Jewish sentiment; and if a person had been executed and his body decomposed, his bones could be interred in his family's tomb:

> R. Meir said: When a man is sore troubled, what says the Shekinah? My head is ill at ease, my arm is ill at ease. If God is sore troubled at the blood of the ungodly that is shed, how much more at the blood of the righteous? Furthermore, every one that suffers his dead to remain overnight transgresses a negative command; but if he had suffered it to remain by reason of the honour due to it, to bring for it a coffin and burial clothes, he does not thereby commit transgression. . . .
>
> When the flesh had wasted away they gathered together the bones and buried them in their own place [the family burying place]. (*m. Sanh.* 6:5-6, Danby trans.)

It took normally about two hours to prepare a body for entombment depending on how many persons were helping with preparations and how elaborate a procedure was followed. That Jesus died a criminal's death does not conflict with his receiving a proper burial according to Jewish tradition: "they may make ready (on the Sabbath or on a feast day) all that is needful for the dead, and anoint it and wash it, provided they do not move any member of it" (*m. Shabb.* 23:5). Therefore everything necessary for a decent burial, including the washing and anointing of a body, as we see in John, was normally possible and within the proper keeping of the law by the Jews. The evangelists, who were familiar with Palestinian conditions and customs, would not have attributed to the women the intention of coming to *embalm* the body of Jesus three days after burial, but only to anoint it according to custom and respect. The intention of the women was in keeping with the ancient Palestinian custom of visiting graves for three days after burial. This custom stemmed from the belief that the soul of the deceased remained in or near the body for three days.[30] The Palestinian custom of bringing spices and ointments for anointing was similar to the modern custom of bringing flowers or wreaths to the graveside of loved ones. Evidence of this can be seen in Josephus's story of the burial of Herod the Great in which there were some five hundred pounds of perfumes that were brought for his burial but were not used to embalm his body (*Ant.* 17.196-99). Crossan's complaint that the amount of spices for Jesus' burial in John not only parallels that of a king but of the divine is without merit.[31]

Although we may agree with Bultmann that according to Mark 15:46 the burial of Jesus appeared complete, do Mark 16:1 and Luke 24:1 really suggest otherwise? It is possible that Nicodemus supplied all the necessary spices for the burial of Jesus and that the women, perhaps unaware of this, only intended to offer their spices and ointments out of love and devotion. This is all speculation, but within the boundaries of custom and activity in the time of Jesus. Whether the women visited the tomb to prepare or simply to anoint the body of Jesus out of respect does not take away from the message of the evangelists that Jesus was buried on the day of his crucifixion. Several motivations for the women coming to the tomb are plausible, but as Bode put it, "the women came and that is enough."[32]

3. Who buried Jesus? The canonical Gospels and the *Gospel of Peter* are unambiguous in their claim that Joseph of Arimathea was responsible for the burial of Jesus, but Acts 13:29 strangely attributes this act to the enemies of Jesus, the Jews. Long ago Hans Grass argued that the Acts account is pre-Lukan and reflects more accurately the burial of Jesus. He concluded that the burial story in all four Gospels is a late tradition and that Jesus was simply placed in a common grave without any special burial preparation because this was the normal procedure for executed criminals in that day.[33] Reginald Fuller concludes that Mark 16:1-8 is more naturally an earlier part of the Gospel tradition (contra Bultmann), and that the burial stories of the Gospels can be explained as a subsequent addition to the original tradition, with the purpose of preventing Jesus from suffering the final shame of an im-

---

30. This tradition is seen in *Gos. Pet.* 8.30 that has the scribes and Pharisees coming to Pilate asking him for a guard to watch the tomb for three days ("give us soldiers that we may watch his sepulcher for three days").

31. Crossan, *Excavating Jesus*, pp. 291-92.

32. E. L. Bode, *The First Easter Morning: The Gospel Accounts of the Women's Visit to the Tomb of Jesus* (Rome: Biblical Institute Press, 1970), p. 173.

33. H. Grass, *Ostergeschehen und Osterberichte* (Göttingen: Vandenhoeck & Ruprecht, 1962), pp. 179-80.

proper burial.[34] He claims that the story of the women coming to the tomb to complete the burial rites was quite in order since, before then, the body of Jesus had simply been taken by his enemies and buried in a common grave. The burial stories in the Gospels, according to Fuller, were an expansion begun by Mark in order to make the final act of hostility toward Jesus one of charity. Mark's claim that Joseph of Arimathea was a respected member of the council and one who was looking for the kingdom of God (15:43) was, according to Fuller, developed later in the Gospel tradition to the point where Joseph was eventually even called a "disciple" (Matt 27:57). He concluded that it was the Markan burial story on which all of the evangelists drew, not the empty tomb story, which was at variance with the rest of the resurrection narratives. Fuller suggests that the difference in the names of the women in the burial and empty tomb stories can be attributed to later attempts to square the empty tomb tradition with the names of the women in the burial story. He also claims that originally only Mary Magdalene went to the tomb (John 20:1) and that when the disciples returned from Galilee after receiving their visions, they heard the report of the empty tomb from Mary Magdalene and they were pleased with the story because it was in accord with their experience.[35] Accordingly, Mary's report was later attached to the passion narrative as a vehicle for proclaiming the resurrection of Jesus.

O'Collins, on the other hand, contends that Luke used an unreliable source in the Acts 13 speech reportedly given by Paul. He also acknowledges the problem in Acts 13:31 (cf. 1 Cor 15:8) that Jesus' resurrection appearance to Paul is not mentioned as it is elsewhere in Acts and in Paul's letters. This passage, according to O'Collins, represents Paul "not as appealing to his own encounter with the risen Christ but as relying exclusively on other witnesses to the resurrection! As Luke fails in this speech to portray accurately the historical Paul, we can hardly insist on the strict reliability of a vague remark about Jesus' burial."[36] Conzelmann accepts the inconsistency, but says that this "pre-Lukan" passage (Acts 13:29) was simply not adopted in Luke's Gospel

---

34. R. H. Fuller, *Formation of the Resurrection Narratives* (London: SCM, 1972), pp. 54-56. Bultmann argued that the story of the women coming to the tomb on Easter morning was secondary because it did not fit with the previous section in Mark. After giving the names in 15:40, 47, it would not be necessary to do so again as in 16:1; also their intention to embalm the body does not agree with 15:46, which gives no indication that the burial was incomplete. See Bultmann, *History of Synoptic Tradition*, pp. 284-85.

35. Fuller, *Formation*, pp. 54-55.

36. O'Collins, *Easter Jesus*, p. 39.

narrative of the burial story. He says that Luke was not aware of the original meaning or significance of this passage and simply included it unwittingly.[37]

Rather than opt for one tradition or another, Bruce claims that it is possible to work out a harmony of the two stories by allowing the enemies of Jesus to remove the body from the cross, as seems likely from John 19:31, and yet to allow Joseph (and Nicodemus) at the same time to take care of the burial itself. This, however, does not seem to solve all of the problems, since Acts 13:29 has the enemies of Jesus not only taking him down from the cross but also placing him in the tomb. Munck calls the final clause of Acts 13:29 a passive construction: "A passive construction is used instead of the active 'they took him down' for the agent might be Romans, the Jews, or the disciples."[38] This, he believes, would allow for the disciples taking care of the burial rather than Jesus' enemies. In the clause in question, however, the participle *kathelontes* ("take down") and the verb *ethēkan* ("place") are both in the active voice, and it would be difficult to argue for a passive construction when there is no passive verb in the whole clause. Also, the disciples (the Twelve) are nowhere in sight in this passage, and Munck's explanation is clearly a stretch. What is more likely is Bruce's argument that both verbs in the passage are "generalizing plurals," that is, Luke does not specifically mean to say that the enemies of Jesus actually buried him.[39] Hanson agrees, saying that Luke's representation of the Jews as burying Jesus is a result of his "condensed style" and not his deliberate intention.[40]

We might further ask, how likely is it that the author of Luke-Acts had Joseph of Arimathea perform the burial rites in one part of his work (Luke 23), but be unaware of this inconsistency in the second part of his work (Acts 13:29), having the enemies of Jesus bury him? A number of alternatives are available to explain the discrepancy between the Gospels and Acts at this point, and I have noted them above. Since Mark does not readily invent names to tell his story about Jesus,[41] it seems likely that Joseph of Arimathea

---

37. H. Conzelmann, *The Theology of St. Luke*, trans. G. Buswell (London: Faber & Faber, 1960), pp. 88, 202.

38. J. Munck, *The Acts of the Apostles*, AB 31 (Garden City, N.Y.: Doubleday, 1967), p. 123.

39. F. F. Bruce, *The Acts of the Apostles: The Greek Text with Introduction and Commentary*, 3rd ed. (Grand Rapids: Eerdmans, 1990), p. 308.

40. R. P. C. Hanson, *The Acts* (Oxford: Clarendon, 1967), p. 143.

41. Richard Bauckham, *Jesus and the Eyewitnesses: The Gospels as Eyewitness Testimony* (Grand Rapids: Eerdmans, 2006), pp. 148-49, table 11, lists these names in Mark and compares Mark's use with Lucian's *Alexander* and Porphyry's *Life of Plotinus*.

was an actual person who served on the council and participated in the decision against Jesus, but probably for the sake of Jewish law regarding the sanctity of the land and appropriate burials even for criminals, he was the one responsible for the burial of Jesus. Because this was the decent thing to do and in keeping with the Jewish law, it may be that Matthew and John concluded that he was a disciple, but Mark and Luke concluded that he was a righteous person seeking to do the right thing according to Jewish law. The unified testimony of all four evangelists about the role of Joseph of Arimathea in the burial of Jesus need not be challenged despite some inconsistencies in details in the burial story, since the evangelists are more agreed on the burial of Jesus than on any other aspect of his death. While this does not settle the case, it does suggest where the burden of proof may lie. Bode suggests that since Joseph of Arimathea did not hold any place of remembrance or honor in relation to the organization of the earliest community of Christians, he might have been regarded as something of an "outsider" and consequently not the kind of person who would likely have been drawn into an invented story.[42]

Geering, on the other hand, argues that because Arimathea is not known as a place from any other source, it was an imagined site like the later Emmaus. The name "Joseph," he says, may have been used to personalize the unknown Jew who was presumed by Mark to have been responsible for the burial of Jesus. He suggests that "Joseph" was used "because of the biblical tradition which told of the care with which Joseph, the patriarch, transported the body of his father all the way back to Machpelah for burial." Geering concludes that the form and content of Mark's burial story is no guarantee of its genuineness and that this "Joseph story" was simply a later addition to his narrative.[43] The location of Arimathea, however, is not as unknown as Geering would have us believe, and certainly not as problematic as the whereabouts of Emmaus. Although it cannot be conclusively demonstrated, many scholars are willing to equate the Greek *arimathaias,* probably from Hebrew *haramatim,* with one of several places, rather than as a figment of the imagination. It is possible to identify Arimathea with *harmathem seipha* (Ramathaim-zophim), the city of Elkanah and Samuel (1 Sam 1:1), near Diospolis in the district of Timnah. The LXX form of Ramathaim is *armathaim.*[44] The basic issue in identifying Joseph

42. Bode, *Easter Morning,* p. 173.

43. L. Geering, *Resurrection: A Symbol of Hope* (London: Hodder & Stoughton, 1971), p. 47.

44. For other possibilities see K. W. Clark, "Arimathea," *IDB* 1:219.

of Arimathea has to do with whether he was indeed a disciple of Jesus (Matt 27:57; John 19:38).

If Joseph was a disciple of Jesus, we must ask why the women did not participate with him in the burial (Mark 15:47; Luke 23:55), since they would presumably have had nothing to fear by doing so. In the Synoptic Gospels, the women are observers of the burial of Jesus, and one gathers that this observation was from a distance. If, on the other hand, Joseph was not a disciple of Jesus, but instead a respected member of "the council" who was anxious to do what was right and proper on the Sabbath day according to Jewish traditions and law, then Acts 13:29 may be right by concluding that the burial of Jesus was performed by his enemies, and the report of the women watching but keeping their distance makes more sense.

The problem here is that if Joseph was not a disciple of Jesus, why would he have provided such an expensive burial place for him (a new tomb and the elaborate preparation of Jesus for burial mentioned in John)? John and Matthew, however, call Joseph a "disciple" of Jesus, and John includes by inference another disciple (Nicodemus) in the burial story. Luke says that Joseph was a member of the Sanhedrin, which makes him both a Jew and one with sufficient clout to ask for the body of Jesus. Joseph of Arimathea may eventually have become a disciple of Jesus, and because of this his actions would have been especially valuable to the evangelists, who wanted to have an adequate preparation of Jesus for burial as a final act of love and respect, but we cannot be sure of this.[45] That he was a righteous man looking forward to the kingdom of God (Mark) may give us the reason that he took a risk ("feared" the Jews, John 19:38) and went to Pilate privately to ask for the body of Jesus. If his concern was preserving the sanctity of the land and therefore wanted to bury Jesus out of respect for Jewish law (Deut 21:22-23), why would he fear the Jews when asking for permission to follow Jewish law in burying a fellow Jew? Likewise, if Jesus were placed in Joseph's family tomb, there is no reason to suppose that the tomb was lost or unknown.

The fourfold testimony of his significant involvement in the burial of Jesus in the canonical Gospels and in the *Gospel of Peter,* I suggest, outweighs the problematic assertion of Acts 13:29 that Jesus' enemies buried him. Whoever buried Jesus, all of the biblical and nonbiblical traditions conclude that he was indeed buried, whether by a member of the Sanhedrin interested in maintaining Jewish purity of the land or by a secret disciple of Jesus. Since

45. For a careful discussion of the Joseph of Arimathea tradition, see Stanley E. Porter, "Joseph of Arimathea," *ABD* 3:971-72.

nothing more is said of Joseph in the rest of the New Testament, he probably had little influence on the emerging life and growth of the early church. The story of Joseph of Arimathea was passed on in the later tradition of the church, not only in the *Gospel of Peter,* but also in the apocryphal *Acts of Pilate (= Gospel of Nicodemus),* where he was arrested for burying Jesus,[46] and he defended himself before the Jewish leaders by indicating how Jesus appeared to him during his (Joseph's) imprisonment (*Acts Pil.* 15.5-6).[47] While this story is certainly legend, it is interesting that Joseph of Arimathea's tradition continued among some of the early Christians, and his legend continued to expand. In the canonical Gospels, however, Joseph is not a legendary figure. He is simply there and providing a proper burial for Jesus.

Other Important Issues

The burial story of Jesus also raises questions about the empty tomb tradition noted in all four Gospels and the *Gospel of Peter.* If no one can be sure that Jesus was buried, then the emptiness of the tomb tradition is also in question. If we do not know where he was buried or even if he was buried, this would call into question the biblical account of the resurrection of Jesus that is witnessed by the empty tomb tradition. On the other hand, affirmation of the empty tomb does not thereby affirm the resurrection of Jesus, as noted above, but only how it got that way. Given current Jewish notions of resurrection from the dead, it is inconceivable that the resurrection of Jesus

46. "We were very angry because you asked for the body of Jesus, and wrapped it in a clean linen cloth, and you placed it in a tomb. And for this reason we secured you in a house with no window, and locked and sealed the door, and guards watched where you were shut up" (*Acts Pil.* 15.5; trans. Felix Scheidweiler, *New Testament Apocrypha,* ed. Schneemelcher, 1:518).

47. After Joseph is arrested and called on to defend himself, the text reads in part: "And Joseph said: 'On the day of preparation about the tenth hour you shut me in, and I remained the whole sabbath. And at midnight as I stood and prayed, the house where you shut me in was raised up by the four corners, and I saw as it were a lightning flash in my eyes. Full of fear I fell to the ground and someone took me by the hand and raised me up from the place where I had fallen, something moist like water flowed from my head to my feet, and the smell of fragrant oil reached my nostrils. And he wiped my face and kissed me and said to me: Do not fear, Joseph. Open your eyes and see who it is who speaks with you. I looked up and saw Jesus" (trans. Scheidweiler, *New Testament Apocrypha,* ed. Schneemelcher, 1:518). See also Brown, *Death of the Messiah,* 2:1232-34.

could have been affirmed and proclaimed in and around Jerusalem if his enemies could have produced the body of Jesus. The author of 2 Maccabees demonstrates the contemporary view that in the *resurrection* life would be returned to the body and that the parts of the body that were dismembered or lost would be regained in the resurrection (see 2 Macc 7:10-11, 23). This is especially clear in the story of Razis tearing out his entrails with the hope that God would restore them to him in the resurrection (2 Macc 14:37-46). In New Testament times, those Jews who held to the notion of resurrection also held to the notion of the resurrection of the body. For them, life after death was a *bodily* existence, and that is what we see both in the Gospels and in Paul especially, as observed above, even if that existence is a *transformed* bodily existence that can suddenly appear and disappear and go through closed doors (1 Cor 15:35-57; Luke 24:31, 36-39; John 20:19). While bodily existence in the resurrection is disputed as a uniform teaching among the rabbis at a later time, this was not the case among Jews who held to the notion of the resurrection of the dead in the time of Jesus.

There are explanations for the empty tomb in the canonical Gospels, namely that the disciples of Jesus stole his body from the tomb (Matt 28:11-15) or someone else removed the body from the tomb (John 20:1-2, 13); but all four Gospels affirm that "he is not here, but has risen from the dead." The explanation for the empty tomb as evidence for the resurrection is mixed with both history and theology and has no exact historical parallels. As noted above, the enemies of Jesus did not question the emptiness of the tomb where Jesus was placed, but only how it got that way. Historians have no adequate means of affirming the early Christian proclamation about the resurrection of Jesus since their experience tells them dead people do not rise and some people have indeed robbed graves from time to time. The early Christians did not use the empty tomb as part of their apologetic for the resurrection of Jesus, but the story was sufficiently embedded in their traditions and it was regularly connected with the resurrection of Jesus and the proclamation about him in the churches. Historically, the emptiness of the tomb was not in question — only how it got that way.

Affirmation of the resurrection of Jesus, however, is not a *historical* statement in the same way that historians understand history, but this does not thereby deny its reality. Christian faith has regularly affirmed what has been beyond the inquiry of historians, namely God's unique activity in history. Historians have several ways to explain the emptiness of the tomb of Jesus, but affirmation of the Christian confession of Easter is not one of them.

Conclusion

Despite several variations in the accounts of the burial story, at least one basic message is found in all of them, namely that it was Jesus of Nazareth who died on a cross and was buried in accordance with Jewish burial practices. Since there was no war or civil uprising going on at the time of Jesus' death, such as we find later during the 66-70 uprising against Rome, it would not have been unusual for Roman authorities to be sensitive to the Jewish concerns about burial practices as we have seen in both Philo and Josephus. The only known ancient text that suggests that Jesus did not receive a proper burial is in the *Apocryphon of James* (5.19-21), which concludes with Jesus saying: "Or do you not know that you have yet to be abused, to be unjustly accused, to be shut up in prison, to be unlawfully condemned, to be crucified <without> reason and to be <shamefully> buried, just like myself, by the evil one?"[48] There is nothing that supports this later tradition about Jesus' burial and nothing that supports that he was shut up in prison either. Since it is late and stands alone in antiquity, it is hardly a reliable witness to the burial of Jesus.

Jesus was taken from the cross and buried by Joseph of Arimathea to complete the requirements of Jewish traditions, but the purchase and use of a linen cloth to do so suggests that Joseph had more than a religious motivation to keep the land undefiled. He was apparently concerned about Jesus himself. It is quite possible that at first Joseph was only an upstanding citizen known for his piety, but not yet a disciple when Mark and Luke had produced their Gospels, though in time he became one (Matthew and John); but it may be that he was never a disciple. The canonical Gospels and the *Gospel of Peter* nevertheless connect Joseph of Arimathea with the burial of Jesus following his crucifixion.

The Gospels also agree that the tomb of Jesus was empty on the morning of the first day of the week — Jesus who was buried was also raised from the dead and his tomb was empty. His body was no longer there. This does not resolve all of the questions in the biblical narratives, but the burial of Jesus is in agreement with the earliest testimony on the matter as well as with early Jewish practices of burial. For those who contend that the burial story was an invention of the church to avoid the final shameful act toward him, it is hard to believe that the act of crucifixion, the most shameful death imag-

---

48. Trans. Einar Thomassen in *New Testament Apocrypha*, ed. Schneemelcher, 1:292. This source is noted in Allison, *Resurrecting Jesus*, p. 359.

inable in the ancient world, could have been surpassed by a shameful burial. Jesus' burial is also in keeping with ancient Roman practices that sought in nonrebellious times to allow Jewish customs of burial on the day of one's death to take place, even for those crucified for crimes of blasphemy according to Jewish beliefs.

As noted above, *historians as historians* cannot affirm Christian beliefs about the resurrection of Jesus since such events are beyond their experience, beyond historical probability, and beyond any rational explanation known among them to explain such nonnatural activity; but does that mean that there is no reality behind the Christian affirmation that God was involved in a unique way in the death and resurrection of Jesus? This is the place where history and theology meet and often conflict, but those who believe in the reality of the existence of a God who is involved in human affairs agree that there is a reality beyond the scope of the historian's craft. The death and burial of Jesus, as well as his empty tomb, however, are arguably historical events that can be debated or challenged, and there is much to support their affirmation. The resurrection of Jesus from the dead, while a matter beyond the scope of historical critical inquiry, is nonetheless at the heart of the Christian faith.

Understanding the Afterlife:
Evidence from the Writings of Josephus

Casey D. Elledge

Among the fascinating variety of afterlife beliefs in the ancient world, the only figure from the first century CE who composed a description of what Jews in Palestine actually believed on this matter is the historian Flavius Josephus (37–post-100 CE).[1] His descriptions, contained in the *Jewish War, Jewish Antiquities,* and *Against Apion,* at once enhance and complicate the study of life after death. On the one hand, Josephus presents a formidable reservoir of descriptive evidence that must be evaluated in any reconstruc-

---

1. On this problem in earlier studies see C. D. Elledge, *Life after Death in Early Judaism: The Evidence of Josephus,* WUNT 2/208 (Tübingen: Mohr Siebeck, 2006); Joseph Sievers, "Josephus and the Afterlife," in *Understanding Josephus: Seven Perspectives,* ed. Steve Mason, JSPSup 32 (Sheffield: Sheffield Academic Press, 1998), pp. 20-43; Adolf Schlatter, *Die Theologie des Judentums nach dem Bericht des Josefus,* BFCT 2/26 (Gütersloh: Bertelsmann, 1932); Roland Bergmeier, *Die Essener-Berichte des Flavius Josephus* (Kampen: Pharos, 1993); H. C. C. Cavallin, *Life after Death: Paul's Argument for the Resurrection of the Dead in 1 Cor 15,* part 1, *An Inquiry into the Jewish Background* (Lund: Gleerup, 1974); Arthur A. Droge and James D. Tabor, *A Noble Death: Suicide and Martyrdom among Christians and Jews in Antiquity* (San Francisco: HarperSanFrancisco, 1992); Steve Mason, *Flavius Josephus on the Pharisees: A Composition-Critical Study,* StPB 39 (Leiden: Brill, 1991); G. W. E. Nickelsburg, *Resurrection, Immortality, and Eternal Life in Intertestamental Judaism,* HTS 26 (Cambridge: Harvard University Press, 1972); Émile Puech, *La croyance des Esséniens en la vie future: Immortalité, résurrection, vie éternelle? Histoire d'une croyance dans le Judaïsme ancien,* 2 vols., EBib 21 (Paris: Gabalda, 1993); Alan Segal, *Life after Death: A History of the Afterlife in the West* (New York: Doubleday, 2004); Claudia Setzer, *Resurrection of the Body in Early Judaism and Early Christianity: Doctrine, Community, and Self-Definition* (Boston: Brill, 2004).

tion of how early Judaism explored the mysteries of death and everlasting life. On the other, Josephus's valuable testimonies on this topic are themselves also highly problematic and further complicate any resultant portrait of the afterlife in prerabbinic times. This is especially the case since the precise conceptual understandings of life after death in Josephus's writings can hardly be corroborated by other ancient evidence for the beliefs of Pharisees, Sadducees, and Essenes. Thus, while Josephus presents an essential piece in the larger puzzle, this piece must be handled with the kind of special care that is sensitive to his own sources of information, historiographical methods, and apologetic tendencies.

When Josephus's testimonies on the afterlife are examined in terms of his own sources, methods, and apologetic tendencies, they yield important evidence for better understanding several broader issues in the study of the afterlife. At the surface level, Josephus's apologetic attempt to render Jewish beliefs about the afterlife in the raiment of Greek philosophy offers a deeper perspective into Judaism's ongoing relationship with Hellenistic afterlife conceptions, even when it does not present an entirely satisfying historical description of actual Jewish beliefs in first-century Palestine. His complete suppression of any explicit reference to physical resurrection, for example, further illustrates the important conceptual impasse that still existed between the resurrection hope in early Judaism and philosophical immortality of the soul among the Greeks. Beyond the glittering surface level of this apologetic portrait, however, the evidence provided by Josephus does attest to the widespread popularity of the afterlife among multiple sectors of Judaism, including especially its apparent role in revolutionary ideologies. The afterlife also frequently serves as the final reward of those who have died faithfully for their adherence to Jewish law. Taken together, his testimonies strongly suggest that hope in the afterlife was a prominent topic of Jewish thought in the late Second Temple period and belongs in any serious attempt to reconstruct its conceptual matrix.

Surveying the Evidence

An inventory of all passages in Josephus that refer to life after death extends significantly beyond his well-known descriptions of the Pharisees, Sadducees, and Essenes. Indeed, life after death counts as a recurrent motif in the portrait of Judaism that runs throughout his corpus, including his catalogue of Jewish beliefs in *Against Apion* (2.217-19) and the speech materials of the

Jewish War (1.648-50; 3.361-82; 6.33-53; 7.337-88). He also calls attention to the importance of immortality and its relation to providence in a brief editorial transition in the *Antiquities* (17.353-54). He even alludes to Abraham's faith in immortality in his account of the Aqedah (1.229-31).

Jewish War

The most frequent references to the afterlife are in the *Jewish War*. In laying out the history leading up to the revolt, near the time of Herod's death, Josephus tells the story of a brief yet powerful "sedition" in which two Jewish teachers exhort their disciples to remove Herod's golden eagle from the temple gate. As an impetus to the dangers they must face in this task, the teachers tell their disciples,

> It is good, if indeed one should be in danger, to die on behalf of the ancestral law. For the soul of those who die in such a way survives immortal, and (their) perception of noble things survives everlasting; but those of a lower mind and inexperienced in their wisdom ignorantly love (their own) soul and choose death by disease before (death) through virtue. (*War* 1.650; cf. 1.653)[2]

According to the teachers, the virtuous embrace death for the ancestral laws of Judaism with faith that their souls will survive in immortality; those who love their own souls, however, are not promised survival beyond a natural death.[3]

Second, in his landmark descriptions of the Jewish sects, Josephus describes the beliefs about death that characterize Essenes, Pharisees, and Sadducees.[4] As is characteristic in the *War*'s version, more detail is invested in

2. Translations of Josephus are mine unless otherwise identified; translations of Greco-Roman literary sources follow the Loeb Classical Library (LCL).

3. For further treatments of this episode, see Bernd Schröder, *Die 'väterlichen Gesetze': Flavius Josephus als Vermittler von Halachah an Griechen und Römer*, TSAJ 53 (Tübingen: Mohr Siebeck, 1996), pp. 35-36; Martin Hengel, *The Zealots: Investigations into the Jewish Freedom Movement in the Period from Herod I until 70 A.D.*, trans. D. Smith (Edinburgh: T&T Clark, 1989), pp. 258-59; Richard A. Horsley and John S. Hanson, *Bandits, Prophets, and Messiahs: Popular Movements in the Time of Jesus*, New Voices in Biblical Studies(Minneapolis: Winston, 1985), pp. 182-85; Elledge, *Life after Death*, pp. 64-67.

4. The scholarship on these descriptions is, of course, vast. Among many fine stud-

the Essenes, whose belief in the immortality of the soul enables them to withstand the torments they endured during the revolt:

> They are despisers of dangers and conquerors of pain by their coura-
> geous resolve, considering death, if it approaches with honor, better
> than immortality. The war against the Romans tried their souls in every
> conceivable way. As they were twisted and bent, burned and broken, and
> forced through all the devices of torture, in order that they might blas-

---

ies that could be mentioned, the following are representative of most critical approaches: Randal A. Argall, "A Hellenistic Jewish Source on the Essenes in Philo, *Every Good Man Is Free* 75-91, and Josephus, *Antiquities* 18.18-22," in *For a Later Generation: The Transformation of Tradition in Israel, Early Judaism, and Early Christianity,* ed. R. Argall et al. (Harrisburg: Trinity Press International, 2000), pp. 75-91; W. Bauer, "Essener," in *Paulys Realencyclopädie der classischen Altertumswissenschaft,* Suppl. 4 (Stuttgart: Metzler, 1914-1972), pp. 403ff.; Günther Baumbach, "The Sadducees in Josephus," in *Josephus, the Bible and History,* ed. L. Feldman and G. Hata (Detroit: Wayne State University Press, 1989), pp. 103-95; Albert I. Baumgarten, "Josephus and Hippolytus on the Pharisees," *HUCA* 55 (1984): 1-25; Todd S. Beall, *Josephus's Description of the Essenes Illustrated by the Dead Sea Scrolls,* SNTSMS 58 (Cambridge: Cambridge University Press, 1988); Bergmeier, *Essener-Berichte;* Christoph Burchard, "Die Essener bei Hippolyt," *JSJ* 8 (1977): 1-41; Elledge, *Life after Death;* Stephen Goranson, "Posidonius, Strabo and Marcus Vipsanius Agrippa as Sources on the Essenes," *JSJ* 45 (1994): 295-98; Gustav Hölscher, "Josephus," in *Paulys Realencyclopädie* 9:1934ff.; John J. Killagen, "The Sadducees and Resurrection from the Dead: Luke 20,27-40," *Bib* 67 (1986): 478-95; Mason, *Flavius Josephus on the Pharisees;* "What Josephus Says about the Essenes in His Judean War," in *Text and Artifact in the Religions of Mediterranean Antiquity: Essays in Honour of Peter Richardson,* ed. S. Wilson and M. Desjardins (Waterloo, Ont.: Wilfred Laurier University Press, 2000), pp. 423-55; G. F. Moore, "Fate and Free Will in the Jewish Philosophies according to Josephus," *HTR* 22 (1929): 371-89; Anthony J. Saldarini, *Pharisees, Scribes and Sadducees in Palestinian Society: A Sociological Approach* (Grand Rapids: Eerdmans, 2001); Kurt Schubert, *Die jüdischen Religionspartien in neutestamentlicher Zeit,* SBS 43 (Stuttgart: Katholisches Bibelwerk, 1970); Daniel R. Schwartz, "Josephus and Nicolaus on the Pharisees," *JSJ* 14 (1983): 157-71; Setzer, *Resurrection of the Body;* idem, "'Talking Their Way into Empire': Jews, Christians, and Pagans Debate Resurrection of the Body," in *Ancient Judaism in Its Hellenistic Context,* ed. C. Bakhos, JSJSup 95 (Leiden: Brill, 2005), pp. 155-75; Morton Smith, "The Description of the Essenes in Josephus and the Philosophumena," *HUCA* 29 (1958): 273-313; Benedict T. Viviano and Justin Taylor, "Sadducees, Angels, and Resurrection (Acts 23:8-9)," *JBL* 111 (1992): 496-98; H. Weiss, "Pharisäismus und Hellenismus: Zur Darstellung des Judentums in Geschichtswerk des jüdischen Historikers Flavius Josephus," *OL* 74 (1979): 421-33; David S. Williams, "Josephus and the Authorship of *War* 2.119-161 (On the Essenes)," *JSJ* 25 (1994): 207-21; idem, "Josephus or Nicolaus on the Pharisees?" *REJ* 156 (1997): 43-58.

pheme their lawgiver or eat something contrary to their customs, they did not submit to either of these things, nor did they once soften before their tormentors or cry. Smiling in their pains and mocking their torturers, they cheerfully released their souls, as though expecting to receive them back again.

For, indeed, this teaching has strength among them: while bodies are corruptible and their matter not enduring, souls persevere, forever immortal. Roaming abroad from the purest heaven, they become entangled in bodies as in prisons, so to speak, having been pulled down by a kind of natural spell, but when they are sent back from the bonds of the flesh, then, as though set free from long slavery, they rejoice and are borne high into the air. Now as for the good, they propound that an abode beyond the sea is set apart (for them), agreeing together with the sons of Greece — a region weighed down neither by rain nor snow nor heat, but the eternally gentle west wind refreshes it, as it blows in from the ocean. But for the wicked, they set apart a dark and wintry recess filled with never ceasing punishments.

It seems to me that according to the same conception the Greeks set apart the Isles of the Blessed for their own courageous (men), whom they call heroes and demigods, and the region of the wicked down in Hades for the souls of the impious, where, their mythologists relate, some are punished, such as Sisyphus, Tantalus, Ixion, and Tityus. In this way, they affirm, first, that souls are everlasting, and then the pursuit of virtue and the prevention of vice. For the good become better throughout life by the hope of reward even after death, and the passions of the wicked are hindered, since they fearfully expect to undergo immortal punishment after death, even if they should escape it in this life. These, then, are the things that the Essenes propose regarding the theology of the soul, lowering an irresistible bait to those tasting even once of their wisdom. (*War* 2.153-58)

This description of the Essenes possesses an intense anthropological dualism of body and soul: the body is "corruptible" and composed of a "matter" that is "not enduring," but the soul "perseveres forever immortal." Souls preexist their physical embodiment, since they dwell in the *Aether*, from which the soul emanates and becomes entangled in human bodies. At death, souls "are borne high into the air" from which they originally descended. As he closes his discussion, Josephus reveals the moral purpose of Essene beliefs in immortality: to exhort their adherents to virtue, while deterring them from vice.

Though it is comparatively brief, Josephus's report on the Pharisees in the *Jewish War* still accentuates their beliefs about the future life:

> And while every soul is incorruptible, only the soul of the good migrates into a different body, but the souls of the wicked are chastised by everlasting punishment. (*War* 2.163)

In this description, Josephus attests something like a return to the body for the righteous; but it is clearly another, a *different,* body than the one that existed prior to death. It would thus be a mistake of terminology to call this a resurrection of the dead in the later rabbinic sense (see below). In the parallel passage in the *Antiquities,* the Pharisees seem consistently to assert an afterlife for the righteous only, while the wicked remain eternally imprisoned (*Ant.* 18.14). A clear contrast appears in the differentiation between other Jewish sects and the Sadducees, who will have nothing to do with these ideas: "And as for the survival of the soul and punishments down in Hades and rewards, they do away with them" (*War* 2.165).[5]

The next attestations of the afterlife occur in two of the most important, and even controversial, portions of the *Jewish War.* After being defeated in battle by the Romans in Galilee, Josephus hides out with his compatriots, who have determined to commit military suicide; and they compel Josephus to join their death pact (3.355-60). In response, Josephus offers a philosophical oration against suicide. After combating arguments in favor of suicide (3.361-69), Josephus affirms his choice to save his life through belief in the soul's divine origin and immortality:[6]

> Now while all people have bodies that are mortal and crafted out of matter, the soul is immortal forever and (it is) a portion of God (that) takes up its abode in bodies. If, then, someone steals or wrongly disposes of (another) man's deposit, then he will appear to be wicked or unfaithful; but if someone casts the deposit of God from his own body, shall he escape the one who is wronged? Indeed, it is considered just to punish fugitive slaves, even if they flee from wicked masters. Do we not then sup-

---

5. Hippolytus's version of the Sadducees offers a fuller rationale for their denial of the afterlife (*Haer.* 9.29). On the possible relationships between Josephus and Hippolytus, see below.

6. On this oration see Tessa Rajak, *Josephus: The Historian and His Society* (London: SCM, 1983), pp. 169-73.

pose that we commit sacrilege, if we flee from the most excellent master, namely God? Do you not know, then, that (as for) those who exit from life in accordance with the law of nature and repay the obligation received from God, when the one who has given (it) chooses to receive (it), theirs is eternal fame, their houses and families are secured, their souls remain pure and obedient, having been allotted (by God) the holiest region of heaven, from which at the revolution of the ages they return again to inhabit undefiled bodies. But as for those whose hands have raged against themselves, darker Hades receives their souls, and God, their father, visits upon their posterity the outrageous pride of their fathers. (*War* 3.372-76)

The soul is an immortal portion of the Deity, "housed" or "inhabiting" a material dwelling, a metaphor that suggests a strong anthropological dualism between soul and body. An ethics also emerges out of this dualism. While the soul is housed in the body, one must preserve the body "according to the law of nature," which means nurturing the body's life and growth into a natural death.[7] Rewards and punishments, in fact, will attend one's treatment of the body. Those who destroy the body will be punished: their souls are absorbed into the darkness of Hades, and God enacts retributive justice against their offspring. The souls of those who revere "the law of nature," however, will ascend to the holiest cosmic regions. Their souls will even be restored to "undefiled bodies" at "the revolution of the ages," a terminology Josephus uses for the future renewal of the cosmos (see below, *Ag. Ap.* 2.217-19).

The significance of these appeals to the future life within Josephus's presentation of Judaism becomes even more conspicuous in Eleazar's ora-

---

7. Studies regarding the controversial nature of suicide in this oration and in the later oration by Eleazar at Masada include the following: Droge and Tabor, *Noble Death,* pp. 86-96; Sidney Hoenig, "The Sicarii in Masada — Glory or Infamy?" *Tradition* 11 (1970): 5-30; Robert Newell, "The Forms and Historical Value of Josephus's Suicide Accounts," in *Josephus, the Bible, and History,* pp. 278-94; K. Kaplan and M. Schwartz, "Freedom, Creativity and Suicide in Greek and Biblical Thought: The Anomaly of Masada," *Journal of Psychology and Judaism* 18 (1994): 205-18; I. Jacobs, "Eleazar ben Yair's Sanction for Martyrdom," *JSJ* 13 (1982): 183-86; Zvi Kolitz, "Masada — Suicide or Murder?" *Tradition* 12 (1971): 5-26; A. Perls, "Der Selbstmord nach der Halacha," *Monatschrift für Geschichte und Wissenschaft des Judentums* 55 (1911): 287-95; David Ladouceur, "Masada: A Consideration of the Literary Evidence," *GRBS* 21 (1980): 245-60; idem, "Josephus and Masada," in *Josephus, Judaism, and Christianity,* ed. L. Feldman and G. Hata (Detroit: Wayne State University Press, 1987), pp. 95-113.

tion at Masada, the climactic speech of the entire *War*.[8] When fear of dying panics many of his listeners, Eleazar turns to a second section in his oration "concerning the immortality of the soul" (περί ψυχῆς ἀθανασίας, 7.341-88). Within this grand oration, appeals to immortality hold a central position. Like the other passages of the *War*, Eleazar's speech envisions immortality as an essential property of the soul:

> From ancient times, right from (their) first awareness, the ancestral and divine words have continually taught us, with our forebears confirming them by their works and intentions, that living is a calamity for human beings, not death. For it is surely (death) that grants freedom to souls

8. The Eleazar oration has been examined in a substantial critical history: Otto Michel and Otto Bauernfeind, "Die beiden Eleazarreden in Jos Bell 7.323-36, 7.341-88," *ZNW* 58 (1967): 267-72; J. Lindner, *Die Geschichtsauffassung des Flavius Josephus im Bellum Judaicum: Gleichzeitig ein Beitrag zur Quellenfrage*, AGSU 12 (Leiden: Brill, 1972), p. 37; Valentin Nikiprowetzky, "La mort d'Eléazar, fils de Jaïre, et les courants apologétiques dans le *De Bello Judaico* de Flavius Josèphe," in *Hommages à A. Dupont-Sommer*, ed. A. Caquot and M. Philonenko (Paris: Adrien-Maisonneuve, 1971), p. 490; Ladouceur, "Masada"; idem, "Josephus and Masada"; Gottfried Mader, *Josephus and the Politics of Historiography: Apologetic and Impression Management in the Bellum Judaicum*, Mnemosyne Sup 205 (Leiden: Brill, 2000), pp. 133-34; Louis H. Feldman, "Flavius Josephus Revisited: The Man, His Writings, His Significance," *ANRW* 21.2 (1984): 763-862; Yigael Yadin, *Masada: Herod's Fortress and the Zealots' Last Stand*, trans. M. Pearlman (New York: Random House, 1966), p. 15; Shaye J. D. Cohen, "Masada: Literary Tradition, Archaeological Remains, and the Credibility of Josephus," *JJS* 33 (1982): 385-405; Harold W. Attridge, "Josephus and His Works," in *Jewish Writings of the Second Temple Period: Apocrypha, Pseudepigrapha, Qumran Sectarian Writings, Philo, and Josephus*, ed. Michael E. Stone, CRINT 2/2 (Philadelphia: Fortress, 1984), pp. 185-232; Rajak, *Josephus*, pp. 80-82; J. van Henten, "Martyrion and Martyrdom: Some Remarks about Noble Death in Josephus," in *Internationales Josephus-Kolloquium*, ed. Jürgen U. Kalms and Folker Siegert, Münsteraner Judaistische Studien 4 (Münster: LIT, 1999), pp. 124-41; Nachman Ben-Yehuda, *The Masada Myth: Collective Memory and Mythmaking in Israel* (Madison: University of Wisconsin Press, 1995); Menahem Luz, "Eleazar's Second Speech on Masada and Its Literary Precedents," *Rheinisches Museum* 126 (1983): 25-43; Morel, "Eine Rede bei Josephus (Bell, Iud. VII 344 sqq.)," *Rheinisches Museum* 75 (1926): 106-7; Elledge, *Life after Death*, pp. 69-73, 117-27, 134-37; Droge and Tabor, *Noble Death*, pp. 86-96; K.-S. Krieger, *Geschichtsschreibung als Apologetik bei Flavius Josephus*, Texte und Arbeiten zum neutestamentlichen Zeitalter 9 (Tübingen: Francke, 1994), pp. 12, 313, 321-25; Newell, "Forms and Historical Value," pp. 278-94; Kolitz, "Masada — Suicide or Murder?" pp. 5-26; A. Schulten, "Masada, die Burg des Herodes und die römischen Lager," *ZDPV* 56 (1933): 24; Norman Bentwich, *Josephus* (Philadelphia: Jewish Publication Society, 1914), p. 134.

and releases them to be set free into their native and pure place, (where) they will be impassible of all calamity. But as long as they are imprisoned in a mortal body and infected with its evils, they are, to say what is most true, dead. For fellowship with what is mortal is unfitting to the divine. Now the soul is indeed able (to do) great things, even as it is imprisoned in the body. For it makes (the body) its own tool for perceiving, impelling it invisibly and leading it on to acts that are beyond mortal nature. But not until (the soul) regains its native region, liberated from the weight that drags it down to the earth and attaches it (there), does it share in a blessed strength and an ability that is not hindered on every side, remaining invisible to human eyes, like God himself. For even while it is in the body it is not seen, since it approaches without appearing and without being seen it departs again, having a single and incorruptible nature that is yet the cause of change in the body. For whatever the soul touches, that lives and flourishes; but whatever it departs withers and dies. So great (a portion) of immortality is there within it. (*War* 7.343-49)

Eleazar claims that these ideas lie at the heart of Jewish ancestral religion. In this philosophy of the afterlife, death will restore the soul to its own pure abode to enjoy powers that are only hindered by life in the physical body. The future life will thus be a return of the soul to its original dwelling place and a liberation from its temporary shelter in the corruptible body. A unique feature of the Eleazar speech is the specific rhetorical *exemplum* the speaker draws from Indic practices of self-immolation:

Let us look to the Indians who devote themselves to practicing philosophy. For these noble men remain alive through the time of life unwillingly, as a kind of necessary service to nature; but they make haste to release their souls from their bodies. Even when no evil presses down upon them or drives them away, because of their desire for immortal life, they tell others beforehand that they are about to depart. No one prevents them, but everyone regards them as blessed, and gives them letters to be carried to their family, so firmly and sincerely do they believe that souls will have an abode with one another. So when they have heard these requests, they give their body over to the fire, as though they were separating the soul from the body in the highest purity, and they die amid the singing of hymns. For their dearest friends bear them on toward death more easily than the rest of humanity (send) their fellow citizens away on

485

a long journey; and while the latter weep over these, the former bless those as having already attained immortal status. Are not we, therefore, ashamed to have lesser wisdom than the Indians? (*War* 7.351-57)

From Eleazar's perspective, the rebels are not dying a rash or unjust death; they are, instead, submitting to the will of heaven in a manner worthy of the Indian sages. What looms throughout the entire speech of Eleazar is, finally, that they are dying by divine necessity (7.358-60, 387). Necessity, in fact, provides the crucial contrast that makes the outcome of Josephus's speech so different from that of Eleazar. To embrace the divine will, death with hope in the future life remains the only option for the rebels (7.325-26, 336, 341, 351, 380, 388).

Finally, Titus himself appeals to similar notions of immortality as he exhorts his soldiers to risk death in battle. This shows that Josephus could attribute to Jews a view of the afterlife that was highly compatible with pagan conceptions. Titus's speech endeavors to show "that it is a beautiful thing to die in glory and how it will not be fruitless for those who first attempt this noble deed." The fruit of heroism will flourish in life beyond death:

> Neglecting to sing just now of death in battle and the immortality that is for those who die in warlike frenzy, I for my part would imprecate death in peace by disease upon those who hold otherwise, whose soul also together with (their) body is condemned to the grave. For who among noble men does not know that *Aether*, the purest element, entertains as strangers the souls that have been liberated by the sword in the battle line from the things of the flesh and sets them up among the stars, (where) they are made visible as noble *agathoi-daimones* and heroes propitious to their own offspring; but subterraneous night obliterates into darkness and deep *Lethe* receives the souls that have dissolved in disease with the body, even if they are especially pure of stains and pollutions, (since they) receive at one and the same time the termination of life and bodies, and yet also of memory. But if death has been spun as a necessity for men, the sword is a nimbler instrument for that purpose than any disease. (*War* 6.46-49)

Like the instructions of the two martyred teachers, Titus envisions the cowardly death as one in which the soul degenerates within the corpse. The souls of heroes, on the other hand, are received into the ethereal regions.

Apotheosized into the stars, they shine forth as astral beings, aiding their off-spring from the heavens. This new existence as divinities *(agathoi-daimones)* serves as a restoration of the soul to its divine status, which it possessed prior to being trapped in the human body (cf. 3.372). The status of the soul as an *agathos-daimon* that blesses its offspring is not to be found among Josephus's descriptions of Jewish figures; and thus, he seems to have crafted this speech with a more dramatically pagan conception of the afterlife, more appropriate to the speaker.[9]

Jewish Antiquities

Throughout the *Antiquities,* hope in the afterlife is largely absent from the treatment of biblical figures, including even Ezekiel and Daniel, where Josephus could have been expected to refer to the afterlife. His treatment of Abraham does, however, contain a substantive allusion to immortality.[10] As he prepares to offer Isaac, Abraham gives a lengthy speech, which alludes to his hope in immortality:

> But since it was by the will of God that I became your father and am now putting you away again to please him, bear the offering nobly. For I am handing you over to God, who deems it worthy now to gain this honor from us, in exchange for the affairs in which he has been my gracious defender and ally. And since you were born [lacuna in the Greek], so now depart from life, not by the common manner, but sent forth by your own father to God, the Father of all, by means of the custom of sacrifice. He, I suppose, judges you unworthy of being released from life either by disease or war or any of the other misfortunes that naturally befall human beings, but amid prayers and sacrifices, he himself shall receive your soul and possess it near himself. And you shall become my guardian and keeper in old age (for which very cause especially I nurtured you) by offering me God in the place of yourself. (*Ant.* 1.229-31)

In this passage, it is possible that Josephus refers to the same tradition, briefly alluded to in Heb 11:19 (cf. Rom 4:17), that Abraham offered Isaac full

---

9. Although cf. *War* 3.372-76, which seems to portray the righteous soul as dispensing benefits upon their earthly offspring, not unlike an *agathos daimon.*

10. Elledge, *Life after Death,* pp. 76-78; Cavallin, *Life after Death,* p. 145.

of hope in life after death. Philo also presents Abraham as a believer in immortality at the death of Sarah (*Abr.* 258).[11] As he prepares to render Isaac back into the hands of God, Abraham's piety is accentuated by prayer, sacrifice, and the hope of immortality for Isaac. The soul is perceived as being separated from the body at death, when it returns to the same God who gave it life (cf. Philo, *Abr.* 258; *Spec.* 3.206-7; Eccl 12:7).[12]

In the *Antiquities*, Josephus reiterates the significance of the afterlife among the Jewish sects. For the most part, these later descriptions in the *Antiquities* assume the more thorough treatments of the earlier *War* and simply summarize them. For this reason, Josephus's description of the Essenes in the *Antiquities* is much abbreviated: "They regard souls as immortal" (*Ant.* 18.18). More substantial interest is invested in the Pharisees, who "have faith that souls have immortal power, and there are punishments and rewards under the earth, for those whose devotion in life has been either virtue or vice. For (wicked souls), there is appointed an eternal imprisonment; but for (good souls), (there is appointed) an easy passage for revivification" (*Ant.* 18.14). In this case, a more detailed description of the Pharisees accentuates their belief in cosmic realms of punishment/reward "under the earth." As for the Sadducees, "the teaching is that souls perish together with bodies" (Σαδδουκαίοις δὲ τὰς ψυχὰς ὁ λόγος συναφανίζει τοῖς σώμασι; *Ant.* 18.16).

In his conclusion to book 17, Josephus comments briefly on the importance of immortality and providence, thus revealing his own philosophical interest in these beliefs.[13] When chronicling the demise of Archelaus and the ominous dreams that foretold it (*Ant.* 17.342-53; cf. *War* 2.112-13), Josephus offers the following commentary:

> Now I have not deemed these matters to be inappropriate to this story, because it concerns the kings and otherwise points toward an example of something resembling the immortality of souls and the foreknowledge of the Deity, who embraces human affairs in his care. (Thus) I considered it acceptable to say these things. As for the one who disbe-

---

11. One may compare passages of the *Testaments of the Twelve Patriarchs*, where the Jewish ancestors are fervent believers in the resurrection hope (*T. Sim.* 6.7; *T. Jud.* 25; *T. Zeb.* 10.1-2; *T. Benj.* 10.6-10).

12. For further comment, see Louis H. Feldman, *Flavius Josephus: Translation and Commentary*, vol. 3, *Judean Antiquities 1-4*, ed. Steve Mason (Leiden: Brill, 2000), pp. 90-92.

13. On the passage see Robert Karl Gnuse, *Dreams and Dream Reports in the Writings of Josephus: A Traditio-Historical Analysis*, AGJU 36 Leiden: Brill, 1996), pp. 194-96; Elledge, *Life after Death*, pp. 75-76.

lieves such things, may he enjoy the profit of his own opinion, but may he not be a hindrance to the one who adds them in the (pursuit) of virtue. (*Ant.* 17.354)

This passage is remarkable in the way that it emerges purely through Josephus's own editorial comments upon his history. This feature of the passage provides a clue to Josephus's own understanding of immortality as affirming a providential order to the events of history and inspiring the pursuit of virtue (cf. *Ant.* 6.328-30; 11.327-29; *War* 7.349; *Ag. Ap.* 1.161-65).

Against Apion

Often overlooked in discussions about Josephus's reports is a brief comment in *Against Apion*. Chronologically, this report is probably the latest of Josephus's public writings on the afterlife. In *Against Apion* Josephus refutes pagan antagonism against Judaism by providing a panoramic summary of its beliefs and practices. As part of this larger survey, Josephus pauses to explain the nature of Jewish beliefs regarding the future life. The reward of those who keep Jewish law is not public recognition, as is the custom among the Greeks. By contrast, the Jews have an entirely different perspective on reward:

> Each man, having his own conscience to bear witness, has trusted — as the lawgiver prophesied, and as God has provided strong confirmation — that, as for those who keep the laws, if it should prove necessary for them to die on behalf of them, God has granted to those who die willingly that they come into being again and receive a better life from the revolution. Now I would have hesitated to write these things, but through certain deeds it became clear to all that many of our own people quite often before now chose, nobly, to suffer many things before speaking even a single word contrary to the law. (*Ag. Ap.* 2.218-19)[14]

Josephus clarifies to his pagan audience that belief in the future life served as a motivation for many of his own people to die for their ancestral laws. A

14. For further commentary on the passage, see John M. G. Barclay, *Flavius Josephus: Translation and Commentary,* vol. 10, *Against Apion,* ed. Steve Mason (Leiden: Brill, 2007), pp. 296-98.

likely source of inspiration for this description resides in the legends of martyrdom in Maccabean lore[15] or even earlier literature.[16] Events within Josephus's own time, in which Jews expressed willingness to die rather than see their laws transgressed, could also have inspired the description.[17] This connection between death for the laws and the afterlife is also a central assumption of Josephus's report on the Essenes (*War* 2.152-53) and the two teachers (*War* 1.650). In contrast with the passages of the *War* and *Antiquities*, this passage never explicitly refers to the immortality of the soul. Instead, the future life is a *palingenesia* (δέδωκεν ὁ θεὸς γενέσθαι τε πάλιν) that God grants those who die for the laws. It as "a better life" to be received "from the revolution" — a reference to the reconstitution of the cosmos that also appears in Josephus's speech at Jotapata.

Cross-Examining the Evidence

Thus Josephus has quite a lot to say about the afterlife. Yet what is the historical quality of these descriptions? Fortunately, Josephus's accounts can be cross-examined by a large amount of contemporary literary evidence in which Jews expressed their hopes regarding the afterlife. As weighed alongside such evidence, Josephus's reports yield a mixed verdict on their historical quality. The principal problem of the descriptions is that in virtually every case, Josephus attributes to the Jews a far more Hellenistic philosophical belief in immortality than other Jewish writings of the age attest.

Bodily Resurrection

His insistent hellenization of Jewish faith in the afterlife is especially apparent in his suppression of physical resurrection. While physical resurrection was by no means the prevailing conception in earlier Judaism, it was still significantly more popular than Josephus's descriptions would attest; and its complete absence is highly conspicuous. A broad diversity of writings dating

---

15. 1 Macc 1:50, 60-64; 2:37-38; 3:59-60; 9:10; 13:1-6; 2 Macc 6:1-11, 27-31; 7:1-42; 14:37-46; *As. Mos.* 9.6; Josephus, *Ant.* 12.279-84.

16. (Pseudo-) Hecataeus 190-92.

17. *War* 1.650-55; 7.323, 326, 385-88; *Ant.* 17.150-59; 18.23-24, 264; *Ag. Ap.* 1.42-43; 2.232-35, 294.

from around 200 BCE through the end of the first century CE supplies a formidable amount of evidence for the popularity of a resurrection of the deceased body.[18] Moreover, other literary evidence for Pharisees, Sadducees, and Essenes defines their beliefs, not in terms of philosophical immortality of the soul, but rather in terms of the resurrection of the body: Hippolytus's Essenes believe that "the flesh also shall be raised and become immortal," and his Pharisees confess to "a resurrection of the flesh" (*Haer.* 9.26-29); the New Testament further defines the beliefs of Pharisees and Sadducees in terms of "resurrection" of the dead, not immortality of the soul.[19] Thus Josephus's evidence is not only conspicuous by its suppression of physical resurrection; but there is, in fact, even counterevidence from antiquity that defines Jewish sectarian beliefs in terms of bodily resurrection, not immortality of the soul alone.

A few of Josephus's references may betray that physical resurrection lies somewhere beneath the artifice of his hellenizing surface description. The closest terminological links between Josephus's descriptions and Jewish resurrection faith may be found in his descriptions of the Pharisees (*War* 2.163; *Ant.* 18.13-14). In *War* Pharisees claim that the "soul" of the good person passes "into a different body" (εἰς ἕτερον σῶμα). Does this return to a different body imply an underlying hope in physical resurrection? In *Antiquities* Pharisees believe that for the souls of the good there is an easy passage for "revivification" (ἀναβιοῦν). The verb he uses to express this idea is cognate with the same expression 2 Maccabees employs to describe a graphically physical resurrection of the dead. Martin Hengel also, perceptively, observes that the same verb is employed to describe the "raising" of a widow's son by Elijah (*Ant.* 8.327).[20] Similar terminology is even used for the Persian magi's

---

18. Dan 12:2-3 ("Many of those who sleep in the land of dust shall awaken, some unto everlasting life and others to everlasting reproach and shame. And the wise shall shine like the shining of the firmament, and those who turn the multitudes to righteousness like the stars forever and ever"); 2 Macc 7:9 ("The King of the cosmos shall raise us up again into an everlasting renewal of life because we have died for his laws"); *4 Ezra* 7.32, 97 ("And the earth shall give back those who sleep within her, and the dust those who inhabit it in silence, and the chambers shall give back the souls that have been entrusted unto them . . . their countenance shall begin to shine like the sun . . . and they shall begin to resemble the light of the stars"); *2 Bar.* 49.2; 51.5, 10 ("For the earth shall surely give back the dead . . . and they shall be made like the angels . . . they shall become equal to the stars"); cf. *1 En.* 22.13; 51.1-2; 58.2-3; 61.5; 4Q521 frgs. 2+4 II 1-12, frgs. 7+5; 4Q385 frg. 2.

19. Mark 12:18-27//Matt 22:23-33; Luke 20:27-40; Acts 23:6-8; 24:15-17; 26:6-8.

20. Martin Hengel, "Das Begräbnis Jesu bei Paulus und die leibliche Auferstehung

beliefs in physical reconstitution of the body in Diogenes Laertius.[21] Such terminological usage may affirm the conclusion of luminaries like Louis H. Feldman and Adolph Schlatter that these are indeed references to the resurrection of the dead.[22] Steve Mason offers a similar conjecture that the return of souls to "undefiled bodies" (*War* 3.374) may assume a resurrection in which the dead will be transformed into a new state of bodily existence, not unlike Paul's language of the "spiritual body" (1 Cor 15:44). Where the Essenes cheerfully release their souls at death "as though expecting to receive them back again (τὰς ψυχάς . . . ὡς πάλιν κοιμιούμενοι)," the same language of "receiving" the dead "back again" is also attested in 2 Maccabees' description of physical resurrection (*War* 2.153-54; cf. 2 Macc 7:11). Once again, belief in the resurrection may underlie these descriptions.

It is ultimately unlikely, however, that in their present form these passages explicitly refer to the resurrection of the physical body. Instead, as Norman Bentwich, Henry St. J. Thackeray, F. F. Bruce, E. P. Sanders, Émile Puech, and others have argued, the report on the Pharisees in *War* 2.163 describes *metempsychosis* — the travel of the soul from one body and its reincarnation into a *different* one.[23] Precisely the same formulation of the soul's

---

aus dem Grabe," in *Auferstehung-Resurrection: The Fourth Durham-Tübingen Research Symposium: Resurrection, Transfiguration and Exaltation in Old Testament, Ancient Judaism and Early Christianity* (Tübingen, September 1999), ed. F. Avemarie and H. Lichtenberger, WUNT 135 (Tübingen: Mohr Siebeck, 2001), p. 162.

21. *Lives* 1.8-9: ἀναβιώσεσθαι . . . τοὺς ἀνθρώπους καὶ ἀθανάτους ἔσεσθαι. Perhaps the belief in physical reconstitution among Persian magi may be anchored to the fourth century BCE by Diogenes's reliance on Theopompus.

22. Feldman, *Jewish Antiquities*, p. 13 n. c; Schlatter, *Theologie des Judentums*, p. 263; Cavallin, *Life after Death*, pp. 141-42; Aimo T. Nikolainen, *Der Auferstehungsglauben in der Bibel und ihrer Umwelt, I: Religionsgeschichtlicher Teil*, Annales Academiae Scientiarum Fennicae 49 (Helsinki: Finnischen Literaturgesellschaft, 1944), pp. 174-75; James D. Tabor, "'Returning to the Divinity': Josephus's Portrayal of the Disappearance of Enoch, Elijah, and Moses," *JBL* 108 (1989): 225-38; Emil Schürer, *History of the Jewish People in the Age of Jesus Christ (175 B.C.–A.D. 135),* ed. M. Black, G. Vermes, F. Millar, and P. Vermes; trans. T. Burkill et al.; rev. ed.; 3 vols. in 4 (London: T&T Clark, 1973-1987), 3:543; N. T. Wright, *Christian Origins and the Question of God*, vol. 3, *The Resurrection of the Son of God* (Minneapolis: Fortress, 2003), pp. 175-77.

23. Bentwich, *Josephus*, p. 117; Henry St. J. Thackeray, *Selections from Josephus* (New York: Macmillan, 1919), p. 159; F. F. Bruce, "Paul on Immortality," *SJT* 24 (1971): 457-72; Beall, *Josephus's Description of the Essenes*, p. 108; E. P. Sanders, *Judaism: Practice and Belief, 63 BCE–66 CE* (London: SCM, 1992), p. 301; Puech, *Croyance*, 2:707; Elledge, *Life after Death*, pp. 48-51.

entrance "into a different body," for example, is attested as standard Pythagorean teaching in a fragment of Posidonius. When describing the Gauls, Posidonius comments on their faith in the afterlife, "For the teaching of Pythagoras has strength among them, that the souls of men are immortal and that throughout an ordained number of years they come to life again (πάλιν βιοῦν), as the soul descends into a different body (εἰς ἕτερον σῶμα)" (Diodorus Siculus, *Libr.* 5.28.5-6).[24]

The reference to a return to a different body in *War* 2.163 would thus have been recognized as standard Pythagorean teaching by Josephus's contemporaries.[25] This increases the likelihood, in turn, that ἀναβιοῦν in *Ant.* 18.13-14 reflects Pythagorean notions of reincarnation and need not rely on 2 Maccabees. The verb, in fact, is frequently attested in the context of Pythagorean/Platonic beliefs in regeneration.[26] Such abundant Hellenistic usage on this point indicates that this passage cannot automatically be read as an easy reference to resurrection, even if genuine hope in the resurrection does ultimately underlie Josephus's description of the Pharisees.[27] The vast majority of references in Josephus also lack the explicit portrayal of God as *auctor resurrectionis,* which one finds in more obvious specimens of Jewish resurrection hope (2 Macc 7).[28] A decisive contrast is provided by *b. Ber.* 60b,

24. Felix Jacoby, *Die Fragmente der griechischen Historiker,* 3 vols. (Berlin: Weidmann, 1923-1958), 2A:303.

25. Elledge, *Life after Death,* pp. 103-5.

26. See Lucian, *Cat.* 13 (ἀναβιῶναί με ἔασον μόνον); *Gall.* 18 (ἤκουσα ταῦτα καὶ ὡς δόχειας ἀναβεβιωκέναι ἀποθανών); *Vit. auct.* 2 (τίς εἰδέναι τὴν τοῦ παντὸς ἁρμονίαν καὶ ἀναβιῶναι πάλιν;); cf. another passage in section 5 of the same work. Mason identifies the causative (τὸ ἀναβιώσκεσθαι) three times in Plato, *Phaed.* 71e, where it appears to be synonymous with πάλιν γίγνεσθαι (72a); Mason, *Flavius Josephus on the Pharisees,* p. 164. Note also that in Plutarch (*Luc.* 18), the noun is used synonymously with δευτέραν τινὰ γέννησιν. More cryptic are Aristophanes, *Ran.* 177, and Appian, *Gall.* 1.3; but both show that the term was so widely reflected in Hellenistic usage that it cannot be exclusively associated with 2 Macc 7. In Philostratus's *Life of Apollonius,* the verb is used to describe mythological rescues from the underworld, which in turn is compared to Apollonius's resuscitation of a young girl (4.45).

27. Likewise, Josephus's language for the Essenes "receiving their souls back again" is also attested in pagan forms of regeneration and is not exclusive to 2 Maccabees. See, e.g., Pindar, *Pyth.* 3.55-56 (ἄνδρ' ἐκ θανάτου κομίσαι); *Nem.* 8.44 (ὦ Μέγα, τὸ δ' αὖθις τεὰν ψύχαν κομίξαι οὔ μοι δύνατον); and (slightly different) Plato, *Phaed.* 107e (ἄλλος δεῦρο πάλιν ἡγεμὼν κομίζει ἐν πολλαῖς χρόνου καὶ μακραῖς περιόδοις).

28. Perhaps the passage in *Against Apion* does, however, envision God's own action in more directly granting a blessed afterlife: "God has granted to those who die willingly

where it is "the Lord, who restores spirits to dead bodies" (המחזטר בשנוף
קפגרים מתים). Ironically, the very belief about life after death that would
become increasingly preferred among the rabbis and was already attested in
2 Maccabees, Daniel, and other writings is consistently evaded in Josephus.
The entire series of descriptions, in the end, has more in common with
Homer, Pythagoras, Plato, Posidonius, and Cicero than with earlier Jewish
writings from Palestine.

Immortality of the Soul in Judaism

By the Hellenistic-Roman eras, the soul and the question of its immortality
had already constituted a major volume in the history of Greek philosophy,
including the views of Pythagoras and Plato, as well as Orphics, Stoics, and
Epicureans.[29] These Greek philosophies deeply impressed the anthropological consciousness of many sectors of Hellenistic Jewry, making it entirely
natural for someone like Josephus to have thought of life and death in
terms of the soul. Philo of Alexandria, Wisdom of Solomon, and
4 Maccabees confirm the attractiveness of the soul's immortality among
Greco-Jewish authors apart from any explicit mention of bodily resurrection. For Philo the virtuous will experience a *palingenesia* at death in which
the noetic element of the soul is reborn into the intelligible world and thus
"rendered immortal" (*Opif.* 135);[30] but souls that pursue temporal goods
will be extinguished.[31] The immortalization of the soul, then, remains con-

---

that they come into being again and receive a better life from the revolution" (δέδωκεν ὁ
θεὸς γενέσθαι τε πάλιν; 2.218-19).

29. Erwin Rohde, *Psyche: The Cult of Souls and Belief in Immortality among the
Greeks,* trans. W. Hillis, International Library of Philosophy, Psychology, and Scientific
Method (London: Routledge & Kegan Paul, 1950); Jan N. Bremmer, *The Early Greek Concept of the Soul* (Princeton: Princeton University Press, 1983); Walter Burkert, *Greek Religion: Archaic and Classical* (Oxford: Basil Blackwell, 1985), pp. 197-99, 293-95; Franz
Cumont, *The Afterlife in Roman Paganism,* Silliman Memorial Lectures (New Haven: Yale
University Press, 1922); Werner Peek, *Griechische Grabgedichte* (Berlin: Akademie-Verlag,
1960); Martin P. Nilsson, "Die astrale Unsterblichkeit und die kosmische Mystik," *Numen*
1 (1954): 106-19; idem, *Geschichte der griechischen Religion,* Handbuch der Altertumswissenschaft 5.2.2; 2 vols. (Munich: Beck'sche, 1974), 1:678-91; 2:231-42, 543-57.

30. Fred Burnett, "Philo on Immortality: A Thematic Study of Philo's Concept of
Palingenesia," *CBQ* 46 (1984): 456.

31. *Opif.* 77; *Gig.* 12-15; *Post.* 39; cf. also *Sacr.* 5; *Leg.* 2.4-55; *Cher.* 75-78, 113-15; *Virt.*

ditional upon human virtue;[32] the punishment of the wicked, on the other hand, is immediate and fully carried out within the human frame.[33] A simpler trust in the soul's immortality punctuates the approach to theodicy found in the Wisdom of Solomon, where "the souls of the righteous are in the hand of God, and no torment will ever touch them. . . . they are at peace. . . . For even if they were punished in the eyes of men, their hope is full of immortality" (3:1-4; revised from NRSV).[34] Despite the fact that *4 Maccabees* depended upon the same martyrological legends found in 2 Macc 7, the former writing self-consciously converted the latter's graphically physical portrait of resurrection exclusively into the idiom of immortality. Its author has preferred to portray the martyrs as making "haste to-

---

205; *QG* 1.16, 45; 3.11; *Somn.* 1.152; *Her.* 45; *Congr.* 57; *Det.* 84; *Spec.* 1.345; *Mos.* 2.288-91; *Plant.* 37. On these passages, see Cavallin, *Life after Death*, pp. 135-40; Puech, *Croyance,* 1:163-66; Émile Bréhier, *Les idées philosophiques et religieuses de Philon d'Alexandrie,* Etudes de philosophie médiévale 8 (Paris: Librairie Philosophique, 1925), pp. 45-66; Erwin R. Goodenough, "Philo on Immortality," *HTR* 39 (1946): 85-108; idem, *By Light, Light: The Mystic Gospel of Hellenistic Judaism* (New Haven: Yale University Press, 1935), pp. 246-56; Harry A. Wolfson, *Philo,* 2 vols. (Cambridge: Harvard University Press, 1948), 1:404-6; Samuel Sandmel, *Philo's Place in Judaism: A Study of Conceptions of Abraham in Jewish Literature* (Cincinnati: Hebrew Union College Press, 1956), pp. 141-85; Wright, *Resurrection,* pp. 144-46; Burnett, "Philo on Immortality," pp. 447-70; Tomas H. Tobin, *The Creation of Man: Philo and the History of Interpretation,* CBQMS 14 (Washington, D.C.: Catholic Biblical Association of America, 1983); Dieter Zeller, "The Life and Death of the Soul in Philo of Alexandria: The Use and Origin of a Metaphor," *SPhilo Annual* 7 (1995): 19-55, who provides a further bibliography on p. 20 n. 7; David T. Runia, *Philo of Alexandria and the Timaeus of Plato,* Philosophia Antiqua 44 (Leiden: Brill, 1986), pp. 330-38.

32. Cavallin, *Life after Death,* pp. 136-37; Zeller, "Life and Death," pp. 24-25.

33. An "apocalypse now and within," according to Zeller, "Life and Death," p. 38.

34. John J. Collins, "The Root of Immortality: Death in the Context of Jewish Wisdom," *HTR* 71 (1978): 177-92; idem, *Jewish Wisdom in the Hellenistic Age,* OTL (Louisville: Westminster John Knox, 1997), pp. 183-86; David Winston, "Wisdom of Solomon," *ABD* 6:120-27; Karina Martin Hogan, "The Exegetical Background of the 'Ambiguity of Death' in the Wisdom of Solomon," *JSJ* 30 (1999): 1-24; Puech, *Croyance,* 1:92-98; idem, "La conception de la vie future dans le livre de la 'Sagesse' et les manuscrits de la Mer Morte: Un aperçu," *RevQ* 21 (2003): 209-32; Maurice Gilbert, "Immortalité? Résurrection? Faut-il choisir?" in *Le Judaïsme à l'aube de l'ère chrétienne: XVIIIe congrès de l'association catholique française pour l'étude de la bible (Lyon, Septembre 1999)* (Paris: Cerf, 1999), pp. 271-97; Wright, *Resurrection,* pp. 162-75; Schürer, *History of the Jewish People,* 3:572; Cavallin, *Life after Death,* p. 127; Nickelsburg, *Resurrection,* p. 81; Matthias Delcor, "L'immortalité de l'âme dans le livre de la Sagesse et dans les documents de Qumrân," *NRTh* 77 (1955): 614-15.

ward death through torture, as if running the path toward immortality"
(ὥσπερ ἐπ' ἀθανασίας ὁδὸν τρέξοντες), inspired to courage by "the immortal soul of piety" (ὑπὸ ψυχῆς ἀθανάτου τῆς εὐσεβείας) within them"
(14:5-6).[35] Perhaps Josephus's descriptions are at least appropriate to sectors
of Judaism in which the philosophy of the soul was exclusively preferred to
the resurrection of the body. Even so, however, his account clearly distorts
the popularity of immortality in philosophically inclined sectors of Judaism by applying it universally to all sectors of Judaism.

Cosmic Immortalization

Where Josephus insists that Essenes and Pharisees envision the soul's travel
to cosmic habitations in the celestial or subterranean realms (*War* 2.153-58;
3.372-76; 7.343-49; *Ant.* 18.14), details may be roughly corroborated by contemporary Jewish writings. This includes both traditions that describe the
cosmic habitations of the dead and those that envision the transformation
of the dead into astral beings. Such beliefs are especially evident among
apocalyptic traditions.[36] Étienne Nodet and others have called special attention to *1 En.* 22 and 102–3 as examples of the kinds of beliefs that may have
motivated Josephus's descriptions.[37] Interpreters have further proposed that
the description of the fate of the wicked dead among the Essenes (*War* 2.155)
may find its counterpart in the *Rule of the Community* 4:11-14, conceivably an
"Essene" writing.[38] One might also conjecture that beliefs in "Paradise"

35. On athletic imagery see David A. deSilva, *4 Maccabees: Introduction and Com-
mentary on the Greek Text in Codex Sinaiticus*, Septuagint Commentary Series (Leiden:
Brill, 2006), pp. 244-45; U. Fischer, *Eschatologie und Jenseitserwartung im hellenistischen
Diasporajudentum*, BZNW 44 (Berlin: de Gruyter, 1978), pp. 98-99.

36. *Pss. Sol.* 3.12 ("those who fear the Lord shall rise up to eternal life, and their life
shall be in the light of the Lord, and it shall never end"); *4 Ezra* 7.97 ("their countenance
shall begin to shine like the sun . . . and they shall begin to resemble the light of the
stars"), *2 Bar.* 51.7-13 ("For they will live in the heights of that world and they will be like
the angels and be equal to the stars. . . . For the extents of Paradise will be spread out for
them, and to them will be shown the beauty of the majesty of the living beings under the
throne, as well as all the hosts of angels"); *1 En.* 104.2 ("now you shall shine like the lights
of heaven, and you shall be seen; and the windows of heaven shall be opened for you").

37. Étienne Nodet, *Baptême et resurrection: Le témoignage de Josèphe* (Paris: Cerf,
1999), p. 232; cf. also Schürer, *History of the Jewish People*, 3:541; P. Grelot, "L'Eschatologie
des Esséniens et le Livre d'Hénoch," *RevQ* 1 (1958-59): 113, 127; Puech, *Croyance*, 2:735-39.

38. John J. Collins, *Daniel: A Commentary*, Hermeneia (Minneapolis: Fortress,

might underlie the reference to the "Isles of the Blessed" in his description of the Essenes. The most primitive portions of the *History of the Rechabites* probably made similar connections between Paradise and the Isles nearer the time of Josephus.[39] Josephus also uses these cosmic motifs to preserve places of retribution for the wicked and reward for the virtuous, as do the apocalypses. Once again, it is possible that ideas of cosmic immortalization in apocalyptic thought underlie Josephus's own translation effort.

Even so, significant differences remain. Although *1 Enoch, 4 Ezra,* and *2 Baruch* can all refer to the travel of the "spirits" of the dead beyond the mortal body, they lack the thoroughgoing anthropological dualism between soul and body that is found in Josephus. Nor do these apocalypses disparage the body as a tomb-like prison of the soul, as Josephus's reports do. Nor does Josephus mention a specific "day of judgment" or "day of the Lord" when the spirits of the dead will finally be judged. Instead, he prefers to describe Jewish beliefs in ways that make them compatible with "the sons of Greece" and their mythological traditions on the Isles of the Blessed, Hades, and the fates of Sisyphus, Tantalus, Ixion, and Tityus in the underworld (*War* 2.153-58). Cosmic immortalization, after all, was not exclusive to Jewish apocalypticism; it was a shared tradition with the Greeks as well (Plato, *Phaed.* 113d-114c).

The Jewish Sects

The New Testament and Hippolytus seem to refute Josephus's claim that the immortality of the soul, rather than resurrection, provided a dividing line among the Jewish sects. Even so, Josephus's general portrait of the popularity of the afterlife among Pharisees and Essenes and its denial by Sadducees can still be affirmed by these other sources. According to the New Testament and Hippolytus, Pharisees affirmed the resurrection of the dead (or flesh) as one of their signature beliefs, while Sadducees defined themselves by their opposition to it.[40] While the Pharisees themselves left behind no self-

1993), p. 398: "Josephus has obviously Hellenized the Essenes for his Roman readers, but there is nonetheless a remarkable degree of correspondence between the two accounts" (of *War* 2.154 and the *Rule of the Community* 4:7-13).

39. James H. Charlesworth, "History of the Rechabites," *OTP* 2:443-61.

40. Mark 12:18-27; Matt 22:23-33; Luke 20:27-40; Acts 23:6-8; 24:15-17, 25; 26:6-8; Hippolytus, *Haer.* 9.26-29.

description of their beliefs on this point, it is hardly a coincidence that both Josephus and Paul, who aligned themselves with Pharisaism, equally affirm a positive hope in life after death.[41] Moreover, the later rabbis whose legal traditions had their origins in earlier Pharisaic interpretation also gravitate consistently toward a belief in resurrection of the dead.[42] In at least one case, denial of resurrection of the dead (תחית המתים) is even prohibited for all Israel (*m. Sanh.* 10:1). Other evidence thus affirms the general portrait that the afterlife had a very positive reception among Pharisees, even if it also highlights how starkly Josephus had distorted their views by suppressing any reference to the resurrection hope.

A similar scenario attends his description of Sadducean denial of the afterlife and postmortem judgment. The New Testament and Hippolytus again affirm the general portrait of Josephus. While Josephus's own description of the Sadducees on this point is unusually brief, the parallel passage in Hippolytus offers a much fuller rationale for their denial of the afterlife:

> And they deny that there is a resurrection not only of flesh, but also they suppose that the soul does not endure. It is only the life; and it is on account of this that man has been created. However, the idea of the resurrection is fulfilled in this: in dying and leaving behind children upon earth. But after death one expects to suffer nothing, either bad or good. For there will be a dissolution both of soul and body (λύσιν . . . καὶ ψυχῆς καὶ σώματος), and man passes into nonexistence, similarly also with the material of the animal creation. (*Haer.* 9.29)[43]

The Sadducean denial of the afterlife was by no means an isolated one, either in Judaism or among the Greeks.[44] Among Jewish wisdom traditions,

---

41. 1 Thess 4:13-18; 1 Cor 15; Phil 3:20-21.

42. *m. Ber.* 5:2; *b. Ber.* 60b; *m. Sanh.* 10:1; *y. Sanh.* 10.1; *b. Sanh.* 11.1; *Gen. Rab.* 14.5; *Lev. Rab.* 14.9.

43. Translation generally follows Alexander Roberts and James Donaldson, eds., *The Ante-Nicene Fathers*, vol. 5, *Fathers of the Third Century: Hippolytus, Cyprian, Caius, Novatian, Appendix*, rev. A. Coxe (1885-1887; repr., Peabody, Mass.: Hendrickson, 1999).

44. See esp. Job 14:1-22; *b. Sanh.* 11.1; *y. Sanh.* 10.1; Plato, *Phaed.* 70a, 86c, 88b; Epicurus, *Letter to Menoeceus* 124-27; *Key Doctrines* 19-21; Lucretius, *De rerum natura* 3.417-62, 624-33, 806-911, 966-1023, 1087-94; Sallust, *Bell. Cat.* 51.20; Pliny, *Nat.* 7.190; Seneca, *Tro.* 371-408; Lucian, *Alex.* 38, 47, 61; Tacitus, *Ann.* 18.1; Diogenes Laertius, *Lives* 10.124-25. On denial of an afterlife see Jocelyn M. C. Toynbee, *Death and Burial in the Roman World*, Aspects of Greek and Roman Life (London: Thames & Hudson, 1971), pp. 34-35; Cumont, *Af-*

both Job (14:1-22) and Ecclesiastes (9:1-12) seem to question the very possibility of a blessed afterlife. As Émile Puech has commented, the monumental Tomb of Jason in Jerusalem may further attest to a denial of a blessed afterlife among the priestly aristocratic classes with whom the Sadducees aligned themselves. In an Aramaic inscription upon the tomb, the burial site has become the "eternal dwelling" of the family, thus accentuating death's finality and the collective unity that the family enjoys in their final resting place.[45] Again, there is strong evidence among other writings that the general portrait of Josephus is accurate regarding Sadducean denial of the afterlife, even if he has neglected to mention their specific opposition to the resurrection of the body. Josephus's description of the Sadducees reminds the modern reader that a positive affirmation of the afterlife was certainly popular in Judaism; however, it was by no means universal, and it could even become a point of controversy among various parties and groups.[46]

A similar verdict may rest upon his portrait of the Essenes. If the Dead Sea Scrolls are viewed as evidence for Essene beliefs, they generally affirm a positive reception of the afterlife, but they do not directly corroborate the specific language, ideas, and concepts found in Josephus's reports. The predominant view of the future life that emerges from the study of Qumran sectarian literature is that the men of the community worship in the presence of angels in a heavenly existence where eschatological life is presently realized in the ritually pure worship of the covenanters.[47] Moreover, escha-

---

terlife in Roman Paganism, pp. 6-12; Richmond Lattimore, *Themes in Greek and Latin Epitaphs,* Illinois Studies in Language and Literature 1 (Urbana: University of Illinois Press, 1942), pp. 74-81; Émile Puech, "Inscriptions funéraires palestiniennes: Tombeau de Jason et ossuaires," *RB* 90 (1983): 483-85; idem, *Croyance,* 1:202-12; K. Strodach, *The Philosophy of Epicurus: Letters, Doctrines, and Parallel Passages from Lucretius* (Chicago: Northwestern University Press, 1963), pp. 58-60; Nilsson, *Geschichte der griechischen Religion,* 2:251-53; C. Segal, *Lucretius on Death and Anxiety: Poetry and Philosophy in De Rerum Natura* (Princeton: Princeton University Press, 1990), pp. 178-86.

45. Puech, "Inscriptions funéraires palestiniennes," pp. 483-85.

46. Setzer, "Jews, Christians, and Pagans," pp. 155-75.

47. 1QS 11:7-9; 1QH 7:17-25; 11:19-23; 14:29-35; 19:10-23; 1QM 12:1-5; 16:15–17:9; 18:6-15. See further John J. Collins, *Apocalypticism in the Dead Sea Scrolls,* Literature of the Dead Sea Scrolls (New York: Routledge, 1997), pp. 110-29; David Aune, *The Cultic Setting of Realized Eschatology,* NovTSup 28 (Leiden: Brill, 1972); Hermann Lichtenberger, "Auferstehung in den Qumranfunden," in *Auferstehung-Resurrection,* pp. 85-88; Heinz-Wolfgang Kuhn, *Enderwartung und gegenwärtiges Heil: Untersuchungen zu den Gemeindeliedern von Qumran mit einem Anhang über Eschatologie und Gegenwart in der Verkündigung Jesu,* SUNT 4 (Göttingen: Vandenhoeck & Ruprecht, 1966), pp. 44-78.

tological punishment and reward are strongly attested (1QS 4:11-14). There is no evidence, however, that this faith was grounded in the kind of anthropological dualism attested in Josephus's description of the Essenes and their belief in the preexistence of souls. Other writings, probably attracted to Qumran from a broader circulation, mention a more explicit hope in resurrection of the dead. The *Messianic Apocalypse* (4Q521) attests expectation of a future resurrection, not the philosophical anthropology that Josephus cites.[48] Moreover, *Pseudo-Ezekiel* (4Q385-388, 391) envisions a reconstitution of physical bodies based upon an exegesis of Ezek 37.[49] Nor does Hippolytus affirm Josephus's description of the Essenes: his Essenes hold fast to the doctrine of the resurrection (*Haer.* 9.26-27), not Josephus's immortality of the soul. The Qumran community further preserved numerous copies of both Daniel and *1 Enoch,* writings that yield crucial sources of reflection on life after death; and it is possible that readers in the community may have interpreted earlier scriptures as referring to some type of life after death, as the author of *Pseudo-Ezekiel* did.[50] The community's actual thinking on this question is likely to be found in a mixed synthesis of beliefs attested in classic sectarian works (1QS, 1QH, 1QM), popular writings gradually adopted from a wider milieu (4Q521; 4Q385-388, 391), and earlier authoritative literature like Daniel and *1 Enoch*. Again, these writings broadly affirm Josephus's general point that the afterlife had a popular reception among Essenes; yet they hardly support in any conceptual detail Josephus's actual description.[51]

48. Puech, *Croyance,* 2:627-92; idem, *Qumrân Grotte 4.XVIII: Textes Hébreux (4Q521-4Q528, 4Q576-4Q579),* DJD 25 (Oxford: Clarendon, 1998), pp. 1-36.

49. Devorah Dimant, "Resurrection, Restoration and Time-Curtailing in Qumran, Early Judaism and Christianity," *RevQ* 19 (1999-2000): 527-48; idem, *Qumran Cave 4.XXI: Parabiblical Texts, Part 4: Pseudo-Prophetic Texts,* DJD 30 (Oxford: Clarendon, 2001), pp. 7-88.

50. The interpretation of Ezek 37 as a text on resurrection of the dead was a popular trend elsewhere in early Jewish and Christian literature (*Liv. Pro.* 3.11-12; *Gen. Rab.* 14.5; *Lev. Rab.* 14.9; Tertullian, *Res.* 29-30; cf. 4 Macc 18:17).

51. As treated in other scholarship, see Puech, *Croyance,* esp. vol. 2; idem, "Messianism, Resurrection, and Eschatology," in *The Community of the Renewed Covenant: The Notre Dame Symposium on the Dead Sea Scrolls,* ed. E. Ulrich and J. VanderKam, Christianity and Judaism in Antiquity 10 (Notre Dame, Ind.: University of Notre Dame Press, 1994), pp. 234-56; Chaim Rabin, *Qumran Studies,* Scripta Judaica 2 (London: Oxford University Press, 1957), p. 73; Kurt Schubert, "Das Problem der Auferstehungshoffnung in den Qumrantexten und in der frührabbinischen Literatur," *WZKM* 56 (1960): 154-67; Sanders, *Judaism: Practice and Belief,* p. 302; Matthias Delcor, *Les Hymnes de Qumran (Hodayot): Texte hébreu, introduction, traduction, commentaire* (Paris: Letouzey et Ané, 1962), pp. 180-84; Geza Vermes, *The Complete Dead Sea Scrolls in English* (New York: Pen-

Other Features

In spite of his grave hellenization of Jewish thought, Josephus does avoid certain radically Greek notions. Animal reincarnation, for example, is apparently avoided in his description of Jewish beliefs.[52] Where Josephus alludes to the "revolution [of the ages]" (*Ag. Ap.* 2.218-19; cf. *War* 3.372), a Stoic conflagration of the cosmos may influence his thinking;[53] and yet he presents a final culmination of the ages more akin to Jewish apocalypticism than to the "eternal return" of Stoicism.[54] One even senses that some of Josephus's de-

---

guin, 1997), pp. 88-89; Wright, *Resurrection*, p. 27; Segal, *History of the Afterlife*, pp. 298-303; James VanderKam and Peter Flint, *The Meaning of the Dead Sea Scrolls: Their Significance for Understanding the Bible, Judaism, Jesus and Christianity* (San Francisco: HarperSanFrancisco, 2002), pp. 245-46; C. D. Elledge, *The Bible and the Dead Sea Scrolls*, SBLABS 14 (Atlanta: Society of Biblical Literature, 2005), pp. 126-28; idem, *Life after Death*, pp. 19-26, 57-63; Stephen Goranson, "Essenes," in *The Oxford Encyclopedia of Archaeology in the Near East*, ed. E. M. Meyers (New York: Oxford University Press, 1997), 2:268-69; Collins, *Apocalypticism and the Dead Sea Scrolls*, p. 110-29; George W. E. Nickelsburg, "Resurrection," in *Encyclopedia of the Dead Sea Scrolls*, ed. L. Schiffman and J. Vanderkam, 2 vols. (Oxford: Oxford University Press, 2000), 2:764-67; Robert B. Laurin, "The Question of Immortality in the Qumran 'Hodayot,'" *JSS* 3 (1958): 344-55; Grelot, "L'Eschatologie des Esséniens," pp. 113-31; Martin Hengel, *Judaism and Hellenism: Studies in Their Encounter in Palestine during the Early Hellenistic Period*, trans. John Bowden, 2 vols. (Philadelphia: Fortress, 1974), 1:196-202; J. van der Ploeg, "The Belief in Immortality in the Writings of Qumran," *BO* 18 (1961): 118-24; Cavallin, *Life after Death*, pp. 60-68; Jan N. Bremmer, "The Resurrection between Zarathustra and Jonathan Z. Smith," *NTT* 50 (1996): 89-107; Harry Sysling, *Tehsiyyat Ha-Metim: The Resurrection of the Dead in the Palestinian Targums of the Pentateuch and Parallel Traditions in Classical Rabbinic Literature*, TSAJ 57 (Tübingen: Mohr Siebeck, 1996), pp. 75-77; Roland Bergmeier, "Die drei jüdischen Schulrichtungen nach Josephus und Hippolyt von Rom: zu den Paralleltexten Josephus, B.J. 2,119-166 und Hippolyt, Haer. IX 18,2–29,4," *JSJ* 34 (2003): 443-70.

52. Plato, *Tim.* 42b-c; 91d; *Phaedr.* 249a-b; *Resp.* 10.620d; *Phaed.* 81e-82a. Jaap Mansfeld notes that it is missing, as well, from Philo: "Heraclitus, Empedocles, and Others in a Middle Platonist Cento in Philo of Alexandria," *VC* 39 (1985): 135, 139.

53. *SVF* 1.522; 2.811; 2.624; Diogenes Laertius, *Lives* 7.156-57; Seneca, *Consolatio ad Marciam* 24-26; Ioannes ab Arnim, *Stoicorum Veterum Fragmenta*, 4 vols. (Leipzig: Teubner, 1905). On this possibility see G. W. Trompf, *The Idea of Historical Recurrence in Western Thought* (Berkeley: University of California Press, 1979), pp. 164-70; Bergmeier, *Essener-Berichte*, p. 64.

54. Elledge, *Life after Death*, pp. 110-16; Mason, *Flavius Josephus on the Pharisees*, pp. 166-67; Hengel, "Das Begräbnis Jesu bei Paulus und die leibliche Auferstehung aus dem Grabe," 162. Perhaps one may compare the attitudes of Origen and Irenaeus toward

scriptions are far more radically and self-consciously hellenized than others. The description of Jewish beliefs in *Against Apion,* for example, is a relatively simple profession of hope that God will grant those who have died for the laws a new existence at the revolution of the ages (2.118-19). This description does not explicitly mention the immortality of the soul and lacks much of the stylized mythological and philosophical ornamentation of Josephus's oration against suicide (*War* 3.372-76), the Masada oration (7.343-49, 351-57), and his description of the Essenes (2.153-58). These limitations to the degree of hellenization suggest that Josephus was gilding over Jewish beliefs with a respectable veneer of Greek thought — and yet even in this very process, his portrait of Judaism still remained somewhat resistant to select features of Hellenistic afterlife conceptions. Indeed, one may perhaps observe in this case that Josephus's hellenization of Judaism is equally characterized by a judaization of Hellenism.

Apology, Ethnography, and Sources

Why would Josephus have remained so insistent about clothing Jewish beliefs about the afterlife in the raiment of Greek philosophy? By his own confession, Josephus writes with the constant awareness that his histories will "go among the Greeks" (*Ant.* 16.174; cf. *War* 1.16); he hopes that "the whole Greek-speaking world will find" his work "worthy of attention" (*Ant.* 1.5-7);[55] and he prides himself on his success in rendering "the learning of the Jews" to all the Greek world: "And I am so bold as to say, now I have so completely perfected the work I proposed to myself to do that no other person, whether he were a Jew or a foreigner, had he ever so great an inclination to it, could so accurately deliver these accounts to the Greeks as is done in these books" (*Ant.* 20.262).[56]

Claiming to balance "the learning of the Jews" with "the learning of the Greeks," Josephus legitimates the methods of his historiography by presenting himself as an erudite cultural translator who could successfully portray Judaism in a manner worthy of the best of Greek and Roman cultural traditions (*Ant.* 20.263-64). With these goals in mind, it is little wonder that

---

Stoic eternal return; see Carsten Peter Thiede, "A Pagan Reader of 2 Peter: Cosmic Conflagration in 2 Peter 3 and the Octavius of Minucius Felix," *JSNT* 26 (1986): 85-87.

55. Translation by Thackeray, LCL.

56. Translation by Whiston.

he has rendered some of the more obscure Jewish beliefs, like the afterlife, in the familiar idiom of Greek philosophical reflection on the soul.

This *interpretatio graeca* was further advantageous since it presented the Jews themselves as possessing a sophisticated and ancient philosophical culture that was analogous to Hellenism.[57] As is well known, the descriptions of the sects even resort to a "three school" typology, allowing the Jewish Pharisees, Essenes, and Sadducees to be compared with the Greek philosophical schools of the Stoics, Pythagoreans, and Epicureans.[58] Josephus makes such comparisons explicit in his own writings, where he directly compares the Pharisees with Stoics (*Life* 12) and the Essenes with Pythagoreans (*Ant.* 15.371).[59] Thus it is entirely appropriate for him to distinguish Jewish beliefs on the afterlife among the three schools, since their Greek counterparts themselves differed considerably from each other on that topic as well.[60]

These methods of cultural translation were not new; instead, they had their precedents in earlier methods of Greek and Roman ethnography, which described the *nomima barbarika* ("barbarian customs") of the ancient peoples whom the Greeks encountered through their imperial conquests. The conceptual distortions in Josephus's account of the afterlife fit well within the larger contexts of ancient ethnography, in which the Greeks could transform the customs of ancient peoples into a fantastic utopia of noble Hellenistic ideals or disfigure them into a dystopia of alien ignorance and corruption.[61]

57. Collins, *Daniel,* p. 398; Segal, *History of the Afterlife,* p. 302: "Josephus was trying to characterize a basically Semitic group to a pagan, philosophically trained readership"; Hengel, "Begräbnis Jesu bei Paulus," p. 162: "Dass er daneben auch einfach von der Hoffnung auf Unsterblichkeit sprechen kann, ist schlicht eine Angleichung an den Verständnishorizont der von ihm erhofften mehr oder weniger gebildeten heidnischen Leserschaft"; Puech, *Croyance,* 2:747-48, 781, 795.

58. Steve Mason, *Josephus and the New Testament,* 2nd ed. (Peabody, Mass.: Hendrickson, 2003), pp. 133-34; Goranson, "Posidonius, Strabo," pp. 295-98.

59. Justin Taylor, *Pythagoreans and Essenes: Structural Parallels,* Collection de la Revue des études juives 32 (Leuven: Peeters, 2004).

60. Elledge, *Life after Death,* pp. 103-5.

61. Robert Drews, *The Greek Accounts of Eastern History,* Center for Hellenic Studies (Cambridge: Harvard University Press, 1973); Sarah C. Humphreys, *Anthropology and the Greeks* (London: Routledge & Kegan Paul, 1978); K. E. Müller, *Geschichte der antiken Ethnographie und ethnologischen Theoriebildung: Von den Anfängen bis auf die byzantinischen Historiographen,* part 2; Studien zur Kulturkunde 52 (Wiesbaden, 1980); François Hartog, *The Mirror of Herodotus: The Representation of the Other in the Writing of History,* trans. J. Lloyd (Berkeley: University of California Press, 1988); Edith Hall, *Inventing the Barbarian* (Oxford: Clarendon, 1989); Albrecht Dihle, *Die Griechen und die*

Some ethnographic portraits of the Egyptians, Gauls, Germans, and Jews even describe the afterlife beliefs of these peoples in hellenizing and perhaps even Pythagoreanizing conceptions. Josephus was, therefore, hardly alone in ascribing Greco-Roman beliefs like Pythagoreanism and the immortality of the soul to other ancient peoples. Herodotus did so when describing the Egyptians (*Hist.* 2.123), Posidonius (Diodorus Siculus, *Libr.* 5.28.5-6) and Caesar (*Bell. gall.* 6.14) when describing the Gauls, Strabo (*Geogr.* 4.4.4) and Appian (*Gall.* 1.3) when describing the Germans, and Tacitus (*Hist.* 5.5) when describing the Jews themselves.[62] Posidonius even explicitly attributes Pythagorean beliefs to the Gauls; and Herodotus seems to hint at the theory that Pythagorean thought had its origins in Egyptian wisdom.

Table 1: The afterlife among the *barbaroi* in ancient historiography

Source	Group	Terminology for Afterlife
Herodotus (*Hist.* 2.123)	Egyptians	"the Egyptians are also the first who reported the doctrine that the soul of man is immortal, and that when the body dies, the soul enters into another creature which chances then to be coming to the birth (ὡς ἀνθρώπου ψυχὴ ἀθάνατος ἐστί, τοῦ σώματος δὲ καταφθίνοντος ἐς ἄλλο ζῷον αἰεὶ γινόμενον ἐσδύεται), and when it has gone the round of all the creatures of land and sea and of the air, it enters again into a human body as it comes to birth; and that it makes this round in a period of three thousand years. This doctrine certain Hellenes adopted, some earlier and some later, as if it were of their own invention, and of these men I know the names but I abstain from recording them."[63]
Posidonius (Diodurus Siculus, *Libr.* 5.28.5-6)	Gauls	"For the teaching of Pythagoras has strength among them, that the souls of humans are immortal and throughout the years ordained they come to life again, as the soul descends into a different body" (ἐνισχύει γὰρ παρ᾽ αὐτοῖς ὁ Πυθαγόρου λόγος, ὅτι τὰς ψυχὰς τῶν ἀνθρώπων ἀθανάτους εἶναι συμβέβηκε καὶ δι᾽ ἐτῶν ὡρισμένων πάλιν βιοῦν, εἰς ἕτερον σῶμα τῆς ψυχῆς εἰσδυομένης).
Caesar (*Bell. gall.* 6.14)	Gauls	"They wish to inculcate this as one of their leading tenets, that souls do not become extinct *(non interire animas)*, but pass after death from one body to another

Fremden (Munich: Beck, 1994); Wilfried Nippel, *Griechen, Barbaren und "Wilde": Alte Geschichte und Sozialanthropologie* (Frankfurt am Main: Fischer, 1990).

62. Elledge, *Life after Death*, pp. 50, 56, 60, 98, 144.

63. Translation by Macaulay.

		(sed ab aliis post mortem transpire ad alios), and they think that men by this tenet are in a great degree excited to valor, the fear of death being disregarded."
Strabo (*Geogr.* 4.4.4)	Germans	"Now they [Druids] and others claim that souls and the cosmos are incorruptible" (ἀφθάρτους δὲ λέγουσι καὶ οὗτοι [Δρυΐδαι] καὶ ἄλλοι τὰς ψυχὰς καὶ τὸν κόσμον).
Appian (*Gall.* 1.3)	Germans	"And they are contemptuous of death through their hope of revivification" (καὶ θανάτου καταφρονηταὶ δι᾽ ἐλπίδα ἀναβιώσεως).
Tacitus (*Hist.* 5.5)	Jews	"They [Jews] think the souls of those killed by battle or torture are immortal: thus, (their) love of procreating, and (their) contempt of death" *(Animosque proelio aut suppliciis peremptorum aeternos putant: hinc generandi amor et moriendi contemptus).*

In describing Jewish piety, Josephus writes within the same tradition of ethnography, which found the best Greek equivalent available for describing the customs of the various *barbaroi* of the ancient world. Since they are also attested in Tacitus, contempt for death and hope in immortality seem to have become familiar ethnographic stereotypes about the Jews by the late first century CE, if not earlier (cf. [Pseudo-] Hecataeus 190-92). In his apology, Josephus maximizes such ethnographic stereotypes about the Jews and other *barbaroi* to his full advantage. What is remarkable about Josephus in this regard is that he, an insider to Judaism, has employed the ethnographic methods of Greco-Roman outsiders, in order to characterize the beliefs of his own people.

Finally, it is equally important to recognize that portions of this ethnographic portrait of Jewish beliefs may already have been available to Josephus in the form of earlier sources for the three Jewish sects. Stephen Goranson, for example, has shown that Pliny's well-known description of the Essenes (*Nat.* 5.73) probably derived from Marcus V Agrippa, who composed a commentary on Judea during the reign of Herod the Great.[64] Josephus too may have utilized earlier sources on the Jewish sects. In the case of the *Jewish War,* the description strikingly parallels, with certain occasional deviation, Hippolytus's description of Pharisees, Sadducees, and Essenes. This includes roughly parallel accounts of the afterlife. A brief citation of their mutual versions of the Pharisees provides an accessible illustration (see table 2).

---

64. Goranson, "Posidonius, Strabo," pp. 295-98.

Table 2: Josephus and Hippolytus on the Pharisees

Josephus (War 2.163)	Hippolytus (Haer. 9.28)
And while every soul is incorruptible, only the soul of the good migrates into a different body, but the souls of the wicked are chastised by everlasting punishment.	These likewise acknowledge that there is a resurrection of flesh (σαρκὸς ἀνάστασιν), and that the soul is immortal (ψυχὴν ἀθάνατον), and that there will be a judgment and conflagration (κρίσιν ἐσομένην καὶ ἐκπύρωσιν), and that the righteous will be imperishable (ἀφθάρτους), but that the wicked will be punished forever in unquenchable fire (εἰσαεὶ κολασθήσεσθαι ἐν πυρὶ ἀσβέστῳ).

The following theories have arisen to clarify the possible relationships between the descriptions of the Jewish sects in Josephus and Hippolytus:

1. *An independent source:* Josephus inherited most of his larger report on the Jewish sects (*War* 2.119-66) from an earlier ethnographic source, as is attested by Hippolytus's independent use of the same account (*Haer.* 9.18-29). This earlier account was either Hellenistic-Jewish in origin or possibly even pagan.[65] Nicolaus of Damascus has been viewed as a strong possibility, when attempting to specify the original source.[66]

2. *Multiple sources:* Josephus inherited multiple sources for each of his reports on the sects and artfully reworked them into their current forms. In this sense, the descriptions are to be considered an eclectic composite of multiple sources, brought together by Josephus himself. Hippolytus, in turn, depended upon Josephus, editing his earlier account.[67]

---

65. Moore, "Fate and Free Will," pp. 371-84; Hölscher, "Josephus," 9:1949; Kaufmann Kohler, "Essenes," in *The Jewish Encyclopedia: A Descriptive Record of the History, Religion, Literature, and Customs of the Jewish People from the Earliest Times,* ed. I. Singer, 12 vols. (New York: Ktav, 1901), 5:224-32; Matthew Black, "The Account of the Essenes in Hippolytus and Josephus," in *The Background of the New Testament and Its Eschatology,* ed. W. Davies and D. Daube (Cambridge: Cambridge University Press, 1956), pp. 172-75; Smith, "Description of the Essenes," pp. 273-313; Ben Zion Wacholder, *Nicolaus of Damascus,* University of California Publications in History 75 (Berkeley: University of California Press, 1962), pp. 70-72; John J. Collins, "Essenes," *ABD* 2:620; Puech, *Croyance,* 2:714-26; Elledge, *Life after Death,* pp. 82-99.

66. Moore, "Fate and Free Will," pp. 383-84; Schwartz, "Josephus and Nicolaus," pp. 157-71; Wacholder, *Nicolaus of Damascus,* pp. 70-72.

67. Bergmeier, *Essener-Berichte,* pp. 114-21; "Die drei jüdischen Schulrichtungen nach Josephus und Hippolyt," pp. 443-70. For arguments that Hippolytus depended upon Josephus and not an independent source, see Burchard, "Die Essener bei Hippolyt," pp. 1-41.

3. *Josephus's own composition:* If Josephus made use of sources at all, this use was far more limited than positions 1-2 will allow. The descriptions in their present form are predominantly his own composition, especially in the report on the Essenes (*War* 2.119-61); and they reflect ideals attested elsewhere in his writings.[68]

A similar source-critical problem is encountered in the correspondences between Philo (*Prob.* 75) and Josephus's description of the Essenes in the *Antiquities* (18.20; cf. 13.171-72), perhaps suggesting that here too Josephus may have utilized earlier sources.[69]

While these source-critical problems remain unresolved in contemporary scholarship, the relationships between the accounts of Josephus and Hippolytus strongly urge the possibility that Josephus could have been working from earlier ethnographic sources about the Jews, sources that he very likely enhanced even further to accentuate the Jewish hope in immortality. Josephus may have been so inspired by what he found in such earlier sources that he broadened the afterlife motif in the major speeches of the *Jewish War* and other accounts in his apologetic portrait of Judaism. If the afterlife had been found in earlier ethnography about the Jews, it provided a stable and effective basis for Josephus's philosophical characterization of his own people to pagan audiences.

As Josephus further developed what he may well have found in earlier literary sources, he seems to have incorporated additional mythological, philosophical, and noble death traditions from Greco-Roman culture. Josephus preserves traditional mythic terminology for the cosmic zones inhabited by the dead, such as "the Isles of the Blessed" (*War* 2.156), "Hades" (2.156, 165; 3.375), and "Lethe" (6.48). Yet one can be even more specific about Josephus's mythological sources when he directly mentions the infernal punishments of Sisyphus, Tantalus, Ixion, and Tityus (2.156), a clear hint that Josephus has in mind the mythological "descent into the underworld" tradition found in the *Odyssey* (11) and other sources.[70] There are

68. Mason, *Flavius Josephus on the Pharisees,* pp. 156-70; idem, "What Josephus Says," pp. 423-55; Williams, "Josephus or Nicolaus," pp. 43-58; idem, "Josephus and Authorship," pp. 207-21.

69. Goranson, "Posidonius, Strabo," pp. 295-98; Argall, "Hellenistic Jewish Source," pp. 75-91.

70. On the "Isles of the Blessed," see further Homer, *Od.* 4.561-69; Hesiod, *Op.* 167-73; Pindar, *Ol.* 2.68-80; J. H. Charlesworth, "History of the Rechabites," *OTP* 2:443-61. On "Lethe" see Plato, *Resp.* 621a; Aristophanes, *Ran.* 186; Lucian, *Dial. Mort.* 13.6; Pausanias,

also strong resonances between Josephus's descriptions and philosophical sources on immortality, as illustrated in Pythagorean, Orphic, Platonic, and other traditions.[71] Legends regarding the noble deaths of philosophical figures like Socrates and faithful Jewish ancestors also provided an abundant reservoir of heroism, which Josephus employs with unrivaled flair.[72] He even utilized the exotic tales of self-immolation among the Indian sages (*War* 7.351-57) that had fascinated the Greeks and Romans for centuries.[73] On the verge of their own death for the laws, Jews faithfully declare their hope in the soul's immortality and final justice, rising to an equal level of philosophical heroism. While the impressive range of these traditions has sometimes prompted scholars to attribute their usage to literary assistants,[74] there is in the end nothing that disqualifies Josephus's own hand from having composed this sophisticated *interpretatio graeca*.[75] Perhaps it is here that Josephus rises to some of his greatest rhetorical achievements as apologist and historian.

Value

Provided that we are able to see through the distortions of his ethnographic and apologetic methods, Josephus should still be regarded as an important

---

Descr. 9.39.8; Virgil, *Aen.* 6.714. On the punishments of Tityos, Tantalus, Ixion, and Sisyphus, see *Od.* 11.576-600; Ovid, *Metam.* 4.458-63; 10.41-44; 13.26; Pindar, *Pyth.* 2.21; 4.90; Aeschylus, *Eum.* 717; Hyginus, *Fabulae* 55; Apollonius Rhodius, *Argon.* 1.759; Pseudo-Plato, *Axiochus* 371a-372. On the divinization (daimonization) of heroes, see Aeschylus, *Pers.* 620; Euripides, *Alc.* 1002; Vergil, *Aen.* 6.129-31; Plutarch, *Rom.* 28.4-8; *Numa* 2.3.

71. On Plato, Pythagoras, and the Stoics in Josephus, see *Ag. Ap.* 1.14, 162-64; 2.14, 161-68, 222-25, 255-61; *Ant.* 15.371; *Life* 12. On possible Platonic influences on Josephus's portrait of the afterlife, see *Apol.* 40c, 40e-41d; *Phaed.* 58e, 62c, 63c, 64c, 66a-d, 67a-d, 70c-76e, 81e, 113d-114c. See also Cicero, *Resp.* 6.13-16; *Tusc.* 1.72; and Seneca, *Consolatio ad Marciam* 24.5; 25.3; 26.6-7.

72. Plato, *Apology*; *Phaedo*; Xenophon, *Cyr.* 8.7.17-21; Cicero, *Tusc.* 96; 2 Macc 7; *4 Maccabees*. See further Sievers, "Josephus and the Afterlife," pp. 20-43; and van Henten, "Some Remarks," pp. 124-41.

73. Arrian, *Anab.* 7.1-3; Aelian, *Var. hist.* 2.41, 5.6; Philo, *Prob.* 14; Plutarch, *Alex.* 69; Strabo, *Geogr.* 15.4; Diodorus Siculus, *Libr.* 17.107; Athenaeus, *Deipn.* 10.437; Lucian, *Peregr.* 25; Cicero, *Tusc.* 2.52, 5.76-79; *Div.* 1.47, 65; Valerius Maximus, *Mem.* 1.8, est. 10.

74. Bergmeier, *Essener-Berichte*, pp. 62-63.

75. Mason, "What Josephus Says," pp. 423-55; Elledge, *Life after Death*, pp. 98-99, 126-27.

witness to the popularity and vitality of the afterlife in early Judaism. Attention to his methods of hellenization and apologetic ethnography requires a reading of Josephus that takes place on two levels. First, when utilizing these passages, one must always remain conscious of the surface level of Josephus's apologetic portrait in which Jewish beliefs have been translated into analogous Hellenistic conceptions. Second, one may therefore more fully appreciate the deeper level of the original forms of Jewish belief that have motivated his elaborate translation effort. In these cases, Josephus presents the Jews to Greeks and Romans as possessing a noble philosophic culture whose beliefs were not so alien to Hellenism, while still remaining as accurate as he could afford to be to the underlying forms of Jewish piety he sought to document.

When reading Josephus on both of these levels, the value and limitations of his testimonies are more fully clarified. One may justifiably read Josephus as maintaining that a confident belief in some kind of life after death characterized most of Judaism. Not only does he portray two of the three leading philosophical sects as confidently affirming the afterlife, but in *Against Apion* he even extends the popularity of the belief to Judaism in general as an expression of its willingness to die nobly for its ancestral laws (2.218-19). One may certainly cross-examine this portrait of the high popularity of the afterlife in Judaism; yet one must equally come to terms with the historical portrait Josephus paints: he regards some form of afterlife as exceedingly popular in multiple sectors of Judaism, and indeed, within Judaism in general. While allowing for the very diverse conceptual expressions that the afterlife actually took in Jewish thought, one can still appreciate their very broad collective appeal in first-century Palestine as Josephus treats the matter. This breadth of appeal further anticipates the favorable reception that the afterlife would receive in both the nascent church and rabbinic Judaism, whose religious traditions were intensively shaped by the very first-century Palestinian context that Josephus describes.

Josephus explicitly associates the afterlife in several cases with Jewish legal piety. Hope in the afterlife was integrally related to faithful adherence to ancestral legal practices and represented the future destiny, especially, of those who died for the laws (*War* 1.650; 2.153-58; cf. 7.351-57; *Ag. Ap.* 2.218-19).[76] This relationship was highly traditional by the time Josephus himself

---

76. On "death for the laws" elsewhere in Josephus, see *War* 2.6, 151-53, 174, 196-98; *Ant.* 12.279-84; 15.280-82; 17.158-59; 18.59, 263-68; *Ag. Ap.* 1.42-43, 191; 2.146, 294. For further comment see C. Gerber, *Ein Bild des Judentums für Nichtjuden von Flavius Josephus:*

wrote. It had already been a central feature of 2 Maccabees, where the dying martyrs repeatedly affirm that physical resurrection will be their destiny precisely because they have died "for the laws" (7:9, 23). Moreover, Daniel's own resurrection prophecy assumes a very similar connection between heavenly exaltation and the faithful deaths of the wise ones "who turned the multitudes to righteousness" (12:3), while suffering death "by sword and flame" (11:33-35).[77] While Josephus adds little that is new to this very traditional relationship between the afterlife and legal piety, he certainly offers new insights into just how popular this traditional conception remained well into the first century CE. Josephus yields a new level of appreciation for the role that the afterlife continued to play in popular Jewish patriotism for adherence to ancestral laws.

In several cases, Josephus associates hope in immortality with ideologies that praised fidelity to God over loyalty to empire. The sociopolitical dimensions of the afterlife have become the focus of several recent studies.[78] From Josephus's point of view, the afterlife provided a powerful appeal to groups who placed themselves at odds with the official political and religious settlement of Roman Palestine. Two teachers defied Herod's policies within the temple precincts with the motivation of a blessed afterlife (War 1.650); the Essenes endured their Roman persecutors through hope in immortality (2.153-58); and Jews in general vowed to die for the laws with hope in a final reward after death (Ag. Ap. 2.218-19). The quintessential icon of revolutionary ideology, Eleazar (son of Jairus) himself, defies the final victory of the Romans through the noble death and hope in immortality (War 7.343-49, 351-57). These episodes from Josephus provide significant insights into how the hope of a blessed afterlife motivated various religio-political movements to offer death-defying resistance to the political authorities of their day. Hope in the afterlife was, therefore, hardly a pious sense of resignation to the existing conditions of an unjust world. Instead, in the hands of some groups, it became a powerful inspiration to offer one's life in resistance and revolt. By claiming that their fallen compatriots now enjoyed a blessed afterlife, Jews further acknowledged a higher norm of divine justice that vindicated those

---

Untersuchungen zu seiner Schrift Contra Apionem, AGJU 40 (Leiden: Brill, 1997), pp. 281-83; Schröder, Väterlichen Gesetze, pp. 35-36; Hengel, Zealots, pp. 258-59; Horsley and Hanson, Bandits, Prophets, and Messiahs, pp. 182-85.

77. Collins, Daniel, pp. 391-93.

78. Wright, Resurrection, pp. 138, 231-33, 728-31; Segal, History of the Afterlife, pp. 315-17; Setzer, Resurrection of the Body, pp. 47-52.

who had died unjustly at the hands of those who held power. Josephus's comments on the Jews are consistent with pagan sources that also regarded the afterlife as possessing a powerful social utility for military heroism.[79]

Josephus himself is a valuable experiment in the state of affairs regarding belief in resurrection in the generation after the temple destruction. In the very generation in which physical resurrection was becoming increasingly standardized in Judaism and Christianity, Josephus has completely veiled any explicit reference to this belief from his Greek and Roman audience. While Judaism could certainly combine immortality of the soul together with physical resurrection of the dead, it is equally important to recognize that crucial conceptual differences also separated these two popular beliefs about the afterlife.[80] As Jon Levenson comments,

> The expectation of an eschatological resurrection coexists easily with immortality so long as the latter is defined as the state of those who have died and await their restoration into embodiment, that is, into full human existence. . . . But if immortality is defined in connection with an indestructible core of the self that death cannot threaten (and may even liberate), then resurrection and immortality are at odds. . . . Whereas history in the classical Jewish vision of resurrection will culminate in God's supernatural triumph over death, this second idea of immortality assumes a very different scenario: individuals at various times and without relationship to each other quietly shed their perishable casings to continue in an unbroken communion with their benevolent creator.[81]

79. See Polybius 6.56.12; Caesar, *Bell. Gall.* 6.14; Diodorus Siculus, *Libr.* 34-35 2.47; Strabo, *Geogr.* 1.19-20; Plutarch, *Mor.* 1104a-b; *Numa* 8; Appian, *Gall.* 1.3; Tacitus, *Hist.* 5.5.

80. Nickelsburg, *Resurrection,* pp. 219-26; Segal, *History of the Afterlife,* pp. 704-18; James Barr, *The Garden of Eden and the Hope of Immortality* (Minneapolis: Fortress, 1993), pp. 94-116; James H. Charlesworth, "Where Does the Concept of Resurrection Appear and How Do We Know That?" in *Resurrection: The Origins and Future of a Biblical Doctrine,* ed. J. Charlesworth et al., Faith and Scholarship Colloquies (New York: T&T Clark, 2006), pp. 1-21; Hengel, *Judaism and Hellenism,* 1:196-202; idem, *Jews, Greeks and Barbarians: Aspects of the Hellenization of Judaism in the Pre-Christian Period,* trans. J. Bowden (Philadelphia: Fortress, 1980), pp. 124-25; Gilbert, "Immortalité?" pp. 271-97.

81. Jon D. Levenson, *Resurrection and the Restoration of Israel: The Ultimate Victory of the God of Life* (New Haven: Yale University Press, 2006), p. 21. See also R. H. Charles, *A Critical History of the Doctrine of a Future Life in Israel, in Judaism, and in Christianity,* 2nd ed., Jowett Lectures (London: Adam & Charles Black, 1913), pp. 155-56.

By suppressing any explicit belief in physical resurrection, Josephus seems intently aware of this conceptual divide. Perhaps he was unusually self-aware that he was writing for an audience whose anthropological consciousness was characterized by views like those expressed in Aeschylus's *Eumenides:* "but when dust drinks in the blood of man, once he is dead, there is no rising again (ἀνάστασις)" (647-48). Josephus's *interpretatio graeca* betrays the important impasse that still existed between Hellenism and Judaism on the question of physical resurrection. In the generation after Josephus, it would remain an obstacle to faith that repeatedly led Christian apologists into contention with their pagan antagonists.[82]

Finally, Josephus seems to have liked the general idea of the afterlife in a more personal way, beyond what he says about the beliefs of other persons and groups. He seems to say as much in *Ant.* 17.354, where immortality of the soul affirms a moral order in which divine retribution governs the cosmos and history. Elsewhere, Josephus adamantly defends this moralizing portrait of history;[83] and a positive hope in immortality only further advances this agenda, encouraging the pursuit of virtue and avoidance of vice (*Ant.* 17.354; cf. *War* 2.157-58). Through the immortality of the soul, the deity's inevitable justice is engrained in the very structure of the created order and the human frame.[84] This concern with theodicy is certainly faithful to other expressions of resurrection, immortality, and everlasting life in early Jewish literature.[85] For the author of 2 Maccabees, the resurrection provided confirmation of God's covenant faithfulness to the Jewish martyrs: "he never withdraws his mercy from us. Although he disciplines us with calamities, he does not forsake his own people" (6:12-17).[86] In the *Messianic Apocalypse* (4Q521), the

82. Justin, *1 Apol.* 8-12, 18-21, 44; Origen, *Cels.* 2.55; 4.58-61; 5.14; 7.28-32, 42-45; 8.54; Minucius Felix, *Oct.* 5.3-4; 8.4, 53; 11.3-8; 12.2-7; 13.4; Tertullian, *Res.* 1; Tatian, *Address to the Greeks* 6; Theophilus, *Autol.* 13; Athenagoras, *Leg.* 36; Clement, *Strom.* 5.9, 103-5.

83. Harold W. Attridge, *The Interpretation of Biblical History in the Antiquitates Judaicae of Flavius Josephus,* Harvard Dissertations in Religion 7 (Missoula, Mont.: Scholars Press, 1976), pp. 165-76.

84. Elledge, *Life after Death,* pp. 137-45.

85. Nickelsburg, *Resurrection;* James H. Charlesworth, "Theodicy in Early Jewish Writings: A Selected Overview," in *Theodicy in the World of the Bible,* ed. A. Laato and J. de Moor (Leiden: Brill, 2003), pp. 470-508.

86. Nickelsburg, *Resurrection,* pp. 92-96; Robert Doran, *Temple Propaganda: The Purpose and Character of 2 Maccabees,* CBQMS 12 (Washington, D.C.: Catholic Biblical Association of America, 1981), p. 53; J. W. van Henten, *The Maccabean Martyrs as Saviours of the Jewish People: A Study of 2 and 4 Maccabees,* JSJSup 57 (Leiden: Brill, 1997), pp. 137-38.

resurrection likewise affirmed that "the fru[it of a good work] . . . will not be delayed" to the righteous forever (frgs. 2 ii+4 10-11).[87] Likewise, for *Pseudo-Ezekiel,* the reconstitution of Ezekiel's valley of dry bones (Ezek 37) posed a crucial answer to the problem of divine justice: "I have seen many in Israel who love your name and walk on the paths of righteousness. When will these things be? And how will they be rewarded for their loyalty?" (4Q385 frg. 2; cf. 4Q386, 388).[88] Immortality further granted to the author of Wisdom of Solomon the hope that God would not overlook the ultimate destiny of the suffering righteous: "The souls of the righteous are in the hand of God. . . . they are at peace. . . . their hope is full of immortality" (3:1-4).[89] Thus, even if Josephus distorted the precise conceptual forms of Jewish afterlife beliefs, he was still true to their religious spirit and enduring relevance.

87. Restoration follows Puech, DJD 25; idem, *Croyance,* 2:629.

88. Dimant, DJD 30, pp. 7-88; idem, "Resurrection, Restoration and Time-Curtailing," 527-48; with John Strugnell, "4QSecond Ezekiel (4Q385)," *RevQ* 13 (1988): 45-58.

89. See Collins, "Root of Immortality," pp. 177-92.

Death and Burial Customs in Earliest Christianity

Konstantinos Th. Zarras

> *Chariton, how are things below?*
> *All dark.*
> *And what about the way up?*
> *A lie.*
> *And Pluto?*
> *A myth.*
> *Then we are done for.*[1]

Viewed from afar, the Holy Land should not have been an easy place to live in the first century CE. When one brings to mind the bloody legacy of Herod the Great, the Roman governors, especially those in power before the war in 66 CE, the numerous attempts at a revolt, as well as the groups of people inspired by haunting visions of freedom and independence, then it becomes obvious that for the people of that tormented land the specter of death in its various forms was absolutely clear and present. In the Gospels and Epistles of the

---

1. Callimachus, *Epigr.* 31; see D. C. Kurtz and J. Boardman, *Greek Burial Customs* (London: Thames & Hudson, 1971), p. 266; or P. W. Van Der Horst, "Jewish Poetical Tomb Inscriptions," in *Studies in Early Jewish Epigraphy*, ed. J. W. van Henten and P. W. van Der Horst (Leiden: Brill, 1993), p. 131 n. 12. Jewish epitaphs offer valuable material on their burial practices too. See L. V. Rutgers, "Death and Afterlife: The Inscriptional Evidence," in *Judaism in Late Antiquity*, part 4, *Death, Life-after-Death, Resurrection and the World-to-Come in the Judaisms of Antiquity*, ed. A. J. Avery-Peck and J. Neusner, HO 1/49 (Leiden: Brill, 2000), pp. 293-310.

New Testament, in the works of the early church fathers and authors, as well as in other texts of the same period or even later, one finds many references concerning their beliefs and customs regarding death and the last rites.

What follows is a brief presentation of those beliefs and ways, focusing only on the most relevant, in the form of an outline — along with some question marks. And as the saying goes, "the text and the spade" are the best companions for biblical research.[2]

Naturally, perhaps the earliest evidence concerning "a Christian view of death" is to be found in the Epistles of Paul.[3] For the author of Hebrews, death was a *hapax genomenon* (9:27); that is, it happens only once, and it was considered to be unnatural and the result of sin (2:14). The primordial disobedience was connected sometimes with the entry of sin, and subsequently of death,[4] into the world of the first humans (cf. John 8:44).[5] After Adam and Eve, all were considered to be affected from that vertical disaster and separated from the Creator: "all have sinned and come short of the glory of God" (Rom 3:23).[6] And it is exactly through the fear of death that humans are capti-

---

2. Cf. V. Tzaferis, *Excavation of Burial Caves at Giv'at ha-Mivtar* [in Hebrew] (1968); B. R. McCane, *Roll Back the Stone* (Harrisburg: Trinity Press International, 2003), p. 35. The examination of the material findings and the literary data — concerning the Jewish tombs in Palestine of the Roman times — has also been called "the promise of the archaeological-literal approach"; see Eric M. Meyers and James F. Strange, "Jewish Burial Practices and Views of Afterlife, and Early Christian Evidences," in *Archaeology, the Rabbis, and Early Christianity* (Nashville: Abingdon, 1981), p. 108.

3. J. Clark-Soles, *Death and the Afterlife in the New Testament* (New York: T&T Clark, 2006), p. 60; and on Paul's views concerning death, pp. 105-6. For a brief yet valuable presentation, see J. J. Collins, "Death and Afterlife," in *The Biblical World*, ed. J. Barton, 2 vols. (2002; repr. London: Routledge, 2004), 2:357-77, esp. pp. 372-73.

4. From Gen 3:19 one infers that death was considered to be universal. Actually, there seem to be two reasons for the existence of death in man's life: "the first states that God made man from the dust of the earth, and to dust he must return (Gen. 2:7; 3:19; Job 10:9)" (*Encyclopedia Judaica*, 16 vols. [Jerusalem, 1972], 5:1419). In Gen 3:22-24 there is a second reason: that of sin. When Adam and Eve lost paradise, they also lost access to the tree of life and thus to eternal life. This stern sentence of death was passed on humanity in Gen 3:19 (see the relevant lemma in *Encyclopedia Judaica*).

5. Also see Rom 5:12; 6:23; 1 Cor 15:21; Jas 1:15. In the *Acts of Paul and Thecla* 17.6 and the *Story of Joseph of Arimathea* 3.3 death is clearly connected to sin.

6. According to 1 Cor 15:21 death entered through a human being and it is through Adam that all humans die (15:22). For Paul, death is deeply rooted in human existence, since it actually started with the loss of communion with God. So death is connected to sin (Rom 5:12; 6:23), and the reign of bodily existence is characterized as "death" (7:24). See also *Acts Phil.* 142.23; *1 Clem.* 2.5.

vated and trapped in the vicious circle of sin and loss, like slaves in bonds.[7] This path of loss is also described in *Did.* 5, where sin equals or results in death. Consequently, death was personified (1 Cor 15:55; also cf. Rev 20:14) and considered to be an enemy, indeed, "the last enemy that will be destroyed" (1 Cor 15:26). In Eph 2:2 this "enemy" is called "the prince of the power of the air, the spirit that now works on the children of disobedience."[8] The one responsible for the continuation or expansion of death was thought to be the devil,[9] but only temporarily, since according to Heb 2:15 the risen Lord would remove this power from his hands.[10] And this would happen through Jesus' own death.[11] The end-of-times process was soon to take place.

It is very interesting that in 1 Cor 15:36 death is depicted as seeding. As the seed is planted, so the dead; and as the plant rises from within the earth,[12]

---

7. Heb 2:15: "and free those who all their lives were held in slavery by the fear of death."

8. In the later apocryphal Greek *Apocalypse of John* (21.11) death is personified as a shepherd in Hades for the sinners. On the issue of authenticity of the NT Apocrypha and Pseudepigrapha, and other similar works, as much as on their role for understanding the evolution of the various Christian beliefs, see the useful work of J. H. Charlesworth, *Authentic Apocrypha: False and Genuine Christian Apocrypha,* Dead Sea Scrolls and Christian Origins Library 2 (N. Richland Hills, Tex.: Bibal, 1998); also, idem with J. R. Mueller, *The New Testament Apocrypha and Pseudepigrapha: A Guide to Publications, with Excursuses on Apocalypses,* Atla Bibliography Series 17 (Metuchen, N.J.: American Theological Library Association and Scarecrow Press, 1987), where one may find a lot of valuable material.

9. In the *Acts Phil.* 110.4, 7 the devil is named as the cause of death.

10. Notice the frequent use of terms related to death and dying in Rom 1:32; 5-8; 6:6; 14:6-15; also Gal 2:19.

11. Cf. Heb 2:14: "Since, therefore, the children share flesh and blood, he himself likewise shared the same things, so that through death he might destroy the one who has the power of death, that is, the devil." In *Trall.* 2.1 Ignatius argued that by believing in Jesus' death, one may escape death; see also *Smyrn.* 3.2.

12. There seems to be Mysteries terminology here, especially from the earlier mythosophic vegetation themes; see M. R. Lefkowitz and M. B. Fant, eds., *Women's Life in Greece and Rome: A Source Book in Translation* (Baltimore: Johns Hopkins University Press, 2005), p. 278, where the dead grain seems to live again in the seed of the next agricultural year, thus referring to Persephone's return to her mother; on the Eleusinian Mysteries see G. E. Mylonas, *Eleusis and the Eleusinian Mysteries* (Princeton: Princeton University Press, 1969); A. C. Brumfield, *The Attic Festivals of Demeter and Their Relation to the Agricultural Year* (New York: Arno, 1981); cf. M. Eliade, *Rites and Symbols of Initiation* (New York: Harper Torchbooks, 1958), pp. 111-13; E. Ferguson, *Backgrounds of Early Christianity* (Grand Rapids: Eerdmans, 1993), pp. 238-42.

so the righteous will be risen "in Christ."[13] Yet it is maintained that real death will not be for all, since "We shall not all sleep, but we shall all be changed" (15:51) and the dead will rise as "incorruptible" (15:52).[14]

According to Tertullian (ca. 210), death is the separation of the soul from the body.[15] The same view is held by Lactantius (ca. 310), too, adding that "death is the dissolution of the nature of living beings."[16] Death was considered to be the ultimate line that separates this world's opportunity for salvation from the total helplessness that follows it. Quoting Lactantius (ca. 285), "a second life is not granted to us," that is why "each result must be brought about in this life."[17] Or, as the *Treatise against Novatian* (*ANF* 5:662-63) has it, "in Hades there is no repentance." All that one can do for one's salvation must be done while in this life; for afterward there can only be Hades and judgment.

There are various ways by which the end of life is denoted in the New Testament. "Falling asleep" (Acts 13:36),[18] having "to depart" (Phil 1:23), losing the "clothes" or going "unclothed" (2 Cor 5:3-4), "putting off this tabernacle" (2 Pet 1:13-14), having "our earthly house of this tabernacle" removed (2 Cor 5:1) are examples of how the various authors portrayed this final act of exodus from the comfortably known.[19]

It is worth mentioning that the book of Revelation also refers to the enigmatic "second death" (Rev 2:11) — that is, second after the temporal first death of the body. For those unjust condemned to remain forever in "the lake of fire," this "second death" was thought to be eternal, signifying the ir-

---

13. The symbol of the seed is also used in the Ethiopic *Apocalypse of Peter* (4:10-13), again in relation to the future resurrection.

14. Phil 3:10, where the faithful are to become *symmorphoi* ("conformed") to Jesus' death, follows in the exact same spirit. It is also interesting that in the *Acts Thom.* 142.22 death is connected to rebirth (cf. 160.9, too).

15. See *A Treatise on the Soul*, ch. 10 (*ANF* 3:228). Unless otherwise specified, all notes are either from Alex. Roberts and James Donaldson, eds., *The Ante-Nicene Fathers*, 10 vols. (repr. Peabody, Mass.: Hendrickson, 1994); or from *Thesaurus Linguae Graece* 8.0 (*TLG*), Silver Mountain Software 1999.

16. *ANF* 7:61. He also says (book 2, "Of the Origin of Error," ch. 13), "We thus define the first death: Death is the dissolution of the nature of living beings; or thus: Death is the separation of body and soul."

17. *ANF* 7:85. See book 3, "Of the False Wisdom of Philosophers," ch. 16.

18. See 2 Pet 3:9; Ps 76:5; also cf. Jer 51:39.

19. In a similar way, in Rom 4:19 and Heb 11:12 the term "dead" signifies the loss of physical strength. In Job 10:21 it is called a journey to the place from where there is no return ("I go whence I shall not return").

revocable separation from God (Rev 20:6, 14; 21:8). Of special importance are the references not only to the death of the body, but to the death of the soul or spirit too.[20] Yet both types of death, physical and spiritual, again came only as a result of sin (Rom 5:12-21)[21] or when the person remains under the power of sin (Rom 8:6; Col 2:13; Eph 2:1, 3). Thus in Eph 2:1[22] the term νεκρούς ("dead") is applied even to those living in sin and so unable to attain the life of the spirit. Especially in Rom 8:6 Paul sharply points to the importance of living in the spirit and distinguishes between the real life and the orientation of the flesh, "For to be carnally minded *is* death; but to be spiritually minded *is* life and peace." Therefore, Paul seems to project or extend the shadow of death on the days of the living too. Subsequently, faith not active in works is characterized as "dead" (Jas 2:17). At the same time, those living not "in Christ," though in life, are considered to be spiritually dead (Matt 8:22; Luke 15:32; John 3:36; 8:24).[23] In a similar manner, all who are not to be redeemed by the Savior are considered to be spiritually dead too (cf. Eph 2:1-3; Col 2:13).

Trying to explain the reason for death, Theophilus of Antioch (ca. 180) compares man to a vessel who has some flaw and now needs to be remade.[24] Only then will it be new and whole, and after resurrection spotless, righteous, and immortal. On the same issue and after connecting death with the loss of immortality, Tatian (ca. 160) maintained that the faithful may conquer death with the power of faith,[25] while for Justin Martyr (ca. 160) death was like a debt that all must pay.[26] For Irenaeus (ca. 180) death was sent from God as a limit to human sin.[27] So death puts an end to human sin by dissolving the

---

20. In general, it is believed that the concept of the immortality of the soul was brought to Israel through the vehicle of Hellenism, esp. Platonism. Cf. A. F. Segal, *Life after Death: A History of the Afterlife in Western Religion* (New York: Doubleday, 2004), p. 367; and on *nefesh* and *ruach*, pp. 142-45.

21. Rom 5:12: "just as sin came into the world through one man, and death came through sin, and so death spread to all because all have sinned."

22. "You were dead through the trespasses and sins."

23. Also, see *Herm. Mand.* 6.2.3 and 8.11.3.

24. *Theophilus to Autolycus* 2.3.26 (*ANF* 2:104-5).

25. *Address to the Greeks* 15 (*ANF* 2:71): "men, after the loss of immortality, have conquered death by submitting to death in faith."

26. See *1 Apol.* 11 (*ANF* 1:166): "also death is a debt which must at all events be paid."

27. See *Haer.* 3.18.7 (*ANF* 1:448): "[man] who had been drawn by sin into bondage, but was held by death, so that sin should be destroyed by man, and man should go forth from death."

body — its very instrument. It is only after death that one may begin to live to God. Of course, the reason for this bodily dissolution was thought to be the first sin of disobedience. Therefore, the body had to be interred to be reproduced or recast anew. Only then would it be pure, incorruptible, and reunited to its soul. Tertullian (ca. 210), too, attributed death to original sin, while teaching that it was by sin that humans deviated from their initial and God-intended process, falling to an unnatural situation.[28] From the start, God created humans as immortal, as is proved by the warning not to eat from the forbidden fruit. Therefore, for Tertullian, death resulted from humans' own choice. If humans had not sinned, death would have remained an unknown. Still, for Methodius (ca. 290) in his *Discourse on Resurrection*, death and body dissolution are compared to the melting down of a statue, while its remolding corresponded to the resurrection.[29] Again, death is connected to the devil and sin, and resurrection to the love of God for his creature.

Of course, it was the narrative about Jesus, who died the death of a human and then was raised to a divine resurrection, that stood at the heart of his early followers' views on death and dying. And the abolishment of death is exactly what they took to be the focus of Jesus' redemptive work. As maintained by Paul again, it was by Jesus' death and resurrection that he defeated death on all levels and dispossessed its sting for all believers.[30] After him all would be able to have life eternal through acceptance of his gospel.[31] Even further, it was believed that this everlasting life was already present to man by faith (John 3:36; 11:25-26), while salvation seemed not only possible but certain.[32] In such a way Jesus is shown to lift the fear of death here and now, though the full extent of his work would take place in the resurrection (2 Tim 1:10).[33] It is interesting that when in the parable of the beggar and the rich man (Luke 16:22-23) the former dies, it is mentioned that he goes to the "bosom of Abraham." By "Abraham's bosom" Tertullian (ca. 207) under-

28. *An.* 52 (*ANF* 3:229).

29. From *Res.* 1.6 (*ANF* 6:365), "For the melting down of the statue in the former case corresponds to the death and dissolution of the body in the latter, and the remolding of the material in the former, to the resurrection after death in the latter."

30. 1 Cor 15:55-57: ποῦ σου, θάνατε, τονίκος; ποῦ σου, θάνατε, τὸ κέντρον; in this way, Christ was considered to be "the first fruits" of all those who have died (15:20).

31. Cf. 2 Tim 2:10: "I endure everything for the sake of the elect, so that they may also obtain the salvation that is in Christ Jesus, with eternal glory."

32. Matt 18:11: "For the Son of Man has come to save that which was lost"; also Rom 5:10, 8:32-35; 2 Cor 5:21; Gal 1:4; 3:13; Eph 1:7; 2:16.

33. Also 1 Cor 15:22, 56-57; Heb 2:14-15.

stands the temporary residence of the faithful that is not in heaven, not on earth, but in the so-called hell.[34] Referring to the martyrdom of Perpetua, Tertullian also states that the only way for the faithful to reach Paradise is by their "own life's blood."[35] Even though both the souls of the righteous and the unjust go to Hades after death, the first are found in a different place, full of light, at the right side of Hades and in the company of angels who fulfill the duty of guarding the souls there. This is the place that according to Hippolytus (*ANF* 5:222) too is called "Abraham's bosom."

As one might expect, these ideas were even older. In his *First Epistle to the Corinthians*, Clement of Rome (ca. 96) maintained that, because of their sufferings, Peter and Paul reached for a glorious abode and that they entered into a place of holiness (*ANF* 1.6; or 5.4 and 7). And Clement of Alexandria (ca. 195)[36] stated that through the cross sunset changed to sunrise and mortality into immortality.[37] Thus, for his audience, death now takes the form of a *dies natalis*, the day of a deathless birth in a totally new scheme of things,[38] constructing a reality to embrace and not to be fearful of.[39] After all, as was

34. *Marc.* 4.34 (*ANF* 3:406).

35. *An.* 55 (*ANF* 3:231). On Perpetua's martyrdom, see Segal, *Life after Death,* pp. 558-60.

36. *Strom.* 1.11.114.4.1-4: "He hath changed sunset into sunrise, and through the cross brought death to life; and having wrenched man from destruction, He hath raised him to the skies transplanting mortality into immortality, and translating earth to heaven."

37. In an impressive way, Ign. *Rom.* 2.2 stated, "It is good to set from the world unto God, that I may rise again to Him" (also 6.2, where entry into "pure light" is mentioned and that "Him I desire" and "Him I seek"). And in Justin, *1 Apol.* 42, it is also mentioned that there is joy in expecting the immortality promised by the resurrected Jesus.

38. See Davies, *Death, Burial and Rebirth in the Religions of Antiquity* (London: Routledge, 1999), p. 196.

39. Referring to the faithful martyrs, Polycarp (ca. 160) writes that they are in the presence of the Lord having become angels (*ANF* 1:197) and relates that the souls of the faithful wait in a better place for the time of judgment. Tertullian (ca. 197) calls Paradise the place of heavenly bliss where the spirits of the saints are gone. In the parable of the beggar and the rich man (Luke 16:22-23), the rich man after death goes to Hades and suffers torments (*ANF* 3:52). According to Justin Martyr (ca. 160), after death the unjust are waiting in a worse place for judgment (*ANF* 1:197). Actually, it was believed that the soul suffers in Hades according to the sin and harm done during lifetime. Here Hades is an intermediate state for the souls of sinners until the final judgment (ca. 210, Tertullian; *ANF* 3:557). It is a deep expanse in the subterranean region that Tertullian calls "a prison" (*ANF* 3:216 and 231). Souls are locked in Hades experiencing either consolation or punishment while waiting for judgment (*ANF* 3:234-35). Hippolytus presents a similar view of the fate of the un-

preached later on in the *Didascalia Apostolorum* (5.7), bodily resurrection was a promise addressed to all men and not only to martyrs or saints.

Of course, at least during its first phases, the early followers of the Jesus movement presented nearly all the characteristics of the "typical Galilean Jews," following the Jewish tradition in all of its ways.[40] Jews and Christians, the "fraternal twins" (term coined by Mary Boys),[41] shared common burial practices, since it is beyond doubt that "the process of the Christian funeral derived essentially from its Jewish origins."[42] As McCane maintains, a shift on the part of the Christians became apparent after the third or fourth century (see below).[43]

In the first century CE the preparations for interring the deceased were called after the Greek term *entaphiasmos,* which Jesus himself seems to use (Mark 14:8). After being washed (Acts 9:37), the body was wrapped or bound in bands (Matt 27:59) usually made of linen (John 11:44).[44] The mouth was closed and the jaw and face were bound up round the head (John 19:40) with a napkin or handkerchief (cf. John 11:44). Perhaps in order to delay decomposition and if they could be afforded, perfumes were applied on the body (John 12:3, 7; 19:39).[45] Those rich, or the persons who had the means, sometimes placed spices between the linen folds too (John 19:40). It is probable that in Mark 14:8, where the woman with the alabaster jar approaches Jesus, there might be an echo of an old royal custom.[46] Aromatic ointments are

righteous: they are brought by the guarding angels to the left and darker side of Hades and they are dealt with as prisoners. There, at the lower scales of Hades, they feel the terrible embrace of the fiery Gehenna, which is in the vicinity. But the worse punishment for them is to be able to see the place of the righteous and the foretaste of bliss that the latter experience, yet not to be able to cross the small distance, for a vast and deep abyss separates the two. See also in *ANF*: Hippolytus, 5:222; Origen, 4:372; Novation, 5:612; Methodius, quoted by Photius, 6:377; Lactantius, 7:217; Arnobius, 6:445; Tertullian, 3:231-35.

40. McCane, *Roll Back the Stone,* p. 83.

41. M. Boys, *Has God Only One Blessing? Judaism as a Source of Christian Self-Understanding* (New York: Paulist Press, 2000), pp. 45 and 48.

42. Davies, *Death, Burial and Rebirth,* p. 198.

43. McCane, *Roll Back the Stone,* p. 110.

44. In a much later work, the *Acts of Philip* (37), right before his death Philip is shown as instructing for preparing his body "with Syriac sheets of paper" and not with "flaxen cloth," because Jesus' body was wrapped in linen; finally, the body should be bound tight with "papyrus reeds" and buried in the church. Forty days of prayer should follow.

45. In older times aromatic incense was burned for the same reason (cf. Jer 34:5).

46. There are instances where a "funeral fire" is mentioned (cf. Jer 34:4-5) or myrrh

also mentioned in Mark 16:1 and Luke 24:1. Similarly, after the burial of Jesus we are told that Nicodemus brought "a mixture of myrrh and aloe, about a hundred pounds," and that they "took the body of Jesus, and bound it in linen cloths with the spices, as the custom of the Jews is to bury."[47] This is one of the most important and earliest references to Jewish burial customs per se.[48] Mary Magdalene and two other women also brought spices for the same purpose (Mark 16:1; Luke 24:1). Similarly, in *Acts Pet.* 40 (11), when Peter dies, Marcellus is mentioned as washing his body with milk and wine, applying aloe and myrrh; and after filling a stone basin with honey, he places him in his own tomb.

Now, from Acts 5:6 and 8:2 one may infer that there was a kind of society or fraternity of young men who used to take over the final preparations on behalf of the deceased person's family. Some professional mourners (cf. Jer 9:17) would arrive at the family house lamenting, weeping, and wailing with loud cries of grief. Quite characteristic is the narrative on the healing of the synagogue ruler's daughter (Mark 5:35-42), in which Jesus found a "crowd making a tumult," weeping and wailing.[49] From the Lazarus narrative (John 11:31), when his sister Mary exits their house, friends and people go with her, "assuming that she is going to the tomb to grieve there."[50] The

---

and fragrances in the case of kings (2 Chr 16:14: "They buried him in the tomb that he had hewn out for himself in the city of David. They laid him on a bier that had been filled with various kinds of spices prepared by the perfumer's art; and they made a very great fire in his honor").

47. John 19:39-40: "They took the body of Jesus and wrapped it with the spices in linen cloths, according to the burial custom of the Jews." In *Apoc. Mos.* 40 the bodies of the deceased Adam and Abel are wrapped in shrouds, anointed with aromatic oil, and then buried in the exact same place of the earth where their clay came from. Angels sprinkled the place with pleasant aromas and the body of Eve received the same treatment. Afterward, God sealed the monument with a triangular seal (42). Finally, archangel Michael instructed Seth (43) to follow the same procedure for all in the future.

48. For burial in Palestine, see Eric M. Meyers, "The Theological Implications of an Ancient Jewish Burial Custom," *JQR* 62 (1971-1972): 98-99. There was a strong belief in the special character of the land, and therefore a strong desire for a burial there; on the importance for someone to be buried in Palestine and not in another place see ibid., pp. 106-7. Also see the very valuable study, yet more general in character, of E. Bloch-Smith, *Judahite Burial Practices and Beliefs about the Dead*, JSOTSup 123 (Sheffield: Sheffield Academic Press, 1992).

49. In Matt 9:23 Jesus "saw the flute players, and the crowd in noisy disorder," while in Mark 5:38 he saw "a commotion, and people loudly weeping and wailing."

50. When Zacharias is killed in *Prot. Jas.* 23, the priests mourn, they tear their

same narrative relates that Mary and Martha were mourning for their brother for four days before the arrival of Jesus (John 11:17-19).⁵¹

Subsequently, a procession was formed that escorted the deceased from the family house to the place of final rest. Usually the body was carried there on a simple bier without a coffin (Luke 7:12-14).⁵² Both Mark 5:38 (on Jairus's daughter) and John 11 (on Lazarus) confirm that at the time funerals took place before sunset and as soon as possible (also cf. tractate *Semaḥot* 9:9), while in *Gos. Pet.* 2.5 and 5.15 the burial of Jesus' body has to take place before sunset. It seems that the custom of immediate burial was widely practiced probably to avoid uncleanness of a ceremonial nature or for hygiene reasons.⁵³ Thus in Acts 5:5-10 both Ananias and his wife are buried almost immediately after their passing.

One would say that so far early followers of the Jesus movement seem to follow the Jewish traditional ways on the topic,⁵⁴ and that seems correct. Yet when Aristides the Philosopher wrote concerning the Christians (ca. 125 CE; see *Fragmenta*, P. London 2486, *Apologia* 15), he offered some important references concerning their funeral practices too.⁵⁵ He mentions that if a poor man among them happens to pass from this world, they give heed to him and see to his burial. In the case of a righteous one, they even rejoice and offer thanks to God. In fact, according to Aristides, they act as if he is emigrating from one place to another, better one. What is more, it is stated

---

clothes apart, and there follows a three-day period of lament (ch. 24). On the problem of death in the Gospel of John, see Clark-Soles, *Death and the Afterlife*, pp. 137-38.

51. Yet see Josephus, *War* 2.1, where a period of seven days is mentioned.

52. In 2 Sam 3:31 King David is mentioned as following Abner's *miṭṭâ* (bier). Concerning Herod's procession, Josephus mentions that Archelaus "brought out all the royal ornaments to augment the pomp of the deceased" (*War* 1.671-73). His bier was made of gold and "embroidered with precious stones"; close to the body came Herod's sons and members of the family, while his guard and other soldiers followed the pomp. On the customs prevailing at Jesus' time also see Geza Vermes, *The Resurrection: History and Myth* (New York: Doubleday, 2008), pp. 12-13.

53. For the biblical background of rapid burial and the climatic reasons, see Meyers and Strange, "Jewish Burial Practices," pp. 96-97.

54. See Justin Martyr, *1 Apol.* 18, 19 (*ANF* 1:168-69); also Tertullian, *ANF* 3:119 and 3:85.

55. Aristides' *Apologia* (Syriac trans.) 15 (*ANF* 9:276-77): "And if any righteous man among them passes from the world, they rejoice and offer thanks to God; and they escort his body as if he were setting out from one place to another near. And when a child has been born to one of them, they give thanks to God; and if moreover it happens to die in childhood, they give thanks to God the more, as for one who has passed through the world without sins."

that they are always ready to offer their souls to their Lord.[56] Quoting from Dionysius of Alexandria (ca. 262), Eusebius also preserves the tradition of the treatment reserved for the very righteous Christians. According to his view, everything seemed to have the nature of a company attending older brothers to the brink of a journey.[57] The following of the deceased by friends and faithful brothers, while singing and rejoicing, is mentioned in the *Apostolic Constitutions* too.[58] In the same instance, Ps 116:15 ("Precious in the sight of God is the death of his saints") is used as a confirmation of all the above-mentioned. Perhaps in accordance with 1 Thess 4:13, Tertullian (ca. 200) too holds that grief in the face of death is needless because of the certainty of resurrection (*ANF* 3:713).[59] And Commodianus (ca. 240), in a more austere way, proposes no grief or black garments, even if the deceased one is a child (*ANF* 4:217).[60] Cyprian (ca. 250), by calling attention to Phil 1:21, moves even further by stating that even when a beloved one is gone, we should rejoice rather than bewail (*ANF* 5:470). In a similar way he goes on to speak against black garments (*ANF* 5:474) too.[61] For him, death was a happy summons, since one may return to Paradise, to the patriarchs, and to the dear ones already gone (*ANF* 5:475). Therefore, sadness should be avoided, since in dying there is peace and the certainty of resurrection (*ANF* 5:548; also 4:346; 5:469-75). In the light of the above-mentioned, it is no wonder that Justin Martyr threw in the emperor's face that by executing Christians he did no real harm to them (*1 Apol.* 45; *ANF* 1:178).

Again, in Justin Martyr we read that Christians would not offer "drink offerings and the aroma of fat to the dead."[62] In a similar manner Tertullian calls "idolatry" the "offerings to propitiate the dead" and uses the same rationale for condemning both the cult of the dead and the worship of idols.[63]

---

56. See *Fragmenta* 15.8.1, where it is mentioned that they are readily available to offer their lives for their belief in Christ *(hyper Christou).*

57. See Dionysius, *Epistle* 12.4-5 (*ANF* 6:108-9).

58. See *Apos. Con.* 6.30.16-17 (*ANF* 7:464), where it is stated that those who have faith in God, even if they will die ("sleep"), they are not dead.

59. *Pat.* 9; also *An.* 56.

60. *Instructions* acrostic 73.

61. See treatise 7, "On the Mortality," 20 (*ANF* 5:474): "departing from us, they precede us as travellers, as navigators are accustomed to do; that they should be desired, but not bewailed; that the black garments should not be taken upon us here, when they have already taken upon them white raiment there."

62. *Apol.* 24.2 (*ANF* 1:171); also, see Tertullian, *Spect.* 13 (*ANF* 3:85 and 119).

63. *Spect.* 12: "Offerings to propitiate the dead then were regarded as belonging to

He also writes (ca. 197) against the use of images of the dead and proposes "no funeral oblations to the departed." From Tertullian (ca. 210) again we learn about the custom of embalming the dead and their subsequent placement in sepulchers and mausoleums (*ANF* 3:565).[64] Tertullian wrote also that Christians did not use frankincense (*ANF* 3:49),[65] and Minucius Felix (ca. 200) relates that they kept ointments only for funeral rites, and they refused to place garlands on their sepulchers (*ANF* 4:179).[66] Half a century later, Commodianus (ca. 240) says that the adornment of a corpse is an error and that all the "pomp of death art" is an exhibition of vanity (*ANF* 4:217).[67] Finally Lactantius, perhaps echoing Tobit (1:16-18), refers to the utmost act of piety, that is, to the burying of the poor and the strangers.[68] The leading principle here is that it is not admissible to allow the desecration of the Creator's image by exposing the dead body to the dogs and the vultures. Their bodies should be buried in order to return to earth, their initial place of origin (*ANF* 7:177).

According to Rowell, Paxton, and Davies, there was no "formal" Christian funeral ceremony "until about the year 900."[69] Nonetheless, elements of last rites are evident in various texts and places. It should be mentioned here that for both Jews and Christians cremation was not an option; and, as was the custom, underground tombs and graves were used for burial places.[70]

---

the class of funeral sacrifices; and these are idolatry: for idolatry, in fact, is a sort of homage to the departed; the one as well as the other is a service to dead men."

64. See *Res.* 27.

65. See *1 Apol.* 42: "We certainly buy no frankincense." Yet, note that in the final part of the *Apocalypsis Esdrae* (33) the use of frankincense is mentioned, while psalms were sung.

66. *Oct.* 12: "You do not wreath your heads with flowers; you do not grace your bodies with odours; you reserve unguents for funeral rites; you even refuse garlands to your sepulchres — pallid, trembling beings, worthy of the pity even of our gods."

67. *Instructions,* acrostic 74: "Alas that the lifeless body should be adorned in death! O true vanity, to desire honor for the dead!"

68. Lactantius calls it "the last and greatest office of piety" (*Inst.* 6.12; *ANF* 7:177), perhaps having in mind the much older burying site at Jerusalem (Jer 26:23), for the burial of strangers there was special providence (Matt 27:7). Similarly, to contribute in the preservation of a prophet's tomb was considered to be an act of piety (Matt 23:29).

69. G. Rowell, *The Liturgy of Christian Burial: An Introductory Study to the Historical Development of Christian Burial Rites* (London: Alcuin Club/SPCK, 1977); also, F. S. Paxton, *Christianizing Death: The Creation of a Ritual Process in Early Medieval Europe* (Ithaca: Cornell University Press, 1990); cf. Davies, *Death, Burial and Rebirth,* p. 191.

70. Also Meyers and Strange, "Jewish Burial Practices," p. 96.

Tertullian (ca. 210) characterized the pagan practice of cremation as "harshest inhumanity" (*ANF* 3:545) and one that Christians should abstain from following (3:228).[71] Minucius Felix (ca. 200) too proposes burial rather than cremation, considering it a better custom (*ANF* 4:194).[72]

In the Old Testament the burial place was portrayed as "the gates of death" (Job 38:17; Ps 9:13; 107:18), and the silence therein was related to the "shadow of death" (Jer 2:6).[73] The burial sites were usually either natural caves or artificial excavations in the side of a hill (cf. Gen 23:9 and 25:9-10; Matt 27:60). During the New Testament era, tombs had the form of cavelike holes dug into cliffs, or just natural caves with a minimum of human intervention. Thus the grave of Lazarus was a cave with a stone protecting the entrance.[74] The entrance was usually closed by a large circular stone *(golal)*, the removal of which required great effort (cf. Matt 28:2; John 11:39).[75] There are numerous finds of this kind in Jerusalem and in many other places in the Holy Land. Therefore, as attested in John (11:38) and Mark (15:46), the burial place was a rock-cut cave with a stone-covered entrance, and archaeological finds confirm Scripture.[76] When Jesus approaches the tomb of Lazarus, he goes near to a "cave," where a rock was rolled in the entrance (cf. also 11:41). In Jesus' own tomb a stone is also rolled (Luke 24:2; John 20:1).[77] Finally, the custom of using family tombs was very old and quite widespread.[78]

71. *Res.* 1.

72. See *Oct.* 34.

73. As to the beliefs concerning afterlife, there was a great controversy on the issue during the first century CE and later on (see Segal, *Life after Death,* p. 385).

74. In John 11:38, "Jesus therefore again being deeply moved within, came to the tomb. Now it was a cave, and a stone was lying against it."

75. A stone in the entrance of a tomb is also mentioned in the *Gos. Pet.* 8 (32) and 12 (53); and *Acts Pil.* 12.1; 13.1; 14.3.

76. The mention of the stone-cut tomb (and the shroud) are also found in *Acts Pil.* 11.3; 5.5-6, while in *Acts John* 111 a tomb is dug by young men.

77. Broshi's very important excavation at St. Helena's Chapel, at the Church of the Holy Sepulchre, brought up (literally) the *Domine Ivimus* inscription, dated to 330 CE. See Magen Broshi, "Evidence of Earliest Christian Pilgrimage to the Holy Land Come to Light in Holy Sepulchre Church," *BAR* 3 (1977): 42-44; also Meyers and Strange, "Jewish Burial Practices," p. 106.

78. Abraham himself purchased the Machpelah cave and clearly wanted it to be his family tomb (see Gen. 23). Later patriarchs followed his example and tried to secure their own final resting place there too (see Gen. 49:29-34; 50:25-26). For the background of the custom to be buried with someone's fathers see Meyers, "Theological Implications," pp. 96-97; also Meyers and Strange, "Jewish Burial Practices," p. 98.

Again, it is almost certain that during the early phases in the development of the Christian funerary customs there was a strong adherence to the Jewish catacomb. As is inferred in the works of Meyers, McCane, and Davies,[79] archaeological remains of Christian burial places are indistinguishable from the Jewish ones.[80] Both Jews and Christians used to bury their deceased either in loculi (6 ft. × 2 ft. × 2 ft.) "cut into the walls of the galleries,"[81] or in cubicula (i.e., chambers with benches over the grave). In many instances there was an attempt to give the structure the resemblance of a miniature temple by adding an arch over the benches (the arcosolia).[82] For a period of time ranging from the second to early fifth centuries, "both religious groups" preferred the loculi, "followed by the *arcosolia,* and then *forma* (straight into the ground), sarcophagi and amphora."[83]

As has been shown,[84] initially both Jews and Christians in Rome (and elsewhere) preferred the catacomb that was located outside the perimeter of the city. That catacomb was also underground. After all, the underground burial was a well-known custom in the ancient Near East, as the burial site (the catacomb) of Beth Shearim, which comes from the same period as the Roman catacombs, may attest.[85]

79. For example, see Meyers, "Theological Implications," pp. 95-119; see also the line of thought in Meyers and Strange, "Jewish Burial Practices," pp. 94-95; and for the discussion on Robert Houston Smith's excavations at Pella, where a Byzantine church and an earlier edifice were found, ibid., 104-5. For McCane see *Roll Back the Stone,* pp. 112-13. For Davies see *Death, Burial and Rebirth,* pp. 195-98.

80. The "little or no consensus among scholars" concerning "the manner of identifying such remains as Jewish or Jewish-Christian" has been already observed in the past, together with the promise of a more optimistic view (see Meyers and Strange, "Jewish Burial Practices," p. 107).

81. L. V. Rutgers, *The Jews in Late Ancient Rome: Evidence of Cultural Interaction in the Roman Diaspora* (Leiden: Brill, 1995), p. xvi; also, cf. Davies, *Death, Burial and Rebirth,* p. 193.

82. A. Ferrua, *The Unknown Catacomb: A Unique Discovery of Early Christian Art* (New Lanark: Geddes & Grosset, 1991), pp. 19-21; B. D. Shaw, "Seasons of Death: Aspects of Mortality in Imperial Rome," *Journal of Roman Studies* 86 (1996): 101; cf. Davies, *Death, Burial and Rebirth,* p. 193.

83. Davies, *Death, Burial and Rebirth,* p. 193. For the basic tomb construction at the time, see Meyers and Strange, "Jewish Burial Practices," pp. 94-95.

84. E. R. Goodenough, *Jewish Symbols in the Greco-Roman Period,* Bollingen Series 37 (New York: Pantheon Books, 1953); Rutgers, *Jews in Late Ancient Rome,* p. xvi; their conclusions presented in Davies, *Death, Burial and Rebirth,* p. 192.

85. Davies, *Death, Burial and Rebirth,* p. 192.

Yet, although Christian catacombs seemed to be identical to the Jewish ones, there were some significant differences.[86] While Jewish catacombs were usually undecorated, Christian ones were adorned with themes taken from the Bible. Even so, sometimes a menorah was found embellishing a Jewish catacomb.[87] There were no mixed burial catacombs; Jews had their own, as did Christians. But with time the "burial ecology of the cities and villages of the Roman Empire" and "funerary architecture" changed considerably in the Christian world.[88] The Roman catacomb was to be abandoned by Christians from the end of the fourth century and "above-ground Christian burial sites . . . began to appear *within the city walls*," signifying the new place of Christianity in the life of the empire.[89]

The practice of secondary burial was very well known (cf. Matt 23:27) too, and the time between the primary and secondary one was a period of grief and mourning.[90] During the first century CE in and around Jerusalem, secondary burial was practiced widely, as archaeological remains — especially the Caiaphas loculus tomb — prove beyond doubt.[91] After all, as is well known, "ossuaries were in wide usage amongst the Jews from the middle of the first century B.C.E. and until the fourth century C.E."[92] Secondary burial might have had the purpose of a kind of preparation for the day of resurrection, and perhaps the vision of the "dry bones" in Ezek 37:1-14 played some role in the development of this custom.[93] Later rabbinic sources relate that the decomposition of the flesh could expiate sin.[94] Therefore, and

86. See Rutgers, *Jews in Late Ancient Rome*, p. 58.

87. Ibid., 56.

88. Davies, *Death, Burial and Rebirth*, p. 191.

89. Ibid., p. 193.

90. Cf. McCane, *Roll Back the Stone*, p. 82. For the second burial, see *Semaḥot* 12:9.

91. Cf. McCane, *Roll Back the Stone*, p. 97. Secondary burial "persisted throughout the Talmudic period" (see Meyers and Strange, "Jewish Burial Practices," pp. 95-96) and it has been suggested that "the custom was well-known in the early Christian era" (p. 96). On the secondary burial see E. M. Meyers, "Secondary Burials in Palestine," *BA* 33 (1970): 2-29; also idem, "Jewish Ossuaries and Secondary Burials in Their Ancient Near Eastern Setting" (Ph.D. diss., Harvard University, 1969); and for the theology implied or supposed by those practices, idem, "Theological Implications," pp. 95-119; and for the details of secondary burial, pp. 108ff.

92. Meyers, "Theological Implications," p. 113.

93. Ezekiel's vision of the "dry bones" is reworked and also presented in the Ethiopic *Apocalypse of Peter* (4.6-9), where archangel Uriel is mentioned as the angel of the resurrection.

94. See *b. Shabb.* 13b; *Qidd.* 31b; *Ber.* 18b; *Sanh.* 47b; also cf. McCane, *Roll Back the*

in concert with the belief in bodily resurrection,[95] the gathering of the bones[96] and the use of ossuaries[97] came as a natural development of the older practice. There is no doubt that earliest followers of the Jesus movement also knew the custom of the marked tomb; they accepted the impurity of the corpse, the perfumes and spices used on the deceased's body, as well as the wrapping and binding, the underground burial place, and the stone in the entrance.

During the first phases of the evolution of the Christian movement, "when Christians were Jews," as a general rule the deceased were placed or kept outside the community limits, thus declaring the "otherworldly" nature of their new "state." Therefore, at least initially, both Jews and Christians seemed to share a common view of the corpse's ritual impurity, and they buried their dead outside the margins of the town or the village. In *m. B. Bat.* 2:9 it is stated that the tomb should be located at least fifty cubits away from the margin of a city or a village. Of course, even to touch a tomb would bring defilement, since not only the corpse itself but also the environs of its final rest were considered to be impure. Consequently, the actual burial site also was thought to be unclean. As a result, in New Testament times the burial places were located outside the periphery of the inhabited area (see Luke 7:12; 8:27; John 11:30), though sometimes they were located in a garden (Matt 27:60; John 19:41; in the OT cf. 2 Kgs 21:26; 23:16). Every year, before the Pass-

---

Stone, p. 43. For the various views on death in Judaism, from the times before the rabbis until the post-talmudic era, see D. Kraemer, *The Meanings of Death in Rabbinic Judaism* (New York: Routledge, 2000).

95. It is believed that "Jewish writers borrowed resurrection of the body from Persia and immortality of the soul from Greece" (Segal, *Life after Death,* p. 394).

96. The bones of the dead were considered to be a manifestation of his soul (Meyers, "Theological Implications," p. 97). An OT origin for the idea of the sanctity of the bones might be found in 2 Kgs 13:21; when a dead man is put into the sepulcher of the prophet Elisha and onto his bones, he revived and stood on his feet.

97. On the history and use of ossuaries, see E. M. Meyers, *Jewish Ossuaries: Reburial and Rebirth: Secondary Burials in Their Ancient Near Eastern Setting,* BibOr 24 (Rome: Biblical Institute Press, 1971). On the ossuaries found in Jerusalem in the mid-twentieth century, whereupon the symbol of the cross (?) was found, and a more critical view — if not down to earth — see Meyers and Strange, "Jewish Burial Practices," pp. 103-4. Also, B. R. McCane, "Bones of Contention? Ossuaries and Reliquaries in Early Judaism and Christianity," *Second Century* 8 (1991): 235-46; idem, "Jewish Ossuaries of the Early Roman Period: Continuity and Change in Near Eastern Death Ritual," in *Encountering the Other: Essays in Honor of Eric M. Meyers,* ed. D. Edwards and T. McCollough (Winona Lake, Ind.: Eisenbrauns, 2006), pp. 239-46.

over, sepulchers were whitened or whitewashed. Underlining the need for tomb marking, the passage in Matt 23:27-29 points exactly in this direction. Jesus' characterization of some of his colloquists as "whited sepulchers" (Matt 23:27, here meaning "hypocrites") is quite telling. Moreover, according to Pseudo-Clementine *Rec.* 1.71, even during the second century Christians referred to the practice of marking tombs for purity reasons. Therefore, McCane has maintained that "for at least the first two centuries" the Christians in Palestine followed the regulations on corpse impurity already prevalent in the area. Change started to be obvious, first "in texts and later in material culture," in the third and fourth centuries.[98]

Together with the rules concerning the impurity emanating from the relic of a once alive and vibrant human, these customs no doubt echoed the fear of the living in the face of an ancient old enemy. The placing of the dead — sometimes of their memory, too — outside the sphere of social life signified an almost apotropaic act of dismissing the dread from the human mind. Therefore, the *polis* of the living was contrasted with the *antipolis* of the dead.

Yet, later on in the *Didascalia Apostolorum* (third century; hereafter *DA*) and the *Apostolic Constitutions* (fourth century; hereafter *Apos. Con.*), one witnesses a definite shift on the grounds of corpse impurity and the social restrictions accompanying it. In *DA* 6.30.30-33[99] it is stated that Christians should not be afraid of corpse impurity, because those baptized "even though they sleep, they are not dead." Actually, in the same work (6.22), the Christian dead were not considered to be impure because it was believed that "they are not dead."[100] Here there is also found precious material concerning the nonpolluting character of the dead, the custom of washing and anointing the dead body, and the mores related to its final place of rest. According to the same source, a vigil was kept, a procession having a priest at its head was formed to escort the deceased to the grave, and all were finalized with a Eucharist, a custom abandoned after the fifth century. The body was placed face up and with the feet toward the east, an expression of the hope to a new birth, clearly an older pagan custom. After the final rites and at appointed times, small congregations would be held to eat, drink, and pray for the memory of the deceased.[101] And in *Apoc. Con.* 6.30, if one touches a

---

98. McCane, *Roll Back the Stone*, p. 115.

99. Here it is stated that not even the bishops are guilty of impurity when they touch a dead man.

100. Also McCane, *Roll Back the Stone*, p. 116.

101. Davies, *Death, Burial and Rebirth*, p. 199.

corpse, there is no need for the purification ritual, because he is not really defiled. So it is probable that perhaps one of the first and most important differences between Jews and Christians arose on the issue of the ritual impurity of a corpse (also cf. Tertullian, *Mon.* 7). This must have been a later development triggered by the Christian views on death and the dead through the speculum of Jesus' death and subsequent resurrection. And again, as McCane maintains, the turning point must have occurred during the third or fourth century.[102]

On the other hand, at the turn of the second century — at least in some parts of the Roman Empire — arose the issue of the burying places for Christians. Tertullian (ca. 212) refers to the commonly heard cry of "no *areae* — no burial-grounds for the Christians."[103] Later on, Lactantius (ca. 310) seems either to verify the tradition passed on by Tertullian or simply to draw from him. The denial of a burial place by Roman authorities is characterized as "madness" and "brutality," while exclaiming, "to deny light to the living, earth to the dead" (*Inst.* 5.11; *ANF* 7:147). So perhaps there was a growing disagreement on that subject. After all, Christians were constantly increasing their numbers and their presence was disturbing — especially when it came to fulfilling the needs of a new society.

Consequently, one may say that at the initial stages of the evolution of the Jesus movement there was a strong adherence to the customs of their Jewish siblings. Yet, later on, in at least two main areas succeeding followers came to focus new attention replete with new content and meaning: it was the way they finally came to perceive death, and eventually, the elevated position of the deceased in their world. An analysis of some of their burial practices, as they are presented in the texts, may lead to the conclusion that eventually death to them was not the tremendous annihilating factor it used to be.[104] It should be emphasized, though, that close to the areas where Christianity was born the necropolises still remained outside the city, and the same principle was followed for the shrines of the saints or martyrs. As already mentioned, according to the traditional Jewish approach, the corpse was considered to be contagious and the world of the dead occupied no prominent status in the eyes of the living. So how did it come to be that the view of the Christians eventually differed so much?

---

102. McCane, *Roll Back the Stone,* p. 112.

103. *Scap.* 3 (*ANF* 3:106).

104. See A. C. Rush, *Death and Burial in Christian Antiquity* (Washington, D.C.: Catholic University of America, 1941); also, Davies, *Death, Burial and Rebirth,* p. 198.

Initially it must have been the interpretation applied to the death of Jesus. And what is most striking — definitely having played a major role in the evolution of the way followers of the Jesus movement viewed death and the dead — is the language Paul seems to use on death and dying. As seen in Paul's theology, being based on the resurrection of Jesus and the resulting view on death, there becomes evident a gradual but impressive shift. Here the centrality of the belief in resurrection acts as an antidote to the paralyzing effect of death on the human soul. Now people — that is, those baptized "in Christ" — could ponder and talk on that most dreadful subject. Balanced or annihilated by the power of the new concept, the subject of death entered into the field of everyday conversation. Paul especially alludes to the meditation on death, but in a manner far too distant from the one proposed by the Greek philosophers *(meleti thanatou)*.[105] As is known, Socrates taught that real philosophers desired or even pursued death, though not the one known to people. In a more impressive way, in *Phaedo* 64a Plato states that the true philosopher studies nothing else than "dying and being dead." In the same dialogue, the "practice of death" while one is alive is called preparation for the true life.[106] In the light of the above, the exhortation to the faithful to ponder on their own exodus from this world in *Acts John* 69 probably carries some special significance. In this way one may attest an attempt to divest death of the power it held on the human mind.

Consequently, it is quite probable that the element that helped bring about the shift was the developing Christian view on the issue of death, a view that ultimately came to differ from the Jewish or the pagan one. Now at the heart of the Christian concept of death came the belief that the dead are not polluting or harmful to the living. And perhaps even from the early phases in the last rites there were elements of a joyful character,[107] and —

105. "To learn to die" was considered to be the true essence of philosophy; see Clark-Soles, *Death and the Afterlife,* pp. 135-36.

106. See *Phaed.* 67e; also 61c-69e and 80c-84b. In their various forms, these beliefs were widespread; they reached the times of Iamblichus (see *Protrepticus* 3) and even later. For the philosophical "practice of death" in relation to Paul's views as well as the examination of Greek sources, see the excellent study of T. Engberg-Pedersen, *Paul in His Hellenistic Context* (Minneapolis: Fortress, 1995), pp. 305-6. In a similar way, "preparing for death" is of utmost importance for Christians (see Irenaeus, *Fragments from the Lost Writings* 11).

107. For the author of the Fourth Gospel, the one who believed had already passed "from death to life" (John 5:24). On death bringing joy even in the material found in the Fourth Gospel, see Clark-Soles, *Death and the Afterlife,* p. 139, where the Epicurean views also are examined.

based on the empty tomb tradition — death might not have posed as the ultimate evil it used to be.[108]

Even more, although the older custom of keeping the necropolis apart and separate from the cities and villages of the living persisted during the initial period, a new praxis came about: that of the *communio sanctorum* (Augustine), from which emerged the concept of connectivity and close relationship of the living with the dead. Thus the dead were gradually deprived of many of their negative aspects and were portrayed as soon-to-be receptacles of their salvation "in Christ." Now they were not just denizens of a dark world, but soon-to-be citizens of the heavenly realm, not to be feared or forgotten, while the community of the *new dead* came to be related in a dynamic way with the community of the living. Gradually but steadily, the two poles approached all the nearer, until the presence of the dead — at least, of some of them — even marked the holy *axis mundi* of the Christian temple or *ecclesia* itself. Occupying a place of equal significance with the living, the venerable dead formed a society akin to the human, leading to "an interpenetration of the two cities,"[109] of the living and the dead. Given the elevated role of the dead in the Christian soteriology,[110] here we witness a new striking example of how theology shaped even the architecture of the poleis of the living.

From this point on, the subsequent "urbanizing of the cities by the dead," resulting from the transference of the burial sites to cemeteries *(koimētēria)*[111] next to the churches *(martyria)*, that is, to the center of the polis, is only one moment away. Moreover, the veneration of the martyrs[112]

---

108. Rush, *Death and Burial*, pp. 170-74.

109. On "the vision of an ideal Christian society re-centered around the dead," see McCane, *Roll Back the Stone*, pp. 127-28.

110. See *Mart. Pol.* 17.3 (*ANF* 1:43), which maintains that on account of the martyrs' "extraordinary affection" for their Lord, believers should love the martyrs as "disciples and followers of the Lord," and wish that they would "be made companions and fellow-disciples."

111. Even the term that came to denote the final resting place, *cemetery,* from Greek *koimētērion,* marks an impressive shift: again, the dead are not really dead, but they sleep or they rest. The literal translation of *cemetery* is *dormitory.* Perhaps, the most important and well-known cemetery found in Palestine that was in use during the Roman times (roughly 100 BCE to 351 CE) is the one at Beth Shearim (Meyers and Strange, "Jewish Burial Practices," p. 93). On the new place of the dead in the lives and lands of the living, see A. Cooper and B. Goldstein, "The Cult of the Dead and the Theme of the Entry into the Land," *Biblical Interpretation* 1 (1993): 201-15.

112. In *Herm. Vis.* 3.1.9 the "place on the right" belongs to the martyrs (see also

became so widespread as to take on the proportions of a new cult of the "successful" dead. The next logical step was toward the mimesis[113] of the martyrs, as new exemplars not only of living but of dying too.[114] Seen in a new perspective, the new dead, the martyrs, carried not the dreadful aspects of the old. They were not part of a decaying world, but active proponents of a new reality. Those dead were worthy of following or keeping near; to stay related to them would help incorporate into the human psyche all the qualities needed for the awaited transition. Needless to say, it is no wonder that the two societies would not stay apart but merged into a novel synthesis, where the once dreadful dead now stood at the very center of their newborn cosmos. This *sympolis (syn-polis)* came to declare both the ascendancy of the new religion over the other propositions, and the elucidation of an otherwise dark issue with a more luminous message at the same time.

9.9.28, where the martyrs are glorified). In addition, see *Mart. Pol.* 2.1-4; 14.2, where he considers himself as blessed because he has reached the point to be among Lord's martyrs; also 17.3. On the nature of early martyrdom, see Davies, *Death, Burial and Rebirth*, pp. 201-16; see also A. J. Droge and J. D. Tabor, *A Noble Death: Suicide and Martyrdom among Christians and Jews in Antiquity* (San Francisco: HarperSanFrancisco, 1992).

113. In *1 Clem.* 45.8 those who remained until their death inherit glory and honor and they remain in the memory of God forever. In *Mart. Pol.* 19.1 it is mentioned that all believers want to imitate Polycarp in his death, for it was in accordance with Jesus' teaching. Therefore, Polycarp crowned his life as an illustrious teacher with a death similar to his Savior (also 2.1). His students would gather at the place where his monument was erected to celebrate the day that he was martyred and the days that the other martyrs died too (18.3).

114. In Ign. *Trall.* 4.2 the author confesses that he desires to suffer, but he does not know if he is worthy to do so. In Ign. *Rom.* 2 he actually wishes not to be saved from martyrdom and lose the opportunity to offer his life on the already prepared "altar," in ch. 6 he is in a hurry to enter the stadium, and in ch. 7 he reports himself ready and eager to die (also 4.1; 5.2-3; 6.2). In *Mart. Pol.* 3.2 too, referring to the martyr Germanicus, it is stated that he himself drew the wild beast near wishing to put an end to his life. Occasionally the church leaders had to warn against the tendency for some to seek and choose martyrdom as a way of facilitating their passing to the new world. Therefore in *Mart. Pol.* 4.1 those who give themselves up to become martyrs are not commended, because no such teaching is found in the Gospel; see also Tertullian, *Instructions of Commodianus* 62.

Burial Practices and Faith in Resurrection

Petr Pokorný

Burial Practices and Interpretation of Death

Burial practices are always somehow linked with the understanding of death and, partially, with hope in death as well. Admittedly, the habits and traditional practices persevere and do not fully correspond to the ideas, thoughts, and theological concepts of the given time, but the links that are present are often quite significant. Generally the burial practices express consciousness of the value of human life, as it was often expressed in myths on the creation of humans. In the time of biblical Israel, in connection with the higher Jewish level of literacy, the value of individual human life was gradually being discovered. One of the best expressions of these feelings and related ideas is the names of the dead engraved or written on graves, urns, or ossuaries. In these examples society recognizes its past and realizes that it consists of different individuals. The fate of the dead is decided not on the level of nature and its vegetative cycle, but by a higher power who is able to deal with the deceased as a person. In contrast, for example, putting the ashes of the deceased into the water, spreading them in the air, or anonymously leaving the corpse in the desert are practices corresponding to a vegetative concept of life. Admittedly, elements of a vegetative rebirth of nature may serve as metaphors of eternal life (resurrection as germination of a grain in 1 Cor 15:36-41); however, the context reveals what is intended.

   On the other hand, overly careful mummification and attempts to preserve the body (and later even the face) of the dead reveal that the afterlife is expected to be of inferior quality to, not the aim of, earthly life. It is a sort of shady counterpart to earthly existence. This applies, for example, to several periods of Egyptian religion.

Since the Hebrew cult of Yahweh is a religion attested and reflected in the texts of the Hebrew Bible, it may be of interest to interpret the burial practices within the corresponding periods of Hebrew religion.

Jewish Burial Practices

The discovery of an ossuary (bone box) with the inscription "James, son of Joseph, brother of Jesus," published in 2002, is an appropriate illustration of the burial practices in Jesus' time. In 2003 Craig A. Evans offered the best overview of the burial practices in Palestine in late antiquity.[1] The graves (the Hebrew word for "grave" is derived from the same root, *qbr*, as the verbal expression for burial)[2] were mostly cut into the rock (in Palestine it was mostly limestone), and they offered space for either several burials (corpses and ossuaries); or, less frequently, they were proposed only as an individual sepulcher. In such a case the grave was often only a shaft in the earth containing a cell for the corpse. The typical phenomenon is the ossuaries (bone boxes), which have been well known since the prehistorical periods. But since Hellenistic times these have been used for family graves by most of the wealthier members of Jewish society. In many graves from the period before about 600 BC the bones of the previously entombed persons were piled in the corner of the grave.[3]

The sepulture itself was important for the dead person and for his or her family. Obviously the hope of the dead was somehow linked with the rest in the grave, which was considered to be something of a house or home. For example, the pious Tobit risked his life when he secretly removed the bodies of his kindred who were murdered by King Sennacherib when Tobit was in captivity in Assyria (Tob 2:16–3:9). This was considered an act of charity on the same level as saving a life by feeding the hungry and clothing the naked (2:17). The origins of the duty to bury the dead reach to prehistoric times and are associated with the cult of the dead. The motivation may have been

---

1. C. A. Evans, *Jesus and the Ossuaries* (Waco, Tex.: Baylor University Press, 2003), esp. pp. 17-30, 90-124.

2. In Greek it was *taphos* for grave and *thaptein* for "to bury."

3. See J. B. Pritchard, ed., *Times Concise Atlas of the Bible* (London: Time Books, 1991), p. 51, on Saul's and David's kingdoms.

different as it stemmed from the idea of the grave as a home and understood death as the aim of the earthly pilgrimage, until the fear of the dead, especially those who died young and might envy the full life of the survivors *(mors immatura)*, became common.[4] Nevertheless, the duty was considered as unconditioned. From classical antiquity we know the story of Antigone, especially as interpreted in the drama of Sophocles. Antigone gave her life, since she decided to bury her brother Polynices against the will of King Creon. In the version offered by Sophocles this is considered to be an act of obedience of divine will and even an expression of the inborn mission of loving the neighbor: "I am born to love (the neighbor)" (*symphilein ephyn*, 523). Therefore the duty of burying is deeply rooted in cultic traditions as well as in moral feeling.

The Jewish burial practices and traditions included the second burial. About twelve months after depositing the corpse in the grave (this short period corresponds to the climatic conditions in Palestine), the relatives gathered the bones and put them into the ossuary (Greek *ostophagos* or *glōssokomos*), a box usually of stone, sometimes of wood, and rarely ceramic, designed so that it could hold even the longest bones. It was possible to plan the second burial in advance. This may be the background of the petition of one potential disciple, who asked Jesus if he could bury his father before joining Jesus and his disciples, as we read it in the source Q (Luke 9:59-60 par.). The import as well as the predictability of such a decision is clearly expressed. Even the mysterious sentence in the answer of Jesus is more understandable: "Let the dead bury their own dead" may have been an allusion to the other dead in the same group grave.[5] It may have been meant metaphorically; nevertheless it is shocking that the answer is principally negative. Jesus said that to proclaim the kingdom of God is more important than to bury the dead. This is a new phenomenon that we have to keep in mind before we draw a theological conclusion from the burial practices and their interpretations.

Jewish Hope of Resurrection in Late Antiquity

In the information about and interpretation of burial practices we often find signs of reinterpretation of traditional habits. In the ancient biblical period,

---

4. H. ter Vrught-Lenz, "Mors immature" (diss., Groningen, 1960), pp. 38-39, 42.

5. Evans, *Jesus and the Ossuaries*, p. 13.

which is reflected in the Pentateuch and most of the earlier prophets, death is the end of life, which, according to the will of God as the Creator, is temporary. The deceased member is honored by later generations as their predecessor in faith who always belongs to God's people as their sleeping part ("or I will sleep the sleep of death," Ps 13:3) in the graves belonging to the same community. The image of Sheol, the pit of the afterlife, is not essential for Israel's faith, and it can be subsumed under the category of the sleep of death.

Nevertheless, Yahweh's faithfulness is as firm as the heavens: "Let me die the death of the righteous and may my end be like theirs!" says Balaam (Num 23:10); "even in death the righteous have a refuge," we read in Prov 14:32.[6] The idea was that life has its final rest as the Jewish week has its final rest with *šabbat*. In Deut 5:14 *šabbat* derived from the exodus; in Exod 20:8-11 it was even derived from the creation of the world. It was a promise of a real rest. We do not know how to imagine such a rest, but we know that it was considered to be an aim of life, not a way toward nothingness.

In addition, there was a hope of rebirth for the people of God as a whole: "Dry bones . . . I will make breath enter you!" (Ezek 37:4b-5). It is not any individual hope, however; it means that the dead get a new role, they are seen in a new context.

The prophetic vision of those "who lead many to righteousness" and will shine like "stars for ever and ever" (Dan 12:3) includes a personal or individual hope only quite indirectly,[7] like the *apotheōsis* in the Greek world. *Apotheōsis* meant that the dead deserved the veneration of the survivors. Personal hope was not the point at issue. For example, the *apotheōsis* of Emperor Titus is depicted on the Arch of Titus in Rome commemorating Roman victory in the Jewish war in AD 70. The intention was to strengthen the empire.

On the other hand the stories about assumption to the heavens of Enoch (Gen 5:24: God "took him," Hebrew *lqḥ*) or of Elijah in 2 Kgs 2:9-12 (*lqḥ*, v. 9) supposed a personal postexistence, and Elijah was expected to reappear in Jesus' time (Mark 6:15; Matt 17:10ff.). Nevertheless, Elijah remained an extraordinary case, as did the supposed resurrection of John the Baptist (Matt 14:2). By the way, the people identified Jesus with both of them (Mark 6:14-15; 8:28 par.). Nevertheless, before the hope of resurrection was

---

6. NIV; despite the problem of the translation of this sentence in the Septuagint, reflected in the standard English translations (e.g., NRSV: "the righteous find a refuge in their integrity"), the Hebrew text is clear.

7. The Milky Way was considered the home of the souls of dead people by the Pythagoreans and Neo-Pythagoreans.

formulated we read a firm expression of personal hope in death in Ps 73:24 ("you will take [*lqḥ*] me into glory") — a surprising proclamation after such deep expressions of the psalmist's despair, so that several commentators consider it a later addition.[8] "My flesh and my heart may fail, but God is the strength of my heart and my portion forever" (Ps 73:26). This is the basis of any further development of resurrection faith: personal communion with the living God, the Creator, cannot be interrupted by the death of the human partner. This can be understood in two different ways.

Anthropology A

From the end of the Hellenistic period we have documents about the resurrection hope for humans in the books of Maccabees, especially 2 Macc 6:18–7:42. Here the resurrection applies to the righteous and pious, but still ordinary people. The brothers who refused to eat the cultically prohibited food (pork) and were sentenced to death declared: "the King of the universe will raise us up to an everlasting renewal of life, because we have died for his laws" (7:9 NRSV); and the third of the seven brothers killed by King Antiochus stretched his tongue and his hands in order that they may be cut from him saying: "I got these from Heaven . . . and from him I hope to get them back again" (7:10-11). The logic of this hope is clear: If the righteous person died confessing God the Creator, God would undoubtedly raise him from the dead in order that he may create a space for his victorious righteousness. The apocalyptic vision of the horizon of history and the expectation of the Last Judgment are common denominators of these expressions of hope in the (mostly postexilic) parts of the Prophets and Psalms.

For our discussion on the significance of burial practices these findings are crucial. What does it mean when the third martyred brother said: "I hope to get them [tongue and hands] back again[9] *(tauta palin elpizō komisasthai)*" (7:11 NRSV)? It may express the idea of a divine restoration of his body, as we meet it in the vision of Ezekiel, where, after the word of the Lord has been prophesied over them, the dry bones of Israel came together and flesh came upon them

8. Not so H.-J. Kraus, *Psalms 60–150*, trans. H. C. Oswald, Continental Commentaries (Minneapolis: Augsburg, 1989), pp. 90-91. For the later impact of the psalm this is unimportant.

9. M. Dommershausen, *1-2 Makkabäer* (Würzburg: Echter Verlag, 1985), ad loc., translates: "hoffe ich sie wiederzuerlangen."

(Ezek 37:1-14). In this case the remnants of the old body become a link between the old and new creations and maybe also a bearer of the identity of the raised from dead with the earthly martyrs. This was the leading anthropology and its consequence for those who die. We do not know whether the fulfillment of this expectation is always (and even in 2 Maccabees) linked with the apocalyptic consummation of this age, the Last Judgment, and the life in the age to come. It is very probable. The core of the later Christian cult of the relics of the saints, even if 95 percent of it may be magic or superstition, still represents the promise as expressed by Anthropology A. Generally, this was the pharisaic anthropology of Jesus' time (Josephus, *War* 2.8.14 §§162-63; cf. Acts 23:8).[10]

Anthropology B

Less popular but still well attested was the understanding of resurrection based on God's grace and his creative act. In *Jub.* 23.30-31 (second century BC) we read: "At that time, the Lord will heal his servants, and they shall rise up and be made whole. And drive out their adversaries, the faithful shall see and be thankful, and rejoice with joy forever. . . . Then their bones shall rest in the earth, and their spirits shall have much joy; and they shall know that it is the Lord who executes judgment, and shows mercy to hundreds and thousands, and to all that love him."[11]

Verse 31 does not relate to the situation before the general resurrection according to the apocalyptic scheme (bones in the earth,[12] spirits living in joy), since verses 30 and 31 describe the situation of the righteous people who were raised from death in parallel sentences, so that the "healed" life of God's servants and the rest of their bones in the earth are parallel phenomena.[13] What is narrated here is mostly called a consequent spiritual solution,

10. For interpretation see esp. N. Gillman, *The Death of Death: Resurrection and Immortality in Jewish Thought* (1997; repr. Woodstock, Vt.: Jewish Lights, 2000), ch. 5.

11. Translation according to Gene L. Davenport, *The Eschatology of the Book of Jubilees,* StPB 20 (Leiden: Brill, 1971), p. 99.

12. As one possibility mentioned by O. S. Wintermute, "Jubilees," *OTP* 2:102; we know such a concept of a preliminary resurrection from the Lukan writings; see P. Pokorný, *Theologie der lukanischen Schriften,* FRLANT 174 (Göttingen: Vandenhoeck & Ruprecht, 1998), p. 102.

13. Similarly H. C. C. Cavallin, *Life after Death: Paul's Argument for the Resurrection of the Dead in 1 Cor 15,* Coniectanea biblica: New Testament series 7/1 (Lund: Gleerup, 1974), p. 37.

but from the text we cannot deduce any immateriality of the servants of God living the eternal life: they will be like infants (v. 28), they will be healed (v. 30), and above all they will drive out enemies, see, give praise, and rejoice. The last argument in favor of this understanding is similar ideas attested by the Essenes in the texts of Qumran (e.g., 1QS XI, 7b-9a): The resurrection for eternal life in a holy congregation of "sons of heaven" that is discussed here is different from what Josephus reported about Essenes as those who teach the immortality of souls (*War* 2.8.11 §§154-58; *Ant.* 18.1.5 §18: "they regard the soul as immortal"). Nevertheless even in such a case the visible material remnants of the dead are of import. They are documents of the value of mortal and temporary human life that may be accepted into communion with God. This is enough for the reverence toward the material remains of the dead.

The Resurrection of Jesus

Christian hope is derived from Jesus' resurrection (1 Thess 1:10; 4:13-18; 1 Cor 15:20), and understanding the logic of this hope may help us define the import of the ossuaries we are discussing.

First, the resurrection of Jesus is exclusively a result of God's activity, as we have demonstrated with anthropology B in Judaism. This applies also for the expected resurrection of the righteous, as we have spoken about in the previous paragraphs. But here it is often explicitly expressed: "And God raised the Lord" (1 Cor 6:14); "And we testified of God that he raised Christ" (1 Cor 15:15). So it is clear that the passive tense ("he was raised," *egēgertai* or *ēgerthē*) appearing in most of the formulae of Easter faith is a *passivum divinum* circumscribing the name of God. The Hebrew equivalent was probably *qûm* (see Mark 5:41-42).

Second, the testimony about resurrection is an indirect deduction. It tries to find the source of the undoubtedly powerful experience of a special post-Easter influence (presence) of Jesus. In the most popular formula of *euangelion* (the gospel), from 1 Cor 15:3b-5, the verb "he was raised" is supported by the clause "he appeared *(ōphthē)* to Cephas and to the twelve." The passive aorist *ōphthē* means "he was seen" or even "he revealed to us." This means that the vision has been interpreted as a consequence of the resurrection. This formulation results from a deduction; it is a kind of interpretation. The resurrection itself is hidden behind a double testimony: the appearance of Jesus as a demonstration of his new presence after the resurrection, and the witnesses (the apostles) who were able to confirm his identity with the earthly Jesus.[14] This is a witness firm in its consequence, but open toward various interpretive anthropological projects. Only the *Gospel of Peter* from the second century dared to create a direct report on the act of Jesus' resurrection in the style of contemporary legends.

Third, what follows is that principally it is possible to express the Easter experience in different ways. "So we proclaim" from verse 11 is a result of an agreement to call it "resurrection." "We" are obviously those who are mentioned in 1 Cor 15:5-8. We can call it a kind of "federation" of Jesus adherents, obviously the most influential grouping. But the editor of the *Gospel of Thomas* would not belong to them. He does not mention the resurrection of Jesus at all; he supposes that Jesus was and is living exclusively in a divine way (*GosThom* Incipit).[15] Human salvation consisted in accepting his wisdom — entering into the spiritual realm of his revelation of divine presence and discovering the divine substance of every human being. We do not know whether the *Gospel of Thomas* would deny the resurrection of Jesus and supposed only his eternal unity with God, or whether its editor would simply stress the present spiritual influence of Jesus and consider the contingent facts mentioned in the formula of the gospel in 1 Cor 15:3b-5 as insignificant. It is also clear that most of the later (post–AD 150) gnostic groups would not join the federation as well.

Fourth, the resurrection of Jesus was not a resurrection in the sense of an extraordinary event in history as the people supposed the potential resurrection of John the Baptist should have been (Mark 6:14b; cf. 8:28). In the oldest texts it is understood as individual anticipation of the apocalyptic resurrection — an anticipation revealing what withstands the judgment of God. The raised Son of God, Jesus, rescues us from the "wrath that is coming," that is, the judgment of God (1 Thess 1:10). The apocalyptic context was dependent on a special mythical worldview, but it offered a good opportunity to express the impact of Jesus on history in general.

Fifth is a caveat: here we are at the very basis of Christian faith. Without this horizon of the Easter gospel it was difficult to keep the teaching of Jesus alive as an intervention in topical problems. It often degenerated into a special wisdom, as it was already with the pre-Markan collection of Jesus' parables (Mark 4:33-34, "he explained everything in private to his disciples")

14. In the Lukan writings the apostles are those who were able to witness the identity of the risen Lord with the earthly Jesus.

15. He is even omnipresent: log. 77; P.Oxy. I,23-30.

or as it is in the *Gospel of Thomas,* as already mentioned. Even some groups of sayings that we know from the source Q were interpreted in an extreme spiritualist and individualist way, as we see in 1 Cor 4:6-13: some Corinthians believed that the promises included in Jesus' beatitudes that we know from the Sermon on the Mount or on the Plain are already fulfilled. They considered themselves kings ("yours is the kingdom of God," Luke 6:20b), rich ("Blessed are you who are poor," Luke 6:20a), and so on. Paul ridicules them ("we are hungry and thirsty"), but the mistrust toward those who quote the sayings of the Lord remained in his heart (cf. 1 Cor 13:2, etc.). Probably they are identical with the people who proclaimed that there is no resurrection of the dead (1 Cor 15:12ff.), since they knew only the spiritual resurrection of the living. Later, in the *Gospel of Philip,* this is expressed in a principal statement: "Those who say that the Lord died first and (then) rose up are in error, for he raised up first and (then) died" (NHC II/3, 56:15b-18).

This way we come to the situation as it was before Mark's Gospel was written: Paul stressed the Easter gospel (he may have known only a limited part of Jesus' traditions), including the death of Jesus. This way he was able to prevent the enthusiasm of the spiritualist and docetic groups.[16] Nevertheless Paul was unable to create a literary genre including the most important traditions about Jesus in a theologically and literarily coherent and attractive way. It was the author of Mark's Gospel who created the "beginning of the gospel." "Gospel" at that time did not denote a book, but was only the oral proclamation about the resurrection as the common denominator of all material about Jesus. "Jesus was raised from the dead" as the original Easter message was understandable only for the followers of Jesus who knew him. Later he had to be introduced in order that the reader may know who he was and what kind of life was rehabilitated by God and has the ultimate (eschatological) future. What Jesus has done becomes now the backbone of history, and all his teaching and behavior are the standard by which to evaluate any interpretation of human activity, human wisdom, and human orientation in history. The story of Jesus as prophet and teacher culminates according to the Markan Gospel by his death, in which he underwent a deep crisis on the cross (so he is near to all humans), but he "saved the others" (Mark 15:31); and by his resurrection he was vindicated by God himself.

To conclude: Mark's collection and selection of Jesus traditions is not only a set of philosophical maxims, it is a cultural, worldly relic of Jesus'

---

16. The stress on the cross helped his followers to cope with the present eschatology of those who are already raised from the dead in the sense of 1 Cor 4; see Col 2:13-14.

story preserved by memory *(anamnēsis, mnēmē, apomnēma)* and conserved by written texts as a literary and theological whole.

The development of early Christian thought enables us to attempt new interpretations of the testimony on resurrection. I have already mentioned that the resurrection of Jesus could have been understood either as an individual extraordinary event or as an anticipated general resurrection (as it is known from some apocalypses). These are two interpretive frames of the same event that are attested by the apostles. Paul would not deny either of the two. His interpretation only excludes the understanding of the resurrection of Jesus as a miracle in the sense of an event that violates the laws of God's creation. "But if we have died with Christ, we believe that we will also live with him" (Rom 6:8).[17] In this respect is the gospel (about Jesus' resurrection) "the power of God for salvation" (Rom 1:16). The resurrection of Jesus complemented the Jewish definition of God as the one "who brought [his people] out of the land of Egypt" (Exod 20) into the "God who raises the dead" (2 Cor 1:9; cf. Acts 26:8). Later the resurrection is considered a counterpart of creation: Jesus Christ is the "firstborn of all creation" and the "firstborn of the dead" (Col 1:15, 18). So the resurrection is a revelation[18] of the deepest (divine) tendency active in history and even in nature (1 Cor 15:35-50; John 12:24). It is not a miracle in the sense of an unnatural phenomenon. We may rather say that resurrection is more natural than all that we may call natural.[19]

The Body, the Empty Tomb, and the Function of Burials

After these general considerations we may define the character of the hope in death according to Christian theology and describe the role of burial practices.

From the discussion about those who deny the resurrection in 1 Cor 15 we may deduce that the restoration of the body *(sōma)* was a necessary part of the Christian concept of resurrection. This does not mean that the resurrection is linked with the biological material of the dead body or that it is a

17. P. Pokorný, "Der Offenbarungsbegriff und die Philosophie," in *Gedachter Glaube: Festschrift für Heimo Hofmeister,* ed. M. Wladika (Würzburg: Königshausen & Neumann, 2005), pp. 169-78.

18. As it is used in Christian dogmatics since the second century AD.

19. Thereby I allude to a thesis of the German theologian Eberhard Jüngel, xx.

spiritual matter: *sōma pneumatikon* in 1 Cor 15:44 does not mean an immaterial body, but a body governed not by sin but by the Spirit of God. It means also that resurrection is a social matter, since "body" in this context is the means of communication: face, voice, hands, and eyes to communicate with one another. The face is even the means of communication with God (1 Cor 13:12). The decisive transformative element of resurrection is a renewed, deeper, and righteous social context in which the transformed person is included. The hope of justice and peace at the end of history and the personal hope in death unite in the Hebrew as well as in the Christian eschatological project of hope. On the one hand is the need of doing something good and just in history and of knowing that one has a future; and on the other hand is the hope that in death the individual human life would not be swallowed by nothingness; these two cannot be separated from each other. I have mentioned the third brother killed by Antiochus. He offered his hands and confessed his firm faith that God gives them new limbs on the day of resurrection. It is interesting to know that even in the *Gospel of Thomas* with its rather platonic anthropology this idea of new extremities is present as a condition of the present rebirth: "When you make . . . a hand instead of a hand and a foot instead of a foot . . . then you will enter the kingdom" (saying 22). This is an expression of a similar hope of resurrection, even if it is not called so and the editor of the *Gospel of Thomas* understood it in terms of his spiritualist anthropology.

What does it mean for the interpretation of death? In the New Testament there are many promises of eternal life, but the new life itself is not described. The promised life obviously does not mean any succession in time; it is rather a more intensive confrontation with God and with other human lives. Theologically there is one basic consequence of our findings, which can be good as interpreted for contemporary people: The individual man or woman can never be considered as a means for reaching some other value (consumer society, classless society, big empire), not even to reach a substantial unity with God. This is different from, for example, the concept of hope in Hinduism and partially also in Buddhism, where humans unite with the deity. In the Bible the hope is not union, but *communion* with God. This is the far-reaching consequence that can be derived from Jesus' teaching as well as from the Easter gospel.

As to the bearer of identity, expressing continuity with the previous life, the earliest Christian texts are not linked with any specific anthropology. The empty tomb of Jesus appears for the first time in Mark 16; in the earlier layers it is not attested, even if in 1 Cor 15 it could have been an excellent argument for Paul in polemics with those who denied resurrection. Even in the Gospel of Mark the witnesses of the burial and even of the empty tomb are women who do not appear in any other post-Easter text. This means that the narratives about the empty tomb are a means of demonstrative expression of the earthly existence of Jesus as God's revelation and of the identity of the present Lord *(kyrios)* with Jesus of Nazareth, but not an argument for his resurrection: the faith in Jesus' resurrection was proclaimed one generation before the first texts speaking about the empty tomb appeared.

This means that even if archaeologists found the ossuary of Jesus (I doubt whether this could be proved, but we have to discuss it theoretically), it would not mean that there is no resurrection. We have already mentioned the B anthropology. But this is not of decisive help for our coping with such a hypothetic possibility. The basis is the fact that all the witnesses understand resurrection as God's act. The identity of a human person is dependent on God's creative memory.

As to the openness of the biblical proclamations of Jesus' resurrection toward various anthropological interpretive frames, the problem is not which anthropology was supposed by biblical witnesses and authors. Their anthropologies may have differed from one another. The problem is rather with our anthropologies and their ability to interpret the biblical witness.

At the beginning I mentioned the saying of Jesus that preferred the proclamation of the kingdom of God to the burying the dead. This means that the burial practices are neither a moral nor a pragmatic priority. Nevertheless they express the reverence toward the men and women who have a specific face and name and are kept in God's memory.

SUMMARY AND CONCLUSION

Polemics, Irenics, and the Science of Biblical Research

James H. Charlesworth

The Jerusalem symposium, whose proceedings are now published, focused on ancient Jewish tombs and burial practices in Judea and Galilee. Our attention was focused on pre-70 archaeological evidence as well as Jewish customs and beliefs. Early Jewish beliefs were sometimes evident from inscriptions and the recorded traditions for secondary burial, but they were usually discerned through a penetrating study of tomb architecture, the use of ossuaries, and contextual features such as loculi, arcosolia, a porch before the tomb, and perhaps a *nefesh* (memorial monument) above it.

While apparently the Maccabeans and Hasmoneans introduced the use of mikvaot, as we know from excavations at Qeren Naftali, Gamla, and Jericho *ossilegium* (ליקוט עצמות) — the practice of gathering the disarticulated bones of the deceased into a box — appears with the rise of Herod the Great (37-4 BCE). Since ossuaries often preserve only portions of the bones of numerous individuals (sometimes over 10 persons), it is unlikely that a Pharisaic belief or hope in individual resurrection prompted the use of ossuaries. If we have recovered the ossuary of Joseph Caiaphas, a Sadducee who did not believe in resurrection, then ossuaries do not by themselves indicate resurrection belief in Judaism. Would early Jews believe that the Creator needed assistance in gathering bones so he could resurrect an individual?

Clearly, the development from corporate solidarity to individualization occurred in Israel before the exile, but the ossuary is not the proof of this development. The importance of the individual in Second Temple Judaism became apparent, in burials, by the use of a *nefesh* on the tomb and most importantly through inscriptions that mention individuals and perhaps their stature or accomplishments.

Most likely ossuaries reflect both Roman influences in Israel-Palestine and the needs of wealthy individuals in Jerusalem and its environs. The manufacture of stone vessels (including the massive stone jars and tables found in the Upper City of Jerusalem) and ossuaries (with sometimes ornate decorations, as in Joseph Caiaphas's ossuary) were dependent on the wealthy in pre-70 Jerusalem and its workshops in the city and nearby.

One of the purposes of the symposium was to clarify the facts about the Talpiot tomb. The facts and the salvage operation of this tomb in a southern neighborhood of Jerusalem are now clearly presented, for the first time, by Gibson and Kloner. The setting of the Talpiot tomb is on a trajectory that leads south and southeastward from the holy temple, past the Tomb of Annas and the other monumental tombs collected in the "Akeldama" cemetery, the tomb of Caiaphas, the Talpiot tombs, to the tomb of King Herod on the Herodium. I imagine this trajectory as the *via sacra* of Second Temple Judaism.

One of the highlights of the symposium is the assemblage of experts from so many divergent fields: DNA, patina analysis, forensic anthropology, geology, archaeology, paleography, epigraphy, inscriptions, prosopography, statistics, imaging, historiography, sociology, theology, Jewish law and halakot, and other scientific methodologies. In 1968, when I excavated on Mount Gerizim, archaeologists worked alone. Now, informed archaeologists depend on insights provided by scientists in virtually all areas of modern scientific research. The archaeologist working alone on a tel has been replaced by teams of experts working collectively and in many places.

The research and reflections in these proceedings are important, indeed extremely significant, for New Testament scholars and Christians. Although many New Testament scholars ignore archaeological research, they will find the present deliberations fundamentally important for New Testament research. For example, one of Jesus' harsh and disturbing sayings receives clarification by the evidence that burial and all the rituals related to it in Second Temple Judaism would take up to a year. Many Jews prepared the deceased for burial, sometimes visited the tomb three days after inhumation, observed the requisite days of mourning, and finally observed secondary burial in an ossuary about one year after the death of the individual. These insights into ancient Jewish traditions help contextualize Jesus' rebuff of a young man who sought to follow him but had just lost his father, asking: "Lord, first let me go and bury my father" (Luke 9:59). Jesus' reply was: "Let the dead bury their own dead" (Matt 8:22; Luke 9:60). This seemingly heartless response, especially when the duty of the son was to honor his father with a respectful burial, now has significant contextualization. Jesus claimed to perceive the imminent dawning of God's rule (the kingdom of God) and demanded full and immediate response in the presence of an urgent call to leave all and follow him. The would-be follower perceived other obligations that precluded him from immediately being Jesus' disciple. Jesus warned that one must not look backward (Luke 9:52), that God is Lord of the living not the dead (Matt 22:32), and now is the moment of decision (e.g., Mark 1:15; 13:28-37; John 5:25).

The chapters in this collection are self-contained and are not written to achieve some putative consensus. Yet they are written with reflections on the work of others, many of them contained in this collection. While experts tend to resist a common consensus, I think the reader will discern reasons why it is unlikely that the tomb or bones of Jesus from Nazareth have been found.

Divergent voices may be heard. Personally, I prefer to contemplate that we are far from a consensus discerning if the Talpiot tomb is related, in any way, to Jesus' family or clan or perhaps to the followers of Jesus. The Palestinian Jesus movement, after Jesus' crucifixion in 30 CE, became centered in Jerusalem. Thus it is pertinent and wise to continue exploring how and in what ways, if at all, Jesus' earliest followers left any evidence of their lives in the Holy Land.

Soon after the symposium, some involved in it suffered ridicule and rejection. Before the symposium, one person had been unanimously offered an honorary degree; afterward, it was withdrawn because of misrepresentations that seemed deliberately to placard him as a heretic. Another articulate scholar was castigated for considering questions and was judged to be one who could have been a luminary in the field.

Why should some Christians anathematize another Christian who stated hypothetically that if anyone could find Jesus' bones such does not disprove, or undermine, resurrection belief or Christian theology? Surely, *fides quaerens intellectum* ("faith seeking understanding"), the Latin dictum from Anselm (ca. 1033-1109) that shapes enlightened Christian orthodoxy, indicates that faithful believers should not judge and castigate someone who explores issues related to faith. The professors in the leading seminaries and divinity schools foster students for a lifetime of learning and the development of a faith that is confident because it has become personal through questioning, studying, and worshiping. Theological professors teach students — and students come to seminaries to learn. Professors implore them to obtain a deeper faith. All professors know that knowledge strengthens faith, and in the words of the scribe who composed the poem that ends the *Rule of the Community,* "Blessed are you, my God, who opens for knowledge the heart of your servant" (1QS 11.15-16).

More than any gathering, the symposium exposed the different tasks of journalists and archaeologists. Some distinguished archaeologists became emotionally distraught as they imagined that journalists were hijacking scholarly debates, perhaps to make money. Too often those asking questions, on both sides, were judged to harbor a secret agenda. Our culture expects journalists to bring us news about developments, recreate a narrative, and entertain us. Journalists are frequently disappointed that scholars and archaeologists speak only to one another and fail to connect the dots to bring attention to an ancient narrative. Scholars and archaeologists disparage journalists who with insufficient data and with unrefined methodologies jump to conclusions and associate a Joseph, Mary, and Jesus with the nativity without perceiving that such common names lead to Jesus' story as much as Jack, Bobby, and Ted in American cemeteries lead to a Kennedy clan. From the sessions of the symposium all of us should have learned better ways to avoid naive gullibility and acidic skepticism.

These polemics have subsided, and we hope that irenics (even respect and admiration) will become more dominant. Archaeologists like to disagree and argue; that is fine. I will never forget hearing how Kathleen Kenyon argued with Roland de Vaux in the Ecole Biblique or how Benjamin Mazar rebuffed Nelson Glueck in the newly opened trenches adjacent to the Temple Mount. These exchanges exploded within a special circle of deep mutual admiration and an unquenching search for more informed answers.

Let us hope that the proceedings of the Jerusalem symposium will produce less fire and more light. I now express my deep appreciations for all who have contributed to these proceedings. They are superb contributions to our complex culture including the academy, church, and synagogue. I salute the skill and devotion of all members of the symposium. I am indebted to each of them for helping me enjoy a learning curve; may those who study the chapters of this collection also enjoy the joy of enlightenment. As Aristotle indicated, one of life's joys is to learn something new.

POSTSCRIPT

What Is the Message of "the Patio Tomb" in Talpiot, Jerusalem?

James H. Charlesworth

When I was in Israel in June 2010, I was invited by the Associated Producers (AP) team to see what had been discovered in East Talpiot by Rami Arav, James Tabor, and Simcha Jacobovici along with the AP team. I was interested in how they were using a custom-made robotic arm outfitted with cameras to explore a first-century tomb (or burial cave). Recently, some individuals have been discussing and blogging through various media about this tomb. With most individuals, I am dismayed by occasional ad hominem comments addressed to some scholars by other scholars.

All of us scholars are disenchanted when archaeological discoveries are presented too sensationally or are used to "prove" the Bible truthful or fallacious. By profession, scholars shun sensationalism and do not feel the need to defend biblical truths. We are dedicated to a means of expression in which certainty appears in a spectrum from "conceivable to probable." Thus it is as absurd to claim with absolute certainty that the Patio Tomb preserves the remains of some of Jesus' first followers as it is unwise to pronounce with equal vigor that such a possibility is unthinkable.

There should be no doubt that this tomb, labeled "the Patio Tomb" (or "Talpiot II"), and the ossuaries still in it date from circa 20 BCE (when the stone industry could produce such artistic works in stone) to 66 CE (when the land of Israel erupted in a revolt against Rome that proved to be devastating).[1] There are doubts, however, about the meaning of a drawing on one of the ossuaries. I now turn to this challenging drawing.

---

1. Ossuaries are found in Galilee and are locally made, but they date only after 70

Associated Producers (AP) commissioned this "museum quality" replica of ossuary 6; it was unveiled at a press conference in Jerusalem, April 4, 2012. The ossuary is still in the tomb. I wish we all could study it.[2] Are six "little fishes" evident near the top and below the lid, or are they enhanced ovals? I do not wish to comment on the image to the right; it is too amorphous. *All photos courtesy of AP.*[3]

Seeing an Ancient Drawing

In June 2010, I visited a housing complex in Talpiot, which is in southeast Jerusalem. I was amazed by what was below an apartment building. I was

---

CE. L. Y. Rahmani chooses 70 CE as the *terminus ad quem* for ossuaries in Jerusalem; this decision is understandable. But, I am convinced that by 66 most stone masons had wandered off to join the revolt. See Rahmani's helpful chart on the distribution and constitution of ossuaries, *Catalogue of Jewish Ossuaries in the Collections of the State of Israel* (Jerusalem: Israel Antiquities Authority, 1994), p. 22, table 1.

2. The chiseled boundaries of ossuary 6 show more care and skill than the two carvings inside the boundary; perhaps two different persons made the carvings. When we can study the ossuary itself, we should search for metal alloy molecules within the tiny "canyons" in the limestone, so as to compare what may be found within the boundary marks with what is within the inside drawings. The comparison may provide evidence of two different workmen or at least different chisels.

3. I am grateful to Felix Golubev for providing me with these images and asserting that none has been altered or "doctored."

looking through a camera on the end of a robotic arm into a pre-70 Jewish tomb. There in the darkness below my feet was an ancient tomb with ossuaries (bone boxes) clearly made before the massive revolt against Rome in 66 CE. As the camera turned, I saw a stone door that sealed the tomb in antiquity. Then the camera moved silently past ossuaries and some bones strewn on the floor of the tomb.

Colleagues near me shouted with excitement as an inscription came into view. Then, not much later, the robotic arm, which was directed by an archaeologist, moved to another ossuary. We could not believe our eyes. We were all riveted to a drawing that ostensibly broke the commandment not to make a "graven image." What was it? What was depicted? What did the inscriber intend to symbolize?

A leading archaeologist and biblical specialist on site first thought the drawing on ossuary 6 depicted a boat. Was it? They unanimously changed their minds when the full image came into view.

Description

First, it is imperative to realize the image is something inscribed by an unskilled hand on limestone. The inscriber did not use a ruler or compass; he seems to have used only a chisel and a hammer. He thus produced a poorly incised freehand ornamentation. We should expect this type of work in and around Jerusalem in pre-70 strata, since Jews were prohibited, and thus had no skills, to depict any likeness in God's creation (recall the opening commandments of the Decalogue). There was also probably no workshop or skilled artisans to help him; and perhaps the image was made without sufficient time.

The long and concave figure is approximately 23 cm long and approximately 15 cm wide at the greatest extremity (the curved "bottom" that is at the top) or 9 cm near the "appendages."[4] The figure merges into a circle on one

4. At this stage, none of us can be precise. We must work with an image taken from a distance and a CGI-generated image created from a composite of several photographs from different angles and in different lighting. The ossuary is still in the tomb. At least no one can debate the provenience of the ossuary. I am trying to discern the tomb in which Sukenik found the ossuary in the Palestine Archaeological Museum; it bears the name "Jesus, son of Joseph." Here are some corrections to Rahmani, *Catalogue*. In no. 222 the Hebrew is backward. In no. 288 the name is "Liezer" (not "Eliʿezer"). In no. 428 the name is "Maryah" (not "Kyria") and "Shimʿon" is scratched out (as is a name in the so-called

The image as seen through the robotic arm
(courtesy: AP)

end and fans out on the opposite end. At the pointed end is a circular shape about 3 cm in diameter. On each side of the figure are lines that appear to be appendages. In the center of the figure are three lines. The section closest to the tip contains square markings while the other two contain something like triangular lines. Halfway between the appendages and the tip is a section that .contains numerous lines drawn at different angles. A series of horizontal lines running perpendicular to the main figure run across the sphere at the bottom. What could this image symbolize, or is it simply a sign? That is, is the drawing a sign that may have been well understood in the first century, or is it a symbol with rich meaning? A sign can mean one and only one thing; a good example is the stop sign. We all know that it means we must stop at that spot.

---

ossuary of Simon of Cyrene). In no. 430 the reading seems to be "Shalom Hallel." The שלם may be uncertain, but הלל seems clear. Recall the name in Jgs 12:13-15: "Abdon son of Hillel." Of course, one immediately thinks of the famous Hillel, the so-called Pharisaic teacher prior to Jesus from Nazareth. In no. 557 the *beth* should not be restored; it should appear with a supralinear circle. I know no better way to honor Rahmani for his superb catalogue than to suggest ways to improve it. (Note that the object to the right of the incised image is another ossuary.)

A symbol must be interpreted and usually has many meanings. Symbols appear in a world of ambiguity and bring with them more than one meaning.[5]

Differing Interpretations of the Drawing

A Nefesh

A *nefesh* is a tomb monument that signals the "soul[s]" entombed. Looking at the image on an unpublished ossuary in Rahmani's *Catalogue of Jewish Ossuaries*,[6] it is easy to imagine the image is a *nefesh*. In both drawings, the "bottom" is concave. Some ossuary images of a *nefesh* do have appendages on their sides that look like spirals. The experts who were studying the Patio Tomb identified a *nefesh* on one ossuary but concluded that the image on ossuary 6 was not a *nefesh*. Nevertheless, it is conceivable that the drawing is, indeed, a *nefesh;* after all, we should admit that the drawing is crude. One problem with the assumption that the image is a funerary monument is that it would be upside down, with the base at the top. Does that seem likely?

An Amphora

The image does appear in some ways like an amphora. It is rounded and has a top. The image has something on each side. Could these be handles? If so, they are not like any known handles on an amphora, whether drawn or part of an amphora itself. Is it possible that retinal retention has elicited these attempts to discern the meaning? If one stares at an amphora, one can eventually see the image on ossuary 6 as an amphora. But is that what the engraver intended? The oval-shaped bottom of the drawing seems too rounded for the base of an amphora. The "handles," moreover, are oddly shaped. Many artisans depicted amphora correctly on ossuaries; why is this image so unlike others?

Any attempt to enter the mind of an engraver in order to discern the

---

5. The serpent can be seen to have about 30 meanings. See Charlesworth, *The Good and Evil Serpent,* Anchor Yale Bible Reference Library (New Haven: Yale University Press, 2010).

6. The ossuary is in the École biblique. See Rahmani, *Catalogue,* p. 32, fig. 30 (drawing of the *nefesh*).

intention of an "artist" borders on unsophisticated methodology, frequently speculating with unexamined presuppositions. To discern what it might mean to a viewer is another matter. Both of the attempts so far rightly assume that ossuaries exist with a drawing of a *nefesh* or an amphora.

A Fish

If this is a fish, it seems crudely drawn and depicted downward. It may well be a fish, if one imagines an unsophisticated attempt. The shape does look like a large fish. The head appears pointed and expands outward toward the center and then slopes inward and down to an elongated "tail." That contour is "fishlike." The tail seems concave like the tail of a fish; it is well drawn but the appendages are poorly indicated. Could they be a crude attempt to depict the fins on a big fish? Had the "artist" ever seen a large fish? If this is a drawing of a big fish, where is the eye and where is the mouth? Perhaps the mouth is at the point near "the bottom," and the eye is a barely visible circle to the left of the "mouth." We will need better images to confirm what some see as a mouth and an eye (but many images of fish have no eye).

Fish do appear as faunal motifs in Jewish art (in synagogal and funeral depictions as well as in zodiacs)[7] and on ossuaries. N. Avigad found, in pre-70 strata in Upper Jerusalem, a stone table with a fish, "the only animal figure to have been found in ornamental use."[8] Rahmani reported that ossuary 348 had a mark that "seems to represent a fish." Is this another example of a fish, and if so, does it merely mean that the one whose bones are inside the ossuary was a fishmonger? According to Neh 13:16, men came to Jerusalem from Tyre (on the coast north of Acco) with "fish" to sell. Rahmani is convinced that the circle on ossuary 140 around "Yeshua'" ("Jesus") is only coincidentally "a fish."[9] Is that discussion closed?[10]

7. As far as I know, all are post-70 CE. See R. Hachlili, "Fish," in *Ancient Jewish Art and Archaeology in the Land of Israel* (Leiden: Brill, 1988), p. 330 and ills. 18 and 19.

8. N. Avigad, *Discovering Jerusalem* (Nashville: Nelson, 1983), p. 168; see ill. 185.4 The mouth of the fish is open and horizontal. There is no reason to imagine that the Jonah story has influenced the artist. But did the image not break the commandment against making graven images?

9. *Catalogue*, p. 140; see p. 113 and pl. 20.

10. P. Figueras disagrees with Rahmani's interpretation. See Figueras, *Decorated Jewish Ossuaries* (Leiden: Brill, 1983); idem, "The Ornamentation of Jewish Ossuaries — Is It Symbolic?" *Archaeologya* 2 (1989): 49-51.

Why has the engraver spent so much time on the lines within the spherical "bottom"? One can count at least 14 strokes. Why? What was imagined?

Without studying the full context of all the inscriptions and the tomb setting, one could easily dismiss the suggestion that someone tried to draw a large fish. The middle section with squares needs explanation. One should be willing to imagine that the image is really an amphora. And staring at it for long periods can convince one it might be a crude attempt at an amphora or a *nefesh*. But something is intended. We should move beyond what it could possibly be and ask what is the intentionality that created this image?

All attempts have so far failed to explain why the drawing is "upside down." But if the Jewish engraver who made this etching had Jonah in mind, then it seems that some answers to our questions are forthcoming. According to the biblical author, Jonah was spat out by the "large fish" unto dry land (Jonah 2:11); that could be depicted by placing a fish upside down. Any other angle would mean that "Jonah" was launched into the air.

But how should we interpret the spherical "bottom"? If the object is "upside down," as almost all seem to agree, then we are looking at the "head" of something, perhaps a fish. Why was so much attention given to the horizontal markings in the round "head"? The author of Jonah also mentions that seaweed was wrapped around Jonah's head: "seaweed [Hebrew *swp*] twined around my head" (Jonah 2:6). Is this concept being depicted? Has the Jewish engraver tried to avoid depicting a face? Has he imagined Jonah's head protruding from a large fish with a tight mouth spitting out Jonah? Any analogies to what someone over three hundred years later than this tomb depicted in a Roman catacomb are too far out of context to warrant discussion. After 70 CE, this image was never seen again until now; hence it is not a model for other imaginative depictions of Jonah being spewed forth from a large fish.

What is meant by the squares inside the image? Could they be an attempt to depict a large fish (Leviathan?) that would have scales and thus be kosher? The only pre-70 CE faunal motif found by Avigad was a fish carved on a stone table; it has etched squares just as on ossuary 6.[11] Could they be an attempt to clarify that the fish is kosher?

Did the inscriber attempt to meld an image of a fish with a *nefesh*? Is there some conflation of symbols? Are there multiple meanings to be contemplated?

---

11. See the image of the fish in Avigad, *Discovering Jerusalem*, ill. 185.4 (opposite p. 168).

If this is a large fish and Jonah is intended, then it is possible to imagine a stick figure inside the fish. If so, the head is absurdly large. Why? Obviously, some Jews imagined the resurrection body to be similar to but different from the fleshy body. Would some early Jews have imagined that a resurrected body would have a large head? Is that the ideal body? We simply need to raise questions and be open to dialogue.

Any scholarly attempt to interpret ancient art should be respected. As Merleau-Ponty pointed out in many books, any refined interpretation demands improving the perception of the one perceiving. And as Polyani showed, all knowledge is personal knowledge. Hence we need each other in a dialogue that appreciates the input of others, whether philologists, archaeologists, biblical scholars, or specialists in ancient art.

As we explore the meaning of the drawing we need to include the inscription on ossuary 5. I sight read the four-line inscription to mean: "Divine Yahweh, who lifts up [or raised up], from [the tomb or death?]."[12] I remain uncertain about the last line and the reading "from" and what is implied. The inscription is impressively chiseled and certainly refers to some Jewish belief in resurrection or the afterlife. Why should this inscription be completely ignored in attempts to understand the drawing?

What type of Jew would have made this inscription and the drawing? A resurrection belief was shared by many early Jews, representing various groups or sects. As I showed in *Resurrection*, resurrection belief means that someone who lived and has died will be raised by God to an eternal existence with God.[13] The belief in a resurrection may be found in some Davidic psalms, but the first lucid (or undebatable) reference to it appears, perhaps ca. 200 BCE, in *1 Enoch*. Then chronologically, the concept appears in Dan 12. in a document probably not composed at Qumran but found there, the belief clearly appears in *On Resurrection* (5Q521) and in *Pseudo-Ezekiel* (4Q385-388). In many works of early Judaism the belief in a resurrection is evident, including Josephus's compositions, *Psalms of Solomon, Life of Adam and Eve,*

12. For an image of the inscription see J. D. Tabor and S. Jacobovici, *The Jesus Discovery* (New York: Simon & Schuster, 2012), p. 91. The inscription may be in alternating languages: Greek, Hebrew, Greek, and Hebrew, meaning: "Divine Yahweh, lift up, lift up." Jim Joyner informs me that the ASOR Blog has a careful study of the possible readings by Richard Bauckham. Richard and I have been discussing the inscription for months; I appreciate his dedication and intensive studies.

13. See J. H. Charlesworth, "Where Does the Concept of Resurrection Appear and How Do We Know That?" in Charlesworth et al., *Resurrection: The Origin and Future of a Biblical Doctrine* (New York: T&T Clark, 2006), pp. 12-17.

4 Ezra, 2 Baruch, 2 Enoch, History of the Rechabites, Lives of the Prophets, 1-
4 Maccabees, Pseudo-Philo, Apocryphon of Ezekiel, Pseudo-Phocylides, Sib-
ylline Oracles, Testament of Abraham, Testament of Job, Testaments of the
12 Patriarchs, Apocryphon of Ezekiel, and *Odes of Solomon.* The belief in resurrection is also found in the *Didache,* the *Hellenistic Synagogal Prayers,* and
the Amidah or 18 Benedictions. According to Hippolytus (but not Josephus),
the Essenes believed in the resurrection of the flesh (*Haer.* 9.27). The Samar-
itans believed that God would summon "his creatures" so that all of them
would "arise in one moment before him" (*Memar Markah* 4.12; cf. also *Yom
ad-Din* 26). Moreover, the concept of a bodily resurrection created and defined the Palestinian Jesus Movement; according to Paul, if Jesus was not
raised by God then "our proclamation is in vain and your faith is in vain"
(1 Cor 15:14). Without any doubt, the concept of resurrection (far more than
a belief in a coming Messiah) brings into perspective the shared beliefs and
hopes within early Judaism.[14]

Are the inscription and the drawing not to be perceived within Jewish
resurrection beliefs? It is as absurd to dismiss the possibility that this tomb
has some relation with the Palestinian Jesus Movement as to claim that it
clearly must be labeled a "Christian" tomb. Emotions are too inflamed by
such unscholarly outbursts.

Regarding Etchings on an Ossuary in "the Patio Tomb"

Now, let us turn, with an open mind, to some etchings inside the drawing, at
"the bottom." Some markings seem to appear on the image near what some
think is the mouth of an amphora or the closed mouth of a "large fish."
When the inscribed drawing is seen as it is on the ossuary (an amphora or a
fish upside down), the etchings look like an inscription in Hebrew.[15] Four
separate markings may be discerned on the stone; each was most likely made
by a hammer and a chisel. I shall begin with the clearest Hebrew letter and

14. But note Sir 10:11; Sirach apparently taught that after death a person inherits
worms. The Sadducees probably denied any concept of resurrection or positive afterlife
(viz., Josephus, *War* 2.165; Acts 23:8).

15. Hebrew letters on ossuaries are notoriously difficult to discern and can be idio-
syncratic. For examples, in Rahmani, *Catalogue,* the *aleph* has no left foot, in no. 483 the
aleph has two left slanted vertical strokes, and in no. 803 the *aleph* looks like an inverted
'*ayin.* In no. 559 the *shin* has only two arms. In no. 571 the "Bar Na?um" becomes possible
if we allow the final *mem* to be two disconnected strokes.

I have been told the following image is not altered or edited *(courtesy: AP).*[16]

16. Felix Golubev sent me this clarification: "Attached are the two best images of the 'Yonah' inscription. One image came from the high definition camera and the other from the fiber-optic video probe. None of these images was altered, enhanced, or even colour corrected. The difference in colour is due to how these two cameras process light. In the HD image, you will notice that the subjects on the left and on the right are out of

564

then move to its right (even though it should be obvious that the letters were written right to left).

The first etching on the left has the unmistakable form of a *he*. The letter is written in three strokes. First, the person drew the horizontal line (the "roof"), and then added the leg to the right and then a shorter, slanted leg to the left. The left leg is well within the end stroke of the horizontal roof. The form of the *he* is typical of pre-70 scripts well known from Dead Sea Scroll manuscripts; examples are plentiful (e.g., 4QDan[b] that dates between 20 and 50 CE). The *he* is similar to many inscriptions on ossuaries.[17] Hebrew *he* represents the English *h*. Anyone who has worked on early manuscripts or pre-70 lapidary scripts should immediately see the *he*.

The meaning of the mark to the right of the *he* is not prima facie obvious. It is one connected stroke as the following image presented here shows (p. 567 below). Conceivably, it can be a *lamed* [= L], but the upper portion of the stroke is too slanted to the left and the lower one appears too long (but the *lamed* appears in various ways prior to 70 CE). The one continuous stroke reminds me of a *nun;* one should be able to discern the turn to the left at the bottom of the stroke. The form is far from clear because the upper portion seems too long; but a lapidary *nun* is not to be confused with the Herodian Formal Book Hand inscribed upon lined leather. For example, in ossuary 571 in Rahmani, the *nun* has a very long bottom stroke and it intrudes underneath two following letters. Perhaps this was caused by the need to inscribe stone with a chisel and the absence of a scribal horizontal line to guide the inscriber for hanging the Hebrew letters. Plus a stick figure and the alleged "mouth of a fish" may be intruding within or causing the elongated *nun*. The form of this *nun* is somewhat similar to the forms in hundreds of Dead Sea Scroll manuscripts; for example, it appears in 4QDeut[j] that dates from about 50 CE (also, in contrast, the Deut ms. represents the Formal Book Hand on leather). The *nun* becomes more likely when one studies that letter on ossuaries.[18] Hebrew *nun* represents the English "N."

The slightly curved scratch to the right of the *nun* is inelegant and some imagination is required (and speculation is frequently the case when studying lapidary scripts).[19] It seems somewhat similar to the *zain* in

---

focus. This is because the HD camera has a shallow depth of field and when you zoom in whatever is in front goes out of focus."

17. For examples, see *Catalogue*, nos. 8, 16, 107, 222, 414, and 730.
18. For examples, see ibid., nos. 12, 68, 107, 270, and esp. 76 and 571.
19. Notice the odd *nun* in ibid., no. 465 (p. 181); it has a long horizontal base that

4QNum[b] that dates from the early first century CE. Most likely the form represents a *waw*. The top of this "letter" may have a "loop" as in the "Loop Mode" of the Herodian Ossuary Script.[20] The form appears similar to the right-curved *waw* in Murabba'at 18 that has been dated to 55 or 56 CE. The curved backward *waw* of *Catalogue*, no. 38, is similar.[21] This Hebrew letter equals the English *w, u,* or *o*.

On first viewing, the next stroke to the right looks like a *zayin*. The top slants downward past the horizontal stroke. On examination, one can clearly see an upper loop to the left of the vertical stroke. The letter may well be *yod* as in the "Loop Mode" form,[22] but the extension to the upper right is problematic. Perhaps the inscriber meant to denote a *yod*. Similar forms with a looped *yod* appear in Rahmani, *Catalogue*, nos. 82, 380, 411, 414, 421, 430 *(bis)*, 435, 559, 603, 705, and 706. This Hebrew letter represents the English *y, i,* or *j*.

Thus from left to right, which is the direction in which English is read, we may discern: HNOJ. Since Hebrew is written right to left, we may recognize: JONH. The "a" vowel did not appear in Hebrew manuscripts until after the seventh century CE. Most likely, therefore, we may comprehend the inscription: "JONAH."[23]

The following high-definition image is not altered or enhanced. Notice that the *nun* is connected and appears to be one angular stroke. Obviously, I never intimated that all the lines in "the head of the fish" are letters; anyone who imagined that I did make such a claim, or that I ignored some lines, simply was dependent on a journalist's summary of my rather lengthy and detailed comments.[24]

---

extends way past the next consonant, supplying "Kynoros." "Aninas" in no. 475 is really "Aniinias."

20. See the example in A. Yardeni, *The Book of Hebrew Script* (Jerusalem: Carta, 1997), pp. 178-79.

21. I am also impressed that this *waw* looks like the *zayin* on ossuaries 74, 75, 82, and 88.

22. See Yardeni, *Book of Hebrew Script*, pp. 178-79.

23. On the name "Jonah," see Rahmani, *Catalogue*, p. 134. It is rare.

24. My reading was announced in the *Globe and Mail* on April 11, 2012. Graffiti on ossuaries are often just scratches; some cannot be deciphered (Rahmani, *Catalogue*, nos. 83, 89, 130). Some inscriptions are curved as in ossuary 6 (*Catalogue*, no. 83). Some graffiti are extremely sloppy (e.g., *Catalogue*, nos. 191, 582, 610, 651, 682, 694, 718, 773). As I have said before, in no. 704 (the famous ossuary from East Talpiot), the name "Yeshua, son of Yehosef," is an educated guess. Debates are focused on the meaning of some inscriptions (e.g., see *Catalogue*, no. 15, and the suggestions of Mayer, Sukenik, Rahmani, Savignac, and Klein). Do the markings on ossuary 33 in Rahmani's *Catalogue* have meanings?

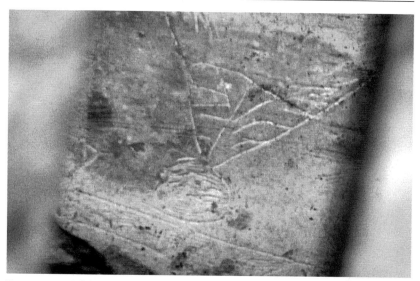

I am open to the suggestion that the "artist" intended an oblate circle to symbolize an eye of the fish and the long line to denote a closed mouth; conceivably he also seemed to depict a stick-figured Jonah (which I will discuss later).
(Image courtesy: AP)

Finally, no assurance is provided for any reading. I am bothered by the
mixing of scripts. The inscriber began with the looped lapidary script and
then continued with forms known from leather manuscripts. Had he been
trained as a scribe? Did he begin with the well-known lapidary script and
shifted to forms with which he was more familiar? The lack of precision in
this inscription is due perhaps to the need to chisel on stone. Were the forms
twisted by the shape of the circular mouth of the alleged fish? Did the inscriber wish to meld the inscription with a stick figure within the mouth?
The Hebrew letters, the image of the stick figure, and the drawing seem to
me to be the same depth and style.

Once again, what about the curving nature of the script? First, one
should not resist the possibility of a script because it is curved; a curved or
waving script is evident on some ossuaries. Second, one should not confuse
a lined formal Herodian script with a lapidary inscription. Even in editing
ancient manuscripts we are forced to work with consonants that are virtually impossible to discern; context alone indicates that a *beth* has masquer-
aded as a *kaph*. An unsophisticated engraver chiseling on stone is not to be
confused with a skilled scribe. Third, the one who made the inscription was

daily familiar with coins bearing curved Hebrew inscriptions. On these coins, the Hebrew letters were rounded and within a curved border as we see with ossuary 6, and resemble the letters that are curved in the putative mouth of a fish.

This reading represents my present speculation and ongoing research. I and all others need to see the ossuary itself or at least a better image of the inscription and the drawing. We are now working with an image that is possibly distorted by a flexible camera. I offer my reading for other epigraphers to discuss. As with many inscriptions, my reading can neither be proved nor disproved.

I am pleased to learn that one of the finest epigraphers in Israel, Robert Deutsch, has no doubt that the inscription clearly reads YONAH. Deutsch sent me this question: "What are statistically the chances for a so-called decoration to look like these four letters?" He answered: "One in over 1 billion." I have been informed that Prof. Haggai Misgav says definitely there are letters, but instead of *yod* and *nun,* he prefers maybe *zayin* and *lamed,* thus ZILA or ZEILA.

The Jonah Stick Figure

Is there a stick figure in the alleged mouth of "the fish"? Along with others who first saw the drawing, I saw what looked like a stick figure inside the fish. I am persuaded that a Jew may have etched a figure inside the so-called fish. It extends downward to become part of the mouth and then protrudes from the "fish" with a bubble head. To the left of the stick figure is a circle that seems intended. Could it be the eye of the fish?

Rahmani interpreted a second-century CE incised drawing as a "featureless human figure(?)."[25] He perceived an outer garment that covered the shoulders and a "peaked cap or hairdo." The figure's "hands are covered by the garment." He wisely reported that this drawing seems to be a depiction of "the deceased and his 'soul,'" since no *nefesh* or contemporaneous tomb structure or tower has "'lattice'-patterned triangles." Rahmani is to be lauded for his reflections and focused imagination. The same applies to what seems to be a stick figure in a "large fish."

---

25. *Catalogue,* pp. 195-96; see the drawing on p. 195 [B]. See pl. 79 with the image in 555:B (detail). The figure does look as Rahmani states. I can discern lines that look like "stick-legs and feet." In the photograph (but not the modern drawing), the garment does look like it is pulled around the shoulders. What looks like an "eye" is only a pockmark in the stone.

Finally, how important is the discovery of ossuaries in the Talpiot Patio Tomb? Will those in the media or academia twist what may be informative in our search for understanding early Jews, including some phenomena perhaps related to Jesus? Can we have a civil and sensitive discussion about a drawing that is clearly Jewish, unique, and pre-70? How do we discern the intended, implied, or attributed meaning of an early Jewish drawing?

If some Jewish engraver intended to depict Jonah and the "large fish," it is prima facie possible that repentance is intended. That seems to be the meaning attributed to Jesus by Luke (ch. 11); and Jonah is still read on the evening of Yom Kippur (the Day of Atonement) to signal the importance of seeking forgiveness before God. If God forgave the heathen, then God will forgive his chosen people, the Jews.

If meaning resides in ambiguity, and all symbols are multivalent, then how can anyone continue to be scholarly while issuing dogmatic pronouncements about the intended meaning or perceived meaning in a symbol?

The Prophet Jonah and Jesus' Followers

Only Luke and Matthew recorded the name "Jonah." How do these evangelists help us in this research? Luke does attribute to Jesus a reference to Jonah and focuses on "the sign of Jonah," denoting the possibility of repentance (Luke 11:29-32).

Did Jesus mean by a "sign" the time for seeking atonement through repentance or resurrection? The latter becomes clear only in Matthew:

> Then some of the scribes and Pharisees answered, saying to him, "Teacher, we wish to see a sign from you." But he [Jesus] answered (and) said to them, "An evil and adulterous generation seeks for a sign; but[26] no sign will be given to it except the sign of the prophet Jonah. For as Jonah was three days and three nights in the belly of the sea monster,[27] so will the Son of Man be three days and three nights in the heart of the earth. The men of Nineveh will arise in the judgment with this generation and condemn it. For they epented at the preaching of Jonah, and behold, something greater than Jonah is here. (Matt 12:38-41)

26. Lit. "and."
27. Or, "large fish."

Matthew claims that as Jonah was three days in the body of the large fish, so Jesus was three days in the body of the earth, and was resurrected by God. These Jewish reflections are from the first century CE, but after 70 CE they were reported by those who claimed to have seen a resurrected Jesus:

> For I delivered to you as of first importance what I also received: That Christ . . . was raised on the third day in accordance with the Scriptures, and that he appeared to Cephas [= Peter], then to the twelve. Then he appeared to more than five hundred brothers at one time. . . . Then he appeared to James, then to all the apostles. Last of all . . . he appeared to me. (1 Cor 15:3-8)

As Pope Benedict XVI states in *Jesus of Nazareth*, although the "essential point is that the Resurrection itself is in accordance with the Scriptures," no scripture passage clearly supplies Paul's text: "There is no direct scriptural testimony pointing to 'the third day.'"[28] Jesus was not three days *and three nights* in the tomb.

On 1 April 2012 in *The Catholic Register*, Michael Swan wrote:

> The idea that this tomb may contain the bones of Jesus is presented as something perhaps scandalous to Christians. The film makers concede there's no way to prove that any particular bones buried in first century Jerusalem belong to any particular person. But even if they could, how scandalous is it? Catholics have always known the resurrection does not refer to a resuscitated corpse. Jesus was resurrected in a spiritual body, just as all of us will be resurrected at the end of history regardless of the decay of our flesh and bones. And of course Jesus' spiritual body is no less real than the body Mary bore in her womb.
>
> Putting aside the scandal that's not really a scandal, The Jesus Discovery does not explore this tomb. It photographs the other tomb, which may belong to Joseph of Arimathea. The idea is that if this second tomb belongs to Joseph of Arimathea it would, based on the Gospel story, bolster the theory that the first tomb contains bones of Jesus, His mother and His brothers.
>
> While we find no hard evidence that the second tomb actually belonged to Joseph of Arimathea, there's lots of circumstantial evidence. It

---

28. Joseph Ratzinger [= Pope Benedict XVI], *Jesus of Nazareth: Part Two* (Vatican City: Libreria Editrice Vaticana, 2011), p. 257.

could be. We also find, carved onto one of the ossuaries, a Christian symbol of the resurrection. It is a depiction of Jonah being spat out by the whale.

What's interesting about this is not whether the ossuary belonged to Joseph of Arimathea or some other wealthy Jew who followed Jesus. What's interesting is that [the] core of Christian belief in years immediately following events we celebrate during Holy Week was resurrection.

Here is another grain of evidence in the mountain of archeological proof which has come to light in our lifetimes that says the first Christians believed what the Church still believes — Christ rose from the dead, and we shall rise with him on the last day.

This feature presents balanced and insightful advice for Christians, and not just Roman Catholics. It is the position that I have taken from the beginning of discussions focused on the Talpiot I tomb. Yet some so-called Christians castigated me; one seminary withdrew a D.D. that had been unanimously offered, claiming that Jesus' bones, if found, would mean the disproval of Christian beliefs. Other Christians wrote, stating that I was a heretic and that Jesus' bones had to be in heaven.

I do not wish to prove them wrong (how could I?). I wanted to be open to reflections that Jesus could have been raised by God and yet his bones could still be in some place on earth. After Jesus' resurrection, according to John, he passed through walls and doors. I doubt that he was doing so with his old bones.

Conclusion

In conclusion, I wish to focus on what is being seen. I am not interested in supporting either the minimalists or the maximalists. I appreciate Crossan's suggestion that exhorts experts to stop bickering and look at the image.[29] I am convinced we should avoid any claims that the image is related to the *ichthys* anagram, which means "Jesus, Christ, Son of God, Savior." That anagram appears much later.

---

29. If it becomes relatively certain that the image was made by a follower of Jesus in Jerusalem, then we should expect him to be very circumspect and careful not to reveal his beliefs. Thus he might have intentionally drawn an image that would be ambiguous. After all, John the Baptizer, Jesus, and perhaps Stephen had been martyred. Was Stephen stoned and buried within the present confines of the Ecole biblique?

I do not see a strong connection between the recent discoveries in Talpiot II and Talpiot I, which was incorrectly (in my judgment) hailed as Jesus' tomb. I am known for concluding that Talpiot I may belong to Jesus' clan or followers. As we seek to discern who is the "Jesus, son of Joseph," that is on two separate ossuaries, we should recall that four men named "Jesus" and three men named "Joseph" served as high priests from about 35 BCE to 64 CE.

Whereas Talpiot I had at least six names etched on ossuaries, Talpiot II has only one ossuary that can be seen with a name: "Mara" in *kokh* two.[30] As we seek to discern the historical and theological importance of all these archaeological discoveries, let us seek to avoid the declarations that has not been fruitful.

Let scholars agree to continue questioning and debating. As we interpret ancient images, none of us can be certain. We come closer to certainty through discussions and open conversations through the usual means of publication. We may part disagreeing. That is fine; and I will never forget Nelson Glueck arguing with Benjamin Mazar beneath the Temple Mount and Kathleen Kenyon blasting Roland de Vaux in the large lecture hall in the École biblique. But they disagreed without jeopardizing the deep admiration they reserved for each other.

Finally, we Christians do not need any proof or support for our commitment to God through Jesus Christ, but we should find inviting the enlightening reflections in windows provided by the Talpiot Patio Tomb. Through them, we may see more clearly the world that shaped the lives and beliefs of luminaries like the Righteous Teacher, Hillel, John the Baptizer, Jesus, Peter, Gamaliel, Paul, and Stephen. What are we now learning about Jewish resurrection faith before the burning of the temple in 70 CE?

Appendix I: Mathematical Computations of Ossuary 6

The numbers of geometric figures across the boundary appear to be consistent; for instance 20 full squares across the top, 20 full sections up the leftmost side, and 20 full sections up the rightmost side. One of the two inner carvings is roughly a rectangle. Evidence of lack of care in carving that rectangle is the fact that the numbers clash. That rectangle has 12 squares

30. The 1981 black-and-white photograph indicates a name on ossuary 4. Amos Kloner reported seeing two Greek names on an ossuary.

across its top (with one of those squares extending to the left, and one of those squares extending to the right of the rectangle). That rectangle appears to have fewer squares along its left side than along its right side, but there is sloppiness along its left side that makes it difficult to count its number of squares (especially when one gets to the 8th square from the bottom of that left side); it appears that there are 11 squares on the rectangle's left side (12, if one double-counts the top square on that column of squares) and yet 12 squares on its right side (13, if one double-counts the top square on that column of squares). That rectangle also has seven squares across its bottom (9, if one double-counts the leftmost and the rightmost square in that row of squares). Thus I would judge that the one who made the borders is not the same person who made the rectangle. The carving of the amphora or fish is also inelegant, but one cannot compare squares, even if (from top to bottom) one could count four, five, seven, and five (?). Did the author intend such different numbers of ornamentation? I think the most likely answer is no; the person simply lacked requisite skill or time. The figures reported here assume that the ossuary was precisely replicated.

Appendix II: Postscript from Professor Rami Arav on 5.6.12

Thank you very much for this detailed article. It is brilliant as always.

Now when you point it out, I see the word "Jonah." How did we miss it immediately when we saw it? It is not only clearly "Jonah," but it is exactly where it is supposed to be. It is not on the top of the ossuary, alluding perhaps to the name of the deceased, or even at the bottom as perhaps a caption, but in the mouth of the fish, in both sides of the stick representing Jonah's body. The inscription could not be better.

I find it very similar to Jewish coins where a name with a title is surrounded by symbols instead of a portrait or a figure (like "Jonathan High Priest and the Head of the Jewish Assembly" surrounded by the cornucopias, or the name Tiberius Caesar surrounded by wreath on Tiberias coins minted by Antipas). You are absolutely correct: Hebrew inscriptions on ossuaries are notoriously difficult to interpret. However, I am pleased my initial guess that it is Jonah is confirmed in this inscription.

Complete Findings From the Patio Tomb

(7 Ossuaries)

7. Plain Ossuary

"After the chamber and the standing pit were hewn, the loculi were cut in a counterclockwise direction, from right to left. The process of burial and reburial was evidently also followed from right to left."

– Rachel Hachlili, "Jewish Funerary Customs, Practices and Rites in the Second Temple Period", Leiden, The Netherlands: Brill, 2005 (p. 56).

6. Jonah image; cross; fish tail

(Ossuary in the back)

1. Highly decorated with "Nefesh"

5. Resurrection inscription

4. Highly decorated (Not fully explored)

(Ossuary in the back)

3. "Mara" inscription

2. Highly decorated

For help in understanding the claims made by the maximalists, here is the data *(courtesy: AP)*

Appendix III

One can appreciate the main reason there is such heat generated by this debate over tombs that may in some way be related to Jesus or his followers. It reminds me of the problems confronted by the great scholar Eliezar Sukenik. The Israeli journalist, Tom Segev, reminds us in his *One Palestine, Complete,* that Colonel Frederick Kisch "immediately demanded that he [Sukenik] deny the story, to avoid giving the impression that Zionists were challenging the status of Jesus' traditional burial site."[31] Kisch, one of the few Jews who joined the British Army and a learned and experienced man with manners of a *diplomat de carrière,* ran the political department of the Zionist Commission. The "story" was Sukenik's discovery of an ossuary bearing the name "Jesus, son of Joseph." Referring to archaeological discoveries on the prop-

31. T. Segev, *One Palestine, Complete: Jews and Arabs under the British Mandate,* trans. Haim Watzman (New York: Metropolitan Books, 2000), p. 302.

erty of A. David Kiraz, Sukenik concluded: "All our evidence indicates that we have in this tomb the earliest records of Christianity in existence. It may also have a bearing on the historicity of Jesus and the crucifixion."³² The luminary and founder of the Ecole biblique, L.-H. Vincent, confirmed that the ossuary did preserve the name "Jesu' son of Yehosef," and that it dated from 150 BCE to 150 CE; but no scientific data connects the name or tomb with "our Savior."³³ A feature on Sukenik's discovery appeared in *Life* (December 22, 1947).³⁴ How and in what ways Sukenik's research is related to Talpiot I and Talpiot II, and the provenience of the ossuary he announced to the world, is worth exploring.

32. Sukenik, *The Earliest Records of Christianity: With a New Introduction by George A. Kiraz* (Piscataway, N.J.: Gorgias Press, 2008), p. 30 [article originally published in 1947].

33. L.-H. Vincent, "Épitaphe prétendue de N.-S. Jésus-Christ," *Rendiconti della Pont. Accad. Rom. Di Archeol* 7 (1931): 215-39; see p. 238.

34. Note the issue appeared just before Christmas. See "A Tomb on the Road to Bethlehem," *Life* (Dec. 22, 1947): 75ff. [I have copies of the article but cannot discern page numbers.]

Selected Bibliography

Blake A. Jurgens and Jon David Shearer III

Attridge, H. W. "Josephus and His Works." Pp. 157-84 in *Jewish Writings of the Second Temple Period: Apocrypha, Pseudepigrapha, Qumran Sectarian Writings, Philo, Josephus*. Ed. M. Stone. CRINT 2/2. Philadelphia: Fortress, 1984.

Aviam, M. "Ossuaries." In *Jews, Pagans and Christians in the Galilee*. Land of Galilee 1. Rochester: Institute for Galilean Archaeology and the University of Rochester Press, 2004.

Avigad, N. "A Depository of Inscribed Ossuaries in the Kidron Valley." *IEJ* 12 (1962): 1-12.

————. *Discovering Jerusalem*. Nashville: Nelson, 1983.

Bagatti, B., and J. T. Milik. *Gli Scavi del "Dominus Flevit,"* part 1: *La Necropoli del Periodo Romano*. Pubblicazioni dello Studium Biblicum Franciscanum 13. Jerusalem: Franciscan Printing Press, 1958.

Barag, D., and D. Flusser. "The Ossuary of Yehohanah Granddaughter of the High Priest Theophilus." *IEJ* 36 (1986): 39-44.

Barclay, J. M. G. *Flavius Josephus: Translation and Commentary*. Vol. 10: *Against Apion*. Ed. S. Mason. Leiden: Brill, 2007.

Bauckham, R. *Jesus and the Eyewitnesses*. Grand Rapids: Eerdmans, 2006.

————. "Traditions about the Tomb of James, the Brother of Jesus." Pp. 61-77 in *Poussières de christianisme et de judaïsme antiques: Études réunies en l'honneur de Jean-Daniel Kaestli et Éric Junod*. Ed. A. Frey and R. Gounelle. Lausanne: Zèbre, 2007.

Baumbach, G. "The Sadducees in Josephus." Pp. 103-95 in *Josephus, the Bible and History*. Ed. L. Feldman and G. Hata. Detroit: Wayne State University Press, 1989.

Beall, T. S. *Josephus' Description of the Essenes Illustrated by the Dead Sea Scrolls*. SNTSMS 58. Cambridge: Cambridge University Press, 1988.

Benoit, P., J. T. Milik, and R. de Vaux. *Les Grottes de Murabba'at*. Discoveries in the Judaean Desert II. Oxford: Clarendon Press, 1961.

Black, M. "The Account of the Essenes in Hippolytus and Josephus." Pp. 172-75 in *The Background of the New Testament and Its Eschatology.* Ed. W. D. Davies and D. Daube. Cambridge: Cambridge University Press, 1956.

Bloch-Smith, E. *Judahite Burial Practices and Beliefs about the Dead.* JSPTSup 123. Sheffield: Sheffield Academic Press, 1992.

Boys, M. *Has God Only One Blessing? Judaism as a Source of Christian Self-Understanding.* New York: Paulist Press, 2000.

Bremmer, J. N. *The Early Greek Concept of the Soul.* Princeton: Princeton University Press, 1983.

Brock, A. G. *Mary Magdalene, the First Apostle: The Struggle for Authority.* HTS 61. Cambridge: Harvard Divinity School, 2003.

Brown, R. E. *The Death of the Messiah: From Gethsemane to the Grave.* 2 vols. ABRL. 1994. Repr. New Haven: Yale University Press, 2007.

Brown R. E., et al., eds. *Mary in the New Testament: A Collaborative Assessment by Protestant and Roman Catholic Scholars.* New York: Paulist Press, 1978.

Bruce, F. F. "Paul on Immortality." *SJT* 24 (1971): 457-72.

Brumfield, A. C. *The Attic Festivals of Demeter and Their Relation to the Agricultural Year.* New York: Arno, 1981.

Burkert, W. *Greek Religion: Archaic and Classical.* Oxford: Blackwell, 1985.

Burnett, F. "Philo on Immortality: A Thematic Study of Philo's Concept of *Palingenesia.*" *CBQ* 46 (1984): 447-70.

Burroughs, D. *The Jesus Family Tomb Controversy: How the Evidence Falls Short.* Ann Arbor: Nimble, 2007.

Carrier, R. "The Burial of Jesus in Light of Jewish Law." Pp. 369-92 in *The Empty Tomb: Jesus Beyond the Grave.* Ed. R. Price and J. J. Lowder. Amherst: Prometheus, 2005.

Carson, M. C. "And They Said Nothing to Anyone: A Redaction-Critical Study of the Role and Status of Women in the Crucifixion, Burial and Resurrection Stories of the Canonical and Apocryphal Gospels." Ph.D. diss. University of Newcastle upon Tyne, 1990.

Cavallin, H. C. C. *Life after Death: Paul's Argument for the Resurrection of the Dead in 1 Cor 15; Part 1, An Inquiry into the Jewish Background.* Lund: Gleerup, 1974.

Charles, R. H. *A Critical History of the Doctrine of a Future Life in Israel, in Judaism, and in Christianity.* 2nd ed. London: Adam and Charles Black, 1913.

Charlesworth, J. H. *Authentic Apocrypha: False and Genuine Christian Apocrypha.* The Dead Sea Scrolls and Christian Origins Library 2. N. Richland Hills, Tex.: Bibal, 1998.

———. *The Good and Evil Serpent: How a Universal Symbol Became Christianized.* Anchor Yale Bible Reference Library. New Haven: Yale University Press, 2010.

———. *Jesus Within Judaism: New Light from Exciting Archaeological Discoveries.* ABRL. New York: Doubleday, 1988.

———. "Prolegomenous Reflections Towards a Taxonomy of Resurrection Texts (1QH^a, 1En, 4Q521, Paul, Luke, the Fourth Gospel, and Psalm 30)." Pp. 237-64 in *The Changing Face of Judaism, Christianity, and Other Greco-Roman Religions in Antiquity.* Ed. I. H. Henderson and G. S. Oegema. Studien zu den jüdischen

Schriften aus hellenistisch-römischer Zeit 2. Gütersloh: Gütersloher Verlagshaus, 2006.

———. "Résurrection individuelle et immortalité de l'âme." Pp. 505-51 in *Histoire du Christianisme*. Vol. 14: *Anamnēsis*. Ed. J.-M. Mayeur et al. Paris: Desclée, 2001.

———. "Theodicy in Early Jewish Writings: A Selected Overview." Pp. 470-508 in *Theodicy in the World of the Bible*. Ed. A. Laato and J. de Moor. Leiden: Brill, 2003.

———. "Where Does the Concept of Resurrection Appear and How Do We Know That?" Pp. 1-21 in J. H. Charlesworth et al., *Resurrection: The Origin and Future of a Biblical Doctrine*. New York: T&T Clark, 2006.

Charlesworth, J. H., and W. P. Weaver, eds. *What Has Archaeology to Do with Faith?* Harrisburg: Trinity Press International, 1992.

Charlesworth, J. H., et al. *The New Testament Apocrypha and Pseudepigrapha: A Guide to Publications, with Excursuses on Apocalypses*. ATLA Bibliography Series 17. Metuchen, N.J.: American Theological Library Association and Scarecrow Press, 1987.

Charlesworth, J. H., et al. *Resurrection: The Origin and Future of a Biblical Doctrine*. New York: T&T Clark, 2006.

Chilton, B. D., and C. A. Evans. *James the Just and Christian Origins*. NovTSup 98. Leiden: Brill, 1999.

Clark-Soles, J. *Death and the Afterlife in the New Testament*. New York: T&T Clark, 2006.

Cohen-Matlofsky, C. "Controverse sur les coutumes funéraires des Juifs en Palestine aux deux premiers siècles de l'Empire romain." *L'information historique* 53 (1991): 21-26.

———. *Les Laics en Palestine d'Auguste à Hadrien: Étude prosopographique*. Paris: Honoré Champion, 2001.

Collins, J. J. *Apocalypticism in the Dead Sea Scrolls*. Literature of the Dead Sea Scrolls. New York: Routledge, 1997.

———. *Daniel: A Commentary*. Hermeneia. Minneapolis: Fortress, 1993.

———. "The Root of Immortality: Death in the Context of Jewish Wisdom." *HTR* 71 (1978): 177-92.

Cooper A., and B. Goldstein. "The Cult of the Dead and the Theme of the Entry into the Land." *Biblical Interpretation* 1/3 (1993): 285-303.

Cotton, H. M., and J. Geiger. *Masada II: The Latin and Greek Documents*. Jerusalem: Israel Exploration Society/The Hebrew University of Jerusalem, 1989.

Cotton, H. M., and A. Yardmen. *Aramaic Hebrew and Greek Documentary Texts from Nahal Hever and Other Sites*. Discoveries in the Judaean Desert XXVII. Oxford: Clarendon Press, 1997.

Crossan, J. D. *The Birth of Christianity*. San Francisco: HarperSanFrancisco, 1995.

Cumont, F. *The Afterlife in Roman Paganism*. New Haven: Yale University Press, 1922.

Davenport, G. L. *The Eschatology of the Book of Jubilees*. StPB 20. Leiden: Brill, 1997.

Davies, J. *Death, Burial and Rebirth in the Religions of Antiquity*. London: Routledge, 1999.

Demski, W., and R. J. Marks "The Jesus Tomb Math." Pp. 113-51 in *Buried Hope or Risen Savior: The Search for the Jesus Tomb*. Ed. Charles Quarles. Nashville: B&H Academic, 2008.

deSilva, D. A. *4 Maccabees: Introduction and Commentary on the Greek Text in Codex Sinaiticus*. Septuagint Commentary Series. Leiden: Brill, 2006.

Dimant, D. "Resurrection, Restoration and Time-Curtailing in Qumran, Early Judaism and Christianity." *RevQ* 19 (1999-2000): 527-48.

Droge, A. A., and J. D. Tabor. *A Noble Death: Suicide and Martyrdom among Christians and Jews in Antiquity*. San Francisco: HarperSanFrancisco, 1992.

Eliade, M. *Rites and Symbols of Initiation*. New York: Harper Torchbooks, 1958.

Elitzur, Y. *Ancient Place Names in the Holy Land: Preservation and History*. Winona Lake, Ind.: Eisenbrauns, 2004.

Elledge, C. D. *The Bible and the Dead Sea Scrolls*. SBLABS 14. Atlanta: Society of Biblical Literature, 2005.

————. *Life after Death in Early Judaism: The Evidence of Josephus*. WUNT 2/208. Tübingen: Mohr Siebeck, 2006.

Eshel, E. "Personal Names in the Qumran Sect." Pp. 39-52 in *These Are the Names: Studies in Jewish Onomastics*. Ed. A. Demsky, J. A. Reif, and J. Tabory. Ramat Gan: Bar-Ilan University Press, 1997.

Evans, C. A. "The Burial of Jesus." Pp. 64-68 in Evans and N. T. Wright, *Jesus, the Final Days: What Really Happened?* Ed. T. A. Miller. Louisville: Westminster John Knox, 2009.

————. *Jesus and the Ossuaries*. Waco: Baylor University Press, 2003.

Ferguson, E., *Backgrounds of Early Christianity*. Grand Rapids: Eerdmans, 1993.

Feuerverger, A. "Statistical Analysis of an Archeological Find." *Annals of Applied Statistics* 2 (2008): 3-54.

Figueras, P. *Decorated Jewish Ossuaries*. DMOA 20. Leiden: Brill, 1985.

————. "The Ornamentation of Jewish Ossuaries — Is It Symbolic?" *Archaeologya* 2 (1989): 49-51.

Fischer, U. *Eschatologie und Jenseitserwartung im hellenistischen Diasporajudentum*. BZNW 44. Berlin: de Gruyter, 1978.

Frey, J-B., ed. *Corpus Inscriptionum Judaicarum*. 2 vols. Rome: Pontificio Instituto di archeologia Christiana, 1936-1952.

Gibson, S. "Is the Talpiot Tomb Really the Family Tomb of Jesus?" *NEA* 69 (2006): 118-24.

Gillman, N. *The Death of Death: Resurrection and Immortality in Jewish Thought*. Woodstock, Vt.: Jewish Light Publishers, 2000.

Goodenough, E. R. *Jewish Symbols in the Greco-Roman Period*. 13 vols. New York: Pantheon, 1953-1968.

Goodenough, E. R. *Jewish Symbols in the Greco-Roman Period*, ed. J. Neusner, abridged ed. Princeton: Princeton University Press, 1988.

Goren, Y., A. Ayalon, and M. Bar-Matthews, "Authenticity Examination of the Inscription on the Ossuary Attributed to James, Brother of Jesus." *Journal of Archaeological Science* 31 (2004): 1185-89.

Goren, Y., A. Ayalon, M. Bar-Matthews, and B. Schilman, "Authenticity Examination of the Jehoash Inscription." *Journal of the Institute of Archeology of Tel-Aviv University* 31 (2004): 3-16.

Greenhut, Z. "The 'Caiaphas' Tomb in North Talpiyot, Jerusalem." *'Atiqot* 21 (1992): 63-72.

Grelot, P. "L'Eschatologie des Esséniens et le Livre d'Hénoch." *RevQ* 1 (1958-59): 113-31.

Habermas, G. R. *The Secret of the Talpiot Tomb: Unravelling the Mystery of the Jesus Family Tomb.* Nashville: Holman, 2007.

Hachlili, R. *Ancient Jewish Art and Archaeology in the Land of Israel.* HO 7/1/2/B4. Leiden: Brill, 1988.

―――. "The Goliath Family in Jericho: Funerary Inscriptions from a First Century AD Jewish Monumental Tomb." *BASOR* 235 (1979): 31-65.

―――. *Jewish Funerary Customs, Practices and Rites in the Second Temple Period.* JSJSup 94. Leiden: Brill, 2005.

―――. "Names and Nicknames of Jews in Second Temple Times." Pp. 188-211 in *A.-J. Brawer Memorial Volume.* ErIsr 17. Jerusalem: Israel Exploration Society, 1984.

Hearon, H. E. *The Mary Magdalene Tradition: Witness and Counter-Witness in Early Christian Communities.* Collegeville, Minn.: Liturgical Press, 2004.

Hengel, M. "Das Begräbnis Jesu bei Paulus und die leibliche Auferstehung aus dem Grabe." Pp. 119-83 in *Auferstehung — Resurrection: The Fourth Durham-Tübingen Research Symposium: Resurrection, Transfiguration and Exaltation in Old Testament, Ancient Judaism and Early Christianity (Tübingen, September, 1999).* Ed. F. Avemarie and H. Lichtenberger. WUNT 135. Tübingen: Mohr Siebeck, 2001.

―――. *The 'Hellenization' of Judaea in the First Century after Christ.* Philadelphia: Trinity Press International, 1989.

―――. *The Zealots: Investigations into the Jewish Freedom Movement in the Period from Herod I until 70 A.D.* Trans. D. Smith. Edinburgh: T&T Clark, 1989.

Hogan, K. M. "The Exegetical Background of the 'Ambiguity of Death' in the Wisdom of Solomon." *JSJ* 30 (1999): 1-24.

Horbury, W., and D. Noy. *Jewish Inscriptions of Graeco-Roman Egypt, with an Index of the Jewish Inscriptions of Egypt and Cyrenaica.* Cambridge: Cambridge University Press, 1992.

Horsley, R. A., and J. S. Hanson. *Bandits, Prophets, and Messiahs: Popular Movements in the Time of Jesus.* New Voices in Biblical Studies. Minneapolis: Winston, 1985.

Horst, P. W. van der. "Greek in Jewish Palestine in Light of Jewish Epigraphy." Pp. 154-74 in *Hellenism in the Land of Israel.* Ed. J. J. Collins and G. E. Sterling. Christianity and Judaism in Antiquity Series 13. Notre Dame, Ind.: University of Notre Dame Press, 2001.

―――. "Jewish Poetical Tomb Inscriptions." Pp. 129-45 in *Studies in Early Jewish Epigraphy.* Ed. J. W. van Henten and P. W. van der Horst. Leiden: Brill, 1993.

Humphreys, S. C. *Anthropology and the Greeks.* London: Routledge & Kegan Paul, 1978.

Ilan, T. *Lexicon of Jewish Names in Late Antiquity.* Part 1: *Palestine 330 BCE–200 CE.* TSAJ 91. Tübingen: Mohr Siebeck, 2002.

―――. "Names of the Hasmoneans during the Second Temple Period." Pp. 497-86 in

The Hasmonean State: The History of the Hasmoneans during the Hellenistic Period [in Hebrew]. Ed. U. Rappaport and I. Ronen. Jerusalem: Yad Ben Zvi and the Open University, 1994.

―――. "Notes on the Distribution of Jewish Women's Names in Palestine in the Second Temple and Mishnaic Period." *JJS* 40 (1989): 186-200.

―――. "Notes on the Spelling of Names in the Second Temple Period." *Leshonenu* 52 (1988): 1-7.

―――. "The Ossuary and Sarkophagus Inscriptions." Pp. 57-72 in *The Akeldama Tombs: Three Burial Caves in the Kidron Valley, Jerusalem*. Ed. G. Avni and Z. Greenhut. IAA Reports 1. Jerusalem: Israel Antiquities Authorities, 1996.

Jacobovici, S., and C. Pellegrino. *The Jesus Family Tomb: The Discovery, the Investigation, and the Evidence That Could Change History*. San Francisco: HarperSanFrancisco, 2007.

Kane, J.-P. "The Ossuary Inscriptions of Jerusalem." *JSS* 23 (1971): 268-82.

Kaplan, K., and M. Schwartz. "Freedom, Creativity and Suicide in Greek and Biblical Thought: The Anomaly of Masada." *Journal of Psychology and Judaism* 18 (1994): 205-18.

Killagen, J. J. "The Sadducees and Resurrection from the Dead: Luke 20,27-40." *Bib* 67 (1986): 478-95.

King, K. L. *The Gospel of Mary of Magdala*. Santa Rosa, Calif.: Polebridge, 2003.

Kloner, A. "A Tomb with Inscribed Ossuaries in East Talpiyot, Jerusalem." *'Atiqot* 29 (1996): 15-22.

Kloner, A., and B. Zissu. *The Necropolis of Jerusalem in the Second Temple Period*. Interdisciplinary Studies in Ancient Culture and Religion 8. Leuven: Peeters, 2007.

Kuhn, H.-W. *Enderwartung und gegenwärtiges Heil: Untersuchungen zu den Gemeindeliedern von Qumran mit einem Anhang über Eschatologie und Gegenwart in der Verkündigung Jesu*. SUNT 4. Göttingen: Vandenhoeck & Ruprecht, 1966.

Kurtz, D. C., and J. Boardman. *Greek Burial Customs*. London: Thames & Hudson, 1971.

Lefkowitz, M. R., and M. B. Fant, eds. *Women's Life in Greece and Rome: A Source Book in Translation*. Baltimore: Johns Hopkins University Press, 2005.

Lemaire, A. "Burial Box of James the Brother of Jesus." *BAR* 28 (2002): 24-33, 70.

―――. "Israel Antiquities Authority's Report on the James Ossuary Deeply Flawed." *BAR* 29 (2003): 50-70.

―――. "Trois inscriptions araméennes sur ossuaire et leur intérêt." *CRAI* (2003): 301-17.

Levenson, J. D. *Resurrection and the Restoration of Israel: The Ultimate Victory of the God of Life*. New Haven: Yale University Press, 2006.

Lewis, N., Y. Yadin, and J. C. Greenfield. *The Documents from the Bar Kokhba Period in the Caves of the Letters: Greek Papyri; Aramaic and Nabatean Signatures and Subscriptions*. Jerusalem: Israel Exploration Society/The Hebrew University of Jerusalem/The Shrine of the Book, 1989.

Lüderitz, G. "What Is the Politeuma?" Pp. 183-225 in *Studies in Early Jewish Epigraphy*. Ed. J. W. van Henten and P. W. van der Horst. AGJU 21. Leiden: Brill, 1994.

―――. *Corpus jüdischer Zeugnisse aus der Cyrenaica*. Wiesbaden: Reichert, 1983.

Lührmann, D. *Das Markusevangelium*. Handbuch zum Neuen Testament 3. Tübingen: Mohr Siebeck, 1987.

Magen, Y. *The Stone Vessel Industry in the Second Temple Period*. Jerusalem: Israel Exploration Society and Israel Antiquities Authority, 2002.

Mason, S. *Flavius Josephus on the Pharisees: A Composition-Critical Study*. StPB 39. Leiden: Brill, 1991.

McCane, B. R. "Bones of Contention? Ossuaries and Reliquaries in Early Judaism and Christianity." *Second Century* 8 (1991): 235-46.

———. *Roll Back the Stone: Death and Burial in the World of Jesus*. Harrisburg: Trinity Press International, 2003.

Mendels, D. "Societies of Memory in the Graeco-Roman World." Pp. 143-62 in *Memory in the Bible and Antiquity*. Ed. L. T. Stuckenbruck, S. C. Barton, and B. G. Wold. WUNT 212. Tübingen: Mohr Siebeck, 2007.

Meyers, E. M. *Jewish Ossuaries: Reburial and Rebirth*. BibOr 24. Rome: Biblical Institute Press, 1971.

———. "The Jesus Tomb Controversy: An Overview." *NEA* 69 (2006): 116-18.

———. "Secondary Burial in Palestine." *BA* 33 (1970): 2-29.

———. "The Theological Implications of an Ancient Jewish Burial Custom." *JQR* 18 (1971-72): 95-119.

Meyers E. M., and J. F. Strange. *Archaeology, the Rabbis, and Early Christianity*. Nashville: Abingdon, 1981. (See esp. "Jewish Burial Practices and Views of Afterlife, and Early Christian Evidences," pp. 92-124.)

Milik, J. T. "Le couvercle de Bethphagé." Pp. 75-94 in *Hommages à André Dupont-Sommer*. Ed. A. Caquot and M. Philonenko. Paris: Maisonneuve, 1971.

Milik, J. T., and R. de Vaux. *Les grottes de Murabba'ât*. DJD 2. Oxford: Clarendon, 1961.

Millard, A. *Reading and Writing in the Time of Jesus*. Biblical Seminar 69. Sheffield: Sheffield Academic Press, 2000.

Misgav, H. "Nomenclature in Ossuary Inscriptions." *Tarbiz* 66 (1996): 123-30, pl. 8.

Mussies, G. "Jewish Personal Names in Some Non-Literary Sources." Pp. 242-76 in *Studies in Early Jewish Epigraphy*. Ed. J. W. van Henten and P. W. van der Horst. AGJU 21. Leiden: Brill, 1994.

Mylonas, G. E. *Eleusis and the Eleusinian Mysteries*. Princeton: Princeton University Press, 1969.

Naveh, J. "Hebrew and Aramaic Inscriptions." Pp. 1-14 in *Excavations at the City of David 1978-1985 Directed by Yigal Shiloh*. Ed. D. T. Ariel. Qedem 41. Jerusalem: Hebrew University, 2000.

Nickelsburg, G. W. E. *Resurrection, Immortality, and Eternal Life in Intertestamental Judaism*. HTS 26. Cambridge: Harvard University Press, 1972.

Nilsson, M. P. "Die astrale Unsterblichkeit und die kosmische Mystik." *Numen* 1 (1954): 106-19.

Nodet, É. *Baptême et resurrection: Le témoignage de Josèphe*. Paris: Cerf, 1999.

Painter, J. *Just James: The Brother of Jesus in History and Tradition*. Edinburgh: T&T Clark, 1999.

Paxton, F. S. *Christianizing Death: The Creation of a Ritual Process in Early Medieval Europe*. Ithaca: Cornell University Press, 1990.

Peek, W. *Griechische Grabgedichte*. Berlin: Akademie-Verlag, 1960.

Peleg, Y. "Gender and Ossuaries: Ideology and Meaning." *BASOR* 325 (2001): 65-73.

Pfann, S. "Mary Magdalene Has Left the Room: A Suggested New Reading of Ossuary CJO 701." *NEA* 69 (2006): 118-24.

Powers, T. "Treasures in the Storeroom: Family Tomb of Simon of Cyrene." *BAR* 29 (2003): 46-51.

Price, J. J., and H. Misgav. "Jewish Inscriptions and Their Use." Pp. 461-83 in *The Literature of the Sages, Second Part: Midrash and Targum, Liturgy, Poetry, Mysticism, Contracts, Inscriptions, Ancient Science and the Languages of Rabbinic Literature*. Ed. S. Safrai et al. CRINT 2/3b. Minneapolis: Fortress, 2006.

Puech, E. "La conception de la vie future dans le livre de la 'Sagesse' et les manuscrits de la Mer Morte: Un apercu." *RevQ* 21 (2003): 209-32.

———. *La croyance des esséniens en la vie future: Immortalité, résurrection, vie éternelle? Histoire d'une croyance dans le Judaïsme ancien*. 2 vols. EBib 21. Paris: Gabalda, 1993.

———. "Ossuaires inscrits d'une tombe du Mont des Oliviers." *LASBF* 32 (1982): 355-72.

Rahmani, L. Y. "Ancient Jerusalem Funerary Customs and Tombs." *BA* 45 (1982): 43-52.

———. *A Catalogue of Jewish Ossuaries in the Collections of the State of Israel*. Jerusalem: Israel Antiquities Authority and Israel Academy of Sciences and Humanities, 1994.

Regev, E. "The Individualistic Meaning of Jewish Ossuaries: A Socio-anthropological Perspective on Burial Practice." *PEQ* 133 (2001): 39-49.

Rohde, E. *Psyche: The Cult of Souls and Belief in Immortality among the Greeks*. Trans. W. Hillis. International Library of Philosophy, Psychology, and Scientific Method. London: Routledge & Kegan Paul, 1950.

Rollston, C. "Inscribed Ossuaries: Personal Names, Statistics, and Laboratory Tests." *NEA* 69 (2006): 125-29.

Rosenfeld, B.-Z. "The Settlement of Two Families of High Priests During the Second Temple Period." Pp. 206-18 in vol. 2 of *Historical-Geographical Studies in the Settlement of Eretz-Israel*. Ed. Y. Katz et al. Jerusalem: Yad Ben Zvi, 1991.

Rowell, G. *The Liturgy of Christian Burial: An Introductory Study to the Historical Development of Christian Burial Rites*. London: Alcuin Club/SPCK, 1977.

Rush, A. C. *Death and Burial in Christian Antiquity*. Washington, D.C.: Catholic University of America Press, 1941.

Rutgers, L. V. "Death and Afterlife: The Inscriptional Evidence." Pp. 293-310 in *Judaism in Late Antiquity*. Part 4: *Death, Life-after-Death, Resurrection and the World-to-Come in the Judaisms of Antiquity*. Ed. A. J. Avery-Peck and J. Neusner. HO 1/49. Leiden: Brill, 2000.

———. *The Jews in Late Ancient Rome: Evidence of Cultural Interaction in the Roman Diaspora*. Leiden: Brill, 1995.

Saldarini, A. J. *Pharisees, Scribes and Sadducees in Palestinian Society: A Sociological Approach*. Grand Rapids: Eerdmans, 2001.

Sanders, E. P. *Judaism: Practice and Belief, 63 BCE–66 CE*. London: SCM, 1992.

Schlatter, A. *Die Theologie des Judentums nach dem Bericht des Josefus*. BFCT 2/26. Gütersloh: Bertelsmann, 1932.

Schröder, B. *Die 'väterlichen Gesetze': Flavius Josephus als Vermittler von Halachah an Griechen und Römer*. TSAJ 53. Tübingen: Mohr Siebeck, 1996.

Schubert, K. *Die jüdischen Religionspartien in neutestamentlicher Zeit*. SBS 43. Stuttgart: Katholisches Bibelwerk, 1970.

Schürer, E. *History of the Jewish People in the Age of Jesus Christ (175 B.C.–A.D. 135)*. Ed. M. Black, G. Vermes, F. Millar, and P. Vermes. Trans. T. Burkill et al. Rev. ed. 3 vols. in 4. London: T&T Clark, 1973-1987.

Segal, A. F. *Life after Death: A History of the Afterlife in Western Religion*. New York: Doubleday, 2004.

Setzer, C. *Resurrection of the Body in Early Judaism and Early Christianity: Doctrine, Community, and Self-Definition*. Leiden: Brill, 2004.

Shanks, H., and B. Witherington. *The Brother of Jesus: The Dramatic Story & Meaning of the First Archaeological Link to Jesus & His Family*. San Francisco: HarperSanFrancisco, 2003.

Sievers, J. "Josephus and the Afterlife." Pp. 20-31 in *Understanding Josephus: Seven Perspectives*. Ed. S. Mason. JSPSup 32. Sheffield: Sheffield Academic Press, 1998.

Sukenik, E. *The Earliest Records of Christianity*, with a new introduction by G. A. Kiraz. Piscataway, N.J.: Gorgias Press, 2008.

———. "A Jewish Burial Cave Northwest of Jerusalem." *Tarbiz* 12 (1930): 122-24.

Tabor, J. *The Jesus Dynasty: The Hidden History of Jesus, His Royal Family, and the Birth of Christianity*. New York: Simon & Schuster, 2006.

Tabor, J. D., and S. Jacobovici. *The Jesus Discovery*. New York: Simon & Schuster, 2012.

VanderKam, J. C. *From Joshua to Caiaphas. High Priests after the Exile*. Minneapolis: Fortress, 2004.

VanderKam, J., and P. Flint. *The Meaning of the Dead Sea Scrolls: Their Significance for Understanding the Bible, Judaism, Jesus, and Christianity*. San Francisco: HarperSanFrancisco, 2002.

Vermes, G. *The Resurrection: History and Myth*. New York: Doubleday, 2008.

Vincent, L. H. "Épitaphe prétendue de N.-S. Jésus-Christ." *Rendiconti della Pontificia Accademia Romana di Archeologia* 7 (1931): 215-39.

Williams, M. H. "The Use of Alternative Names by Diaspora Jews in Graeco-Roman Antiquity." *JSJ* 38 (2007): 307-27.

Wolfson, H. A. *Philo*. 2 vols. Cambridge: Harvard University Press, 1948.

Wright, N. T. *Christian Origins and the Question of God*. Vol. 3: *The Resurrection of the Son of God*. Minneapolis: Fortress, 2003.

Yadin, Y. *Masada: Herod's Fortress and the Zealots' Last Stand*. Trans. M. Pearlman. New York: Random House, 1966.

Yadin, Y., and J. Naveh. "The Aramaic and Hebrew Ostracon and Jar Inscriptions." Pp. 1-68 in *Masada I. The Yigael Yadin Excavations 1963-1965 Final Reports*. Jerusalem: Israel Exploration Society and Hebrew University, 1989.

Yardeni, A. *The Book of Hebrew Script*. Jerusalem: Carta, 1997.

—————. *Textbook of Aramaic, Hebrew and Nabataean Documentary Texts from the Judaean Desert and Related Material.* Jerusalem: Hebrew University, 2000.

Zerubavel, Y. "Antiquity and the Renewal Paradigm: Strategies of Representation and Mnemonic Practices in Israeli Culture." Pp. 331-48 in *On Memory: An Interdisciplinary Approach.* Ed. D. Mendels. Bern: Peter Lang, 2007.

Zias, J. "Human Skeletal Remains from the Mount Scopus Tomb." *ʿAtiqot* 21 (1988): 97-103.

Made in the USA
Columbia, SC
28 August 2022